Reinhold Nïebuhr

HIS RELIGIOUS, SOCIAL, AND POLITICAL THOUGHT

EDITED BY

CHARLES W. KEGLEY

Reproduced by permission of
The Pilgrim Press

Wipf and Stock Publishers
150 West Broadway • Eugene OR 97401
2001

Wipf and Stock Publishers
199 W 8th Ave, Suite 3
Eugene, OR 97401

Reinhold Niebuhr; His Religious, Social, and Political Thought
By Kegley, Charles W.

ISBN 13: 978-1-60899-128-0
Publication date 9/24/2009
Previously published by Pilgrim Press,

CONTENTS

PREFACE TO THE SECOND EDITION

WHAT accounts for the fact that the thought and writing of Reinhold Niebuhr maintains and even increases in influence whereas that of most of his contemporaries in religious, social, and political thought decreases? Its integral merit? Its profundity? Its range? Its distinctiveness? Its volume—he published for six decades, from 1911 to 1971? Clearly, all these and more. There is not one essay in the first edition of this book which can be ignored by today's authors; the same is true of Niebuhr's reply to his critics in this volume. In addition to updated essays by John Bennett, Arthur Schlesinger, Jr., and Kenneth Thompson, there are new interpretations by Ronald Stone and Richard Fox. The bibliography, which ended with 1952 in the first volume, is here completed by D. B. Robertson, who has published a separate book including a bibliography, listing of translations of Niebuhr's major works, and books about Niebuhr.

The theological, philosophical, and political world needs, almost desperately, to take into account the wisdom of Niebuhr and to reread *his* replies to his interpreters. My hope is that, short of hearing his voice, serious minds the world over will re-encounter his contributions.

The public may need to be reminded of the aims and unique structure of *The Library of Living Theology* of which this is the second volume (the first, *The Theology of Paul Tillich,* has also just been published by The Pilgrim Press with new contributions and a complete bibliography). This *Library* is parallel to *The Library of Living Philosophers*, now in two score volumes. Each volume in these *Libraries* includes (1) an intellectual autobiography; (2) essays on the major aspects of the subject's work, written by leading scholars; (3) a "Reply to his Critics" by the theologian/philosopher; and (4) a complete bibliography of the subject's writings. Both series have met with world-wide acclaim.

The Library of Living Theology interprets "theology" very broadly. It includes not only dogmatic, biblical, and confessional theology, but empirical theology or what some would call "philosophy of religion." Still further, there is no intention to confine the *Library* to the Western, Judeo-Christian tradition. The criteria for choosing the subjects—e.g., Brunner, Bultmann, Wieman, Nygren—are "aliveness," creativity, and individuality of thought. Tillich and Niebuhr are prime examples.

These volumes have been described as religious and theological in subject matter, philosophical and analytical in method and approach. The aim is to provide a real meeting ground for some of the keenest intellects of our age. Accordingly, they may serve as an agency not only of enlightenment but also of mutual understanding and good will.

CHARLES W. KEGLEY

PREFACE TO THE FIRST EDITION

The dominant motif of our age, as Alfred North Whitehead has pointed out, is science, and two characteristics associated with the scientific mentality are change and specialization. Such an age demands, of anyone who would interpret and criticize its methods and goals, discernment and comprehensiveness.

Reinhold Niebuhr, writing and speaking from the religious point of view and as an American, has exhibited these qualities and has performed this service for almost half a century. There are very few parallel personalities who have at once interpreted and influenced the thought of a variety of fields in this era. The fact that in the sphere of religion one can count, throughout the world, such men on the fingers of one hand is itself worth pondering.

Such considerations render superfluous any defense for including Reinhold Niebuhr in this series; the essays in this volume, by world scholars of different faiths and fields of study, eloquently document the point. Clearly, Niebuhr himself demands to be interpreted and evaluated. The interpretation is the more appropriate because the mass and variety of his writings make it unlikely that the general reader, even if he is intelligent and conscientious, can take the time and effort to study all or even most of the contributions cited in the bibliography at the close of this volume. Were he to make this his goal, he soon would be liable to think that Niebuhr's mind, like Stephen Leacock's hero, mounts his horse and rides off in all directions at once—speaking with insight here on the arts, there on social and political issues, in still another place on perennial theological questions. Hoping, of course, that readers will be led directly to Niebuhr's own writing, one has a right to ask how the abler minds of our age understand and evaluate his thought. This is precisely the service that the present volume attempts to perform.

The diversity of writing referred to above is in part responsible for the divergence in the title of this volume from the form set by its predecessor. Pondering the nature both of Niebuhr's work and of these essays of interpretation and criticism, it appeared that the orientation suggested by the title is more appropriate than one which fixes attention primarily on "theology."* A simultaneous consideration from another angle supports this: Professor Niebuhr has repeatedly expressed his hesitation at being called a theologian and in having his thoughts analyzed and criticized as a theology. The disclaimer makes sense on two scores, (*a*) because in fact he has not primarily operated, as teacher and writer, in what academically is considered the field of systematic theology as compared with the historical, Biblical, and functional fields and (*b*) because, as already pointed out, one of his distinctive contributions is that he has applied theological or "Biblical" insights to many aspects of contemporary life. The special title therefore is a tribute to, and not a criticism of, his undisputed rôle in *The Library of Living Theology.*

The several references to "critics" and to "criticism" also call for comment. The reader can scarcely fail to recognize, as he examines almost any of the essays on aspects of Niebuhr's thought, that the authors have taken seriously the editorial demand to "pull no punches." In many cases they have demanded clarification on specific issues; in many others they have put their finger on vital elements in his thought, including the methodology behind it, and have said, "Thou ailest here." This precisely is what is wanted; it offers the subject of the volume an unparalleled opportunity to clarify his thought and to defend himself. It is particularly gratifying, therefore, that in his "Reply" to interpreters and critics, Professor Niebuhr is dealing with men in philosophical, political, and social as well as religious fields, for instance, and of non-Christian as well as Christian, Jewish and Roman Catholic as well as Protestant standpoints.

This meeting of minds would have been even richer had certain other leaders of thought in our time found it possible to participate. Karl Barth, Martin Buber, and Arnold Toynbee have expressed their genuine regret in not being able to accept the editors' invitation to participate in this volume. To critics who, as in the case of *The Theology of Paul Tillich,* point out that this or that person's views would have added greatly to the illumination, the advance reply to be made is that one probably agrees, none the less, that it

* See the General Introduction.

is kinder to tell you who does engage in the inquiry than to indicate, save in the exceptions noted, who would not or could not.

Regarding this participation, moreover, it is a particular cause for satisfaction that in this volume there is a cross-fertilization of minds at the summit, if a Churchillian figure may be used. In these pages the incisive judgments of the subject of Volume I, Paul Tillich, and of the subject of a future volume, Emil Brunner, elicit a written "Reply" from Reinhold Niebuhr. Here is free and responsible inquiry and criticism at its best—and the reader will perceive at once the candor and vigor of the engagement. Philosophy of religion and theology will neither become impotent nor be ignored in such an atmosphere.

To fix upon the order of the essays was exasperating, and it is hardly possible to defend that order against all criticism. It is necessary, however, to explain the rationale of that order, even though most readers will read the various essays in the order of their own interests. The volume opens with the statements of two scholars who were (Tillich) and will be (Brunner) the subjects of other volumes. The notion, then, is that the reader can ponder Niebuhr's thought in the sequence in which he revealed his mind. Now as Professor Brunner correctly says in his essay, Reinhold Niebuhr first came to the world's attention as a critic of social conditions. Hence we ought first to examine his social thought, and more especially as a Christian ethicist, proceeding from this to the political sphere. Because of the major shift which occurred, the background and relation of his thought to liberalism may then be pursued. After this, one is ready for two groups of essays, the first of critical exposition, the second dealing chiefly with criticisms and questions, though all of these, of course, shed increasing light on his total thought. Inevitably classification breaks down because the studies overlap. Above all, no judgment of relative importance or merit is intended in the order.

Certain additional aspects of the theological work of Reinhold Niebuhr admittedly claim consideration. One is especially aware, for instance, of his rôle in ecumenical thought and life. His contributions have been immense, and a study of the meeting of minds between him and the leaders of the Continent, the British Isles, and the East would be fruitful. There is something of this, of course, in the present essays, but it was impossible to obtain an explicit study of the ecumenical aspect of his work.

Particular thanks are due to Professor Robertson for his patience and thoroughness in preparing the bibliography. Limitations of space required moderate condensation, but the bibliography probably stands as the best available to the time of this publication, and as such it should be unusually valuable for future research. At several points Professor John Bennett, in his customarily modest but clear-headed and valuable way, made helpful suggestions about several matters; they are gratefully acknowledged, though he is not responsible, of course, for whatever weaknesses may here appear.

Finally, a personal word of gratitude should be expressed for the fact that this particular volume meets the full structural demands of *The Library of Living Theology*. As his friends know, Professor Niebuhr recently suffered a period of grave illness. At one time we feared that we should never have his Autobiographical Statement and his Reply to his interpreters and critics. Happily we have not only these but also the expectation of years of productivity by a mind singularly endowed and a personality which, as one who has worked with him in producing this volume knows, is very rich in the Christian graces.

CHARLES W. KEGLEY

I

INTELLECTUAL AUTOBIOGRAPHY OF REINHOLD NIEBUHR

INTELLECTUAL AUTOBIOGRAPHY

It is somewhat embarrassing to be made the subject of a study which assumes theology as the primary interest. I cannot and do not claim to be a theologian. I have taught Christian Social Ethics for a quarter of a century and have also dealt in the ancillary field of "apologetics." My avocational interest as a kind of circuit rider in the colleges and universities has prompted an interest in the defense and justification of the Christian faith in a secular age, particularly among what Schleiermacher called Christianity's "intellectual despisers." I have never been very competent in the nice points of pure theology; and I must confess that I have not been sufficiently interested heretofore to acquire the competence. De Tocqueville long since observed the strong pragmatic interest of American Christianity in comparison with European Christianity; and that distinction is still valid. I have been frequently challenged by the stricter sects of theologians in Europe to prove that my interests were theological rather than practical or "apologetic," but I have always refused to enter a defense, partly because I thought the point was well taken and partly because the distinction did not interest me.

The first formative religious influence on my life was my father, who combined a vital personal piety with a complete freedom in his theological studies. He introduced his sons and daughter to the thought of Harnack without fully sharing the liberal convictions of that theologian. I attended the college and seminary of my denomination. The little college had no more than junior college status in my day, and I was not interested in any academic disciplines. The seminary was influential in my life primarily because of the creative effect upon me of the life of a very remarkable man, Dr. S. D. Press, who combined a childlike innocency with a rigorous scholarship in

Biblical and systematic subjects. This proved the point that an educational institution needs only to have Mark Hopkins on one end of a log and a student on the other.

After completing my studies at the denominational college and theological seminary, I completed my graduate training at the Divinity School of Yale University. I remember particularly two teachers who influenced the course of my development. Professor Porter was at that time the New Testament theologian. His lucid and comprehensive exposition of New Testament theology made a tremendous impression, and the notes I took in his classes are the only school notes I still preserve.

Professor Macintosh, the systematic theologian, opened the whole world of philosophical and theological learning to me, lent books to me out of his own library, and by his personal interest inspired a raw and timid student who had made his first contact with a great university. Professor Macintosh was a great authority on the problem of knowledge and had written a most comprehensive survey of epistemological theories. I was thrilled at first with this encyclopedic knowledge; but, unfortunately, in time the philosophical theories bored me, though I was subsequently to discover that Macintosh's challenge of the age-old alliance between the Christian faith and philosophical idealism was important. Incidentally my brother, H. Richard, who came to Yale as a mature person some ten years later, profited much more than I could, in my youthful awkwardness, from Yale. Ultimately he became an associate of Professor Macintosh on the Yale faculty. He was always a few paces ahead of me in theological development; and all my life I have profited greatly from his clearer formulation of views I came to hold in common with him. Since he did not share my political interests and activities, which were the source of my first disillusionment in nineteenth-century religion, my political experience was obviously not the only road back to faith, though it was important to me personally.

Family needs (my father had died just before my entrance into Yale) and my boredom with epistemology prompted me to foreswear graduate study and the academic career to which it pointed, and to accept a parish of my denomination in Detroit. According to the rules of our denomination, a young ordinand was at the disposal of the Home Mission Board for two years after ordination. The board picked a newly organized parish for me in Detroit.

The automobile industry, particularly the Ford Motor Company, was just beginning its rapid expansion, which was to make Detroit the motor capital of the country. During my pastorate of thirteen years in the city, Detroit was to expand from a half to a million and a half population. The resulting facts determined my development more than any books which I may have read. For on the one hand, my congregation grew from a handful to eight hundred souls. An English friend, looking at the American scene through European perspectives, has described my parish as a "slum parish." It was, as a matter of fact, situated on the spacious West Grand Boulevard, and it numbered in the flock everything from auto workers to two millionaires. On the other hand, the social realities of a rapidly expanding industrial community, before the time of the organization of the workers, and under the leadership of a group of resourceful engineers who understood little about human relations, forced me to reconsider the liberal and highly moralistic creed which I had accepted as tantamount to the Christian faith. Incidentally, all the speeches of the Divinity School Commencement, including a little junior effort of my own, in June of 1914, celebrated an optimistic faith which was to be challenged by the outbreak of the European War during that very summer. But it wasn't the then distant war so much as the social realities in Detroit which undermined my youthful optimism. My first interest was not so much to challenge the reigning laissez-faire philosophy of the community as to "debunk" the moral pretensions of Henry Ford, whose five-dollar-a-day wage gave him a world-wide reputation for generosity. I happened to know that some of his workers had an inadequate annual wage, whatever the pretensions of the daily wage may have been. Many of them lost their homes in the enforced vacations, which became longer and longer until the popular demand for the old Model T suddenly subsided, and forced a layoff of almost a year for "retooling."

The realities were brought home to me particularly when the A.F. of L. held its annual meeting in the city and threatened to organize the auto industry. The threat was an idle one, for the old craft unions could not succeed in organizing modern mass-production industries with an aristocracy of skilled workers and a mass of semi-skilled mechanics. The labor organization of the industry had to await the C.I.O. industrial unions over a decade later. But this did not prevent the Detroit Board of Commerce from branding the A.F. of L. as communistic, and from putting pressure on the churches to cancel invitations which had been extended to Labor-convention speakers. The incident vividly portrayed the irrelevance of the mild moralistic idealism, which I had identified with the Christian faith, to the power realities of our modern technical society.

Meanwhile the war was dissipating other illusions of the nineteenth-century world view which informed American Christianity. But I was influenced in my disillusionment more by local than by international experience. In my parish duties I found that the simple idealism into which the classical faith had evaporated was as irrelevant to the crises of personal life as it was to the complex social issues of an industrial city.

Two old ladies were dying shortly after I assumed charge of the parish. They were both equally respectable members of the congregation. But I soon noted that their manner of facing death was strikingly dissimilar. One old lady was too preoccupied with self, too aggrieved that Providence should not have taken account of her virtue in failing to protect her against a grievous illness, to be able to face death with any serenity. She was in a constant hysteria of fear and resentment. While my own simple idealism would have scarcely been equal to the test of facing the ultimate issue, I found myself deeply disturbed by the fact that faith was evidently of so little account in the final test. The other old lady had brought up a healthy and wholesome family, though her husband was subject to periodic fits of insanity which forced her to be the breadwinner as well as homemaker. Just as her two splendid daughters had finished their training and were eager to give their mother a secure and quiet evening of life, she was found to be suffering from cancer. I stood weekly at her bedside while she told me what passages of Scripture, what Psalms and what prayers to read to her; most of them expressed gratitude for all the mercies of God which she had received in life. She was particularly grateful for her two daughters and their love; and she faced death with the utmost peace of soul.

I relearned the essentials of the Christian faith at the bedside of that nice old soul. I appreciated that the ultimate problem of human existence is the peril of sin and death in the way that these two perils are so curiously compounded; for we fall into sin by trying to evade or to conquer death or our own insignificance, of which death is the ultimate symbol. The Christian faith holds out the hope that our fragmentary lives will be completed in a total and larger plan than any which we control or comprehend, and that a part of the completion is the forgiveness of sins, that is, the forgiveness of the evils into which we fall by our frantic efforts to complete our own lives or to endow them with significance. I was conscious of the nobility which was the fruit of the simple faith of a simple woman; and that was not the only time in parish duties in which I learned the meaning of Christ's prayer: "I thank Thee, Father, that Thou hast withheld these things from the wise and prudent and revealed them unto babes." As for the difference between the faith of the two old ladies, outwardly so similar until submitted to the ultimate test, we in the churches ought to admit more humbly than is our wont that there is a mystery of grace which no one can fathom. "Two women will be grinding at the mill. The one will be taken and the other left." The Church is a curiously mixed body consisting of those who have never been shaken in their self-esteem or self-righteousness and who use the forms of religion for purposes of self-aggrandizement; and of the true Christians who live by "a broken spirit and a contrite heart." Whether we belong to this latter group, which makes up the true but invisible Church, no one but God can know. Facing the test of death is obviously more important than I had imagined in the days of my simple "moralism." But I have noted, in these latter days of Christianity's struggle with Nazi and Communist idolatries, that defiance of malignant evil, involving the peril of death, is also a test which proves some obscure saints to be true conquerors, while others less obscure may fail mysteriously to pass the test. Indeed, one must come to the conclusion that none of us can be certain whether we have the faith or the courage to pass any final test. "If any man stand let him take heed lest he fall."

My early writings were all characterized by a critical attitude toward the "liberal" world view, whether expressed in secular or in Christian terms. There was, as a matter of fact, little difference between the secular and Christian versions of the optimism of the nineteenth-century culture. For years I commuted, as it were, between ecclesiastical and academic communities. I found each with a sense of superiority over the other either because it possessed, or had discarded, the Christian faith. But this contest was ironic because the viewpoints of the two communities were strikingly similar, and both were obviously irrelevant to the ultimate realities, whether in terms of mankind's collective behavior or in terms of individual man's ultimate problems.

I note to my embarrassment that my criticisms could not have been very thoroughgoing because they revealed so many vestigial remnants of the culture which I ostensibly criticized. Thus I joined and ultimately became the head of the pacifist organization, the Fellowship of Reconciliation. I did write an article for the *Atlantic Monthly* in this period on the topic "A Critique of Pacifism." In this article I proved the political irrelevance of absolute pacifism and revealed myself as a proponent of "pragmatic" pacifism. But this form of pacifism, while provisionally valid in the sense that any wise statesmanship will exhaust every possibility of accommodating competing interests in order to avoid violent conflict, is nevertheless a dubious compound of the prudential ethics of a commercial civilization and the absolute demands of the Gospel ethics, which has not, and cannot have, a direct relevance to the problem of the accommodation of interests from which we must extract a proximate justice amid the complexities of social life. Secondly, I followed the fashion of the "social gospel" school Christianity in criticizing the individualism and the optimism of the old liberalism, sometimes by appropriating the collectivism and the catastrophism of Marxism. My first major work, entitled *Moral Man and Immoral Society,* was not uncritically Marxist, but it does reveal a failure to recognize the ultimate similarities, despite immediate differences, between liberal and Marxist utopianism. I was instrumental in organizing the Fellowship of Socialist Christians in the late twenties, a group to which I owe much, and the development of which, from a rather tentative Marxist orientation to a position which was equally critical of both Marxist and liberal illusions, has been admirably charted by Professor Hutchison in the symposium *Christian Faith and Social Action.* This development was hastened by the contact which I and other members of the group had with the growing ecumenical movement beginning with the World Conference on Church, Community, and State in Oxford in 1937.

I became a member of the faculty of Union Theological Seminary in 1928, largely at the instigation of my friend Sherwood Eddy, who persuaded the seminary faculty to call me to a Chair of Christian Ethics. This was a hazardous venture, since my reading in the parish had been rather undisciplined and I had no scholarly competence in my field, not to speak of the total field of Christian theology. My practical interests and the devoting of every weekend to college preaching prevented any rapid acquisition of competence in my ostensible specialty. It was therefore a full decade before I could stand before a class and answer the searching questions of the students at the end of a lecture without the sense of being a fraud who pretended to a larger and more comprehensive knowledge than I possessed. Meanwhile, the pressure of academic discipline and my companionship with the distinguished members of the Union faculty did serve to introduce me to the main outlines of Biblical faith and to the classical texts of Christian theology. I am, however, surprised to note in retrospect how late I was in studying the thought of Augustine carefully. The matter is surprising because the thought of this theologian was to answer so many of my unanswered questions and to emancipate me finally from the notion that the Christian faith was in some way identical with the moral idealism of the past century. It is difficult to know whether the criticism of both liberal and Marxist views of human nature and history was prompted by a profounder understanding of the Biblical faith; or whether this understanding was prompted by the refutation of the liberal and Marxist faith by the tragic facts of contemporary history which included two world wars and the encounter of a liberal culture with two idolatrous tyrannies, first Nazism and then Communism, resting respectively upon the foundations of moral cynicism and moral utopianism. About the circular relation between the presuppositions of faith and the facts of experience I must say more presently.

When I was invited to give the Gifford Lectures in 1939 at the University of Edinburgh, I chose the only subject which I could have chosen, because the other fields of Christian thought were beyond my competence. I lectured on "The Nature and Destiny of Man," comparing Biblical with classical and modern conceptions of human nature and destiny. Later I incorporated studies undertaken for the Lyman Beecher Lectures at Yale, the Warrack Lectures at the Scottish Universities, and a lectureship at the University of Uppsala in Sweden, in a volume entitled *Faith and History.* Since these studies are but an elaboration of the second part of my Gifford Lectures, the reader would be fair in concluding that I have not, in years of theological study, proceeded very far from my original ethical and apologetic interests.

In these works I was concerned to prove that modern versions of man's nature and fate were at once very different from, and yet very similar to, interpretations found in classical idealism, and that the Biblical view of man was superior to both classical and modern views. The intellectual pilgrimage which these succeeding volumes reveal shows that I began to criticize liberal viewpoints from a

Marxist perspective in the first instance, and that I learned gradually to subject both viewpoints to a Christian criticism. I learned increasingly to value highly, rather than be apologetic for, the unique emphases of Biblical faith.

The thesis which I developed in my Gifford Lectures prompted a rather extensive debate and was challenged from various standpoints, which it may be interesting to enumerate:

A. I was criticized by both secular and Christian liberals for my preoccupation with the Christian doctrine of sin, and my alleged overemphasis on the corruption of human nature. I must plead guilty to this charge in the sense that it was a long time before I paid as much attention to the Christian conception of the cure as to the diagnosis, to "grace" as well as to sin. But even if I had not made this mistake, the criticisms would have been made; for it would not have been possible to challenge the sentimentalities of our culture from the standpoint of a Christian realism without becoming exposed to this criticism.

In the field of speculation about God, the crux of the issue between Biblical faith and the various philosophies is whether it is respectable to think of God as a person who wills and loves, when the philosophies find the concept of personality to be too ambiguous to ascribe to the divine nature. They therefore content themselves with equating God with some rational structures of existence or with an undifferentiated ground of being, which is at once the fullness and the absence of being. In the field of speculation about human nature, the crux of the issue is whether the distinctive marks of man as a unique creature shall be so defined that the proofs of his "dignity" are also the proofs of his virtue; or whether his dignity shall be defined in terms of the radical character of human freedom. In the latter case his dignity would have the same ground as his destructiveness or his sin.

When we speak of man's "radical" freedom, we do not suggest that his creaturely limitations should be obscured: he is subject to the necessities of nature, of sexual and racial limitation, of geography and climate, and of the dominant drives of his own creaturely nature. His freedom must be defined as "radical" to indicate that, when man rises above the necessities and limits of nature, he is not inevitably bound in his actions to the norms and universalities of "reason." Therefore the growth of his power and freedom over nature does not make for freedom over self and does not automatically make for wider interests and more inclusive harmonies. It is the absurd notion of modern liberalism, both Christian and secular, that the Christian estimate of man's sinfulness is determined by the Biblical account of the fall of Adam, and that it can be dismissed by anyone who does not find this primitive account credible. Actually, the estimate is supported by overwhelming evidence taken both from a sober observation of human behavior and from introspective analysis. The latter evidence is important because it reveals that the self as subject, as distinguished from the self as object of thought, is not some universal and rational self but is always, even in its height of self-transcendence, a particular self; and that this self is even more inclined to be preoccupied and anxious about its position and prestige than the self which is engaged in its affections and responsibilities. On the other hand, the various forms of secularism, whether naturalistic or idealistic, have such a unanimously favorable opinion of human virtue because the naturalists regard man as an object in nature who can be manipulated to desire and seek "socially approved" ends; while the idealists, after the manner of classical philosophy, place the root of evil in the impulses of the body, and expect "mind" to come into progressive control of the infra-rational impulses. Only the Biblical-Christian view sees that the evil in man is at the center of the self, and that it involves all his unique capacities of freedom which endow him with "dignity" and make him, though a creature, also a creator.

Though I have meditated on these issues for some time, I have only recently come to realize fully why the dramatic-historical account of the Bible (about which an earlier generation of modern theologians have been unduly apologetic) should give a truer view of both the nobility and the misery of man than all the wisdom of scientists and philosophers. The fact is that the human self can only be understood in a dramatic-historical environment. Any effort to co-ordinate man to some coherence, whether of nature or of reason, will falsify the facts; because the self's freedom, including both its creative and destructive capacities, precludes such co-ordination.

For this reason the age-old alliance between a Christian and a rational humanism, having its foundation in the classical and Biblical roots of our culture, must continue to be an uneasy one. Professor Bultmann's recent suggestion of a common defense of a humanistic culture against its foes had more plausibility in the days of the Nazi peril than in this day of Communist idolatry. For Communism manages to threaten the dignity of the human spirit on the basis of an ostensible devotion to the dignity of man. For that matter bourgeois naturalism is very confused on the ultimate issues. It talks endlessly of the "dignity" of man which a democratic society must guard and cherish. Yet it also thinks of man as no more than an object in nature which it is possible, scientifically, to "manipulate."

B. Many secular critics and some Christian ones were dumbfounded by an attack upon modern liberal culture, particularly from a Christian standpoint. For a secular culture agreed with the French Enlightenment in regarding religion as the chief support of a traditional society; it therefore believed secularism to be the foundation-stone of a democratic one. There is a measure of truth in this estimate which Catholicism systematically obscures: it cannot acknowledge an incapacity for refashioning the static and aristocratic culture into the modern dynamic and fluid one. Particularly in America, where the viewpoints of the French Enlightenment and the idealism of sectarian Christianity became strangely compounded, the achievements of a liberal culture and society seemed very impressive: It had emancipated the individual from irrelevant social restraints and inequalities; it had unloosed the initiative of the common man, particularly in economic pursuits, and had harnessed the forces of nature so that hitherto unknown standards of well-being could be achieved; it had established a democratic political order and vanquished ancient tyrannies. In America the wide opportunities of an advancing frontier and of a consistently expanding economy had destroyed class distinctions, and had made the "liberty, equality, and fraternity" of the French Revolution seem to be a present reality and achievement. The sentimental views of human nature were so endemic in a liberal culture, and its democratic achievements were so great, that it became popular to regard mild illusions about human virtue as prerequisites for democratic success. During a decade of devotion to causes of democratic justice, I was often falsely accused of being a "reactionary" on the ground that Christian faith must naturally lead to conservatism; or I was mildly reproved for devotion to democracy in contradiction to my religious convictions, which my friends were willing to tolerate in view of the fact that they did not lead to dire results which some predicted, while my critics sometimes held that a provisional or imaginary devotion to democracy must not obscure the alleged peril of such men as myself to the democratic cause.

This suspicion of Christianity despite generations of exertion by devotees of the "Social Gospel" must be regarded as very strange. But it must be remembered that the proponents of the Social Gospel were not under suspicion, because they did not believe in "sin"; and they had in any case a faith which did not differ too grievously from the main outlines of the "American dream." Naturally I had not only critical but sympathetic reactions to the political implications of the theology I attempted to propound, particularly from historians and political scientists. It is significant that these two academic disciplines are most critical of the illusions of our culture, probably because they are closest to the historical and political realities which refute modern illusions. Some of the political scientists have not, operating under the one-dimensional presuppositions of naturalism, been able to avoid the pitfall of a morally nihilistic realism as they sought to counter the errors of modern idealism. Our practical statesmen have in fact extracted a wiser balance between idealism and realism from their practical experience than our academics; and so has the traditional "man in the street." Whatever may be the achievements of sociology and psychology, they have, on the whole, covered the field of political analysis with sentimentality and confusion, probably because they are so intent on being as scientific as the natural sciences, and so foolishly hopeful that a technical age will be able to master the vast realm of historical vitality by the same methods which it used to "manage" nature.

The achievements of a liberal culture are naturally not as impressive, and its self-assurance not as complacent, at the end of two world wars and confronting the dread prospect of an atomic conflict, as they were in the heyday of its triumphs. But there are always some proponents of a credo and defenders of a culture whose defense becomes the more desperate as evidence multiplies that its foundations are inadequate and its conclusions in conflict with the experiences of life.

C. The criticism of a liberal culture from distinctively Christian presuppositions, and the defense of the faith through an analysis of the inadequacy of the modern liberal and Marxist alternatives, were subject to two contrasting criticisms from the secular opponents of Christianity and from the Protestant, chiefly Continental, theologians.

The illusion that it is possible to have an empirical inquiry without a framework of guiding presuppositions is so widespread, particularly in America, that it is regarded as outrageous to criticize a culture from the standpoint of "dogmatic," that is, Christian, presuppositions. "Dogmatic" presuppositions are presumably ruled out in a "scientific" inquiry, particularly explicitly religious ones; for has not every religion been relegated to an *überwunderner Standpunkt* by modern culture? These prejudices are the fruit of our culture's naïve belief that the scientific elements in an examination of the human scene are more true the more they can imitate the "methods" of the natural sciences. Actually, no empirical observation is possible without a conceptual framework. And every rational framework points beyond itself to some framework of meaning which cannot be simply identified with rational coherence. In the natural sciences the analysis of efficient causes requires only one presupposition of faith: namely, that the operations of reason are relevant to the processes of nature; that consequently, as the Renaissance was so proud to discover, "mathematics unlocks the mysteries of nature." The necessary presupposition, in other words, is that the universe is orderly, and the sense of order in reason is relevant to it. But every historical event or series of events requires a more specific framework of meaning than the mere idea of a rational order. This is so because historical events do not follow each other in a "necessary manner" either in the form of necessity in which the scientist analyzes them empirically by repeating an experiment frequently enough under identical conditions to be able to predict its future events, or in the way that metaphysics would define necessity on the basis of logic, affirming that because a thing or event belongs to a certain category of objects or processes it must necessarily share in the attributes or destiny of that category. In the world of human events and history, events are related to each other in a system of multiple causation; and the human agent enters the causal chain continually as one of the causes, having a freedom which makes his action unpredictable despite his obvious relation to the necessities of nature. Therefore it is not possible to find anything following "in a necessary manner" in the vast phantasmagoria of history, and among the dramatic encounters between men and nations. It is possible to predict that a little bear will grow into a mature bear, fulfilling the potentialities of bearhood in a predictable manner. But when a little child grows to maturity it fulfills potentialities in a predictable manner on the one hand, yet on the other, its character is formed by wholly unpredictable reactions to family traditions, to childhood experiences, and to the virtues and weaknesses of its parents. The dramas of life and history may be analyzed, and analogies and recurrences in and between various sequences may be scientifically established. But any definition of the meaning of any sequence will be determined as much by the framework of meaning upon which the inquiry is initiated as upon the evidence adduced. For the correlations of sequences are so various that a rational sense of order cannot compel any particular conclusion. Thus modern culture, which imagines itself engaged in a purely "scientific" analysis of historical events, invariably betrays that a faith is guiding its inquiry, which is something more than the faith of the natural scientist in the orderliness of nature. And the faith determines the conclusions which the scientist reaches, though he assumes that these conclusions are the fruit of his empirical inquiry.

The faith of modern man contains two related articles: the idea of progress and the idea of the perfectibility of man. The latter is frequently the basis of the former article. Man is regarded as indeterminately perfectible because it is not understood that every growth of human freedom may have evil as well as virtuous consequences. The root of this error is that reason is identified with freedom, and it is not seen that reason may be the servant, rather than the master, of the self. This essential religion of modernity is no less "dogmatic" for being implicit rather than explicit, and it is no more true for being arrayed in the panoply of science.

Any encounter with the essential religion of a secular age must penetrate through the confusions which have been created by equating history with nature and meaning with rational intelligibility, and implicit though highly questionable dogmas with the prestige of science. The fact that the Communists should adorn their more explicit dogma with the prestige of science provides modern liberal culture with a caricature of its own beliefs.

D. My apologetic pursuits were challenged from an opposite standpoint by theologians, particularly of the Barthian persuasion. Was not this analysis of the human situation and the refutation of modern estimates of man's nature a tortuous and ineffective return to the Christian faith? they asked. Their point was that whether or not one accepts the Christian faith is a mystery of grace because there is no way of compelling faith rationally. Since it governs the conclusions at which one arrives, ostensibly by experience, there is no way of using experience to determine faith. These criticisms from opposing viewpoints prompt me to expand and defend my conception of the circular relation between faith and experience.

Since a guiding presupposition, held by faith, acts as a kind of filter for the evidence adduced by experience, it would seem that the theologians are right, and that the modern scientists are wrong in making "experience" a final arbiter of truth. But the matter is more complex. Guiding presuppositions do indeed color the evidence accumulated by experience; but they do not fully control experience. Presuppositions are like spectacles worn by a nearsighted or myopic man. He cannot see without the spectacles. But if evidence other than that gathered by his sight persuades him that his spectacles are inadequate to help him see what he ought to see, he will change his spectacles. We have recently had a symposium of confessions by ex-Communists who revealed how they arrived at their Communist faith, how their faith colored all their judgments, and how they became gradually aware that experience controverted the Communist faith. Thereupon they disavowed it and felt that sight had returned to blind eyes. Modern secularism results from the disavowal of traditional Jewish and Christian faiths on what seems to be the incontrovertible evidence of experience. These faiths assumed a mystery of a person and a will behind the observable phenomena of the world. Science proved these phenomena to be related to each other in sequences of efficient causation, and the metaphysicians discerned higher rational essences above the level of efficient cause. It seemed unnecessary to bother with a realm of mystery in the face of this evidence, particularly since religion had discredited itself by neglecting the coherences of natural causes in which science is interested. Consequently it presented an obscurantist view of a world governed by divine caprice. The evidence against traditional religion seemed the more compelling because modern man was too preoccupied with the practical affairs and the promises of a technical culture to delve either into the mysteries of human selfhood or into the corresponding mysteries of the supernal. Therefore various types of "secularism" which regarded the whole of reality as self-explanatory and self-fulfilling, and which interpreted man in terms of his relation either to the realm of reason or to the realm of nature, seemed to have compelling evidence in their favor. Traditional and historic religions seemed passé. It is therefore necessary to recount the experiences of modern man which are most obviously at variance with this modern picture of the human enterprise. My critics may be right in suggesting that the mysteries of good and evil in man's collective life are not the best evidences for proving the modern religion of reason and nature to be mistaken. At any rate, men are always subject to individual experiences of sin and death on the one hand, and of grace on the other hand, which invalidate the modern secular view. Indeed, I must confess that my dominant political interests may have prompted me to engage in this analysis of man's collective life. But in self-defense I must insist that modern man's collective history, embodying as it does both the earlier dreams of happiness and universal harmony through the progressive mastery of both nature and history by the "methods of science," and the contemporary disillusionment, is pretty conclusive evidence that there was something wrong with the spectacles through which modern man looked at himself and his world.

The refutation of one set of presuppositions does not, of course, rationally compel men to accept an alternative faith. Indeed, we have already confessed that no ultimate sense of the meaning of life is rationally compelling. Our apologetic task as proponents of the Christian faith must include the analysis of experience which proves alternative faiths to be mistaken. The apologetic task has the object of inducing the confession: "Lord, to whom shall we go? Thou hast the words of eternal life." But we must recognize that not only is no faith rationally compelling but that there is a special difficulty with reference to the Christian faith which would seem to make it quite unacceptable to men schooled in the ethos of a scientific culture. That difficulty arises from the fact that the Christian faith distinguishes itself from other forms of faith by its greater degree of explicitness. There is a difference between the implicit faith that some system of nature or reason embodies ultimate meaning, and the Christian faith which apprehends a realm of mystery above and beyond the ascertainable structures of the world. This is explicit faith because it is recognized that meaning must be discerned in the mystery above the rationally intelligible structures of existence.

There is a dimension of human existence which makes all purely rationalistic interpretations, not to speak of purely naturalistic ones, inadequate. That is the dimension of the eternal in the human spirit, which reveals itself in the capacity of the self to transcend not only the processes of nature but the operations of its own reason, and to stand, as it were, above the structures and coherences of the world. Whenever typically modern men become conscious of this dimension and seek for an interpretation of life which will do justice to this dimension, they elaborate a mystical doctrine in addition to their rationalistic one. We think of Bertrand Russell's now famous *Mysticism and Logic* and of Santayana's *Platonism and the Spiritual Life;* and more recently of Aldous Huxley's elaboration of classical mysticism in his *The Perennial Philosophy*, and Walter Stace's escape from pure naturalism in his discovery of an eternal realm in his *Time and Eternity*. It is evidently more respectable philosophically to delve into a realm of pure mystery (about which nothing can be said but that it is at the same time the fullness of being and the absence of being) than to accept the Christian affirmation that the mystery of the divine has been disclosed and transmuted into meaning by historical revelation. The alternative of classical mysticism seems to remain more attractive, even after it becomes apparent that, in doing justice to one aspect of human experience—the sense of the eternal dimension in the human spirit—it falsifies another experience: namely, man's uneasy conscience, his awareness that in the ultimate instance he is judged for making too much of himself. This experience is interpreted by mysticism as a judgment upon all temporal particularity, including man's own individuality. By the definition of mysticism, only the undifferentiated unity of the divine is good, while all particularity is evil. The sin of man is thus absurdly interpreted as an ontological fate, whereas every experience must persuade us that our conscience is uneasy not because we are egos but because we are egotists. Man is, in short, misunderstood as seriously in mystical as in idealistic or naturalistic philosophy. The unity of his life in body, soul, and spirit is destroyed, and the meaningfulness of his existence in history is annulled. He is asked to engage in disciplines which will eliminate his particular selfhood, a futile procedure because man is an integral unity in his particularity and indeterminate freedom.

The philosophies which emphasize ontological categories, whether in naturalistic, idealistic, or mystical terms, in short, annul man in his undoubted historic existence. Man is primarily a historical creature. He plays his role against some ontological background, but his real milieu is history. History is a curious mixture ontologically, with elements of time and eternity in its composition. The validity of Christianity is inextricably bound up with the idea of the historical character of man. The preference of the "wise and prudent" for ontological religions represents the mind's abhorrence of the incredibilities of history. The Christian faith asserts about God that He is a person and that He has taken historical action to overcome the variance between man and God: "God was in Christ reconciling the world unto Himself." Both propositions are absurd from a strictly ontological standpoint. Ontology has persistent difficulty with the concept of God's personality. The concept of the person is loaded with connotations of finiteness and can therefore not be ascribed to God. Has not Bradley, *inter alia,* proved beyond peradventure that if God is "absolute" He cannot be a person? This philosophy involves itself in an absurdity in the effort to escape an absurdity; it defines God in terms of all kinds of " absolutes"; but its God lacks the simple majesty of the freedom which man undoubtedly has. May not this difficulty be due to the fact that the concept of "personality" is itself a rational absurdity? For we can define the structure of human personality and the freedom which rises indeterminately above structure; but we cannot find a system which will do justice to both structure and freedom.

The second affirmation asserts that God has taken historical action to heal the breach between man and God. This affirmation is just a little more absurd than the original diagnosis of the human situation, that man is at variance with God not by ontological fate but by historical guilt. There is no way of validating such a proposition philosophically, or of proving that in the ultimate personal encounter between man and God there can be forgiveness of sin and unburdening of the burden of guilt to a repentant heart. The only validation of such a proposition is the repentance and the new life which must obviously result from genuine repentance.

The whole of modern theology in its various aspects is involved in the effort to reduce the absurdity of the idea of God involved in history and taking action in historic terms. This is done by reducing the message of the Bible to "eternal principles" of ethics or of ontology. Thus Harnack characteristically defines the "essence of Christianity" as the affirmation of the "transcendent value of the individual" (a proposition which Christianity does not affirm but takes for granted) and the brotherhood of man in love (whereas Biblical faith derives the injunction that we love one another from the original historical affirmation that God, in Christ, loved us). In the desperate effort of the modern Christian to make his faith acceptable to the intellectual scruples of modern men, he reduces it to ontological absurdities or to ethical truisms. These also become absurd when, for instance, the love commandment is interpreted as a simple possibility by modern Christian moralism.

We are confronted with the fact, in other words, that man evidently is a historical creature and that any reduction of religion to ontological and non-historical proportions obviously denies or obscures some element or dimension of his complex nature. On the other hand, a religion of history and revelation in history is not acceptable to the "wise and prudent" of our generation. To judge from Christ's observation, it has not been acceptable to the wise of any generation. In this situation it would be foolish to predict some easy return to the faith by this generation even if the alternative faiths of modern secular liberalism and Marxism have proved to be erroneous and involved in incredible utopian illusions which are either dangerous or pathetic; while the only other alternative which seems available to the "wise and prudent" is a form of mysticism which annuls the meaning of history and runs counter to modern man's creative involvement in historical problems.

While Christian apologists cannot hope for too much success, it has become progressively clearer in my mind, since I wrote my several books, what line the apologetic venture of the Christian Church should take. I hope to follow out this line in the years of activity still allotted to me. We must make it clear that the concepts of both personality and history are ontologically ambiguous. Personality, whether God's or man's, is defined only in dramatic and historic encounter. Though these dramatic and historical media of personality are not inherently "irrational," they are not subject to the ordinary "scientific" tests of rational intelligibility. Nothing in history follows as it does in nature or reason, "in a necessary manner." The personality is bound by historical destiny rather than by natural or ontological necessity. The revelation of "God in Christ," for instance, is a force of destiny for the community of faith which has been gathered by that revelation: the Christian Church. The Church does not exist to propound eternal ethical truths, though it significantly regards the "love of Christ" as normative for human existence. But the truth in Christ cannot be speculatively established. It is established only as men encounter God, individually and collectively, after the pattern set by Christ's mediation. The creative consequences of such encounters, the humility and charity of true repentance, the absence of pride and pretension, must be the proofs that there has been an encounter with the only true God and not on the one hand with an idol of our own imagination who is invented to establish some interest of ours; and not on the other hand with a vast ocean of fullness and nothingness which condemns our individuality and particularity in a judgment in which the whole of history is also annulled. The encounter between God and man, as the encounters between men in history, must be by faith and love and not by the discovery of some common essence of reason or nature underlying individuals and particulars.

It is perhaps significant that among artists, dramatists, novelists, and poets, there have always been some who understood the Christian faith, while philosophers and scientists found it difficult to respect it intellectually. The former had an artistic understanding of the dramatic and historical which was less evident among the wise men who were prompted by nature and inclination to reduce all of life to its causalities and rational coherences.

In my opinion, a defense of the Christian faith as ultimately true must include a more generous and humble recognition than has been our wont of the falsehoods and corruptions which may use a final truth as their instrument in actual history. The liberal church has made one admission and sought to correct one traditional error of historic Christianity: its cultural obscurantism. In fact the liberal church has been so conscious of this error that it has been in danger of dissipating Christian truth in its effort to correct it.

The fact is that an obscurantist attitude toward the disciplines of science and philosophy and an irresponsible attitude toward the whole task of analyzing the various structures of existence, whether in geology, biology, astronomy, or any other realm of being, are a recurring evil in Christianity. Christian faith is still suffering from the obscurantist effort to guard its truths in an age of Darwinian science by defying the undisputed evidences which honorable and honest scientists have adduced. One still feels the force of Huxley's scorn against the dishonesties of the religious polemicists.

The obscurantism of historic faiths is aggravated by the fact that a type of religious orthodoxy betrays man's natural skepticism about the truths of love and faith, and also the natural human inclination to avoid a genuine encounter with God, by transmuting *Heilsgeschichte* into a series of miraculous events, miraculously attested, so that one need not appropriate them existentially, but merely claim some special knowledge of historical miracles. It is incidentally one of the minor trials of one who is engaged in a polemic against liberalism in theology to be described on occasion by ignoramuses, including even college presidents, as a "neo-fundamentalist." One cringes at such a description, for it shows that our culture knows of no distinctions short of the difference between the modern credo and a graceless and obscurantist version of Christian orthodoxy.

In addition to the obscurantist corruption, we must admit that there is no guarantee in any theology or form of worship that a community of faith, which intends to bring men into contact with the true God, may not be used for essentially idolatrous purposes. Men may use it to claim a special alliance with God against their foes. We must confess the significance of the long history of religious fanaticism, and must admit that a religion which has triumphed over idolatry in principle may in actual fact be made an instrument of partial and interested perspectives. Without such an admission the humility of a genuine scientist and the measured common sense of the man of affairs, who knows his ends to be in conflict with other legitimate ends, are superior to the wisdom of Christians.

There are other corruptions which must be more fully admitted. Christianity is, in principle, a religion of the spirit rather than of law. We are warned to "stand fast in the freedom with which Christ has set you free." St. Paul means that no meticulous obedience to specific moral standards can be a substitute for the self's encounter with God, in which the pretensions and the pride of the self are broken and it is set free of self and sin. But actually the excessive conventionality, the frantic respectability, and the devotion to the minutiae of propriety in historic Christianity stand in sharp contrast to the "love, joy, and peace" which characterize a genuine conversion. They sometimes compare unfavorably with the freedom of the best secular idealists.

In short, a genuine Christian apologetic must be prepared to bring the judgment of Christ to bear as rigorously on the household of faith as upon the secular and the pagan world, even as the prophets of Israel were as severe in mediating the divine judgment upon Israel as upon Babylon.

The statement of my present interests has already taken too much time in an account which was meant to chronicle my spiritual pilgrimage. I must close with an expression of gratitude to the many friends, unknown and known, who have helped me to come into a fuller knowledge of the "unsearchable riches of Christ," and by expressing the hope that I may still have time to correct the many inadequacies in my witness.

REINHOLD NIEBUHR

UNION THEOLOGICAL SEMINARY
NEW YORK CITY

II

ESSAYS OF INTERPRETATION AND CRITICISM OF THE WORK OF REINHOLD NIEBUHR

1

Richard Wightman Fox

WHO CAN BUT PROPHESY?—THE LIFE OF REINHOLD NIEBUHR

1

WHO CAN BUT PROPHESY?—THE LIFE OF REINHOLD NIEBUHR

It is a rare student in the 1980s who has heard of Reinhold Niebuhr. But from the 1920s to the 1950s he was the talk of many campuses across the country, an itinerant preacher who drew thousands to chapels that on other Sundays sat mostly empty. Of course Niebuhr was well-known to statesmen, politicians, labor activists, journalists, intellectuals, and to a trans-Atlantic reading public outside the university and the church. But his true forum was the college pulpit circuit, which he joined in the early 1920s thanks to Sherwood Eddy's encouragement and financial largesse. It was fitting that one of his last lengthy public talks, in his seventy-fifth year, was his 1967 address on Vietnam to Union Theological Seminary students, whom he held alternately in stitches and in rapt silence.

Niebuhr's unusual rapport with the young provides one important clue to his character. In his dealings with other people, whether great or ordinary, mature or fledgling, he was a pure democrat, incapable of condescension. The adulation of others genuinely embarrassed him. Those he found it hardest to stomach were the ones who put him on a pedestal. With students, especially those with earnest, pointed questions, he found himself thoroughly at home. Like him, they were oblivious to social form, and not given to polite acquiescence. Like him, they were uncynical, willing to believe that commitment mattered, eager to put their abundant energy to work.

That single word—energy—takes us closer than any other to an understanding of Niebuhr the person. The testimony of those who knew him is unanimous. None ever knew another remotely like him. Other vigorous, intense, charismatic preachers, political organizers, religious thinkers, or social critics crossed their paths, but "Reinie"—they shake their heads and smile—was different. It was not just that he managed to play all four of those roles instead of one or two of them. It was his utterly unique form of energy. He did not just radiate energy, like some tranquil sun; he pumped it out like a steaming, churning power plant. He was electric, incandescent, possessed. He was in perpetual motion, unable to rest.

Students in his office at Union Theological Seminary sat before a caged animal who paced with long strides through clouds of cigarette smoke from one corner to the other. He had to be up and about. Forty or more weekends a year, for more than a quarter-century, he bolted from one state to another, preaching at colleges, addressing student conferences, conferring at political meetings. His packed suitcase sometimes sat poised beside him in the classroom. A delayed train or airplane drove him to distraction. He constantly checked his watch. There might not be enough time.

No one who heard his sermons ever heard his equal. His imposing six-foot two-inch frame rocked, his arms gyrated feverishly, yet this was no pulpit act. He was the same out of the pulpit, in the classroom, at a political meeting. His face contorted, his shiny pate glowed, his hawk-nose thrust itself forward, seemingly on the verge of flight. His voice quaked with the force of his gospel message: now a faint whisper, his index finger to his lips; now a tentative query, his hands stroking the backs of his ears; now a thunderous tirade, his arms whirling. The pleasure of pronouncing the Word was at times so intense it was as much a form of pain. In later years the energy consumed by a single sermon left him limp, exhausted to the point of collapse.

One major problem that Niebuhr's biographer must confront is that in his maturity he was too busy, too driven, to pause for self-observation. Unlike his younger brother Helmut and older sister Hulda, he was not—despite his prolonged reflection upon the mystery of human selfhood—an introspective soul. Like his older brother Walter, the only one of the four children who did not follow their father into a professional religious career, he was a doer, a hustling man of the world. Perhaps his frantic style of life was chosen partly as a means of avoiding the personal probing that led both Helmut and Hulda at one time or another into deep depression.

In later life he showed little interest in mapping the course of his personal journey. Autobiography, he insisted repeatedly, was dishonest, pretentious, narcissistic. When one editor persuaded him in the 1950s to attempt a "Later Leaves," modelled after his earlier diary *Leaves from the Notebook of a Tamed Cynic* (1929), the plan fizzled: Niebuhr's brief manuscript was dull, meandering, and pocked with factual errors about himself. Even his "Intellectual Autobiography" written for the first edition of this volume is strikingly reticent about the personal formation, "family needs," and psychological predilections that lay behind his career choices and intellectual development. It is entirely fitting that the first four words of his essay are, "It is somewhat embarrassing."

"The first formative religious influence on my life was my father," Niebuhr wrote. But Gustav Niebuhr was much more than a "religious" influence. He was a commanding presence in whom Reinhold as a young boy caught a glimpse of the man he wished to be. When he was ten years old, in 1902, his father—who had just assumed a major pulpit in Lincoln, Illinois and the directorship of the town's modern hospital—asked him what he wanted to be when he grew up. "A preacher," Reinhold replied with no hesitation. Gustav asked him why. "Because," Reinhold replied, "it is the most interesting job I know of." A half-century later Niebuhr recalled the incident in an interview and explained that what he had really been thinking, but had not dared reveal, was that his father was the most interesting man he had encountered.

It was common knowledge among the other children in Lincoln that Reinhold was headed for the ministry. Florence Denger, a family friend slightly older than he, remembered him later "as a bright eager boy with a zest for life. His face was usually wreathed in smiles, he was a battery of energy, he was very popular with young and old alike in the church and he never left any doubt in anybody's mind that he would be a preacher. We all took it for granted." Unlike Helmut, Reinhold was not shy, withdrawn, or pensive. Nor was he always respectful of adults. "I remember when I was a guest in the Niebuhr home," Florence Denger recalled, "Reinie was imitating peculiarities of some member of the church. I laughed heartily, although I was old enough to know better. His mother frowned on this kind of thing but I noticed his father smiling slyly behind the book he was reading. Another time a crowd of young people went out to the Chautauqua on the closing day for a picnic. The session had just closed and the last speaker had been very pompous and over-developed in the stomach. Reinie, skinny fellow of about 13, got up on the platform, with all the pompousness of the speaker, walked back and forth with his stomach sticking out, used all the same pompous phrases until the rest of us were in stitches. He was always the life of the party wherever he was, but we all still knew he was going to be a preacher."[1]

It is scarcely surprising for a ten-year-old boy to be captivated by his father. Nor is it remarkable that he should have found his father the most interesting man in a small, central Illinois town with barely 10,000 residents. What is striking is that Niebuhr made a firm career decision before adolescence and before acquiring any experience of the outside world. It never occurred to him to doubt his chosen path. Unlike Walter, who rebelled against his father's worldview, and Helmut, who entered the ministry only after lengthy soul-searching, Reinhold pursued his goal with relentless determination. He was a compulsive worker even as a child; family friends constantly remarked that he had the same drive and inexhaustible energy as his father.

Gustav, for his part, could not hide his enthusiasm for this bright, spontaneous, but always disciplined child. His other children must certainly have suffered when Reinhold alone was brought, as an adolescent, into his father's study for confidential discussions about the future of his father's own ministry. "I have a very vivid memory," Niebuhr reminisced in 1953 "of the impression he made upon me in consulting me about whether or not he should accept a call to a church in another town." There is no doubt that Reinhold was the apple of his father's eye. In all likelihood Reinhold picked up subtle signals of his father's feelings about him even before adolescence, signals that led him inexorably to the selection of his father's calling. In a real sense he was the chosen son.[2]

In 1907, after completing the ninth grade at Lincoln High School, Niebuhr left for Elmhurst, the "pro-seminary" of the German Evangelical Synod of North America, where he spent three years specializing in extra-curricular activities. The teaching was so poor, the curriculum so antiquated, that Niebuhr's education suffered a serious setback. Elmhurst completely neglected the sciences, and

[1] Florence Denger to D. B. Robertson, January 28, 1959. Letter in possession of Robertson.

[2] *The Reminiscences of Reinhold Niebuhr* (New York: Columbia Oral History Research Office, 1972), p. 1.

gave English and modern history short shrift. Even the Latin instruction was abysmal, which infuriated the teen-aged Niebuhr since Elmhurst prided itself on its classics program. He proceeded to mount an effort to sack the Latin teacher, an effort which, thanks to his father's active support, met with success. But whatever organizational and political experience Elmhurst gave him, it "cheated me out of an education," as he later put it. Throughout his life he regretted his lack of scholarly training. As a genuinely self-taught thinker he was sometimes defensive about his poor preparation in so many subjects, about never having gone to college, and never even completing a general high school education. Sometimes his defensiveness expressed itself in enraged replies to public criticism of his writings; at other times, it was displayed in more temperate expressions of "embarrassment" at being taken as a "theologian," or as an "author," or as an "intellectual."

In 1910 Niebuhr began his three-year program at Eden Seminary, from which his father had graduated in 1885, four years after leaving Germany for the United States. Eden was still a heavily German institution, but since his father's day a single native-born American faculty member had been appointed. Professor Samuel Press, whom Niebuhr dwells upon with great feeling in his "intellectual biography," was the first member of the Eden faculty to teach his courses in English. Press was a powerful role model for an adolescent German-American who was acutely conscious of how incompletely acculturated he was. Press was living proof that one could be thoroughly American and attain a respected position within the Evangelical Synod, precisely the goal that Niebuhr had set.

In the spring of 1913, as he was preparing to graduate from Eden and looking forward to departing for graduate work at Yale in the fall, his father was stricken suddenly with an attack of diabetes and died a few days later. Gustav was only 50, and he left his widow Lydia, aged 43, with no continuing means of support. She had been a full-time parish assistant to him, as she had previously been to her own father, the Rev. Edward Hosto, another minister of the Evangelical Synod. Lydia was eager to have Reinhold proceed to Yale Divinity School for further study, but she was also determined to have him return to the Midwest thereafter to take up a pastorate. She made it clear that her own well-being depended upon taking up once again the work to which she was accustomed. This "family need," to which Niebuhr referred obliquely in his "intellectual autobiography," had a good deal to do with his lack of enthusiasm about pursuing the Ph.D., although it is not at all clear that Yale would have permitted him to continue after the M.A. Since his grades were not outstanding—perhaps because of his constant worry about his mother and about his finances in addition to his general lack of academic preparation—there was even some opposition in the Graduate School to offering him the M.A.

It was at Yale, where despite a modest scholarship he was quite poor, that Niebuhr first realized the financial potential of his writing. One of his course papers, "The Paradox of Patriotism," won the third prize of $200 in the student essay contest of the Carnegie Endowment for International Peace in 1915. One ten-page essay had earned him the equivalent of two or three months of a Synod minister's salary. From this point on Niebuhr never let his pen rest. For several years the torrent of articles was published for the most part in denominational organs, but occasionally he would receive both wider recognition and what seemed to him at the time to be big money—like the $60 from the *Atlantic* for "The Failure of German-Americanism" in 1916. Certainly Niebuhr's literary output stemmed primarily from his desire, or perhaps compulsion, to transmit a message, to influence his contemporaries inside and outside the church. But to understand both the enormous quantity and the specific character of his production—disproportionately short pieces, quickly produced and (when purchased at all) quickly paid for—one must grasp the fact that in his young adulthood, when his literary habits were formed, he was financially strapped and the main support for his mother.

It was also at Yale that Niebuhr made his initial, and very difficult, psychological move beyond the confines of the German Evangelical Synod. The Yale experience convinced him, if he was not already convinced before going east, that his preaching career would take him into the cosmopolitan, liberal Christian community. That was not a simple step for a young man who not only dependent upon the Synod for his future employment but was also linguistically and culturally on the boundary between German-America and Anglo-America. His letters from New Haven to Professor Press, to whom he turned for advice and fatherly encouragement, are poignant expressions of the transformation he was undergoing. On March 2, 1914, his first year at Yale, he wrote to Press about his academic difficulties, his financial problems, and his general feeling of inferiority. "I feel all the time like a mongrel among thoroughbreds and that's what I am," he lamented. He proceeded to reflect that he probably ought not to spend a second year at Yale, since "I am forgetting my German fast. Not because I don't read but because I never speak it. I'm afraid I won't have any German left by the end of next year." But then Niebuhr lets loose a whole reservoir of dammed-up feelings.

> But at that I've about made up my mind that I will have to do most of my work in English. I'm tired of this half-way business. . . . I've made up my mind that I must master one language to some degree at least. I can't master both and so I've cast my lot with the English. I have therefore applied myself to the English classics quite diligently lately. What do you think of my desertion?[3]

Niebuhr was crying out for Press to release him from his residual fear of abandoning his childhood world, his father's culture. He knew Press would provide that support, but he had to solicit it explicitly, in writing, to cross the psychological barrier.

It soon became clear that Niebuhr's decision "to cast my lot with the English" was a personal turning-point with momentous political and ecclesiastical consequences. When he arrived at Detroit's Bethel Evangelical Church in August, 1915, England and Germany had been at war for a year. Several of his first cousins and uncles, dozens of his more distant kin, were under arms in the Kaiser's forces. Along with his brother Walter, Reinhold was determined to help counter-balance all those Niebuhr forces on the German side. Walter left Lincoln to serve as a war correspondent in Europe, and later produced anti-German films for the government's Committee on Public Information. Reinhold did his part by pushing the cause of Americanization in the Evangelical Synod, and by branding as "unpatriotic" those Synod officials who were insufficiently zealous in dissociating themselves from Germany.

Niebuhr's first act as pastor at Bethel was to propose to the church council, at its meeting of September 7, 1915, that English services be held every week, not just every other week. The council accepted the suggestion, as it did his proposal a few months later that the church buy English hymnals. But despite the changes Niebuhr was dissatisfied with his lot at Bethel, as he disclosed to Professor Press in a letter of November 3, 1915. "Contrary to what

[3] Niebuhr Papers, Library of Congress, Washington, D.C.

I had been led to expect," he complained, "the congregation is three-fourths German so that after spending two extra years in English study I am forced to take a church more German than most of the Eden graduates get and have to throw all my ambitions of perfecting myself in English to the winds." His negative feelings about his parish extended to the Synod as a whole, which to his mind was hopelessly unAmerican and even unChristian on the war question. "The German propaganda is so hysterical among many of our ministers that largely by reaction I am getting to be a violent American patriot. . . . There is no real interest in the welfare of this country and no genuine American patriotism."[4]

As the war progressed, Niebuhr spent less and less time at Bethel. It was his mother's expertise at parish management that made his prolonged absences possible; it was the tedium of day-to-day parish work and his determination to bring about basic changes in the Synod that made his absences necessary. He wanted to abolish the use of German in the liturgy and to eliminate the word "German" from the Synod's name, causes that he trumpeted on his frequent speaking tours as secretary of the Synod's War Welfare Commission. By 1918 his correspondence with Synod officials had reached a shrill, vituperative pitch. "In both Elmhurst and Eden," he informed the Rev. John Baltzer, the Synod's President-General, "there is an attitude of sneering contempt for the American participation in the war. . . . As an American patriot it hurts me to hear young men of the second and third generation pour contempt on everything the nation does and is. . . . The faculties ought to have a word of warning not to discourage patriotism and inculcate disloyalty."[5] To the Rev. J. H. Horstmann, editor of the Synod's English-language *Evangelical Herald*, he wrote, "If you do not know I shall inform you that there are a large number of men in our church who are sincerely for America, for America so devotedly that they would gladly lay down their lives for her, and so thoroughly American in their viewpoint that your attempts to invest every issue with a subtle pro-German bias infuriates them."[6] Later in 1918 Niebuhr's efforts were rewarded when the leadership voted to eliminate the

[4] *Ibid.*

[5] April 26, 1918. War Welfare Commission Files, Eden Theological Seminary, Webster Groves, Mo.

[6] September 27, 1918, *Ibid.*

"German" in the Synod's name, and when Bethel, along with many other congregations, voted to eliminate the use of the German language.

The boundless zeal of both Reinhold and Walter for the American cause was much more than a political commitment. It was an anxious effort to achieve, to dramatize for themselves and for others, their firmly American identities. For the rest of his young adult life Reinhold would be quick to defend his loyalty to America. His persistent insecurity on the subject of nationality colored his personal and political relationships, as well as his ethical and theological judgments, for years to come. In particular, it made him hesitate before joining the legions of liberal Protestants who in the 1920s and early 1930s embraced the cause of pacifism. Even when, after his tour of Germany in 1923, he agreed to call himself a pacifist, there was a strong air of ambiguity about his commitment. In the deepest recess of his mind he continued to associate pacifism with disloyalty. He never overcame the sentiment to which he gave voice in his *Leaves from the Notebook of a Tamed Cynic* (a mysterious title apparently chosen not by Niebuhr but by the publisher): "I cannot bring myself to associate with the pacifists. Perhaps if I were not of German blood I could. That may be cowardly, but I do think that a new nation has a right to be pretty sensitive about its unity."[7] Likewise a young man who was psychologically a new "American" could be expected to be sensitive about his own feelings of nationality.

By the early 1920s the mature Niebuhr was quite recognizable: constantly on the road, captivating packed auditoriums of college students, producing reams of editorials and articles for the *Christian Century* (where his unsigned editorials began to appear in the fall of 1922) and other publications, pontificating on every subject from the cult of the automobile to the British tariff, garnering a national reputation as a peerless preacher. Charles Clayton Morrison, who opened the pages of his *Christian Century* to him, and Sherwood Eddy, the wealthy YMCA organizer who subsidized his lecture tours, share the credit for putting him prominently on the national liberal Protestant stage. They were only two of the many older men who, like Press before them, glimpsed the genius in Niebuhr, befriended him, and facilitated his entry into wider and wider worlds.

[7] Reinhold Niebuhr, *Leaves from the Notebook of a Tamed Cynic* [Chicago, 1929], Cleveland: Meridian Books, 1957, p. 32.

Ironically, Niebuhr was a significant and well-known figure in national Protestant circles before he was in Detroit itself. It was only after 1925 that his opposition to the Ku Klux Klan and to Henry Ford, his defense of the trade union movement, and his chairmanship of the Mayor's Inter-racial Committee put him squarely in the local public eye. At the same time, he began to take greater interest in Detroit, from which he had absented himself whenever possible during the previous decade. Having established himself as a national figure he could perhaps more easily spend time immersing himself in local issues. And as one who now labelled himself a "socialist," he wanted to grasp the realities of industrial capitalism at first hand. In Detroit the dynamics of capitalist expansion—exponential profits for the few, financial insecurity for the many—were clearly evident. Moreover, Bethel itself was no longer a small German-American parish; it was now a cosmopolitan, middle-class church of several hundred members in a large facility on a major Detroit boulevard. Its pastor was by definition a community force to be reckoned with.

Niebuhr's move in 1928 from Detroit to New York's Union Theological Seminary is usually interpreted as an inevitable step up from the provincial outback to the cosmopolitan nerve center of the nation, a natural jump for a man on his way to greater distinction. But from Niebuhr's standpoint at the time the decision was far from inevitable; he had great difficulty making up his mind. Not only was he beginning to exercise real influence in Detroit, but his mother had a secure existence there as his assistant. Leaving Detroit, he well knew, would break her heart. On the other hand, his finances were as usual in very poor shape. A professor's salary, though scarcely high, would improve on what he earned as a minister, and it would also allow more time to write and speak, including the entire summer. Still he could not decide. It was not until Sherwood Eddy—who had been trying for years to get him to move to New York where the YMCA had its headquarters—came up with an irresistible package deal that Niebuhr announced his readiness to pick up stakes.

Eddy and his YMCA associate Kirby Page had earlier made it clear to Niebuhr that he could come to New York as associate editor of the monthly *World Tomorrow*, a radical pacifist journal that Eddy was subsidizing and Page was editing. Niebuhr wanted badly to obtain that kind of literary outlet—a magazine in which he could write whatever he wished whenever he wished—but he could not support even himself, much less his mother, with such a position. Eddy then approached Henry Sloane Coffin, President of Union Theological Seminary, to see whether Harry Ward, Professor of Christian Ethics, could use a colleague in that field. Ward, himself a leftist, was delighted at the prospect of acquiring such a dynamic socialist clergyman, but Coffin assured Eddy that Union lacked the funds for such a slot. Eddy replied that money was no obstacle. Coffin, who had heard Niebuhr preach at student conferences in 1926 and 1927, had, like everyone else, been awed. He was the opposite of a leftist, but he was a shrewd judge of men and grasped immediately, as Morrison of the *Christian Century* had years before, what Niebuhr had to offer him. What Niebuhr offered was far more than a radical political perspective; it was an unparalleled capacity to inspire young minds and attract them to Union Theological Seminary.

Niebuhr claims in his "intellectual biography" that Eddy persuaded the seminary faculty to call him to a Chair of Christian Ethics, but he leaves out the important information that it was Eddy who paid his entire salary for the first two years. And it was Coffin who pushed the highly irregular appointment (not to a "Chair," but to a half-time associate professorship) through a contentious faculty meeting by one vote. Some faculty members, renowned scholars in their fields and in some cases elegant gentlemen of good breeding, were appalled at the prospect of this uncouth preacher with no scholarly credentials and a heavy midwestern accent joining their ranks. But Coffin, whose blood was as blue as anyone's, was committed to moving Union away from the emphasis on research and scholarship that his predecessor Arthur McGiffert had pursued. He knew that Niebuhr was the man to put preaching and the pastoral vocation on the map at Union. The prospect of half-time teaching at Union and half-time editing at the *World Tomorrow* persuaded Niebuhr that he could no longer avoid transplanting himself and his mother.

Coffin was right about Niebuhr's appeal to students, who immediately flocked to his side and took to addressing him, in a stark departure from Seminary tradition, as "Reinie." They surrounded him at dinner in the refectory and sat in circles around him in the common room afterwards, as he smoked, gesticulated, and held them spellbound with machine-gun commentary on the events of the day. What Coffin could not have anticipated was Niebuhr's growing commitment to the socialist cause. It was one thing for a professor of ethics to spout idealistic platitudes about a future society based on brotherhood. Coffin could put up with that. What he and several of the seminary's wealthy Presbyterian trustees had difficulty tolerating was Niebuhr's decision, after becoming a member of the Socialist Party in the fall of 1929, to run for the New York State Senate on the Socialist ticket in upper Manhattan in 1930.

Later Niebuhr would imply that he had been put on the ballot without his consent while on a trip to Europe, but contemporary evidence makes clear that he chose to run and campaigned hard. His showing was acceptable for a non-Presidential year. He got 1480 votes (4.5 percent) and the Party rewarded him with a prized place on its 1932 Congressional ticket. Again Niebuhr campaigned hard, both for himself and for other candidates on the ticket. He spoke at major mass rallies and harangued passers-by on windy street corners. It was a year of severe depression and the Socialists expected massive support and even a few victories. But Niebuhr's 3550 votes (4.4 percent) actually amounted to a decline of Socialist strength in Manhattan's 19th District; in 1930 the Socialist candidate received 4.8 percent in losing to the same Democrat, Sol Bloom, who beat Niebuhr. The result was an embarrassment for Niebuhr—who did not run again—and a severe disappointment for the party.

Niebuhr's poor showing shocked his Socialist friends, but it was nothing compared to the blow inflicted by the release the following month of his *Moral Man and Immoral Society*. Most of his Socialist friends, such as Norman Thomas, were liberal Protestant pacifists and contributors to or supporters of the *World Tomorrow*. *Moral Man* was a straightforward repudiation of the pacifism they represented; some of them took it as a personal betrayal which they could never forgive. With men such as Kirby Page, John Haynes Holmes, and Charles Clayton Morrison, who had been among his biggest boosters, his relations were never the same. The book was not just a departure from Niebuhr's own earlier ideas or from the liberal Protestant tradition, but an abrupt dismissal of the circle of colleagues he had cultivated since the early 1920s.

The combined effect of his electoral failure and his alienation from his former friends led Niebuhr to withdraw increasingly from Socialist activities. For a time he actually took a more radical turn; throughout 1933 he issued a series of "catastrophist" proclamations that led some readers to imagine he was on the road to Communism. His Taylor lectures at Yale in April, 1933, which formed the basis of *Reflections on the End of an Era* (1934), were explosive: he raged for three days about the decadence of American culture and predicted the immediate collapse of bourgeois civilization. But when *Reflections* appeared the following year it became clear that what had collapsed was not bourgeois civilization, but Niebuhr's own confidence about the adequacy of his radical vision. On one level his most radical book, it was on a deeper level an announcement that Niebuhr was searching for a more "conservative" religious faith that could supply a firm foundation for radical political action.

It was at this point, as Niebuhr began to reflect systematically upon his own political experience of the previous five years, that he became a religious thinker as such—even, despite his later, repeated disclaimers, a theologian. He had committed himself to a systematic inquiry into the "truth value" of Christian "myths," the central concern of his work from *An Interpretation of Christian Ethics* (1935) to *Beyond Tragedy* (1937) and *The Nature and Destiny of Man* (1941, 1943). He was not rejecting politics, not even radical politics. But he understood that to maintain his political commitment he needed a more secure philosophical and religious base. Gradually he came to realize what his brother Helmut (who now called himself Richard) had been telling him since the publication of *Moral Man*: he had rightly asserted that human society could never be transformed into perfect community, but he had not yet taken seriously enough the imperfectability of the human self and the radical transcendence of God. With the prodding of Richard—the only critic who could speak bluntly to Reinhold and be listened to—Niebuhr worked out his distinctive stance. Only a Judeo-Christian standpoint, he came to argue, could both spark commitment to working for justice in society and provide an ultimate perspective from which that commitment could be criticized. This resolution of his personal dilemma became the basis of the many-sided, frenzied career of his maturity; political activism (especially his chairmanship of the Union for Democratic Action, precursor of the A.D.A., and his leadership role in New York's Liberal Party), journalistic analysis of current events (his editorship of *Radical Religion, Christianity and Society*, and *Christianity and Crisis*), and philosophical and theological reflection upon the self and the dramas of history in his later books.

But the reckless abandon with which he pursued that career, his total neglect of his personal health, brought him at age 59 to an abrupt halt. Beginning in February, 1952 a series of small neurological attacks left him partially paralyzed in his left arm. But even more damaging, they left him with only a fraction of his former energy. He had never had a hobby, had never learned to relax or go on vacation; he had completely identified his life with his work. Now he was forced to sit still, to save his strength for the one or two hours a day when his body would respond to his still fiery will. Where before he tended to equate the Old Testament with the prophets (Amos was his favorite), he now had to grapple with Job. There could have been no greater test of his faith; at times the depression seemed overwhelming.

It was in that painful period that Niebuhr composed his "intellectual autobiography," and it is in the context of his struggle with an unwilling body that one critical passage of that essay must be read. The most personal section of the essay by far is not the opening three pages that pass briskly over his family and educational background, but his relating in classic New Testament fashion of a parable of "two old ladies" he had known at Bethel. Each of the women was facing death, but only one of them was confronting it with faith. The faithful old lady lived by "a broken spirit and a contrite heart"; she was a sign of "a mystery of grace which no one can fathom." Niebuhr was yearning for that serenity, praying for the capacity to "accept those things that cannot be changed," but he found it only occasionally. He frequently doubted whether he was capable of the faith in the face of adversity that marked the "true Christians," "the true but invisible Church" whose membership was known only to God.

Near the end he found a place of tranquility to which he gave expression in his frequent correspondence with his dearest friend, Bishop Will Scarlett, whom he had met during his first tour of Germany in 1923. The two old men buttressed their faith in God by voicing their gratitude for the precious things they had been given. Niebuhr repeatedly gave thanks for his wife Ursula, who had subordinated her own theological career to his, and nursed him continuously since 1952. And he thanked God for friends like Will, who was "full of grace." "We agreed," he wrote Will in 1968, "that neither of us feared death. I can only hope that if I go first you will say a prayer at my funeral, even though I cannot promise, because of increasing weakness, to return the mutual service of friendship. You have been a source of grace to all of us. The Lord be with you and with us my good friend, in this year and in the years to come."[8] On Friday, June 4, 1971, two days after Niebuhr's death, 87 year-old Will Scarlett drove alone from his home in Maine to the First Congregational Church in Stockbridge, Massachusetts to bid him farewell. He was unable to say a prayer himself at the memorial service, but he heard Rabbi Abraham Heschel express it for him and the other 200 mourners: "Revered, beloved Reinhold: In the words of the psalmist,

> You are the fairest of the sons of men,
> Grace is poured upon your lips
> Therefore God has blessed you forever.

RICHARD WIGHTMAN FOX

REED COLLEGE
PORTLAND, OREGON

[8] January 4, 1968, Niebuhr Papers.

2

Ronald Stone

THE CONTRIBUTION OF REINHOLD NIEBUHR TO THE LATE TWENTIETH CENTURY

2

THE CONTRIBUTION OF REINHOLD NIEBUHR TO THE LATE TWENTIETH CENTURY

REINHOLD Niebuhr Place is a two-block street in New York City running from Columbia University between Union Theological Seminary and Barnard College to the Inter-Church Center and Riverside Church. All these institutions felt the presence of Reinhold Niebuhr, but Union Theological Seminary has taken as its address Broadway at Reinhold Niebuhr Place. It was uniquely his place. He labored there on behalf of the church for four decades teaching Christian ethics. It was his basic community from which students, influenced by him, spread throughout the world. From there he wrote, founded voluntary associations for social action, and left to preach across the nation.

Although Niebuhr often castigated the church for an otherworldly mysticism neglecting the needs of people or for a sentimental activism neglecting the depths of the Christian faith, the church was his primary instrument of change. His essays and books sometimes were addressed to the intellectual despisers of religion, but often were addressed to the devout. He gained fame for his social wisdom, but his daily work was the preparation of ministers for their tasks.

His theology of the church was shaped by his Reformed-Lutheran heritage and the Congregational polity of the United Church of Christ and by his ecumenical commitments. Service for the Federal Council of Churches and its successor, the National Council of Churches, was matched by efforts to shape the World Council of Churches' social thought. His ecclesiology remained congregational and conciliar, leaving Roman Catholics and Episcopalians to doubt the seriousness of his ecclesiology. He understood the high claims for the church preferred by those in the Catholic traditions, but his own preference stayed closer to that of low-church polity. When asked about the social location of Reinhold Niebuhr, it is necessary to recall what he did. He taught ministers. This vocation is more important than class analysis in explaining his position. One could say he was a middle class intellectual, but first he had experienced the genteel poverty of the parsonage of his parents, and his social attitudes were established in his early ministry at Bethel Church in Detroit. The students he taught at Union were not anticipating lives of affluence, and Union's policy of paying all full professors equally meant that his own income was never at the level of the more prestigious pastors nor of the higher paid professors at wealthy universities. So while correlating his social thought with perspectives shaped by class analysis may inform an analysis of his thought, the commitment to theological scholarship for the equipping of the American churches is more fundamental to understanding his contribution.

The recognition of Niebuhr's primary work as a theological educator brings into perspective both his ministry at Bethel Church in Detroit (1915–1928) and his critique of American religion. At Bethel he learned of the inadequacies of his liberal theological education in dealing with social conflict, economic injustice, and international strife. During the rest of his life as a theological educator he labored to join Christian faith to a realistic analysis of people and society. This led him to criticize sharply the inadequacies of American spiritual life as one training seminarians to correct those deficiencies.

THE WEAKNESS OF AMERICAN RELIGION[1]

Niebuhr deplored the lack of vitality in American religious life, particularly his own Protestantism. His criticism of Roman Catholicism mellowed since the 1930s when Roman Catholicism made tragic political alliances in Europe. He welcomed the reforming spirit of the Second Vatican Council, but was not surprised when the curia delayed the implementation of reforms. Shortly before his death,[2] he noted particular signs of vitality in Dutch Roman Catholicism and urged American Catholics and Protestants to take note. His treatment of Judaism emphasized its rigorous re-

[1] Pages 4–29 are a contemporary editing of pages 219–240 of Ronald Stone, *Reinhold Niebuhr: Prophet to Politicians* (Nashville: Abingdon Press, 1972).

[2] Reinhold Niebuhr, "Toward New Intra-Christian Endeavors," *The Christian Century,* LXXXVI (December 31, 1969), 1622–67.

sponse to problems of social justice. Protestantism, however, was his inspiration and target of attack.

He confided that on Christmas Day in New York he liked to attend the Cathedral of St. John the Divine.[3] The liturgical services preserved the drama of the high holidays of the Christian year better than most preaching. His tendencies toward improving the worship of his own Protestantism were deepened by his marriage to Ursula Kempel-Compton in Winchester Cathedral.

He recorded the engaging dialogue between his Anglican wife and himself over the relative merits of Protestant preaching services and Anglican liturgical services. Ursula usually had the edge because of her background and greater interest in art and culture. Also, her interest in religion was more radically involved in acts of devotion than was his activist Protestantism. In an essay,[4] she reveals deep faith and rigorous scholarship, demanding that religion's strength be evaluated by its own intrinsic value. Reinhold would agree, but she would dismiss the pragmatic criteria quicker than he would.

Long before the recent liturgical renewal, he attacked the sentimentality and awkwardness of common patterns of worship. He enumerated some of his charges:

1. The pastoral prayer is both too long and too formless. . . .
2. Without the discipline of traditional and historic prayers there is a tendency to neglect some of the necessary and perennial themes of prayer. . . .
3. The language of the prayers of common worship is either too common, too sentimental, or too extravagant. . . .
4. The use of Biblical ideas in prayer is necessary not merely to purify the expressions but to correct the thought. . . .
5. The free worship tends to be too personal in every respect. . . .
6. The reading of the Scripture in Protestant worship leaves much to be desired. . . .
7. The participation of the congregation in the worship service is too minimal. . . .
8. Choir music in the nonliturgical churches and in some liturgical ones is still affected by the sentimentality which began to corrupt religious music in the latter part of the last century. . . .[5]

[3] D. B. Robertson, ed., *Applied Christianity*, p. 29.

[4] Ursula M. Niebuhr, "The Testing of Our Calling," in Martin Caldwell, ed., *Lift Up Your Hearts* (New York: Morehouse-Gorham Company, 1956), pp. 35–53.

[5] Robertson, ed., *Applied Christianity*, pp. 57–63.

Niebuhr often criticized American Protestantism for its disunity. He labored hard in the ecumenical movement, but felt that the Protestant churches seeking unity had delayed too long. In 1924 he criticized those who boasted of the churches moving together.

> The church has lost the chance of becoming the unifying element in our American society. It is not anticipating any facts. It is merely catching up very slowly to the new social facts created by economic and other forces. The American melting pot is doing its work. The churches merely represent various European cultures lost in the amalgam of American life and maintaining a separate existence only in religion.[6]

The major reason he wanted more unity among the churches was so that each tradition could borrow the elements of the fullness respective groups had preserved. The spectacle of competition among the denominations was a scandal. He rejected, however, arguments for unity based on notions of a united front against Catholicism or of more power and prestige.

He also criticized American churches for failing to provide moral leadership because spiritual vigor and social intelligence were missing in American Protestantism. People needed to be confronted with the ethic of love so that the essential selfishness and poverty of American life could be exposed. The church did not have to become a political agency, yet must be involved in the contentious issues of American common life. Reinhold Niebuhr was a true son of the Social Gospel movement. He articulated the relevance of the gospel to American social problems. In his writings on the churches' need for an adequate social ethic, his dual attitude of love for and critique of the church is most obvious. He was a Protestant clergyman with his whole heart, but delivered scathing criticisms of the church's failure to fulfill its ethical tasks. His book, *Man's Nature and His Communities* leveled its strongest criticism at the self-righteousness religious communities encouraged. Religious self-righteousness and strictly legalistic moral codes sealed off the gates of grace and vital ethical concerns. The ideal of humility was lost by the tendency to reinforce community mores. Instead of becoming a constant source of community renewal, religion had obscured the need for it.

[6] Niebuhr, *Leaves from the Notebook of a Tamed Cynic*, p. 90.

THE LIFE OF FAITH

Niebuhr's *The Nature and Destiny of Man* is a bold book which makes far-reaching claims for the truth of the Christian life. A contemporary reader of the book, however, is helped by reading two of Niebuhr's essays[7] on the role of myth and symbol in religious language. The essays make clear the roles of the disciplined religious imagination and the poet writing theological prose.

Faith does not mean belief for Niebuhr. It involves belief, but is more a state of trust that there is meaning in human existence and in one's own existence. The content of that meaning is perceived for Niebuhr through Christ as the symbol of a trust that one is forgiven and affirmed by the source of one's being. The contradictions of human life, dependent on standing simultaneouly in nature and history but refusing to be at home in either, cannot be overcome. However, they can be accepted and one can live in trust. The trust for Niebuhr (who stands in immense debt to Luther), is never secure in this life. One has faith and yet does not securely possess it. In thinking one has control of the situation through faith, one falls into spiritual pride.

Niebuhr lived since his illness in 1952 with an awareness of the radical contingency of his own life. For the last decade, his life and comfort depended on the sacrifice and love of his wife, whose ministering to his needs witnessed to human love at its best. Minor strokes reminded him regularly of the closeness of death. He talked with friends about his approaching death without fear while revealing impatience about his inability to contribute more to struggles for justice.

His inaugural address at Union in 1930 on the spiritual life of modern man[8] emphasized the incompleteness and confusion of modern life. Promethian technology contained within itself possibilities of evil as well as good, and to regard it as essentially self-correcting and beneficent was naive. Modern humanity's anxieties and illusions prepared it poorly for the crises of communal life. Niebuhr believed one needed faith in the essential purposefulness of life and in the forgiveness of failures. The faith could not

[7] "Faith as the Sense of Meaning in Human Existence" and "The Truth in Myths," in Ronald Stone, ed., *Faith and Politics*, pp. 3–31.

[8] *Ibid.*, pp. 67–76.

be in outworn creeds but on a restatement of the symbolic affirmations of Christian faith.

An adequate restatement of Christian faith for Niebuhr combined poetry and moral insight. Our moral efforts depend upon our convictions that they are not irrelevant to the deeper purposes of life. Expressions of the purposes of life are better stated in poetry or Biblical metaphors. Philosophy, for Niebuhr, has its place and needs to be combined with the imagination of the poets and prophets to discipline their insights.[9] Vital religion depends upon its ethical rigor, and religion properly interpreted furnishes a basis of hope for moral heroism.

Religious faith frees people to accept the finiteness of their lives, but still to live with a sense of basic trust. It promotes concern for the well-being of the neighbor which, when defined in terms of love, has no arbitrary limits. It provides a theological pattern for thinking about humanity and society. Faith is incomplete and cannot claim to possess that sureness of life and meaning which is beyond history. The life of faith cannot be validated; it can only be lived. The quality of the life is the ultimate test, but no Christian can claim righteousness without becoming self-righteous. Close to the center of the life of faith is a humility which cannot, by its nature, be claimed as evidence for the truth of the faith. A cautious, careful New Testament scholar remarked to a former student, "If I had the power to canonize only one Christian, I would make Reinhold Niebuhr a saint. He is a grace-filled man."[10]

GOD AS THE SYMBOL OF ULTIMATE MYSTERY AND MEANING

Niebuhr often uses the term *God* in his writing. But, beyond asserting that God is the creator, redeemer, and judge known most clearly through Jesus Christ, he is not precise about what he means by the term. The infrequency of rigorous discussions of God in his hundreds of articles and over a score of books is striking. Similarly, there is no adequate writing by others of his thought on God. This volume, for example, also did not include an essay on his doctrine

[9] *Ibid.*, p. 73.

[10] W. D. Davies, a remark made at the Pittsburgh Festival of the Gospels, April 10, 1970.

of God.[11] The paucity of analysis reflects Niebuhr's refusal to equate God with rational structures of thought. His emphasis on the freedom and person of God encouraged him not to develop a doctrine of God. God, as doctrine, was outside his usual frame of reference.

Niebuhr's attack on the death of God theologians in 1966 reveals the essential meaning of God to him.[12] He objected to their failure to suggest viable alternative schemes of meaning for the symbols they were asserting had died and suspected they were attacking literal readings of symbolic assertions. Such attacks were beside the point. In Niebuhr's opinion, their misuse of Tillich said more clearly that Tillich had died than that God had. Niebuhr pointed out that the Tillich to whom Thomas J. Altizer and William Hamilton had dedicated their book[13] had insisted that all propositions, either affirmative or negative, about God's existence were irrelevant. God was not subject to the categories of existence.[14] Niebuhr asserted that there was a realm of mystery which secularism could not express. Also there was, as people of faith knew instinctively, a universe with an order and a purpose. The concept of God expressed better than any alternative way of speaking both the mystery and the meaning. He wrote:

> The very word *God* represents both the unknowable "X" of mystery and the fullness of meaning—perhaps the "God the Father Almighty, Maker of heaven and earth" of the Christian creed and the "King of the world" of Jewish faith. . . .[15]

Niebuhr often returned to Alfred N. Whitehead's model of God as the principle of creation as a way of speaking about God's creative role. He regarded Whitehead as stating metaphysically what the person of faith knew intuitively about the dependence of the world upon God, but did not enter into the metaphysical subtleties of the issue. It was enough to have a unity of mystery and meaning in particular entities. Niebuhr's interests were not in metaphysical arguments but in human problems. However, inas-

[11] Charles W. Kegley and Robert W. Bretall, eds., *Reinhold Niebuhr*. (New York: The Macmillan Company, 1956).

[12] Stone, ed., *Faith and Politics*, pp. 3–13.

[13] Thomas J. Altizer and William Hamilton, *Radical Theology and the Death of God* (New York: Bobbs-Merrill, 1966).

[14] Stone, ed., *Faith and Politics*, p. 4.

[15] *Ibid.*, p. 5.

much as one's thoughts and illusions about the gods are important human problems, scholars interested in Niebuhr will puzzle over this deficiency.

God, for Niebuhr, remains the hidden God. "He is *Deus Absconditus*."[16] The divine cannot be reduced to the categories of a particular philosophy or doctrine. God is radically different from all expectations and interpretations. Yet, the covenants, laws, prophets, psalmists, and, ultimately, Christ indicate God's graciousness and purposes for humanity.

Niebuhr uses the word *God* in different ways in his preaching and teaching, tending to use it as a symbol rather loosely. Like the Old and New Testaments, he did not analyze language about God but related his faith in God to perplexing issues of human justice, meaning in history, and human suffering. The three motifs of God's action most meaningful to Niebuhr were creation, judgment, and redemption.

The role of God as creator is important as humanity is ultimately dependent upon God. An individual cannot complete oneself and all human experience contains an overtone of the dependence upon God. Here, Niebuhr reveals his continuity with Schleiermacher. He understands this human experience as that which Schleiermacher named "unqualified dependence" (*schlechthinnige Abhängigkeit*).[17]

Pointing to the redemptive work of God in human life was the primary task of the church. In an address prepared for the World Council of Churches' Assembly in Evanston, Illinois in 1954, he wrote,

> It is in the light of this overwhelming testimony in history to this truth, first discerned by the prophets and then conclusively proved in Christ's revelation, that we insist that the church's duty is to point to God, our creator, judge and redeemer, as the source of our peace, rather than to any human virtue or power.[18]

Before being understood as redeemer, however, God must be known as judge. Niebuhr holds that people generally have an experience of being judged from beyond themselves, a more ultimate judgment. Biblical faith presupposes this sense of judgment

[16] Niebuhr, *Faith and History*, p. 103.
[17] Niebuhr, *Nature and Destiny*, I, 128.
[18] Reinhold Niebuhr, "Our Dependence Is on God," *The Christian Century*, LXXI (September 1, 1954), 1034.

dependent on a transcendent God. God as the standard of universal judgment beyond any particular human understanding of moral law is exceedingly important to Niebuhr. There is a standard beyond human standards. The sense of moral rigor in Niebuhr's thought is so strong because he firmly believes that human morality is an approximation of God's will. Finally, moral standards are rooted in a sense of ultimate concern. God is not only the one upon whom we depend, but also is the troubler of our consciences.

There are intimations of God as creator, judge, and redeemer in human experience, filled out for Niebuhr in qualities of biblical neoreformation theology. His own confidence in God was seldom if ever shaken. His quoting of John Baillie on the reality of God applies to his own life:

> "No matter how far back I go, no matter by what effort of memory I attempt to reach the virgin soil of childish innocence, I cannot get back to an atheistic mentality. As little can I reach a day when I was conscious of myself but not of God as I can reach a day when I was conscious of myself but not of other human beings." *Our Knowledge of God*, p. 4.[19]

God is a hypothesis without which Niebuhr's analysis of the human condition is inadequate. God is the symbol of unity, purpose, moral seriousness, and graciousness as being constitutive of reality itself. Only in God are the ideal and the real united. From a sense of the presence of God came Niebuhr's freedom to analyze the situation in the world so powerfully.

THE RELEVANCE OF THE SOCIAL ETHIC

Reinhold Niebuhr's thought and action affected American religion and politics significantly. Scholars in both disciplines take his thought seriously, and have admitted the impact of his life on their work. Still, the relationship of his Christian faith to his practical politics has remained a puzzle to some. The most direct connection between faith and politics for him is social ethics. Social ethics for Niebuhr is research and teaching that relates theology to the disciplines of the social sciences and religion to the problems of community life.

Social ethics depends upon theology for its sense of meaning in history and for its conception of the deeper dimensions of life. It relates these theological insights to the questions raised by political

[19] Quoted in Niebuhr, *Nature and Destiny*, I, 127.

science or sociology. When pushed as to the exact connection between his faith and his political philosophy, he replied:

> I would say that man's collective life is related to his stature as a human being. This stature is best grasped by the spirit of true humanism, which in the phrase of my friend Jacques Maritain means a humanism in which the human spirit transcends nature and history. In that sense a religious viewpoint is relevant to all the moral problems of the individual and of society.[20]

How relevant is Niebuhr's social ethic to contemporary life? Niebuhr regarded *relevance* as adequacy to inform and to fortify one about contemporary problems as a test of any social philosophy or theology. Scholars agree his thought was relevant to the problems of the 1930s, 1940s, and 1950s. Even a historian as critical of Niebuhr as Walter LaFeber admits his influence:

> Not since Jonathan Edwards' day of the 1740's had an American theologian so affected his society and, like Edwards, Niebuhr emphasized the role of sin and sinful power in that society.[21]

During the 1960s he was counselor to students, faculty, and statesmen. He was honored by the Presidential Medal of Freedom in 1964 and a banquet at which Vice President Hubert Humphrey called Niebuhr the most influential preacher of his time. But, is Niebuhr's thought relevant to the late twentieth century?

LOVE AND JUSTICE

The key to understanding Niebuhr's ethic is the dialectical relationship between love and justice. Love, for Niebuhr, is the way people would live together if they were not selfish and sought to fulfill the greatest good for their neighbor. Love is an outgoing acceptance of the other and a seeking of the other's good. The model of love is the ethic of Jesus. We live under two commandments: to love God and to love the neighbor. The love for God is more an act of adoration and trust, while the love for neighbor is to treat the other as one would have oneself treated. For Niebuhr, love is the motive for social action and the greatest state of mutuality between two people or among those of a group.

[20] Ronald Stone, "An Interview with Reinhold Niebuhr," *Christianity and Crisis*, XXIX (March 17, 1969), p. 52.

[21] Walter LaFeber, *America, Russia, and the Cold War, 1945–1966* (New York: John Wiley and Sons, 1967), p. 40.

God's justice or the perfect state of justice would not differ greatly from love. However, justice for Niebuhr usually refers to a state of harmony among people in which the values of freedom and equality are fulfilled to the degree possible under the given conditions. Justice depends upon the interests and the capacity of individuals and groups to agree on a tolerable solution to their inevitable conflicts. Justice refers to the agreed-upon rules for settling conflicts and to the more ideal, transcendent standards.

Love refers to the possibilities for human mutuality always relevant to any social situation as inspiration and critique. Justice refers to the degree of love that can be achieved under the pressures of conflicting interests among those who pursue their own advantage at the cost of the greater social good. Love motivates the search for justice, and in history love reaches further than justice. Love cannot be substituted for justice in society, for people need rules to maintain community life. Justice at its best utilizes power to enforce its judgments for the social welfare of all; love at its best is willing to sacrifice the self for the other.

Niebuhr mines Western philosophical traditions so that principles of social wisdom can be reformulated for contemporary life. Niebuhr rejects the notion that there are reliable laws to furnish universal and eternal ideals for human society. Scripture, reason, and nature do not provide universally valid concepts of justice for all time. Humanity, in its freedom, changes its communities and itself. The double love commandment presupposes this freedom, but particular formulations of principles of justice reveal the particular historical contingencies of the formulators and must be revised in each new era. Of course, there is wisdom in the natural law traditions. Humanity continues to transform its present societies by reference to new standards beyond present societies. However, one is not free to escape historical contingencies by reference to an eternal natural law. What were claimed as natural laws were human and historical products.

As with truth, humanity both has justice and cannot grasp it. If justice is the harmony which preserves the vitalities of the participants or the approximation of full human community under the conditions of sin, it is a transforming process which ought not be halted. Humanity from time to time possesses a tolerable degree of justice, but it criticizes the tolerable settlement and moves toward a fuller community.

Because justice implies a balance or a harmony, it is not found without order in society. An order may be unjust if it maximizes force to gain consent to its existence. Most orders imply some approximation of justice; justice implies order. In Western democratic society, the principles relevant to a just order are primarily liberty, equality, and tolerance.[22] The three principles, in Niebuhr's understanding, complement one another.

The understanding of justice not only as an ideal but finally as a harmony reinforced by a balance of power relates Niebuhr's ethic directly to politics. In a society in which the important decisions are made through political action, to pursue justice means to engage in politics. The struggle for justice is the struggle for power, in part. Justice without power is a vague ideal; power without justice is either chaos or tyranny. Given Niebuhr's understanding, politics is not strange ground for a Protestant social moralist; rather, it is his proper field of study.

Since his acceptance of the New Deal, Niebuhr's social ethic has been articulated in terms relevant to the American political process. He did not advocate a displacement of that system, though he often severely criticized it. He regarded most revolutionary rhetoric as irrelevant to the hard choices confronting the American public, but his social ethic does not eliminate the possibility of sanctioning revolution. He did not oppose revolutionary movements throughout the world, and some contemporary theologians of revolution have found Niebuhr's thought helpful in Latin America.[23] His ethic is controlled by love, and so concrete human needs and lives take priority over conceptual schemes for a new society.

His thought most consistently is revolutionary Calvinism. He believed seventeenth-century Calvinism, particularly when mixed with sectarian radicalism, produced the greatest social fruits of Protestantism's history.

> Perhaps the most impressive social ethic of the churches of the Reformation was that which developed in seventeenth-century Calvinism.

[22] Niebuhr usually writes of two regulative principles including only liberty and equality. This is true because during much of his career it seemed as if the struggle for tolerance had been won. The writing in *Nature and Destiny*, II, 220–43, places tolerance in the center of his thought and reinforces the view that it deserves a place with liberty and equality as a regulative principle.

[23] E.g., "Niebuhr's writings made such a profound impression on me and proved so valuable in my work in Latin America." Richard Shaull, "Christian Realism: A Symposium," *Christianity and Crisis*, XXVIII (August 5, 1968), 177.

This form of Calvinism revealed itself in the struggles with Catholic princes in Scotland and Holland and in the Cromwellian revolution in England. It laid the foundations for a free society and for toleration in the religious sphere, without which a modern pluralistic national community would not be possible. . . . It is the only form of Protestant social ethic which I find congenial to present perplexities.[24]

Love is expressed socially through justice evaluated in terms of pragmatic calculation. His bias is toward thorough change, as no situation perfectly embodies justice and we continually reach for better communities. However, the reaching for fuller justice is resisted. The choice of tactics for achieving justice where justice is resisted is a pragmatic or prudential affair which grounds its politics (but not its goals) on what is possible.

HOPE AND SOCIAL ETHICS

The question of whether Niebuhr was overly pessimistic arose afresh in the late 1960s with the emergence of the theology of hope. Jürgen Moltmann argues that there is hope beyond our powers, expressing a radical trust in the Easter faith. God can create a new future out of the abyss.[25] Rubem A. Alves, a Brazilian, hints that the problem with Niebuhr's thought is that it is too anthropological and does not trust enough in the "messianic thrust of God's activity."[26] Further development of his argument can be anticipated. Harvey Cox's *The Secular City* and his *Feast of Fools*[27] glorify optimism. The latter argues for the projecting of models of utopian thought while the former was an example of utopian writing itself.

In a symposium on Christian realism held in 1968, those most eager to move beyond Niebuhr to new forms of political imagination and more hopeful attitudes toward social life included Tom Driver, Richard Shaull, and Harvey Cox. All felt that realist analysis promoted despair or defeatism. Ironically, in 1968, Niebuhr as an old man kept fighting for what he believed to be the best political

[24] Reinhold Niebuhr, "The Problem of a Protestant Social Ethic," *Union Seminary Quarterly Review*, XV (November, 1959), 5.

[25] Jürgen Moltmann, *Theology of Hope* (New York: Harper & Row, 1967), and *Religion, Revolution and the Future* (New York: Charles Scribner's Sons, 1969).

[26] Rubem A. Alves, *A Theology of Human Hope* (Washington: Corpus Books, 1969), p. 181.

[27] Harvey Cox, *The Secular City* (New York: The Macmillan Company, 1965), and *The Feast of Fools* (Cambridge: Harvard University Press, 1969).

choice available to the country long after some of the more youthful hopeful theologians had despaired. Committed to Eugene McCarthy early in the campaign, after the Chicago convention he supported his old liberal ally, Hubert Humphrey. Many of the younger liberal theologians could not distinguish sufficiently between Richard Nixon and Hubert Humphrey to participate actively in the election. It is too early to mediate a debate between Reinhold Niebuhr and the theologians of hope. The questions, however, cause a renewed interest in what Niebuhr said about the possibilities of renewal of human community. A picture of Niebuhr's reflections on hope within man's social life can be seen in an early 1930s debate with his brother, *The Nature and Destiny of Man* and Niebuhr's commitment to social action.

Niebuhr's major hope was in a fulfillment beyond history. Human history, by definition, would remain fragmentary and incomplete. The problem of the hopefulness of history became an issue between Reinhold and his brother H. Richard, and they debated the issue in the pages of *The Christian Century*.[28] In 1932, Reinhold was more inclined to urge the United States to an activist role regarding Japan's aggression than was H. Richard. Beneath their political disagreements were several theological issues. The Niebuhr brothers were sometimes unable to interpret accurately each other's thought, and the exchange in *The Christian Century* reveals several misunderstandings. H. Richard's criticism of Reinhold's view of history as tragic was, however, justified. Reinhold had written: "To say all this is really to confess that the history of mankind is a perennial tragedy; . . ."[29] H. Richard replied:

> History is not a perennial tragedy but a road to fulfillment and that fulfillment requires the tragic outcome of every self-assertion, for it is a fulfillment which can only be designated as love. . . .
>
> For my brother, God is outside the historical processes. . . . But God, I believe, is always in history.[30]

[28] H. Richard Niebuhr, "The Grace of Doing Nothing," *The Christian Century,* XLIX (March 23, 1932), 378–80; Reinhold Niebuhr, "Must We Do Nothing?" *The Christian Century,* XLIX (March 30, 1932), 415–17; H. Richard Niebuhr, "The Only Way into the Kingdom of God," *The Christian Century,* XLIX (April 6, 1932), 447.

[29] *Ibid.,* p. 417.

[30] *Ibid.,* p. 447.

He understood his brother's position as being more idealistic and, consequently, regarding the reality of history as being tragic. He understood himself to be a "bit pantheistic" with more of a hope in the divine creative process and a better future emerging out of the present.

Reinhold Niebuhr's view of history mellowed with time; the categories of irony were substituted for the emphasis upon tragedy. Both Niebuhr brothers had hope. Reinhold's hope, however, was more inclined to be a fulfillment beyond history. In his address prepared for the World Council of Churches at Evanston he returned again and again to hope. The hope is not in the divine creative process, or the newly emerging order, or man's involvement in shaping his destiny. The hope is in God's triumph at the end of history. He wrote:

> Therefore we are saved, not by what we can do, but by the hope that the Lord of history will bring this mysterious drama to a conclusion, that the suffering Christ will in the end be the triumphant Lord.[31]

Reinhold labored with tremendous strength and determination for numerous political and social causes. If H. Richard had greater hope for society, still Reinhold labored more realistically within the given political alternatives to improve society. Love rather than hope was the major motivation for his action.

Examining *The Nature and Destiny of Man* indicates that the claims of the theologians of hope do not add much substance to Niebuhr's model. Rewriting the second volume during World War II, he wrote:

> The new world must be built by resolute men who "when hope is dead will hope by faith"; who will neither seek premature escape from the guilt of history, nor yet call the evil, which taints all their achievements, good. . . . History moves towards the realization of the Kingdom but yet the judgment of God is upon every new realization.[32]

The central purpose of the philosophy of history he presented was to unite Renaissance and Reformation insights. He regarded the Reformation pessimism about historical possibilities as extreme. Reformation pessimism needed to be corrected with valid insights of Renaissance optimism like the following:

[31] Niebuhr, "Our Dependence Is on God," *The Christian Century,* XXXV (September 1, 1954), 1037.

[32] Niebuhr, *Nature and Destiny,* II, 285–86.

> Life in history must be recognized as filled with indeterminate possibilities. There is no individual or interior spiritual situation, no cultural or scientific task, and no social or political problem in which men do not face new possibilities of the good and the obligation to realize them.[33]

On the other hand, the Reformation understanding that history did not complete itself also needed to be protected.

His attack was leveled against a sentimental optimism of a relatively untroubled bourgeois culture. The attack strikes readers sobered by events as realistic. Faithfulness to his writings forces interpreters of Niebuhr to note passages like the following:

> There is no limit to either sanctification in individual life, or social perfection in collective life, or to the discovery of truth in cultural life; except of course the one limit, that there will be some corruption, as well as deficiency, of virtue and truth on the new level of achievement.[34]

The structure of the first volume of *The Nature and Destiny of Man* suggests a point of criticism on this issue. In a theological understanding of humanity, the concept of original righteousness is as important as the concept of original sin. Only a dialectical relationship of the two can adequately express the dynamic of the Christian view of self if either symbol is used. The first thing a theologian should say about humanity concerns original righteousness. Niebuhr reversed the order. The three chapters in the volume on the doctrine of sin have received most attention. Given Niebuhr's assumptions about too easy a conscience of the contemporary he was addressing, the emphasis made sense. Forty years later, a guilt-ridden and despairing generation finds an overemphasis upon sin and needs the dialectic changed by a prior emphasis upon creative possibilities.

Feminist critique of his doctrine of sin shows that the emphasis in his work was drawn from the experience of the assertiveness of the male-dominated culture of the mid-twentieth century. Pride was a primary expression of unbelief in the political actors he focused on and in the religious and political movements of the twentieth century. But from an interpretation of women's experience, the will to power and egoistic self is not a universal experience. In fact the self that does not dare to develop itself is more

[33] *Ibid.*, p. 207.
[34] *Ibid.*, p. 156.

characteristic of sin in women argues Judith Plaskow.[35] Her point that a theology of human nature will have to take fuller account of feminine experience than Reinhold Niebuhr's did is sound.

Niebuhr's work was to help Protestants and others engage in action for a more just society. His participation in and commitment to the process of social action imply, as his writings confirm, that society could be meaningfully improved. There were no given limits on what humanity could accomplish except that people would not eliminate their creative and corrupting egoistic drives. Social action requires hope but Niebuhr resisted illusory hopes. Between illusion and despair was a hope-filled reading of events in which to engage oneself. The discipline of social ethics implies hope, though it does not commit one to the boundless optimism of the Social Gospel. The movement of social ethics from the way things are to the way they ought to be implies hope and action. Niebuhr refuses to close the future. However, no utopian schemes can seal humanity off from continuing to realize and to violate dreams for human community.

RACE RELATIONS: AMERICAN DILEMMA

Niebuhr worked in the struggle for the rights of black Americans throughout his ministry. His analysis accepted the stubbornness of white Americans to surrender privilege, and he saw the roots of racial prejudice in the foundational sin of pride. Grace and experience could overcome prejudice in individuals, but social reorganization was necessary to eliminate the structured expressions of sin in the society. Five examples of his dealing with the malignance of racial pride reveal the essential outlines of his response to the issue and suggest ongoing strategies for the late twentieth century.

RACE RELATIONS IN DETROIT[36]

Racial conflict broke out in the streets of Detroit in 1925. Black immigration from the South had increased the population from 10,000 at the end of World War I to 80,000 in 1925, and the massive migrations still lay ahead.

[35] Judith Plaskow, *Sex, Sin and Grace: Women's Experience and the Theologies of Reinhold Niebuhr and Paul Tillich* (Washington, DC: University Press of America, Inc., 1980).

[36] Pages 30–33 are a contemporary editing of pages 31–34 of Stone, *op. cit.*

Niebuhr accepted the chairmanship of the Mayor's Race Committee despite the complaint from some of his fellow pastors that a Christian minister should not cooperate with a mayor with such a shady political record. The vice-chairman of the group was Bishop William T. Vernon of the African Methodist Episcopal Church. The committee included lawyers, representatives from Ford Motor Company, physicians, and other leaders in Detroit. Fred M. Butzel provided much of the leadership of the committee and became a lifelong friend of Niebuhr. Niebuhr often used Butzel as an example of the vitalities of prophetic Judaism.

The committee was one of many twentieth-century race relations committees unable to translate its findings into needed reforms. The committee did, however, base its recommendations on a study by the Detroit Bureau of Governmental Research, and its findings in 1926 were farsighted. It called for the creation of a permanent race commission to combat prejudice through education and through the exercise of control over public agencies. The report also called for several immediate changes in practice in the municipal government, business, education, welfare agencies, recreational opportunities, and in real estate practice.

The report of the committee reveals at places a note of paternalism toward blacks; it recommends a plan of education to help them keep their neighborhoods in attractive condition. That recommendation was followed by, "A similar emphasis upon the personal appearance and demeanor of colored people and their children is equally desirable."[37] Probably some conservative on the committee insisted on that sentence, but it is strange to see it in a report of a committee Niebuhr chaired. On the other hand, attitudes toward race have changed abruptly in the last few years, and some of Niebuhr's own writing on race is almost as badly dated. In a 1944 book he suggested the need to give blacks full credit for their native abilities and specifically mentioned only "artistic gifts."[38] The report also failed to wrestle significantly with white ownership of black slum housing.

The committee faced forthrightly the racism in the police depart-

[37] *Report of the Mayor's Committee on Race Relations* (Detroit, 1926), p. 4.

[38] Reinhold Niebuhr, *The Children of Light and the Children of Darkness*, p. 141.

ment and called for the immediate transfer from black[39] neighborhoods of prejudiced police and for intensive efforts to hire more Negro police. Most of the public services to the Negroes were found to be inadequate and recommendations for changes were made.[40]

In industry, discrimination by employers and unions was reported, but the committee trusted to the example of the success of nondiscriminatory employers and unions for the promotion of change. Employers were urged to hire more blacks and to promote them, but the lead sentence of that section of the report set the tone: "The progress of the Negro in the industrial life of the city, following the large migrations since the war, has been most creditable."[41]

The committee studied the churches and recommended several actions: (1) the Negro churches should organize an interdenominational organization; (2) the interdenominational agency should combat "irresponsible religious organizations which enjoy a mushroom growth in the city";[42] (3) white churches should help Negro churches financially. The recommendations on the churches were confined to bureaucratic details of only incidental significance to Detroit. In a 1957 address to graduating seniors at Union, Niebuhr castigated the church for being slower than the state in desegregation.

The report by 1982 standards was very mild and innocuous. It did, however, put an official voice of criticism against most of the structures of Detroit. Its proposals for reform were stronger than Detroit in 1926 was willing to put into effect. The report reveals the mind of a representative group of the Detroit establishment more clearly than the particular convictions of its chairman.

MORAL MAN AND IMMORAL SOCIETY

The oppression of the black American illustrated the thesis of Niebuhr's 1932 book very well. Race commissions like the one he had chaired in Detroit did not touch the basis of economic and political disfranchisement. Structured inequality reigned.

[39] The committee did not use the terms black or racism which have meanings in 1982 which were unknown to the committee in 1926.

[40] *Report of the Mayor's Committee*, p. 15.

[41] *Ibid.*, p. 13.

[42] *Ibid.*, p. 14.

If the black race waited for the moral maturity of the white race to grant them human rights they would wait forever. He wrote:

> The white race in America will not admit the Negro to equal rights if it is not forced to do so. Upon that point one may speak with a dogmatism which all history justifies.[43]

He found Gandhi's strategies of nonviolent coercion suggestive. Violent rebellion by an outnumbered and outarmed minority was hopeless. But the spiritual solvent of nonviolent coercion could, he thought, reduce the brutal response of the white majority. A combination of moral and economic pressures had advantages in winning the place of human dignity that the nation confessed it prized for all. Social ignorance and economic self-interest were against change to improve the situation of the blacks, but the tactics of nonviolent coercion showed promise for the American situation. He wrote prophetically in 1932:

> The emancipation of the Negro race in America probably waits upon the adequate development of this kind of social and political strategy.[44]

Urging boycotts against banks, stores, public service corporations which practiced discrimination, he also suggested nonpayment of taxes in states which discriminated against black education.

Religion could make a great contribution to the development of nonviolent resistance. Here the religious convictions of the common humanity of oppressed and oppressor could create attitudes which would reduce cruelty. Attitudes of repentance could be nurtured by religion, and community across social conflict could be seen by religiously informed imaginations.

> One waits for such a campaign with all the more reason and hope because the peculiar gifts of the Negro endow him with the capacity to conduct it successfully. He would need only to fuse the aggressiveness of the new and young Negro with the patience and forbearance of the old Negro, to rob the former of its vindictiveness and the latter of its lethargy.[45]

Social imagination inspired by religion and nonviolent resistance inspired by necessity were the combination he hoped to see emerge.

[43] *Moral Man,* p. 253.
[44] *Ibid.,* 254.
[45] *Ibid.*

Years later these words were read and pondered by Martin Luther King, Jr., who began to have his view of humanity sobered as a theological student when he studied Niebuhr. *Moral Man and Immoral Society* became the only book mentioned in King's writings more frequently than Walter Rauschenbusch's *Christianity and the Social Crisis.* [46] Before King would study Niebuhr and almost a quarter of a century before the nonviolent revolution led by King would achieve some of the gains Niebuhr hoped for, Niebuhr had another project.

THE DELTA COOPERATIVE FARM

Sherwood Eddy's response to the eviction of tenant farmers he found living in tents, shacks, and caves in the South was to found the Delta Cooperative Farm. Reinhold Niebuhr became chairman of the board, and from 1936 into the early forties he labored to finance and organize this inter-racial community in the Delta of Mississippi. On the farms economic cooperation between the races was achieved as poor whites and poor blacks labored together to throw off the tenant farming system. To Niebuhr, this cooperative movement seemed "the most significant experiment in social Christianity now being conducted in America."[47] Over against a system that in some ways was more dehumanizing than slavery the cooperative movement tried to give the poor economic power which was a prerequisite to liberty. "Freedom that has no economic base is a bogus freedom."[48] He regarded whites and blacks together as a Christian proletariat. The established church turned from them, but lay Christians were organizing the Southern Tenant Farmer's Union and joining relevant Biblical passages to their cry "Land to the Landless."

Eddy summarized the principles of the movement as efficiency through the cooperative principle, participation in a socialized economy and the rights of collective bargaining, interracial justice,

[46] See: Kenneth L. Smith and Ira G. Zepp, Jr., *Search for the Beloved Community: The Thinking of Martin Luther King, Jr.* (Valley Forge: Judson Press, 1974) for the best discussion of King's thought and his relationship to Reinhold Niebuhr.

[47] Reinhold Niebuhr, "Meditations from Mississippi," *The Christian Century,* LIV (February 10, 1937), p. 184.

[48] *Ibid.*

and "realistic religion as the social dynamic."[49] The farm was essentially a Christian cooperative movement.

The hostility of the racism of the delta, the difficulty of operating a Christian cooperative in a secular-capitalist economy, and rivalry with the Southern Tenant Farmer's Union eventually led to the dissolution of the cooperative with the tenants becoming landowners. A medical facility continued, and there is evidence that the Delta Cooperative Farm "provided inspiration for several of the experiments in community rescue which Franklin Roosevelt undertook in the later years of the New Deal."[50]

Niebuhr's apology for the Delta experiment used moral arguments against racism, but argued that moral suasion has to be joined with economic power to liberate the poor from racism and exploitation. The project received aid from the Niebuhr-founded Fellowship of Socialist Christians as did the Southern Tenant Farmer's Union and the Fellowship of Southern Churchmen. The founding and labor on behalf of these organizations is vital in understanding Niebuhr's social ethic. Voluntary institutions were part of the tradition of social Christianity he had inherited from Calvinistic social ethics and an essential part of his social strategy. All of these were parachurch organizations which could take on ministry in areas in which the official church was reluctant to move or in ministries to which the establishment church was opposed.

MARTIN LUTHER KING, JR.

The distance of Martin Luther King, Jr. from Niebuhr involves his black experience, his continued loyalty to the tradition of liberal Boston personalism, his more muted critique, and his tendency to use eschatology more as a spur to social action than as a limiting concept against social utopianism. However, their deep mutual respect and their alliance in the fight against racism and the Vietnam War should be noted.

Andrew Young made the point in a testimonial dinner for John C. Bennett:

[49] Sherwood Eddy, "The Delta Cooperative's First Year," *The Christian Century*, LIV (February 3, 1937), p. 139.

[50] Paul Merkley, *Reinhold Niebuhr: A Political Account* (Montreal: McGill-Queen's University Press, 1975), p. 256.

I want to begin by saying that there was always a misunderstanding of what Martin Luther King was about. I remember one night when somebody came at him with some of the philosophical presuppositions of strict Gandhian nonviolence, and he responded about three o'clock in the morning with the most brilliant lecture I had ever heard on *The Nature and Destiny of Man,* Reinhold Niebuhr, and the thinking of John Bennett and *Christianity and Crisis.* He reminded us that he had done his Ph.D. thesis on Paul Tillich, and you realized how everything he did was formulated much more out of a sense of Christian realism and out of the historic Black reality of the Christian Church in the Southern part of the United States than I think the press ever really understood.

We always tried to make nonviolence something that was very idealistic and ethereal and for the saints to live by, and never really understood as Dr. Niebuhr said as far back as *Moral Man and Immoral Society,* that nonviolent power and economic withdrawal would be the means that the Black community might eventually use to gain justice.[51]

King deepened his social thought in the struggle, but his "realistic pacifism" is very close to Niebuhr's Christian realistic advocacy of nonviolent resistance. Niebuhr supported King's struggle and was jubilant over his victories. Much of what he had hoped for in 1932 was realized by King in the 1950s and 1960s. The structure of King's ethic hung on love, justice, and power as did Niebuhr's; the differences between them faded as Niebuhr referred to King as "the most creative Protestant, white or black."[52] In Niebuhr's estimation, King combined idealism and realism appropriately and in Niebuhr, King found concepts that made sense of the heartrending struggle of the civil rights movement.

Niebuhr supported students and faculty from Union Theological Seminary in their direct action in the civil rights movement. He was saddened that his own physical condition prevented him from more active participation.

LATER REFLECTIONS

Niebuhr's realism led him to expect "slow erosion of racial prejudice."[53] He welcomed the courts' attempts to desegregate the schools, but he expected community pressures to delay the process.

[51] *Christianity and Crisis,* XXXI (May 3, 1971), p. 80. Quoted in Smith and Zepp, p. 72.

[52] D. B. Robertson, ed., *Love and Justice,* p. 20.

[53] Reinhold Niebuhr, *Pious and Secular America,* p. 82.

He understood the Supreme Court's decision to be reflecting the rising social consciousness of the country on human rights, but he expected local communities to find ways of evading the mandate of the courts. More than two decades after the 1954 decision, community resistance in the North as well as the South supports his analysis of the deep rootedness of prejudice and the creative but limited role of law in changing mores.

His critique of the lack of creative action in the community was especially sharp on the church. The church's universal mission was falsified as it remained more segregated than theater, public accommodations, and athletics. The local control of the Protestant churches rendered them less able to desegregate than the Roman Catholic churches. Neither law nor religion could overcome the bigotry of the nation, but still he saw progress being made though slowly.

His last major essay[54] on race located the slowness to integrate in the idealism of the country which obscured the roots of prejudice in human sin. Both its secular and religious idealism contributed to a self-righteousness which did not understand the fury of oppressed minorities. He concurred with the report of the National Advisory Commission on Civil Disorders which located the sources of the rage of the riots of 1966–68 in the poverty, poor housing, and unemployment of the blacks in the United States. The "helplessness of the black minority is due to a complacent self-satisfaction about our American democracy."[55] He traced this self-satisfaction from the country's founding documents to the current complacency about black deprivation. Only a total national response could deal with the black poverty which was the national shame.

The churches had failed to transcend the barriers of race in their own life and also they had not criticized the country's idealistic complacency concerning "the horrible injustices to its Negro minority."[56] As he called for a program to combat racism, he urged the church to witness to transcendence across racial lines with various organizational steps. He pleaded for programs that at that time had possibilities of legislative implementation: the negative income tax, scholarship programs, anti-poverty programs, and

[54] Reinhold Niebuhr, "The Negro Minority and Its Fate in a Self-Righteous Nation," *Social Action* (October 1968) Vol. XXXV, No. 2, pp. 53–64.

[55] *Ibid.*, p. 55.

[56] *Ibid.*

endorsed the Commission's recommendations for new national priorities in the new administration.

However, Niebuhr's plea in 1968 for new priorities regarding race were to be ignored as his endorsement of Hubert Humphrey for the Presidency was rejected by liberal admirer and conservative opponent. With Humphrey's defeat, policies of benign neglect were implemented, the black community could not organize around leadership to replace the assassinated Dr. King, and the beneficent intentions of the Carter administration could not overcome inflation and unemployment which ravaged the black community. The dilemma continues.

Niebuhr's strategies for countering racism from 1925–1971 included: moral teaching, education, economic boycott, study commissions, civil rights legislation, cooperative economic organization, anti-poverty legislation, church action, writing, rallies, and demonstrations. The black church overcame partially its other-worldly piety and led the action, here and there the white churches responded creatively, still integration of the churches moved ahead slowly. The reuniting of the above strategies as appropriate for the 1980s with religious imagination remains the task of the churches. The realism of both King and Niebuhr demanded that this be done to emphasize the economic empowerment of the black community.

PEACEMAKING AND REALISM

Reinhold Niebuhr's many debates with Christian pacifists and his polemics against idealists in politics have obscured his commitment to the search for peace. His fate is not too different from that of Hans Morgenthau whose passion for peace is seen in the title of his famous text, *Politics Among Nations: The Struggle for Power and Peace.* Power was central to international politics for both Niebuhr and Morgenthau, but their goal was peace. Both opposed vigorously the United States' war in Vietnam. The other direct use of U.S. military force abroad during Niebuhr's later years was President Johnson's intervention in the Dominican Republic, and Niebuhr opposed that in print also.[57]

Still the major critique of Niebuhr's public policy positions resides in his thought regarding the Cold War. Probably only consistent

[57] "Caribbean Blunder," *Christianity and Crisis* (May 31, 1965), Vol. 25, No. 9, pp. 113–114.

pacifists would decry his support of the United States' participation in World Wars I and II. Opinion divides around the support for the United States' position in the Korean War. Walter LaFeber regards Niebuhr as one of the main systematic thinkers who contributed to the philosophy of the American cold warriors. His *America, Russia, and the Cold War* attributes immense influence to Niebuhr in shaping the American thinking about the Cold War.

A fellow theologian, John M. Swomley, accuses Niebuhr of providing "the religious rationale for the military foreign policy that created the contemporary American empire and the policy of global intervention culminating in the war in Vietnam."[58] Building on the insight of Charles West, he suggests that Christian realism served an ideological role in justifying American empire. The record shows that Niebuhr consciously provided rationale for competition with the Soviet Union while he explicitly attacked the Vietnam policy. One of his most famous essays, "The King's Chapel and the King's Court," explicitly attacked the attempt by the Nixon administration to religiously legitimize its policies.[59]

He had hoped during World War II for post-war cooperation among the allies, but tensions between the U.S.S.R. and the Western allies convinced him during the war that both sides would try to advance their own interests. The collapse of the wartime alliance led him to regard the Soviet Union as a dangerous opponent. Its creed and policies led him to believe that it was important to rally the United States to assume responsibility after the war and to oppose the presumed ambitions of the Soviet Union. The role of Niebuhr in leading American liberals to oppose Communism is well known. As he had provided arguments for the opposition to Nazism before and during World War II, he supported opposing Communism.

He perceived the process of maintaining competitive existence between the U.S. and the U.S.S.R. as necessary to maintaining peace. "There cannot be war between us without mutual annihilation. There must not be war."[60] He envisaged the competition

[58] John M. Swomley, *American Empire: The Political Ethics of Twentieth Century Conquest* (London: The Macmillan Company, 1970), p. 34.

[59] *Christianity and Crisis,* XXIX (August 4, 1969).

[60] "After Sputnik and Explorer," *Christianity and Crisis* (March 4, 1958) reprinted in Ernest W. Lefever, *The World Crisis and American Responsibility* (New York: Association Press, 1958), p. 126.

extending for decades or even longer. There could be no resolution through war, but neither partner in the competition could be expected to surrender its respective myths or ideologies. Wise statesmanship was the most important element in maintaining the uneasy partnership in preventing nuclear war. He had no great confidence in education, cultural exchanges, religious impulses, or disarmament plans to eliminate the competition of two continental empires competing for influence and interests in the world. This view of the world, essentially of two nuclear armed scorpions locked in a small battle, was not a world he would have wished for but it was the world he perceived. It was also a world subjected to the winds of revolutionary demands flowing through the undeveloped world, and a world made more dangerous and unified by technological development.

He warned of the danger of the U.S. overreliance on military power. The tendency to build defense pacts in Asia revealed little understanding of the political complexities there. Military force could be effective in crises, but without political forces of cohesion military force could accomplish little. Overreliance on military power was a temptation to a nation as wealthy as the U.S., but it could contribute to our political embarrassment. Military force for Niebuhr was a means of last resort, but the American temptation was to use it as a meat-axe where subtlety was called for. The understanding of the needs of a population required wise statecraft not primarily military power.[61]

The real task of preserving the nuclear stalemate rested in the political sphere. He noted that technical miscalculation might bring about the nuclear catastrophe, but his primary concern was in political miscalculation. A defeat in some vital area of competition might tempt one side or the other in hysteria to resort to nuclear weapons. This I think was the central reason for his continued reference to the "balance of power" in the post-World War II situation. He often described it as a "nuclear umbrella"; competition could go on, but it must be limited so as not to threaten the vital interests of the other party. Of course, it was not balance of power in any prenuclear meaning of the term, but an arrangement, ironically stumbled into which was not securing peace in any deep sense, but at least the avoidance of the nuclear holocaust.

[61] "The Limits of Military Power," *The New Leader* (May 30, 1955). Reprinted in Lefever, *op. cit.*

He rejected the notion of "winning the cold war," and I do not think he ever entertained the idea of "rolling back Communism" as John Foster Dulles had dreamed of briefly. Without war and without hysteria, he counseled the United States to meet the Soviet challenge.

> World peace requires that the dynamic of this strange political movement be contained, its ambition to control the world be frustrated, and its revolutionary ardors be tamed by firm and patient resistance.[62]

Niebuhr regarded the complex and threatening post-war world as requiring "shrewder calculations of both ideological and power factors than we are accustomed to give them."[63] How shrewd was Reinhold Niebuhr? Was he just commenting on the world in countless editorials, articles, and numerous books on empire, power, American history? Or was he trying to have a political effect? I think he was being very political in his writing. He wrote in a major essay on the theory of international politics:

> If power is identical with authority, it follows that the climate of a culture of its "ideology," which sanctions a particular type of authority, is really the ultimate source of power.[64]

Niebuhr knew that the facts did not interpret themselves. The complexities of the international world had to be reduced to be graspable and put into perspective to become politically relevant. Niebuhr did not write much about method in either theology or international politics. But what he wrote about myth, symbol, and ideology reveals that he knew that in their articulation resided power. The articulation was itself a creative act even as it remained loyal, to the best of one's ability, to the materials being discussed. Millions of events were occurring in the world but he would write "Thus modern history is fated to be governed by the contrasting myths of the two superpowers, . . ."[65] He knew that these myths were not easily changed and that he was powerless to affect the mythology or perspective of the Soviet Union. He did set out to affect the mythology of the United States and to affect the perspective of the United States in its understanding of the Soviet Union.

[62] *Faith and Politics,* p. 215.
[63] *Ibid.,* p. 211.
[64] *Ibid.,* p. 203.
[65] *Ibid.,* p. 236.

So his critics who accuse him of presenting an ideology for United States' participation in the Cold War are correct. The perspective he presented, however, was one of a precarious partnership between the two countries in preserving a nuclear peace while struggling elsewhere. The struggle Niebuhr envisaged was primarily ideological. Finally, authority rested on a governing group's ability not only to ensure order but to deliver or promise a tolerably just society.

In the ideological struggle he felt that the United States with its ties with previously colonial powers and its own problems of race and social justice was at a temporary disadvantage in the developing world. However, the creed and actual accomplishments of Marxism were so badly flawed that he believed that patient resistance would eventually encourage other governments to find their own solutions without succumbing to alliances with Communist powers.

Technological aid and economic aid were among the major contributions the United States could make to the health of the developing nations. In 1962 he would regard the ability of a democratic process to provide funds for aid as "the litmus test of the capacity of a democracy to survive in the contest."[66]

Elsewhere, I have criticized Niebuhr's overly optimistic expectations for the Alliance for Progress.[67] It is unfortunate that his critic, John M. Swomley, Jr.,[68] takes part of the paragraph in which he is arguing for a strong interventionist policy in Latin America in the terms of the Alliance for Progress as evidence of the advocacy of imperial self-interest, and neglects to mention that his use of economic power was for attempted land reform and education. For the sake of changes in the oligarchic practices of Latin America he urged intervention, overriding liberal reservations about anti-imperialism. To Niebuhr, the United States was an empire in a struggle. Critics often seem to find fault with Niebuhr as if he were responsible either for the empire or the struggle. Certainly his views shaped our perspectives on the empire and the struggles, but they are rooted in reality as well as perspective. A sympathetic reading of Reinhold Niebuhr's writing finds him urging a cautious policy of statecraft, the upbuilding of the developing world, a nuclear partnership, a decrease in American reliance on military

[66] *Ibid.*, p. 218.
[67] *Reinhold Niebuhr: Prophet to Politicians*, pp. 207–210.
[68] *American Empire*, p. 35.

power, outright rejection of U.S. policy in Vietnam, and a struggle to criticize and replace political leadership responsible for it.

Competitive coexistence in Niebuhr's perspective called for ideological debate. Hence, while he tried to clarify and reform American ideology by interpreting its religious and secular elements, he criticized the pretensions and illusions of Marxism severely. This criticism of Marxism can be seen as fueling the cold war. However in Niebuhr's perspective, it was exactly the ideological debate that needed to be carried on in order to follow Senator Fulbright's idea of not trying "to redress ideological deficiencies with military power."[69] He feared the dominance of the military-industrial complex and criticized its dominance of the United States economy and resisted journalistically some of its demands for new systems.[70]

Doves in the peace movement will probably never be at ease with Niebuhr. He had been president of the pacifist organization, the Fellowship of Reconciliation, and editor of the pacifist newspaper, *The World Tomorrow*. His resignation from the F.O.R. in the depression had been over the possibility of sanctioning the use of violence by the workers in defense against capitalist owners in American industrial strife. His pacifism proved to be a pragmatic preference for nonviolent means of social change, and it could not be absolutist. Eventually with Augustine he came to believe that the peace of the world was defended by violence or the threat of violence. So in 1948 he joined the debates over U.S. foreign policy with an article in *Life* entitled "For Peace We Must Risk War." Statecraft would seek to broaden national interest to a wise view of the broader world interest and attempt to reconcile the two, but force remained a means of last resort. Hawks could never be content with Niebuhr either. In World War II he argued against unconditional surrender, attacked the policies of massive bombing of German cities, sponsored German refugees and German political groups in the United States working for moderation in the treatment of Germany, and helped defeat the "Morgenthau" plan for reducing post-war Germany to a pastoral economy. With Augustine, he believed peace to be among the highest achievements, but to preserve it required a mixture of means including political authority which relied both on agreement and force.

[69] "An Interview with Reinhold Niebuhr," *Christianity and Crisis*, XXIX (March 17, 1969), p. 51.

[70] *Ibid.*

On questions of disarmament, then, he was not a dreamer. His own history had witnessed the difficulty of disarmament plans in the early twentieth century. The ban on nuclear testing he regarded as a great achievement as he thought the negotiations to stop the anti-ballistic missile race were a gain. The non-proliferation treaty seemed to him of dubious worth because it represented the satiation of the "haves" and the repression of the "have nots."[71] Community had to precede disarmament or, at least, accompany it in its formation. The formation of that community was significantly begun in the work of UNESCO in which he served as a United States delegate, but finally it required the moderation of the revolutionary ardor of Communism, the development of the third world, and wise statecraft on the part of the Atlantic Alliance. So there was no guarantee of peace.

The building of community as seen in the work of UNESCO was flawed. The flaws revealed the spiritual nature of contemporary humanity. Modern humanity had to find ways of continuing to build community across international borders and to avoid discouragement when it failed to complete the tasks. His comment on UNESCO stands as his attitude toward the building of world community.

> Here is an organization which seeks to realize the impossible: a world community. It must not regard this end as a simple possibility; but neither can it dismiss the task as an impossibility. It stands, therefore, constantly at the final limit of the human situation where the possible and the impossible are curiously intermingled and where it is difficult to distinguish between God's and our possibilities.[72]

BEYOND RELIGIOUS SOCIALISM

The practical problems of auto workers in Detroit inspired Niebuhr's interest in political economy and led him to criticize the moral pretensions of the Ford Motor Company. The needs of rural sharecroppers led him to experiment with a cooperative means of economic organization. The plight of the unemployed in the depression inspired his constant work for economic reform in the 1930s. He approached economic issues as a Christian social ethicist, and his writing on economic matters often was dealing with the history of Christian ethics in relationship to the rights of property

[71] *Ibid.*

[72] "Peace Through Cultural Co-operation," *Christianity and Crisis* (October 17, 1949), Reprinted in Lefever, pp. 111–112.

or the various forms of social organization. In analyzing wages paid to the workers at Ford Motor Company or in formulating and raising a budget for the Delta Cooperative Farm, he became very specific. The tendency to abstraction led him, however, often to contrast Karl Marx's thought with Adam Smith's and not to enter into much detail in the intermediate realm of economic theory where crucial issues were being fought.

John C. Bennett, Arthur Schlesinger, Jr., and Kenneth Thompson have all analyzed Niebuhr's relationship to socialism thoroughly. There is little to be added.[73] The practical origins of his interest in economics helps to explain the infrequence of his post 1940s work on economics. He became interested in economics to advance the cause of the workers, and with the victories of labor during the New Deal his interest in economics declined. The winning of the right of labor to organize and bargain was a fundamental victory which changed the country. With their victory, the socialist option lost its power. In a tribute to Norman Thomas he could not refrain from pointing out the irrelevance of socialist faith to the American scene. Though he had broken with socialism as a party movement over its foreign policy, the reason for dismissing socialism after the war was hidden in the tribute to Thomas: "The organization of unorganized workers changed the social and moral climate of American industry more than the nationalization of the means of production could ever have done."[74] He had worked hard for socialism and his commitments to many aspects of its intended reforms continued. His developing theological work led him to develop his own form of Christian pragmatism on economic issues. He remained sympathetic to socialist critiques of American culture. He recognized in the 1950s the extent to which business passions contributed to a banalization of American culture, and left pockets of poverty in the country. But against his friend and former socialist ally, Eduard Heimann, he defended Christian pragmatism in the absence of persuasive argument that some other inclusive theoretic system could better analyze American ills or propose remedies.[75]

[73] Paul Merkley's study *Reinhold Niebuhr* presents the most complete account of the incessant activity of Niebuhr for socialist causes and my earlier work *Reinhold Niebuhr: Prophet to Politicians* demonstrates the evolution of his thought regarding socialism and Marxism.

[74] "Norman Thomas: Incarnate Conscience," *Christianity and Crisis,* XXIV, No. 23 (January 11, 1965), pp. 271–272.

[75] "Commentary," *Social Action* (January, 1957) XXIII, No. 5, pp. 12–14.

The failure of religious socialism and political socialism in the United States left him without a developed alternative policy. He never returned to the analysis of economic reality with the same energy that he had exhibited as a socialist. In policies to deal with the remaining pockets of poverty, he favored New Deal type policies in the Kennedy and Johnson administrations and regarded the old laissez-faire capitalism as dead. He still regarded a policy of government activism as necessary to correct the inequities of the racial problems.

To refer to the American system in 1964 as "free enterprise" was to render a mythical account which obscured the realities of the mixed economy.[76] Though no longer favoring nationalization of industry, Niebuhr wanted a recognition of the government, management, labor alliance. A progressive income tax, tax on estates, government regulation, and government planning regarding the economy had been partially won through the New Deal and near the end of his life with a Republican administration accepting most of the New Deal gains and advocating a negative income tax he did not fear a return to laissez-faire economics. Generally his post-war writing on economic thought reflects the same pattern. The United States had been blessed through the wealth of a continent to rise to affluence. The affluence had obscured the need for social reform and allowed the creed of Adam Smith to live longer in the United States than Europe. But experience refuted both Smith and his alternative, Marx, and the United States had tolerably corrected its injustices while avoiding the perils of the collective power of the Marxist state. Strong governmental leadership was still necessary to correct disproportionate economic power. His practical concerns were represented by the two organizations he was instrumental in forming, the Liberal Party and the Americans for Democratic Action.

His references to a tolerable justice being achieved in the United States referred to the legitimization of labor power and did not sanction complacency in the struggle to win economic rights for those excluded. He assumed the ongoing interventionist policy of the government to limit freedom in the marketplace for the sake of justice. Liberty and equality were both regulative principles; neither was to be absolute. He feared the military-industrial complex and

[76] *Faith and Politics*, p. 246.

was not optimistic about limiting its influence in the economy or on the government.

On economic matters, only general guidelines of moral advice for the late twentieth century can be derived. First, economic policy must be guided by the political process practiced aggressively and democratically for the benefit of those who have not. In his own time those were the workers, the minorities, and the developing peoples of the third world. He assumed rather than advocated that the American middle class would protect its own interests, and he hoped that through the political process this interest would be generously adjusted to the wider interests. Nostalgia for laissez-faire capitalism was to be expected, but it was largely irrelevant to the agenda of the technological nations of the developed world. Mixed economies were the best adjustment to Western history and needs and governmental processes to eliminate the effects of poverty and protect against undue centralization of economic power were required.

The return of a modified laissez-faire direction in economic thinking since his death, the curtailing of the government's regulatory powers, and the tilting of government policies to favor the privileged will probably tempt some to use Niebuhr and particularly his critique of socialism as ideological justification for these directions. Nothing could be further from his intentions. In his revision of his thinking, he made clear that his conception of human nature was intended to reinforce progressive movements in the society.

> A realist conception of human nature should be made the servant of an ethic of progressive justice and should not be made into a bastion of conservatism, particularly a conservatism which defends unjust privileges.
>
> I might define this conviction as the guiding principle throughout my mature life of the relation of religious responsibility to political affairs.[77]

BEYOND REINHOLD NIEBUHR

Niebuhr knew that his work was limited to his historical situation. Christian social ethics continues to develop attempting to relate the eternal gospel to the contingent facts of history. He did not seek disciples, and I doubt that he ever hoped that his work would be more than a chapter in Christian social thought. He hoped it was a relevant chapter, but that very relevance was limited to time and place.

[77] Niebuhr, *Man's Nature and His Communities,* pp. 24–25.

I believe the claims that his work had the most important impact on social thought and public policy of any Christian thinker of our time. His task was to persuade Christians and fellow travelers of Christians to translate their faith into socially responsible action while helping them to avoid illusions and to see the dangers of American pride. The pride and illusions of white American decision makers was particularly his target. He analyzed their egoism, urged them to accept and defend their freedom while promoting equality and freedom for the wider human community. Out of that wider community have come criticisms of his work which I think he would now graciously accept. Liberation theologians of the third world, of the American black community, and of the women's movement have all noted deficiencies from their own perspectives. Much is obscured by condensing these criticisms, but I think they all point toward one tendency.

Niebuhr saw the failure of the human community fundamentally in terms of the lack of trust which was expressed in prideful self-assertion of the powerful. He generally did not speak about the lack of trust which led people to surrender to oppression. He saw sin in the oppressors and may have neglected the aspects of the human condition which led the oppressed to accept their oppression and to become defective in their humanity. In one sense this was a wise emphasis, but in another expression it does not meet the human experiences of minorities, women, and the poor who need resources to develop their confidence to win for themselves a fairer place in the human community. Those groups suffer from the pride of the powerful as Niebuhr saw. But they also suffer from their cooperation with the oppressor. Niebuhr did not emphasize the sin of the oppressed which helped hold them in bondage. Valerie Saiving Goldstein has argued that women suffer more from the "underdevelopment or negation of the self" than from pride or will to power.[78] Similar perspectives have been developed from black and third world theologies. In short, Niebuhr's emphasis upon the sin of the anxious, powerful male decision maker obscured other human experiences which also reinforced the unjust social situation. Niebuhr's category of sin as sensuality has possibilities for meeting the need; at least it reveals he knew of the surrender of freedom as well as its prideful assertion. But even development of this category could not fulfill

[78] Valerie Saiving Goldstein, "The Human Situation: A Feminine View," *Journal of Religion*, XV, No. 2 (April, 1960), p. 109.

the need for a theology which would help people understand their apathy, self-abnegation, conformity, and passivity. Black power and conscientization have attempted to awaken people to throw off this denial of self which reinforces their oppression.

Still we wait for the fuller development of an activist Christian social philosophy which will explore the roots of apathy as brilliantly as Niebuhr explored the human pathology expressed by pride. Such an analysis would enable the teacher of theological students to explain not only the illusions and corruption of the powerful but the roots of apathy in the powerless and show us how to overcome the apathy as well as to combat the pride.

RONALD STONE

PITTSBURGH THEOLOGICAL SEMINARY
PITTSBURGH, PENNSYLVANIA

3

Emil Brunner

SOME REMARKS ON REINHOLD NIEBUHR'S WORK AS A CHRISTIAN THINKER

3

SOME REMARKS ON REINHOLD NIEBUHR'S WORK AS A CHRISTIAN THINKER*

FIRST I should like to say a word of heartfelt thanks for the great things God has accomplished in the United States and in the world at large through his servant Reinhold Niebuhr. It was in the autumn of 1928 that I first met Reinhold, at an evening discussion group after a lecture I had given at Union Seminary in New York. There were three of us (the third being Professor Van Dusen, now president of the seminary) who sat together and discussed the theme of original sin. At that time both Karl Barth and I were known to these men in little more than name only. What I had said in my lecture about sin led to an animated and passionate discussion. The concept of sin in those days had almost disappeared from the vocabulary of enlightened theologians. But I sensed how this basic term seemed to stimulate Niebuhr and set fire to his imagination. Since then this concept has become one of the main pillars of his thought structure. Soon after that my lecture was published under the title "The Theology of Crisis"—a lecture which for many was their first introduction to the new theology called "the dialectical theology" in Europe, while in America it became known mostly as the "Barthian theology." Since then I have collaborated with Reinhold Niebuhr in many ecumenical study groups, and I can be cheered by the constant growth of friendship and sympathetic understanding between us. This friendship belongs among the most precious experiences of my life.

Other writers in this book will evaluate the theological revolution in the United States which is bound up with the name of Reinhold Niebuhr. The label "neo-orthodoxy" is rather unfortunate, since in

* Translated by Robert W. Bretall.

all the world there is nothing more unorthodox than the spiritual volcano Reinhold Niebuhr. For most people "orthodoxy" means something like spiritual conformism, while Niebuhr is a true son of independent non-conformism. The term "radical-Protestant" would suit him very much better. The return to Reformation ways of thinking and a protest against the ruling thought patterns of his age are equally characteristic of him.

Theologically he has no doubt learned most from the dialectical theology, which for him was more understandable, more accessible, and more easily digestible in my version than in Karl Barth's. But Niebuhr has made out of the dialectical theology something quite new, something genuinely American, while translating its concepts from the theological language into that of the philosophy of culture and social criticism, and kindling them with his prophetic spirit. In his hands the new theological concepts were used to throw a light upon the spiritual and social framework of modern civilization and lay bare its fundamental flaws and errors. By virtue of an unusual facility for dealing with the abstractions of cultural history he succeeds in relating social facts, cultural principles, and spiritual tendencies to the teachings and the concerns of Christian faith. Thus he makes clear the essence of both the present-day world and the Christian faith. With him theology broke into the world; theology was no longer quarantined, and men of letters, philosophers, sociologists, historians, even statesmen, began to listen. Once more theology was becoming a spiritual force to be reckoned with. Reinhold Niebuhr has realized, as no one else has, what I have been postulating for decades but could not accomplish to any degree in an atmosphere ruled by abstract dogmatism: namely, theology in conversation with the leading intellects of the age.

Compared with this enormous achievement of Reinhold Niebuhr's, anything that might be criticized in his interpretation of the Christian faith is insignificant. On my own initiative I would not have spoken on this subject, but I have been urged to do so by the editors of this volume, by some of the important contributors, and by Niebuhr himself. Let me ask, however, that the following remarks be taken in the spirit of questions addressed to Reinhold Niebuhr and not as criticism from a pretended superior. Please take into consideration also that at the present moment I am not able to support my objections by reference to the writings of Niebuhr himself.

1. Reinhold Niebuhr's first and most passionate concern was the

criticism of American social conditions. The protest of the simple workingman against the exploiting of his labor by the capitalist—this protest found in Niebuhr a persuasive and clearsighted spokesman. He became the critic of a social order (be it noted, at a time *before* that peaceful revolution which we know as the "New Deal") which had created on the one hand the gigantic wealth of the multimillionaire and on the other hand the abominations of the city slums. That Niebuhr, with all the passionateness of his nature and his unbounded fighting spirit, never became an agitator even in the most heated of his assaults, and that he never abandoned the high plane of his spiritual calling, must be considered a high tribute to this fiery spirit. Always he was concerned for human dignity and for justice. All the more surprising is it, therefore, that Reinhold Niebuhr has never worked out a clear concept of justice whereby the difference between the demands of justice and those of the supreme ethical norm of love might be understood. If one uses the term "justice," intending it to be distinguished from the "agape" of the New Testament (which for Niebuhr also is the highest norm), then one is duty-bound to say exactly what this "justice" is as distinguished from love. Niebuhr has taken occasion publicly to dissociate himself from the traditional "natural law" doctrine, because for him this is inseparably bound up with the Aristotelian-Thomistic system, and anyone who is somewhat familiar with the history of the "natural law" philosophy will understand this reservation on the part of a New Testament-oriented thinker. All the more urgent, however, becomes the question what "justice" could mean to a Christian who wants to distinguish it from the supreme ethical norm of love. It is certainly not acceptable to dispose of this attempt by branding it as "sub-Christian," as was done by a critic of my book *Justice and the Social Order* who is very close to Niebuhr. Niebuhr himself is clear on the fact that justice is not the same thing as love, but that justice is the proper norm for the social order. All the more necessary might it be to make clear what justice is as distinguished from love and in what relation justice stands to love, the sovereign norm for Christian ethics.

This deficiency explains a second point—the criticism that has often been leveled against Niebuhr's social ethics. Brilliant as Reinhold Niebuhr is in his analysis of existing social conditions or of historical movements and cultural trends, this critical analysis seldom gives rise to definite, concrete ethical postulates for social action. We who, in various ecumenical study groups, often marveled at the brilliance of his analyses, nevertheless noted time and again this deficiency between criticism and construction. And the reason for this is evident: the lack of an adequate concept of justice.

By this, however, we do not mean the kind of theory against which Niebuhr is always—and rightly—at war: that is, a system of "natural law" made up of timelessly valid ethical demands. Anyone, however, who in the name of justice offers a critique of social issues or of political policy is thereby under obligation not only to state what he means by "justice" but also what concrete choices are demanded in the name of this "justice" that he is talking about. Moreover, he must be able to make clear the relationship of these obligations posed by justice to the supreme ethical principle of love.

2. Another point that I should like to bring up here lies in quite a different realm, yet it is just as important as the foregoing in relation to Niebuhr's critical analyses of society and human culture. It is greatly to this theologian's credit that he aimed his guns at the optimistic American progress-philosophy at a time when on the whole it was still largely unchallenged. With Niebuhr this assault was made from two positions: first of all from his widened Christian understanding of sin, but then also from the standpoint of Biblical eschatology. As regards the first, one of my pupils, Hans Hoffmann, has set forth the whole of Niebuhr's thought from the standpoint of his understanding of sin, and this presentation of it has met with complete approval from Niebuhr himself. This work has been published as a dissertation of the University of Zurich. The Christian concept of sin is indeed one of the cornerstones of this structure of thought.

On the other hand, it would be difficult to determine just what Reinhold Niebuhr means by his equally crucial concept of the Biblical "eschatological symbol." Clear it is that this concept is of central import for his understanding of history, as he has made particularly clear in his book *Faith and History*. The reader of this book, however, remains in some uncertainty as to just what kind of a reality is designated by this concept. Certainly Niebuhr is fully justified in employing the concept of "symbol" for the eschatological sayings of the Bible. Herein he has anticipated much of what the Continental theology is now accomplishing under the key word of "demythologization" (R. Bultmann). As over against a literalistic fundamentalism which uses the Bible as a "paper Pope," it is certainly valid to emphasize that the eschatological sayings of the Bible are to be understood as symbolical. On the other hand, as over against Bultmann's elimination of the "mythical" sayings of Biblical eschatology, Reinhold Niebuhr would no doubt stress the point that these symbols are not to be eliminated but are, rather, to be taken seriously as symbols. But what kind of reality lies hidden beneath these symbols? Is it an everlasting life, for which we should hope in the hour of death? Is it the fulfillment of the Biblical expectation of the kingdom of God?

We quite understand and appreciate Niebuhr's oft repeated assertion that he is not a theologian in the sense of a doctrinal systematizer even though he has never disputed the necessity of such systematization. "It's just not my job to go into these questions." On the other hand, does one not have a right to expect of every thinking Christian —and *a fortiori* of every Christian thinker—that he be cognizant of what he has to hope for in Christ? To what extent there stands behind Niebuhr's "eschatological symbols" a *reality*, and what kind of reality—or whether perhaps these eschatological symbols are merely "regulative principles" in the Kantian sense—these are questions on which we should like to have him make a definitive pronouncement.

3. A third point of criticism I should like to mention with circumspection and with great hesitancy, in the hope that it will really be understood as a question only—to which this very book may well supply the answer. With us European scholars it is customary to give our readers some information as to the sources of our thought. Not infrequently we are somewhat pedantic—perhaps even somewhat fussy—with our references and our footnotes, but on the whole this European tradition still seems to me to be praiseworthy. On this point Reinhold Niebuhr leaves much to be desired. This is of significance chiefly as one tries to understand the connection between European and American thinking. Already I have read works on Niebuhr which gave not so much as a single word of intimation that he might have learned something from contemporary European thinkers. Herein Niebuhr himself is not entirely without fault. To give just one example, which happens to be close to me personally: In reading the first volume of his most significant work, the Gifford Lectures on *The Nature and Destiny of Man*, I was somewhat astonished to find no mention of the fact that in this work Reinhold Niebuhr had been strongly preoccupied with certain ideas which I had put forward in my book *Man in Revolt* in the year 1937, that is, four years before the publication of the first volume of Gifford

Lectures. This was all the more surprising to me inasmuch as Niebuhr had informed me personally by word of mouth in the year 1938, just as he was beginning to prepare those lectures, that my book was claiming a great deal of his attention. Nor am I the only one who has wondered about Niebuhr's silence on this point. It may seem petty to bring such a criticism to bear on so monumental a work, in addition to which it may look like an author's wounded vanity. Nonetheless I venture it, because something very much more is at stake: namely, the danger of a false picture of theological development in our time, not to mention the danger of a false "Continentalism," which is especially imminent today in view of the supremacy of America as a world power. Niebuhr's achievement as a thinker is so great and so indisputably original, that any admission of his having learned this or that from anyone would not endanger his reputation.

And yet—what does all this amount to compared with the debt of thanks which not only American theology, and not only Christendom, but the world at large owes to Reinhold Niebuhr? I sincerely hope that the day is not far off when at last it will be recognized in Europe, even in Germany, how very much we all have to learn from this impassioned Christian thinker. And in the days to come, should the German publishers continue to withhold from us the translation of his complete works, then it should be made clear to every student of theology at least, that he owes it to himself to learn English in order to get acquainted with Reinhold Niebuhr. It is very much to be hoped that the present volume will help to overcome the inexcusable neglect which in Europe, at least in the German-speaking countries, has marked the reception of this mighty interpretation of the Gospel for our time.

EMIL BRUNNER

INTERNATIONAL CHRISTIAN UNIVERSITY
TOKYO, JAPAN

4

Paul Tillich

REINHOLD NIEBUHR'S DOCTRINE OF KNOWLEDGE

4

REINHOLD NIEBUHR'S DOCTRINE OF KNOWLEDGE

The difficulty of writing about Niebuhr's epistemology lies in the fact that there is no such epistemology. Niebuhr does not ask, "How can I know?"; he starts knowing. And he does not ask afterward, "How could I know?", but leaves the convincing power of his thought without epistemological support. This certainly appears as a great advantage if one compares his writing with that of some theologians of the last generation who never liberated themselves from the bondage of the methodological question. But it also has the danger of every omission, that the omitted element reappears under a disguise in another place. I believe that this place is Niebuhr's doctrine of reason, and that the disguise in which the epistemological question appears is his rejection of the ontological question within theology and the exclusiveness with which he confronts Jewish and Greek thought, retaining only the former as theologically sound. I shall deal with these three points in Niebuhr's thought, and in doing so I shall enlarge upon my "Reply" to his criticism of my own thought in the first volume of this series.

When Niebuhr criticizes Aristotle's description of man as a rational animal, he presupposes a concept of reason which has been peculiar to us since the middle of the nineteenth century but which is far removed from the classical concept of reason as it appears, for example, in Stoicism. We may call the latter the logos-type of reason: reason seen as an element within the divine life, the principle of his self-manifestation to himself and to everything separated from him. Reason in this sense is the universal power of form and meaning. It is present in the structures of reality and in the structures of the mind which correspond with one another, and which make knowledge and aesthetic intuition, ethical insight and political justice possible. Such reason is divine in its essential nature and does not admit any confrontation with faith. Reason in this sense (as logos) is the principle of that which creates faith: namely, revelation.

In his valuation of ancient and modern philosophers Niebuhr does not distinguish this "high" concept of reason from the "low" concept of reason: namely, the calculating type of reason. If we call this type "low," it is not meant in a depreciating sense. For calculating reasoning is as old as man's ability to make a tool, and there is no man as man before the first tool was made. Aristotle, as well as Hegel, gives a large place to this calculating reason. But they do not identify it with the logos type of reason, with reason in its divine nature. In the attacks of the eighteenth-century philosophers on the distortions of the religious and political traditions, the classical concept of reason was still alive, and was applied as a critical standard against these distortions. The passion for justice against the infamies of a tyrannical church was rooted in the awareness of ultimate principles which are given to man by his very nature. This "critical reason" of the "enlightened" philosophers was a derivative of reason as logos. Slowly, however, this foundation disappeared. Reason was reduced to the cognitive function. It became technical reason: scientific, calculating, arguing. Niebuhr is right when he denies the ability of reason, in this sense, to attain knowledge of God. This is not only impossible; it is also religiously condemnable because it represents an attempt of man to force God down to man through cognitive endeavor. But Niebuhr is wrong when he asserts that this is all one can say about the relation of reason to man's knowledge of God. For reason is more than arguing reason.

Perhaps Niebuhr could agree with the distinction of the two types of reason and try to find another term for the logos type of reason: for example, as he once suggested to me, the term "spirit." But "spirit" unites power with meaning and is creative, whereas reason is only the structure of meaning. Yet beyond this terminological question he would say that reason, even if it were essentially God-related, is now corrupted in man's fallen state together with his whole being. There again I would agree. But corruption is not annihilation. Corruption presupposes the reality of that which is corrupted. Revelation does not replace reason, but it overcomes the corruption of the rational structure of man and his world. Faith is not an act beside or against reason; rather it is the state of the rational person in which he is grasped by that which reestablishes reason in its integrity. In this sense faith is rational; it is reason moved and shaped by its own divine depth.

Such a description stands against both supranaturalism and naturalism. In Niebuhr's struggle against the naturalistic standpoint one often feels that he himself is not free from supranaturalistic elements. This is understandable if one considers his great and successful fight against naturalistic (and idealistic) methods in theology. It weakens the power of this fight, however, if naturalism is simply negated and not also affirmed as a necessary criticism of the two-worlds type of supranaturalism. The transcendentalism of Niebuhr's interpretation of man and history would gain in strength if that which is beyond human possibilities and historical progress were understood as the depth-dimension of ourselves and our world. In a different terminology one could say that the elements of ancient dualism which crept into Christian thought, and which were never completely removed, not even in the Reformation, have prevented Niebuhr from accepting the principle of the "coincidence of the opposites" which is expressed both in the philosophy of the Renaissance (Nicolaus Cusanus) and in the theology of the Reformers (Luther): the divine does not constitute a realm above life, but a dimension of life.

The epistemological difference indicated here is best visible in the treatment of the concept of paradox. Niebuhr likes to call the Christian paradox "impossible possibility." In terms of pure logic this is a nonsensical combination of words. In terms of theological insight it can express the real and only Christian paradox: namely, that the principle of the divine self-manifestation, the divine logos, has appeared without restriction in the life of an individual person. It can express the surprising, unexpected fact that the eternal unity between God and man has appeared under the conditions of man's radical estrangement from God. The term "paradox" should never be used for a meaningless combination of words, but only for this fact and its implications. "Impossible possibility" ceases to be irrational and becomes genuinely paradoxical if the hidden adverb and adjective are added and if one reads "humanly impossible divine possibility." The term "paradox" in this non-irrational sense should be used only for the appearance of essential God-manhood under the conditions of existence; that is, for the appearance of Jesus as the

Christ. And there should be no confusion between the mysterious and the paradoxical or between the dialectical and the paradoxical: The mysterious is the depth of reason, the infinite and the inexhaustible ground of being and meaning; the dialectical is every description of a life process, including the divine life. Therefore the trinitarian formulas are dialectical. The word "paradox" should be reserved for the assertion that the Logos became manifest in the life of a historical person who for this reason is called the Christ. Such epistemological distinction would have prevented the impression Niebuhr has made on many people that he is an irrationalist. This impression is wrong; but it is caused by Niebuhr's predilection for a paradoxical language even when a dialectical, and this means rational, language would have been more adequate. The paradox is not created by reason, but reason can receive it without being destroyed. And reason can show the place of the paradox and its relation to other forms of religious expression.

II

The second place in Niebuhr's thought where a hidden epistemology may be observed is his struggle against ontology within the Christian framework. He understands ontology as a way of reducing the dynamic-dramatic history of creation, fall, salvation and consummation into a static system which is determined by rational necessity. If this were the case, if ontological categories did deprive God, man, and the world of freedom and chance, if fall and salvation were necessary structures of reality, Niebuhr's rejection of ontology would be justified. This is especially clear if one considers the way in which he uses with increasing emphasis the term "self" in order to describe the nature of man and his relation to God. Self is dynamic acting in time; it has freedom, it can contradict itself, it can be changed and saved, it can relate itself to God. All this is true and is very well stated in Niebuhr's writings. The centered self is the condition not only of freedom but also of a world with which the self is correlated. Criticism of Niebuhr's philosophy of the self is necessary only when he confronts his philosophy of the self with a philosophy of being. But there is no necessary conflict between them, for the self has being and God has being. One cannot escape the question of being by speaking of "self." The special kind of being which has a centered self is embedded in the whole of being. Its relation to God, moreover, is not the relation to another self but to the ground and aim of every self. For both reasons the ontological question cannot be avoided. He who says that God is, and says this as a theologian, must also say what this "is" means, if applied to God. So long as one remains in an unbroken mythological symbolism, such a question would not be asked. Yet in the moment in which one forms concepts like *self* and *dynamics* and *history*, one has left the innocence of mythological imagination and must answer the question of God's being in contrast to any finite being. And the distinction of different kinds of being is a matter of ontology.

Let us now look at the arguments which have convinced Niebuhr of the inevitable dangers of ontological thought in theology. The basic argument follows directly from his understanding of reason. If ontology were a work of calculating reason, its place in theology could be only instrumental, like the rules of formal logic which the theologian should use, as must anyone else. But if ontology means more than this, it must influence the content of theology itself. And it is this possibility of which Niebuhr is afraid and which actually creates a very serious problem. For the way in which philosophers deal with being as being is a matter of ultimate concern; it has an open or hidden religious character. If this is the case, moreover, is it not unavoidable that the content of ontology clashes with the content of revelation?

Niebuhr tries to show this inescapable conflict in the following ways: Being, according to his understanding, is necessarily static because it abstracts from everything finite and changing. This may be the case in some types of ontological thought. But it is not true of the predominant trend in ontology. Being should be understood as the power of being, and even more dynamically expressed, as the power of resisting non-being. Such was the meaning of those who answered the question what kind of being God has with the assertion that he is being itself and not *a* being. Ontology, making this assertion, puts into conceptual form the Christian confession of God the almighty. If being is understood as the power of being, the contrast between static and dynamic disappears, and the God who is the Lord of time and history is both, always beyond change—otherwise he could not be the Lord of that which changes—and always participating in change; otherwise he could not direct that which changes. There again ontology conceptualizes the Christian confession to God's providential acting in history and personal life. Niebuhr is afraid that ontology removes the freedom of the individual self, including the drama of fall and salvation. Even freedom, however, has an ontological standing. It is never absolute but is always united with destiny. It is freedom within a frame of given factors. If a theologian uses the term "freedom," he cannot avoid the question of the ontological place of freedom within the whole of being. And if he gives any kind of answer to this question he ontologizes, as Niebuhr does, when he rightly binds freedom to the centered self as we experience it in ourselves. "Centered self" or even simply "self" are ontological concepts. They describe one structure of being in distinction from other structures, the most important one for us who are this structure, but not the only one. Niebuhr, in speaking of "the self," ontologizes against his own will.

If freedom has an ontological status and is correlated with destiny, the question of the fall can find an ontological answer which does not destroy the genuine meaning of the Biblical myth as Niebuhr fears. Everything man as a centered self does has the double character of responsibility and necessity. There is destiny in everything we decide in freedom. And there is freedom in everything we experience as destiny. In this way—which is an ontological way of speaking—both the individual and the universal character of man's estrangement from God are preserved, and it is not necessary for the theologian to repeat the myth of the fall which he otherwise understands as myth. He does not need to be afraid of removing the seriousness and irrationality of sin by describing the sinful state in terms of being.

Lastly, Niebuhr, like many other Protestant (not Catholic) theologians, is afraid that the assertion that God is being itself implies the denial of the personal God and makes a person-to-person relation between man and God impossible. This fear would be justified if the assertion that God is being itself were not only the first, as it must be, but also the last statement about God. But there are many more statements, such as, God is life and love and spirit, all of which are derived from revelatory experiences and all of which can be expressed ontologically. The personal character of God is no exception. It makes the person-to-person encounter between God and man possible; but it excludes the assertion that God is *a* person.

It seems to me that the substance of Niebuhr's theology would not be changed by the admission that in every theological assertion an ontological assertion is included, and that it is one of the tasks of theology to elaborate explicitly its implied ontology.

The lack of such an admission and, more important, the lack of such an elaboration make the approach to Niebuhr's thought often unnecessarily difficult for people who examine it "from outside." They do not see how far away from any mechanical supranaturalism and from any authoritarian Biblicism Niebuhr's thought actually is.

III

It is in the same vein that Niebuhr emphasizes increasingly the conflict between the Jewish and the Greek elements in Christian thought, trying to remove the latter and to strengthen the former. One easily sees that in this attitude Niebuhr follows the Neo-Kantian, Ritschlian theology which he has otherwise radically rejected. As for Harnack, the Greek mind is intellectualistic, so for Niebuhr it is rationalistic (in the sense of technical reason). It is now largely acknowledged that in the Hellenistic period in which Judaism and Christianity encountered Greek thought, the Greek mind was neither intellectualistic nor rationalistic, but mystical and longing for a way of salvation. "Gnosis" is not detached knowledge but insight on the basis of union. Even in the earlier periods of Greek philosophy this interest was at least as strong as the purely scientific one. And Niebuhr himself saw this fact when he discovered the significance of the Greek tragedy for a Christian doctrine of man. For it is impossible to separate Greek tragedy in its essential nature from Greek philosophy. Both are creations of the Apollonian-Dionysian spirit which has made the Greeks Greek.

Niebuhr, like Ritschl and Harnack, explains the acceptance of Greek concepts by the early Church as a necessary adaptation of the Christian message to the minds of those whom it wanted to reach. Such adaptation is a part of every missionary work and was done in relation to the different nations and cultures which Christianity encountered. But the case of Greek philosophy is different. Adaptation is not amalgamation. Christian theology, moreover, amalgamated Greek concepts with its message. The reason for this was that in Greek thought something universally valid had appeared which Christianity could not disregard and without which it would not have been able to express itself in a universal fashion. The question of being is as essential for human nature as the question of God, and the Logos in which the structure of being appears in reality as a whole, as well as in the human mind, is valid for every human being. Therefore it was not an accidental adaptation but a substantial necessity when the early Church related the Greek quest for ultimate reality to the Christian quest for salvation.

If one speaks of the Jewish element in Christianity, one must make a distinction between forms of expression which are generally Semitic and especially Israelitic on the one hand, and that which has been done to these forms by the revelatory experiences of the religious leaders of Judaism, on the other hand. When Christianity broke through the shell of Judaism, Christianity was liberated from bondage to the Israelitic type of Semitic culture and religion. Therefore Christianity cannot give a preference to the Jewish in contrast to the Greek encounter with reality. It transcends this contrast. But the Old Testament is more than a document of Israelitic culture and religion. It is also a document of the revelative events which happened and were received within this culture and religion. These events have drawn Israelitic forms of life and thought into the history of revelation and salvation, the center of which is the appearance of the Christ. The symbol of "Christ" itself belongs in both the Semitic-Israelitic culture and the history of revelation in Judaism and Christianity. The Christian Church was instinctively aware of this situation: it used the term "Christ" with its dynamic-historical implications; but it used other terms also, most important of which was the term Logos, which is essentially strange to Israelitic forms of thought and imagination. The contrasting of Jews and Greeks by Christian theology in order to affirm the former and to reject the latter is misleading and inadequate from Niebuhr's own point of view. He never would accept an absolute claim of any culture, not even the Jewish culture over against other cultures. No one has emphasized more strongly than he that the Christian message transcends every culture and every religion. He would contradict himself in the center of his thought if he tried to tie Christianity to the forms which have been created by Israelitic culture and Jewish religion.

This brings my short essay to an end. It contains more discussion than exposition. Descriptions of Niebuhr's thought are given in many places in this book. The preceding discussion is a continuation and a summary of many theological disputes I have had with my great friend, to whom I owe more for life and thought than I can express in this place.

PAUL TILLICH

HARVARD UNIVERSITY
CAMBRIDGE, MASS.

5

John C. Bennett

REINHOLD NIEBUHR'S SOCIAL ETHICS

5

REINHOLD NIEBUHR'S SOCIAL ETHICS

REINHOLD NIEBUHR'S social ethics are close to the center of his thought. The center is doubtless to be found in his theology; but, more than with other theologians, his theology has developed in response to his reading of contemporary history and to his reflections upon his own social and political responsibility in that history. His thought as a whole is a unity. His theology is in immediate control over his social ethics; but there is here no one-way deductive process, for in large measure his theology has developed as he has sought answers to problems which first became acute for him as a teacher of ethics and as a participant in public affairs. Both his theology and social ethics have deep roots in personal faith, in what he calls "Biblical faith." This personal faith, about which he is generally reticent, is best expressed in his prayers and in his sermons. The unity of his thought can be seen in the way the same central convictions appear in many different types of writing, in his formal books, in his sermons, and in his countless articles and editorials. One unusual characteristic of his writings is the way in which he expresses the same insight sometimes in the context of explicitly Christian theology and sometimes in articles in secular journals without any such Christian reference.

To understand Niebuhr's thought we must move back and forth between his books, which provide the theological frame for his thought, and his articles and editorials, which show his response to contemporary events. The chief reason for this is that the dialectical structure of his thought as a whole often leaves us with a delicate balance between opposite positions which are brilliantly criticized, and it is only in the light of his concrete decisions for action that we can be sure where his emphasis finally lies. These concrete decisions are found chiefly in his articles and editorials. They reveal a man who in practice spends very little time in a state of dialectical balance but who comes down frequently on one side or another of particular issues. The dialectic still shows through in the accompanying ideas which qualify his decisions without annulling them.

There is some importance in the fact that though Niebuhr is regarded as above all else a theologian, he has never been a teacher of systematic theology and has never had to develop a rounded system of doctrine. His elaboration of theology has always been an avocation professionally, as his teaching has been in Christian ethics from the beginning of his academic career. In fact, his actual chair is a chair of "applied Christianity," though such a chair is seldom occupied by a thinker with as many theologically sophisticated reservations about the application of Christianity. This somewhat accidental aspect of his professional life has had some influence on the emphasis within his theological writings, and it is partly because of it that we find him elaborating the Christian doctrine of man and the Christian view of history rather than, for example, the doctrine of God or Christology.

The changes in Niebuhr's social ethics between the 1920's and the 1950's are very striking. I shall have to deal with them, though other chapters in this volume go into more detail concerning the development of his economic and political theory. He does not help his interpreters very much by explaining how his thought has moved from book to book or from period to period. Every book or article or sermon seems to be a fresh attack on an old problem, and usually it is written as though it were his first! I believe that the essential structure of his social ethics took permanent shape during the late thirties and early forties, the period of his most intensive theological activity, when he wrote *The Nature and Destiny of Man.* His chapter "The Kingdom of God and the Struggle for Justice,"[1] in the second volume of that book, represents the continuing structure of his social ethics as well as anything that he has written. Since that was written (the preface is dated January, 1943), he has changed his opinions concerning the application of Christian ethics to particular problems, but I do not think that the style of his thought has changed fundamentally. In the subsequent period the reader can find clear indications of the general direction of his thought con-

[1] Chap. IX.

cerning such concrete applications in *The Children of Light and the Children of Darkness,* published in 1944, his only systematic study of social ethics. I believe that there is a clear line from that little book to his most recent summary of his views, which may be found in the concluding chapter of the symposium *Christian Faith and Social Action.*[2]

I have said that Niebuhr's social ethics are immediately controlled by his theology. This is especially true of his doctrine of man and of his understanding of justification by faith. I mention these doctrines for emphasis, but they cannot be isolated from the context of the Biblical faith in God who transcends history but who is active in history as creator, judge, and redeemer. Niebuhr continually contrasts Christianity with religions which have no important place for history and for which there can be no religiously based social ethics. So, deeper than every other theological influence on his social ethics is his doctrine of God and of the relation of God to history. The presupposition of his emphasis on justification by faith is his belief in the revelation of God in Christ, though his Christology is never fully elaborated. Niebuhr has little patience with metaphysical theories concerning the incarnation and even less with any conception of the incarnation which is used as the basis for a doctrine of the Church as the extension of the incarnation. His thinking about Christ is centered in the cross, understood as the revelation of the forgiving love of God in relation to man's sin. Against this background I shall try to show how Niebuhr's thinking about man and about justification influences his social ethics.

In general we can say that Niebuhr's theological teaching about human nature determines the limits of what should be attempted in society and that it is one of the factors which determine the direction of ethical action. Niebuhr's wisdom about human nature and especially about the behavior of nations and other social groups is one of the most important sources of his influence, especially of his influence outside Christian circles. He has extraordinary perception of the complexity of human motives and of the relation between morality and interest and power in society. There are many people, especially in academic circles, who rejoice in Niebuhr's diagnosis of the historical situation but who have no interest in or at least no

[2] Ed. John A. Hutchison (Charles Scribner's Sons, 1953). The chapter is entitled "Christian Faith and Social Action."

belief in the Christian gospel which Niebuhr seeks to relate to that situation.

The development of Niebuhr's conception of man in theological terms was the result of continuous interaction between his growing understanding of Biblical thought and classical Christian theology, especially the theology of Augustine and Luther, and his practical disillusionment concerning first liberal and then Marxist interpretations of man's historical development. He was never an uncritical liberal believer in progress or an uncritical Marxist, but it took him years to see through the illusions of both. Marxism helped him to recognize the illusions of liberal progressivism, and classical Christian theology helped him to see through the illusions of Marxism. We must remember, however, that this development of thought took place amidst events in which he participated and which were also disillusioning. His theological work probably hastened the process of disillusionment; it certainly provided a frame within which he was able to understand it. During the past twenty years his social ethics have been developed with constant reference to the dangers of a false idealism or utopianism. His continuous criticism of liberal progressivism which assumes that history is itself redemptive, of Communist utopianism, of optimistic political pacifism, of projects of world government which are set forth as solutions by constitutional fiat of the international problem—this is always based ultimately on the Christian doctrine of man. These criticisms limit the range of the social choices which he regards as defensible. He sees in such false idealisms not merely harmless illusions which should be avoided if one is not to be disappointed, but in some cases an escape from urgent responsibilities and in other cases the source of the most destructive forms of idolatry and of cruel fanaticism.

I have said that the doctrine of man provides both limits and direction for social ethics. These limits are themselves a form of direction. They steer us away from the effort to find absolute solutions and instead influence us to emphasize what he calls proximate solutions. The very avoidance of the idolatry and fanaticism which accompany absolute solutions is no mere negation, because it is the condition for the releasing of the constructive and cooperative elements in the human situation.

One of the great misinterpretations of Niebuhr is the idea that he is the great pessimist of modern theology. His polemics against the absolutistic optimists of various kinds have given him that reputation. But the other side of the matter is that he has very persistent hope that if men avoid these great illusions they will be able to deal constructively with their problems. In addition to warnings against hopeful illusions, he has a balanced view of human nature which supports hope. He says: "Sanctification in the realm of social relations demands recognition of the impossibility of perfect sanctification."[3] That sentence as well as any other in all of his writings states Niebuhr's relationship to our hopes and fears for society. Niebuhr's vocation has been to make way for such solutions of our problems as are possible by clearing away the idealistic and utopian illusions which have flourished among religious liberals and secular intellectuals. Today in many circles he has largely won that battle (helped, of course, by events), and it may be easier to see his thought in true perspective.

One of the most interesting examples of the bearing of Niebuhr's doctrine of man upon social ethics is his famous dictum about democracy: "Man's capacity for justice makes democracy possible; but his inclination to injustice makes democracy necessary."[4] That reveals the essential balance of his thought, which is as far from cynicism as it is from utopianism.

Closely related in Niebuhr's thought to the doctrine of man is the doctrine of justification. The former is the source of our idea of the limits and the direction of our social purposes. The latter is the source of motive and morale for ethical living amidst the moral ambiguities of historical existence. The believer in the absolutely ideal goals which were thought to be within reach was buoyed up by his expectations. But such expectations cannot long be the source of motive or morale if Niebuhr is right about the conditions of our life. His own sober but hopeful expectations are probably more important for morale in practice than he recognizes. I have always wondered if one element in his own feeling about life which adds its own quality to his thought is not a hidden disappointment that the perfect goals are not within reach. Many of us would be so much relieved, if we believed that approximate justice were not too far away, that our thought would be less influenced by the haunting disappointment that perfect justice would still elude us, than is the case with Niebuhr. It may be true that the vigor of Niebuhr's at-

[3] *The Nature and Destiny of Man,* II, 247.

[4] *The Children of Light and the Children of Darkness,* p. xi.

tacks on perfectionism comes partly from the fact that he has always been much tempted by it. He preserves the perfectionist element in Christianity in his own statement of the nature of Christian love, in his way of interpreting the relation of Christ to historical forms of power,[5] and in the tribute that he pays to the perfectionist forms of pacifism which make no claims for the applicability of pacifism to political life.

There are nuances in Niebuhr's thought in this area which are not often communicated to others, but they are not essential to an understanding of the relation of the doctrine of justification to his social ethics. It is this belief about justification which enables a Christian to act in a sinful world, to do the next best thing even though it involves participation in the corporate evil which produces real conflicts of conscience. Action within the ambiguous political struggles for social justice created for Niebuhr the great spiritual problem of the 1930s. Since the outbreak of the Second World War he has increasingly emphasized the morally tormenting conflicts connected with the violence of overt international war or with the risks which attend every policy in the period of the cold war between East and West. He has summarized the significance of the doctrine of justification in these words:

> Justification by faith in the realm of justice means that we will not regard the pressures and counterpressures, the tensions, the overt and the covert conflicts by which justice is achieved and maintained as normative in the absolute sense; but neither will we ease our conscience by seeking to escape from involvement in them. We will know that we cannot purge ourselves of the sin and guilt in which we are involved by the moral ambiguities of politics, without also disavowing responsibility for the creative possibilities of justice.[6]

In his emphasis upon justification by faith in relation to social ethics Niebuhr resembles Emil Brunner, who bases the whole ethic of *The Divine Imperative* on that doctrine. But I believe that Niebuhr is never as satisfied as Brunner seems to be that a particular policy at a given time is the will of God. Nor does the receiving of the justifying grace of God enable Niebuhr to move ahead with as untroubled a conscience. One of his favorite texts in the New Testament is Paul's words about being "perplexed, but not driven to despair" (II Cor. 4:8). Those words state well Niebuhr's own feel-

[5] *The Nature and Destiny of Man,* II, 72. [6] *Ibid.,* II, 284.

ings after he has been helped by the Gospel to take action in spite of the conflicts of conscience which usually accompany social decisions.

There is a great difference in the way in which Niebuhr's writings about these two doctrines have been received. There are many who see the point of what he says about human nature but who have no way of making contact at all with the idea of justification. This is especially true of those outside the Church whom he has influenced, but it is also true of many liberal Christians who have hardly heard of this doctrine of justification by faith until recent years. Niebuhr says little to bring pressure on those who accept his diagnosis to give more attention to his presentation of the Christian gospel. In the short run these can be separated in such a way that anyone who learns from the diagnosis can go quite far with it in reconstructing his thought. Individuals, depending on their special experiences, can make all sorts of combinations of ideas. But Niebuhr believes that these two aspects of his teaching are ultimately interdependent. If one faces the truth about the human situation, about oneself, with full honesty and realism along the lines suggested by Niebuhr's doctrine of man, it is difficult to live with what one sees unless there is some understanding of justification or forgiveness. The depth of the problem is often hidden because there are resources of grace that are not labeled with the usual theological labels. This is one factor which keeps Niebuhr from driving through the logic of his position at this point. There are occasions on which the problem appears with full clarity. One such occurred when a group of British air-force fliers in the Second World War refused to take communion because of their own moral revulsion against what they had done as a matter of duty. Niebuhr saw in this case how much they suffered because they had no understanding of justification.[7]

LOVE AND SOCIAL ETHICS

Niebuhr's ultimate reference in ethics is always to the perfect love revealed in the cross of Christ, the suffering love of one who sought nothing for himself, the love that is directed toward all neighbors. This is the pinnacle of ethics, the nature of the divine perfection in the light of which all of our moral achievements are judged. This is one of the points at which Niebuhr always underlines the perfectionist element in Christianity. This perfect love is what he has

[7] *Christianity and Society*, Summer, 1943, p. 3.

called an "impossible possibility."[8] This means that, while love is never fully embodied in any human motive or human action, it remains relevant as a standard for both motive and action. It is relevant because we are judged by it and because, if in humility before God we avoid the pretensions which most seriously distort our life, we are able to approximate such love. The chief warning must always be that whenever we do approximate it, at that moment even the best that we do is in greatest danger of corruption.

How is it possible to move from this perfect love to social ethics? The title of Niebuhr's early and most provocative book, *Moral Man and Immoral Society,* suggests too sharp a contrast between personal and social ethics even for his own thought at the time. The immorality is in man and is not a product of social institutions. Yet Niebuhr has always been impressed by the aggravated form of the moral problem whenever the relations between social groups with power are involved. He sees far greater possibilities of self-deception in connection with such group behavior. In his first book he emphasized difficulties of group morality which have always had an important place in his social diagnosis. The absence of direct personal experience of the effect of group behavior on others is one factor.[9] There is also the fact that "the ethical attitude of the individual toward his group easily obscures the unethical nature of the group's desires."[10] The moral impulses of the individual are often satisfied by his loyalty to the group and he easily becomes uncritical of the group's behavior. Put beside these factors the endless capacity to cloak group behavior with false idealism, with all manner of rationalizations and ideologies, and we have an adequate explanation of the aggravation of moral problems in the relations between groups. The possession of the various forms of economic and political power greatly increases the range of temptation and the capacity to do objective harm. The fact that groups live much longer than individuals enlarges the possibility of cumulative wrong. It is true that public morality may be above that of many individuals and that there are selected groups which may raise indefinitely the level of the life of their members; but it is large-scale political and economic groups which are here in view. Even the most morally sensitive individuals find that as citizens and as members of economic

[8] *An Interpretation of Christian Ethics,* pp. 117ff.
[9] *Does Civilization Need Religion?* pp. 125–126.
[10] *Ibid.,* p. 131.

groups such as corporations or labor unions they face more limited moral possibilities than they do in their personal relations.

There is always in Niebuhr's mind an uneasy relationship between the ethic of love or the Kingdom of God and all concrete action in society. He says: "The fact is that the Kingdom of God represents a final and absolute possibility which is, in some respects, equally distant from all political programs because all of them involve elements of coercion and resistance which are foreign to a commonwealth of pure brotherhood and love."[11] Here is an example of the background of perfectionism to which I have referred. If Niebuhr said only that, he would be no different from the early Barth who could have no ethic for social institutions or policies. But there is great importance in the words "in some respects." They keep such sentences from canceling out the very great emphasis on the relevance of the Christian ethic for society. The major reason for the recurrence of such sentences in Niebuhr's writings is found in the next sentence in this passage: "The real problem for the Christian is not how anyone as good as he can participate in unethical political activity but how anyone as sinful as he can dare to set himself as a judge of his fellow men." Here we have a warning against self-righteousness which is a constant refrain in all of Niebuhr's writings. He has never found a way which is satisfactory even to himself of relating the real and often overwhelmingly important moral differences between men and between social institutions or programs and the religious dimension which keeps them all under judgment so that there is never a place for self-righteousness. He struggles with this problem in the section on "the equality of sin and the inequality of guilt" in the first volume of *The Nature and Destiny of Man,*[12] but the result hardly does justice to his own thought.

Here is one of the most clearly dialectical elements in Niebuhr's thought. He refuses to let go of the ideal of equal judgment upon all social achievements as a warning against the self-righteousness which threatens to pervert the highest achievements, and he is no less concerned to preserve the relevance of the Christian ethic to all political and social life. I think that we can keep these two things together if we realize that each serves a purpose of its own. The relevance of the ethic gives direction to both motive and decision, and this is never canceled by the emphasis upon the equality of all

[11] *Christianity and Society,* Spring, 1938, p. 1. [12] Pp. 219–227.

things human before the divine judgment. The latter is corrective teaching which keeps the belief that some actions are better than others from leading to the kind of pride which corrupts what is good in those better actions. This religious corrective is quite as important for social ethics as the positive ethical directive which Niebuhr finds in Christian teaching. At least this can be seen to be true if we accept Niebuhr's conviction that the most destructive social evils come when the assurance that one possesses the perfect program or policy destroys charity and tolerance and the capacity for self-criticism.

Christian love is related to our social decisions by way of such general ethical principles as justice and order and freedom. These are not static principles, and the way in which they should be related to one another in concrete situations is as varied as each situation is unique. They are not distinctively Christian principles, but they are forced upon us inevitably by reflection upon the conditions of our life. Love cannot repeal them and love cannot work apart from them. Love obligates us in each situation to find the best pattern for the ordering of society in terms of these principles.

These general principles are not ultimately in conflict with one another, but there is usually tension between them and often it is necessary to give priority to one of them. Toward the end of the Second World War, for example, Niebuhr emphasized the primary importance of developing some kind of stable order in the world following the war. He referred to the experience of Lincoln with his emphasis upon saving the Union as instructive in dealing with international relations. Lincoln found that only by abolishing slavery could he save the Union. Niebuhr says of Lincoln's experience: "This is a nice symbol of the fact that order precedes justice in the strategy of government; but that only an order which implicates justice can achieve a stable peace. An unjust order quickly invites the resentment and rebellion which lead to its undoing."[13] He frequently criticizes the tendency in some forms of Christian orthodoxy, especially in Lutheranism, to stress order at the expense of justice. He traces this to a one-sided pessimism in Luther's view of human nature. Such pessimism may cause us to fear anarchy above all else and to assume that the maintenance of whatever order exists is preferable to the risk of anarchy. More recently Niebuhr has emphasized the error in the one-sided libertarianism in America which

[13] *The Children of Light and the Children of Darkness*, p. 181.

gives priority to freedom, especially in the form of economic individualism, and neglects not only justice but any direct concern for community.

Niebuhr carries on a continual debate with both legalists and moral relativists. He recognizes the claim of these broad principles; but always above them for him stands the "law of love." But every system of social morality which is based upon the idea that there are universal laws which are known in advance and which control the relationship of love to these principles in concrete situations fails to recognize the dynamic character of history and the unique elements in most situations. Here we find one of Niebuhr's chief criticisms of Catholicism. He believes that Catholic moralists tend to absolutize aspects of medieval culture in their interpretations of natural law. He believes that they are far too rigid in their application of the natural law to the endless complexities of social life. In his polemics against the Catholic conception of natural law he often seems to reject natural law altogether, but he draws back from that conclusion and presents at times a critical conception of natural law or a real Protestant substitute for natural law.

The following is a typical statement of his position: "There must be some way of resolving this debate between legalists and relativists which will refute the legalists whenever they make too sweeping claims for fixed standards of conduct and which will, at the same time, avoid an abyss of nihilism on the edge of moral relativism."[14] In this context he emphasizes the law of love as the protection against moral relativism. But he also recognizes that there is limited truth in the natural-law conception, that there is a "permanent structure of human personality"[15] and that there are moral principles which are known apart from revelation. He is as impatient with Karl Barth as he is with the Catholics. He writes: "Karl Barth's belief that the moral life of man would possess no valid principles of guidance if the Ten Commandments had not introduced such principles by revelation is as absurd as it is unscriptural."[16]

So much of Niebuhr's writing is polemical that he cannot usually be understood unless what he says is interpreted in the light of the position which he is attempting to correct. Very often he overcorrects, and his own real emphasis will then be seen by comparing his polemics against one position with those against the opposite

[14] *Faith and History*, p. 173. [15] *Ibid.*, p. 180.
[16] *The Nature and Destiny of Man*, II, 254.

position. The dialectical structure of his thought is favorable to this polemical method of overemphasis. The best way of discovering his essential position is to see where he comes down in terms of a concrete decision for action.[17]

One of the distinctive elements in the structure of Niebuhr's thought is his method of relating love to the essential social principles which I have discussed and to all the prudential considerations which emerge in concrete situations. As I have said, he thinks of love in terms of radical self-giving. This is the nature of Christian *agape* in its perfection, and "the law of love" in these radical terms is always relevant as an ultimate guide and as a basis for judgment. It is very difficult to find a clear line connecting this perfect love with social ethics. Niebuhr helps us at this point by developing the conception of mutual love. This is the form of love which is in varying degrees present in human relations, especially personal relations. Mutual love is not based upon calculation concerning degrees of actual reciprocity. It develops in relationships where such reciprocity does exist or where it can be expected to exist, but it goes far beyond any bargaining attitude. It intends faithfulness and sacrifice for those who are loved without self-centered calculation. There is therefore an element of *agape* in mutual love. On the other hand mutual love is nourished by those relationships in which reciprocity is possible and even expected.[18]

I believe that in Niebuhr's formal analysis of love there is a missing link as we seek to relate love to social ethics. This missing link is presupposed in his thought as a whole, and yet I do not find it clearly described or clearly related to the types of love which he emphasizes. Mutual love is the form of love that is closest to social ethics, but this concept does not describe the kind of love which is often present in connection with the larger problems of society where the element of mutuality is lacking. We have here something

[17] In a recent article Niebuhr applies his ideas about fixed and one-sided conceptions of the moral law that bedevil the present international situation. He writes: "This matter is the more important for that majority among us who know that we face two problems in our generation rather than one: the avoidance of war and resistance to tyranny. The 'pure' idealists are always tempted to war against communism in the name of justice or to come to terms with it in the name of peace. The ideals of these contrasting idealists may be purer than ours. We cannot claim greater moral purity; but perhaps we may claim to possess a wisdom which is more relevant to our two-pronged predicament."—*Christian Century,* Dec. 2, 1953, p. 1388.

[18] *The Nature and Destiny of Man,* II, 68–70.

that has *agape* in it but which is not pure *agape*. It is a real caring for the welfare and dignity of all of our neighbors, even those whom we never see, those who may live as vast multitudes on other continents or those who may actually be opponents or enemies. Our attitude to these people may seldom involve full self-giving, but it may involve many degrees of the willingness to pay a price when the welfare of others is at stake. Love in this sense is closer to justice than any other form of love. It means the willing of justice for others. It means sensitive concern for the development of structures of social life which are essential to the welfare of people everywhere. Love of this kind has often been expressed in the willingness to make sacrifices to prevent tyranny from being fastened on some other community. It has often been present in those who have endured the hardships of military service and of actual warfare. The fact of violence does not cancel the element of *agape* in this love. This love is seen in countless ways among men of conscience who really give themselves to the task of making human relations "a little more tolerable and slightly more just."[19] Christians have no monopoly of it; indeed, one of the unusual characteristics of Niebuhr's thought is that he is often less inhibited in recognizing the purity of such love among non-Christians than he is in the case of those who because they are Christians seem to him to have greater moral pretensions and sometimes more theological rationalizations for escaping from the demands of love. All that I have said about love in this sense pervades Niebuhr's thought, but it is not clear how it is related to *agape* or to mutual love.

Niebuhr's conception of the relationship between love and justice is extraordinarily many-sided. There is no more fruitful analysis in all of his ethical writings than his discussion of this problem. All ideas of justice are for him both negated and fulfilled by love. Justice is in part an embodiment of love wherever there are complex human relationships. And yet every idea of justice and every structure of justice is capable of being corrected and raised to a higher level by love. Justice always involves an element of calculation of interests. It has to do with permanent obligations and with impartial methods of determining rights and interests. Justice for Niebuhr is never far from equality. Equality in the sense of impartiality in the determination of needs and rights is an essential aspect of justice; but even more, though justice does not involve a legalistic effort to

[19] *Ibid.*, II. 197.

impose equality on society, it should keep all unequal conditions under rigorous criticism. Even though it may be granted that some inequalities of privilege should go with inequalities of function, the tendency is for all beneficiaries of inequality to exaggerate the case for their special privileges. As he says: "They will seek to hide the historic fact that privileged members of the community invariably use their higher degree of social power to appropriate an excess of privileges not required by their function and certainly not in accord with differences of need."[20] He goes so far as to say that "equality as a pinnacle of the ideal of justice implicitly points toward love as the final norm of justice; for equal justice is the approximation of brotherhood under the conditions of sin."[21]

I have depended here on Niebuhr's discussion of the subject.[22] I think that his analysis in that book is still true to his thought. There is a difference today in that he is more willing to accept social inequalities than he was fifteen years ago because he is more fearful of the threat to efficiency and to freedom if efforts are made to impose equality on society.

LOVE, JUSTICE, AND POWER

There are two emphases in Niebuhr's discussion of the relation between love and justice which, in the sharpness and clarity with which they are presented, seem to me to be distinctive. The first is that justice must always be thought of in dynamic terms, and that love can always raise justice to new heights. There is an indeterminateness about the possibilities of transforming justice by love. Love makes our consciences more sensitive to the needs of others, especially to the needs of those who have been neglected or exploited. The vast body of social legislation in recent years in many countries is an embodiment of justice. It became possible partly because of the political and economic pressures of groups that have been at a disadvantage, but also because there has developed in society at large, even among privileged classes, a more sensitive social conscience. Those who think of Niebuhr as chiefly the great discoverer of sin fail to realize how much credit he gives to the effect of this sensitized conscience upon society. He never thinks of it as working alone, for always its effectiveness depends upon its interaction with the political pressures to which I have referred.

The other emphasis in Niebuhr's conception of the relation be-

[20] *Ibid.*, II, 255. [21] *Ibid.*, II, 254. [22] *Ibid.*, Chap. IX.

tween love and justice is his conviction that love never takes the place of justice even under the best possible human conditions. He often uses relations within the family to illustrate this. He says: "Even the love within a family avails itself of customs and usages which stereotype given adjustments between various members of the family in such a way that each action need not be oriented by a fresh calculation of competing interests."[23] This is the result of sin; but I think that he would admit that it is also the result of human finiteness. Generally accepted structures and habits of justice, even in communities which are bound together in considerable measure by love, reduce the occasions for conflict, and for the wear and tear which are present even in good human relations. Also, there are no institutions and no communities which are so good that power does not tempt those who hold it to take advantage of others, perhaps in quite subtle ways. This is true of families and churches and academic communities and of any other forms of association which might be mentioned. To try to live entirely by love and to discard all structures of justice is to run a great risk of destroying love. There are, of course, occasions on which love should break through the best structures of justice to take account of a new and unrecognized need, and on which all calculation of rights and interests should be discarded. The fact that the willingness to do that is present in reserve is one of the characteristics of love which gives a different quality to human relations in any community, even though it is self-defeating to found those relations on such spontaneous love alone.

A large part of Niebuhr's thought about the application of social ethics to concrete situations is concerned with the relation between justice and power. The strength of the egoism of all social groups is such that the power of every group needs to be checked by the power of those of whom it is tempted to take some advantage. The struggle for justice consists largely in the effort to increase the power of the victims of injustice. But the victims themselves will always be tempted by their new power. Sometimes they are driven by blind fury which must be checked or by false idealism which gives them an excuse for cruel and unjust methods for the realization of their goals. Nations in their wars for justice or against unjust aggression are involved in the same temptations as social classes, with even greater opportunities for self-deception. The great difficulty is that

[23] *Ibid.*, II, 248.

there is no agency with power which stands impartially above these conflicts, for every such agency gets its power from particular groups whose interests are involved in the conflict. This is patently true in the international sphere. To some extent it is true in a more disguised way in the case of the power conflicts within a nation, though Niebuhr today is more willing than he was in the 1930s, when he was most influenced by Marxism, to grant that a national government may succeed in representing a sufficient variety of interests and a sufficient sense of national community to be able to transcend the egoism of a particular class.

He sees no escape from this constantly changing and often partly hidden conflict between groups with power. Today he would put less emphasis than formerly on the purely economic aspect of this conflict, and given a tendency for power to balance power, he finds the conflict of power both modified and transcended in many ways. Without this tendency toward balance there can be little justice. But this tendency is compatible with the development of moral resources in a community which keep its life from being a naked power struggle. In our own highly pluralistic society the fact that most people participate in many different non-economic and non-political groups is of great importance. Even where the power conflicts are sharpest it is possible for men to respect one another as persons and to remain aware of common interests, common traditions, and common loyalties. When law represents these forms of awareness, it can greatly modify the way in which citizens use their power. Love working within the hearts of people can do much to strengthen the common loyalties, to raise the moral level on which power still adjusts itself to power, and to develop within the community many kinds of personal relationships in which such love is directly expressed. It cannot be said too often that all of these problems of justice become at least manageable if the various groups and parties do not cloak their struggles for power with self-righteous illusions.

DEVELOPMENT OF NIEBUHR'S THOUGHT

In the development of Niebuhr's thought about social ethics there have been remarkable changes, though there has been no change either in his conception of the relative importance of the Christian's social responsibility or in his habit of viewing social problems with a sharp realism. Changes in his theology have greatly altered the basis of his judgments and have given him a quite different understanding of the Gospel. These changes in theology have interacted with changes in the historical situation and, as a result, between the 1920s and the 1950s we find him making profoundly different judgments about pacifism, about the Marxist view of history, about Socialism and Capitalism as economic systems, about problems of political strategy. And yet, readers of *Leaves from the Notebook of a Tamed Cynic*, published in 1929 and reflecting his outlook during the previous fifteen-year period, will find far more of the same spirit and of the same habit of mind which they know in him today than he himself will recognize.

Niebuhr's social outlook was formed originally in large measure by the tradition of the liberal Social Gospel. He was brought up in the Evangelical Synod, now a part of the Evangelical-Reformed Church of which he is a minister. It was the transplantation to America of the Prussian Union Church which contained Lutheran and Reformed elements. This meant that for him Luther was a stronger influence than was the case with most American Protestants. I have often thought that this fact may have made him responsive to elements in Luther's faith and theology which have always been completely alien to most American Protestants. These very elements of Luther's thought later modified his theology and his understanding of the relation between the Gospel and social ethics, but without changing his essential social concern. So, for Niebuhr there were early theological influences which, when he had time to reflect on them, brought a different shading into his understanding of the Christian social teaching than can be expected from those who have always lived on soil prepared chiefly by Calvinism or by various forms of the sectarian version of Christianity. I think that it is in part this influence from Luther which has made it difficult for Niebuhr to communicate his convictions about perfectionism or about law and grace to the majority of Christian liberals in this country.

The Detroit of 1915 gave Niebuhr many targets for his Christian indignation. This early exposure to American industrialism in the raw (long before the days of the Ford Foundation!) was a decisive factor in the development of Niebuhr's social ethics. In his *Leaves from the Notebook of a Tamed Cynic* he writes often about the greed and blindness of the industrial overlords and of the lack of social imagination among the middle classes generally. The following is a typical passage: "Look at the industrial enterprise anywhere and you find criminal indifference on the part of the strong to the fate of the weak. The lust for power and the greed for gain are the dominant note in business. An industrial overlord will not share his power with his workers until he is forced to do so by tremendous pressure. The middle classes, with the exception of a small minority of intelligentsia, do not aid the worker in exerting this pressure. He must fight alone."[24]

In the 1950s he modified his judgment of the American businessman and the middle classes, and his support of the workers became more qualified because of the power of their unions; but these changes are largely the result of changes in the situation.

Other chapters in this volume emphasize the changes in Niebuhr's theology and indicate how these changes have affected his attitude toward the Social Gospel. He came to stress the extent to which the liberal Social Gospel identified Christianity with the religion of social progress. As early as 1932 he wrote sharply about the limitations of the Social Gospel, criticizing Walter Rauschenbusch. He agreed with Rauschenbusch's criticisms of social institutions and accepted his objectives, but he believed that Rauschenbusch shared the liberal illusions about the possibility of building a new society through education and moral persuasion. He said: "Rauschenbusch had a holy zeal for a social ideal which was essentially socialistic. But he had no conception of the class struggle." Niebuhr found that the whole liberal movement in religious as in secular educational circles reflected a middle-class optimism which was conditioned by the fact that the middle classes had little firsthand contact with the more intolerable injustices in society.[25]

He wrote in 1935 of liberal Christianity: "Its Kingdom of God was translated to mean exactly that ideal society which modern culture hoped to realize through the evolutionary process. . . . The Christ of Christian orthodoxy, true mythical symbol of both the possibilities and the limits of the human, became the man of Galilee, symbol of human goodness and human possibilities without suggestion of the limits of the human and the temporal—in short, without the suggestion of transcendence."[26] In 1954 he writes of the Social Gospel in the context of the catastrophes and perils of our age: "The 'social gospel' was informed by the ideals and illusions of a 'liberal'

[24] P. 94. [25] *World Tomorrow*, Sept. 21, 1932.
[26] *An Interpretation of Christian Ethics*, p. 15.

age which could not cope with these dread realities and possibilities."[27]

He has generally admitted freely the contribution of the Social Gospel in correcting the individualism of American Protestantism. His own thought would be profoundly different if there had been no liberal Social Gospel. The Social Gospel was one of the forces which prepared much of the leadership of American Protestantism to encourage the Labor movement in its struggles to exist and then to achieve a position of considerable power in the economy. The same Protestant leaders were prepared by the Social Gospel to support the New Deal reforms even though many of the Protestant Churches were predominantly Republican and though their members most often voted against the New Deal. Niebuhr's criticism of the liberal theology which was generally associated with the Social Gospel did not prevent him from working with liberal churchmen with whom he agreed on immediate social goals. I think that he was often more at home, however, with Jews and secular idealists who shared many of the illusions common among Christian liberals but who did not give to them a Christian sanction.

In what follows I shall consider two major changes in Niebuhr's thought. The first is the change connected with the issue of pacifism. The second is the change from the strong support of Socialism under definitely Marxist influence to his present pragmatic outlook which constitutes a rejection of any doctrinaire views concerning economic institutions. I shall deal in more detail with the pacifist issue because the development of his thought here is closer to the inner structure of his social ethics. I shall say something about the effect of the second development upon his method of thinking but leave the details to be discussed by Professor Schlesinger.[28]

THE PACIFIST ISSUE

Niebuhr was once counted a pacifist. He was for several years national chairman of the Fellowship of Reconciliation. (From this vantage point the mystery deepens when we find that at that time the executive secretary of the Fellowship was J. B. Matthews!) I cannot find that Niebuhr was ever in theory consistently an absolute pacifist. He did share the general revulsion that followed the First World War. He was convinced of the futility of international war. His own pacifism was based on the belief that in all conceivable circumstances

[27] *Christianity and Crisis,* March 22, 1954. [28] See Chap. 5.

war would be the greatest evil, a belief which could be defended very easily before the development of aggressive totalitarianism. There was, moreover, in the background of Niebuhr's thought a perfectionism for which all forms of coercion created a serious problem.

The break with pacifism became clear in 1932. It came in the context of political coercion in the class struggle rather than in the context of international war. Niebuhr at that time was under stronger Marxist influence than at any other time in his career. His long-standing realism about the moral limitations of large-scale power groups was greatly sharpened by his study of Marxism and by his observation of events during the period of the depression. The criticism of pacifism came with his emphasis upon the idea that there was no intrinsic moral difference between violent and non-violent resistance. He wrote in 1932: "The differences are pragmatic rather than intrinsic. The social consequences of the two methods are different, but the differences are in degree rather than in kind. Both place restraint upon liberty and both may destroy life and property. Once the principle of coercion and resistance has been accepted as necessary to the social struggle, and pure pacifism has thus been abandoned, the differences between violence and non-violence lose some of their significance though they remain important."[29]

There seems to be here a kind of watershed between pacifism and non-pacifism in Niebuhr's mind, and from 1932 until the present time Niebuhr has been known very widely as the sharpest critic of pacifism in the American church. Just before the Second World War he was largely instrumental in founding *Christianity and Crisis* in order to counteract the pacifist trend in the Church and especially the curious combination of pacifism with isolationism resulting from the fact that both were concerned to avoid involvement in the war in Europe.

The first full statement of his criticism of pacifism is in *Moral Man and Immoral Society* (1932), a book which marks the beginning of his break with both pacifism and liberal theology in the Church. We find here an elaboration of the idea that there is no intrinsic difference between violent and non-violent resistance.[30] Many Christian pacifists had identified themselves with Gandhi because they believed that he had given them a *political* alternative to the Marxist approach to class conflict and to the conventional military approach to international conflict. They transferred to Gandhi's program the

[29] *World Tomorrow*, Sept. 21, 1932. [30] Chap. 9.

absolute claims which had been associated with Christian non-resistance. This confusion for years aroused in Niebuhr something like wrath. He rejected it first because he saw only a difference in degree between non-violent resistance, which was often the more successful form of coercion, and violent resistance. But later he came to emphasize the irresponsibility in relying on non-violent resistance when there was no ground to believe that it would be successful in preventing the spread of totalitarian tyranny. It could only be successful when those who are resisting have a potential ally in the consciences of their opponents, as was the case in Gandhi's struggle against the British.

Niebuhr in 1932 placed strict limits around morally permissible violence. He said: "If violence can be justified at all, its terror must have the tempo of a surgeon's skill and healing must follow quickly upon its wounds."[31] He emphasized the great moral superiority of non-violent resistance in terms of its consequences where such resistance was possible. He says: "Non-violent coercion and resistance, in short, is a type of coercion which offers the largest opportunities for a harmonious relationship with the moral and rational factors in social life."[32] His interest here was in the possibility of violent resistance in the interests of justice in the class struggle. He was still highly dubious concerning the possibility of justifying international war. His mind changed only as the actual alternatives in the world became limited to surrender to the expanding totalitarianism on the one hand and violent resistance by nations resulting in war on the other.

All of this discussion of pacifism has been carried on against a background of conviction concerning the place of absolute non-resistance in Christian ethics. He believed that perfect love does involve such non-resistance. In *Moral Man and Immoral Society* he says: "Nothing is clearer than that a pure religious idealism must issue in a policy of non-resistance which makes no claims to be socially efficacious. It submits to any demands, however unjust, and yields to any claims, however inordinate, rather than assert self-interest against another."[33] That theme recurs throughout most of his writings.

In his *The Nature and Destiny of Man* he says that the perfection of Christ was dependent on the fact that he was not involved in any

[31] *Moral Man and Immoral Society*, p. 220.
[32] *Ibid.*, p. 251.
[33] *Ibid.*, p. 264.

power conflicts.[34] This has always seemed to me to be precarious because it indicates that Christ could only be perfect by being free from the temptations which accompany the moral responsibilities of most other men. This idea does play a very important part in Niebuhr's social ethics. It enables him to have great respect for those forms of pacifism which do not confuse Christian love with a political program, which do not regard the cross as a strategy that can be expected to lead to a non-violent victory over opponents. He has always rejected the idea of the cross as a "success story." He prefers the more consistent sectarians, especially the stricter Mennonites, who do not expect to change the course of history, to the Quakers, who have generally held to an optimistic view of man and history and who usually believe that they do have a clue to a strategy which will avoid violence and at the same time restrain conquerors and oppressors.[35]

Niebuhr has always believed that the more consistent Christian pacifists had a constructive vocation in the Church. He wrote in 1940 about the witness of the pacifist: "We who allow ourselves to become engaged in war need this testimony of the absolutist against us, lest we accept the warfare of the world as normative, lest we become callous to the horror of war, and lest we forget the ambiguity of our own actions and motives and the risk we run of achieving no permanent good from this momentary anarchy in which we are involved."[36] But he always reminds the pacifist that his testimony will be more effective if the pacifist himself is free from self-righteous illusions, if he does not claim to be free from the moral dilemmas in which the Christian non-pacifist must admit that he is involved.

Niebuhr's polemic against pacifism reached its height in the late thirties when the world was threatened by Nazi tyranny and the politically minded pacifists were making it difficult to see clearly the nature of the threat and were placing obstacles in the way of resisting it. Some of them were making common cause with the pro-Munich conservatives in Britain and with the "America First" movement in this country. Niebuhr was a great admirer of George Lansbury, the British Labor leader, a devout Christian pacifist whom Niebuhr regarded as a saint. When Lansbury died in 1940 Niebuhr wrote an editorial combining appreciation for his personal qualities with criticism of his political judgment. He said that Lansbury's Christian

[34] II, 72. [35] *Reflections on the End of an Era,* pp. 111–112.
[36] *Christianity and Power Politics,* p. 31.

idealism in combination with the opportunism of the Tories had made "Britain impotent before advancing German aggression and made the war inevitable." He said of Lansbury that the last years of his life "were spent in the futile attempt to prove that the dreadful realities of a decadent Europe were not real."[37] In the same issue of this journal he had an editorial attacking American Christians, especially the *Christian Century,* for failing to see that tyranny can be as destructive as war.

Niebuhr saw in the readiness of many American pacifists to make common cause with isolationists on the ground that the latter were seeking to keep America out of war the final absurdity to which pacifists' illusions led. But more than pacifist illusions were involved. As he wrote six months before Pearl Harbor: "A religious perfectionism which shuns the realities of politics in one moment and embraces the sorriest political relativities in the next is the natural fruit of decades of sentimentality in which religious absolutes were regarded as easily achieved goals of political justice."[38]

Niebuhr did not advocate American entrance into the war even while he was criticizing the pacifists for failing to see the issues at stake in the war. He believed that America could not enter the war even after the invasion of western Europe by the Germans because we were not united as a nation. Our interests as a nation were ultimately at stake but they were not immediately at stake, and we could not expect our people to be united in war. The nation in 1940 did not "feel that coincidence of vital and ideal interests which alone prompts nations to enter such a horrible carnage with comparative unanimity."[39] He believed that entry into the war in 1940 would so divide the nation that we might lose our liberties through the effort of the majority to coerce the minority into support of the war. This argument of Niebuhr's is an example of the way in which he usually weighs considerations of justice with considerations of prudence. To disregard prudence in such a situation is to find oneself responsible for catastrophes which in the end may lead to greater injustice.[40]

The rejection of pacifism, especially in its political form, is based primarily on Niebuhr's doctrine of man. In an open letter[41] to

[37] *Christianity and Society,* Summer, 1940, p. 3.
[38] *Christianity and Crisis,* June 16, 1941.
[39] *Christianity and Society,* Summer, 1940.
[40] Cf. Chap. 6 by Professor Thompson.
[41] *Christianity and Society,* Summer, 1940, pp. 30–31.

Richard Roberts, one of the pacifists whom he most respected, Niebuhr emphasized the failure of pacifists to do justice to the Reformation doctrine of justification by faith, substituting for it a sectarian perfectionism which believed "that divine grace actually lifts man out of the sinful contradictions of history and establishes him above the sins of the world." The illusion which he saw in the pacifist case is that the pacifist believes that he can avoid sin in the situation if he resolutely refuses to engage in violence. He said to Dr. Roberts, "Your difficulty is that you want to try to live in history without sinning." But in failing to do what can be done to "preserve some relative decency and justice in society against the tyranny and injustice into which society may fall," the pacifist himself is involved in sin. If he would only recognize this and then make his choice of a pacifist policy as the lesser evil in the circumstances, but not as a sinless policy, Niebuhr would not be able to use this theological argument against him.

Sometimes in his arguments with the pacifists Niebuhr seems to move too easily from the idea that sin is universal to the conclusion that war as a particular expression of sin is justified. But always in the background there is the assumption that war, horrible as it is, may be preferable to surrender to a totalitarian system. Without that judgment, or an equivalent judgment drawn from circumstances, the use of the general fact of sin as a justification for support of war is beside the point. Pacifists usually have concentrated on the human consequences of war for so long that they are not quite as sensitive to the human consequences of totalitarianism. Also, they are often prevented by their more optimistic view of man from recognizing the extent of malignant power in such a system as National Socialism, or with some important differences in Stalinism. Pacifists often seem to be driven by their special interest to paint a prettier picture of the foe than the facts support. They combine this with a tendency to exaggerate the darker side of their own society. So, the comparative judgments that are made in any given situation concerning the degree of evil in the consequences of war versus those of tyranny and the possibilities of improving by peaceful means the injustices on either side of a conflict are essential to the argument.

The doctrine of man cannot of itself lead Niebuhr or anyone else to reject pacifist conclusions in every case. It would not be impossible for him in principle to decide that in some other situation war was the greater evil. If he did so, unlike the pacifists against whom he argues, he would doubtless be aware of the moral ambiguities in his case. In recent years the horrors of atomic warfare have not shaken his belief that pacifism as a universal law is wrong. They have, however, created for him, as for most other Christians, an almost intolerable dilemma. If this kind of power exists at all, it is right that nations should be able to protect themselves against it. Yet if they ever have to use hydrogen weapons as part of a program of defense or of threatened retaliation as itself a measure of defense, the result would be violence without any moral limits. Niebuhr in his criticism of obliteration bombing in the Second World War has always protested against this in principle. His predicament is shared by all who are not absolute pacifists; and if the absolute pacifists are wrong in not accepting the judgment that the readiness to use atomic weapons in retaliation may actually prevent war and hence prevent their use, then they may be advocating a policy which would make atomic war more probable. Whether this judgment about the effects of such a policy is right or not is a precarious psychological and political judgment, but Christian theology may prepare us to accept the fact that both pacifists and non-pacifists are in this moral predicament.

Niebuhr during the Second World War became one of the most influential representatives of a kind of Christian non-pacifism which was in sharp contrast to the outlook of Christians in the First World War. It was not new in history, but in the modern period of wars fought by whole nations for ideals it came as an extremely important corrective. As Herbert Butterfield has shown, it is these wars for righteousness which have generated the most fanatical self-righteousness on the part of nations.[42] Niebuhr ceaselessly applied his warnings against self-righteousness to the nation. He never regarded the war as a "holy war" and he saw great ambiguities even in the justice on our side. He sought to keep the methods of warfare under criticism and he signed the report of the Federal Council's Commission on the Church and the War in the Light of the Christian Faith which greatly emphasized this responsibility of the Church. In accordance with his theological convictions he saw the war as the result of corporate sins in which our nation shared. No one could have been more opposed to National Socialism, but he saw how far our own policies had contributed to its rise.

One of the most significant aspects of his attitude toward the war

[42] Herbert Butterfield, *Christianity, Diplomacy and War* (Abingdon-Cokesbury Press, 1954), Chap. 3.

was his own close relations with the anti-Nazi Germans, both exiles and those who remained in Germany. This helped him to avoid the "unconditional surrender" psychology, and he became one of the chief advocates of a moderate policy in regard to Germany as soon as the war ended. He wrote a great deal about a peace of reconciliation during the years immediately following the war. Much of this writing was in secular journals and contained no reference to Christian theology. It was obvious to those who knew his thought as a whole that what he said which made his thought different from that of many secular liberals with whom he agreed on other subjects came from assumptions about the pride and guilt of nations, about vindictiveness and forgiveness, which would not have come to have as clear a meaning for him had it not been for the context of Christian faith.

THE SOCIALIST ISSUE

A second major transition in Niebuhr's social ethics was from a Christian socialism which was based upon a general acceptance of the Marxist view of historical developments and of social strategy to the acceptance of a mixed economy and of a pragmatic view of social and political strategy. This transition is important for his whole method of thinking about social issues. Much of the change came from his quickness to learn from history; but as I have said before, the interaction between his growing interest in and knowledge of the theology of Augustine and the Reformation and his response to changing events gives us the real explanation of the changes in his thought. He was not merely reflecting the changes in external circumstances, for he was digging more deeply at the same time into the history of Christian thought.

Niebuhr's confident acceptance of most of the Marxist diagnosis of the historical situation and of the Marxist solution of the problems of what seemed to be a decaying Capitalism is to be found in two books written in the early thirties, *Moral Man and Immoral Society* and *Reflections on the End of an Era.* The files of *Radical Religion,* for which he wrote most of the editorials from 1935 until the period of preoccupation with international issues in 1939, yield most interesting and, from the vantage point of the present, surprising material on this earlier phase of his thought. We must remember that the period of Niebuhr's critical "Christian Marxism" was the period of the Great Depression. During that period he used Marxism as an instrument for the criticism of liberal social Christianity; but soon he used his deepening knowledge of Christian theology as the main instrument for the criticism of Marxism.

I have used the word Marxism rather than Socialism because Niebuhr went far beyond the acceptance of Socialism as a social goal or as a morally preferable alternative to Capitalism. He believed that the Marxist view of the historical process was largely correct during the period of Capitalism, though he acknowledged the Marxist illusions about the world after the revolution, illusions which soon came to be, in his view, the major source of the evil of Communism.[43] I should say now for the benefit of any reader who does not read further that before 1940 Niebuhr became one of the sharpest critics of Communism and one of those who stood most firmly against any co-operation with Communists long before the "cold war." Today Communism has no opponent in this country who knows how to deal it a deadlier blow on the intellectual and spiritual level.

Niebuhr's complete rejection of Capitalism and his advocacy of Socialism as an alternative began earlier and lasted longer than the influence of the Marxist view of history and strategy, i.e., from the beginning of his professional life until as late as 1948. During the 1930s especially he wrote about Capitalism with prophetic derision and often expressed his belief that Capitalist institutions were the most putrid aspect of a decaying civilization and the oligarchs of the business world the chief examples of social stupidity.

In 1935, in a book on Christian ethics which shows the beginning of Niebuhr's more distinctive theology, we find a clear statement of the adequacy of Marxism as an analysis of "the technical aspects of the problem of justice." He says that "every event in contemporary history seems to multiply the proofs of its validity." At that time he also said that "the program of Marxism" will "merely provide the only possible property system compatible with the necessities of a technical age." But he believed then that "it is rather tragic that the achievement of a new property system as a prerequisite of basic justice should be complicated by the utopian illusions of Marxism on the one hand and the moralistic evasions of the mechanical problem by liberal Christianity and secular liberalism on the other."[44] From this book to the present, emphasis upon the illusions of Marxism is an

[43] *Christian Realism and Political Problems*, Chap. 3.

[44] *An Interpretation of Christian Ethics*, p. 185.

essential structural element in his thought, and each year he comes to see more clearly their destructive effect.

The quarterly *Radical Religion* (its name was changed in 1940 to *Christianity and Society*) was started in 1935. In this journal Niebuhr was to write his least inhibited comments on events. He summarizes in an initial editorial his outlook at that time on Marxism. He used Marxism to criticize the sentimentality of liberalism. He does not expect "the conception of love, held by oligarchs of a civilization, to qualify or challenge the power which they hold." This leads him to accept the class struggle as diagnosis and as strategy with few qualifications. He goes on to say: "We believe that a capitalistic society is destroying itself and yet that it must be destroyed, lest it reduce, in the delirium of its disintegration, our whole civilization to barbarism. We believe that the social ownership of the means of production is the only basis of health and justice for a technical age. We believe that such a society can be established only through a social struggle and that in that struggle we ought to be on the side of the workingman. In these things we support socialism wholeheartedly."[45]

Until 1939 he continued to emphasize this point of view. During that period he retained some confidence in the Russian experiment and even gave some support to united-front movements until the Hitler-Stalin pact in 1939. During that period he was extremely patronizing toward the New Deal. As late as 1939 he wrote of the New Deal: "We have discovered a medicine, in other words, which wards off dissolution without giving the patient health."[46] His break with the Socialist party on international policy gave him no place to go politically except the Democratic party, but in 1940 he was still hoping that in four years or eight there would be a "genuine farmer-labor party."[47] He was quite sure in 1940 that "nothing is more obvious than that socialism must come to America through some other instrument than the socialist party."[48]

During the next five years changes in emphasis were coming into his thought. He was gradually becoming disillusioned about Russia and about united fronts and he was gradually becoming more sympathetic with the pragmatic approach of the New Deal. The war

[45] *Radical Religion*, Autumn, 1935.
[46] *Christianity and Society*, Spring, 1939.
[47] *Ibid.*, Summer, 1940. [48] *Ibid.*

years turned his attention to other problems for the most part. The results of his period of most intensive theological reflection, when he was writing *The Nature and Destiny of Man*, also came to give him a somewhat different perspective on the issues of economic change and practical politics.

PRESENT TRENDS

By 1946 the profound changes in his thinking about the economic order and political strategy were clarified. From that date until the time of writing this chapter we have the development of a quite new phase of his thought, involving a break with Socialism as a system, the acceptance of the New Deal and the Fair Deal as the pattern of a creative revolution in America, the acceptance of a very much broader base than even "workers and farmers" for a progressive political strategy combined with a readiness to criticize both workers and farmers, the elaboration of a pragmatic method of social change. One of the key factors was his application of his doctrine of man more fully to the idea of combining political and economic power in the same hands. His visit to England in 1949 caused him to become vividly aware of the problems of incentive and bureaucracy under Socialism. His change of thought can be seen in his criticism of the British health program on his return to this country. He accepted most of it, and what he said would have given no comfort to the American Medical Association. But he did put his finger on a real weakness which stemmed from what Niebuhr regarded as a doctrinaire approach to human nature. He believed that the British Socialists shared the Marxist illusion that there are limits to "human needs, desires and ambitions." He then said: "Human beings are on the whole too thoughtless to justify a community in allowing them to set their own limit on demands which they may make of a public servant. . . . The service must be essentially free; but some system of graduated payments above specified minimal limits will have to be found."[49] It is not surprising to find him saying at about this time: " 'Christian Socialism' is no longer a viable compound."[50]

For at least a quarter of a century Niebuhr's thinking about society was controlled by a quite consistent scheme of Socialism. As a consistent scheme this has been broken, though he has retained some of the Socialistic criticisms of Capitalism and some of the institutional goals of Socialism. The abandonment of Socialism was in

[49] *Ibid.*, Autumn, 1949. [50] *Ibid.*, Summer, 1949.

the first instance the result of particular disillusionments. The success of the piecemeal and experimental changes in the American economy began to impress him greatly after 1940 as offering a possible alternative to the Socialist pattern.[51] But there was something deeper at work. His doctrine of man was never really consistent with democratic socialism which had too optimistic an attitude toward the problem of incentive and toward the tendency to unite economic and political power. Also, his own rejection of fixed social laws which came out much earlier in his criticism of the Catholic doctrine of natural law really applied to his own conception of fixed Socialistic goals for society.

Niebuhr makes frequent use of the word "pragmatic" to describe his new method of social thinking now that he has abandoned what he now regards as a falsely doctrinaire Socialistic approach. This pragmatism is not relativistic except when it comes to concrete decisions, and these are more controlled by the particular situation than was the case when he was inclined to read the situation through a Marxist view of what the situation was expected to be. I think that openness to the possible uniqueness of each historical situation is the new element in his thought which is most important. However, he knows that there is no situation in which one should not seek to have embodied some combination of the principles of justice and order and freedom to which I have referred. All of the ethical resources which I have described in the first part of this chapter are available for his more pragmatic type of social thinking. Love remains the ultimate source of both direction and judgment. His view of human nature remains essentially the same and helps him to avoid the destructive illusions which he has long seen to be the chief social dangers. He now realizes that even democratic socialism has operated as a source of illusions because it gave people a false picture of the situation in which they had to act and promised that if they concentrated on the solution of one problem, other problems would not get out of hand in the process. The abandonment of Socialism means that he must look again at the actual situation and work at the

[51] In the same number of *Christianity and Society* in which he wrote an editorial entitled "We Need an Edmund Burke," he also has an editorial acclaiming evidence that had just been published concerning changes in the distribution of income in the direction of greater equality between the years 1929 and 1946. He concludes this editorial with these words: "Surely this is a very considerable revolution. It may be more drastic in its consequences than some more advertised revolutions in Europe" (Summer, 1951).

same time on a wider range of problems. This approach denies him the kind of security which his earlier social thinking seemed to offer, but it is actually more consistent with his own long-standing view of the dynamic and the precarious character of historical existence.[52]

In this most recent phase of his thought he has begun to elaborate a more flexible social philosophy which has great bearing on his social ethics. Now the stress is on the distribution of economic power rather than upon Socialistic planning, upon avoiding pretentious schemes to be imposed on society by "abstract modes of social engineering."[53] He now speaks respectfully of the historical sense of British conservatism at its best, and the name of Edmund Burke appears more and more often. He makes no system of conservatism, either, and insofar as Burke represented a defense of the *status quo,* insofar as he failed to see the creative contribution of democracy based upon the participation of all citizens, Niebuhr would not regard him as a guide. The influence of Niebuhr's disillusionment with collectivistic schemes is to be seen in this tribute to Burke's conservatism: "It is therefore intent upon developing politics as the art of the possible, being cautious not to fall into worse forms of injustice in the effort to eliminate old ones."[54]

There is some danger in ending on this note because it may seem that Niebuhr has merely substituted a conservative creed for the radicalism of his earlier career. This is certainly not true. He presupposes the gradual but radical changes in the American economy which American conservatives often regard as "creeping socialism." He is completely opposed to the doctrinaire individualism which has become the American form of the "conservative creed." He sees the illusions in all ideological defenses of privilege as much as ever. He is now prevented by his very principles from spelling out a full-length alternative to Socialism or to individualistic Capitalism, but he continues to keep all positions under the criticism of a radical social ethic. The issues of this decade are much vaster and more fateful than those in the periods in which economic schemes seemed

[52] Niebuhr uses more than he explains what I am calling his pragmatism. The best references for it are the final chapter in the symposium *Christian Faith and Social Action*, pp. 225–242, and his own *Christian Realism and Political Problems,* Chaps. 1, 6, 7. I am indebted to a B.D. thesis in the Union Theological Seminary Library by Albert Fay Hill entitled "The Pragmatic Element in Contemporary Christian Economic Thought."

[53] *Christian Realism and Political Problems,* p. 72.

[54] *Ibid.*

to hold the key to history. The old controversies over economic systems are overshadowed by the immense spiritual and political problems which now face us. Niebuhr, as far as social institutions are concerned, still puts his chief trust in democracy as the method by which opposing interests and viewpoints are adjusted. The one condition for the successful working of democracy[55] has remained the same in Niebuhr's thought for twenty years: it is the avoidance of self-righteous illusions.

In recent writings Niebuhr makes clear that he cannot be classified with the "new conservatives" who also appeal to Burke. He says, after referring to the confusion in current discussion of conservatism and liberalism: "The confusions arise not because realistic liberals fail to be uncritical of the moral defects in any *status quo,* whether feudal or capitalistic, but because scholars, like Russell Kirk, who have discovered the realism of an Edmund Burke always tend to mix this realism with an uncritical acceptance of inequality, conformity, and the current balance or equilibrium of power in any social scene."[56] Elsewhere he says in criticism of Russell Kirk that "he assumes that there is authentic conservatism in the mere desire to preserve the *status quo* of the American paradise; and he rather uncritically seeks to relate this American conservatism with a British conservatism that is rooted in the aristocratic tradition and has none of Kirk's prejudices against the Welfare State."[57]

JOHN C. BENNETT

UNION THEOLOGICAL SEMINARY
NEW YORK CITY

[55] Note one of his most recent statements concerning democracy in his *Christian Realism and Political Problems,* p. 17: "We have all felt that a democratic society was most compatible with the Christian faith, but a pietistic inheritance in our evangelical tradition persuaded us that its chief virtue was its safeguarding of the individual. We should realize in this age of the rise of noxious political religions that it has another great resource from the standpoint of the Christian outlook. It provides checks and balances upon the pretensions of men as well as upon the lust for power; it thereby prevents truth from turning into falsehood when the modicum of error in truth is not challenged and the modicum of truth in a falsehood is not rescued and cherished."

[56] *Christianity and Society,* Winter, 1954–55, p. 3.

[57] *New Republic,* July 4, 1955, p. 11.

AFTERWORD: 1982

During the 1950s Reinhold Niebuhr was known for his sophisticated Christian anti-Communism. This part of his social ethics influenced students and churches, but it also had public importance because he helped to provide the rationale for the nation's policies in the early period of the cold war. In 1953 he expressed his most negative position on Communism in an article entitled "Why Is Communism so Evil?"[1] A gradual modification of his position became noticeable as early as 1958. I shall trace the stages of this modification.

In his 1953 article Niebuhr said that Stalinism as totalitarian repression was a natural outgrowth of the absolute utopianism in Marxism, and this he regarded as the root of the evil in Communism. Communism, he said, was not malignant in its intention, as was National Socialism, but this very fact made it the more dangerous. Its universal ideals gave Communism an appeal in Asia, Africa, and Latin America that National Socialism with its racism could never have had. The reason that utopianism is the root of so much evil is that believers are sure that they alone have the key to utopia and feel justified in using any means to gain or use power in the short run because of expected future gains for humanity. This view of an absolute Communism that could not be expected to change for the better dominated Niebuhr's thought for several years.

After Stalin's death and after Khrushchev showed signs of being more pragmatic, Niebuhr hinted that Soviet Communism might possibly become less rigid. Niebuhr's early diagnosis of our situation in the cold war was guided by the perception of "the fact that we are embattled with a foe who embodies all the evils of a demonic religion."[2] Yet it was characteristic of Niebuhr that he thought this very fact tempted us to be very self-righteous, and that is the root of another kind of evil.

It is surprising to find him saying as early as 1958 that "the fate of the world depends upon our capacity to leaven the lump of our own orthodox conceptions of an unchangeable Communist ortho-

[1] First published in *The New Leader* it is included in *Christian Realism and Political Problems* (New York: Scribner, 1953).

[2] *Christianity and Crisis,* February 8, 1954.

doxy."[3] In 1959, in his most thorough study of international relations, *The Structure of Nations and Empires,* he holds out the possibility of our sharing the world with the Soviet Union "without bringing disaster on a common civilization." On our part he hopes for "a less rigid and self-righteous attitude toward the power realities of the world and a more hopeful attitude toward the possibilities of internal development in the Russian despotism."[4] The words, "share the world," which today seem very pretentious, reflect his belief that there was for each superpower what he called "hegemony" over a large part of the world.

I am not sure how much Niebuhr ever moved away from this bipolar view of the world. He realized the legitimacy of nonalignment and the constructive contribution of nonaligned nations. One element in his hope for changes in the Soviet Union was that he was much impressed by the role of the Central Committee after Stalin's time, which for him was a step away from the much hated one-man despotism of Stalin, and he speculated concerning analogies for this development in the history of political freedom in the West. He was especially shocked by the invasion of Czechoslovakia in 1968 and said that "the present triumvirate of Kosygin, Brezhnev, and Podgorny seems no less devoted to Communist orthodoxy."[5] Though there have been improvements for most citizens since Stalin's time, the most hopeful changes have not been in the Soviet Union but in other Communist countries such as Hungary, Poland, and Yugoslavia. Also, the fact of diversity among Communist nations, including the split between the Soviet Union and China, offers some of the opportunities that Niebuhr hoped for in all that he says about changes in the Soviet Union.

In the years that followed, Niebuhr continued to hope for changes in Communism though he never ceased to look upon the Soviet Union as our country's great adversary. He has been criticized for being the one who more than anyone else provided Christian legitimization of the Cold War. It would give us a fairer view of Niebuhr's thought and of the policies he recommended from 1953 to 1971 if we bring together here the ways in which he showed independence of the prevailing stance of Americans in the Cold War.

He always warned against American pretensions and self-

[3] *Ibid.*, April 28, 1958.
[4] Scribner, 1958, p. 282.
[5] *The New Leader,* November 18, 1968.

righteousness while supporting American hegemony in the "free world." He also came to emphasize the view that the United States does not have a political and economic alternative that would be relevant to conditions in most of the Third World countries. He grew pessimistic about the possibility of establishing democratic institutions in nations that had never gone through the cultural and spiritual preparations for them that have been so important in the West. He said in 1967: "I think that it is also fantastic that we regard democracy as a universal option for all people. That is as fantastic in its way as is the Communist dogma and Utopianism."[6] He still regarded democracy as a most desirable goal for all people, and in the same context he reiterated his famous statement about the necessity of democracy for justice from his *The Children of Light and the Children of Darkness.*[7]

Niebuhr never shared the prevailing policy toward Communist China, and as early as 1954 said that we should be willing to accept China in the United Nations. He regretted our alliance with Chiang Kai-shek. In 1966 he wrote about our "neurotic darkness about China."[8] He always insisted on the necessity of coexistence with the Soviet Union and continually criticized the self-righteous ideological conflict as a danger to peace, self-righteous on both sides. He questioned the Cuban policy, which is still with us.[9] Believing in a military balance, he opposed too much reliance on the military and sought to prevent provocative approaches to the Soviet Union. He opposed Lyndon Johnson's intervention in the Dominican Republic.[10] While he gave the Central Intelligence Agency credit for some important accomplishments, he shared the general liberal distrust of it. He not only emphasized such glaring failures as the Bay of Pigs episode but also criticized the efforts to use student organizations, called official explanations a whitewash, and expressed satisfaction that the students were not corrupted. All of these positions on cold war issues add up to a considerable modification of the conventional cold war stance.

A major change in Niebuhr's outlook came in connection with the

[6] Dialogue between Reinhold Niebuhr and Hans Morgenthau, *War/Peace Report,* February 1967.

[7] Scribner, 1944, p. xi.

[8] Letter dated March 14, 1966 in *The New York Times.*

[9] *Christianity and Crisis,* May 15, 1961 and April 2, 1962.

[10] *Ibid.,* May 31, 1965.

Viet Nam War. This also was gradual, and it led to a parting of the ways among those who had been influenced by Niebuhr's political realism. His writings about the war caused one of these, Paul Ramsey, to say that Niebuhr was writing as though he had never read Niebuhr.[11] Ramsey was one of many who continued to regard themselves as true followers of Niebuhr, who on the Viet Nam War and on other issues maintained the hard line on the Soviet Union and Communism of which Niebuhr had become critical.[12] Many others, including this writer, welcomed the changes in Niebuhr's outlook. Some of them have gone beyond any position that can be attributed to him in their openness to leftist movements in the Third World. It is common now to contrast Niebuhr's Christian realism with Latin American liberation theology.[13] Critics of liberation theology see in it signs of the utopianism which Niebuhr so passionately rejected. Many who share his criticism of utopianism discount its importance as a determinative factor in liberation theology and see the commitment of those theologians to revolutionary change as justified in view of the desperate situation of a majority of the people in many Latin American countries.

Concerning the Viet Nam War, Niebuhr originally believed that our presence in Indochina was justified in order to resist the expansion of Communism. He soon became disillusioned by the succession of governments in South Viet Nam and decided that we were trying to do the impossible: not only to defend a nation but to create one. He regarded the governments on both sides as tyrannies we should not support. He came to be horrified by the cruelty and destruction of the war. He came to give moral support to the antiwar movement in our country. Perhaps the clearest statement of the position to which he finally came is expressed in the foreword to a pamphlet containing speeches delivered at Riverside Church on April 4, 1967. At those meetings, Martin Luther King came out most strongly against the war. Niebuhr wrote:

> My illness prevented me from attending the meeting, but I am deeply persuaded by its concern about our bloody, costly, and essentially futile

[11] In 1981 he said that he had been mistaken and that Niebuhr had been wiser than he earlier about the war.

[12] *Christianity and Crisis,* March 20, 1967.

[13] The most thorough attempt to compare Reinhold Niebuhr's thought with liberation theology is Dennis P. McCann: *Christian Realism and Liberation Theology* (Orbis Books, 1981).

involvement in a civil war in Viet Nam. Some of our citizens regard our involvement as an expression of our sense of responsibility, but we are among those who regard it as an example of the "illusion of American omnipotence."

There is no doubt that Niebuhr's earliest reason for opposing the war in Viet Nam was his belief that we were doing something that could not be done. He came to criticize the bombing of civilians and he approved movements that combined belief in the war's costly futility with moral outrage concerning our destruction of Viet Nam. That moral concern was much emphasized in the speeches for which he wrote the foreword. Future studies of Niebuhr may give a clearer sense of the relative force of these two motives for opposing the war. It must be remembered that Niebuhr died before the full human cost of the war to us and the Vietnamese was known.

Niebuhr went beyond anything I have so far quoted regarding the cold war in general in an article in 1969.[14] I was surprised to read that he even said that now he "must ruefully change that decade old opinion in regard to Barth's neutralism." (His criticism of Barth had been bitter.) And then he went on to say: "I must admit that our wealth makes our religious anti-Communism particularly odious. Perhaps there is not much to choose between Communist and anti-Communist fanaticism, particularly when the latter, combined with our wealth, has caused us to stumble into the most pointless, costly, and bloody war in our history."*

Closely related to Niebuhr's thinking about the relations between the United States and the Soviet Union was his attitude toward nuclear weapons and the possibility of nuclear war. I do not think that there was much development in his thought since my original

[14] *The Christian Century,* December 31, 1969, quoted in an article by Tracy Early in *Christianity and Crisis,* April 7, 1981.

* There is a significant contrast between two books about Niebuhr's thought including the thought of his last years: Paul Merkley's *Reinhold Niebuhr: A Political Account* (McGill-Queens University Press, 1975) and Ronald Stone's *Reinhold Niebuhr—Prophet to Politicians,* (Abingdon Press, 1972). Stone's chapter, "The United States' Role in International Politics Since World War II" gives a more balanced view of Niebuhr's role in the cold war than Merkley's exposition, and I have been influenced by it. His reporting of Niebuhr's debates with colleagues about the Suez crisis in 1956 illumines his way of working on a controversial issue, and it reflects his commitment to Israel which was an unchanging element in his approach to foreign policy.

chapter was written. I emphasized then that the horror of nuclear war did not make him a nuclear pacifist. He believed that it was essential to possess nuclear weapons to deter the other side from using them. The balance of terror and the "nuclear umbrella" were often mentioned as the best safeguard against nuclear war. He even referred to " 'the balance of terror,' by the grace of which we have a precarious peace."[15]

In the years that followed, these ideas kept recurring. He was convinced that both superpowers had as a common purpose, indeed as a common necessity for survival, the prevention of nuclear war. He wrote about the dreaded possibility of nuclear war with a good deal of hope because of his confidence in the effectiveness of deterrence. His realism did not tempt him to despair. He knew that it was possible to stumble into nuclear war through a technical or political "misadventure," but he felt that as long as the balance of terror was fairly stable this was not a danger on which to dwell.

In 1958, in commenting on Henry Kissinger's suggestion that tactical nuclear weapons be used as a substitute for all-out nuclear war, Niebuhr stated that these weapons would be as destructive as the bomb that fell on Nagasaki. He drew back from the idea of such a limited war, not so much because he feared that it would not remain limited but because in itself such a war would be so horrendous. In the context of the use of such weapons, he wondered "why our leaders were so complacent about the fact that physical survival seemed now to mean our moral annihilation." He added: "For even without the hydrogen bomb, a dozen Nagasaki bombs in Europe and Asia would mean the destruction of any moral claim for our civilization."[16]

Those words introduce an idea that next to the idea of deterrence seemed to be his most important consideration about nuclear war. Suppose deterrence fails and a nuclear attack comes and we retaliate, what would be the moral situation? He raised the question in 1961: "Could a civilization loaded with the monstrous guilt (connected with a nuclear catastrophe) have enough moral health to survive?"[17] With his friend and fellow political realist, Hans Morgenthau, he agreed in raising this question with an implied moral judgment.

[15] Reinhold Niebuhr and Alan Heimert, *A Nation So Conceived* (Scribner, 1963) p. 152.

[16] *Christianity and Crisis,* January 6, 1958.

[17] *Christianity and Crisis,* November 13, 1961.

Morgenthau was even more emphatic.[18] Neither of them faced the question of how much risk of becoming involved in nuclear war we should take in any confrontation with an adversary, with or without use of conventional military force. Perhaps no one except an absolute pacifist can really face the question in advance of the situation that would call for an answer. If that is true, it reveals a dimension of the nuclear dilemma that is in itself not often faced.

I heard Niebuhr say (twice, I think) that if a nuclear attack came he hoped that he would be among the first to be killed because he could not take responsibility for decisions that might follow. (This is confirmed by June Bingham in her life of Niebuhr, *Courage to Change.*)[19] That is very honest, but it throws no light on what should be done; it makes one think that nuclear war would be beyond the limits of any defensible ethical decision. I shall not speculate on what Niebuhr would think today when the emphasis on deterrence is less dependable than it was in his lifetime and when the idea that, in the hope that nuclear war could be kept limited, nuclear weapons might be used to come out ahead of an adversary has considerable military support.

As one reads the writings of Reinhold Niebuhr in the years after this volume was first published, his preoccupation with foreign policy and global politics stands out above all other concerns in social ethics. This is so much the case that Paul Merkley in his significant study of Niebuhr concludes that he and his liberal, reformist circle had become convinced that domestic problems had in principle been solved. This obviously was not true of the problem of racial justice, which Niebuhr at times referred to as America's gravest problem. Merkley even refers to "a pattern of increasing complacency about domestic affairs traceable in the Niebuhr canon from 1945 onward to at least the eve of his death."[20] There may have been the idea that economic problems had been solved in principle with a mixed economy since the changes needed required nothing radically new. But there were also two other factors: the preoccupation with global problems to which I have referred and the serious limits to direct involvement in public activities because of his illness that began in 1952. Merkley is very sympathetic with Niebuhr's basic theology and ethics, but I can understand how an

[18] *Commentary,* September and October 1961.
[19] Scribner, 1961, p. 386.
[20] *Reinhold Niebuhr, A Political Account,* pp. 177–178.

outside critic (from Canada) who is somewhat to the left of American liberals would make this judgment. After Niebuhr rejected socialism and identified himself with the welfare state and with pragmatic political and economic strategies, it did appear that the direction of economic change was clear. I doubt if Merkley realizes what a continuing struggle it has been in this individualistic country to continue in the direction in which Niebuhr believed. Today this is clearer than Niebuhr ever could have expected! His favorite word "precarious" applies to his own successes in the struggle for economic justice.

Niebuhr's outlook on economic problems in his last years is well stated in a 1957 article: "Adam Smith contributed mightily to a free society, but he almost wrecked that society with the unfulfilled promise that justice would flow inevitably from freedom. Karl Marx contributed mightily to a just society by his practical understanding of the realities of power in an industrial age but he laid foundations for a new despotism by not understanding these realities well enough. Fortunately, we are living in a day in which healthy nations do not concern themselves too much with the dogmas of either Smith or Marx but profit by the truths they have winnowed from the errors of both."[21]

I concluded my original chapter with comments on the tendency to classify Niebuhr as one of the "New Conservatives" of that period. He had been writing favorably of Edmund Burke's emphasis on organic change in a community guided by values in a national tradition and of his fear that a new imposed scheme would, as Niebuhr said, "fall into worse forms of injustice in the effort to eliminate old ones." But he found in both Burke and the New Conservatives too much of a tendency to rationalize the *status quo*, too much complacency about inequalities, and an inadequate appreciation of the values of democratic participation.

Today there is a new generation of Neo-Conservatives, some of whom claim Niebuhr as the first Neo-Conservative. I do not think this group is more correct in claiming Niebuhr than were their predecessors. One area of difference is that they represent an unnuanced anti-Communism and anti-Sovietism that is certainly out of line with the developments of Niebuhr's thought on those subjects I have traced here. They stress far more than he ever did the role of

[21] *The New Leader*, December 23, 1957.

military power in their support of our present unprecedented peacetime military build-up. On domestic issues their celebration of American capitalism, which they would free from most governmental intervention, is alien to Niebuhr's acceptance of a mixed economy which included those non-capitalistic elements that make the capitalistic elements more tolerable.

Though in his writing he was preoccupied with other issues, there is no reason to believe that he ever ceased to believe in equality, not as a law but as a regulative principle by which all structures of justice should be judged, or that he ever lost his habit of exposing the destructive self-interest in the defenses of privilege. All his life he had been a biblical preacher who saw society always under both the transcendent judgment and the mercy of God. One of his last articles in *Christianity and Crisis,* "The King's Chapel and the King's Court"[22] (prompted by President Nixon's Sunday worship services in the White House), showed that the spirit of the prophets was still with him. His quotation from Amos, "but let justice roll down like water, and righteousness like an ever-flowing stream," fits Niebuhr's world but is out of place in the world of New Conservatives.

Niebuhr's deep commitment to racial justice fit each stage of the struggle for it during his lifetime. Before there was a Civil Rights movement, Niebuhr in his ministry in Detroit had been a pioneer on racial issues; he had early in his career been active in support of the Fellowship of Southern Churchmen, the Southern Tenant Farmers' Union, and of the Cooperative Farm in Mississippi. This commitment continued during the later period in which a new generation of black people created the aggressive Civil Rights movement of the 1950s and 1960s. That was a time for activists, for demonstrations and freedom rides, for martyrs and for imprisonments. Niebuhr's illness made the activist role impossible, but he wrote strong editorials in support of the Supreme Court's decision in Brown v. Board of Education in 1954, in support of the most far-reaching initiatives of Kennedy and Johnson, in support of the activists when victimized, in support of the Civil Rights Act of 1965, and in calling attention to the plight of young unemployed blacks trapped in ghettoes in spite of many good changes in the law.

One interesting sign of his capacity to share the feelings of

[22] August 4, 1969.

young and militant blacks is that after reading James Cone's *Black Theology and Black Power*[23] he wrote to me about his warm approval of the book, but commenting that Cone did not do full justice to the forms of integration that had been achieved. He expressed satisfaction that Cone was joining the Union Seminary faculty. Niebuhr always gave strong support to Martin Luther King. His special emphasis on the wisdom of King's strategy of nonviolence reminds us of his early tendency to recognize the positive role of nonviolence even while criticizing the view that held it was the strategy for all situations.

He said in words that look beyond King and the Civil Rights movement of the 1950s and 1960s: "The impatience of the Negro will not subside until the last vestiges of inequality have been removed. Revolutions do not stop half way."[24] That passage is a good one with which to conclude; it helps us to realize vividly that Niebuhr's criticism of inequalities—racial and economic—never ceased. This is a moment when it is much needed.

JOHN C. BENNETT

PRESIDENT EMERITUS
UNION THEOLOGICAL SEMINARY
NEW YORK CITY

[23] New York: Seabury Press, 1969.
[24] *Christianity and Crisis,* July 8, 1963.

6

Paul Ramsey

LOVE AND LAW

6

LOVE AND LAW

THROUGHOUT the writings of Reinhold Niebuhr there are strictures against the theory of natural law in Roman Catholic moral theology and the form it has sometimes taken in Protestant thought. There are also strong commendations of this view, with the plain implication or statement that some revision of the traditional concept of natural law is valid and necessary for the elaboration of a Christian ethic relevant to all the concrete problems of the moral life. And in his recent volume of essays one deals profoundly and at length with the issue of "Love and Law in Protestantism and Catholicism."[1] Because of the importance of the relation between love and the natural moral law both for personal and for social ethics, what Niebuhr has to say on this subject needs to be singled out for special consideration. Such an undertaking has also a practical significance for the present-day theological situation, since there are a number of persons, more or less of the neo-orthodox persuasion, who appear resolved to swelter out the present moral crisis with their own personal decisions impaled on the point of the existential moment or suspended wholly within a solution of justification by faith.

I. THE NATURAL LAW FOR FREEDOM

Fortunately or unfortunately, we today have a way of finding out whether anything akin to the traditional theory of natural law still remains central in a man's thought or to what extent this still governs what he has to say about man and morals. We can compare him with a viewpoint which in fact drops out altogether every remnant of the natural law and breaks decisively with the Western tradition in this regard: the viewpoint of atheistic existentialism. By contrast with Jean-Paul Sartre, the divergence of views among

[1] *Christian Realism and Political Problems,* Chap. 10.

Christian theologians appears as only family quarrels over the *meaning* of the natural law or the moral law God gives us for living in his human family.

Sartre quite rightly points out that according to traditional theism "the individual man is the realization of a certain concept in the divine intelligence."[2] This was the import of the doctrine of creation, and of the theory of natural law built upon it. By contrast Sartre may also help us to realize what has been insufficiently acknowledged: that some view of the essence of man is also implied in God's purpose for his creatures in their final redemption seen in Christ. Whether the stress be placed on creation or on redemption, man has in either case an essential nature. The "essentialist" tradition was only cowardly attenuated, according to Sartre, in all non-religious views of natural law or theories of *a priori* values. He breaks decisively with all this, and instead begins with bare existence.

Man only is. He is not this or that *kind* of being. Having no essence *behind* him or *before* him which defines what he ought to be, the individual man defines himself by his own engagement in choice. *Opto ergo sum.* "Man is nothing else but what he makes himself."[3] Man creates himself by the limitless rebounding effect of his own self-understanding. "Not only is man what he conceives himself to be, but he is also what he wills himself to be after this thrust toward existence."[4] For Sartre "there is no explaining things away [or, dropping out that last pejorative word, there is no explaining things] by reference to a fixed and given human nature."[5] "Man makes himself. He isn't ready-made at the first. In choosing his ethics he makes himself, and force of circumstances is such that he cannot abstain from choosing one."[6] Choice creates value and essence. There is no pre-existent value or essence or structure of reality or God which justifies choice; and it would be fruitless to try to justify by a value the action which alone creates the value. Man is a free, self-manufacturing being whose freedom "in every concrete circumstance can have no other aim than to want itself."[7]

It is true that by probing to a freedom whose only aim is to want itself, Sartre here discovers a kind of limit: "When in all honesty, I've recognized that man is a being in whom existence precedes essence, that he is a free being who, in various circumstances, can

[2] *Existentialism* (New York: Philosophical Library, 1947), p. 15.
[3] *Ibid.*, p. 18. [4] *Ibid.*, p. 18. [5] *Ibid.*, p. 27. [6] *Ibid.*, p. 51.
[7] *Ibid.*, p. 53.

want only his freedom, I have at the same time recognized that I can want only the freedom of others."[8] But this shows that even a man who takes the most extreme measures to lighten the boat by emptying it of every concept that hampers free movement by legitimizing only some forms of conduct must still remain in the boat. To think at all about the nature of man Sartre must think with essences, even if that be only the thought that man essentially consists of an entirely dynamic and limitless freedom. However radically reshaped, here surely there is a modicum of the natural law. It may even be affirmed that any conception of the nature of man is so far a conception of the natural law. This becomes even more evident in the universal principle that individual freedom which can have, because of its self-creative nature, no other aim than to want itself is implicitly obliged at the same time to recognize that it can want only the same freedom for others. So hard it is as to be well nigh impossible to break with the Western tradition of moral theology without standing on its shoulders!

Nevertheless, a comparison of atheistic existentialism with the theistic existentialism of Reinhold Niebuhr (if this be an apt way to characterize his view) shows how vastly more the latter is dependent upon the essentialist tradition and the theory of natural law. Or rather, it shows how his judgments are grounded in the same facts of moral experience and truths grasped by reason (or by reason illuminated by revelation) which were enshrined, with more or less adequacy or inadequacy, in this ancient teaching. Without blurring any distinctions or overlooking the additional complexity which Niebuhr rightly points out, we can see that he is actually proposing an interpretation of the nature of man and of the natural moral law which enters into continuing conversation with all the other viewpoints of this type that have been under the sun.

Readers of any of Niebuhr's books need not be reminded that he too believes that there is no explaining things by reference to a fixed and given human nature. Man is largely what he becomes; he isn't ready-made at the first. There are no fixed structures of nature or reason or history which man does not transcend by virtue of his spiritual freedom. What Niebuhr actually objects to when he rejects the idea of natural law is the view ordinarily associated with it, that human nature conforms wholly to stable structures and nicely reposes within discoverable limits. The thread running through Nie-

[8] *Ibid.*, pp. 54–55.

buhr's criticism of naturalism, rationalism and romanticism in *The Nature and Destiny of Man* is his contention that man's self-transcending freedom rises above the limits or even the vitalities of physical nature and above the patterns of reason or the uniquely individual organic structures discovered by romantic idealism. Man stands before possibilities for action which are not to be calculated in terms of the potentialities of a fixed essential nature of any sort. His freedom means that his self-understanding affects what he is or is to become; and he grasps after possibilities envisaged only when, from the heights of self-transcending consciousness of himself and the present historical actuality, he seeks to reshape both himself and his social environment.

Is not such a dynamic interpretation of the indefinite possibilities of human freedom just as reasonable a conception of the nature of man as more static interpretations of his essence, and insofar does it not like them entail a (revised) conception of the natural moral law? The answer to this question, often explicit and certainly implicit in Niebuhr, is Yes.

To parley this issue at the summit, it is noteworthy that Niebuhr contends that for such a free spirit as man love is the law of life. In the search for ethical principles, as well as in other areas of his thought, Niebuhr's apologetic procedure is the technique of demolition. This is to say, he attempts to show that all other views of the moral life fail by not taking fully into account the dimension of freedom or self-transcendence in man. In a sense this is a negative method; but, as Socrates long ago discovered, significant and rich conclusions may be drawn from a negative voice. Thus, something like the older conception of natural law might be established by reference not to man's sense of justice but to his "sense of injustice," or the basic judgment that some situations are not meant for man nor he for them. Likewise love is the moral law for man, whose nature is what is indicated in Niebuhr's writings; and his way of pointing us to this conclusion is by showing that the natural moral law elaborated in the philosophies of naturalism, rationalism, and so on, fails and must fail to captivate and fulfill the special dimension of freedom in man's essential nature. Among the ruins of these systems love still stands as the relationship in life which was meant for man and for which man was intended. Despite the complexities that arise when we later consider the relation of love to the structures of nature and reason, and despite the fact that love at its pinnacle requires a heroic self-sacrifice which finds a nesting-place in human history only at the foot of the Cross, what can be more grounded in "Nature" than the assertion that man is made for life-in-community whose quality is love?

There is in nature or reason, for Niebuhr, no form or structure to which the self ought to return from its freedom; but this is true because the dimension of freedom already points the self toward a more ultimate harmony. "While egotism is 'natural' in the sense that it is universal, it is not natural in the sense that *it does not conform to man's nature,* who transcends himself indeterminately and can only have God rather than self for his end."[9] Similarly an ethics built mainly upon certain fixed structures of human nature is "not natural in the sense that it does not conform to man's nature" as indeterminate freedom. Therefore, "the law of love is the final law for man in his condition of finiteness and freedom because man in his freedom is unable to make himself in his finiteness his own end. The self is too great to be contained within itself in its smallness."[10] Although the self does not get beyond itself radically and into a relationship of love simply by taking thought, in its freedom the self is always already so far beyond itself that it cannot without damage to its essential nature return and live within "the cask of self stopped with the bung of self."[11] *Agape* is "the final law of human existence because every realization of the self which is motivated by concern for the self inevitably results in a narrower and more self-contained self than the freedom of the self requires."[12]

This is not, as for Sartre, a mere implication that one should want the freedom of others drawn from the primary and logically more ultimate fact that he always aims at his own freedom. It is rather the heart of the matter, based on the human essence in existence, or on the fact that man is made in his created freedom so that he comes to fruition only in convenant with others and in steadfast love for them. His transcendent freedom is *in order to* love; and love is ordained as the law for his life in freedom. "Materially," that is, in its content, love is the chief part of the natural moral law; and consonant with the dynamic nature of freedom this is a dynamic conception of the moral law. Love contains no code or fixed form to be imposed upon human freedom. Nor is it the law for life only in some super-

[9] *Christian Realism and Political Problems,* pp. 129–130.

[10] *Faith and History,* p. 174.

[11] Ibsen, *Peer Gynt.*

[12] *Faith and History,* p. 175.

natural realm. It is rather, as Principal Micklem suggests, "more like that *vis sanatrix naturae* whereby a body that is injured seeks to adapt itself to the unforeseen circumstances and to regain health, or like that law or instinct whereby if an ants' nest is disturbed its denizens set about its restoration. It is a binding obligation to loyalty under all circumstances. But, since circumstances are infinitely variable, it is neither positive Divine law nor a code. But it is in some sense law and obligatory in principle upon all men; it belongs therefore to the nature of man."[13]

Of course these analogies are drawn from biological nature, and only *mutatis mutandis* do they become illuminating for the realm of human freedom. There is also another law in our members which wars against the law in our minds. Of course, we are now speaking only of the material content of the moral law; and it need not be supposed, as the foregoing quotation might suggest, that human nature possesses self-curative powers in this respect. Because of that other law that holds sway within, the resources for living as we ought may flow only from common grace and the grace of the Gospel —and beyond the power, the grace of forgiveness to bring in us the halt, the lame, and the blind. Nevertheless, when by sin freedom injures itself and its life in love, there still remains a silent pressure toward love as the *vis sanatrix naturae* in the very constitution of man's transcendent spiritual freedom determining the *direction* in which alone health is to be found. Love belongs therefore to the nature of man. From thus defining the essence of man we at once define the natural norm for man. Niebuhr validates "the law of love as a vision of health which even a sick man may envisage, as the original righteousness which man does not possess but which he knows he ought to possess."[14]

The fact that Niebuhr is saying something not unlike this is shown also by the common ground between his thought and the impressive evidence from psychotherapy that man's most fundamental need, in sickness or in health, is to have the strength to love. In a review of Erich Fromm's *Man for Himself*, Niebuhr expresses succinctly the self's freedom and the consequent moral law: "The self in its freedom is too great to be contained within the self in its contingent

[13] Nathaniel Micklem, *Law and the Laws* (Edinburgh: W. Green & Sons, Ltd., 1952), pp. 108–109.

[14] *The Nature and Destiny of Man,* I, 287. Cf. also his use of the analogy with health at the beginning of the section "The Locus of Original Righteousness," *ibid.*, pp. 276–277.

existence. It requires an object of devotion beyond itself, and an indeterminate field of fellowship." Such a statement is clearly grounded in a more adequate understanding than Sartre's (or, as we shall see, than Fromm's) that love is, materially, the law of life. "Actually the Christian view is based," writes Niebuhr, "precisely upon an estimate 'of the proper functioning of our total personality' which Fromm regards as the hallmark of humanistic ethic."[15]

Because of the significance of such statements as the above, it may be suggested that much would be gained from saying that love with its indeterminate possibilities is Niebuhr's radical revision of the conception of the natural law for human personality with its indeterminate freedom. The gain which results is not merely a clarification of terms, or the consequence that hereby Niebuhr's ethics is clearly set in definite continuity with every other attempt under the sun to rest morality upon some conception of man's essential nature and in direct engagement with these other viewpoints. The result will also be to remove some unnecessary complexity and paradoxicality from his own thought. For it will be seen at once that in defining the material content of man's whole duty there is no such thing as love beyond all law.

The essay on "Love and Law" consists of a discussion of "love as law and love at the limits of law and love beyond the limits."[16] As far as I can see, "love at the limits of law" is never given further conceptual definition. The essay is therefore a discussion of "love as law" and "love beyond the limits of law." *Subjectively,* of course, these are the exact terms in which the problem can be stated. It is the problem of the relation between duty and inclination, or between love as a commandment and the spontaneity of the grace to love. Subjectively there is in human experience such a thing as "love beyond law." This was perhaps better expressed in an earlier book:

> Now love implies an uncoerced giving of the self to the object of its devotion. It is thus a fulfillment of the law; for in perfect love all law is transcended and what is and what ought to be are one.
>
> To command love is a paradox; for love cannot be commanded or demanded. To love God with all our hearts and all our souls and all our minds means that every cleavage in human existence is overcome. But the fact that such an attitude is commanded proves that the cleavage is

[15] *Christianity and Society,* Spring, 1948, p. 27. [16] *Loc. cit.*

not overcome; the command comes from one side of reality to the other, from essence to existence.[17]

Subjectively there is tension between love as law and love beyond law. But the author puts this issue largely behind him after the second section, which is five pages long. The same is not the case materially. When from the third section onward in this essay Niebuhr turns to an attempt to define the content and meaning of Christian ethic, he delineates four points concerning the indeterminacy of love and of human freedom. In each case he confuses the subjective with the objective problem, and this leads him mistakenly to call these instances of the material transcendence of love over all law. Since he believes that in fact these points of indeterminacy correspond to the character of human freedom, and knows that ultimately the natural law has to be defined in terms of man's essential nature, he cannot with consistency affirm that, materially speaking, love ever goes beyond law. Consequently he hedges: "This first element in the indeterminacy of love has already been described as being, *in one respect at least,* within the limits of law. *For it describes the sum total of all our obligations to our fellowmen without specific detail. It is thus the summary of all law.*" "Law *in the determinate sense* must stop with distributive justice." Heedless love "cannot be separated from the realm of natural love by a neat line. It transcends the line of natural love. Yet without an element of heedless love. . . ." "Yet even forgiveness comes *partially* into the category of love as law." The context here makes it plain that materially forgiveness falls within love as law, while only subjectively does it transcend law: "Our forgiveness of our brethren is primarily *a grateful response* to God's forgiveness." "This kind of love is a matter of law in the sense that the essential nature of man, with his indeterminate freedom, requires that human relations should finally achieve such intimacy," that is, materially indeterminate love is the law of life. "But it is also a matter of grace because no sense of obligation can provide the imagination and forbearance by which this is accomplished," that is, subjectively love never flows from law but from beyond it.[18]

Thus are the "dialectical relationships" multiplied, or at least the expression of them rendered unclear, by failure to carry through

[17] *An Interpretation of Christian Ethics*, pp. 209–210.

[18] *Ibid.*, pp. 155, 159, 162, 165, 168 (italics mine).

terminologically the actual reconstruction of the theory of natural law in terms of love. Freedom and love as corresponding nature and norm belong within the essentialist tradition of moral theology despite the difference from traditional views. This is especially true if Niebuhr allows that natural reason may know of love as the requirement of freedom. There would perhaps be something lost in "dialectic" brilliance but substantial gain in clarity of thought if the revision of the traditional theory of natural law were made more explicit. Moreover, his other writings support this, in that he does not elsewhere toy with the idea that *materially* love transcends its status as the law for man's existence in freedom.

Incidentally, the author's brief remarks about Kierkegaard in this essay are wrong for the same reason. He accuses Kierkegaard of presenting "a legalistic version of universal love in his *Works of Love*."[19] It is true that Kierkegaard in one chapter rhapsodizes about the word "shalt" in the love-commandment. But this is because he knows that love is the highest law, not materially beyond all law. His "second ethic" transcends abstract Kantian norms or the universalities of traditional natural law based on the fixed structures of human nature (these are "suspended" in *Fear and Trembling*). Where Kierkegaard is weak, and where Niebuhr proves most helpful, is in clarifying the relations between love, the natural law for freedom, and the "first ethic" based on determinate aspects of human nature and society. These tensions fall within the totality of the natural law as now re-viewed; they do not fall between the natural law (or love as law) and love beyond law. It is also inaccurate to say that Kierkegaard would have us regard "the loved self as anonymously as possible." He suggests that in Christian love we "close our eyes" to every selfish preferential relationship and then open them and "love the man we see," that is, our neighbor in all his concreteness and full identity. Kierkegaard is right in thus defining the material meaning of the law of love. He is weakest, and here again Niebuhr proves most helpful, in clarifying the relations between such love as the law of life and the intimate, preferential loves which clothe us in daily life. But this is a problem which falls within the totality of an ethics built upon the law of nature or on an estimate of the proper functioning of human personality.

No more words should be written on the subject of Christian ethics

[19] *Ibid.*, p. 158.

unless it is right to separate the material from the subjective problem of love and law. If we persist without this distinction Augustine's *On the Spirit and the Letter* will haunt our dreams. For it is the letter of the Gospel and not the old law only which kills. Love as law or duty condemns our actual inclinations. In this sense any actual love goes by the Spirit beyond law. Yet in the material sense love is the law of life and not more than the law; and this is the concern of Christian ethical analysis.

II. THE LAW FOR MAN AS A DETERMINATE CREATURE?

The relation between Niebuhr's thought and traditional moral theology based on the known structures of human nature is indicated by his own summary: "What is usually known as 'natural law' in both Christian and Stoic thought is roughly synonymous with the requirements of man as creature, and . . . the virtues, defined by Catholic thought as 'theological virtues,' that is, the virtues of faith, hope and love, are the requirements of his freedom and represent the *justitia originalis*. . . . There is no uncorrupted natural law, just as there is no completely lost original justice."[20] We have considered love as the natural law for freedom, and turn now toward what is more familiarly known as "natural law" or "the requirements of man as creature." By this characterization Niebuhr can only mean the requirements of man insofar as he is a determinate creature living within social and historical structures, since the freedom by which he exceeds these limits is also finite, creaturely freedom. Both these aspects of the natural moral law, as it is modified and understood in Niebuhr's thought, belong inseparably together and constantly interplay with each other. A typical passage illustrating this interaction is found in the essay on "Love and Law in Protestantism and Catholicism":

> These points of indeterminacy in the law of love correspond to the indeterminate character of human freedom. Insofar as man has a determinate structure, it is possible to state the "essential nature" of human existence to which his actions ought to conform and which they should fulfill. But insofar as he has the freedom to transcend structure, standing beyond himself and beyond every particular social situation, every law is subject to indeterminate possibilities which finally exceed the limits of

[20] *The Nature and Destiny of Man*, I, 280–281 *et passim*.

any specific definition of what he "ought" to do. Yet they do not stand completely outside of law, *if law is defined in terms of man's essential nature. For this indeterminate freedom is a part of his essential nature.*[21]

Thus sometimes Niebuhr allows that, insofar as man has a determinate structure, it may be possible to state the "essential nature" of human existence in these respects and to gain some understanding of the natural law for man as a determinate creature—subordinate, of course, to the law of love. Yet sometimes he makes the sweeping assertion that "fixed historical structures and norms . . . *do not in fact exist*" and that therefore "the moral certainties of natural law in Catholic thought are *all dubious.*"[22] The issue here raised really cannot be left vague by merely qualifying the strictures and saying that traditional natural law is "less valid" than was supposed or that "both Catholic and Reformation thought are *too certain* about the fixities of the norms of law."[23]

Niebuhr writes:

> The development of natural law theories in Christianity has been criticized as an apostasy from the Christian ideal of love. But all such criticisms are informed by a moral sentimentalism which does not recognize to what degree all decent human actions, even when under the tension and inspiration of the love commandment, are in fact determined by rational principles of equity and justice, by law rather than love.[24]

Are we, then, to take most seriously Niebuhr's commendation of the theory of natural law? If so, this means that there are two inseparable but distinguishable sources and bases for the first principles of human conduct: there is first, love as the norm for freedom in view of the fact that "the quintessence of a human personality is never in time or historic actuality" or contained in determinate structures.[25] Then secondly, there are principles based upon definition of the human essence insofar as man does have his being within determinate limits. *Together* these would comprise the entire natural law or the revised equivalent of it in Niebuhr's thought.

Or on the other hand, are we to pay more attention to the other aspect of his thought? Man's life in time itself seems subject to the all-embracing flux of historical change. In addition, human self-

[21] *Loc. cit.*, pp. 154–155 (italics mine).
[22] *Ibid.*, p. 172 (italics mine).
[23] *Ibid.*, pp. 172, 173 (italics mine).
[24] *An Interpretation of Christian Ethics*, p. 144.
[25] *Ibid.*, p. 83.

transcendence and freedom are capable of unsettling every determinate structure and setting it in motion and commotion. Moreover, sin obscures our vision of the essential nature of man and leads us to mistake for the moral law structures destined only to last for a day. On this interpretation there is only one fundamental principle for Niebuhr—the law of love itself, which, since it stands in relation to the very essence of man, we have called the natural law. "It is true that reason discloses the 'moral law,'" writes Niebuhr, and then goes on to explain: "It reveals, or at least suggests, the total field of life in which obligation moves."[26] Principles proximate to this are the equivalent, not of the older natural law as one element in his thought, but of the *jus gentium* or *jus civilis*. Proximate principles then are *applications* of the natural law, which requires that freedom have an indeterminate field of fellowship, to certain conditions of fact. In paying tribute to the traditional theory of natural law, it may be said, Niebuhr does not mean to affirm that there actually is a secondary source of *first* principles. He means only to emphasize the necessity of keeping love relevant to actual life, and to say that when love goes in search of a social policy and into action, it gives rise to more specific principles or schemes. Thus reflection upon the concrete situation is only a secondary source of *secondary* principles. This traditionally was not the role of natural law but of the *jus gentium,* or with greater particularity, the *jus civilis.* As Maritain sums up: "The Law of Nations, or the common law of civilization, deals, like natural law, with the rights and duties which follow from the first principle in a *necessary* manner, but this time *supposing* certain conditions of fact." And "*positive law* (statute law), or the body of laws in force in a given community, deals with the rights and duties which follow from the first principle, but in a *contingent* manner, by virtue of the determinate ways of conduct."[27] It may be instructive to try this second interpretation on for size, to see whether proximate principles in Niebuhr are not more correctly to be regarded as applications of his first principle (freedom and love), "this time supposing certain conditions of fact," or as "determinate ways of conduct" related contingently to contingent factors and not to any fixed or determinate mode of man's being in the world.

However, before undertaking in the next section to substantiate

[26] *Ibid.*, p. 203.

[27] Jacques Maritain, *The Rights of Man and Natural Law* (New York: Charles Scribner's Sons), 1943, p. 70.

this interpretation, a small degree of truth should be noted in the first. Niebuhr criticized modern relativists for not recognizing a permanent structure of human personality because of "their obsession with the changing aspects in the human situation."[28] But he ordinarily needs only a single sentence to draw up the bill of particulars. He cites the practical universality of the prohibition of theft and murder, and even then points out that these are minimal requirements. (Sometimes he suggests that these, too, have their source in love.) Announcing that, despite his freedom, man is "a creature of nature who is subject to certain natural structures," he affirms at once that "these natural structures have negative rather than positive force."[29] Then with bewildering rapidity the reader finds himself back in the midst of the other dialectic—against the fixed structures of natural law. Still, that one sentence will have made plain that the minimal, negative, and most universal aspects of morality are grounded for Niebuhr in certain immutable aspects of human existence, and that here man's knowledge of nature and norm supplements the law of love. At only one other point do I find that Niebuhr actually defines the determinate character of human nature to any significantly greater extent. Objecting to Bertrand Russell's views on sex morality, Niebuhr writes that he "obviously disregards one important immutable aspect of the human situation, namely, the organic unity between physical impulses and the spiritual dimension of human personality. This organic unity means that sexual relations are also personal relations."[30] This aspect of the natural moral law for man as a determinate creature was applied with telling effect by Niebuhr in his analysis of the Kinsey reports,[31] and it was central in his analysis of sexuality in relation to sin and anxiety in the first volume of the Gifford Lectures. This comprises a by no means small and insignificant purchase upon traditional notions of natural law. Still, one cannot escape the conclusion that Niebuhr's frequent tributes to the meaning he still finds in natural-law theory outnumber and outweigh his actual use of such determinate moral knowledge, and are therefore largely verbal. Likewise, his criticism of relativism's stress on novelty and creative emergence somewhat disguises—but for the law of love—his own.

[28] *Faith and History,* p. 180. [29] *Ibid.,* p. 174.

[30] *Ibid.,* p. 181.

[31] "Kinsey and the Moral Problem of Man's Sexual Life," *An Analysis of the Kinsey Reports . . . ,* ed. Donald P. Geddes (New York: E. P. Dutton & Co., 1954), Chap. IV.

Niebuhr may be quite correct in finding few immutable norms for man's moral behavior, or in relating all principles to the law of love rather than allowing them to stand on their own base. This chapter is concerned only to clarify and interpret his views on love and law, and not to defend a greater use of the supposed findings of the traditional theory unrevised. One step in the direction of properly grasping Niebuhr's thought is to understand love as the natural law for freedom. Another is to understand that what he often calls natural law, or its equivalent in his thought, is not that at all, but an application of the fundamental law of love. This has to be qualified only to the extent that we have now indicated an actual spelling out of the determinate structures of human existence.

The best summary of Niebuhr's position on the issue now under consideration is his statement:

> There is not much that is absolutely immutable in the structure of human nature except its animal basis, man's freedom to transmute this nature in varying degrees, and the unity of the natural and the spiritual in all the various transmutations and transfigurations of the original "nature."[32]

Because of the unity of the spiritual and the natural, or of indeterminate freedom with the determinate in man, men are always engaged in introducing creative emergents (as well as sinful elements) into the "various historic configurations of human vitality."[33] Freedom endows all natural impulses with new dimensions, and transmutes and transfigures almost every given structure. Therefore every norm which seems to be validated by experience or to be expressive of something immutable about the human essence "must be held with some degree of tentativity and be finally subordinate to the law of love."[34]

III. JUS GENTIUM JUS CIVILIS

Several times in *An Interpretation of Christian Ethics,* which contains the justly celebrated chapter on "The Relevance of an Impossible Ethical Ideal," Reinhold Niebuhr remarks that love and even minimal standards of justice "logically" involve each other and are "organically" related.[35] These words do not throw much light. More illuminating is the statement, also repeated in several forms, that

[32] *Faith and History,* p. 183.
[33] *Ibid.,* p. 182.
[34] *Ibid.,* p. 183.
[35] *An Interpretation of Christian Ethics,* for example, pp. 105, 110, 111.

"every moral value and standard is *grounded in* and *points toward* an ultimate perfection of unity and harmony not realized in any historic situation," or that a "minimal standard of moral conduct is *grounded in* the law of love and *points toward* it as ultimate fulfillment."[36] While establishing the transcendence of love, he also seeks to point out the relevance of the transcendent as "both *the ground* and *the fulfillment* of existence," as "*a basis* of even the most minimal social standards," "not only as *the source* of all norms of justice, but as an ultimate perspective by which their limitations are discovered."[37]

Now the statement that justice "points toward" and finds "fulfillment" in love suggests that justice itself may properly be grounded in structural reason and nature, independent of love which transcends these things. Justice, then, would stand on its own base, even though it reaches up toward heaven and is subject to Heaven's judgment. This seems to be Niebuhr's view or at least his expression, when he discusses the relation of justice to love in the chapter titled "The Kingdom of God and the Struggle for Justice" in his Gifford Lectures.[38] There, without indicating any perceptible difference, he passes from "the practical universality of the prohibition of murder," one of the minimum, negative requirements which form, as we have seen, the determinate natural moral law, to "essentially universal 'principles' of justice"; and he counts heavily on the evidence that "both 'equality' and 'liberty' are recognized in Stoic, medieval and modern theories of natural law."[39] Does this mean that here at last he elaborates more fully what comprises the determinate natural law? This conclusion might be drawn from the fact that the emphasis falls on natural or historic achievements of justice "approximating" or "pointing toward" love; and from the fact that (although he does say that "systems and principles of justice are the *servants* and *instruments* of the spirit of brotherhood insofar as they extend the sense of obligation toward others"[40]) there is not nearly so much said about love as the "ground," "basis," and "source" of justice as is the case in *An Interpretation of Christian Ethics.*

The question at this point is not whether all men possess some "sense of justice," but whether their sense of justice is mediate or immediate—whether, in short, the sense of justice is grounded in

[36] *Ibid.*, p. 106 (italics mine). [37] *Ibid.*, pp. 105, 107, 140 (italics mine).
[38] *The Nature and Destiny of Man,* Vol. II, Secs. II and III.
[39] *Ibid.*, II, 254. [40] *Ibid.*, II, 248.

man's sense of the love-requirement upon his freedom or grounded in itself by virtue of what he knows concerning the natural requirements of his determinate nature and the fixed structures of human relationships. The earlier book, *An Interpretation of Christian Ethics,* spells out the way "justice" stems from "love" as well as how justice (be it dependent or independent in origin) points toward and approximates the law of love; and this viewpoint, I believe, is most characteristic of Niebuhr's thought in general. Love as "ground," "source," "basis" suggests the relationship in the traditional theory between natural law and the principles men may devise for applying the fundamental law (love) to actual existence. "Reason, in short, discovers that life in its essence is not what it is in its actual existence, that ideally it involves much more inclusive harmonies than actually exist in history. This is what the Stoics meant by the natural law."[41] This is also, in large part at least, what Niebuhr means by love and the vision of the ideal possible for man in the moment of transcending himself and his world.

The author also sets up a scale comprised of several terms: love, freedom, equality, equal justice (which in his usage sometimes leans toward transcendent equality, sometimes toward concrete justice), justice, and "schemes" of justice. Read in one direction—in the order given—love is the ground, source, and basis of these proximate principles. Read in the reverse direction, these proximate principles point toward love as their end and fulfillment as well as critical standard. They represent "an ascending scale of moral possibilities in which each succeeding step is a closer approximation to the law of love."[42] The latter reading, in the ascending direction, would have to be regarded as primary for certain purposes *if* Niebuhr believes that these more particular principles are actually grounded in some sort of natural law for man as a determinate creature within the structures of nature, reason, or history; and this would then be moral knowledge, supplementing that gained in freedom, of man's destiny for an indeterminate life-in-love.

It is significant that in the order of validation or justification, the opposite or descending order is the one adopted: love is the source and ground, and these other directives follow from it.

The ideal possibility for men involved in any social situation may always be defined in terms of freedom and equality. Their highest good consists

[41] *An Interpretation of Christian Ethics,* p. 205.
[42] *Ibid.,* p. 110.

in freedom to develop the essential potentialities of their nature without hindrance. . . . Since human beings live in a society in which other human beings are competing with them for the opportunity of a fuller development of life, the next highest good is equality; for there is no final principle of arbitration between conflicting human interests except that which equates the worth of competing individuals.[43]

In other words, since love requires that human life be affirmed, the positive freedom to possess the affirmed fruition is the first implication and—in a world of competing claims—equality of opportunity is the second implication drawn from the law of love itself.

Infrequently Niebuhr states that in drawing these conclusions reason is simply at work building a coherent system of relationships. Such statements occur when, reversing the direction, he is concerned to point out how rational consistency "points toward" love as its end and fulfillment:

Reason tries to establish a system of coherence and consistency in conduct as well as in the realm of truth. It conceives of its harmonies of life with life not only in ever wider and more inclusive terms, but also works for equal justice within each area of harmony by the simple fact that the special privileges of injustice are brought under rational condemnation for their inconsistency. Under the canons of rational consistency men can claim for themselves only what is genuinely value, and they cannot claim value for any of their desires if they are not valuable to others besides themselves. Reason thus forces them to share every privilege except those which are necessary to insure the performance of a special function in the interest of the whole. A large percentage of all special privilege is thereby ruled out by the canons of reason.[44]

To the contrary, it is perfectly possible for reason (unless under the sway of love and the conviction that all persons are equal before God—and sometimes even then) to imagine a much more coherent world without the principle of equality than with it, according to some of the hierarchical arrangements or caste systems which have been the system of coherence in actual existence at most times and places.

Moreover, *if* only the "canons of reason" are here at work according to the intrinsic requirements of any viable social structure, and *if* Niebuhr is here elaborating the parallel in his thinking to the natural law for man as a determinate creature, then he proves to be

[43] *Ibid.*, p. 147.

[44] *Ibid.*, p. 204.

more the rationalist than Maritain the Thomist. For in his latest statement, Maritain defines our way of knowing the fundamental law as "knowledge *through inclination*" and not through reason.[45] This is to say, man's sense of justice consists of his inclination toward that which is suitable to the human essence, and his sense of injustice arises from disinclination to that which is averse to his essence. And Maritain declares flatly that "the *only* reason on which the natural law depends is divine Reason,"[46] not human reason at all. The actual situation, I suggest, is that there is a close parallel between what Maritain means by knowledge through inclination (or disinclination, for example, our innate horror when confronted by unheard-of evils in the world such as genocide) and Niebuhr's belief that because of freedom and man's self-understanding in the moment of transcendence "all human life is informed with an inchoate sense of responsibility toward the ultimate law of life—the law of love."[47] This is not known by discursive reason, but it is for Niebuhr the natural law based on a radically different conception of the quintessence of human nature. On the other hand, the principles of equal justice, which are arrived at discursively or by immediate inference from the law of love, correspond closely to Maritain's definition: "A precept which is *known through rational deduction, and as a conclusion conceptually inferred* from a principle of natural law, is part of *jus gentium.*"[48]

The fact is that in his *An Interpretation of Christian Ethics* Niebuhr has taken the position indicated as a possibility in the essay we have had occasion before to comment on: "It may well be," he writes, "that everything defined as the 'sense of justice' is an expression of the law of love within the limits of law."[49] Numerous passages in the earlier book make this his evident view. A few of these may be cited here, since it is of considerable importance to establish once for all that the relevant principles of social ethics have their ground and source in the law of love, and not in the concession of a degree of validity in the older forms of natural law nor simply as the products of technical reason contriving temporary "schemes" of justice:

[45] Jacques Maritain, *Man and the State* (Chicago: The University of Chicago Press, 1951), pp. 91, 94, *et passim.*

[46] *Ibid.*, Footnote 13, p. 98 (italics in the original).

[47] *An Interpretation of Christian Ethics,* p. 112.

[48] *Op. cit.,* Footnote 13, p. 98 (italics in the original).

[49] "Love and Law in Protestantism and Catholicism," *loc. cit.,* p. 152.

Equality is always the regulative principle of justice; and in the ideal of equality there is an echo of the law of love, "Thou shalt love thy neighbor AS THYSELF." If the question is raised to what degree the neighbor has a right to support his life through the privileges and opportunities of the common life, no satisfactory, rational answer can be given to it, short of one implying equalitarian principles: He has just as much right as you yourself.

Since the law of love demands that all life be affirmed, the principle that all conflicting claims of life be equally affirmed is a logical approximation of the law of love in a world in which conflict is inevitable.

As the ideal of love must relate itself to the problems of a world in which its perfect realization is not possible, the most logical modification and application of the ideal in a world in which life is in conflict with life is the principle of equality which strives for an equilibrium in the conflict.

Equal justice remains the only possible, though hardly a precise, criterion of value. Since no life has value if all life is not equally sacred, the highest social obligation is to guide the social struggle in such a way that the most stable and balanced equilibrium of social forces will be achieved and all life will thereby be given equal opportunities.[50]

Evidently these are not conclusions drawn by pure reason discerning, at least with "partial validity," the fixed structures of human existence. Nor are they the product merely of technical social reason contriving schemes of equilibrium while blind to the ultimate moral law. What are they then, if not principles which follow "in a necessary manner" from reflecting upon the nature of man as man and the love-requirement of his quintessential freedom, but "this time *supposing* certain conditions of fact, as for instance the state of civil society or the relationships between peoples"? Freedom, equality, justice—these are universal principles, "at least insofar as these conditions of fact" in which the fundamental law has to be applied "are universal data of civilized life." They are, in fact, the *jus gentium* or "the common law of civilization."[51]

It ought to be noted that Niebuhr locates equality in the realm of (relevant) transcendence, along with the law of love:

[50] *An Interpretation of Christian Ethics*, pp. 108, 149, 150, 196.

[51] Cf. Maritain, *The Rights of Man and Natural Law*, p. 20 (italics in the original).

> Equality, being a rational political version of the law of love, shares with it the quality of transcendence. It ought to be, but it never will be fully realized. . . . The ideal of equality is thus qualified in any possible society by the necessities of social cohesion and corrupted by the sinfulness of men. It remains, nevertheless, a principle of criticism under which every scheme of justice stands and a symbol of the principle of love involved in all moral judgments.[52]

Yet equal justice comes closer to existence than love; and to point this out Niebuhr even uses the opposite language and denies it transcendence: "The principles of equal justice are thus approximations of the law of love in the kind of imperfect world which we know and not principles which belong to a world of transcendent perfection." His meaning, clearly stated on the same page, is that "the ideal of love and the ideal of equality . . . stand in an ascending scale of transcendence to the facts of existence."[53] This in turn means that in Niebuhr's view the notion of equality "presupposes competition of life with life" or "a recalcitrant nature which must be brought into submission to it"; and that the ideal of love "presupposes the resolution of the conflict of life with life, which it is the concern of law to mitigate and restrain."[54]

When Neibuhr corrects the lack of precision in equality and justice as criteria of value so as to apply them to more particular historical situations, he discovers of course that "so many contingent factors arise in any calculation of the best method of achieving equal justice that absolute standards are useless"[55]—this is to say, useless in that they provide no detailed map of the historical terrain. But this does not mean that principles have been abandoned as no longer relevant. It means only that a man is now engaged in applying them. He has, in short, entered the realm of *jus civilis* where he must deal, as Maritain says, "with the rights and duties which follow from the first principle, but in a *contingent* manner, by virtue of the determinate ways of conduct set down by the reason and will of man when they institute the laws and give birth to customs of a particular community."[56]

Not noticing clearly enough that his thought actually follows the traditional ordering *jus naturale*—*jus gentium*—*jus civilis*, Niebuhr

[52] *An Interpretation of Christian Ethics*, p. 109.
[53] *Ibid.*, p. 149. [54] *Ibid.*, pp. 149, 150. [55] *Ibid.*, p. 196.
[56] *Op. cit.*, p. 70 (italics in the original).

makes the mistake of interpreting his accommodation to historical contingency and relativity as a revision of the distinction between absolute and relative natural law. He points out correctly that the so-called relative natural law was an adjustment of moral requirements to human *sinfulness*. He criticizes the unqualified and absolute nature of this distinction between the two laws because it removed to too great a distance the ferment of the absolute ideal and led to complacent acceptance of arrangements based on inequality:

> The difficulty in the Christian application of the theory of natural law . . . is to be found in the undue emphasis placed upon the relative natural law which was applicable to the world of sin, as against the absolute natural law which demanded equality and freedom.
>
> The principle of equality was thereby robbed of its regulative function in the development of the principles of justice. It was relegated to a position of complete transcendence, with the ideal of love.[57]

Such relegation either of love or of equal justice is always a disastrous mistake. But when Niebuhr restates the truth there is to be found in this distinction between absolute and relative natural law, he explains its meaning in terms of the adjustment of the moral law more to the *contingencies* in historical situations than to the sinfulness of man:

> A rational analysis reveals both the ideal possibility and the actual situation from which one must begin. In that sense there are really two natural laws—that which reason commands ultimately and the compromise which reason makes with the *contingent* and arbitrary forces of human existence.[58]

This is not what was ever meant by two natural laws, one absolute, the other relative. It is however what was meant by *jus civilis*. There is then in Niebuhr only one natural or essential law, the absolute law of life (love); and there are principles of equality and justice by which love takes shape for application to historical situations; and finally there are relative schemes of civil law and economic and other institutions which fully embrace the particularities in various constellations of human relationships in history. His aim is so to relate the principle of equality to the law of love on the one hand and to the problems of relative justice on the other, that complacent con-

[57] *An Interpretation of Christian Ethics*, pp. 144, 146.
[58] *Ibid.*, p. 147 (italics mine).

servatism may be avoided, and man's allegiance to existing schemes of justice be always in danger of being set in motion toward some higher possibility. One might therefore summarize the meaning for Niebuhr of the sense of inequality or injustice, whether taken most generally or most particularly, as the reaction of love to everything which is not love. For everything defined as the "sense of justice" is an expression of love with greater specification as law.

In some of Niebuhr's later writings there may be detected a tendency to skip over the correlation of love with freedom, and following that with equal justice, and to pass at once to the way in which man's indeterminate freedom shatters every structure in history and escapes all fixed norms. This leaves him in a poor position for showing, as he is fond of saying, that "the final dyke against relativism is to be found, not in these alleged fixities, but in the law of love itself."[59] At one point in his "vindication of democracy and critique of its traditional defence," for example, the author says: "One of the facts about man as man is that his vitalities may be elaborated in indeterminate variety. . . . It is man's nature to transcend nature and to elaborate his own historical existence in indeterminate degree."[60] These statements, which the author deliberately juxtaposes with Maritain's definition of natural law, are to be recognized, of course, as Niebuhr's central affirmation about the nature of man: freedom. But in this context he is concerned to point out the negative consequences of transcendence and not the positive requirement of "an indeterminate field of fellowship"—what freedom wrecks and not what freedom works through love. Freedom, of course, remains an ultimate; and the author has the positive and worthy intention of vindicating democracy. But "social freedom" proves to be as indeterminate and limitless as the ontological freedom on which it is based.

This becomes clear when the author asks "the final question to confront the proponent of a democratic and free society": "whether the freedom of a society should extend to the point of allowing these principles to be called in question." He answers that "the ultimate freedom of a democratic society" requires that "not even the moral presuppositions upon which the society rests are withdrawn from constant scrutiny and re-examination."[61] We must tread cautiously

[59] "Love and Law in Protestantism and Catholicism," *loc. cit.*, p. 173.
[60] *The Children of Light and the Children of Darkness*, Footnote 8, pp. 77–78.
[61] *Ibid.*, pp. 68, 74.

here, for what Niebuhr says is mostly valid. He does point out that "every society needs working principles of justice [are they not in the earlier book much more than mere working principles?], as criteria for its positive law and system of restraints. . . . But every historical statement of them is subject to amendment."[62] Certainly no "historical statement" or "scheme" of justice ought to go long without amendment, on account of both the vested interests and the limited imagination of any historical epoch. But this is a far cry from saying that the "moral presuppositions upon which society rests" are never to be withdrawn from constant scrutiny and reexamination—if this means not to find out better what these presuppositions require in a new day but to call them fundamentally in question and to challenge them. Such unlimited freedom means unlimited war, or a perpetual and unqualified inclination thereto, among all us Hatfields and McCoys; and there would then have been found no positive basis for community.

Of course, Niebuhr cannot adhere consistently to this answer even with regard to the single presupposition he has in mind in this context: If "the freedom of society" is really vindicated and "*made necessary* by the fact that human vitalities have no simple definable limits,"[63] then here is a moral presupposition so firmly grounded that objection to it by the primitives of our time ought not to be genially tolerated, even though particular proposals for adjudicating between freedom and order may be multiplied without number. It may be suggested that if what Niebuhr wrote earlier in *An Interpretation of Christian Ethics* about love as the law for freedom, and about positive freedom as love's first discernment concerning the neighbor's need, and equal justice as the next following perquisite, were all brought fully into relation to this issue, his answer would gain still greater substance and clarity. For there he wrote of "equal justice" as "the simplest of all moral principles" and said:

> That principle has been operative in all the advances made by human society, and its application to the modern social situation is obviously valid. In a struggle between those who enjoy inordinate privileges and those who lack the basic essentials of the good life it is fairly clear that a religion which holds love to be the final law of life stultifies itself if it does not support equal justice as a political and economic approximation of the ideal of love.[64]

[62] *Ibid.*, p. 71. [63] *Ibid.*, p. 77 (italics mine). [64] P. 131.

Yet this is Niebuhr's viewpoint in books later than the one on Christian ethics. The chapter "Beyond Law and Relativity" in *Faith and History* says in effect that there is one only natural and essential law; the rest is application:

> The principles of "natural law" by which justice is defined are, in fact, not so much fixed standards of reason as they are rational efforts to apply the moral obligation, implied in the love commandment, to the complexities of life and the fact of sin. . . . Any definition of moral rules beyond the minimal obligation of the self to the neighbor are discovered, upon close analysis, to be rational formulations of various implications of the love commandment rather than fixed and precise principles of justice. . . . Equality stands in a medial position between love and justice. . . . Thus equality is love in terms of logic. But it is no longer love in the ecstatic dimension. . . . Therefore equal justice is on the one hand the law of love in rational form and on the other hand something less than the law of love.[65]

Likewise, in Niebuhr's latest volume of essays there is a passage in the chapter on "Augustine's Political Realism" that is obviously his own viewpoint and which may be regarded as a *précis* of the foregoing. He is speaking of the "sense of justice" on the part of various interest-groups in a nation, and then declares that the "spirit of justice is *identical* with the spirit of love except at the highest level of the spirit of love, where it becomes purely sacrificial and engages in no calculation of what the due of each man may be. . . . Certain 'principles' of justice, as distinguished from formulas or prescriptions, were indeed operative, such as liberty, equality, and loyalty to covenants; but these principles will be recognized as no more than the law of love in its various facets."[66]

IV. THE MEANING OF CHRISTIAN LOVE

There may be readers who will be of the opinion that the foregoing interpretation has leveled the towering summits of the Niebuhrian mountain range, with its gathering storms and lightning flashes, to about the height of the mountains Wordsworth loved best. What has happened, they may ask, to the pinnacle of self-

[65] Pp. 188–190.

[66] *Christian Realism and Political Problems,* p. 135. Although at its highest level the spirit of love is heedless of the self's due, it may be questioned whether love ever "engages in no calculation of what the due of each man may be."

sacrificial love which seems in its ecstatic heroism and spontaneous heedlessness to be such an "impossible possibility" for men and nations?

Two main interpretations of the meaning of Christian love are contending for acceptance in present-day theological discussion. One is the view that the primary meaning of love is to be found in self-sacrifice. This is Niebuhr's position, and he believes the critical relevance of such love to ordinary human motives is to be found in the fact that "without an element of heedless love every form of mutual love would degenerate into a calculation of mutual advantages, and every calculation of such advantages would finally generate resentment about an absence of perfect reciprocity."[67] In demonstrating that such a redemptive relationship exists between self-sacrificial love and all forms of mutual love, Niebuhr has been accused of holding a conception of mutual love that is "neither mutual nor love." Theologians who raise this objection themselves are in general adherents of the second interpretation of the intrinsic meaning of Christian love. They believe that "community," or the highest and truest form of mutual love itself, is the basic notion in Christian ethics. In support of this viewpoint one might cite the notion of "covenant-community" so fundamental in Biblical ethics, and the New Testament *koinonia,* the "fellowship" of the early Christian *ecclesia,* or the "kingdom of God" interpreted as "the beloved community" in which God's will reigns.

A notable example of the latter interpretation of the meaning of love is Daniel Williams's Rauschenbusch Lectures *God's Grace and Man's Hope*[68]—a book which otherwise shows so much acceptance of Niebuhr's general analysis that many readers may not have noticed the most signal difference. Williams describes our present human situation with its omnipresent evil and distress admixed with good as "the embattled reign of Christ."[69] The meaning he assigns to this New Testament concept, however, may more adequately be expressed as "the embattled reign of mutual love." "Community," he writes, is the "order which is sought by love"; and "the one absolute demand is that we serve the growth of community."[70] "Here, then, is the distinctive task of Christian social philosophy: to raise in every social order the question, 'What is its consequence

[67] "Love and Law in Protestantism and Catholicism," *loc. cit.*, pp. 160–161.
[68] *Op. cit.* (New York: Harper & Brothers, 1949).
[69] *Ibid.*, pp. 133ff. [70] *Ibid.*, pp. 151, 152.

for the community of mutuality among men?' "[71] In passing, and if it be a virtue that the task be "distinctive," one might conclude that this has not been adequately defined by the category of mutuality, since utilitarians and self-realizationists and many another type of social philosophy propose for themselves the same task. Among these schools, and between them all and a Christian ethic of "community," there may remain significant differences; but are they fundamental enough to warrant the use here of "the embattled reign *of Christ*" as a religious label for the notion of mutuality common to them all?

When Williams asserts that "actually all love does combine the desire *of the self* with the good of another,"[72] he is right in one sense of the ambiguous genitive case he uses, in another wrong. "The desire of the self" contains two possible meanings which should be sharply distinguished: the self's desire for its own good and the self's desire for the good of another. Either may be the self's desire or the desire of the self. All love does actually express the self's desire and some love combines the self's desire with the good of another, but not all love combines the self's desire for its own good with its desire for the good of another: only mutual love sets out to do this. And if Niebuhr is correct, such love will fall short of mutuality unless it lives under the tension, correction, and constant redirection by a love that combines the self's desire, heedless of the self's own good, with the good of another. Doubtless every self is or ought to be, to borrow Tillich's phrase, "a centered self"; but not self-centered or centered only on mutuality—nor through mutual or communal love centered at the same time on one's own good and the good of another by some sort of calculating reciprocity.

Daniel Williams asks "the simple question, 'What is the good which the spirit of *agape* seeks—what does Christian love intend?' " and answers, "The Kingdom of God." Again, these Biblical expressions have already been loaded with the meaning he takes from them—when he concludes that "in intention universal mutual love and sacrificial love are one, for what is intended is the mutual good of all." He sees plainly enough that mutual love is not intrinsically self-sacrificial; yet it readily becomes so, for where and whenever this kingdom of mutuality "is really intended, the self is ready to sacrifice anything for that good except the good itself."[73] Mutual love becomes sacrificial only under the present conditions of Christ's

[71] *Ibid.*, p. 168. [72] *Ibid.*, p. 71 (italics mine). [73] *Ibid.*, pp. 75, 76.

"embattled reign." It is always sacrificial because of the omnipresence of evil in human history, and this, we may readily believe, is no momentary state of affairs. Still, mutuality is the very substance of love, while sacrifice is—in the philosophic sense of the word—only an "accidental" part either of the intention or of the behavior of love. Under the present conditions of history, self-sacrifice becomes a "universal property" of mutual love, but this still is a "property," not the essence of the matter.

By contrast, Niebuhr believes that the motive and direction of Christian love is essentially sacrificial, at its highest heedless of self and containing none of the self-referential motives which are co-present with other-regarding motives in mutual love. Surely this is the more correct reading of Biblical and New Testament ethics. While the national life of the people of the Old Testament was based on covenant, this covenant among men was in turn measured by the standard of the extraordinary righteousness of God. God's *hesed*, or his steadfast faithfulness to men even when there was on their part no returning love, gave the standard for the covenant. This was, so to speak, the cement of community. And we know well enough what was the basis of the New Testament *koinonia*. Here there was plenty of mutuality and strong visible bonds of community, of course; but the supporting substance of this was another sort of love which gave definitive meaning to the *agape*-community of the early church. When the scripture enjoins: "Let love be among you," it does not mean, "Let 'among-you-ness' be among you." It is one thing to say "Let mutual love be mutual," and quite another to say in the New Testament meaning of the word, "Let *love* be mutual." For the love in question takes its measure from Christ's love for the Church when he "gave himself up for her," nourishing and cherishing her more than his own life (Ephesians 5:25–29). It is one thing to say, "Have a mutually loving mind among you," and quite another to say, "Have *this* mind *among* yourselves, which you have in Christ Jesus," for the apostle goes on to explain the meaning of such love in terms of One who "emptied himself" (Philippians 2:5–8). When Jesus said to his disciples, "A new commandment I give to you, that you love one another," so far that was no new commandment; and it only became a new word when he went on to explain the love wherewith they were to love one another: "Even as I have loved you, that you also love one another" (John 13:34).

Notice that "mutual love" or any other sort of love may be the attitude of only one party to a relationship and not of the other. Therefore it is a significant moral injunction to say, "Let mutual love be *mutual*" (or let enlightened selfishness be mutual, or let Christlike love be mutual). Niebuhr certainly grants that mutual love is a genuine sort of *love*, and he is considering the more perfect instances in which it may be truly *mutual*, before subjecting it to criticism. His position may be put in this way: There must be present some degree of the sort of love which is heedless of the question whether it is mutual or not and which nevertheless affirms the being and well-being of the other, or else a person whose attitude toward another includes that other's good (whether out of mutual love or a wise egoism) will sooner or later begin to wonder whether his own good is in turn included in the attitude of the other to the same degree, and thus human community will finally end in resentment about the *possible* absence of perfect reciprocity and in mutual recriminations over the possible or actual lack of mutuality from the other's side.

A few of Niebuhr's definitions lend support to the charge that his conception of mutual love is "neither mutual nor love." Criticizing reductive substitutes for suffering love in modern liberal Christianity, he describes these surrogates as on "the level of mutual love *or the love which calculates its relations to others from the standpoint of its own need of others.*"[74] Mutual love, he writes in his most extended discussion of this issue, is "always arrested by reason of the fact that it seeks to relate life to life from the standpoint of the self and for the sake of the self's own happiness."[75] This attitude may be mutual enough, yet it is certainly not love but a wise self-love. Here mutual love has already suffered alteration. However, Niebuhr's real definition, perhaps regrettably not used frequently enough, is qualitatively higher than this. For example, he writes that "mutual love (in which *disinterested concern for the other* elicits a reciprocal response) is the highest possibility of history; . . . such love can only be initiated by a type of disinterestedness (sacrificial love) which dispenses with historical justification."[76] In other words, both mutual and sacrificial love are types of "disinterested concern for the other," which is simply to say both are genuine love. But

[74] *Faith and History*, p. 178 (italics mine).

[75] *The Nature and Destiny of Man*, Vol. II, Chap. III, p. 82.

[76] *Ibid.*, Vol. II, Chap. IX, p. 247 (italics mine), where he is summarizing his earlier discussion (Vol. II, Chap. III, pp. 81–90) of the relations between the two loves.

mutual love *also* intends the elicitation of a favorable self-referential response, and without the element of sacrificial love may soon *come* to depend on such a response; while sacrificial love intends the good of the other even in face of the necessity of sacrificing the response. What Niebuhr says of the initiating and redemptive relation between sacrificial and mutual love remains true when the latter is taken in its best possible meaning: "The consequence of mutuality must, however, be the unintended rather than the purposed consequence of the action. For it is too uncertain a consequence to encourage the venture towards the life of the other."[77]

Nevertheless, something may be lost from sight in our passion for distinction among different types of love. In speaking of "mutual" and "sacrificial" love there is danger that the adjective may overpower the substantive in our understanding of the terms. Niebuhr suspects that this is the case with mutual love in the first step in its inevitable declension from disinterested concern for the other. The good of the beloved, and not "community" as Williams apparently believes, is what love seeks. The one absolute demand is that we serve the growth of the neighbor God gives us; that we bend and redirect community to serve this end, and not that we serve "the growth of community." Love is just love, the genuine article, for which perhaps one univocal word should be reserved. The word "love" is surely not deserving of use for the self's relation to itself; and what makes the term inappropriate for use in this connection is its univocal meaning no matter what adjectives are attached to it; namely, love is a bond of life with life by which one person affirms the being and well-being of another.

There is also some evidence that the primary meaning of love has been outweighed by the adjectives Niebuhr uses. He speaks of "heedless," "suffering," "self-sacrificial" love. There can be no frontal objection to these descriptions of the *inner* attitude by which a person cleaves to the other. But without a whole cluster of other qualifications they too readily imply *rigor mortis* at the very heart of love, and soon may be taken as literal descriptions of the *external* behavior love will adopt on all occasions, or *should* adopt if only it were strong and pure enough. No doubt love is "heedless"; but there is also nothing more heedful, careful, and flexibly wise than

[77] *Ibid.*, Vol. II, Chap. III, p. 82 (italics mine). Cf. also *Faith and History*, p. 185.

love. No doubt love "suffers" all things; but also love rejoices with those that rejoice. Love proves willing to sacrifice the self to the needs and good of neighbors and companions in God; but love also endures in the very loving. In his *Commentary on Galatians* (6:2) Luther writes that love is not merely "to wish well one to another, but for one to bear another's burdens; that is, to bear those things which be grievous unto you and which you would not willingly bear. Therefore Christians must have strong shoulders and mighty bones, that they may bear flesh, that is, the weakness of their brethren; for Paul says that they have burdens and troubles." But Christians need more than strong shoulders and mighty bones to bear flesh. They need also wide and sensitive hearts to rejoice in another's small joys, unenvious hearts to rejoice in his great ones, and powerful currents of vitality within themselves to embrace as their own all things human. If they are to bear flesh they must also bear those things which may surprise them with sudden and unexpected joy in another's good fortune. All this is by no means lacking from Niebuhr; and he certainly believes that love is spontaneous, even ecstatic. Yet one suspects that "sacrifice" and "suffering" tend to overcome affirmation of life in the meaning of love, and that when these are then soon rated as the clearest evidence of the presence of love in the heart, Niebuhr gains too easy a victory, and by a somewhat mistaken strategy, in his campaign to demonstrate the (relevant) *impossibility* of love. Love is mainly intent on the good of another. It is not intent on the *overt* sacrifice or the suffering this often entails, any more than it intends the mutuality that sometimes (perhaps often) follows.

For surely it must be said that Niebuhr exaggerates the "impossibility" of such a reconciling love among men, under the momentum of his polemic against a sentimentalism which supposes it to be too easily possible. No doubt such love fully and constantly incarnate in a human life ends, as he says, upon a Cross out on the edge of human history. Yet we are here dealing with the motive or intention of the act, and not only with external acts of visible self-sacrifice. Just as love which is mutual in essence or intention becomes sacrificial even in spirit only by "accident," so it ought to be said that a love whose essential spirit and intention impels one, heedless of self, steadfastly to affirm the well-being of another requires the actual act of self-sacrifice only when the occasion warrants it in terms of actually advancing the neighbors' good. The numerical infrequency of self-sacrifice open to external view does not necessarily indicate the absence, much less the impossibility, of the motive of self-giving love in the mundane lives of ordinary people, who may not have found in themselves the strength for martyrdom simply because they have not found reason for it or a situation actually calling for it. No doubt self-giving love sometimes expresses itself in actual sacrifice of self and of one's life, and most often weakness or selfishness holds us back from such a course. But there is also no doubt that self-sacrificial love ought often to "sacrifice the sacrifice," and then only weakness or selfishness or simply conformity to what our own bravado has led people to expect of us would plunge headlong on toward actual sacrifice. It must never be forgotten that Christian ethics casts *no more* suspicion upon the motive that may lead a man to stay at his post and "sacrifice the sacrifice" than it does upon the motive that may lead to giving one's body to be burned—and, of course, no less.

This is especially significant for the morality—or the immorality—of group actions. Niebuhr is fond of saying that the action of nations can never go beyond the area where there is actual congruence between national self-interest and concern for the needs of other peoples or of the world community (although the latter motive widely held by a people may make them and their statesmen more enlightened and inclusive of the good of other nations when deciding what is in their own national interest). The implication is that it is always a defection from the ultimate ideal, and proof of the impossibility (though not of the irrelevance) of love in inter-group relationships, for us never to be able to point to a national policy which persists in going beyond national self-interest. This may be true; and it is the case that nations never commit suicide—except by living below, not beyond, the limits of group self-interest. By measuring the facts of history against the law of love, Niebuhr arrives at his celebrated "relevant impossibility." This is stated in a typical passage:

> Only a forgiving love, grounded in repentance, is adequate to heal the animosities between nations. But that degree of love is an impossibility for nations. It is a very rare achievement among individuals; and the mind and heart of collective man is notoriously less imaginative than that of the individual.[78]

[78] *An Interpretation of Christian Ethics,* pp. 128–129.

Nevertheless, this analysis leans toward error because Niebuhr switches too easily from the delineation and castigation of the motives of men and nations to the data supplied by their external conduct and (with little or no warrant from our religious ethics) finds in the latter evidence of the nature of the former.

Two things should be pointed out in this connection: One is that there is no such thing as "the mind and heart of collective man," but only individual men and women engaged in collective action by means of a gradation of leaders who also are individuals with a mixture of motives in what they do in public and in private life. Although people always act together upon a stage set by the nature and momentum of their traditions and heritage, at the moment of action and in their public no less than in their private capacities people may be just as loving, forgiving, repentant and imaginative as nature and grace enable them to be. Perhaps there are no saints in private or in public. Nevertheless, what they, or we of mixed motives, should do overtly is another matter. For what sort of behavior or public policy self-giving love will lead men to undertake may be quite the opposite of what they would do were they alone involved in the issue. As one Irishman said to his friend with whom he was discussing the problem of evil in the world: "Faith, and there be many things which God does in his official capacity which he wouldn't think of doing as a private individual." This is also true of the statesman—not only regrettably but because whatever love requires for the preservation of human life in the world must be done. Perhaps where we fall short of the ideal of love in private and in public life is a subject that should only be approached confessionally, throwing the mantle of charity over the sins of others, as Luther said, and not curiously spying them out, much less laying down in advance for them or for ourselves how far sin must abound.

The second point is that it is exceedingly doubtful if ever nations *ought* to allow themselves to be nailed to a cross. Or, expressed more accurately since only individuals bear personal responsibility, it is doubtful whether the leaders or citizens of a nation *ought* ever to read from the law of love, which defines the ideal motive for their conduct in their public capacities no less than in private, the conclusion that they should render functioning in these capacities no longer possible for themselves or others by voluntary suicidal abandonment of the system of vocations in which God has placed them in responsibility. This judgment is not just a matter of collective self-interest or the group will-to-live, which (while necessary) is then subject to either cynical or redemptive wholesale criticism by the theologian in the light of the transcendent possibilities of self-sacrifice. Since self-giving love is a matter of motive and not first of all of external action, defining its own hard course of action, sometimes to the death and sometimes to stick to one's post, are not nations, in the light of their total task in behalf of their own people and all the future generations and their possible contribution to the community of mankind, duty-bound to "sacrifice the sacrifice"? At least we can all be thankful that Themistocles persuaded the Athenians to use the funds from a newly discovered vein of silver in their mines, not for democratic distribution and consumption, but for building a stronger navy by which they were able to hold off the power of the despotism from the East for a few more decades in which Greek culture came to flower. Whether or not there was a Marshall Plan for strengthening the Ionian isles we need not inquire; but if there was, this was not only called for by a wise collective egoism assisted *up to that point* by genuine-enough concern for the Ionians; nor was it simply demanded by concern for the Ionians *enlarging* the Athenians' conception of their own actual interests. It was called for also, as we can see from the perspective of a later age, by a concern to affirm the being and well-being of others and by the performance of an actual historic mission. The Athenians might conceivably have been unmindful of their own interests and thereby not mindful enough of their vocation in the world.

The point is not that the motive of love can ever be taken alone, any more than self-interest can, but that we ought not to say that only the admixture of collective self-interest prevents love in group action from leading on to overt self-sacrifice. It is true that Christianity has enlarged the field of concern to the Christian statesman's vocation, particularly with regard to including the enemy. But unless we are to say that the enemy always truly needs to succeed in aggression, we ought not to say or seem to say that it is only our own inevitable self-interest or some mysterious limit upon collective action in history, and not also our best judgment (very possibly mistaken) about what the enemy and all the rest of the world need, which demands that he be resisted. Just as sin is so inevitable that it is bound to happen, likewise the neighbor-claims which surround the Christian statesman and define for him his duty are so inevitable and numerous that it may be that he is always bound to sacrifice sacrifice, regardless of what he might be willing to do were his own life alone at stake. This may be the primary motive for what he does, and not just the desire to stay in office as the political leader of a collectively selfish people. Niebuhr is right in pointing out that individuals hear and heed the call of their appointed opportunity for actual sacrifice of life more often than groups do (perhaps the latter never). He is wrong in implying that this is always because of the greater strength of collective self-interest or necessary lack of creative imagination in public policy-makers, and not quite possibly also because statesmen and citizens see that for them *as such* there is no such responsibility and for their groups no such appointment.

At one point Niebuhr nearly cuts through the Gordian knot he himself has tied. Since, he writes, an unconditional perfection in history is impossible,

> *it is not even right* to insist that every action must conform to *agape*, rather than to the norms of relative justice and mutual love by which life is maintained and conflicting interests are arbitrated in history. *For as soon as the life and interests of others than the agent are involved in an action or policy, the sacrifice of these interests ceases to be "self-sacrifice."* It may actually become an unjust betrayal of their interests.[79]

Pondering this paragraph will suggest its own revision and improvement as a Christian analysis of the statesman's or the citizen's vocation. What can be more "right" and "conformable to *agape*" than a wise concern for the life and interests of others? Here plainly Niebuhr derives a too literal, external description of acceptable Christian action from what was never meant for such, that is, the test of conformity to *agape;* and this makes necessary his recourse to relative justice and mutual love for deciding what is actually right. Yet the passage shows also that *agape* itself, and not just these lower, less transcendent standards, requires that the interest of all involved in the policy be not "unjustly," that is to say *unlovingly,* betrayed.

No doubt cleavages and tensions remain. If perfect love means the cessation of all inner contradictions within the self, and the overcoming of all conflicts and tensions between the self and the other and between one group and another, by the complete obedience of all wills to the will of God,[80] that will have to wait on heaven

[79] *The Nature and Destiny of Man,* Vol. II, Chap. III, p. 88 (italics mine).
[80] *Ibid.,* Vol. II, Chap. IX, p. 246.

or the age in which the kingdoms of this world become the kingdom of Christ—and also where there will be neither marrying nor giving in marriage. We were not appointed to be first-coming, or second-coming Christs who will close the books on God's historical calling to the nations. Yet we are called to readiness to let love reign; and in face of the requirement of simple discipleship Niebuhr's rigid dualism between "within history" and "beyond history," or between what may be true "in principle" and "in fact," may prove more disastrous than all the supposed rigidities of the traditional theory of natural law, since the former places limits upon God's *agape* and providential redemptive power while the latter only indicates a recalcitrance in the human nature and history which are subject to redemption. As for what we wayfaring men do exteriorly in private or in public capacities, let not him who does this despise him who does that, "for God has welcomed him. Who are you to pass judgment on the servant of another? . . . Let every one be fully convinced in his own mind. . . . So do not let what is good to you be spoken of as evil. . . . The faith that you have"—and the love that you have—"keep between yourself and God; happy is he who has no reason to judge himself for what he approves. . . . For whatever does not proceed from faith"—and love—"is sin" (Romans 14:3, 5b, 16, 22, 23).

V. FAITH AND REASON IN LOVE

The question which next arises is this: How does Niebuhr, and in his view mankind, know that love is the norm for human life in freedom? Is it entirely from a reasonable "estimate of the healthful functioning of total human personality"? Is it the positive conclusion that remains after showing that no other view proves suitable to the full measure and the indeterminate possibilities of human freedom? If so, then love is established as the moral law, as Maritain says of his own more traditional viewpoint, *"from the simple fact that man is man,* nothing else being taken into account"—although the natural law is now one single norm and no longer to be defined as an "*ensemble* of things to do and not to do" which follow from the fact that man is man in logically necessary fashion.[81] More correctly stated for Niebuhr, love is known to be the moral law for freedom by a man's reflection upon *himself*, or by an act of self-understanding. For Niebuhr locates *the consciousness of* original

[81] Jacques Maritain, *The Rights of Man and Natural Law*, p. 63 (italics mine).

righteousness "in the self in the moment of transcending itself."[82] He writes: "Reason itself is not the source of law, since it is not possible to prove the self's obligation to the neighbor by any rational analysis which does not assume the proposition it intends to prove. Yet reason works helpfully to define the obligation of love in the complexities of various types of human relations."[83] By this he means discursive, contriving reason or the sort of reason which applies the law of love in principles and schemes of justice. This does not exclude but calls for an act of reasonable self-understanding which apprehends the law of love itself.

There are still would-be system-builders who may be heard to say rather petulantly that Niebuhr is an anthropologist or social analyst or psychologist and not, after all, a theologian. I would insist that at all points he is at the same time a rational analyst of human nature and a Christocentric theologian. There is in his thought a constant dialogue between man's knowledge of himself and the moral law when he views himself in the moment of self-transcendence or when studying alternative interpretations of his historical existence on the one hand, and on the other the knowledge that comes from encounter with the revelation in Christ and from viewing himself in the mirror of the Word. For this reason, having associated the Christian view closely with humanistic ethics in attempting to estimate the proper functioning of total human personality, he goes on to point out that "the Christian view recognizes that it is not easy to measure our total personality. . . . The self, as interested participant, is always involved in these processes; this is why self-knowledge is more ambiguous than the proponents of scientific objectivity in the study of human nature realize, and why self-love is more dubious than Dr. Fromm realizes."[84]

Yet there is a remaining ambiguity—perhaps a necessary one —in the uses of autonomous reason and Christonomous reason in discerning the law of love. The notion of constant "dialogue" between them just suggested may help somewhat—but only somewhat, since this tells us nothing of the contributions of each to the conversation. Niebuhr's own terms are not much better for what the revelation does to "accentuate," "clarify," and make "fuller" our

[82] *The Nature and Destiny of Man,* I, 277.
[83] *Faith and History,* p. 193.
[84] Review of Fromm, *Man for Himself. Christianity and Society,* Spring, 1948, p. 27.

natural self-knowledge and knowledge of the moral law.[85] Would the best thing be to rewrite him as more explicitly an Augustinian on this point: *Fides praecedit rationem, nisi credideritis non intelligetis, credo ut intelligam, fides quaerens intellectum?* This would mean that reason does not of itself alone discern that love is the natural moral law for freedom, but nevertheless that when we begin by faith we, that is, our reasons, do end in sight of this truth. Thus it would be *illuminated* reason that knows the self and freedom's requirement; yet, as Augustine believed, these would be truly known, and by reason. Such an interpretation to a degree runs counter to the credit assigned by Niebuhr to the powers of autonomous reason in anthropological and social and self-analysis. Is his procedure of joining to the extent he does in dialogue with secular rationalistic viewpoints to be taken as only an apologetic method, or as an indication of the balance between faith and reason in his own thought? If the latter, faith would appear as much more a dialogic supplement to reason than a corrective and redirection of reason from the beginning and throughout all the notes in the scale, as it was in Augustine. Perhaps the truest description would be to return to the notion of dialogue, and to stress the degree to which faith and reason each *confirms* what the other discerns of how love is native in the land of human freedom, while faith "firms up" and enlarges what self-consciousness alone would experience as the claims of others.

At the summit of love as a self-giving affirmation of the being and well-being of another, perhaps we can better delineate the problem of faith and reason raised by Niebuhr's ethical position. Reason, he says, or man's self-awareness in the moment of self-transcendence, has an "inchoate" knowledge that love is the law of human life, or that only an indeterminate field of fellowship really corresponds to the dimensions of freedom. This awareness is "accentuated," "clarified," "made full" by the revelation.

There are three possibilities as to how this should be understood, of which the second should be chosen (if the first two exhaust the alternatives) or (if they do not) the third should be chosen as both

[85] *Inter alia*, p. 290 of Vol. I of *The Nature and Destiny of Man*, where he considers and partially rejects (or rather only partially accepts) the view that not by natural endowment does man learn that faith, trust, and love are the requirement of human freedom.

closer to the truth of the matter and also most accurately and consistently representing Niebuhr's point of view.

1. It may be that man has an "inchoate" knowledge of the requirement of *self-sacrificial* love, or that he dimly knows that he should heed not his own but his neighbor's good. If this be what Niebuhr means, then the revelation enters into "dialogue" with natural knowledge of the moral law; and, while we cannot separate their distinctive contributions to the ongoing conversation but must confine ourselves to saying that faith "accentuates" what reason already forecasts, both or both together come to the same conclusion: namely, that such love as was seen in the flesh in Jesus Christ is the very *imago Dei* or essence of our common humanity. On this interpretation, Niebuhr's position would be un-Augustinian in crediting so much to natural knowledge unillumined by precedent faith. At the same time it would be quite authentically Augustinian in refusing to remove from reason's sight any of the ultimate meaning of Christian faith or ethics (as St. Augustine in the *De Trinitate* still sought to understand what he began and continued in by believing, rather than separating a number of mysteries as a supplement altogether beyond reason). For this combination of motifs I can think of no better word than ceaseless dialogue; and this may appear to be what Niebuhr is saying in the main when both his autonomous anthropological analysis and his Christocentric moral theology are viewed together.

2. Perhaps a more definite meaning should be precipitated out of these words "inchoate" for natural knowledge and "accentuation" or "clarification" for the revelation, or put in their place. It may be that in his free spiritual self-awareness man has a sense of *mutual* love, and that only by faith in Christ does he know himself to be judged in terms of the *self-giving* love which seeks to save him at such cost. This then would be the distinction between love as the natural law naturally known and love as the revealed law of life; and a reconstruction of the truth there was in the traditional distinction between infused love and the other theological virtues "living beyond reason," and natural love and the natural virtues "living within reason." But for knowing ourselves as known by such love we would not know that any such love were required of us, nor would we know the fulfillment of our own human essence as that in covenant-love we should adhere to the well-being of another with such costly

fidelity. The continuity that may exist between this love and the community of mutuality adumbrated by nature and reason can still be emphasized. Yet the contribution of faith and reason to morality through their dialogue with each other would be more clearly indicated or confessed. Moreover, it hereby becomes evident that at every point faith precedes reason if reason ends in sight of sacrificial love.

The former of these two possibilities seems more explicit in Niebuhr when he is at work seeking to show that Christian ultimates are fulfillments of the truth there is in secular outlooks, and the latter when he is seeking to show that Christian love is the correction of the defects in secular alternatives. Yet it may be that he actually makes substantially more use of the rationally persuasive power of *mutual* love in all these polemics, while only tangentially indicating the bearing of self-sacrificial love. His review of Fromm's book, already cited, may be taken as an example of the problem.

There Niebuhr was able to correct the self-regarding imbalance in the psychologist's opinions about the source of love for others in proper love for self. The theologian's agreements and disagreements with the psychologist are quite revealing of how each may have arrived at his respective estimate of the healthful functioning of total human personality. The two are wholly in agreement in regard to the futility of moral pronouncements for securing obedience to the law of love. But there is a subtle and significant difference which springs from the fact that the psychologist, in Niebuhr's opinion, does not adequately grasp the truth that the human personality needs to abide in love and affirm the being and well-being of another. Fromm approaches the problem obliquely from the point of view of the self's own love or hatred for itself and so never quite arrives at the center of the issue, which is the bond of love itself, or else he gets there only indirectly. If man is made for covenant, then the relationships comprising his "indeterminate field of fellowship," and the defects in them, may be grasped from either end—either from the side of the self or from the side of the other. Or better, both must be held together. Fromm, however, affirms that the self's love for itself must come before he can have the strength to love another, just as some form of self-hatred precedes hatred for others. This slant only reveals that he does not really understand that the self lives always in relationship. Thus Niebuhr writes:

> From the Christian standpoint the self-hatred which is supposed to make love impossible is actually the consequence of a too anxious pre-

> occupation with self. The self-love which is supposed to make the love of others possible is actually the by-product of a genuine self-giving. Fromm is quite right in seeing that it is not possible to move from self-hatred to love by moral injunction.
>
> Actually both admonitions, that the self ought to love itself and that the self ought to love others, are spiritually impotent. An insecure impoverished self is not made more secure by the admonition to be concerned for itself; for an excessive concern for its security is the cause of its impoverishment. Nor is it made secure by the admonition to love others because that is precisely what it cannot do because of its anxiety about itself. That is why a profound religion has always insisted that the self cannot be cured by law but only by grace; and also why the profoundest forms of the Christian faith regard this preoccupation as not fully curable and therefore as requiring another kind of grace: that of forgiveness.[86]

On the face of it this sounds like an unqualified reference to intentionally self-sacrificial love, or to a "genuine self-giving" of which proper self-love is only a by-product. Unquestionably Niebuhr's view is grounded in a more adequate understanding that love is, materially, the law of life. Is he therefore relying on an "inchoate" knowledge of this as the essential truth about human interrelatedness on the part of the psychologist and in the minds of his readers?

On the other hand, may not the excellence and persuasiveness of this brief analysis actually silently depend upon the concept of mutual love common to them both? For mutual love also would indicate a correction of Fromm's unbalanced concern for the isolated individual's self-love or self-hatred—unless they are correct who say that what Niebuhr *calls* mutual love is neither mutual nor love. At another place in his writings Niebuhr makes substantially the same criticism of the psychologist's views. He says that Fromm

> fails to measure the freedom of the self in its dimension of transcendence over self, which makes it impossible for it to be rich within itself. Whatever spiritual wealth the self has within itself is the by-product of its relations, affections and responsibilities, of its concern for life beyond itself.[87]

But it is significant that this contention was put forward after a paragraph in which Niebuhr cited various ways in which Christian *agape* has been attenuated into forms of mutual love and rational-

[86] *Christianity and Society*, Spring, 1948, pp. 27–28.
[87] *Faith and History*, p. 177.

prudential ethics. His disagreement with Fromm is elaborated in order to illustrate the fact that "even when the norm of love is thus reduced to the dimension of a prudential ethic, it falls under the stricture of modern psychiatry." In other words, any genuine conception of the bond of love as the norm for human life (and mutual love is one such conception) is able to correct the defects of an overly individualistic concern for the health of the private person who, apart from prior relation to life beyond himself, is trying to muster the strength to be able to love.

The true situation may, then, be this: The operational concept in Niebuhr's position when he is engaged in dialogue with secular points of view is mutual love "accentuated" by self-giving love, or self-sacrificial love in "organic" relation to other types of love; and this arises from a more fundamental inward encounter between self-sacrificial love and the love of mutuality, or from a perpetual dialogue of faith with reason. The review is an excellent illustration of the effectiveness of what Niebuhr regards as the actual relationship between self-sacrificial and mutual love. It shows that because of the element of heedless love controlling his own thinking about man and morals, he was able to point out Fromm's failure to give heed to perfect reciprocity. It shows that mutual love of itself has not the power for long to sustain true mutuality; and that unless people love one another beyond the point of being concerned about mutuality, then a love which at first was really mutual tends to degenerate into calculations about which party is most given to the community between them or gives most to the other. This soon leads to actual withdrawal from the bonds of mutual love, which becomes evident whenever the first concern is to calculate how a person needs first to love himself properly and then go on from there to engage his own being intimately with the being of another.

In short, we have here an instance in which Niebuhr was able to out-think the secular psychologist, as St. Augustine out-thought the pagans, not necessarily because of greater rational powers or perception of what rational self-awareness adumbrates as the law of life, but because of love- or faith-illuminated reason. Thus he is able to a great degree "to heal the wounds inflicted by man on himself and on his life-in-community in modern times and, by transcending while still doing justice to the elements of truth contained in philosophic and psychological theories of man and society, to revive and give direction to the expiring spiritual ideals of the contemporary period."[88] More important than what happens verbally is what may happen in actual life. In order to maintain a person's stance or mode of existence in the world under the full sustaining, transforming, and redirecting impact of the love of Christ, it seems that much would be gained from clearly acknowledging the difference between his own ordinary sense of justice or sense of the meaning of love and the meaning of love which Christ brings to life.

The dilemma in which we now find ourselves in seeking a sound interpretation of Niebuhr's viewpoint, and of the truth of the matter, can be resolved in some measure by following a suggestion made in the preceding section of this chapter. The expressions for love which set the terms of the problem need to be *de-adjectified*, for the predicates of love are threatening to obscure the substantive. Love is simply love, the genuine article; and it intends the good of the beloved one and not the response of mutuality; it intends the good of the other and not its own actual self-sacrifice or suffering. It is the *neighbor*, and not mutuality or heedlessness or sacrifice or suffering, who stands ever before the eyes of love. This leads us to formulate a third possible interpretation of Niebuhr's viewpoint, and of the situation with regard to faith and reason in love.

3. It is simply love that is known as the norm for human existence by the self in the moment of self-transcendence and self-understanding. And in Christ we have revealed not another sort of love, nor for that matter a "pinnacle" of love, a species of love that can be clearly demarked from other classes of the same genus. The revelation shows us just the meaning of love itself. This is why Niebuhr must speak of an "inchoate" natural knowledge of the law of love and of the "accentuation" of this by revelation. Every effort to clarify the situation by stressing the predicates "mutual" and "sacrificial" only obscures the substance of the love-relation and gives rise to the first two alternatives we have considered. In these terms, indeed, there is ground for supposing *either* that self-understanding apprehends, albeit dimly, the requirement of suffering love (thus making revelation only a companion in dialogue with reason) *or* that natural knowledge goes only as far as mutual love (thus making revelation a supplement or radical redirection of human self-understanding). In these terms Niebuhr can be interpreted both ways.

[88] Cf. Charles N. Cochrane's tribute to St. Augustine in his *Christianity and Classical Culture* (Oxford: Clarendon Press, 1940), p. 360.

He does say that "the ethical norm of history as comprehended by the 'natural' resources of man, by his sober examination of the facts and requirements of life in human society, is *mutual* love."[89] Yet among "the natural resources of man" is the capacity to transcend both himself and history; and in the moment of self-transcendence Niebuhr locates *the consciousness of* original righteousness, which means the law of love—love substantive, the genuine article. While he sometimes inadequately and less typically defines mutual love as the effort to relate life with life from the point of view of the self, on the other hand he declares that while "non-Christian conceptions of love do indeed seek to justify love from the standpoint of the happiness of the agent," still "the freedom of man is such that he is not without some idea of the virtue of love which does not justify itself in terms of his own happiness."[90] Shall we call this a higher definition of mutual love or a dim awareness of the requirement of suffering love? The answer to this question is Either, or better, Neither, for the awareness is just of the requirement of love itself. And in an ironic note directed against Brunner he attributes to children a sense of justice and of equality in which they "may lack proper reverence for the Creator of inequalities; but on the other hand they have certainly never heard of, or been spoiled by 'Stoic rationalism.' "[91] We have already seen that the sense of justice and the norm of equality are nothing less than human nature's sense of love taking shape for application.

In the revelation of suffering love in Christ visibly sacrificing himself, we stand face to face not with the revelation of another or specially self-sacrificial sort of love, nor with a fast-bounded species of love which then must be brought into some relationship with another type of love which naturally commends itself to us, nor even with a "pinnacle" of love which goes so far beyond the love we know as to amount to a difference in kind. We stand before love itself. Here existing human beings meet essential humanity undistorted, for Christ is, as Berdyaev says, the truth about freedom. The contrast between us and Him is so great, not because true love in us is admixed with other types of love structured in history, but because true love in us is mixed with no love at all, with what is not properly love at all. Such an encounter supplies our deepest need, for in all our so-called loves we underestimate how far we have

[89] *The Nature and Destiny of Man,* Vol. II, Chap. III, p. 81 (italics mine).
[90] *Ibid.,* p. 84, Note 16.
[91] *Ibid.,* p. 255–266, Note 8.

come short of love; "we underestimate how far we have come short of what is necessary for a genuine understanding of the other party's case." At our natural best we still may not understand our neighbor nor be able to feel with him, because we do not know that we have to "give something of ourselves in order to achieve real apprehension."[92] We have not broken through the sound barrier of self, and yet we think we love. This does not only fall short of suffering love, it falls short of love. In the visibly suffering love of Christ we know that God gives something of himself in order to break through the barrier and to take upon himself a genuine understanding of the other party's case. If any one imagines that he knows something of love in his own life and has stepped existentially over to the side of another, from encountering Christ he may discover that he does not yet know as he ought to know (I Cor. 8:2).

PAUL RAMSEY

DEPARTMENT OF RELIGION
PRINCETON UNIVERSITY
PRINCETON, NEW JERSEY

[92] Herbert Butterfield, *Christianity, Diplomacy, and War* (New York: Abingdon-Cokesbury Press, 1938), p. 8.

7

Arthur Schlesinger, Jr.

REINHOLD NIEBUHR'S ROLE IN AMERICAN POLITICAL THOUGHT AND LIFE

7

REINHOLD NIEBUHR'S ROLE IN AMERICAN POLITICAL THOUGHT AND LIFE

AMERICAN liberalism—if by liberalism we assume the tradition of Jefferson and Jackson—has retained through American history a constancy of political purpose while undergoing a succession of changes in philosophical presuppositions. The generation which fought the American Revolution had, on the whole, a realistic image of human limitation. "Every man by Nature," said a petition from Pittsfield, Massachusetts, in 1776, "has the seeds of Tyranny deeply implanted within."[1] This realism pervaded the sessions of the Constitutional Convention in 1787, dominated the *Federalist Papers*, ruled the thought of such Jeffersonians as James Madison, and was still to be found in such Jacksonians as Nathaniel Hawthorne.

But early in the nineteenth century a new and more cheerful estimate of human potentiality began to suffuse liberal thought. The rising optimism about man derived from many sources: from the new mystique of democracy and the common man, welling up from the American and French Revolutions; from the beneficent and harmonizing role newly assigned to individual self-interest by the laissez-faire economics of Adam Smith; from the passionate new romantic faith in human innocency, in self-reliance, and in the perfectibility of man, a faith stimulated by English poetry, French political theory, and German philosophy; and, above all from the new circumstances of life and opportunity in nineteenth-century America. It has become fashionable in a more somber age to patronize or ridicule this optimism. But it is hard to deny that it was more

[1] Oscar and Mary F. Handlin, *Commonwealth, a Study of the Role of Government in the American Economy: Massachusetts, 1774–1861* (New York: New York University Press, 1947), p. 5.

true to the needs of American life than the mechanical and exaggerated pessimism of the increasingly sterile Calvinism it displaced, and harder to deny that it released the energy of the nation to serve invaluable political and social ends.

If the tragedy of the Civil War momentarily disturbed this optimism, the extraordinary economic expansion of the years after the war quickly quenched any nascent doubt or disillusion. Andrew Carnegie's interpretation of human evolution would have served for liberals and conservatives alike. "Man was not created with an instinct for his own degradation," Carnegie wrote, "but from the lower he had risen to the higher forms. Nor is there any conceivable end to his march to perfection. His face is turned to the light; he stands in the sun and looks upward."[2] In much this mood, American liberalism marched through its Populist and Progressive phases. The faith even survived, in important aspects, at least, the agony and slaughter of the First World War.

For an important segment of the liberal community, optimism after World War I found its warrant in two converging streams of thought. One was the Social Gospel. The other was the social application of the instrumentalist version of American pragmatism, associated with John Dewey. While differing in their origins, both currents of thought combined to vindicate a common attitude toward man and society—a radiant sense of optimism and of hope, a conviction of the manageability of human tensions and the plasticity of human nature. In this sanguine climate, the old liberal optimism acquired new religious and scientific guarantees.

By 1920 the Social Gospel had, of course, a long history. Beginning in the eighties as the beleaguered conviction of a disreputable minority, it had sought to rescue nineteenth century Protestantism from its individualistic and reactionary interpretation of Christianity and to restore contact with the working classes. By the first decade of the twentieth century, it had won its way to respectability within the Protestant churches. And by this time Walter Rauschenbusch, its most penetrating theologian, had begun his work of systematizing its implications for traditional Christian thought. For Rauschenbusch the conception of the Kingdom of God was central in an approach both to religion and to society; the Kingdom represented not just the final end of man but man's historical hope. "Does not

[2] Andrew Carnegie, *Autobiography*, ed. John C. Van Dyke (Boston: Houghton, 1920), p. 339.

the Kingdom of God consist of this," Rauschenbusch asked, "that God's will shall be done on earth, even as it is now in heaven?" The Kingdom meant, he said, "a growing perfection in the collective life of humanity, in our laws, in the customs of society, in the institutions of education, and for the administration of mercy." The Kingdom was "humanity organized according to the will of God"; it would be "brought to its fulfillment by the power of God in his own time." This would require first, faith; then knowledge, "a scientific comprehension of social life"; then, as Rauschenbusch, a convinced socialist, concluded, a revolutionary mission and a dedicated class: "If the banner of the Kingdom of God is to enter through the gates of the future, it will have to be carried by the tramping hosts of labor."[3]

Rauschenbusch had no naïve expectations that social change would abolish the sinfulness of man; he never wholly lost his tragic sense. But many followers of the Social Gospel read his affirmations more enthusiastically than they did his reservations. After the First World War, it was widely believed in Social Gospel circles that the Kingdom of God could be realized on earth, within history; that its laws were identical with the laws of human nature and society; that the Christian ethic and the commandment of love were directly applicable to social and political questions; and that Christian policies offered practical alternatives to secular policies in specific situations. Charles M. Sheldon's question—"What would Jesus do?" —was considered the key which would unlock social and political perplexity. Such a document as the report of the Federal Council's Committee on the War and the Religious Outlook, *The Church and Industrial Reconstruction* (1920), provided a measured but unambiguous summation of the Social Gospel premises:

Mankind in all its relations . . . must be organized according to the will of God, as revealed in Christ. The entire social order must be Christianized. The world as a whole is the subject of redemption. . . . By the Kingdom Jesus means a social order which is not merely of man's devising, but which it is God's purpose to establish in the world. . . . Is such an ideal practicable? Beautiful though it be, can it ever be anything more

[3] D. R. Sharpe, *Walter Rauschenbusch* (New York, The Macmillan Co., 1942), p. 62; V. P. Bodein, *The Social Gospel of Walter Rauschenbusch* (New Haven, Yale University Press, 1944), p. 2; Rauschenbusch, *A Theology for the Social Gospel* (New York, The Macmillan Co., 1917), p. 142; *idem, Christianity and the Social Crises* (New York, Book Stall, 1907), p. 194; *idem, Christianizing the Social Order* (New York, The Macmillan Co., 1912), p. 449.

than another Utopia? To this question the Christian answer is definite and unmistakable. This ideal can, indeed, be realized.[4]

Politics, in short, could incarnate the absolute.

Nor was the task of applying Christian law to immediate problems deemed overly difficult. Christianity seemed not only transcendent; it was utilitarian. It was not only the religion of ultimate judgment and repentance; it also, properly interpreted, had the immediate answers on prohibition, foreign policy, wages-and-hours legislation and universal military training. And, as Rauschenbusch had suggested, sociology might further mitigate the conflicts of social policy. Scientific studies of social issues, undertaken in the light of the Christian ethic, would show how the simple moralism of the Gospels would resolve the complex issues of industrial society. "There is every reason to believe," observed officials of the Federal Council in 1928, "that science can now adopt social ideals as specifications of a great task to be accomplished for humanity and proceed by the scientific method to assist in evolving a new industrial order which shall be increasingly characterized by righteousness and peace."[5]

As for individual human beings, they were essentially mild, good, and reasonable, and would in time respond to the sociological argument, especially when fortified by the Christian appeal. The parable of the leaven explained how the principle of love would gradually conquer an evil world. The Kingdom of God was thus identical with historical progress. Neither egoism in man nor power in society need be serious obstacles; they could be by-passed by following the path of love in human relations, of non-violence in political relations, and of pacifism in international relations. For most of the Social Gospel, the onward march of democratic idealism would assure the Kingdom. For the radical minority, the Kingdom was the classless society of Marxist anticipation, to be won by the tramping hosts of labor.

The Social Gospel thus supplied democratic idealism with a religious sanction. At the same time, John Dewey was providing it

[4] Pp. 6, 9, 32.

[5] Labor Sunday Message, *Federal Council Bulletin,* Sept., 1928; see the discussion in D. B. Meyer, "The Protestant Social Liberals in America, 1919–1941," Ph.D. thesis, Harvard University, pp. 247–249. I am indebted to Mr. Meyer's brilliant thesis both for information and for insight concerning Reinhold Niebuhr and his place in the development of Protestant social thought.

with a humanistic and secular rationale. In a series of influential books in the twenties Dewey affirmed in naturalistic terms the capacity of man to achieve beneficent social change through education and experiment. Social progress could be reliably attained, Dewey emphasized, by the planned and experimental techniques which had won such brilliant success in the natural sciences. In fine, the organized social intelligence could be counted on to work out definitive solutions to the great political and economic issues.

If all this was so, why was society still so far from man's ideal? The answer, Dewey suggested, was primarily ignorance, which made man unaware of his potentialities, and prejudice, which prevented him from acting scientifically to realize them; the answer, in short, was the cultural lag. And as the remedy for ignorance was education, so the remedy for prejudice was science.

These views, it is obvious, ran closely parallel to the Social Gospel. Indeed, Robert E. Fitch has recently argued that Dewey should be considered "the Last Protestant."[6] Dewey's individualism, his rationalism, his belief in the primacy of experience, his faith in education and in tolerance, his utopianism—all these, in a sense, might be taken as Protestantism at the end of its journey. Certainly the social philosophy of Dewey and the commandments of the Social Gospel fused happily in a common conviction that human and political tensions, however widespread or exasperating, could be dissolved in the end by reason or by love. The result was a prevailing liberal climate which Reinhold Niebuhr impatiently sought in 1936 to reduce to a set of propositions:

a. That injustice is caused by ignorance and will yield to education and greater intelligence.

b. That civilization is becoming gradually more moral and that it is a sin to challenge either the inevitability or the efficacy of gradualness.

c. That the character of individuals rather than social systems and arrangements is the guarantee of justice in society.

d. That appeals to love, justice, good-will and brotherhood are bound to be efficacious in the end. If they have not been so to date we must have more appeals to love, justice, good-will and brotherhood.

e. That goodness makes for happiness and that the increasing knowledge of this fact will overcome human selfishness and greed.

[6] R. E. Fitch, "John Dewey—The 'Last Protestant,'" *Pacific Spectator,* Spring, 1953. Reinhold Niebuhr, in reviewing Dewey's *A Common Faith,* suggested that Dewey's credo came "closer than Dr. Dewey is willing to admit to the primary tenets of prophetic religion." *Nation,* Sept. 26, 1934.

f. That wars are stupid and can therefore only be caused by people who are more stupid than those who recognize the stupidity of war.[7]

This was the developing atmosphere of American liberalism when in 1915, at the age of twenty-three, Niebuhr, fresh from the Yale Divinity School, came to a small church in industrial Detroit. Spurred by vigorous and incisive intelligence, he combined his pastoral duties with eager attention to the intellectual challenges and controversies of the day. The wretchedness of life on the industrial frontier quickened an already live interest in social problems. Niebuhr was, in a real sense, the child of the Social Gospel. He was soon serving on the Mayor's Commission on Inter-racial Relations and on the Detroit Council of Churches' Industrial Relations Commission. He became a member of the Fellowship for a Christian Social Order and of the Fellowship of Reconciliation. He was active in the Federal Council; he was a circuit rider to the colleges and universities; and he was a prolific contributor to the *World Tomorrow* and the *Christian Century*. He responded deeply to the social passion; and his first book, published in 1927—*Does Civilization Need Religion?*—while critical of easy assumptions concerning the capacity of people or of institutions to transcend self-interest, was still safely within the Social Gospel presuppositions.

In a similar—if less demonstrable—sense, Niebuhr was a child of the pragmatic revolt. Nature had made him an instinctive empiricist; he had sharp political intuitions, an astute tactical sense, and an instinct for realism; and his first response to situations requiring decision was typically as a pragmatist, not as a moralist or a perfectionist. He shared with William James a vivid sense of the universe as open and unfinished, always incomplete, always fertile, always effervescent with novelty. Where James called it a "pluralist universe," Niebuhr would call it a "dynamic universe"; but the sense of reality as untamed, streaming, provisional, was vital for both. Similarly both revolted against the notion that this unpredictable universe could be caught and contained in any closed philosophical system. The burden of James's polemic was against the notion that there was any human viewpoint from which the world could appear as an absolutely single fact; the crudity of experience, said James, remained an eternal element of experience. Similarly Niebuhr: "A

[7] Niebuhr, "The Blindness of Liberalism," *Radical Religion*, Autumn, 1936. Hereafter all citations will be to writings of Niebuhr unless otherwise attributed.

perfectly consistent world view is bound to outrage some actual facts in the life of nature and the history of man." For James monism and absolutism were the end, the miserable culmination of what he dismissed as "tender-mindedness"; and for Niebuhr: "The universe is simply not the beautiful Greek temple pictured in the philosophy of the absolutists and monists."[8] Where James would accept the intractability of experience and the incompleteness of perception as the essence of reality, Niebuhr, committed to ultimate explanation, developed the category of "paradox" to deal with the antinomies which had formed the substance of James's "radical empiricism." The device of paradox would become a central tactic of Niebuhr's Christian pragmatism.

Thus Niebuhr came to intellectual maturity under the influence both of the Social Gospel and of pragmatism. But, where Dewey and the social passion had agreed on the fundamentals of social strategy, Niebuhr, in the course of the twenties, began to detect a difference between what he called the "prophet" and the "statesman"—the one committed to God, the other to the sinful world. The ethic of Jesus and the dictates of pragmatic wisdom, instead of coinciding, seemed almost at times—and necessarily so—to point in opposite directions:

> It may be well for the statesman to know that statesmanship easily degenerates into opportunism and that opportunism cannot be sharply distinguished from dishonesty. But the prophet ought to realize that his higher perspective and the uncompromising nature of his judgments always has [*sic*] a note of irresponsibility in it. Francis of Assisi may have been a better Christian than Pope Innocent III. But it may be questioned whether his moral superiority over the latter was as absolute as it seemed. Nor is there any reason to believe that Abraham Lincoln, the statesman and opportunist, was morally inferior to William Lloyd Garrison, the prophet. The moral achievement of statesmen must be judged in terms which take account of the limitations of human society which the statesman must, and the prophet need not, consider.[9]

This insight foreshadowed a fundamental criticism of the prevailing liberal ideology. Without escaping the influence either of the Social Gospel or of pragmatism, Niebuhr was beginning to lose his loyalty to the current formulations of both. The Social Gospel lacked for him a sense of the relative; pragmatism lacked a sense of the absolute; their value came, not in their agreement, as in the prevalent ideology,

[8] "A Religion Worth Fighting For," *Survey Graphic*, August, 1927.

[9] *Leaves from the Notebook of a Tamed Cynic*, pp. xii–xiv.

but rather in their discord; they seemed fruitful, not as a harmony, but as paradox.

Niebuhr's philosophy always bore to a degree the imprint of events; this was to be an essential source of its strength and its relevance; and his development in the twenties was visibly spurred by the crises of his experience. The aftermath of the First World War was one experience driving him to re-examine the bases of his conviction. He had supported the war, honestly if without great enthusiasm ("I think that if Wilson's aims are realized the war will serve a good purpose. . . . If we must have war I'll certainly feel better on the side of Wilson than on the side of the Kaiser"). But by 1923 he was prepared for "the whole horrible truth about the war"; "every new book," he said, "destroys some further illusion." The war, as he later wrote, "made me a child of the age of disillusionment." It convinced him that religion could be effective only if it resisted the embraces of civilization.[10]

Detroit left its mark too. More and more the "simple little moral homilies" he preached in accordance with the social passion seemed irrelevant to the brutal facts of life on the industrial frontier. Such sermons assuaged individual frustrations perhaps, but they did not change human actions or attitudes in any problem of collective behavior "by a hair's breadth." By 1927 Niebuhr was criticizing "modern religious liberalism" for its "sentimental optimism" which still spoke of "the essential goodness of men without realizing how evil good men can be." For all its partial acceptance of the thesis of the cultural lag and its tendency still to conceive religion as morality, *Does Civilization Need Religion?* sought none the less to re-establish transcendent religious perspectives. The Christian absolutes, far from fitting smoothly into everyday life, were "always a little absurd"; the relationship between the ultimate and the historical was one of tension rather than harmony; still, Niebuhr felt bound to assert, "reality slowly approaches the ideals which are implicit in it." Yet, for all these gestures to moralism, *Does Civilization Need Religion?* was a book shot through with premonitions and misgivings over the prevalent liberal creed.[11]

The depression accelerated the process of change. Rauschenbusch

[10] *Leaves*, pp. 14, 42; "What the War Did to My Mind," *Christian Century*, Sept. 27, 1928.

[11] "Ten Years That Shook My World," *Christian Century*, April 26, 1939; "A Religion Worth Fighting For," *loc. cit.; Does Civilization Need Religion?* pp. 44–45.

had written that he could hear human virtue cracking and crumbling all around in the panic of 1893. For Niebuhr, now translated from the Detroit parish to the Union Theological Seminary in New York City, the economic collapse came as a conclusive refutation of liberal hopes. His book of 1932—*Moral Man and Immoral Society*—was a somber and powerful rejection of the Social-Gospel-Dewey amalgam, with its faith in the politics of love and reason. To the champions of the Social Gospel he denied that the law of love could ever achieve social perfection; to the followers of Dewey he denied that expert knowledge could ever achieve impartial wisdom. Individual egoism, he asserted, was not being progressively checked by either "the development of rationality or the growth of a religiously inspired goodwill."

Scientific intelligence and moral piety, said Niebuhr, could not abolish social conflict; and those who would stake all on rational and moralistic methods ignored the limitations in human nature which must finally frustrate their efforts. An effective theory of politics must take account not only of the possibilities but of the weaknesses of man, especially the weaknesses of men in their collective behavior. The Kingdom of God would "never be fully realized" on earth; coercion was the necessary instrument of social cohesion; the realm of love was one thing and the realm of power another. Each, Niebuhr emphasized, must be approached in its own terms: "Better to accept a frank dualism in morals than to attempt a harmony between the two methods which threatens the effectiveness of both."[12]

What the Social Gospel and Dewey had joined together Niebuhr now sought to thrust asunder: love was the strategy of religion, pragmatism the strategy of society. In place of the older social passion he now affirmed what he called "Christian radicalism." His new formulations emerged in part from the discussions in the Fellowship of Socialist Christians, founded in 1930; in 1935 the Fellowship acquired its organ in *Radical Religion* (later *Christianity and Society*). For the Christian radicals the Kingdom of God was "final and absolute"; it was in some respects "equally distant from all political programs." The Kingdom offered not alternatives but perspectives; it would be a check not on policies but on pride; a source not of directives but of humility and contrition. The law of love, Niebuhr contended in *An Interpretation of Christian Ethics* (1935), was relevant not as a possibility but precisely as an impossibility: the

[12] *Moral Man and Immoral Society*, pp. xi–xii, 21, 271.

tension between the unconditioned and the relative created the need and the opportunity for the grace of God. Yet the remoteness of the Kingdom of God by no means relieved Christians of the responsibilities of acting in history and in terms of the relativities of society. And political action, if perseveringly directed toward justice, could be a form of service to God. "The Kingdom of God is not of this world; yet its light illumines our tasks in this world and its hope saves us from despair."[13]

Thus proximate political action was a Christian duty. Niebuhr vigorously attacked interpretations of the Christian religion which denied "the meaningfulness and importance of man's temporal existence, of his life in this body, of the vicissitudes of his social history, of the victories of good and evil in the rise and fall of empires and civilizations." Man remained the child of God, and no evil in human nature could completely destroy the image of God in him. Yet "we are men and not God and we have to act even though we know that we are and will be proved by subsequent history to be sinful men in action." So no acts could escape the stain of self-interest and sin. Politics thus must always involve a choice between evils. "We use evil in every moment of our existence to hold evil in check." And political achievement must in consequence always be limited, fragmentary and incomplete. "Historic reality is never self-explanatory or self-sufficient. Both the ground and the goal of historic existence lie beyond itself. . . . What is in history is always partial to specific interests and tainted by sin." Next to rejecting the human condition in favor of the absolute, there could be no worse error than in identifying the absolute with contingent philosophies or programs. The role of prophetic religion was to guide men in a mood of dialectical humility between the twin disasters of utopianism and defeatism, trusting in the end to the judgment and mercy and grace of God.[14]

Niebuhr's Christian radicalism thus constituted a fundamental critique of the liberalism created by the fusion of the Social Gospel and Dewey. In the political field Niebuhr rejected the Sermon on the Mount for pragmatism; even the choice between violence and non-violence in social change, he asserted, was purely an expedient choice. But pragmatism had its limits: social redemption was im-

[13] "Socialist Decision and Christian Conscience," *Radical Religion,* Spring, 1938; "The Hitler-Stalin Pact," Fall, 1939.

[14] "Christian Radicalism," *Radical Religion,* Winter, 1936; "Socialist Decision and Christian Conscience," *loc. cit.;* "Pacifism and Sanctions," *loc. cit.;* "Marx, Barth and Israel's Prophets," *Christian Century,* Jan. 30, 1935.

possible within history; the realm of power and sin was eternally under the judgment of the absolute; ultimately he rejected pragmatism for the Gospel. Thus he retained both the divine purpose and the pragmatic method which had characterized the liberal amalgam. But he sought to save each from the other by affirming the separateness of both.

If the politics of love was now rejected as confusing and irrelevant, how would the politics of power equip moral man to approach the problems of immoral society? Here Niebuhr's thought suffered a profound split of its own. He rendered two answers to this question—one on the level of strategy, the other on the level of tactics—and assumed that the two answers were identical. It would take him more than a decade before he finally perceived that they were different.

His first answer derived from his conviction that power conflicts were the basic elements of history. Both the Social Gospel and Dewey had minimized the significance of power.[15] But for Niebuhr, power was the characteristic object of that imperialistic egoism which was man's ineradicable failing. "All life is an expression of power"; therefore all political calculations had to begin and end with power. So long as power remained in society, mankind could obviously never escape the necessity of endowing those who possessed it with the largest measure of ethical self-control. But that would not, said Niebuhr in *Moral Man,* "obviate the necessity of reducing power to a minimum, of bringing the remainder under the strongest measure of social control; and of destroying such types of it as are least amenable to social control. For there is no ethical force strong enough to place inner checks upon the use of power if its quantity is inordinate." He quoted Madison with approval: "The truth is that all men having power ought to be distrusted." But where did this analysis lead? If social cohesion were impossible without coercion, and coercion impossible without injustice, if self-interest could not be checked without the assertion of conflicting self-interest, what were the prospects for social harmony? If this analysis were right, Niebuhr concluded,

[15] In the case of Dewey exceptions should be made for his wartime essays "Force, Violence and Law," *New Republic,* Jan. 22, 1916, and "Force and Coercion," *International Journal of Ethics,* April, 1916. Both are reprinted in *Characters and Events* (New York: Henry Holt & Co., 1929). But the essence of the argument—"squeamishness about force is the mark not of idealistic but of moonstruck morals"—was ignored in his writings of the twenties.

"an uneasy balance of power would seem to become the highest goal to which society could aspire."[16]

On the level of strategy the balance of power in one form or another remained—and remains still—Niebuhr's answer to the problem of achieving a tolerable society. "The force of human egoism and the limits of the human imagination will make the struggle against the abuse of power a perpetual one," he wrote in 1933, "and will confront every society with the treble problem of decentralizing power as much as possible, of bringing power under social control and of establishing inner moral checks upon it." The urgent need, he repeated in 1934 in *Reflections on the End of an Era*, was for a political theory which would be radical "not only in the realistic nature of its analysis but in its willingness to challenge the injustices of a given social system by setting power against power until a more balanced equilibrium of power is achieved."[17]

But the statement of the end could not, for a Christian realist, solve the problem of means. The next question was what to do in America of the 1930's to attain the "more balanced equilibrium of power." And in the area of immediate action Niebuhr, under the pressure of depression, found himself deeply attracted both to the diagnosis and to the prescriptions of Marxism. Liberalism, he crisply declared a few days before the inauguration of Franklin D. Roosevelt, was a "spent force." If anything was clear in March of 1933, it was "that capitalism is dying and . . . that it ought to die." Capitalist society could not reform itself from within; "there is nothing in history to support the thesis that a dominant class ever yields its position or privileges in society because its rule has been convicted of ineptness or injustices. . . . Next to the futility of liberalism we may set down the inevitability of fascism as a practical certainty in every Western nation."[18]

The apocalyptic mood was dominant in *Reflections on the End of an Era*. The book throbbed with urgency and foreboding. The sickness of capitalism, Niebuhr said, was "organic and constitutional"; it was rooted in "the very nature of capitalism," in "the private ownership of the productive processes." There was no middle way;

[16] "Politics and the Christian Ethic," *Christianity and Society*, Spring, 1940; *Moral Man*, pp. 164, 232.

[17] "Optimism and Utopianism," *World Tomorrow*, Feb. 22, 1933; *Reflections on the End of an Era*, p. 230.

[18] "After Capitalism—What?" *World Tomorrow*, March 1, 1933.

economists like Keynes might offer their advice, but they could not hope to arrest the drift toward fascism; "the drift is inevitable." The only hope was the socialization of the economy; but the rise of fascism seemed to guarantee that "the end of capitalism will be bloody rather than peaceful." Marxism thus came to seem to Niebuhr "an essentially correct theory and analysis of the economic realities of modern society," correct in its theory of class conflict, correct in regarding private ownership of the means of production as the basic causes of economic crisis and international war, correct in insisting that "communal ownership of the productive process is a basic condition of social health in a technical age."[19]

The appeal of Marxism to Niebuhr was a measure of his recoil from the optimism and moralism of Christian liberalism. One great attraction of the Marxist analysis was evidently its catastrophism. Rebounding from the liberal belief in the inevitability of progress, Niebuhr was all too susceptible to an equally extreme belief in the inevitability of catastrophe. The recurrence of the "end of an era" formula in his writings of the thirties suggests his shocked fascination with the possibility of some basic turn, some drastic judgment in history. He found the Marxist appreciation of the "fact of judgment and catastrophe in history . . . closer to the genius of Hebrew prophecy than liberalism, either secular or religious"; the notion that unjust civilizations would destroy themselves seemed only a secularized version of the prophecies of doom in which the Old Testament abounded.[20]

Thus, as Marxist catastrophism countered liberal optimism, so Marxist cynicism about the power of self-interest countered liberal sentimentalism and idealism; so Marxist collectivism, with its understanding of the need for community, countered liberal individualism; so Marxist determinism, with its sense of the implacability of history, countered the naïve liberal faith in the perfect plasticity of man and society; so the Marxist commitment to the working class countered the self-righteous complacency of the middle class. Above all, the historical and economic analysis of Marxism seemed to make in-

[19] *Reflections*, pp. 24, 30, 53, 59; "Russia and Karl Marx," *Nation*, May 7, 1938; "Socialist Decision and Christian Conscience," *loc. cit.* (see footnotes 13 and 14).

[20] "Marx, Barth and Israel's Prophets," *loc. cit.;* see also "Christian Politics and Communist Religion" in John Lewis, *et al.*, eds., *Christianity and the Social Revolution* (New York: Charles Scribner's Sons, 1936), especially pp. 461–463.

creasing sense in what appeared to be an era of disintegrating capitalism.[21]

Yet Niebuhr's allegiance to Marxism was always strictly limited; and, though he was willing at various periods to consider tactical collaboration with the Communists, he never had illusions concerning the perils in their version of the Marxist faith. The fundamental Communist error, in his view, was a new form of the liberal heresy: that is, the Communists found the Kingdom of God *in* history; they perceived in the Soviet Union the incarnation of the absolute. If the liberals were soft utopians, the Communists were hard utopians. For a season, while writing *Moral Man and Immoral Society,* Niebuhr regarded this Communist error as an indispensable myth, "a very valuable illusion for the moment; for justice cannot be approximated if the hope of its perfect realization does not generate a sublime madness in the soul." But on reflection the madness generated by Communism seemed to him less sublime than sinister. Indeed, he had already (in 1931) written about "The Religion of Communism," suggesting that "only a sentimentalist could be oblivious of the possibilities of Napoleonic ventures in the forces which are seething in Russia." By 1933 he explicitly repudiated the note of tolerance for myth on which *Moral Man* ended. By 1935 he could write ruefully: "I once thought such a faith to be a harmless illusion. But now I see that its net result is to endow a group of oligarchs with the religious sanctity which primitive priest-kings once held."[22]

His other basic objection to Communism arose from his theory of power. Not only did Communist utopianism breed fanaticism and tyranny, but Communist economic reorganization gravely jeopardized the conditions of freedom. If power remained the central fact of society, and the desire for power man's ineradicable failing, then the destruction of economic privilege could hardly be expected to alter human nature to the degree that no one thereafter would desire to make selfish use of power. "The abuse of power by communistic bureaucrats is very considerable," he wrote in *Moral Man,* "and is bound to grow as the purer revolutionary idealists are sup-

[21] For Niebuhr's retrospective accounts see "Communism and the Clergy," *Christian Century,* Aug. 19, 1953; "Liberals and the Marxist Heresy," *New Republic,* Oct. 12, 1953.

[22] *Moral Man,* pp. 276–277; "The Religion of Communism," *Atlantic Monthly,* April, 1931; "Optimism and Utopianism," *World Tomorrow,* Feb. 22, 1933; "Religion and Marxism," *Modern Monthly,* Feb., 1935.

planted by men who have consciously sought for the possession of power. . . . If the Russian oligarchy strips itself of its own power, it will be the first oligarchy of history to do so." In *Reflections* he made the indictment even more specific. The attempt to establish "an economic equilibrium through social ownership," he warned, might well create "a new disproportion of power. . . . The new and stronger centres of political power will be new occasions for and temptations to injustice." By 1938, after the Moscow trials, he would state the viewpoint of "modern Christian Socialists" in blunt terms: "They want to equalize economic power but not at the price of creating political tyranny in a socialist society. They do not trust any irresponsible power in the long run, whether it is wielded by priests, monks, capitalists or commissars."[23]

He thus saw a profound contradiction between the Communist reality and his basic conviction that "all justice in human society rests upon some kind of balance of power." But, while excluding Communism, he apparently saw no contradiction between his demand for a social balance-of-power and democratic socialism. Throughout the decade of the thirties, the socialization of property seemed to him, not of course (as it did to some of his Social Gospel friends), the means of ushering in utopia or of establishing the Kingdom, but still the top pragmatic priority in order to achieve "a tolerable equilibrium of economic power." "We need more Christians," he cried in 1937, "who see how absolutely basic a revolution in the property system is for the sake of justice." Socializing the means of production remained for him, in a favorite phrase, "a primary requisite of social health in a technical age."[24]

In this respect Niebuhr and Dewey, despite their differences in presupposition, had no differences in program. For all their professed dislike of doctrine, they were both in this period staunch economic doctrinaires. For all their rejection of closed abstract systems, each saw the contemporary American problem in closed and abstract terms. The passionate champions of experiment, both flatly condemned the most massive and brilliant period of political and economic experimentation in American history. With a supreme

[23] *Moral Man*, pp. 164, 193; *Reflections*, pp. 243–244; "The Creed of Modern Christian Socialists," *Radical Religion*, Spring, 1938.

[24] Editorial comment on Dwight J. Bradley, "Radicalism and Religions of Redemption," *Radical Religion*, Spring, 1938; "Ten Years That Shook My World," *loc. cit.*; review of *Toward a Christian Revolution*, *Radical Religion*, Spring, 1937; "Socialist Decision and Christian Conscience," *loc. cit.*

political pragmatist as President, and with the most resourceful and creative economic and legal pragmatists of the time seeking patiently and tirelessly to work out a middle way between *laissez-faire* and collectivism, neither the secular pragmatist nor the Christian pragmatist managed to work up much interest. The pragmatic philosophers, abandoning pragmatism to Franklin D. Roosevelt, retreated precipitately to their own crypto-utopias. In the case of Dewey, it should be said that his disdain for the New Deal and his commitment to socialization proceeded naturally enough from his disregard for power in society and from his faith in human rationality and scientific planning; but for Niebuhr, who was realistic about man and who wanted to equilibrate power in society, the commitment to socialization was both the price of indifference to the achievements of piecemeal reform and a symptom of despair. Where Dewey spurned the New Deal because of his optimism about man and his belief in science, Niebuhr seemed to spurn it because of his pessimism about man and his belief in catastrophe.

Early in 1935 Niebuhr took an inventory of the resources of the American democratic tradition. Middle-class politics—by which he evidently meant party politics—seemed to him hopeless, "rushing us at incredible speed from the futilities of Rooseveltian 'liberalism' to the worse confusion of a political program concocted by a radio priest and a Louisiana 'kingfish.'" The New Deal continued to figure in his writings of the period as an image of incoherent and aimless triviality; and his attitude toward what was going on in Washington in these days remained singularly lacking in concreteness and even in curiosity. This was, no doubt, because he had excluded the middle way, so to speak, by definition. Liberalism, after all, was "spent," and there was evidently no point in wasting time examining its works. Keynes, Stuart Chase, Sir Arthur Salter might insist on the necessity for democratic planning; but "the imperilled oligarchy of our day, though it may pay lip service to the sweet reasonableness of their counsels, drifts nevertheless toward fascism"; and the drift was inevitable.[25]

The "paradox" was, of course, that at these very moments the imperilled oligarchy was being forced by effective democratic government to accept measures of regulation and reform which would avert fascism and lead to recovery. But Niebuhr, blinkered by doc-

[25] "Our Romantic Radicals," *Christian Century*, April 10, 1935; *Reflections*, pp. 45–46, 53.

trine, scornfully rejected in practice the very pragmatism he called for in theory. The nation, he said after the 1936 election, when he supported Norman Thomas, "has chosen a messiah rather than a political leader committed to a specific political program; and unfortunately the messiah is more renowned for his artistic juggling than for robust resolution."[26] The possibility that "artistic juggling" might be the strategy by which social power could best be distributed and balanced was not then to be considered.

Niebuhr's attitude toward the New Deal seems to have been further influenced by his indifference to New Deal economics. Like Dewey, he wrote with earnest conviction on economic questions without adequately informing himself on the issues of economic policy. Indeed, like the British Socialists of 1930, he seemed almost to feel that, if socialism was excluded, one had to play the capitalist game according to strict capitalist rules; the choice was between nationalizing everything and balancing the budget; the power and resources of fiscal policy in a capitalist economy did not figure in his calculations. Thus his writings of the middle thirties showed a curious but persistent concern with the unbalanced budget and the terrifying size of the annual deficits (which actually only once—1936—exceeded $4 billion in Roosevelt's first two terms). During the recession of 1937–1938, caused in great part by the reduction of government spending, Niebuhr actually urged an *increase* in taxes, which would, of course, have only reduced further the government's contribution to the economy. In 1939 he denounced deficits as a form of insulin, a medicine "which wards off dissolution without giving the patient health." And the incurable experimentalism of the New Deal clearly seemed to him to stand in sorry contrast to the clear-cut logic of socialism. Roosevelt was concededly "better than most of his reactionary critics," said Niebuhr in 1938. "But no final good can come of this kind of whirligig reform." "If that man could only make up his mind to cross the Rubicon!" Niebuhr added. "A better metaphor is that he is like Lot's wife. Let him beware lest he turn into a pillar of salt."[27]

The Rubicon metaphor suggested the either-or approach which Niebuhr still maintained in face of the New Deal assumption that

[26] "The National Election," *Radical Religion*, Winter, 1936.

[27] "The Political Campaign," *Radical Religion*, Autumn, 1936; "The Administration and the Depression," Winter, 1937; "Roosevelt's Merry-Go-Round," Spring, 1938; "The Domestic Situation," Summer, 1938; "Nicholas Murray Butler," Fall, 1938; "New Deal Medicine," Spring, 1939.

the mixed economy was a better means of equilibrating power than was socialism. For Roosevelt, of course, the problem was not to cross the Rubicon but to navigate up it. And in time the relative success of New Deal improvisation, especially in contrast with the melancholy results of Communist logic, began to force Niebuhr to re-examine his political presuppositions; perhaps the reflections on the end of the era had been premature. The attack on socialism in Bertrand Russell's *Power* in 1938 plainly touched an exposed nerve. In 1939, considering the question whether the capitalist system could not be made to work, Niebuhr surprisingly confessed, "It would be rather rash to give an unequivocal answer," even adding that socialists should prefer a solution of the New Deal type to a general breakdown. A year later he frankly said that "if socialization of economic power is purchased at the price of creating irresponsible and tyrannical political power, our last estate may be worse than the first." Social justice, he declared, could be achieved only if social forces were allowed considerable freedom of challenge and maneuver through an unremitting process of "political pressure and counter-pressure."[28] When in June, 1940, Niebuhr resigned, after a dozen years, from the Socialist party, it was the ratification of inner reservations which had made him a keen critic of the party's policies and leadership for the three years preceding. In November, while still viewing himself, in some sense, as a socialist and still insisting on "a genuine farmer-labor party" as one of "the inevitabilities of American politics," to be anticipated in 1944 or 1948, he nevertheless cast his first vote for Franklin D. Roosevelt and the Democrats.[29] After the election he joined with a group of ex-Socialists and New Dealers in founding the pragmatically oriented Union for Democratic Action.

It cannot be said, however, that domestic economic policy was the decisive reason for Niebuhr's rejection of the Socialist party and his new approval of Roosevelt. What was decisive was the issue of foreign policy, growing in size and urgency as Nazi aggression began to remake the map of Europe. Here the Socialists, committed largely to isolationism, and the Protestant ministry, committed to some degree to pacifism, seemed to show in a dismal and devastating way

[28] "Anatomy of Power," *Nation*, Oct. 1, 1938; review of Ezekiel's *Jobs for All*, *Radical Religion*, Spring, 1939; "A New Name," Winter, 1940; review of Eliot's *The Idea of a Christian Society*, Winter, 1940.

[29] "An End to Illusions," *Nation*, June 29, 1940; "The Socialist Campaign," *Christianity and Society*, Summer, 1940.

the consequences of moralized politics. In contrast, the canny and opportunistic political realism of Roosevelt gained new stature in his eyes; rather than merely an artistic juggler, Roosevelt now seemed almost to have the dimensions of a great democratic leader.

Niebuhr had not always approved Roosevelt's attempts to build up American armed strength against fascism. In 1937 he assailed Roosevelt's naval program as "sinister"; "this Roosevelt navalism," he said, "must be resisted at all costs." The next year he called the naval program "the most unjustified piece of military expansion in a world full of such madness"—in short, evidently worse than Nazi rearmament. But after Munich it seemed to him that even world war might be better than the extension of Nazi tyranny. By 1940 Niebuhr was prepared to make magnanimous reparation. Roosevelt "anticipated the perils in which we now stand more clearly than anyone else," he wrote. "In fact there are few among us who did not make unjustified criticisms of his preparedness program, which subsequent events have proved to be conservative rather than hysterical."[30]

The pacifist program, on the other hand, now seemed to concentrate in itself all the errors of liberalism which Niebuhr had castigated for so long. It refused to accept the existence of power; by refusing to use power, it bowed out of the field of political responsibility; by retreating from responsibility, it dodged its Christian duty; and it did all this under the cover of an intolerable self-righteousness. Pacifism might be necessary as a witness and reminder of absolute perspectives; but it could well be disastrous if it sought to intervene in pragmatic politics and to demand "all kinds of fatuous political alternatives." In *Christianity and Power Politics* (1940) he attacked the versions of Christian and secular perfectionism which placed a premium upon non-participation in conflicts; this was a "very sentimentalized" form of the Christian faith, and at variance with the profoundest insights of the Christian religion. The effort to reduce the peace of the Kingdom of God into a simple historical possibility, he added, inevitably invited surrender to evil as the price of avoidance of conflict. "In waging the war and in building the peace," he said in 1942, "we need the idealism of the Christian gospel to save us from cynicism and complacency. But we also need the realism of the Christian faith to save us from sentimentality. In America at

[30] "Brief Comments," *Radical Religion,* Winter, 1937; "Brief Comments," Spring, 1938; "Willkie and Roosevelt," *Christianity and Society,* Fall, 1940.

least the dangers of a perverse sentimentality have been greater than the perils of cynicism."[31]

In 1939 Niebuhr had delivered the Gifford Lectures at Edinburgh. Suitably revised and expanded, they appeared in the two great volumes of 1941 and 1943 which made up *The Nature and Destiny of Man.* Here his politics, as they had emerged from his experience of the 1930s, took their place in the full setting of his religious conviction. "We know," he wrote, "that we cannot purge ourselves of the sin and guilt in which we are involved by the moral ambiguities of politics without also disavowing responsibility for the creative possibilities of justice."[32] As for democratic politics, he now found their essence in "the pressures and counter pressures, the tensions, the overt and the covert conflicts by which justice is achieved and maintained." This acceptance of conflict as the consequence of power and antidote to it would stand in sharp contrast to some of his fellow Socialist Christians, such as Paul Tillich, who as late as 1953 would regard the "competitive society" as a basic threat to personality and community and call for "social transformation."[33]

What Niebuhr meant was spelled out in more detail in the West Foundation lectures at Stanford in 1944, published the next year under the title *The Children of Light and the Children of Darkness.* Here he wrestled once again with his old commitment to the socialization of property. The Marxist theory was correct, he still felt, in emphasizing the "social character of industrial property"; but perhaps socialization was "too simple a solution"; and he now questioned the Marxist assumption that it would "destroy all disproportions of economic power in the community." How, indeed, could one socialize property "without creating pools of excessive social power in the hands of those who manage both its economic and political processes"? Even if social ownership were more efficient, it might be wise to sacrifice efficiency "for the sake of preserving a greater balance of forces and avoiding undue centralization of power." He was still not sure; the "logic of history" still seemed to him behind proposals for socialization, but "the logic is not unambiguous." And he later

[31] "Christianity and the World Crises," *Christianity and Society,* Fall, 1940; *Christianity and Power Politics,* ix–x; "The Churches and the War," *Town Meeting of the Air,* Aug. 27, 1942.

[32] *The Nature and Destiny of Man,* II, 284.

[33] Paul Tillich, "The Person in a Technical Society," J. A. Hutchison, ed., *Christian Faith and Social Action* (New York: Charles Scribner's Sons, 1953), pp. 144, 152.

underscored the ambiguities of this historical logic by arguing that the two prerequisites for a free society were that there should be equilibrium among class forces, and that the equilibrium should be dynamic, gradually shifting "the political institutions of the community to conform to changing economic needs and unchanging demands for a higher justice."[34] This sounded a good deal more like the mixed economy and open society of the New Deal than like socialism.

The retreat from socialization was visibly reducing the gap between the ends and means of his social thought in the thirties. Yet he was still reluctant to identify the more appropriate means in concrete economic and political terms. In 1944 he voted for Roosevelt; but again foreign rather than domestic policy was dominant. In 1947 the Fellowship of Socialist Christians changed its name to Frontier Fellowship. "We continue to be socialists," Niebuhr explained, "in the sense that we believe that the capitalist order of society stands under divine judgment and that there is no justice in modern technical society without a completely pragmatic attitude toward the institution of property. It must be socialized wherever it is of such a character that it makes for injustice through inordinate centralization. . . . [But] the most dangerous error is the centralization of both economic and political power in the hands of a communist oligarchy."[35]

In the thirties the Socialist party had been Niebuhr's political outlet, but during the war he had worked through UDA, and after 1947 he became a leading figure in Americans for Democratic Action, a group of pragmatic liberals opposed to all dogmatisms, conservative, socialist, or communist, and dedicated to piecemeal and gradual reform. In 1948 he voted for Truman. And by 1949 he was prepared to accept the logic of his "completely pragmatic attitude." There was, he said, "a bare possibility that the kind of pragmatic political program which has been elaborated under the 'New Deal' and the 'Fair Deal' may prove to be a better answer to the problems of justice in a technical age than its critics of either right or left had assumed." Democratic socialism, even in its British version, seemed to him encumbered with dogmas almost as confusing as the dogmas of the plutocracy. The "unplanned improvisations of our early New Deal" now seemed more likely than conservatism or socialism to "grow into

[34] *The Children of Light and the Children of Darkness*, pp. 74, 76, 78, 80, 82, 102.

[35] "Frontier Fellowship," *Christianity and Society*, Autumn, 1948.

a purposeful pragmatism" which would make "a significant contribution to the cause of democracy."[36] It turned out not to have been necessary to cross the Rubicon after all; "whirligig reform" now seemed a viable middle way.

Niebuhr's subsequent writings elaborated this general position. When Frontier Fellowship dissolved into Christian Action in 1951, the single economic plank in the new statement of purpose only pledged government action "to maintain a high and stable level of economic activity"[37]—a position so vague that a conservative Republican would have little difficulty in accepting it. A crucial chapter of *The Irony of American History* (1952) was entitled "The Triumph of Experience over Dogma." He now could speak of "our success in establishing justice and insuring domestic tranquillity." We have, he wrote, achieved such social justice as we possess in the only way justice could be achieved in a technical society: "we have equilibrated power. We have attained a certain equilibrium in economic society itself by setting organized power against organized power. When that did not suffice we used the more broadly based political power to redress disproportions and disbalances in economic society." It had been, he concluded, "a pragmatic approach to political and economic questions" which would have done credit to Edmund Burke.[38] At long last the two halves of Niebuhr's social thought were together; Christian radicalism had given way, so to speak, to Christian realism; his old demand for a social balance of power had finally found its objective correlative in public policy.

Having resolved the inner contradiction in his social thought, Niebuhr was now able the better to resolve his ambivalent relations to the two creeds from which he had drawn so much strength and which he had subjected to such devastating criticism. I suggested earlier that he was, in a sense, the child both of the Social Gospel and of pragmatism, but that he had profoundly resisted the attempts

[36] "Plutocracy and World Responsibilities," *Christianity and Society*, Autumn, 1949.

[37] "Christian Action Statement of Purpose," *Christianity and Crisis*, Oct. 1, 1951.

[38] *The Irony of American History*, pp. 89, 101; see also Niebuhr's most recent and critical reconsideration of Marxism and democratic socialism, "The Anomaly of European Socialism," *Christian Realism and Political Problems*, pp. 43–51; and his vigorous affirmation of the necessity for limited government intervention in economic life along mixed-economy lines, "Coercion, Self-Interest and Love," in K. E. Boulding, *The Organizational Revolution* (New York: Harper & Brothers, 1953), pp. 228–244; also his "Christian Faith and Social Action," Hutchison, ed., *Christian Faith and Social Action*, pp. 225–242.

of the Social Gospel to annihilate the relative, as he had profoundly resisted the attempts of pragmatism to annihilate the absolute. By 1952 the old battle with the moralistic simplicities of the Social Gospel seemed to have come to an end. Reviewing the familiar defects of the Gospel, Niebuhr now dismissed them as "minor when its achievement is recognized: it delivered American Protestantism from meeting complex ethical problems of a technical civilization with an almost completely irrelevant individualistic pietism and moralism."[39]

The issues with pragmatism remained more tense and complex. Niebuhr had never ceased his polemic against Dewey—against the illusions of "social science" and the supposition that "scientific" analysis of society could produce impartial and uncontaminated results.[40] When empiricism mistook a finite for an absolute perspective, it sinned; and its sin, in Niebuhr's view, could be fraught with perilous consequence. Yet Niebuhr continued to maintain just as resolutely the supremacy of the pragmatic method in the world of contingent decision and action. Relativism was, of course, the inevitable result of his belief that original sin tainted all human perception and knowledge. The absolute was thus, by definition, unattainable; so mortal man's apprehension of truth had to be fitful, shadowy and imperfect; he saw through the glass darkly; nor could there be a worse expression of human self-righteousness and self-deception than the attempt to endow fragmentary and corrupt perceptions with objectivity and certitude.

The great lesson of prophetic religion, he often remarked, was to show "how relative all human ideals are." Against absolutism he insisted both on the "relativity of all human perspectives" and on the sinfulness of those who claimed absolute validity and divine sanctions for their opinions. He declared himself "in broad agreement with the relativist position in the matter of freedom, as upon every other social and political right or principle."[41] In the thirties it had been the gospel-minded of the left who contended most aggressively that the Kingdom of God existed on earth and who sought to hypostatize the finite into the absolute. When, in the late forties and early fifties, the main religious pressure came from the right, Niebuhr valiantly turned to oppose the attempts to identify capi-

[39] "The Protestant Clergy and U.S. Politics," *Reporter*, Feb. 19, 1952.

[40] Cf., e.g., "Faith and the Empirical Method in Modern Realism" and "Ideology and the Scientific Method," *Christian Realism*, pp. 1–14, 75–94.

[41] "Marx, Barth and Israel's Prophets," *loc. cit.*; "Moral Rearmament," *Radical Religion*, Fall, 1939; "The Limits of Liberty," *Nation*, Jan. 24, 1942.

talism with Christian truth or to transform necessary pragmatic resistance against Communist aggression into a "holy war" against Communism.

In pointing to the dangers of what Mr. Justice Jackson has called "compulsory godliness,"[42] Niebuhr once again argued that "religion is so frequently a source of confusion in political life, and so frequently dangerous to democracy, precisely because it introduces absolutes into the realm of relative values." Religion, he warned, could be a source of error as well as of wisdom and light; its proper role should be not to endorse but to question; to inculcate, not a sense of infallibility, but a sense of humility. Indeed, "the worst corruption is a corrupt religion."[43]

He still defended the line between pragmatism and faith—the lines designed to keep the absolute out of the relative but at the same time to prevent the relative from mistaking itself for the absolute. In the immediate past it had seemed most important to hold this line against the simplistic followers of Dewey who wanted to sacrifice the absolute to the relative. But in the early fifties Niebuhr found himself equally involved in holding the line against the simplistic believers in religion who wanted to sacrifice the relative to the absolute.

The penetrating critic of the Social Gospel and of pragmatism, he ended up, in a sense, the powerful reinterpreter and champion of both. It was the triumph of his own remarkable analysis that it took what was valuable in each, rescued each by defining for each the limits of validity, and, in the end, gave the essential purposes of both new power and new vitality. And he did this not alone in his books and articles, but in his life. No man has had as much influence as a preacher in this generation; no preacher has had as much influence in the secular world. His own authentic humility, his deep awareness of the moral precariousness of historical striving combined with his moral resoluteness about the immediate issues, the range of his compassion, the honesty of his wrath, the spontaneity of his unselfishness, and the sweetness and grandeur of his character—all these qualities succeeded in making manifest and vivid, as no mere sermons or essays could, the image of Christian man.

It was almost as much his personality as his writing which thus

[42] In his dissenting opinion in *Zorach* v. *Clauson,* 343 U.S. at 325.

[43] Letter to the Editor, *Reporter*, May 27, 1952; "Prayers and Politics," *Christianity and Crisis*, Oct. 27, 1952; comment on book jacket of R. L. Roy, *Apostles of Discord* (Boston: Beacon Press, 1953).

helped accomplish in a single generation a revolution in the bases of American liberal political thought. A culture which had staked too much on illusions of optimism found itself baffled and stricken in an age dominated by total government and total war; history had betrayed its votaries. Defeatism and despair might have been a natural reaction to so devastating a disillusion—a natural reaction in the world of philosophy, at least, even if reflexes of survival would have guaranteed resistance in the world of politics.

But if history refuted democratic absolutism, the resources of democratic pragmatism turned out to be greater than many people—including Niebuhr himself in certain moods—had imagined. And his "vindication of democracy and a critique of its traditional defenders" turned out—in another "paradox"—to be the supreme interpretation of the pragmatic economies and politics of the thirties for which, at the time, he had so little use. Thus Niebuhr showed that the refutation by history of democratic illusions need not turn into a refutation of democracy; that the appalled realization that man was not wholly good and reasonable need not turn into a repudiation of man as wholly evil and impotent; that men and women could act more effectively for decency and justice under the banner of a genuine humility than they had under the banner of an illusory perfectibility. His penetrating reconstruction of the democratic faith—in the context of Roosevelt's brilliant invocation of democratic resources against the perils of depression and war—absorbed and mastered the forces of disillusion and preserved the nerve of action. With his aid, that faith emerged from two anguished decades far better armed than before against future ordeal and challenge.

It was, I have said, the achievement both of Niebuhr the moral and political philosopher and of Niebuhr the man. If his searching realism gave new strength to American liberal democracy, or, rather, renewed sources of strength which had been too often neglected in the generations since the American Revolution, his own life and example have shown in compelling terms the possibilities of human contrition and human creativity within the tragedy of history.

Arthur Schlesinger, Jr.

Harvard University
Cambridge, Mass.

AFTERWORD: 1982

For Reinhold Niebuhr, history was best read in the dry light of irony. By irony he meant the chronic disjunction between human purpose and social result, a perennial miscarriage of hope in which the person or community involved bears a share of responsibility for the contradictory outcome. As a connoisseur of ironies, he would doubtless find sardonic pleasure in the vicissitudes of his own reputation over the quarter century since the first edition of this book appeared.

I shall discuss three influential recent perceptions, or misperceptions, of Niebuhr as a political thinker: the old left's view that Niebuhr was the philosopher of the Cold War; the new left's view that he was the enemy of revolution; and the neo-conservative view that he was the original neo-conservative. All these views find footholds of a sort in his writing. None, I believe, does justice to the essential character of his political and social convictions.

In the 1960s, revisionist historians of the Cold War, their belief in the innate depravity of American foreign policy now richly confirmed by Vietnam, assigned Niebuhr a major role in shaping the anti-communist mood of the 1940s and 1950s. This was because of his espousal of the "realist" analysis of world affairs and his advocacy of a demonic view of the Soviet Union.

Niebuhr did indeed, along with Hans Morgenthau, George Kennan and Walter Lippmann, reject the old Wilsonian assumptions about American virtue and the moral character of foreign policy, affirming instead national interest and the balance of power as the key to international relations. Some revisionists blamed the realist critique of moralism and legalism for what the historian Christopher Lasch called in 1965 "the cult of the hardboiled" in American political discourse.[1] The realist school was further charged with undermining that kind of old-fashioned American idealism (associated, for example, with Henry Wallace) that might have averted the Cold War.

[1] Christopher Lasch, *The New Radicalism in America,* 1889–1963 (New York: Random House, 1965), p. 289.

According to the revisionist indictment, not only was Niebuhr thus held to minimize the role of ideals in foreign policy, but his theory of Soviet communism as irremediably evil abolished hope of accommodation and made the Cold War inevitable. "In seeing the cold war as a struggle between Marxist 'despotism' and the 'open society' of the West," as Lasch wrote in 1965, "Niebuhr was . . . playing off one myth against another. Even during the Stalinist period, the distinction between 'despotism' and the 'open society' was hardly an accurate description of the difference between Russia and America; by the fifties and sixties it has become completely unreal."[2]

The diplomatic historian Walter LaFeber summed up the case: "As the Cold War heightened, Niebuhr stood ready with an explanation and a solution. . . . Niebuhr's work provided points of departure for criticizing Wallace, condemning Communism, formulating a Europe-first policy, and rebuilding Germany. Most important, he provided a historical basis and rationale for the tone, the outlook, the unsaid, and often unconscious assumptions of this period."[3]

There is some validity to these charges. Niebuhr unquestionably believed that Western resistance was essential to preserve the balance of power and prevent Soviet domination of Europe. "Russian truculence," he wrote in 1946, "cannot be mitigated by further concessions."[4] "We must be ready to risk war," he wrote during the Berlin Blockade two years later, "rather than yield to Russian pressure."[5] Niebuhr very likely underestimated the extent to which the Soviet Union was acting on defensive and local grounds. Still any country's security "requirements" are, as Americans well know, elastic. Can anyone be sure that Stalin's aims would have stayed local and limited had western counterpolicies not developed—had there been no Truman Doctrine, no Marshall Plan, no NATO, no rearmament, no response to the Berlin blockade or to the invasion of South Korea? In his opposition to the Staliniza-

[2] *Ibid.*, p. 301.

[3] Walter LaFeber, *America, Russia, and the Cold War, 1945–1966* (New York: Wiley, 1967), p. 41.

[4] Reinhold Niebuhr, "The Fight for Germany," *Life*, October 21, 1946.

[5] Reinhold Niebuhr, "For Peace, We Must Risk War," *Life*, September 20, 1948.

tion of western Europe, Niebuhr may have contributed to the Cold War. But it is by no means obvious that the maintenance of a balance of power in Europe was a mistake.

Niebuhr's demonic theory of communism raises more troubling questions, though his formulations in these years become more understandable if the contemporary reader substitutes "Stalinism" for "communism," which is what Niebuhr meant. The forms of communism arising in decaying agrarian societies were, in Niebuhr's view, something different from Soviet communism. His detestation of Stalinist practice was unrelenting, but hardly in itself a cause for retrospective embarrassment. His theory of Stalinism, however, went too far in postulating a radical, monolithic, invariant totalitarian essence, immune to human incompetence and to historical change. In this regard, he shared the illusion of the day, powerfully rendered by George Orwell in *1984* (1949) and by Hannah Arendt in *The Origins of Totalitarianism* (1951), that totalitarianism was an absolute rather than a relative phenomenon and involved a change in phase from all existing societies.

For all this, it is hard to sustain the notion of Niebuhr as the philosophical godfather of the Cold War. Far from defining the contest in the style of John Foster Dulles as a battle between good and evil, Niebuhr could write as early as 1946, "We are not really good enough for this struggle, and I can well imagine that such scruples may be at the basis of the motives of men like Wallace. No culture or civilization is as good as it pretends. But . . . we do face once more [as during the Second World War] the distinction between relative justice and tyranny."[6]

As the Cold War developed, Niebuhr grew increasingly alarmed over the delusions generated by excessive American power. "If there is anything that we can contribute from the standpoint of Christian faith to a nation as powerful as ours," he wrote in 1952, "it would be a sense of its impotence and lack of majesty before the Supreme Majesty which governs the nations. . . . Nothing is more dangerous to a powerful nation than the temptation to obscure the limits of its power. It will be our undoing if we imagine ourselves the masters of contemporary history."[7]

[6] Niebuhr, "Fight for Germany."

[7] Reinhold Niebuhr, "The Limits of American Power," *Christianity and Society*, Autumn, 1952.

In *The Irony of American History*, published in 1952 at the height of the Cold War, Niebuhr reaffirmed his demonic view of communism but at the same time carried further his warnings to the United States against the danger of trying to play God to history. Acutely apprehensive about the "deep layer of Messianic consciousness in the mind of America," Niebuhr feared that Americans were growing "too secure in both our sense of power and our sense of virtue." He was much concerned with finding means to discipline both American power and American emotion. Inordinate anti-communism seemed a particular threat.

"Hatred disturbs all residual serenity of spirit and vindictiveness muddies every pool of sanity. . . . Our foreign policy is thus threatened with a kind of apoplectic rigidity and inflexibility. Constant proof is required that the foe is hated with sufficient vigor. . . . A frantic anti-communism can become so similar in its temper of hatefulness to communism itself."

"If we should perish," he wrote in the last lines of the book,

> the ruthlessness of the foe would be only the secondary cause of the disaster. The primary cause would be that the strength of a giant nation was directed by eyes too blind to see all the hazards of the struggle; and the blindness would be induced not by some accident of nature or history but by hatred and vainglory.[8]

The Irony of American History contains nearly all the essential points in the latter-day critique of America's Cold War conviction of national righteousness and its obsessive hatred of the communist enemy. Soon Niebuhr modified his abstract theory of an unchanging Soviet communism and restored the Soviet Union to the realm of historical permutation and vicissitude. While he never abandoned his realist analysis of foreign affairs, this analysis became the vehicle for ever-sharpening criticisms of messianic delusions in American foreign policy; in fact, such delusions were more vulnerable to questions about national interest than to questions about national ideals.

"President Johnson and Secretary Rusk," Niebuhr observed, "are

[8] Reinhold Niebuhr, *The Irony of American History* (New York: Scribner, 1952), pp. 69, 134, 146, 170, 174.

very Wilsonian in their idealism,"[9] and it was the anti-Wilsonian school that mounted the most effective attack on the premises of the Indochina War. Rather than encouraging extravagant and global use of American power, the realist analysis insisted on a due and prudent relationship between American actions and American interests. As for Niebuhr himself, far from being the philosopher of the Cold War, he became a powerful and penetrating critic of what he deemed unnecessary excesses arising in the wake of a necessary defense of democratic societies. "Our record as a righteous nation," he wrote in one of his last pieces, "has proved so filled with error that, obviously, we must stop thanking God we are not like other nations."[10]

While revisionist historians of the old left were portraying Niebuhr as an intellectual villain in their Cold War melodramas, the Niebuhrian outlook was subject to attack from another quarter—from the outburst of assertion and emotion among young people in the 1960s. This new left could hardly have been more anarchic in its medley of views and practices. But the rebel young had in common certain guiding assumptions. Tormented by injustice at home and a ghastly war abroad, they proclaimed the unalloyed goodness and virtue of spontaneous humanity, applied simple moral judgments to complex political situations, argued for the instant solubility of social problems, and announced the irrelevance of history.

These were in more romantic and violent forms the utopian, perfectionist, and moralistic illusions that Niebuhr had so unsparingly criticized in his polemical days. It was characteristic of him that now, instead of denouncing the young for ignoring his wisdom, he awaited the fragments of insight that he felt must be seeking outlet in the general din. "I have a negative reaction," he said in 1966, "to the negative interpretation of youthful irresponsibility and delinquency, though I know there is some truth in it."[11]

Niebuhr was not an issue for the rebel young, who preferred

[9] Reinhold Niebuhr, "The Social Myths in the 'Cold War,'" *Journal of International Affairs*, xxi (1967).

[10] Reinhold Niebuhr, "Redeemer Nation to Super-Power," *The New York Times*, December 4, 1970.

[11] John Cogley, "An Interview with Reinhold Niebuhr," *McCall's*, February 1966. See also Reinhold Niebuhr, "Thinking Aloud: Indicting Two Generations," *New Leader*, October 5, 1970.

epiphanies to arguments and rarely read books anyway. The explicit repudiation of Niebuhr came rather from the theology-of-hope school, objecting to Niebuhr's emphasis on the need to balance social forces, his acceptance of proximate solutions and his resignation to the frustrations of history. This controversy has produced a most able and thoughtful book—Dennis P. McCann's *Christian Realism and Liberation Theology: Practical Theologies in Creative Conflict* (Maryknoll, New York, 1981)—and requires no further discussion here.

Was Niebuhr, in his recoil from catastrophic remedies, the original neo-conservative? Certainly he has been embraced latterly by people of the right. Jimmy Carter, the most conservative Democratic President since Grover Cleveland, used to present himself as a Niebuhrian, though his repertoire consisted of a single sentence: "The sad duty of politics is to establish justice in a sinful world." It is hard to reconcile Carter's alleged Niebuhrianism with his repeated statement that his aim was "a government that is as good and honest and decent and competent and compassionate and as filled with love as are the American people"[12]—a description Niebuhr would have dismissed as hopeless sentimentalism.[13] [See Schlesinger letter.]

The bizarre invocation of Niebuhr by the conservative economist George Gilder on the last page of his hymn to human greed *Wealth and Poverty* makes even less sense. Quoting, or rather garbling, the passage from *The Irony of American History* that begins "Nothing that is worth doing can be achieved in our lifetime," Gilder concludes: "These are the fundamental laws of economics, business, technology, and life. In them are the secret sources of wealth, and poverty."[14]

Ernest Lefever and Michael Novak at least had read Niebuhr with care before they began to claim him as the father of neo-

[12] See Jimmy Carter, *A Government as Good as Its People* (New York: Simon and Schuster, 1977), *passim.*

[13] This is a misquotation of Niebuhr's remark: "To establish justice in a sinful world is the whole sad duty of the political order." He wrote this in "The National Preaching Mission," *Radical Religion,* Spring 1937; and it may be found in H. R. Davis and R. C. Good, eds., *Reinhold Niebuhr on Politics* (New York, 1960), p. 180.

[14] George Gilder, *Wealth and Poverty* (New York: Bantam paperback, 1981), p. 315. The passage misquoted is from *The Irony of American History,* p. 63.

conservatism—in effect, as an unrepentant Cold Warrior, a stalwart champion of capitalism and, were he around, a sympathizer with South Africa and supporter of American intervention in El Salvador. No doubt Niebuhr's Christian realism contains many "conservative" elements—his disbelief in human perfectibility and in the inevitability of progress, his rejection of political rationalism and abstract idealism, his skepticism about the superior virtue of the oppressed, his understanding of the uses of power and of the occasional need in history for military action, his sense of the organic character of social change, his ironic awareness of the perverse consequences of human decisions, his profound conviction of the limits of human striving. Yet it is necessary to put the word "conservative" in quotation marks, because these are equally elements in post-Niebuhrian liberalism. Each one of the "conservative" points against the virtue and wisdom of the people strikes with even greater force against any elite ruling in the name of the people. As Niebuhr wrote in one of his most famous sentences, "Man's capacity for justice makes democracy possible; but man's inclination to injustice makes democracy necessary."[15] Niebuhr's method was to use "conservative" arguments to make a stronger case for "liberal" policies.

Nothing is more futile than trying to predict how people now dead would have responded to some later contingency; it is hard enough to predict the reactions of living people. But it is difficult to imagine Reinhold Niebuhr as a neo-conservative champion of privilege, pomposity, complacency and self-righteousness in the conduct of public affairs. His response to the civil rights struggle, the Indochina War, and the disaffection of the young shows that to the end of his life he continued to draw liberal conclusions from Augustinian premises. His remark of 1960, though in a narrower context, expresses, one believes, his deepest conviction: "When I find neo-orthodoxy turning into sterile orthodoxy or a new Scholasticism, I find that I am a liberal at heart."[16]

The ironic experience, Niebuhr wrote in *The Irony of American History,* takes a variety of forms. One form he noted especially, because he found it hard to fit into the Christian pattern of irony, is

[15] Reinhold Niebuhr, *The Children of Light and the Children of Darkness* (New York: Scribner, 1944), p. xi.

[16] Harold E. Fey, ed., *How My Mind Has Changed* (Cleveland: Peter Smith, 1961), p. 117.

when "our very virtues become the occasion for mistrust against us."[17] Among his supreme virtues were his instinct for the ambiguity of history, his sensitivity to changes in the historical equilibrium, and his abiding desire to defend liberty by maintaining a balance of ideas and structures in an imperfect world. These virtues enable commentators of diverse persuasions to seize on one or another partial aspect of the thought in order to embrace or condemn the thinker. What is essential, however, is to recall the unswerving passion of the man himself for individual freedom, for social justice, and for fairness in human and social relations.

ARTHUR SCHLESINGER, JR.

ALBERT SCHWEITZER PROFESSOR IN THE HUMANITIES
THE GRADUATE SCHOOL AND UNIVERSITY CENTER
OF THE CITY UNIVERSITY OF NEW YORK

[17] *Irony of American History*, p. 162.

8

Kenneth Thompson

THE POLITICAL PHILOSOPHY OF REINHOLD NIEBUHR

8

THE POLITICAL PHILOSOPHY OF REINHOLD NIEBUHR

THE prevailing mood toward political philosophy of much of contemporary American political science is one of undisguised hostility. Modern critics find philosophy wanting because of its unscientific character and its alleged irrelevance to the urgencies of modern life. Philosophers are identified as political metaphysicians who cling tenaciously to outworn dogmas and illusions. In this context, it is significant that a scholar whose writings have earned him widespread acclaim as America's foremost contemporary political philosopher is hailed for the relevance of his thought at the same time that he rejects the scientific pretensions of modern culture. Indeed, it is the first step in understanding the essence of Reinhold Niebuhr's political philosophy to perceive the relationship between his profound practical insights and his rejection of scientism, which he defines as the blind worship of the methods of the natural sciences as ends in themselves. In making a frontal attack on so-called scientific investigations of human relations, Niebuhr works out an alternative approach to the problem. This approach leads him to a rediscovery of dimensions of political life which our culture for the most part has obscured and ignored.

I. THE SCIENTIFIC METHOD AND POLITICAL PHILOSOPHY

Fundamentally, Niebuhr's approach to political realities has two aspects which constitute its negative and positive content. Negatively, he turns aside from the ground on which most contemporary thought is founded. Positively, he ultimately constructs a theory with its roots in the bedrock of politics. In contrast to most social scientists, including some noted social philosophers, Niebuhr is unwilling to concede that the physical sciences provide the sole possibility of progress and growth. It is true that the hallmark of our culture is its conscious revolt against historic restraints, whether religious or secular, upon free scientific inquiry. Niebuhr's criticism is aimed at the social scientist's unqualified trust in the scientific method and not at its legitimate functions. He concedes that "modern social and psychological sciences have been able to teach us a great deal about man and his community."[1] In spheres where judgments are frequently swayed by powerful ideological sentiments, empirical studies of reality are essential as the basis for political choice. Today, for example, the strident debate between the spokesmen for extreme free enterprise and extreme collectivism can be moderated only through "the resources of an inductive rather than a deductive social science."[2] Such a pragmatic and empirical approach prefers not to deal in general terms with questions like property or planning. It insists upon examining more limited and practical questions, such as the role of property in an agrarian as against an industrial society, the argument for the socialization of coal compared to that of steel in Britain or the effects of governmental interference on the railroads as compared to the utilities. By means of these inquiries "significant decisions between competing systems . . . [can] be constantly reviewed empirically and amended in the light of new evidence."[3] It should be obvious that Niebuhr has subjected social and economic realities to this kind of review throughout his professional career.

Yet it is also obvious, in spite of his recourse to empiricism in politics, that Niebuhr's position regarding the place of the vaunted scientific method is almost unqualifiedly critical. In his view, scientific studies of human behavior are embarrassed by at least five illusions or fantasies. The first fantasy is the myth of a presuppositionless science. Objective social science today is given the wholly imaginary character of an approach characterized by the quest for autonomous, incontrovertible, and self-evident facts. In practice, responsible scholars have learned the impossibility of giving form or meaning to any social research in the absence of a framework or rough outline

[1] *Christian Realism and Political Problems*, p. 3.
[2] Niebuhr, "Christian Faith and Social Action," in *Christian Faith and Social Action*, ed. John Hutchison, p. 233.
[3] *Ibid.*

for organizing their research. Ironically enough, modern social science itself is grounded in certain stubborn and inflexible assumptions which more often than not determine the focus of scientific inquiry and affect its conclusions. The idea of progress and of the perfectibility of man is the lodestar of contemporary social science. It is almost universally assumed that a better and more scientific world will provide tools for erecting general theories that will be more precise and thus permit man to solve his problems once for all.

Another fantasy grows out of the concealment of all those conclusions which fail to conform to the facts. Modern culture, despite its scientific progress, has been caught in some obvious miscalculations. The brave new world of the twentieth century which rationalists of the eighteenth century predicted if men would only disavow their otherworldly illusions scarcely resembles utopia. Such contradictions and errors inherent in a rationalist and scientific approach probably stem from the dual meaning of "scientific." On the one hand, science as empiricism means humility before the facts; on the other hand, science as rationalism may mean the invoking of logical coherence as the test of truth. The two connotations may stand in contradiction because the test of rational coherence prompts men to deny obvious facts if they appear to violate the tenets of coherence.[4]

A third fantasy of present-day social science involves the position of the social observer. In contrast with the physical scientist, the observer of the human scene is at the same time agent and observer. Whereas the natural scientist has only a stake in the discovery of truth, say, regarding cancer, the judgment of the student of society is beclouded by ideological taint, national loyalty, and social and economic status. He cannot be fully objective, for his observations arise from his place in history and his responsibilities to a particular society and group. Not pure mind, but the self with its interests and capacity for rationalization, is the agent of the scientific method, and no perfection of method can coerce these passions. Only when the observer is removed from his subject in time and place, as in certain historical studies, does this problem become less acute.

A fourth fantasy of the scientific approach results from modern conceptions of causation and prediction which ignore the complexity of causation and the intervention of contingent factors in history,

[4] *Christian Realism and Political Problems*, p. 4.

including the human agent. Prediction which is the cherished goal of social scientists is possible in terms of rough probabilities. But Niebuhr maintains: "In both nature and history each new thing is only one of an infinite number of possibilities which might have emerged at that particular juncture. It is for this reason that, though we can trace a series of causes in retrospect, we can never predict the future with accuracy."[5] There are recurrences and cycles in history, but a strong leader, an economic catastrophe, or the juxtaposition of novel forces may channel history in unexpected ways. Moreover, in contrast to the scientific laboratory, nothing is exactly repeated in history. Analogies which infer that a policy pursued, say, in the Roman Empire prior to its decline and fall will, if followed in the present, expose man to a similar fate are erroneously conceived in at least two basic respects. First, given the infinite variety of causal sequences to which every event is related, some other correlation of cause and effect based on another principle of interpretation might be equally plausible. Second, given the uncontrolled character of social inquiry and the interplay of multiple causes, judgments which are inevitably value judgments based on historical analogy can neither be proved nor refuted with the certainty of the physical sciences.

The fifth and perhaps the most persistent illusion is the conviction that science is "the profoundest, because it is the latest, fruit of culture."[6] Auguste Comte's conception of the history of culture as the movement from a religious to a metaphysical to a scientific age is partly true insofar as it correctly describes certain major historical tendencies. But as the value judgment of our culture endlessly prompted us to assert that the latest attainments are the wisest, it is of doubtful validity. For modern culture, in its preoccupation with methods and details and in its confidence that the human situation remains ambiguous only because of a residual ignorance which scientific discovery is certain to correct, has inevitably been shallow and barren in confronting the fundamental issues. In opposition to Comte, Niebuhr proposes that there must be a movement from science to philosophy to counteract the movement from philosophy to science; and from this point the controlling aim of his approach becomes the recovery of the wisdom of philosophy and the humility

[5] *Christianity and Society*, Vol. X, No. 2 (Spring, 1945), p. 4.

[6] Niebuhr, *Faith and History: A Comparison of Christian and Modern Views of History*, p. 53.

and magnanimity of a transcendent religion. His writings on contemporary affairs find him delving beneath the surface of events to expose a general principle which he seeks to integrate into the framework of a general political and social philosophy. In this way he departs from the scientific approach which avowedly eschews such analysis and generalization for the collection and classification of data within sharply defined limits.

II. THE EVOLUTION OF A POLITICAL PHILOSOPHY

If the negative side of Niebuhr's approach to the study of politics constitutes a more or less severe indictment of the blind acceptance of the scientific method, the negative side of the substance of his philosophy derives from his investigation, application, and eventual rejection of the dominant contemporary political creeds of liberalism and Marxism.

The odyssey of Niebuhr's political thought begins in the third decade of the twentieth century, taking as its first pathway a rather conventional liberalism. Next comes a period in the thirties when his criticism of Marxism is not wholly convincing for himself or for others, especially as a basis for concrete political judgment. The last or most recent stage of his journey roughly coincides with the period before and after the Second World War. Here we witness the triumph of a pragmatic conception of politics cast in the mold of the classic principles of Western statesmanship but seeking ultimately to transcend them.

At every stage this development has been rooted in personal experience, including the impressions of an informed student of contemporary history. Beyond this, the existential quality of Niebuhr's philosophy has supplied at least a partial corrective to the coercive influence of every form of political dogma. He has checked his premises against historical developments, and his fascination with higher principles has been curbed by political experience. In its three major periods his philosophy has reflected, to a greater or lesser degree, events of the outside world which prompted a drastic reexamination of some of his fundamental assumptions. Hence change and growth, and not a foolish consistency, appear at first glance to be the dominant characteristics of his approach. We shall discover, by exploring in greater detail the three stages in Niebuhr's political thought, to what extent this is true and to what extent his basic assumptions remain unchanged. It goes without saying that each dominant stage merges imperceptibly into its successor, and the abrupt shifts which a division into periods implies are not readily ascertained.

It has been argued that Niebuhr's theology was most responsive to the influence of liberal Protestantism before 1932. In the same way, from 1915, when he completed his studies at Yale Divinity School, to 1932, when he published *Moral Man and Immoral Society*, his political philosophy most nearly approximated twentieth century liberalism, especially in its practical consequences. For during this period there is evidence that the political program of liberalism, with its tenets of support for the League of Nations, racial tolerance, and sympathy for labor unions, coincided with Niebuhr's views. More important, he accepted many of the liberal philosophical assumptions which he was later to question or abandon. Witnessing the harmful effects of the American industrial system on the laboring class of Detroit during his pastorate there, he sought liberal solutions to specific problems which arose. He criticized Protestantism for stressing metaphysics at the expense of social ethics at a time when the massive and impersonal scientific world required new light on the problem of social injustice no less than on the conflict and reconciliation of religion and science.

As early as 1929, Niebuhr expressed his doubts on some basic liberal tenets, and by the time of the publication of *Reflections on the End of an Era,* in 1934, this critical approach had reached its full growth. In 1936, in his journal, he enumerates six articles of the liberal creed which blind it to the real world. He suggests that liberalism fervently believes that: (1) Injustice is caused by ignorance and will yield to education and greater intelligence; (2) Civilization is becoming gradually moral; (3) The character of individuals, not social systems, will guarantee justice; (4) Appeals to brotherhood and good will are bound to be effective in the end, and if they have been ineffective to date we need only more and better appeals; (5) Goodness makes for happiness, and increased knowledge of this will overcome human selfishness; (6) War is stupid and will yield to reason.[7]

The failure of liberalism results from its blindness to "the perennial difference between human actions and aspirations, the perennial

[7] *Radical Religion*, Vol. I, No. 4 (Autumn, 1936), p. 4.

source of conflict between life and life, the inevitable tragedy of human existence, the irreducible irrationality of human behavior and the tortuous character of human history."[8]

Liberalism which is steeped in faith in man's capacity to subdue nature, in his essential goodness, and in human history takes on all the attributes of a religious creed. Niebuhr concludes that this condition constitutes a disease particularly difficult to cure because the afflicted are classes who imagine they are unusually robust and clear-eyed. In other words, liberalism is inapplicable to problems of our day because of its naïve picture of man and the political order and because it has become a passionate ideological justification for the selfish pursuits of the dominant middle class. One part of this criticism adumbrates the need for a philosophy which will not be refuted by political experience; the other part suggests that Niebuhr's impatience with liberalism is informed and inspired by Marxist assumptions. It is these assumptions with which he is to grapple for part of a decade before casting them irretrievably aside.

In the late twenties and early thirties, Niebuhr's appetite for social realism fed on his growing disenchantment with liberalism and the consequent appeal of Marxism. The defects of the one appeared at this time to be the strengths of the other philosophy. Liberalism had failed to relate the individual organically to society; Marxism made society the beginning and the end. Liberalism maintained that the individual through maximizing self-interest would miraculously serve the interests of all; Marxism showed that this was in practical terms a middle-class ideology. Liberalism concealed the conflicts of interest which prevail in all communities; Marxism laid bare the struggles which went on between diverse social and economic classes. Liberalism insisted that justice could be attained through the automatic working of a free economic system; Marxism proclaimed that injustice was inevitable as long as economic inequality prevailed. It was Niebuhr's opinion in 1932 that Marxism "made no mistake in stating the rational goal toward which society must move, the goal of equal justice, or in understanding the economic foundations of justice."[9]

However, despite the impact of such insights, Niebuhr has always been uneasy about the most fundamental Marxist assumptions and conclusions. In the first issue of *Radical Religion,* he observes that an appraisal of socialism raises many questions which cry for an

[8] *Ibid.* [9] *Moral Man and Immoral Society,* p. 165.

answer. Take the issue of a materialistic interpretation of history. If the materialistic interpretation is rejected unqualifiedly, we shall have dismissed a valuable insight. Marxism has rediscovered a truth that lies at the heart of prophetic religion: namely, that man's cultural, moral, and religious achievements are never absolute but are colored by human finiteness and corrupted by human sin. Yet whoever accepts Marxism unreservedly does violence, among other things, to the dialectic between nature and spirit and between freedom and necessity. Niebuhr warns young American parsons reacting to the sentimentalities of liberalism not to capitulate to Marxist dogma lest they find that their liberal faith of a not very unique Christian quality is being supplanted by a radical faith more realistic in its analysis of immediate social issues but even less Christian in its total insights into life.[10]

Marxism proves an ally, but a transient one, in Niebuhr's attack on the liberal approach to the problem of justice in society. Liberalism hopes to solve the great issues by asking people to be more kind and loving; Marxism knows that justice cannot be established without a struggle in which the interests of the victims of injustice are set against the beneficiaries of injustice. For Niebuhr in 1935, however, this Marxian insight represents no more than a partial perspective which is weakened by Marxism's utopian faith that such conflicts will end with the destruction of capitalism. He distinguishes between the capitalistic aggravation of the problem of justice and its perennial nature in all human societies. The struggle for power will go on in some form or other in all societies. The Marxist illusion results from equating class conflict with human rivalry, whereas Niebuhr conceives of the struggle for power endlessly elaborating itself as an expression of human finitude and sin.[11]

It is fair to say of Niebuhr that he at no time accepted the Marxist critique of liberalism indiscriminately or without serious criticism. However, it would serve no point to infer that its influence or importance was negligible for his thought. Coming at a time when the deep gloom of a major depression cast its heavy shadow over the intellectual world, Marxist estimates and predictions gained credence in ever widening circles. The conception that capitalism was destroying itself and must be destroyed to make way for the social ownership of the means of production which furnished the only basis

[10] *Radical Religion,* Vol. I, No. 1 (Autumn, 1935), p. 3.
[11] *Ibid.*

of health and justice in a technical age was based on the objective social and economic situation as Niebuhr and others viewed it at the time.[12] If he adjusted his position to fit the unfolding realities of American economic life more quickly than most social observers, it is also the case that precisely for Marxist reasons he misunderstood the pragmatic character of the social revolution of the New Deal. At a time when President Franklin D. Roosevelt was painfully effecting a compromise program based on social aspirations shared by Niebuhr, the political philosopher found the politician hesitant, vacillating and halfhearted. Perhaps no other error in Niebuhr's thinking has influenced so profoundly the development of the last stage of his philosophy.

Moreover, the genuine peril attaching to the combination of economic and political power was frequently underestimated in this period. In 1932 he refers to a prophecy of Bertrand Russell that some form of oligarchy is inevitable in a technological age, and asks himself whether a communistic or capitalistic oligarchy would be more onerous. Probably in the long run, if Russell's prediction is right, the communistic oligarch would be preferable. For in Niebuhr's view: "His power would be purely political, and no special economic interests would tempt him to pursue economic policies at variance with the national interest."[13] Today he most emphatically refutes this point. In retrospect he confesses: "It was not realized that even a democratic socialism might face problems of preserving incentives in a completely collectivist economy and would betray the perils of the concentration of economic and political power in the hands of a bureaucracy even when held in a democratic framework."[14]

From much the same standpoint, Niebuhr's criticism and rejection of Marxism reflect the history of the times. To be sure, it was on grounds of philosophy and not experience that he expressed his first doubts. As early as 1936, he decried as a pathetic illusion the Marxist conception of the nature of man. For Marxism, man was a being who would be transfigured with the withering away of the state. For Niebuhr, the illusion that the classless society would eliminate the problem of power was as utopian as the sentimentality of liberalism. A second point on which he was critical at an early date concerned the Russian experiment. In 1936 he took exception to the book *Soviet Communism: A New Civilization,* by the Webbs. He

[12] *Ibid.*, p. 5. [13] *Moral Man*, p. 90.

[14] *Christian Faith and Social Action, loc. cit.*, pp. 227–228.

criticized its confusion of legal structures and precepts with political facts. The Webbs' study resembled a discussion of municipal government in New York City which omitted any reference to Tammany Hall. By 1939 there was no disputing the evidence in this sphere. Marxism's "notion that evil would disappear once capitalism is destroyed is just as completely negated by the facts in Russia, as the liberal notion that education can lift men completely out of their economic circumstances and prompt them to act as discarnate spirits, filled with goodwill alone, is negated in our society."[15]

Beyond this, however, Niebuhr's perception of the demonic character of Marxism as a secular religion represents a later phase of his criticism. Time and again in the thirties he intimated that Marx, who had caught a glimpse of the truth, had confused the issue by attributing fundamental problems to special causes. Yet it was not until the forties that he wrote: "The deepest tragedy of our age . . . is that the alternative to capitalism has turned out to be worse than the disease which it was meant to cure."[16] This failure, he finds, is a natural consequence of Marxist illusions and not a corruption of Marxism by Stalinism. It results from ascribing all human virtue to a single class, the proletariat, and all human evil to a single institution, private property. Not only is each of these assumptions false, but in juxtaposition they are mutually contradictory. The one assumes that the "good society" will come about purely through an economic change, for man is the inexorable product of natural forces. However, the proletariat acting independently of economic forces on the basis of the utmost rationality is chosen to preside with absolute power during the transition from the old society to the new awe-inspiring classless society. These two illusions constitute the deadliest errors of Marxist apocalyptic thinking, for they give divine sanction, free from popular influence and control, to one technique of social reform, one guaranteed solution of the socio-ethical problem, and one group which alone is untarnished by sin. The messianic character of Soviet communism and its absolute totalitarianism are therefore not accidental but follow inevitably from its premises. A partial truth confused with the whole and administered by a class posing as the surrogate of God becomes a universal creed under which cruelty, injustice, and violence become legitimate instruments of the historical process.

[15] *Radical Religion,* Vol. IV, No. 2 (Spring, 1939), p. 8.
[16] *Ibid.,* Vol. XIII, No. 4 (Autumn, 1948), p. 5.

Marxism, therefore, which by its illumination of liberalism's worst illusions caught Niebuhr's imagination, ends by erecting laws and precepts more evil and terrifying by far. It is hardly surprising that Niebuhr, twice disillusioned, should embark in the thirties on the mission of discovering a viable theory of politics. In this quest he retains certain perennial truths inherent in liberalism and Marxism but unencumbered by their worst fantasies. Liberalism, for example, provides certain moral objectives which serve as the gentle civilizers of politics in our society. Together they make up what Niebuhr calls the spirit of liberalism, which is older than bourgeois culture. They include a spirit of tolerance and fairness without which life is reduced to an almost consistent inhumanity. Freedom or liberty is another moral and political objective which the spirit, if not the middle-class application and interpretation, of liberalism bequeaths to Niebuhr's thought.

In the same way Marxist philosophy, although rejected more completely and emphatically than liberalism, remains as at least a residual element of his approach. The three insights from Marxist thought which, if properly interpreted, appear most enduring include its emphasis on the social dimension of life and the collective fate of man's existence which for Niebuhr implies a responsibility to seek justice at the national and international level. He adds, however, that these organic forms of life will not yield to the efforts of collectivists or idealists to coerce them into new mechanical or artificial molds. Second, Marxism requires that the political and economic structure of human communities be taken seriously. It rejects the belief that structures are of no importance so long as good men operate these systems and structures. Third, as against the liberal concept of an easy harmony of interests Marxism postulates the idea of the class struggle. Niebuhr finds this last idea unacceptable unless expanded to embrace all political struggles which endlessly go on as the sole means of righting the balance between the victims and the beneficiaries of injustice.

We have concentrated until now on the earlier stages of Niebuhr's thought, which reveal a characteristic analytical method. Whether Marxism or liberalism or the scientific method be the target, Niebuhr probes to the heart of an intellectual trend or culture to grasp and expose the peculiar idea or assumption which holds it together. One obvious consequence is to limit his role primarily to that of social critic. The negative content of this approach has led some observers to say that Niebuhr's only contribution is that of penetrating critic. At some time before the Second World War, however, the more positive side of his approach was becoming increasingly apparent. His first step was to make more explicit his theory of human nature. In this undertaking Niebuhr has more in common with the traditional political philosophers than with many of his present day contemporaries. The practice of rooting political theory in political institutions and processes, rather than probing deeper to the level of human nature, belongs mainly to the last few decades. Contrariwise, Niebuhr explicitly assumes that an understanding of political phenomena, whether international or domestic, is inseparable from a clear picture of human nature. The impetus for turning to this problem results more from practical reasons than any aesthetic longing to build a complete system of political thought. For Niebuhr in the thirties frequently asks: "Is it possible to lead man out of social confusion into an ordered society if we do not know man a little better than either Marxians or liberals know him?"[17] Man has never more completely misunderstood himself, especially in terms of the tension between his finiteness and freedom. This is perhaps the spur to which Niebuhr has responded throughout his mature writings. If there is a single strand of his thought which runs like a red thread from his liberal to his pragmatic phases, it is awareness of the rock-bottom problem of human nature.

The Gifford Lectures, begun at the University of Edinburgh in the spring of 1939 as war clouds hovered over Europe and completed in the autumn as the threat became a dreadful reality, represent their author's most systematic attempt to demonstrate the need for and broad outlines of a realistic theory of human nature. The lectures begin: "Man has always been his most vexing problem. How shall he think of himself?"[18] Any affirmation he makes involves him in contradictions. If he stresses man's unique and rational qualities, then man's greed, lust for power, and brute nature betray him. If he holds that men everywhere are the product of nature and are unable to rise above circumstances, he tells us nothing of man the creature who dreams of God and of making himself God and whose sympathy knows no bounds. If he believes man is essentially good and attributes all evil to concrete historical and social causes, he merely begs the question; for these causes are revealed, on closer scrutiny,

[17] *Ibid.*, Vol. IV, No. 2 (Spring, 1939), p. 8.

[18] Niebuhr, *The Nature and Destiny of Man*, I, *Human Nature*, 1.

to be the consequences of the evil inherent in man. If he finds man bereft of all virtue, his capacity for reaching such a judgment refutes the terms of his judgment. Such baffling paradoxes of human self-knowledge point up the vexing problem of doing justice at one and the same time to the uniqueness of man and to his affinities with nature. Only a theory inspired by a knowledge of both qualities can be adequate. "The obvious fact is that man is a child of nature, subject to its vicissitudes, compelled by its necessities, driven by its impulses, and confined within the brevity of the years which nature permits its varied organic forms, allowing them some, but not too much, latitude. The other less obvious fact is that man is a spirit who stands outside of nature, life, himself, his reason and the world."[19] Modern views of man which stress exclusively his dignity or his misery are fatuous and irrelevant chiefly because they fail to understand the dualism of man's nature.

The classical view of man is convinced that man must be understood primarily in terms of his uniqueness and reason. Mind is sharply distinguished from body. Reason is the creative principle which is identical with God. Mind is good whereas the body is evil. Niebuhr is forever impatient with classical rationalism which, he maintains, naïvely believes that reason can subdue man's evil natural impulses. In fact, however, reason itself has been corrupted and since the time of the Fall guides men indiscriminately toward evil as well as toward virtue. Therefore any ethical dualism which implies that by reason alone man can transcend his selfish nature is wholly illusory. It may be that Niebuhr does injustice to classical rationalism by implying that liberalism, which overestimates man's creative potentialities and understresses his destructiveness, derives from "the triumph of the modernized classical view of man."[20] Some classicists argue that he overlooks the realistic and pessimistic tone of Greek thought which clearly is missing from all modern views. However, Niebuhr, it must be noted, concedes that Greek drama is self-consciously aware of the tragic element in life even though it has no positive solution for the problem of evil.

In opposition to classical thought, Niebuhr restates the main elements of the Christian view of man which rationalists and naturalists overlook. Man is a unique mixture of spirit and nature; he is in nature yet he transcends it. The ambiguous and dialectical interpenetration of those two elements is a clue to the mystery of human

[19] *Ibid.*, I, 3. [20] *Ibid.*, I, 5.

personality. The spirit is limited by nature, and nature is spiritualized. The human spirit reflects the image of God and stands outside the self and the world in its capacity of self-transcendence. According to the Bible, man "to understand himself . . . [must] begin with a faith that he is understood from beyond himself, that he is known and loved of God and must find himself in terms of obedience to the divine will."[21] This faith makes it possible for him to relate himself to God without pretending to be God, and to accept his distance from God without believing that his evil nature is caused by this finiteness.

Yet this high estimate of human nature enjoys a paradoxical relationship with the low estimate of human virtue in Christian thought. Man in fact is a sinner not because he is physical or finite or because his impulses are evil but because he refuses to admit his "creatureliness." He is not divided against himself as good mind and evil body. Rather by the wrong use of his freedom and his rebellion against God, evil is installed at the very center of personality: in the will. "Man . . . is a sinner . . . because he is betrayed by his very ability to survey the whole to imagine himself the whole."[22] Or, put another way: "The freedom of his spirit causes him to break the harmonies of nature and the pride of spirit prevents him from establishing a new harmony. The freedom of his spirit enables him to use the forces and processes of nature creatively; but his failure to observe the limits of his finite existence causes him to defy the restraints of both nature and reason."[23] Man's ambiguous and contradictory position at the juncture of freedom and finiteness, of spirit and nature produces in him a condition of anxiety. He is anxious because he is conscious of the imperialism of others while secretly aware of some of the metes and bounds of his own finiteness. Yet "he is also anxious because he does not know the limits of his possibilities."[24] Anxiety may theoretically be overcome by perfect faith in the ultimate security of God's love, but perfect faith for mortal man is not an actual possibility. Insofar as man cannot trust God's love he seeks security by his own deeds, thus pretending to be self-sufficient in the triumph over finiteness and human limitations.

For our purposes, the most important observable expression human anxiety takes is politically in the will-to-power. Man shares with animals their natural appetites and desires and the impulse for survival. Yet, being both nature and spirit, his requirements are

[21] *Ibid.*, I, 15. [22] *Ibid.*, I, 17. [23] *Ibid.* [24] *Ibid.*, I, 183.

qualitatively heightened; they are raised irretrievably to the level of spirit where they become limitless and insatiable. "Man being more than a natural creature, is not interested merely in physical survival but in prestige and social approval. Having the intelligence to anticipate the perils in which he stands in nature and history, he invariably seeks to gain security against these perils by enhancing his power, individually and collectively."[25] To overcome social anxiety, man seeks power over his fellows, endeavoring to subdue their wills to his lest they come to dominate him. The struggle for political power is merely an example of the rivalry which goes on at every level of human life. The tragic paradox of the quest for security is that power, the main instrument of political security, can itself never guarantee security. Those who attain the advantages of great power might be assumed to have conquered insecurity. However, "the more man establishes himself in power and glory, the greater is the fear of tumbling from his eminence. . . . The will-to-power is thus an expression of insecurity even when it has achieved ends which . . . would seem to guarantee complete security. The fact that human ambitions know no limits must therefore be attributed . . . to an uneasy recognition of man's finiteness, weakness and dependence, which become the more apparent the more we seek to obscure them. . . . There is no level of greatness and power in which the lash of fear is not at least one strand in the whip of ambition."[26]

The human predicament has roots primarily in the security-power dilemma. Weak men and nations assume that if they had more power they would be more secure. Yet "the more power an individual and nation has, the more of its life impinges upon other life and the more wisdom is required to bring it into some decent harmony with other life."[27] In the political arena groups are motivated, much as individuals, to seek dominion over one another. In 1944 Niebuhr answered the criticism that labor was jeopardizing the common interest by pressing its cause when he said: "It is silly to talk of the danger of pressure groups. Labor has merely fashioned its own political power inside the Democratic party."[28] The various groups or corporate entities in society compete for power in the manner

[25] Reinhold Niebuhr, *The Children of Light and the Children of Darkness*, p. 20.

[26] *The Nature and Destiny of Man*, I, *Human Nature*, 193–194.

[27] *Christianity and Society*, Vol. XI, No. 3 (Spring, 1945), pp. 7–8.

[28] *Ibid.*, Vol. X, No. 2 (Winter, 1944), p. 7.

of the individuals who compose them. Their success is dependent on their unity and vitality, for "in politics, as in warfare, numbers without cohesion and organization count for nothing."[29] Power is the organization of factors and forces which are impotent without organization. Some group or coalition emerges as the holder of a preponderance or a balance of power. It assumes the responsibility for government or the administration of the system wherein the power struggle continues. This group, in turn, is supplanted by another, and the endless and inescapable conflict goes on. Effective limits on the struggle, especially among larger groups, are usually far more modest than is widely understood. "In the field of collective behavior the force of egoistic passion is so strong that the only harmonies possible are those which manage to neutralize this force through balance of power, through mutual defenses against its inordinate expression, and through techniques for harnessing its energy to social ends."[30] For Niebuhr the limits of human imagination, the easy subservience of reason to the passions, and the persistence of collective irrationalism and egoism make social conflict inevitable in human history, probably to its very end.

Moreover, the possibility of force or resort to coercion is present in all social conflict. "The threat of force, whether by the official and governmental representatives or by the parties to a dispute in a community, is a potent instrument in all communal relations."[31] Coercion is inevitable and universal in even the most intimate community, the family. There it is expressed in the position of the father and his capacity for imposing his will upon his children. Political power represents a special form of coercion, for it rests on the ability to use and manipulate other forms of social, economic, and religious power for the purpose of organizing and dominating the community.

Furthermore, Niebuhr notes the ferocity and intensity of the struggle among groups, when compared to the rivalry of individuals, stemming from the tendency of groups such as the nation to express both the virtue and selfishness of their members. One consequence of modern mass society has been to thwart the attainment of personal security and the satisfaction of basic human aspirations, especially for particular groups. Frustrated individuals strive to fulfill themselves vicariously by projecting their ego to the level of the

[29] *Ibid.*, Vol. XII, No. 1 (Winter, 1946), p. 8.
[30] Niebuhr, *An Interpretation of Christian Ethics*, p. 140.
[31] *The Nature and Destiny of Man*, II, *Human Destiny*, 259.

national ego. In mass society collective attainments offer possibilities of self-aggrandizement which individual pretensions no longer serve. At the same time, appeals are made to the loyalty, self-sacrifice, and devotion of individuals in the group. In this way social unity is built on the virtuous as well as on the selfish side of man's nature; the twin elements of collective strength become self-sacrificial loyalty and frustrated aggressions. From this it follows that politics is the more contentious and ruthless because of the unselfish loyalty of the members of groups, which become laws unto themselves unrestrained by their obedient and worshipful members. Group pride is in fact the corruption of individual loyalty and group consciousness; contempt for another group is the pathetic form which respect for our own frequently takes. The tender emotions which bind the family together sometimes are expressed in indifference for the welfare of other families. In international society a nation made up of men of the greatest religious goodwill would be less than loving toward other nations, for its virtue would be channeled into loyalty to itself, thus increasing that nation's selfishness. The consequence for Niebuhr's political theory is his conclusion that "society . . . merely cumulates the egoism of individuals and transmutes their individual altruism into collective egoism so that the egoism of the group has a double force. For this reason no group acts from purely unselfish or even mutual intent and politics is therefore bound to be a contest of power."[32] Relations among such groups must always be essentially political and not ethical, and the study of political science becomes the study of the objective distribution of power.

III. THE UNSOLVED PROBLEM IN NIEBUHR'S POLITICAL PHILOSOPHY

For a professor of social ethics such a picture of social conflict and endless strife can obviously not remain the whole story. The burden of the analysis to this point construes politics as an irrational realm in which the elements of conflict and rivalry almost completely overshadow those of co-operation and mutuality. At this point, however, Niebuhr, having laid bare the bitter and tragic facts of power, sets about to transcend them. His mind's ascent from the depths of human selfishness and sin to the bright summit of tran-

[32] Niebuhr, "Human Nature and Social Change," *Christian Century,* L (1933), 363.

scendent faith traverses the rough crags and peaks along which are strewn the remnants of earlier philosophical enterprises. In one sense, Niebuhr can with justice maintain that he makes this perilous ascent within another dimension; his religious faith frees him from the need for having illusions about human nature at the same time that it prevents him from making these realities normative. The Christian, he argues, lives in a deeper dimension than the realm in which the political struggle takes place. Yet it is the relevance—or irrelevance—of this deeper dimension to concrete political problems which is sometimes ambiguous and unclear. Indeed, the unsolved problem in Niebuhr's philosophy arises precisely from this crowning point in his thought. Aware that any criticism may merely betray the limits of my own intelligence and faith, I propose nonetheless to examine, finally, what appears to me the most fundamental problem in Niebuhr's political philosophy.

It is obvious that Niebuhr's writings are filled with realistic reminders of the recalcitrance of men and nations to all attempts to transform them and alter their natural impulses and inescapable self-love. Friction, rivalry, and competition for power are universal; the best men can hope for is an armistice from overt conflict and a balance of power that ideally becomes part of organized government based on a total equilibrium of forces. But lust for power, if universal, cannot be normative, for man is also a being who transcends himself indeterminately and is saved only as love draws him beyond self-love. Niebuhr disavows the sentimental perfectionism of some forms of liberal Protestantism and the utopianism of liberalism and Marxism which overlook the persistence of egotism and self-interest. However, he warns simultaneously that to hold up man's selfish qualities as a final imperative is to dispense with all ethical standards and thus to suffer the paralyzing consequences of nihilism or cynicism. He finds in the law of love the sole proof against this peril; love provides foundations for a final standard against which interest and power can be measured, beguiled, harnessed, and deflected for the ultimate end of creating the most inclusive possible community of justice and order. The Christian in society must be ready to use interest and power for an end dictated by love without becoming complacent about the evil and injustice inherent in the pursuit of partial ends. Love and power in tension make up the dynamic field of a transcendent ethic.

Paradoxically enough, Niebuhr's effort to relate an absolute love ethic to the hard realities of politics is the source of his deepest insights and his most misleading political estimates. Creatively he shows that love serves the prophetic function of inspiring self-criticism of political actions. It is of course obvious that there can be no true political order unless there is moral consensus based on the calculation and discrimination of mutual and common interests. Yet reason which must find points of coincidence between the interests of the self and of others is so deeply involved in the conflicts and ideologies of men and nations that it cannot be truly objective and discriminating. It is at this point that the possibility exists of love's moderating the pursuit of interest by creating a spirit of contrition which can break some of the pride of the implacable contestants and introduce the conditions essential to perception of the fragmentary character of human values and interests. Theoretically, at least, compromise becomes plausible when the pretensions of the individual and collective ego are laid bare and the dishonesties of conflict are indicated. Love assists in the identification of mutual interests which reason corrupted by passion might otherwise obscure. Love provides the ultimate end and law of life to which social conduct must aspire and with which it is eternally in tension.

At a more proximate level, reason and morality qualify and mitigate the political struggle by tempering power with justice. Men have a residual capacity for justice and order; government expresses the community's desire for justice no less than the will-to-power of an oligarchy. Even hypocrisy is essentially the tribute which an unjust oligarchy, claiming responsibility for the common good, oftentimes pays to justice. It is of course essential that the student of political morality be alerted to the evils inherent in self-interest when cloaked with the pretensions of ideals. In the most recent pragmatic phase of his political writing, Niebuhr has warned against the uncritical acceptance of too inclusive and abstract programs which fail to take account of the endless contingencies of history and become screens for particular interests in society or, alternatively, "ideologies of conscience." In the face of these hazards, moral choices are none the less possible, based on proximate normative principles, like justice and order, which with the rising middle class were expressed in terms of "natural liberty." Because of the historical relativity of socio-moral choices, a newer era has called for greater emphasis on equality and collectivism, and these values are, in turn, being re-examined today. Significant decisions between competing moral and political systems are continually being made in history; and Niebuhr offers as concrete examples the triumph of the rising middle class over monarchical absolutism, which for him was morally right as well as historically inevitable. Niebuhr is confident that general values are at stake in almost every political struggle, that nations in particular run the risk of viewing as absolutes the proximate values embodied in their cause, but that values no less than interests must be measured as they relate to the welfare and justice of a larger community.

Niebuhr's clear emphasis on reason and general moral values not only makes his philosophy more satisfying than the moral views of other political realists; it has also been the occasion for confusion and ambiguity in his analysis and thought. Much as Niebuhr may stress that the absolute ethic of love is essentially irrelevant to practical politics, and that selfish nations often confound their own cause with higher principles of justice, he in fact introduces abstract principles into the political arena as a measure of behavior and success. He judged the New Deal against the background of its achievement of proximate goals such as equality and social justice, obscuring its character as a moderately progressive, pragmatic political movement. He railed against those who asked for an armistice in the Second World War and maintained that conflict in any age, individual as well as collective, is not frequently resolved without an obvious victory and a patent defeat. And in 1945 he confused the abstract principles of British socialism with the realities of foreign policy by announcing that Labor's victory "puts a stop to Churchill's abortive efforts to keep discredited monarchs on the throne in Greece and Italy. . . . It will most probably contribute to the invention of a *modus vivendi* between Russia and the western world and thus reduce the peril of a third world war."[33] Niebuhr until very recently has dealt with the problem of negotiations less creatively than other realistic observers partly because he has approached the whole problem less in political than in abstract ideological terms. Not until late in 1953 do his writings indicate full and unqualified appreciation of, for example, Winston Churchill's conception of the elements of diplomatic negotiation.

It would seem that the fundamental defect of Niebuhr's political philosophy which he has somewhat belatedly discovered and transcended is that for which he has criticized so unsparingly both

[33] *Christianity and Society*, Vol. X, No. 4 (Autumn, 1945).

liberal and Marxian thought. In seeking to apply an absolute ethic however indirectly to politics, he has in the past disregarded or underestimated the iron law of politics and the enduring truths of foreign policy. Sometimes by translating the problems of politics to a higher theological or philosophical level he has begged the vital questions essential for the school of the statesmen. For example, other observers have argued that political leaders might be less unjust if they recognized the inevitable moral ambiguity of their deeds. If Niebuhr accepts this truth—and who can doubt that he does—he dilutes its importance when he writes: "Power cannot be evil of itself, unless life itself be regarded as evil. . . . According to Christian faith perfect power and goodness are united only in God. But this is not because life is inherently evil; but because all power in history is partial."[34]

These peculiar contradictions and uncertainties which accompany Niebuhr's heroic attempt to transcend the egocentricity of politics are also manifested in the content and meaning he gives to political idealism and political realism. Most students in the field recognize idealist approaches as those which look for conditions and solutions which are supposed to overcome and eliminate the selfish instincts of man. Realism on the contrary takes self-interest for granted and seeks in the improvement of society to work with men and political forces as it finds them. No serious student of Niebuhr's thought can be unaware of his essential and inevitable political realism. But in his concern that ethical values be affirmed, he questions whether realism itself is enough. Its inadequacies arise from its involvement in the grime and heat of the world's struggle and its unwillingness to be deflected from immediate issues and duties. It stands on the abyss of cynicism and is oblivious to spiritual perspectives. Yet humanity has been endlessly prompted by conscience and insight to visions of perpetual peace. For Niebuhr this attests to the soul's rebellion against the fate which binds man's collective life to the world of nature. Such a vision can be kept alive only when permitted to over-reach itself. Realism can be indicted on the three counts that it ignores the ultimate ideological dimensions of political struggles, that it is affronted by genuine principles and standards of justice, and that it frequently accepts the inevitability of war. Niebuhr's heaviest blow is his claim that the fatal sin to which real-

[34] *Ibid.*, Vol. VIII, No. 1 (Winter, 1943), p. 10.

ism is constantly tempted is to make that which is universal in human behavior normative as well.

The test of a scientific theory is its capacity for bringing order and meaning to a mass of data which would otherwise remain unrelated. It is legitimate to ask whether idealism and realism as defined and applied by Niebuhr contribute to this purpose. Realistic political scientists conceive of politics, as distinct from economics or aesthetics, as the pursuit of interest defined in terms of power. Niebuhr's definition is less precise and more subject to ambiguity. He considers political realism as the disposition to take into account all factors in a social and political situation which offer resistance to established norms. But what are these norms? What reference do they have to concrete political situations? Is it not true that norms like *equality* become in the political arena objects of endless contention, rationalization, and self-deception which have confounded the philosophers who strive to advance abstract political judgments? What, for instance, does the norm *justice*, which Niebuhr construes as requiring that each man be given his due, mean in practical terms? What are the standards by which to determine what is "due" labor or management in every situation? It is this kind of question which troubles some of Niebuhr's most devoted students.

Beyond definitions, Niebuhr's application of the concepts of realism and idealism is so inconsistent, polemical, and vague as to drain them of much of their content, meaning, and usefulness. Realism at one time or another is said to imply postwar diplomatic policies ranging from preventive war to naïve demands for a peaceful settlement with the dynamic world communist movement, or from indifference to the ideological dimensions of conflict to an exaggerated awareness of national deceptions and pretensions. In fact, for Niebuhr political realism refers to conduct on a continuum ranging from cynicism to sheer utopianism. Yet common sense would seem to tell us that opposites cannot be examples of the same thing and that something must be wrong with a theory which has no other standard than popular claims for what is a realistic policy. Perhaps if Niebuhr's definitions of philosophical tendencies were more sharply drawn he would not flounder, as these examples seem to indicate, in the application of political realism. For in truth the realist conception of politics as a clash of interests presupposes neither a naturally harmonious world nor the inevitability of war. Instead it asserts that at some stage in the political struggle interests must be identified, adjusted, and accommodated or, failing this, statesmen must go on to redefine their nation's hierarchy of interests in order that mutually antagonistic interests may, if possible, be made more compatible. Because Niebuhr is disposed ultimately to treat with politics in at least proximate moral terms, he confuses, ignores, or underestimates the elements of this process and thus misunderstands the demands of realism. His failure to perceive the clash of historic Russian interests with Europe's interests or his inclination to rank other things as more vital led him to predict in the Winter, 1944 issue of *Christianity and Society* that geographic propinquity and common sympathy for revolutionary ferment would encourage Russo-European relations more intimate in character than Europe's relations with the United States.

The lessons of history attest that interest can be transcended not by abandoning or even enlarging it; it can be overcome only through promoting in concert the interests of a number of groups or nations which through the impact of history may discover new interests that they may eventually come to hold in common. Moral principles can become the polestar for the conduct of foreign policy only if they are filtered through the circumstances of time and place. They must be derived from political practice and not imposed upon it. We have a right to ask of our national leaders a kind of cosmic humility regarding the moral actions of states. If realism strives to guard against over-rating the influence of moral principles upon politics, it does so because this humility is so frequently the missing factor.

Edmund Burke, perhaps the greatest of English-speaking political philosophers, has added to the West's repository of political wisdom a concept which Niebuhr understands but has sometimes overlooked.[35] Prudence, not justice, is first in the rank of political virtues; she is the director, the standard, the regulator of them. Metaphysics cannot live without definition; but prudence is cautious how she defines. Yet if Burke is wiser in perceiving and applying this truth, Niebuhr perhaps is bolder, sees life in dimensions that are deeper, and in the end may emerge more creative in his agonizing appraisal of the roots of the moral problem. Moreover, while Burke essen-

[35] *The Works of The Right Honorable Edmund Burke*, 4th ed. (Boston: Little, Brown, and Company, 1871), IV, 80–81.

tially expresses the genius of a nation or people, Niebuhr just as obviously transcends our scientific era. If beyond this he fails to transcend the eternal and tragic paradoxes of politics, he clarifies and illuminates the problem as does no other contemporary social philosopher.[36]

KENNETH THOMPSON

POLITICAL SCIENCE DEPARTMENT
NORTHWESTERN UNIVERSITY
EVANSTON, ILLINOIS

[36] I am especially indebted to Professor Harry R. Davis, of Beloit College, Wis., whose brilliant dissertation (University of Chicago, 1951) provides a most extensive and sympathetic analysis of Professor Niebuhr's political thought.

POSTSCRIPT: 1982

I remember a comment in the late 1950s by Walter Lippmann following a conference of theorists of international politics: "How many generations will it be before we see Niebuhr's equal again." Reinhold Niebuhr, making his first trip to Washington since the onset of his illness in 1952 had joined Lippmann, Hans J. Morgenthau, James Reston, George F. Kennan, Arnold Wolfers, Dean Rusk and others for a day-long conversation on foreign policy. His limited strength required periodic absences from the conversations. Yet, Lippmann's comment provides testimony that Niebuhr's commanding presence dominated their debate.

Why had Niebuhr emerged as first among equals? If the conference had been held earlier, a factor would surely have been his rhetorical skills but by 1959 illness had taken its toll. I had jotted down a few observations concerning the participants. "Niebuhr had the historian's command of the facts. He illustrated the precept of his favorite American statesman, Abraham Lincoln. The first step in moral and political judgment is to ascertain the plain facts of the matter." Moralists and theorists, for the most part, are impatient with long and painful pursuit of facts. Perhaps for this reason, statesmen and policymakers have little time for the more simple-minded moralists. Contemporary policymakers were not impatient with Niebuhr; surely one reason was his mastery of practical realities and the facts.

In my notes, I find a second reference to the uniqueness of Niebuhr's approach. He understood a distinction of classical political philosophy between theoretical and practical knowledge. Niebuhr was at home in the theoretical world of the philosopher, the theologian, and the philosopher of science, but he recognized this was not the world of the politician or statesman. Contemporary philosophers and scientists call for the *application* of philosophical and scientific principles to rid the world of the indeterminacy of politics. Niebuhr gave short shrift to this notion polemicizing against Huxley's scientific humanism at UNESCO and the over-sanguine views of some atomic scientists that their methods would bring peace. The source of the scientist's illusion was failure to understand political responsibility. The politicians' oath of office pledged them to preserve the union and denied them the freedom of international science. To suppose that the political process could be transformed through applying the scientific method was greatly to misunderstand practical politics. Politics had its own requirements for Niebuhr, a lesson he derived from first-hand experience.

At the same time, Niebuhr resisted arguments that absolutes from philosophy or theory could, with certain modifications, provide the basis for political decisions. While he agreed with the classicists that politics involved action in the practical realm, he disagreed that abstract doctrines of natural law or any other self-contained system of thought offered guidance for politics. Thus, on one front he engaged in intellectual encounters with philosophers and scientists who described politics as nothing more than applied philosophy while on the other he confronted natural law thinkers seeking to translate political and moral absolutes into practical politics. Because of his respect for facts he considered himself an empiricist but an historical empiricist not a social science or behavioral empiricist. He appropriated some of the insights of those with whom he did battle while consistently trying to preserve the integrity of his own political theory.

It was Niebuhr, conspicuous as a lone theologian among the theorists who met in Washington, who was first to insist that no single overarching norm in international politics provided the basis for evaluating and judging all other norms. This viewpoint set him apart from those who saw freedom or security or justice as the controlling objective of American foreign policy. He concurred with Justice Holmes' phrase: "People are always extolling the man of principle but the superior man is the one who knows he must find his way in a maze of principles."

In the last years of his life, this viewpoint separated him both from anti-communists and anti anti-communists. He resisted the attraction of political slogans in part because he held himself close to the facts of the situation which did not yield to facile slogans. The fabric of his normative thought had many strands. He understood that moral and political objectives compete with one another. Especially in his later years, he came to believe that one can be for or against movements and policies without embarking on a crusade. Some explain this belief by his illness, but I observed that a deepening political wisdom and the end of early illusions were the wellsprings of the change in his approach.

With the passing of the years, international politics for him became increasingly complex and intractable. He recognized that nation-building in Asia was different in kind from reconstructing the nations of Europe. He expressed moral outrage at the prospect of nuclear warfare and would surely have aligned himself with those who urge continued negotiations for arms control. Yet, one cannot forget that he favored the testing of the hydrogen bomb saying that those responsible for national security had to consider the development of every means of self-preservation.

In my last conversation with Hans J. Morgenthau before his death, he expressed his concern about the arms build-up of the Soviet Union and its intentions in Afghanistan and the Middle East. My guess would be that Reinhold Niebuhr would have shared this anxiety and concern. As political realists, both thinkers expected to confront shifts and turns in foreign policy. Circumstances influenced his thought. It will not do in tracing Niebuhr's view of the Cold War to imply he was hawkish in the late 1940s and dovish after Vietnam. He was for containment when the momentum of Soviet expansionism was the threat. Whether the issue was negotiation over Germany or the thinning out of forces in the center of Europe, his response was that the time was not ripe; the Communist dynamism had to run its course. Then in the 1950s, he began to write about potential changes in the Soviet system and the decline of revolutionary ardour and he grew more sympathetic to negotiations. What he would say today about a super power which had attained at least nuclear parity while growing increasingly anxious because of encirclement by unfriendly powers is difficult to project. One can only speculate that his answer would be less hawkish and provocative than the early rhetoric of the Reagan administration but stronger than the language of those who proclaim there is neither a military nor political threat from the Soviet Union. Soviet behavior, not a change of heart, influenced the changes in Niebuhr's political analysis.

The late Herbert Butterfield in calling on the West "to take a chance for peace" in relations with the Soviet Union added that only a strong Western leader was capable of such an initiative, a Bismarck or a Kissinger, not a parson who would "give everything away." One reason the little group of international theorists assembled in Washington had respect for Niebuhr was his political toughness. He understood that power was inevitably at the center of the political equation but power for him was more than military strength or force. Power was the health of the whole society or the body politic; force was analogous to the fist. Prestige was also an element of power and resulted in part from a nation's reputation for justice. Given his wider definition, power was a primary determinant of success or failure in foreign policy. He came to accept the reality of power because of the origins of World War II and the failure of the allies to construct an effective balance of power against Hitler.

With all his political toughness and his acceptance of the reality of power, Niebuhr had empathy and compassion for the mass of struggling humanity. His personal philosophy about those in need carried over into his view of less privileged peoples and nations. Niebuhr was ahead of his time in his insistence that for nations on the verge of famine, enfeebled by poor health and ravaged by poverty, democracy was a luxury. But when the people of less developed countries gave tacit consent to the legitimacy of a regime, they were taking a first small step toward government by the consent of the governed. Because he understood the trials and tribulations of poor people, Niebuhr, more than any other political realist, had sympathy for the new nations. Yet he was never as sanguine as the development people with whom I worked in technical assistance that the American example had much relevance for the problems of the Third World. He saw Britain and some of the European nations as having more to offer. Nor did he see the

United Nations as the source of much hope, although he was more optimistic about its economic and social activities than its role as a peace and security agency in the Cold War. He sought to understand the desperate need of peoples whose culture was not his own but whom he recognized as God's children. His compassion left its imprint.

Finally, Niebuhr's uniqueness amongst the theorists in Washington stemmed from his profound understanding of the tragic element in politics and the enduring conflict between morality and power persisting until the end of history. Popular theorists too often have had a penchant for "the quick-fix," embodied for some in an interdependent world, for some in collective security and for others world government. What a contrast to Niebuhr's uncompromisingly realistic view of politics. With all the conversation that went on that day in Washington about deterrence, conflict resolution, peacekeeping, security forces and the United Nations, I retain the memory of Niebuhr's firm and unflinching view of people and politics.

KENNETH W. THOMPSON

DIRECTOR, WILLIAM WHITE BURKETT CENTER
UNIVERSITY OF VIRGINIA
CHARLOTTESVILLE, VIRGINIA

9

Richard Kroner

THE HISTORICAL ROOTS OF NIEBUHR'S THOUGHT

9

THE HISTORICAL ROOTS OF NIEBUHR'S THOUGHT

REINHOLD NIEBUHR is not merely and not primarily a systematic theologian; he is rather, and first of all, an ethical teacher, a religious politician, and most of all a prophetic preacher. The historical roots of his thought are therefore widespread. They embrace not less than the whole tradition of Western civilization. There is hardly any great figure or any important school or movement of the past that has not affected his mind at least to a certain degree and that has not left some traces on his thought. All theological doctrines from that of the apostle Paul to those of Schleiermacher and Ritschl may be called the roots of his thought; but he is also tinged or even formed by the main political and social, scientific and literary upheavals and revolutions. It is therefore extremely difficult to single out of this enormous range certain special thinkers or ideas and to identify them specifically as the historical roots of his own doctrines.

Moreover, a man of genius never depends upon any of his predecessors in a narrow sense; he never imitates models or feels bound by labels and designations, least of all a man so rebellious and radical at heart as Niebuhr. He has never been afraid of any catchword and never has stuck to any slogan. He is rather seeking God and the truth by sincerely investigating the facts at his disposal and by searching himself, as his early "notebook" shows. He adopts whatever he deems right or profound even from sources he dislikes, and he rejects whatever seems wrong or weak to him, even when it comes from authorities recognized or from men esteemed by him. There is no historical personality he would not occasionally criticize or repudiate; there is no historical hero he would not dare to blame, if some aspects or utterances appear blameworthy in his view.

There is no loyalty that would deter him from protest, when a higher loyalty seems to demand a protest.

I

The man of genius does not rely upon any previous opinion, principle, or doctrine; but neither is he without deep historical roots. In the case of a Christian theologian these roots are naturally inseparable from his religious faith. The Bible and especially the New Testament are therefore the central and fundamental sources upon which Niebuhr's thought draws. What he often calls "the ethics of Jesus," that is, the ethics of spiritual love, is the solid ground on which he stands as a religious personality; it is also the goal toward which he moves and toward which he would lead mankind—the absolute measurement of all his judgments and of all his counsels. In this respect he feels in full agreement with the whole tradition of Christianity, although he would, of course, discriminate between the several branches of the body of Christ and their various ethical, social, political, philosophical, and intellectual programs and principles.

What characterizes Niebuhr's Protestantism best is his ever growing emphasis upon those elements in the ethics of Jesus which the great Reformers, particularly Luther, stressed in their campaign against Rome. In this respect his position has been rightly called neo-orthodox, although this catchword is not at all adequate, since his orthodoxy, as has been well noted, is very unorthodox indeed. For in spite of his loyalty to the original spirit of the Gospel and the Reformation theology, Niebuhr is also a thoroughly modern thinker, sensitive to all the social problems of our present situation and fervently seeking for their solution.[1] In this he is not at all a conservative, but rather a revolutionary and progressive Christian leader whose roots are as much in our world of today as they are in the remote past.

Niebuhr's thought is the result of an attempt to apply the standards and principles of the Gospel ethics to the situation in which we find ourselves in the middle of the twentieth century. While on the one hand his ultimate loyalty is to the ancient religious sources, he has always the pressing task of the day before his eyes and seeks

[1] "Ideals are neither challenged nor applied, if they are not finally embodied in concrete proposals for specific situations."—*Does Civilization Need Religion?* p. 119.

the means to discharge this task in the spirit and according to the rules and norms of these sources. Eternity and the instant meet in his mind, and out of this creative tension is born the energy and the courage of everything he preaches and teaches. It is this rare and precious combination which makes his thought and every utterance remarkably prophetic in the Biblical sense of this word. If one compares him with men like Barth and Brunner, he appears to be rooted in the present moment, while they seem to be theoretical and academic dogmatists. He is interested not in purely theoretical questions, but in the solution of urgent social and political problems. To educate, to reform, to guide and to warn Christians everywhere, but especially those in his own country, he uses the great store of his learning and the powerful capacity of his thinking.

The two powers in his breast, the fundamental faith and the temper of modernity, inevitably clash sometimes; his early diary notes show that they produced an earnest combat in his youth. Fundamentalism and rationalism, traditionalism and liberalism, conformism and skepticism fought each other in his mind before he reached the balance of maturity. This inner struggle is one of the springs of his dialectical method, just as this method is the final response to that inner antagonism. Niebuhr is essentially and intrinsically a "tamed cynic" or a converted liberal, as he is also a conservative with a drop of socialism or a Lutheran with an open eye for the reasons why Marxism arose and conquered half of the world today. This *concordia discors* or *coincidentia oppositorum* may be an inheritance of his German ancestors, racial and spiritual, but it may also be the outcome of an accurate insight into the actual forces of reality—it may correspond with the true constitution of reality after all. In any case it testifies to the sincerity as well as to the sagacity of Niebuhr as a thinker.

The double root of his thought makes Niebuhr a representative of the epoch often called the Age of Industrialism or of technical civilization. For the historical understanding of Niebuhr's views it is important to know that his mind was formed during his Detroit years when he preached to a community of industrial workers and became acquainted with the sorrows, hardships, and struggles of that group. His keen realism originated from this experience. It tempered but never obscured his ethical and spiritual idealism. It developed the awareness of life's constant tragedy, but it also mobilized the forces which can overcome or at least mitigate the effect of those ineradicable evils which make for the origin of such tragic sufferings.

In 1925 he wrote in his diary: "It seems pathetic to me that liberalism has too little appreciation of the tragedy of life to understand the cross and orthodoxy insists too much upon the uniqueness of the sacrifice of Christ to make the preaching of the cross effective."[2] The social ills he saw at Detroit taught him that human sin is a far more serious fact than liberalism would think, and a much more mysterious one than rationalism would admit. Niebuhr belongs to the illustrious group of those writers who called attention to the alarming illusions of bourgeois society regarding the moral progress of mankind and its potential capacities in overcoming "original sin." The great poets of the nineteenth century who first recognized those illusions, men like Dostoevsky, Ibsen, Zola, Strindberg, and others, may be classed therefore amongst the historical roots of his thought. Unamuno's stirring book on *The Tragic Sense of Life* also had a considerable influence upon his philosophical views, as had the pessimistic announcement of *The Decline of the West,* by Oswald Spengler, although he of course could not accept the naturalistic trend of its philosophy. Perhaps Melville's *Moby-Dick* also impressed itself upon his mind, since this book also pointed to the tragic features in man's destiny and exposed his self-styled righteousness. Like Melville, Niebuhr is convinced that "all human sin seems so much worse in its consequences than in its intentions."[3]

However, Niebuhr is not a pessimist any more than he is an optimist. In striking contrast to Schopenhauer or Spengler, and more akin to Dostoevsky and Unamuno, Niebuhr firmly believes that there is a position "beyond tragedy." Although man can never rid himself of the "foul taint" of his race, as Kant calls original sin, there is a spiritual power that can reconcile man with himself, when God accepts man, in spite of his default, by the saving grace mediated through Christ. This victorious faith conquers the perplexities of experience, as it is also enlightens the mind encountering the complexities of history. "The moral purpose is at the heart of the mystery"[4]—of this Niebuhr had never the slightest doubt.

[2] *Leaves from the Notebook of a Tamed Cynic,* p. 85.
[3] *Ibid.,* p. 43.
[4] *Ibid.,* p. 55.

II

Among theological thinkers of the nineteenth century Kierkegaard must be mentioned as a powerful source of Niebuhr's theology. Although there was probably not much in Kierkegaard's writings that would have been completely new to Niebuhr, still the brilliance of all that they contained and expressed could not fail to leave traces in a mind as well prepared as that of Niebuhr to receive the message of the Danish poet and prophet. When the antagonism of polar extremes had torn him and had prompted him to seek a unification, in Kierkegaard he met a similar struggle and a bold answer to his questions. The tragic confusions and ambiguities of modern life were not dissolved by the dialectic of Kierkegaard any more than by any other theologian, but they were at least fully understood, and what was more, they were regarded as the necessary presupposition for the understanding of the central truth of the Christian faith.

Niebuhr could therefore hail in Kierkegaard a companion of his own inner plight and of his spiritual uncertainty. What Kierkegaard calls "the paradox" exactly articulated the feeling that the Christian message cannot be rationalized without losing its deepest meaning and its most precious truth. If there were no impossibility of thinking out the eternal verities of faith by means of scientific or speculative reason, if there were no paradox at the bottom of revelation, then the Bible would be the most pointless and indeed worthless of all books and the high regard in which it has been held by so many generations of believers would be the greatest of all riddles; indeed, this would be in itself the greatest paradox. Then the drama of Jesus Christ would be nothing more than a bad satire. If such a cynical view was not acceptable, then the doctrine of Kierkegaard pointed to the true center of faith.

Kierkegaard justified and expressed Niebuhr's own deepest convictions. In him he found arguments triumphantly defeating all theological liberalism without reviving magic or superstition. From him he could learn how to avoid scientific or speculative rationalism without being trapped by obscurantism or fundamentalism. Kierkegaard could reassure him that all the store of modern knowledge about nature and all the subtleties of metaphysical systems did not match the "foolishness" of God any more than ancient philosophy had been able to do.

Niebuhr can be called a Christian existentialist on better grounds than either Jaspers or Marcel, for Jaspers explicitly rejects and denounces religious revelation as a source of truth, while Marcel, though a devout Catholic, makes little use of Scripture in his philosophy. Quite independently of continental "crisis-theology" Niebuhr developed his own scheme of an existential interpretation of Biblical revelation. He was, however, informed by Kierkegaard about the mystery of human selfhood. Kierkegaard, he says, has interpreted the human self "more accurately than any modern, and possibly than any previous, Christian theologian."[5] These words demonstrate how highly he esteems this doctrine. He finds it attractive because it takes into account the dialectical status of man based both upon man's self-alienation from his divine origin and upon his longing for reconciliation with his supreme judge.

The self is mysterious because it transcends itself, although it can never surmount its human limits. It is infinite and yet forever prohibited from re-entering paradise by its own efforts. It is the image of God, and yet corrupted. It is free, and yet in bondage to sinful desires and ambitions. It is consequently ambiguous in all its aspects and manifestations. It has to rely, therefore, on the equally mysterious and yet revealed forgiveness offered by Jesus who is the Christ. With respect to the doctrine of sin, Niebuhr is more in agreement with Kierkegaard than he is with Calvin.[6] Calvin does not recognize the intrinsic inevitability of sin, but regards it as "adventitious," as something accidental, whereas Kierkegaard acknowledges that sin cannot be separated from man, since even Adam was a potential sinner whom temptation disclosed as such. Nevertheless Kierkegaard left room for man's freedom and responsibility in succumbing to temptation; he did not confuse the inevitability of sin with a natural causality or an ontological necessity. Sin can be imputed to man only because his will is free, but his power to resist temptation is finite; so he falls, not because he lacks freedom of decision, but rather because he owns this freedom but does not own sufficient ability to withstand the lure of the devil. Kierkegaard renewed this ancient doctrine of sin, but in an ingenious modern fashion, by introducing a psychological "explanation" which Niebuhr accepted.

Ultimately original sin is mysterious; no doctrine can ever account for the fact that man is a potential or actual sinner. But even so,

[5] *The Nature and Destiny of Man*, I, iii. [6] *Ibid.*, I, 243.

Kierkegaard argued that there is a psychological explanation concerning the condition under which man falls. This explanation does not make sin a natural necessity, but it does to a certain degree comprehend its origin. The condition rests upon man's double nature as both animal and spirit. This double nature causes a state of inner uncertainty or a lack of inner balance which Kierkegaard calls "anxiety." This instability exposes man to temptations. As an animal man is like any other creature, prompted by his nature to seek the fulfillment of his impulses and desires. As a spirit he is called upon to be perfect and holy as God is. Stretched between the two poles of his existence, man lives in dread because he feels that his natural resources are not sufficient in all cases to subordinate the animal to the spirit within him. This anxiety is the soil from which sin easily sprouts.

Niebuhr also found his dialectical thinking confirmed by Kierkegaard. Whereas Hegel had used dialectic in order to conceive the Absolute, Kierkegaard used it in order to demonstrate that the Absolute can never be conceived by human reason. In this respect Kierkegaard was, and Niebuhr consequently also is, though only indirectly, a successor of Kant. Hegel believed in the eventual solution of the dialectical contradictions in a rounded system. Kierkegaard derided and scorned this attempt. Those contradictions, he agreed, do not exist in the mind of God but only in our mind because it is finite. But the impossibility of solving the ultimate contradictions is spiritually acceptable, although it is logically frustrating. For reason encounters an insurmountable barrier when it tries to comprehend ultimate truth, and this barrier in turn makes faith legitimate and necessary. In its own way faith is the adequate response of a sinful creature toward his holy creator and supreme judge.

Niebuhr also agrees with Kierkegaard's doctrine of the "leap." There is an infinite distance between man and God which can be traversed by God only, and not by man. This leap makes revelation necessary as well as comprehensible. On the part of man only despair and contrition can prepare for the reception of forgiving grace and the transformation of his sinful state into membership in the kingdom of divine love.

In more recent times Niebuhr seems to assume a somewhat more critical attitude toward Kierkegaard's doctrine of the discontinuity between man's understanding and things divine. In a chapter of his latest book[7] he emphasizes the perils of overstressing the incoherence and irrationality of the Christian faith in its relation to the facts of nature and history. The Existentialists have made manifest this danger by abusing Kierkegaard's theory of the "Absurd" to validate their own fantastic views. "Kierkegaard," he argues here, "exploits the inner contradiction within man as being a free spirit and a contingent object too simply as the basis of faith." He goes too far in deducing from the impossibility of understanding God's transcendent nature the "passionate subjectivity" of religious truth. Under this cover all kinds of error and arbitrariness may intrude into the interpretation of the ultimate issues in social and political life. In this connection Niebuhr severely criticizes Karl Barth's position.

III

There is another thinker who preceded Kierkegaard in many respects and who has also to be reckoned as a predecessor of Niebuhr: Blaise Pascal. His profound doctrine of man expressed in the style and scientific manner of another period and of another religious creed are nevertheless ideas akin to those of Kierkegaard. He too stressed the paradox of God and man in their relation to each other; he too pointed to the contradictory nature of human selfhood in his famous statements about the greatness and smallness of man's intellectual capacity to know the All and yet to be like nothing in comparison with an infinite intellect. It is this Pascal whom Niebuhr likes to quote and whom he highly regards. It is the Pascal who so brilliantly characterizes man's strength and weakness at the same time, who demonstrates that the glory of man is matched by his misery, his nobility by his basic corruption. Niebuhr's Pascal is the penetrating critic of reason who discovered and laid bare the limits of human knowledge long before Kant did so, and who propagated a logic of the heart which would interpret the significance of spiritual love in all matters concerning ultimate truth.

Niebuhr's Pascal is the man who has written: "There are only two kinds of men, the righteous who believe themselves sinners; the rest, sinners who believe themselves righteous," an apothegm about which Niebuhr remarks: "Pascal does not fully appreciate, at least as far as this statement is concerned, how infinite may be the shades of awareness of guilt from the complacency of those who are spirit-

[7] *Christian Realism and Political Problems,* pp. 75ff., 191f.

ually blind to the sensitivity of the saint who knows that he is not a saint."[8] This remark shows in what sense Pascal may be called a root of Niebuhr's thought and at the same time in what sense Niebuhr has refined Pascal's thought.

Niebuhr's Pascal is the ethical thinker who knows it is divine grace alone that can save man from pride, and not discourses on humility which "are a source of pride to the vain and of humility in the humble."[9] He is the forerunner of Kierkegaard in that he anticipated the insight into the logical absurdity of the doctrine of original sin.

From Pascal the lineage of Niebuhr's spiritual ancestry leads back to the great Reformers. The dependence upon Reformation theology is evident in every book and every line Niebuhr has written. As his church unites the tradition of the Lutheran with that of the Reformed Church, so his thought unites what he deems true in both Luther and Calvin. It would be difficult to decide which of the two he regards more highly or from whom he more frequently or more heavily draws inspiration. To neither does he subscribe unconditionally. He agrees, however, basically with both of them.

Luther more than Calvin was a mystical and a dialectical thinker who repudiated rationalism to such an extent that he could assert: "Nothing more pernicious and Satanic has been or ever will be on earth" than—Aristotle! Although Niebuhr most certainly would not consent to such a statement, there is a definite Lutheran trend in his writings. On the other hand he feels much more affinity with the political and social views of Calvin. Even in his first publication, *Does Civilization Need Religion?*, he confronts the two reformers and describes Calvinism as more *weltfreundlich* (dealing with secular affairs in a sympathetic mood) in contrast to Luther's *Weltfeindlichkeit* (hostility to the world), and leans to the first, although he sees the merits of the second also. This corresponds to his central attitude which seeks a "point of contact" between the ethic of Jesus and the needs of modern society, and yet preserves the Pauline position which he sees revived by Luther more than by Calvin. "Religion is at once the necessary part and the potential foe of moral life."[10] Or as he phrases the same idea in a later book: "The

[8] *The Nature and Destiny of Man*, I, 257.

[9] Pascal, *Pensées*, no. 377; *The Nature and Destiny of Man*, I, 202.

[10] P. 116. The most explicit discussion of the Reformers' theology is included in *The Nature and Destiny of Man*, Vol. II, Chaps. VII and VIII.

kingdom of God, in his view [the view of Jesus], will be established not by the goodness of loving men but by the grace of God. Yet there are glimpses of the eternal and the absolute in human nature."[11]

IV

Tracing Niebuhr's historical roots further back, we must pay attention to Augustine, who is in many respects the predecessor of the Reformers as well as of Pascal and Kierkegaard, and therefore also of Niebuhr, who is the present representative of this illustrious series of thinkers. "It must be recognized that no Christian theologian has ever arrived at a more convincing statement of the relevance and distance between the human and divine than he," says Niebuhr with respect to Augustine. "All the subsequent statements of the essential character of the image of God in man are indebted to him," he continues, thereby expressing his own indebtedness. Niebuhr, like this great ancestor of his, is a Christian philosopher of man in the first place and a systematic theologian only in the second place. Perhaps our cultural situation today has some resemblance to that of the Patristic Roman Father. Like him, we live at the edge of tremendous upheavals—social, political, cultural, and spiritual. Like him we face the degeneration of a splendid epoch which has produced many classical works of art and which has enriched mankind by an enormous progress in scientific knowledge. Like him we must fear that this epoch has come to an end and that the future will not be as creative in this respect as the past has been. Like him we believe that religious life was dim in those creative centuries and that only now have we come to see the truly spiritual values. Like him we hope that the grace of God will allow us to transform the world in the direction toward which the Gospel leads mankind. Like Augustine, Niebuhr would apply the ethic of Jesus to the new tasks and necessities arising out of the new situation. The necessity both of negation and of reaffirmation is the reason that he holds tenaciously to the Augustinian thesis that "the world is always something of an armistice between opposing factions."[12]

Augustine did not stress the paradoxical element within Chris-

[11] *Reflections on the End of an Era,* p. 283. See also *The Irony of American History,* pp. 49ff.

[12] *Discerning the Signs of the Times,* p. 187. See also *The Nature and Destiny of Man,* II, 272f.

tianity as much as Pascal and Kierkegaard did; even so, it is obtrusive enough in the *City of God.* The state is a devilish institution, but it is nevertheless also an instrument in the hand of God. This Augustinian note dominates Niebuhr's thought. Like Augustine, Niebuhr would accommodate Christian love to the necessities of political life. Although he, not less than his Roman ancestor, insists upon the infinite chasm between God and the world, he would constantly seek ways and means to overcome that chasm and to propose measures for a better world.

Niebuhr feels, I would presume, the deepest affinity for one feature in Augustine which has often been called his "inwardness"—that participation of the heart in his thinking, that primacy of faith in his philosophy; in other words, that existential trend which enabled Augustine to lay stress upon Biblical concepts instead of expressing those concepts in speculative terms. Augustine applied the "logic of the heart" before Pascal proclaimed this logic as the only one well adapted to the exigencies of theological problems.

Niebuhr especially praises Augustine's doctrine of sin. While Augustine, he says, failed to understand the Pauline doctrine of grace, he anticipated the Reformers' conception of sin. He realized "that it is not finiteness but the 'false eternal' of sin . . . which brings confusion and evil into history."[13]

As the roots of Kierkegaard point back to Pascal and the Reformers and finally to Augustine, so the roots of Augustine must be sought in the theology of the apostle Paul, where we therefore have to seek the deepest roots of Niebuhr's theology also. When he preached (for the first time, I suppose) on the word of the apostle: "We preach Christ crucified, to the Jews a stumbling-block and to the Gentiles foolishness, but to them that are called, the power of God and the wisdom of God," he put down the note: "I don't think I ever felt greater joy in preaching a sermon."[14] And one of his more recent essays[15] ends with another word of Paul often quoted by Niebuhr in sermons with great fervor and enthusiasm: "Whether we live, we live unto the Lord; and whether we die, we die unto the Lord: whether we live therefore, or die, we are the Lord's."

The subtlety of Niebuhr's analysis, the penetrating acuteness, the

[13] *The Nature and Destiny of Man,* I, 158.

[14] *Leaves from the Notebook of a Tamed Cynic,* p. 83.

[15] "Religion and Modern Knowledge," in *Man's Destiny in Eternity,* The Garvin Lectures (Boston: The Beacon Press, 1949).

sagacity of his thinking, the predilection for antithetical concepts testify to the similarity between the logical method of Paul and Niebuhr. The basic Paulinism of his thought enables him to strike down the pretensions of modern ideologies, which seek to reform society and state, as if the injustice and misery inherent in human institutions and laws could be erased by a change of economic or racial politics. This Paulinism shows him that although reforms are necessary and desirable, they can improve the conditions of men only if they are undertaken in the spirit of humility and in the conviction that nothing can endure without the help of God, and that the fundamental ambiguities and confusions are too deep-seated in man ever to be overcome by his own efforts alone. Paul appears in Niebuhr's mirror, therefore, as far as the historical scene of cultural and political achievements is concerned, as a gloomy prophet. The Cross, as propounded by Paul, is according to Niebuhr "a scandal from the standpoint of any common sense or rational ethic which seeks to establish the good in human relations by some kind of, or discrimination between, competing interests."[16]

V

Finally let me add a word about Niebuhr's relation to Greek antiquity. Without any doubt his thought and diction could never have taken shape if they were not rooted in this ancient soil of our civilization. In spite of the great contrast between paganism and Christianity which is so central in Niebuhr's work and personality, and although Niebuhr is in mind and heart an ardent disciple of Christ and Paul, still he is not untouched by the Greek inheritance of our culture. Ever since the Renaissance resuscitated the ideals and ideas of antiquity, the classical element cannot be wholly eliminated from any profound thought uttered in the Western world.

It is the paradoxical feature of Protestantism since its rise that on the one hand it repudiated the spirit of the Renaissance; on the other, however, it was itself at least partly rooted in this very spirit, and is in some degree its outcome. Both Reformation and Renaissance have in common that they opposed the medieval synthesis of ancient culture and Gospel, of Romanism and Christ, of Caesar and God. But the reasons that they opposed that synthesis were contrary: the Renaissance wanted to renew ancient culture set free from the bondage to Christ, while the Reformation wanted to renew

[16] *Faith and History*, p. 171.

the Gospel disengaged from the fetters of Greek philosophy and from the imperialism of the Roman Church. Nevertheless, the Reformation itself took its strength, at least insofar as historical circumstances are concerned, from the individualism of the Renaissance, its new-born sense of freedom and its passion to go back to the sources.

The thought of Reinhold Niebuhr reflects this dialectical situation more than the work of most other Christian theologians because of his profound sincerity and self-criticism. He knows very well that there is this duality in his spiritual inheritance, although of course he would always subordinate Athens to Jerusalem, philosophy to theology, the affairs of the world to the counsel of God's prophets and the ethic of Jesus.

If I am not mistaken, there is a development in Niebuhr's thought in this respect: there is an ever growing stress upon the Pauline aspects and prospects, or an ever increasing emphasis on the ideals of the Reformation in contrast to those of the Renaissance. His earlier books seem to be less outspoken in rejecting secular considerations than are the later ones. In *Does Civilization Need Religion?* (1927) the dialectical, paradoxical, existential tones and overtones are not yet as apparent as they are in the period of his mature works. His faith and thought in the earlier period are still somehow tinged by elements of cultural and intellectual tendencies which later vanish. In the beginning of his career he still believed that metaphysics is an indispensable factor in or for religion, that the ethics of love is a kind of idealism, that there is no chasm between religious and poetic imagination, and that Christology is altogether outmoded.

It is true that all these features are from the beginning counterbalanced and offset by others which intimate the future development in advance, by slightly "orthodox" leanings and sturdily defended Pauline notes. But in 1928 he can write what he would probably disavow today: "In my creed the divine madness [a Platonic reminiscence!] of a gospel of love is qualified by considerations of moderation which I have called Aristotelian, but which unfriendly critics might call opportunistic."[17] The Greek vein of his sympathies was more clearly seen at that time than it is today. But even so, it has never disappeared completely. He will always, I think, preserve a vestige of what he once called "Greek caution."

[17] *Leaves from the Notebook of a Tamed Cynic,* p. 195.

Although Niebuhr knows well that Greek wisdom is foolishness in the eyes of God, and that Greek strength is weakness, nevertheless he also knows that Western civilization and Western Christianity are somehow bound up with that foolishness and weakness. He still knows and appreciates Aristotelian "moderation," but he no longer has to fear that critics may call his position opportunistic, since "orthodoxy" has become so prevalent in the meantime that the slogan "neo-orthodoxy" is now more to be feared.

Whereas Kierkegaard had to protect himself against the reproach of the world by writing incognito, Niebuhr disclosed from the start frankly and frequently his intimate apprehensions and inclinations. He could do so because there is no inner split in his personality, for all his stress upon human ambiguities and paradoxes. His historical roots and his own individuality are in full harmony, which is to a great extent the result of his own labor and conscience. He need not suppress the Greek element within his mind, but can admit it freely, because he is not an "ecclesiastical dogmatician" but a cultivated Christian of the twentieth century who has succeeded in bringing about a personal synthesis of Greek wisdom and Christian devotion.

I wonder whether Socrates, the greatest representative of irony the world has ever seen, does not also belong—in a hidden and subtle sense—among the spiritual ancestors of Niebuhr. In any case Niebuhr's view of man, in its deeply ironical, humble, and humanely pious character, is not altogether remote from the mild humor and the self-abnegating purity of heart in that strange Athenian who anticipated by centuries some of the ethical rules of the Gospel. I wonder too whether the Greek tragedians did not also convey something to Niebuhr that lives again in his comprehension of man—some insight into that inevitable tragedy of man which the Christian has to acknowledge in order to understand fully the darkness and the brightness of the Cross on which Jesus hung.

Richard Kroner

Temple University
Philadelphia, Pennsylvania

10

Daniel D. Williams

NIEBUHR AND LIBERALISM

10

NIEBUHR AND LIBERALISM

Every theologian interprets the Christian faith from a standpoint in which his own cultural heritage plays a formative rôle. Reinhold Niebuhr's theology has arisen within American Christianity in its liberal period. But he is our foremost critic of "liberal Christianity." No theme recurs more frequently in his writing than the polemic against "liberal culture" and against the liberal Christianity which he regards as having capitulated to that culture. It is due more to Niebuhr's influence than to that of any other single thinker that liberalism in America has come to a period of radical self-examination. In consequence, for many there now must be a re-establishment of faith on other than liberal foundations.

Niebuhr's evaluation of liberalism is not exclusively negative. He sees modern liberalism as the heir of the discovery of creative possibilities in human nature in the Renaissance, and he has stated the central problem of his theology as an attempt to combine the insights of the Renaissance and the Reformation.[1]

The fundamental problems which Niebuhr sets out to solve are the characteristic problems of liberalism: the discovery of the meaning of the Bible beyond a literalistic orthodoxy, the establishment of the practice of tolerance, the relating of the Gospel to cultural movements and the search for its intelligibility in relation to human experience, the discovery of the theological basis of democracy. Certainly these are the problems which liberal theology has raised and left for the "post-liberal" work of theologians such as Niebuhr. When we examine now Niebuhr's relation to liberalism, we do not hold up "liberal theology" or "the liberal spirit" as the norm by which his thought is to be tested. Christian faith transcends every culture in which it may be expressed. No theology of great stature

[1] *The Nature and Destiny of Man*, II, 207.

like that of Niebuhr's can be forced into the position of dependence upon a single cultural outlook. Still, it remains true that his thought bears a special relationship to liberalism, for his early thought was formed by liberalism, and he has developed his own theology largely by working out his criticism of liberal presuppositions. Therefore, by examining his relationship to liberalism we have one way of getting at the meaning of his theology. Further, an inquiry into Niebuhr's critique of liberalism raises some of the questions which to me, at least, remain unanswered in his own theology.

I propose, then, to ask what Niebuhr means by liberalism and liberal Christianity, to summarize briefly his evaluation of them, and then to ask what light this view of liberalism throws upon the method and content of his theology.

I. NIEBUHR'S METHOD OF INTERPRETING LIBERALISM

When we ask what Niebuhr means by the "liberalism" and "liberal Christianity" he criticizes, we have to take account of his method of characterizing broad cultural movements and theological positions. He views the history of human thought as exhibiting a series of "types" of outlook. He arranges these according to certain key concepts and problems in which he is interested. For example, he distinguishes between "classical" and "modern" cultures according to their views of time, and contrasts both of these with the "Biblical" view of time. Again, he classifies modern philosophies as "vitalistic" or "idealistic" as they find their principle of meaning in nature or in spirit. Thus Niebuhr is not so much concerned to trace nuances of meaning in different philosophies, or to work out the complex lines of historical development. He is rather an apologist and critic who tries to get directly at the basic principles by which various faiths grasp the meaning of life.

This "typological" method seems to me one of the major reasons that Niebuhr's cultural criticism has been so effective. His great genius in using the method permits him to go swiftly to the heart of a vast and complex cultural movement, to lift out the central idea which gives it its drive, and which also betrays in many cases its weakness. Though the method produces a considerable oversimplification, it permits the discovery and concise statement of fundamental issues. Its disadvantage is that it permits Niebuhr to deal with the point of view he is criticizing by using its most exaggerated, and sometimes even its most fatuous, expressions to represent the entire position. It is so important to understand this method as Niebuhr uses it in dealing with liberalism that I illustrate the point by quoting one paragraph in which Niebuhr sums up the kind of liberal Protestant faith which he rejects:

> The mystery of creation is resolved in the evolutionary concept. "Some call it evolution and others call it God." The Bible becomes a library, recording in many books the evolutionary ascent of man to God. Sin becomes the provisional inertia of impulses inherited from Neanderthal man against the wider purposes of mind. Christ is the symbol of history itself, as in Hegel. The relation of the Kingdom of God to the moral perplexities and ambiguities of history is resolved in utopia. The strict distinction between justice and love in Catholic thought is marvelously precise and shrewd compared with the general identification of the *agape* of the New Testament with the "community-building capacities of human sympathy." (Rauschenbusch) This reduction of the ethical meaning of the scandal of the Cross, namely, sacrificial love to the dimensions of simple mutuality imparts an air of sentimentality to all liberal Protestant social and political theories.[2]

Now this paragraph tells us what Niebuhr sees in liberalism, especially its limitations. But what liberalism is he looking at? Hegel cannot be reduced to these dimensions. Neither can Rauschenbusch. Niebuhr himself once refers to Albrecht Ritschl as "the most authoritative exponent of liberal Christianity."[3] But there is not a single statement in the above paragraph which can possibly be said to represent Ritschl's view. He could hardly be thinking of Ritschl here, nor could he be thinking of his own teacher, D. C. Macintosh, whose *Social Religion* he has also characterized as a representative statement of liberal Christianity. His statements would have to be radically qualified if he tried to document them from the thought of his late colleague Eugene W. Lyman or that of Robert Calhoun. He rarely discusses in any detail the thought of Josiah Royce or William Ernest Hocking, both exponents of versions of liberal Christian faith. In short, the "liberal Protestantism" which Niebuhr is getting at is not to be found in this "pure form" in the more adequate expressions of liberal theology. I do not mean that it does not exist. It certainly does exist in naïve simplicity in much popular

[2] "Coherence, Incoherence, and Christian Faith," *Journal of Religion*, Vol. XXXI, No. 3 (July, 1951), p. 162.

[3] *The Nature and Destiny of Man*, I, 178.

Christianity, and in the extreme views of a few theologians. The point is that Niebuhr here gives exaggerated statement to what he regards as the essential tendency and outcome of all liberal faith. He exposes the heart of the issue about moral progress in history which is the central difficulty of liberalism. The danger in the exaggeration is that some of the truth for which liberalism contended may be overlooked. I believe this to be the case in Niebuhr's critique of liberalism. But first we must see what his main theses about it are.

II. WHAT NIEBUHR MEANS BY "LIBERALISM"

Our main concern is with "liberal Christianity," but Niebuhr sees liberal Christianity as having very close connections with liberal culture, so we must examine his characterization of both.

Liberal culture is essentially the spirit and outlook of the middle classes in the modern period. It is a phenomenon of the ascendancy of the bourgeois. The most characteristic idea of the liberal is his faith in historical progress. The values which are usually placed foremost as criteria of progress are individual freedom and the practice of tolerance.[4] John Locke, John Stuart Mill, and John Dewey are among the typical interpreters of the liberal faith in its widest context.

Niebuhr sees liberal Christianity as a phase of this cultural liberalism. He says, "Christian liberalism is spiritually dependent upon bourgeois liberalism and is completely lost when its neat evolutionary process toward an ethical historical goal is suddenly engulphed in social catastrophe."[5] The liberal faith is the child of the age of reason, and Thomas Jefferson is one of its most characteristic prophets.[6]

Behind this characterization of liberalism as a function of class structure is Niebuhr's indebtedness to the Marxist analysis of society. Especially in his *Reflections on the End of an Era* he tends to look at liberal politics and social philosophy with the presuppositions of a modified Marxism. He never accepted the Marxist oversimplification of its picture of society; but he found a large element of truth in it, and he accepted its catastrophic view of history. In the light of this doctrine of historical conflict, he criticized liberal programs which hoped to avoid class conflict through amelioration. At the same time Niebuhr has always regarded dogmatic Marxism

[4] *Reflections on the End of an Era,* p. 88. [5] *Ibid.,* p. 135.
[6] *An Interpretation of Christian Ethics,* p. 170.

as falling into the characteristic errors of liberal culture when it absolutizes the rôle of one class as the bearer of perfect justice and looks forward to a utopia in which all historical injustices and contradictions will be overcome.

Christian liberalism then for Niebuhr is that phase of modern Christianity which has taken over from the Enlightenment a conception of man's goodness and his potentiality for moral improvement, and which has reinterpreted the Gospel according to rational methods, and with a system of values which includes individualism, tolerance, and progressive achievement of a free and just order of society. Wherever we encounter the belief that "all social relations are being brought progressively under the law of Christ," and wherever we see the Christian Gospel expressed as a moral pronouncement which can be made intelligible as a purely rational ethical ideal, there we have encountered the liberal Christian spirit as Niebuhr sees it.[7]

III. THE CRITICISM OF LIBERALISM

"The real basis for all the errors of liberalism is its erroneous estimate of human nature."[8] This is the key point of Niebuhr's attack. Faith in man's reason, in his goodness, and in his power to overcome the limitations of existence has led liberalism to a view of the progressive fulfillment of good in history which simply does not conform to the facts of experience. "There is not a single bit of evidence to prove that good triumphs over evil in this constant development of history," declares Niebuhr.[9]

When we seek the explanation of the naïve optimism of liberalism, we are led by Niebuhr to several important historical insights and judgments. In the first place there is the expansive period of modern economic and political life in which new freedoms were won by the rising classes. Men in the more favored groups at least

[7] *Moral Man and Immoral Society*, p. xxi.

One of Niebuhr's characteristically pungent descriptions of Christian liberalism is the following:

"This 'pure Gospel' which we claim to have rescued from the obscurantists and dogmatists, including St. Paul, is little more than eighteenth-century rationalism and optimism, compounded with a little perfectionism, derived from the sanctificationist illusions of sectarian Christianity" ("Christian Moralism in America," *Radical Religion*, Vol. 5, No. 1, 1940, p. 19).

[8] *Reflections on the End of an Era*, p. 48.

[9] "Ten Years That Shook My World," *Christian Century* (April 26, 1939), p. 544.

were easily persuaded that the possibilities of overcoming threats to man's happiness or success were unlimited. The liberal mind usually went on to trace the evil in human life to specific causes which time or effort could eliminate, such as outworn and unjust institutions, or the remnants of animal nature yet to be sloughed off; or, in the case of the Marxist, all evils were derived from the character of the economic order. Niebuhr sees all this as a naïve judgment on the historical realities, for there is nothing to prevent new sources of evil from emerging.

Even more important than the optimistic social climate is the error in the understanding of the nature of man. The problem of evil in human nature lies precisely in the character of man as a being who in reason and imagination can transcend particular historical circumstance. This higher capacity of man offers no guarantee of victory over evil. It is the source of the profoundest evils in human life. It is in the corruptions of the life of the spirit that sin lies. Man who sees beyond himself becomes anxious about his ultimate being and security. He falls into the sin of identifying some particular interest or vitality with God, or he seeks redemption by trying to establish himself and his partial values more securely than in fact they can be established.

Here Niebuhr's critique of liberalism reaches its prophetic height. He sees the liberal spirit in both its secular and its Christian forms as essentially a sentimental obscuring of the truth. But behind that sentimentality there lies that which the Christian Gospel enables us to expose: man's sin of thinking of himself as possessing disinterested good will and as able to solve his problems, perhaps with the help of God, but with progressive expansion of human powers. Thus man denies his dependence on the mercy of God who transcends all historical processes, and whose work of redemption must be fulfilled at the end of history or "beyond history." Liberal optimism has the sin of pride in it.[10]

In refuting specific liberal claims Niebuhr points out how ambiguous are the instruments and powers in which men have put their faith. Scientific knowledge does not give man control over himself. It can become the means of inhuman exploitation and the imposition of tyrannical power. The development of high civilization does not remove the threat of fanatical tribal idolatry. Consider the emergence of the Nazis in Germany. The development of demo-

[10] *Faith and History*, p. 85.

cratic processes of persuasion is extremely valuable; but it may lead men to feel that they are free from the temptations and brutalities of conflict when actually they have only covered them up. One reason modern men have felt more "humane" is that they have transferred their vices to larger and larger groups.[11] Beneath the façade of peaceable economic relations there lies a struggle for power which may erupt into overt conflict.

Neither secular nor Christian liberalism has really understood man because of their failure to see the full dimension of his being. Niebuhr sees man as rooted in nature, subject to the power and vicissitudes of finite existence. Man's mind enables him to transcend time to a limited degree, and it permits him to organize his experience into wider and wider circles of coherence. Yet mind is not the full height of man. Man transcends *himself;* this is spirit. He is aware of a mystery beyond all rationally determinable coherence. He can imagine possibilities beyond the given order of things. The self then is a three-dimensional reality. Niebuhr turns this analysis against liberal faith in reason. It is just because man lives both in the depths of nature and on the heights of spirit that his deepest anxieties arise. The corruption of the self affects the whole man. He falls into the sins of pride or sensuality precisely to escape the threats which his peculiar situation involves. Liberals generally have assumed that mind can lift man beyond the frustrations of nature, and seize control of history. But they forget that mind itself is limited in its reach, and is subject to the corruptions of fear and pride.

Niebuhr's interpretation of the liberal confidence in reason is so fundamental for understanding both his criticism of liberalism and his own theological method that we need to examine an additional aspect of it here. One of the themes which runs through his work is that liberal culture has not understood the organic unities of life because reason does not offer an adequate grasp of organic processes. He makes this point in connection with his analysis of individualism in liberal culture. "The organic character of the individual's relation to society can be comprehended and illumined by an adequate mythology, but hardly by rationalism, for reason mechanizes human relations."[12] The rationalistic approach leaves the in-

[11] I heard Dr. Niebuhr make this point in a lecture. I do not know whether he has written it.

[12] *Reflections on the End of an Era*, p. 93.

dividual rootless. He is bound to his neighbor only by mechanically defined contracts which envisage no deeper participation in concrete community. Reason in ethics reduces all moral issues to a matter of calculated prudence. This is what Niebuhr means by the failure of "mutuality" as an ethical ideal. In "mutuality" the ethical goal leads to the satisfaction of the other's interests only so long as mine are taken care of. Liberalism therefore misses the meaning of sacrificial love in the Gospel. It reduces the Cross to a "success story." It cannot understand the radical giving of the self beyond any visible or historical reward.[13]

Niebuhr's judgment on rationalism in ethics has therefore an intimate connection with his insistence that our interpretation of the Christian faith must keep a tension between faith and reason in which the ultimate mysteries of faith are expressed in mythical symbols, for only in myths of creation and redemption has Christian faith been able to express its truth and yet preserve the realm of mystery and the appreciation of organic realities within and beyond the coherences and processes of nature.[14]

Liberal theory has led to one very nearly fatal consequence in Western civilization, as Niebuhr sees it. Those who rely on rational persuasion have weakened themselves before the attacks of the forces which would destroy the free society. He charges liberals with failing to realize the significance of Hitler's movement, because there was nothing in the liberal view of history which comprehended the possibility of a Hitler.

This point about liberal reliance on persuasion is of course directly related to Niebuhr's rejection of his early commitment to pacifism. He has come to analyze the problem of power in history in terms which lead to a complete rejection of the pacifist ethic as a sufficient strategy for dealing with social problems. In *Moral Man and Immoral Society* he argued that the refusal of exploited classes to use coercive means betrayed society into the hands of oligarchs. Bourgeois liberalism contributed to the betrayal by putting too great reliance on the power of rational ideals to cure social injustice. The error of Christian liberalism here was doubly serious, for it "appropriates the prestige of the religiously inspired absolute ethic of Jesus for the ideals of prudence which have developed in a com-

[13] *Moral Man and Immoral Society*, p. 263.

[14] "The Truth in Myths" in *The Nature of Religious Experience* (New York: Harper and Brothers, 1937).

mercial civilization." Niebuhr is here thinking of the way in which the claim of absolute disinterestedness may cloak private interest and satisfy the privileged by reducing Christian ethics to a "prudent and utilitarian altruism."[15]

Much of Niebuhr's polemic against the social policy of Christian liberalism is directed at Christian pacifism. He recognizes, of course, that not all Christian liberalism has taken the pacifist position; hence I shall not dwell here on his arguments against pacifism. It is probably true that some of the extreme things Niebuhr says against liberalism in ethics are colored by the fact that he is thinking primarily of liberal pacifism. He does believe that no Christian liberalism has really resolved its dilemma between reliance on the persuasive power of ideals and the necessities of coercion in securing justice. Christian liberalism has not known how to relate its view of the ethic of Jesus as a program for direct social action to the necessities of social existence. Hence it makes pragmatic concessions to the use of violence, or tries futilely to justify strategies of non-violence on practical grounds. Niebuhr believes that the liberal position actually came to bankruptcy in dealing with the ethical problem.[16] It has simply not understood the full dimensions of the Christian's ethical situation as he stands between the absolute ethic of Jesus and the requirements of social strategy in a sinful world.

In sum, Niebuhr sees all liberalism as lacking in depth of understanding of who man is and what his problems are. "The liberal soul," he says, "is pedestrian and uninspired. Its moral philosophy is always utilitarian and practical. It avoids the fanaticism and passion of the servants of the absolute and goes about its business to tame life and bring larger and larger areas of human society into its circles of humane good will and prudent reciprocity."[17]

IV. THE WORTH OF LIBERALISM

Niebuhr argues against liberalism from a broad base of rational and ethical criticism, as well as from strictly Christian premises. He does not affirm a simple Christian orthodoxy or an exclusively Biblical norm against liberalism. He argues from within a framework which is largely dominated by the liberal problems, including the relation of reason to revelation and the relation of the Gospel to

[15] *Reflections on the End of an Era*, pp. 268–269.
[16] *An Interpretation of Christian Ethics*, p. 179.
[17] *Reflections on the End of an Era*, p. 261.

social ethics. He sees positive values in the liberal outlook, and his own method is dependent on the liberal achievements.

There are values in the liberal spirit of tolerance. Reason has its rights and its constructive function. Niebuhr says, "The extension of rational justice and the encouragement of a tolerant attitude toward life is the very essence of liberalism."[18] Coupled with tolerance is liberalism's outstanding achievement of the "discovery and affirmation of the rights of the individual."[19] Reason has played a part in the discovery of the worth of the individual and is necessary to the achievement of tolerable justice in human relations. The very reliance on reason does tend to achieve something of a balance of power.[20] The liberal spirit in morals is of most value in working out pragmatic adjustments within a fairly stable situation. It does not know so well how to cope with major upheavals and conflicts.

Christian liberalism rightfully used scientific reason to destroy crude supernaturalism in the understanding of nature. Science discloses a realm of law in the processes of nature, and theology must respect this aspect of the truth in its doctrine of God's action. Liberalism applied the scientific historical method to the records of Christian origins. This was necessary as a criticism of pre-scientific supernaturalism, and it had important ethical results. It saved the Christian mind from the error of making an inflexible and infallible law out of the historically conditioned precepts in the Biblical record. Thus liberalism recognized the law of love as the final norm for Christian ethics; and it made possible in principle the criticism of every historical dogma and ethical system.[21] Niebuhr's own critical method in theology which allows him to reject the absolutizing of any single theological doctrine is certainly in the liberal spirit, even though his ultimate presuppositions about Christian knowledge look for truth beyond the realm of rational intelligibility.

Most important of all in Niebuhr's positive appreciation of liberalism is his assertion that liberalism was right in declaring the relevance of Christian love to social issues even though it understood this relationship far too simply. He acknowledges a "prophetic element in the passion for justice in eighteenth and nineteenth century moralism."[22] Niebuhr is never more blunt than he becomes

[18] *Ibid.*, p. 252. [19] *Ibid.*, p. 88.
[20] *Moral Man and Immoral Society*, p. 237.
[21] "Ten Years That Shook My World," *loc. cit.*
[22] Title essay in *Christian Faith and the Common Life* (Chicago: Willett Clark & Colby, 1938), p. 91.

when he criticizes theological ethics which try to keep the realm of law and social order sharply separated from the imperatives of the Gospel. He once wrote against a view which upheld such a separation: "Any judge who seeks the aid of psychiatric specialists to understand the causes of the criminal's wrong doing and thus to mete out punishment with an eye to his reformation is closer to the Kingdom of God than this theological pessimism."[23]

This positive appreciation of the worth of relative moral gains in social action enters directly into Niebuhr's conception of the authority of the Biblical revelation. The issue is whether Christian ethics is to be allowed to derive some supplemental insight from cultural standards. Niebuhr believes that Christianity must recognize such insight and allow it to supplement the ultimate standards derived from the Biblical faith. One of the essays which reveals most vividly Niebuhr's appreciation of cultural values comes in his discussion with Karl Barth about the authority of the Bible. Niebuhr argues that the exclusively Biblical approach to every moral issue which he finds in Barth prohibits any attempt even to discuss Christian ethics with non-Christians. It leads to a "torturing" of Biblical texts to prove that certain newly discovered values, democratic ideals for example, were there in the Bible all the time. Niebuhr declares that it was modern secular culture which first granted women full recognition as persons. "There are certain insights about the political order which come to us in the same way from modern secularism, despite its libertarian or equalitarian tendencies."[24] He concludes that the Christian's appropriation of the mind of Christ requires a continual analysis of values discovered in human experience. In the end all cultural insights and ethical systems raise problems which cannot be solved apart from the standpoint of faith in God's sovereignty over history which is revealed finally in the Cross. Once this truth of faith is apprehended, we may be brought to a fuller coherence in our understanding of life, though it is the kind of coherence which acknowledges ultimate mystery beyond any definable structure of intelligibility.[25] Niebuhr is further agreeing with one point for which Christian liberals have contended when he acknowledges that a "hidden Christ operates in history," so that some men come to the truth He reveals outside Christian culture.[26]

[23] *Ibid.*, p. 89.
[24] Reinhold Niebuhr, "An Answer to Karl Barth," *Christian Century*, Vol. 56, No. 8 (Feb. 23, 1949), p. 236.
[25] *Faith and History*, p. 165.
[26] *The Nature and Destiny of Man*, II, 109n.

Yet in spite of its elements of permanent validity, liberal culture, both in its secular and Christian expressions, remains in Niebuhr's eyes inadequate to preserve the very values it cherishes. The preservation and renewal of what is good in civilization depend upon its establishment on the foundation of the Christian faith which apprehends the true depth of man's problems and the source of his ultimate redemption.

V. THE CENTRAL THEOLOGICAL ISSUE

It is necessary to confine my critical questions to the problem of the liberal theology itself rather than to try to deal with the whole of Niebuhr's critique of liberal culture. It must surely be allowed that Niebuhr has raised the crucial difficulty in the liberal theology, that is, the question of whether the course of history exhibits any such progressive movement toward redemption as the liberal theologians held. He has shown that the "long run of history" is a false asylum for refuge from the realities of historical evil. He believes that the meaning of redemption in Christian faith must be expressed in symbols which point beyond history to a fulfillment which is disclosed and promised by the revelation in Christ but which lies in a realm that transcends the ambiguities of temporal human existence.

Since Niebuhr holds that an interpretation of redemption as progressive fulfillment of the Kingdom of God in history cannot be sustained, has he put in its place a more adequate expression of the Christian faith that redemption is accomplished through the goodness and power of God revealed in Jesus Christ? It is in relation to this question that I wish to make my critical remarks. Liberal theologians were trying to formulate and protect the truth that God does achieve his redemptive purpose in the concrete transactions of his dealing with his creatures. Niebuhr has shown that this faith was formulated too simply and superficially in the liberal period. But it is worth asking whether in his tendency to look mainly at the more exaggerated expressions of liberal optimism he may not have overlooked the significance of the preservation of this central Christian theme, that God does transform human life. It is Niebuhr's own doctrine of the actuality of redemption which remains less clear and convincing than it might be.

I restrict my comments to three points: (*a*) Niebuhr's conception of the meaning of history; (*b*) his view of God's action in history, and especially of the significance of God's suffering; and (*c*) his conception of the ethical decisions which Christians must make in this kind of history.

VI. THE RELATION OF MEANING TO HISTORY

No term appears more frequently in Niebuhr's writing than "meaning." What Niebuhr seeks in the Biblical revelation is its "meaning," that is, the truth which cannot be literally defined in a text, but which constitutes the revelation which comes through Christ. In that revelation, he says, the "meaning of man's historic existence is fulfilled."[27] Again, he views history since Christ as "an interim between the disclosure and the fulfillment of its meaning."[28] Obviously this is a key term; but I know of no place where Niebuhr isolates it for analysis. What is the "meaning of meaning" for Niebuhr?

The term seems to be used in two ways. Often it refers to any realm of coherence or order. It can designate ethical principles as relevant to moral behavior, or it may refer to scientific theories. Any system of principles or any orderly relationship has "meaning."

But there is another and more fundamental usage. Meaning signifies the victory of good over evil. Further, meaning usually refers to the completion of this victory. This completion involves both God's judgment upon history and his mercy overcoming its evil; but both of these constitute the complete victory over evil.

There is no single text which clinches this interpretation, but a careful reading of the Gifford Lectures and *Faith and History* seems to support it. History has a "true meaning" which is contradicted in part by actual history, but which nevertheless is the reality which "bears history."[29] The Christian revelation in all its aspects "points to the impossibility of man fulfilling the true meaning of his life."[30]

Niebuhr has a Calvinistic doctrine of meaning. God's sovereignty asserted in complete victory over evil is the very meaning of meaning itself. My comment here is that this gives a clue as to where Niebuhr's real divergence with liberal theologies of history comes.

[27] *Faith and History*, p. 139.

[28] *The Nature and Destiny of Man*, II, 13. Cf. his statement in the same book that if the idea of progress were to be rejected, "the whole liberal structure of meaning would collapse" (p. 240).

[29] *The Nature and Destiny of Man*, II, 51, 61. On p. 61 Niebuhr seems to equate "eternal meaning" with eternal purpose and power.

[30] *Ibid.*, p. 98. Cf. p. 67: "History is meaningful but its meaning is threatened by meaninglessness."

He finds meaning ultimately only in complete victory over evil. Therefore history depends upon something "beyond history" for its meaning; because there is no complete victory in history. Profound liberalism always regards the struggle with evil as meaningful in itself. Some liberalism, it is true, found meaning in history only by believing in a complete victory over evil in time, the building of the Kingdom of God on earth. But the more realistic element in the liberal spirit was not so concerned about complete triumph. Can we not believe in an actual redemptive working of God in history without falling into the utopianism which Niebuhr rightly exposes and rejects?[31]

VII. HOW DOES GOD REDEEM MAN?

The central theological issue is the account to be given of God's redemption wrought in Jesus Christ. Niebuhr's position I take to be this: God has disclosed both his wisdom and power in Jesus Christ; but this very disclosure required Jesus' disavowal of historical power in order that he could express the disinterestedness of the divine love. What his life and death shows is that God suffers and takes up into himself the sin of man. In the light of this revelation men can be brought to repentance. By discovering that God suffers for them they have discovered the reality of his forgiveness. But they have also been freed from the false notion that the meaning of history can be fulfilled in history. They come to hope for and expect a completion of life "beyond history." This hope enables them to live in history a life of serenity and creativity.

Now what I should like clarified is the relation of God's action in Christ to this beginning of redemption in history. It is the question of Niebuhr's view of the relation of time to eternity. Put in another way, it is the question of whether *God has a history*, so that He fulfills the meaning of life in a real history of redemption. Or is the ultimate "meaning" of life something beyond concrete action and events?

Sometimes Dr. Niebuhr seems to argue in a way which separates God's mode of being sharply from the actualities of existence. He seems to think in a Kantian framework in which God is a reality behind the phenomena. Here it makes sense to talk of something "beyond history," for this means beyond time and space and beyond

[31] Royce, Whitehead, Dewey, Ritschl, Wieman are examples of liberals who could not be said to hold the simple utopianism which Niebuhr criticizes.

the whole phenomenal order. Redemption in history therefore means that in Christ we know a symbol or pointer which permits us to anticipate a fulfillment beyond all events. History continues on its own tragic and ambiguous way forever; but its meaning lies in another realm of being.

But there is much in Niebuhr's writing which does not seem to be in harmony with this Kantian metaphysic. Take these sentences from *Faith and History:*

> The climax of the crucifixion and resurrection thus becomes not merely the culmination of the whole series of revelations but the pattern of all subsequent confrontations between God and man. They must contain the crucifixion of self-abandonment and the resurrection of self-recovery. Men must die to sin with Christ and arise with him to newness of life.[32]

This surely is the language of concrete events. It speaks of the new life of the Christian as something begun here and now through God's present working. And it seems to say that this confrontation of God with the sinner is a real event for God also.

Another passage is relevant here. Niebuhr speaks in *Faith and History* of the "transfiguration" of nature and history. What is this transfiguration? Is it an event? Is it something that God actually accomplishes in history? In Christ, Niebuhr seems to say, this transfiguration has begun. But if that is so, then the Christian lives not merely in an interim before the fulfillment of history's meaning, but he already participates in a new history which has begun with the transfiguration of the old.

In his discussion of the resurrection Niebuhr again comes close to this view when he places the resurrection "in a different order of history than the story of the crucifixion."[33] But surely this "different order" is still a history, and not "beyond history." And again we cannot overlook such a striking affirmation as this: "The goodness of Christ must be embodied in the stuff of history."[34]

We cannot claim, and Dr. Niebuhr has made us see this clearly, that this transfiguration which God accomplishes removes all evil from life. History is full of unresolved issues of injustices and broken projects. But if this second interpretation be correct, then redemption is something in history and not beyond it. The problem is to understand the relation between two aspects of our actual history: the ongoing of human events with all their mixture of good and evil,

[32] P. 149. [33] *Faith and History*, p. 147. [34] *Ibid.*, p. 213.

and the history of God's redemptive activity culminating in Christ and continuing in His Church. It seems to me this is the way the Bible views the matter. The Bible sees these two histories as finally one; for there is one God and one creation, and real history is simply the story of God's dealing with his creation.

A closely related theme in Niebuhr's theology of redemption concerns the meaning of the suffering of God. He says that the Christian answer to the problem of life is that "a suffering divine love is the final coherence of life."[35]

Surely, however, a suffering love is not "beyond history." Love suffers precisely because it is engaged in this kind of world. When Niebuhr says that redemption consists in the agony of existence being "taken up into the divine life," then he is hardly saying something different from what liberal theology declared when it found the meaning of life in the history of the actual dealings of God with men. The doctrine that God deals with sin and evil in part by suffering their consequences in love does not lead to a simple utopianism. Indeed, it excludes utopianism. The meaning of life lies in participation in the whole drama of God's working and in dependence on the sustaining reality of his forgiveness. It is true that this leaves many questions unanswered about future events, about the meaning of life in God beyond death, and about the last things. But whatever good we hope for in this realm beyond our sight, it is not something outside the history of God's redemptive working but an actual fulfillment within that history.

My question to Dr. Niebuhr, then, is, How does he conceive the relation between what he refers to as "beyond history" and God's suffering and redemptive working in history? If he asserts God's actual transforming power in history, then it seems to me that his view comes close to what a realistic liberal theology of history would be. But if Niebuhr holds that we must think of a "three-storied" system of meaning, in which the realms of nature, history, and beyond history are somehow ultimately separate, then I have to say I do not believe that this is the way the Bible regards God's relationship to time and His creation, or that an adequate Christian interpretation of God's saving work in Christ can be put in this way. It seems to me to be an imposition of a Kantian epistemology and a Greek metaphysics on the Bible's dynamic conception of time as the form of the concrete encounter between God and man.

[35] "Coherence, Incoherence, and Christian Faith," *loc. cit.*, p. 159.

VIII. MUTUAL AND SACRIFICIAL LOVE

The question about Niebuhr's critique of liberal ethics with its definition of love as mutuality can be put more briefly, because it is closely bound up with the distinction we have been examining between what is in history and what is beyond history.

It is not valid, Niebuhr holds, to regard the love which is revealed in Christ as a simple possibility for human action. It requires a heedlessness of self-interest which sinful man in his anxiety and sin is not able to achieve. But more than this: it is not possible on the grounds of purely historical observation and experience to justify complete self-giving, for history does not prove that such sacrificial love ever receives an adequate response, or that it leads directly to the fulfillment of good. Niebuhr therefore holds that we must distinguish mutual love which seeks a community in which each is fulfilled through what he gives and receives, from sacrificial love which transcends all requirements of reciprocity. It gives itself up for the other. Since mutual love can be shown by rational historical analysis to be the highest ethical possibility which can be explicitly justified on the basis of reason and experience, and since sacrificial love transcends all such rational justification, we can see that Niebuhr's distinction between history and what is beyond history has its ethical relevance. Although sacrificial love cannot maintain itself in history, it is yet essential to bring the ultimate judgment of the spirit upon all human ethics. Once sacrificial love is understood by faith, it has power to qualify, purify, and renew man's ethical life, which always tends to bog down in calculated systems of mutual harmony.

I have the same difficulties with this distinction between two kinds of love that I do with the distinction between history and what is beyond history. It seems to me to leave the Christian with two kinds of obligations, one to honor the good in the world, even his own good, the other to obey the spirit of sacrificial love which cannot take account of his own good. This leaves the Christian caught between two worlds which have two differing ultimate norms, and therefore distraught and divided in all ethical decision.

The issue here is what it is that love rightly intends and seeks. Is it a good which lies beyond history and therefore beyond any envisaged fulfillment of the person who loves? Or is it a real community of good in which all life, including my own, is intended to share? There is a Christian ethical tradition from St. Augustine to present-day liberal theories of mutuality which says that love is one because its object is one. What love seeks is the full community of each with all. It may be remarked here that profound liberal ethical theories never defined mutuality as a simple calculation of mutual reward. Such systems as Wieman's have held that the new community of life which love seeks requires the transformation and the continual sacrifice of the present good to which the self clings.

Now Dr. Niebuhr always affirms that Christianity does not require the annihilation of the self or its interests. "It is . . . not the highest perfection for man to achieve a unity of his being from which all natural and historical vitalities have been subtracted. The highest unity is a harmony-love in which the self relates itself in its freedom to other selves in their freedom under the will of God."[36] But he believes that while the ultimate goal of the spirit of love is fulfillment for the self, this cannot be the *intended* goal; because as soon as we intend our own good we have lost the freedom from self-interest which can enable us to enter into the fulfilled community. Thus he wishes to leave the paradox of losing one's life and saving it a real paradox which defies strict rationality, but which describes the reality of the human situation.

My difficulties come at the point where we try to pass from this paradox as Niebuhr interprets it to our making concrete decisions in history. Shall one honor the demand of sacrificial love and become an ethical absolutist, recognizing that the proximate problems of society cannot be directly solved in this way? Or shall one be guided by the demands of mutual love and justice, which may include justice even for oneself? How can this be decided? How is *agape* as the ultimate norm related to a sense of responsibility for the proximate problems of human life and history?

Surely if relative justice and systems of mutuality are good, and if the self is not to seek its own annihilation, then *for the sake of love* we must undertake to construct communities of good in history in which we can share. Cannot the labor leader who fights for justice for his own union have a Christian vocation to do so? Surely it is not only the ethical absolutists who have a vocation to express the love we know in Christ. But if this be the case, then there cannot be an absolute distinction between sacrificial love and mutual love. Christian love must involve the seeking of community of life, and in the end must be one love which embraces all possible good.

[36] *The Nature and Destiny of Man,* II, 94–95.

Certainly there are levels of community, and no historical community adequately expresses love. Perhaps it is almost impossible for any human life fully to express the full meaning of love. But the love revealed in Christ does lead us to seek a fulfillment of all life in the relationship which God intends. There is no way to that fulfillment apart from a continual self-giving. But it is giving for the sake of the Kingdom of God which includes all good.

In any case, if my question is a legitimate one, perhaps Dr. Niebuhr would restate his conception of the way in which we move from the distinction between mutual and sacrificial love to concrete and responsible Christian decisions in history.

IX. CONCLUSION

There are, I have argued, two insights in the liberal tradition which must be brought within an adequate Christian theology. One is that God's dealing with man is a matter of concrete events, of processes of personal confrontation and renewal. The other is that Christian love has its unity in the truth that God intends a community of all life, and that this love is the basis for the vocation of the Christian in the midst of the ethical struggles and dilemmas of history. I am not quite sure whether to interpret Dr. Niebuhr more in the light of the Kantian and Platonic strains of his thought in which he distinguishes between history and a realm beyond it, or whether to emphasize those tendencies which seem to be closely akin to the most realistic liberalism when it has asserted God's present redemptive action in history.

I close with a personal confession. Whenever the case is argued for a more positive view of redemption in history, Dr. Niebuhr's theology comes to trouble and disturb. For he has shown how every theology which has tried to affirm unambiguously a conception of God's redemptive action in history has ended by sanctifying some partial cultural or religious perspective. He has uncovered the pervasiveness of sin and the persistence of self-centeredness in the Christian life. He makes us wonder whether the paradoxes and radical distinctions which he holds between what is possible in history and what is possible only beyond it may not be necessary warnings against this inevitable tendency to allow the hope of redemption to hide the depth of human corruptibility.

In any case we can be grateful that one of the most discerning of all interpreters of the Christian faith has brought a whole generation to see more clearly the full dimensions of sin and reconciliation. We can be grateful also that liberal Christianity helped to provide the freedom and the critical methods by which its own most trenchant critic has sought to establish the values achieved by liberalism upon firmer Christian ground.

DANIEL D. WILLIAMS

FEDERATED THEOLOGICAL FACULTY
UNIVERSITY OF CHICAGO
CHICAGO, ILLINOIS

11

Alan Richardson

REINHOLD NIEBUHR AS APOLOGIST

11

REINHOLD NIEBUHR AS APOLOGIST

The title of this essay must in one sense be considered misleading. An apologist in the strict meaning of the word is one who seeks to make sympathetic contact with the thought of his age with a view to commending Christian truth to his contemporaries and defending it against hostile criticism. It is clear that Reinhold Niebuhr does not set out in the deliberate fashion of other apologists to do this. He is far too critical of the presuppositions of our age to be a conventional apologist. If we are looking for an epithet by which to describe him, the word that comes to mind is not "apologist" but "prophet." In an important sense a prophet's function is exactly the opposite of an apologist's: instead of making sympathetic contact with the thought of his age the prophet is compelled by an inner necessity to criticize and reject it. A prophet will not compromise with the accepted thought forms and presuppositions of his day, since they appear to him to be idolatries; he exposes their inadequacy and hypocrisy, and he remorselessly drives those who will listen to his proclamation to seek for new and more adequate forms of understanding. Niebuhr is clearly a prophet in this sense: in an age of the dominance of the categories of "liberal" and "evolutionary" thinking he has compelled serious-minded people to criticize their assumptions and to look for new and deeper ways of understanding their experience.

But there is a sense in which the prophet inevitably performs the work of an apologist, whether he intends to do so or not. The prophet by the startling and compelling quality of his utterance arrests men's attention and compels them to consider afresh the basic truths of the Biblical revelation and their implications for the life of man and of society. Through genuinely prophetic utterance in this sense many who have come to regard Christianity as an outworn and conventional platitude are persuaded to reconsider their attitude and re-examine the content and significance of Christian belief. In this way they may come to see that the platitudes which they formerly judged to be the sum-total of Christianity are in fact not Christian faith at all, but merely the conventional evasions of it. This is precisely what has happened to many thoughtful people through the work of Reinhold Niebuhr. What they had formerly dismissed as sentimentalism or bourgeois ideology they have been made to realize is not Christianity at all, and they have been led to see that the insights of Biblical faith have an existential relevance to their own condition and to the condition of the society in which their lives are set. It may be true that the number of those who have been thus awakened by Niebuhr to a new and realistic awareness of the nature of Christian truth is not very large; but in matters of this kind the size of the prophet's following is not important; in every age it is only a handful of thoughtful people who create the "climate of opinion" and shape the outlook of the oncoming generation. In this secondary sense Niebuhr is of very great significance as a Christian apologist, and it is for this reason that it is permissible and indeed requisite that in any serious consideration of his work as a whole this aspect of his achievement should receive due recognition.

In an age in which the chief categories of thought were those of evolutionary optimism, Niebuhr grew to maturity and began his work. "Jesus was the great believer in man," wrote T. R. Glover in a book which sold in its thousands. Christianity was widely held to be the perfection of human idealism, and its strength was thought to lie in its appeal to all that was good in human nature. If Niebuhr had been an apologist in the normal meaning of the word, he would have sought to build on the apparently solid foundation thus provided by liberal thought for the superstructure of the Christian religion. Here we see nicely illustrated the perennial temptation which besets the apologist: he is continually tempted to acquiesce in current assumptions and to draw them into a Christian synthesis of the "best" elements in the thought of his age. If space permitted, one could illustrate the process from the work of all the great Christian apologists down the ages: Aquinas's building upon the new and fashionable Aristotelian categories of the thirteenth century renaissance; Joseph Butler's appeal to the deistical presuppositions of eighteenth century rationalism; and so on. In the twentieth century there were scores of would-be apologists who believed that by "liberalizing" the Christian faith it was possible to convince the modern mind that Christianity was not merely intellectually respectable but was demonstrably the best possible hypothesis for the explanation of all the riddles of the universe. On the continent of Europe, however, the liberal-Protestant outlook collapsed as a result of the experiences of the years after 1914, and new prophets like Barth and Brunner arose to demolish the ruins. In England to a limited extent the national Church, with its Book of Common Prayer and its Catholic tradition, had resisted the encroachments of the liberal flood tide; but, generally speaking, the triumph of "progressive thinking" was complete in the Anglo-Saxon world.

What was needed in the years which followed the First World War was not an apologist who would make "sympathetic contact" with the liberal categories of thought, but a prophet who would sweep them out of the way. How and why Reinhold Niebuhr became that prophet it is not our task to determine. A prophet arises suddenly, unpredictably, miraculously, as God sends his word. Those who have read that moving autobiographical writing *Leaves from the Notebook of a Tamed Cynic* (1929) will have some inkling how a prophet may be raised up in our times. So far from serving an apologetic purpose, Niebuhr's earlier writings cut the ground from underneath all the Christian apologetical writers then in vogue. To many Christian readers Niebuhr's writings seemed to deny the very foundations upon which a Christian philosophy or apologetic could be built. Their dearest assumptions concerning man's perfectibility, his kinship with the divine, his natural goodness, were all demolished with ruthless iconoclasm. *Moral Man and Immoral Society* (1932) seemed to many Christian leaders, especially to those of the older generation, to be the outpouring of a cynical and perverse spirit, very far removed from the benevolent and sanguine serenity which was held to be the hallmark of a truly Christian mind. It seemed hard to the complacent liberal Christians of the period to be told that their ideals and aspirations were illusions; and it was cold comfort to hear that nevertheless such illusions were necessary to social well-being. To know that one's ideals were illusory and yet to be told that the only possibility of achieving even a distant approximation to them lay in a deceitful assertion of their truth seemed to many to be a counsel of despair. Yet amongst thoughtful men and women outside the Christian fold this shattering of the complacency and escapism of much contemporary Christian preaching and writing compelled at least a respectable listening, even if it did not convert. And there was a whole generation of young Christians in the thirties, especially in Britain, which was avid to hear Niebuhr's prophetic word. Niebuhr himself seems at the earlier stage of his work to have expected little success from his efforts as an apologist. In the preface to *Reflections on the End of an Era* (1934) he wrote:

> The effort to combine political radicalism with a more classical interpretation of religion will strike the modern mind as bizarre and capricious. It will satisfy neither the liberals in politics or religion, nor the political radicals, nor the devotees of traditional Christianity. These reflections are, therefore, presented without much hope that they will elicit any general concurrence. Perhaps they may help a little to shake the easy faith by which modern liberalism lives and through which the tragic facts of contemporary history are obscured.

Similarly in the sphere of ethics Niebuhr does not build upon contemporary assumptions but, on the contrary, overthrows them. It was generally assumed by the liberal-Christian moralists that all one had to do in order to be perfect was to obey the simple ethical injunctions of the Sermon on the Mount. "If only" everyone would do unto others as he would be done by, then the Kingdom of God would have come. Against liberal simplicities of this order Niebuhr's polemic was devastating. Negatively his strictures have been influential; nowadays we rarely hear the claim that the "ethics of Jesus" can be simply "applied" without compromise amidst the complexities of modern life, or that our social problems can be solved by better education, or that man's innate goodness is able of itself to overcome the evil within and around him. Of course, many other factors beside the polemics of Niebuhr have been at work to produce the more sober estimate of ethical possibilities which is prevalent today; but it may be confidently affirmed that in this respect the teaching of Niebuhr has exerted a powerful influence upon the thought of our age. More positively it may be asserted that Niebuhr has performed a most valuable apologetic service in emphasizing the God-centered character of the moral teaching of Jesus. It is the demand of God that is the basic truth in the ethical sphere. God's demand is an absolute, uncompromising, unattainable demand, which leaves no room for self-satisfaction or ease of conscience, and which, just because it is a demand for what is impossible, forces men to see that their basic problem is religious rather than moral, that it concerns their relationship with God rather than their attainment of virtue. To make this fundamental New Testament truth apparent, not merely in academic discussion but in terms of the actual everyday life of the modern world of social, industrial, political, and international affairs, is perhaps, though indirectly, the most important long-term objective of Christian apologetics today. For today people are more interested in living than in theories, and they will see truth in its impact upon the world of real life long before they will recognize it in the writings of the academics or even in the expositions of the preachers. To make people listen to what Christ has to say about morality, not because they have an interest in "religion," but because they are concerned about men at work or at leisure—this is surely the most valuable apologetic there is in our day.

Niebuhr's apologetic is mainly concentrated upon the practical, the ethical, and the social; in this regard it is specially adapted to the dominant interests of twentieth century men. His approach, for instance, to the philosophy of history, about which he has written much, is largely practical. That is to say, he comes to the question of history not with the synoptic comprehension of a Toynbee, nor yet with the speculative concern of a Collingwood, but rather in the challenging spirit of a Biblical prophet: one will best understand history and its meaning in the effort to change it. To stand aside from the course of events and to contemplate them in a disinterested attitude is to forego the possibility of understanding and interpreting history. History is understood only from within, from the standpoint of the mind which knows that "thus saith the Lord." As beings involved in history yet transcending history, it is only in the actual business of living in *this* particular moment in history and yet acting upon history from beyond it that we can find in it a meaning which the speculative study of history does not disclose. Hence it is that the question about what one ought to *do* in the social process or in this political situation here and now is never far away from Niebuhr's discussion of the meaning of history. And hence also the characteristically Niebuhrian concept of the divine activity in history is always near the center of interest: God is not a kind of third force in history over against nature and man; he is the Lord who is encountered in every historical situation, who is obeyed or disobeyed in every contingency, and who yet is the Sovereign Controller of the whole historical process. He is for Niebuhr as essential to the meaning of history as he was for the Hebrew prophets. His sovereign will is inevitable in all our affairs, and man possesses freedom in historical choices not because God has abdicated in favor of human free will and left history to go its own way, but because God and man encounter each other in a complex struggle in which even man's opposition to God's will is one of the means by which God's purpose is achieved. This is the Biblical conception of history, and Niebuhr's significant contribution to theology is not simply to restate academically what this Biblical conception is but to show how our own history, the tragic world history of this present generation, dramatizes in the newspaper headlines the Biblical insight into the nature of human existence.

This is a type of apology which reaches those who are interested not in theories and speculations but in persons and politics, in the actual fate of individuals and groups, of (let us say) Poland or democracy, of Hiroshima or private enterprise. It exhibits the relevance of faith in God on a level altogether different from that of the endless quest of the philosopher to discern a pattern in the historical process by means of an academic study of history. The search for patterns in history involves the assumption that there is rationality in the course of human affairs and perhaps also in the universe itself, while the denial of patterns involves the assertion of irrationality. Niebuhr starts not from an assumption but from real life as he has found it, and there he discovers a paradoxical admixture of rationality and irrationality. Not only are there coherences in human experience but there are also non-personal "vitalities" which limit the rational will which seeks to control them. Consequently every "turning point" of history is a point at which rationality and mystery intersect, and the irrationality, the mysterious non-intelligibility, is just as important as the rationality. Liberal utopianism, which stresses rationality, and naturalistic cynicism, which exaggerates the irrationality, are alike shown to be inadequate to account for the strangely equivocal compound of malleability and intransigence which is called history, that is, for the wretchedness and greatness of our human condition.

Niebuhr's appeal as an apologist lies in his honest refusal either to rationalize the stark incoherences of human existence in some academic theory of metaphysical idealism or on the other hand to deny the basic coherences of our experience in the interest of some irrationalist or existentialist view of the type which is nowadays so fashionable. Most people do in fact find life to be an encounter between rationality and irrationality, and an apologetic which sought to explain away either of these sides of our experience would appeal rather to a passing mood than to a truly reflective mind. It is the clearness of his recognition of this essentially paradoxical character of our experience which makes Niebuhr the apologist of our day who, above all others, can lead those who are passionately concerned about the condition of man in society up to the point at which the paradoxical and supra-rational affirmations of the historic Biblical and Christian faith may be seen to be profoundly relevant to the situation. The doctrines, for example, of the Trinity and the Atonement can be perceived to be the clues which make the drama of human existence intelligible to those who will commit themselves in faithful obedience to the demand and promise of the Gospel. In thus avoiding the temptation to explain away the paradox of human experience, Niebuhr at the same time escapes the danger of reducing the Christian faith to an unmysterious, rational theology: his awareness of the incoherences of our life saves him from all forms of simple rationalism, while his perception of life's coherences prevents him from yielding to a theology of despair. The refusal to oversimplify the complexity of human experience leads to a recognition of the true depth of Biblical-prophetic theology. From this theological vantage ground Niebuhr is able to step back into the world of politics and ethics and show how Christian insights can illuminate the strange compound of altruism and egoism, of hope and despair, of high promise and tragic failure, which forms the very substance of human life.

It would have been so fatally easy for Niebuhr, having once seen through the illusions of liberal rationalism, to have rebounded to the opposite extreme and embraced an irrationalist existentialism, as the protagonists of the "dialectical theology" on the continent of Europe had already done. To have done so would have soon become fashionable, and, as we have noted, the desire to be à la mode is the besetting temptation of the apologist. Niebuhr's strength was that right from the beginning of his work he was able to see that the defects of one way of thinking are not valid reasons for embracing its opposite. The mistakes of idealistic rationalism or the misplaced confidence of liberalism in the objectivity of its own judgments is not a justification for making a passionate subjectivity the sole test of truth. A philosophy which embraces the inner contradiction within man as its clue to understanding possesses no real criterion for discriminating between one *summum bonum* and another: an existentialist may be a Christian, a non-Christian, a Catholic, a Protestant, a Nazi or a nihilist. There must be some criterion beyond a passionate subjectivity. Barth, Bultmann, and Marcel must presumably have some reasons for distinguishing themselves from Heidegger and Sartre. Niebuhr sees clearly that subjectivity, however passionate, is not enough; there are those who are temperamentally inclined to prefer the passionate worship of an idol to the conventional worship of the true God, but Niebuhr holds that it is both possible and desirable to avoid each of these attitudes. He prefers a Christian realism which speaks of both the coherence and the incoherence of life as ordinary men and women experience it, and this means that Niebuhr can be an apologist for the Christian faith in a way in which Barth, for example, cannot.

A comparison at this point between Niebuhr and Barth may perhaps be instructive. Barth is compelled to renounce the task of apologetics because revelation is for him a kind of flash of lightning in the dark night of human ignorance: we see its brilliance and are almost blinded by it, so that we no longer see the stars by which we had formerly determined at least the points of the compass. Revelation, that is to say, does not illumine human wisdom, but negates it. Hence for Barth there is no connection between the absolute righteousness of God and the relative justice that is so precariously attained in the political and ethical life of human societies. For Barth the righteousness of God is revealed from heaven against all unrighteousness of men in such a way that there is no light which lighteneth every man, no general revelation at work in all of the civilizations known to Professor Toynbee, by which they may attain for a season an unstable approximation to a divine law of justice. Hence there is no apologetic task to be attempted by the theologian, for there is no *logos* in man to which the divine *Logos* may be commended by human words. As Niebuhr writes:

> This means that the whole commerce between the foolishness of the Gospel and the wisdom of the world, between faith and culture, is disavowed. . . . One could not, for instance, from this standpoint engage in a debate with psychologists on the question of what level of human selfhood is adequately illumined by psychiatric techniques and what level

of the self as subject and free spirit evades these analyses. Nor could one debate with social scientists on the possibilities and the limits of a rational justice in human society.[1]

It is, of course, precisely in this area of the debate with psychologists and social scientists, and with serious students of the human sciences generally, that Niebuhr has done the work of an apologist, and done it supremely well. He has demonstrated the relevance of Christian insights in these spheres by taking them seriously up to the point at which they become conscious of their own limits and at which they seem to stand in contradiction to one another. He has been able to do this because, unlike Barth, he has not been hampered by an arbitrary and strictly heretical—self-chosen—theory of revelation, which reacted from liberal rationalism into an extreme Kierkegaardian subjectivity. By remaining loyal to the classical Christian doctrine of revelation, best stated in our times under the headings of "general" and "special" revelation, Niebuhr has avoided both Scholastic (Thomistic) and liberal rationalism without being driven to the opposite extreme of subjectivist irrationalism. Therefore he has been able to find a point of connection with those who, by the grace of God in general revelation, are able to discern certain levels of truth and who may yet, by the grace of God in special revelation, be led to the fuller knowledge that is possible to those who see by means of the "true light."

By thus entering into debate with thoughtful non-Christians, Niebuhr the apologist has been able to show those who are inclined toward rationalism that the human situation is more complex than any scheme of rational meaning which has yet been devised to comprehend it; and in his discussions with the naturalists he has been able to show grounds for holding that current attempts to evaluate human selfhood in terms of the coherences of nature are misinterpretations of the unique character of human freedom. He has then been able to go on to show that there is a possibility of transforming the natural stuff of social and political life by the grace and wisdom of the Gospel. Thus he could present in modern situations the Biblical conception of the encounter with God in human history as the source of the true hope that may be found amidst the tragedy of the human existence. All this constitutes a powerful apologetic which reflective modern people, who have glimpsed something of the dignity and

[1] *Christian Realism and Political Problems*, p. 182.

wretchedness of the human existence, are able to appreciate. To those who are dissatisfied with the pious simplicities of conventional pulpit oratory, such an approach brings an entirely new dimension of religious understanding and ethical discrimination. In this way Niebuhr's prophetic insight is transmuted into first-rate contemporary Christian apologetics, not only in his better known volumes but also in some scores of briefer and more ephemeral articles in the secular as well as the religious press. It is an apologetic which has on the one hand saved countless ardent young people from the shallows and disillusionments of liberal utopianism and on the other hand won very many others from either the fanatical idolatry of Marxism or the cynical despair of nihilism.

There are, however, as was only to be expected, some fields within the total area of Christian apologetics in which the contribution of Niebuhr is less incisive. He has written much about the connection between faith and history, and on this topic he has, as we have noted, much to teach us. He is vividly aware of the importance of history as the sphere of the saving encounter of man with God and as the *locus* of the Biblical revelation. At one crucial point in the discussion he becomes uncharacteristically reticent. Much of the Biblical narrative involves the miraculous, and it is not clear what is Niebuhr's final attitude toward miracle. On this matter his apologetic appears to falter. It is uncertain from his writings whether he would dismiss miracle, after the manner of Bultmann, as merely a mythological means of bringing out the significance of the historical. Those who follow the current fashion of "demythologizing" the Gospels would say, for example, that the Feeding miracles in the four Gospels are merely mythological means of representing and emphasizing the truth that Jesus is the Bread of Life, or that the Resurrection story is only a mythological attempt to stress the significance of the triumphant death of Christ. There are passages in his writings in which it is inconclusive whether Niebuhr subscribes to some such view. He is impressed (as who could fail to be?) with the accumulated evidence of natural science that the realm of natural causation is more closed, more rigid, than the pre-scientific Biblical writers were aware. Though he holds it reasonable in the light of modern science to accept many of the Gospel miracles of healing, Niebuhr is tempted to believe (with Bultmann) that there is much to be gained by dissociating the historical basis of Christian faith from any divine miraculous interventions in the realm of natural causation (for example, the Virgin Birth or the physical Resurrection). But at the same time he is aware of the grave dangers involved in this type of solution of the problem; there is the danger of turning Christianity into a new Gnosticism, a way of salvation for such as can understand the philosophy of Heidegger. Niebuhr therefore rejects such a solution, but one suspects that he is unable confidently to put forward any other or more satisfying answer to the problem because (like Bultmann) he retains a lingering respect for the methods and assumptions of an old-fashioned liberal type of Gospel-criticism. Accordingly he seems to suppose that Christian scholars who preach the Gospel to ordinary people must necessarily practice some doctrine of reserve, "as deceivers and yet true"; they must preach as history what they know to be merely symbolical. Thus:

> The message of the Son of God who dies upon the cross, of a God who transcends history and is yet in history, who condemns and judges sin and yet suffers with and for the sinner, this message is the truth about life. It cannot be stated without deceptions; but the truths which seek to avoid the deceptions are immeasurably less profound. Compared with the Christ who died for men's sins upon the cross, Jesus, the good man who tells all men to be good, is more solidly historical. But he is the bearer of no more than a pale truism.[2]

It would appear that Niebuhr holds that the critical study of the Gospels reveals the "liberal" Jesus as a genuinely historical figure, and that one must therefore somehow make a leap of faith to some presumably non-historical Christ of faith. But surely the progress of New Testament research in the twentieth century has utterly disposed of the liberal picture of Jesus as in any way historical. The liberal Jesus was a figment of the liberal imagination, the reflection of the liberal critic's own face at the bottom of the well. The only Jesus known to contemporary historical and critical scholarship is the Christ of the apostolic witness, the very Jesus who healed the sick, raised the dead, and himself was raised from the dead on the third day. There is no other *historical* Jesus. The apologist today can say with confidence, as Loisy said to Harnack, "To history thou hast appealed; to history thou shalt go." There is no need to practice deceptions, however pious, in the matter of the miracles of Jesus or in the matter of his Resurrection. Bultmann, the critic who starts from the positivistic assumption that the miraculous is incredible, can

[2] *Beyond Tragedy*, pp. 20f.

rescue the saving truth of the Gospel from the consequences of the skeptical presuppositions only by restating it as an existential Gnosis. But it is the exigencies of the liberal philosophy which have driven him to this desperate expedient. Niebuhr, who has analyzed so brilliantly the process of rationalization which goes on in the mind of the historian, should have followed the logic of his own investigation to an altogether different conclusion from that of Bultmann.

There is nothing in Niebuhr's own analysis—at least as one reader understands it—to account for the hesitation and (to speak plainly) equivocation which appear in so much of his writing upon the historicity of the Gospel. Take, for example, the penultimate paragraph of Niebuhr's last book:

> The situation for faith is only slightly altered by the new [modern scientific] picture of a quasi-autonomous nature, created by God, not maintained by his fiat from moment to moment. No sign can be given but that of the prophet Jonah, by which Jesus meant the sign of death and resurrection. This is to say, whenever the vicissitudes from which the self, either individually or collectively, suffers are appropriated by faith as divine judgments and not as meaningless caprice, they result in the love, joy and peace of a new life.[3]

These words would seem to mean that "the sign of the prophet Jonah" is concerned with the general ethical message about a metaphorical death and resurrection as a means of attaining love, joy, and peace. They do not apparently refer to the specific, once-for-all death of Jesus Christ, the Son of God, under Pontius Pilate, and to the specific Resurrection of this same Jesus Christ on the third day. Or do they? We cannot tell. Is the "solidly historical" Jesus still the bearer of no more than a pale truism?

Niebuhr urges that there are no simple solutions to such problems as these, and of course he is right. There are no simple solutions, but there are clear issues. Into these issues, however, we can here inquire no further. But one thing must be said. Christians may hold that, for instance, the stories of the Creation and Fall of Man in Genesis I–III are not literally true, but it is misleading to speak of them as myths unless the word is carefully defined. There is in them an element of historicity or factuality which cannot be surrendered without exchanging the historic Christian faith for a theistic philosophy. God *did* create the world; man *has fallen* from grace: these

[3] *Christian Realism and Political Problems,* p. 190.

assertions are not myths in any sense of the word. When Christian writers speak loosely of the Genesis stories as myths, what they really mean to say is that they are mythological ways of expressing things that really did take place. It is only the *form* of the Genesis stories which is mythological. But when the apostolic witnesses assert that Jesus died and rose again, they mean to assert that these events really did happen: they may (and do) bear profound symbolical meaning as pictures or "myths" of our existence as a divine-human drama of death and resurrection, but if they are "only myths" the Christian religion becomes a different thing from what it has been since the days of the apostolic preaching. If the Resurrection of Christ is not a historical event but only a profound myth, that is, a representation created by the poetic imagination of the true meaning of life, then a kind of Christian philosophy and a kind of Christian religion might still conceivably be true, even though the original apostolic witnesses were mistaken about the very facts around which the poetic imagination played and out of which it built its myth. But then Christianity would be an imaginative religious interpretation of the world, which would differ from the historic Christian faith as poetry differs from history and as religion differs from Gospel. It would not be the historic apostolic faith, because the latter was from its birth the proclamation of the Resurrection of Jesus Christ. If God did not vouchsafe to the world the sign of the Resurrection, he is a very different God from the God of the Christian revelation: amongst other differences he is a God whose truth can be expressed in pale truisms. Modern New Testament research, however, has discovered nothing to suggest that the apostolic witnesses were mistaken about the cardinal affirmations of the Gospel, and the apologist need not retreat to his philosophical bastions until his historical defenses have been successfully assailed. A premature withdrawal from the front line of defense is the strategy of the defeatist. The historic Christian faith will survive the onslaughts of modern positivism as it has survived many earlier challenges. In these days we must be especially heedful of Luther's warning not to defend the Christian faith so that it collapses.

ALAN RICHARDSON

DEPARTMENT OF THEOLOGY
UNIVERSITY OF NOTTINGHAM
ENGLAND

12

William John Wolf

REINHOLD NIEBUHR'S DOCTRINE OF MAN

12

REINHOLD NIEBUHR'S DOCTRINE OF MAN

NIEBUHR'S most significant contribution to the restatement of Christian theology in our generation is his exposition of the doctrine of man. Unlike systematicians like Aquinas or Barth who cover the whole corpus of Christian truth by the method of a *Summa,* Niebuhr makes one doctrine, brilliantly plumbed to its depths, the basis of his whole thought. Articulated in terms of man's relations with his fellow men, the doctrine of man is determinative for his social ethics and for his interpretation of the meaningfulness of history. Concentrated in terms of personality, and brought into correlation with the historic Christian revelation, it defines his understanding of Christology, atonement, and eschatology. Other contributors to the volume will develop Niebuhr's rendering of these doctrines, for this essay must focus on some of the points in his doctrine of man detached (and thereby inevitably somewhat impoverished) from its context in the whole of his thought.

An interesting history of the development of Niebuhr's doctrine of man could be written, from the predominantly sociological critique of man's situation in *Moral Man and Immoral Society,* with its somewhat Marxist overtones and "liberal" theological presuppositions, through the greater dependence upon historic Christian revelation in *An Interpretation of Christian Ethics,* to a definite anti-Marxist, anti-fundamentalist, anti-nineteenth century theological polemic in *Beyond Tragedy* and *Christianity and Power Politics.* Such a survey, which is beyond the scope of this chapter, might illuminate nuances in his present positions. It might also explain why many of the criticisms still heard about Niebuhr have lost most of their significance in the course of his own development. This chapter must, however, confine itself to the more recent statements of his thought and primarily to the Gifford Lectures which he significantly entitled *The Nature and Destiny of Man.*[7] Later works have more amply illustrated, but not essentially modified, his basic contentions in the Gifford Lectures. It is primarily on this ground that the critics must fight.

I. HIS THOUGHT FORMS

At the very beginning of an exposition of his doctrine of man a difficulty is encountered which makes his thought unacceptable to many. In his own words, it is "dialectical thought." That is to say, he believes that most of the deeper truths about man, history, and reality must be stated in such a way as to do justice to contradictory or seemingly contradictory aspects of reality. To many rationalists or even to empiricists who absolutize the principle of logical consistency and coherence, this approach is self-contradictory and "nonsense." Even those who, trained by Hegel, will patiently endure the statement of preliminary contradictions in the pattern of thesis and antithesis in order to find logical simplicity in the synthesis (usually somewhat mechanically ground out) part company with Niebuhr when the hoped-for resolution is not forthcoming. Niebuhr's only answer to these criticisms, and, quite apart from the special content assigned to his pattern of thought, the answer of all who hold to the Christian faith in its Biblical dimensions, must be, "There are more things in heaven and earth, Horatio, than are dreamt of in your philosophy." This preliminary agreement that his method of thought is well adapted to the complexity of reality itself and to the Christian answer to this complexity does not justify every special use made of it. "Dialectical thought" can become as mechanical as the rationalistic pattern of simple declarative sentences pruned by canons of logical consistency and coherence. A somewhat stylized Niebuhrian analysis of a human problem is to state two opposite facets of the problem, then to reduce each further to negative and positive elements, to correlate the sub-negation of the basic affirmation with the sub-positive of the basic negation, then to show how the Christian answer meets these complexities, but only in the wholeness of the problem; for once any one element of the Christian answer is emphasized at the expense of some other facet, distortion occurs. This pattern is the framework for Niebuhr's analysis of man's sin and his goodness in the light of grace which both represents God's forgiveness and his empowering of man. This procedure offends both secular rationalists whose systems would be destroyed by an acknowledgment of the full complexity of the issue and Christian rationalists or institutionalists who wish to advertise a patent medicine of simple formula suitable for all complaints. Much criticism of Niebuhr is based upon an isolated statement of one of his positions naïvely, or perhaps sometimes deliberately, detached from its full context in a total system of relationships. Perhaps a better phrase than "dialectical thought" would be "relational thought."

II. FAITH AND EXPERIENCE

What are the sources of Niebuhr's doctrine of man? Obviously they are two: an analysis of the human situation integrated with the insights of Christian revelation. There are theologians who make the exposition of their doctrines of man much easier by developing one or the other of these sources in isolation or, if conjoined, in simple temporal sequence. Personalists like Brightman attempt an analysis seemingly quite apart from the presuppositions of Christian revelation. Barth scornfully rejects the philosophical approach and offers an anthropology based, he believes, upon the pure Word of God. Aquinas defines man and his essential structures in almost purely Aristotelian categories of "nature" and "reason," and then invites belief in a revelation of "grace" not contrary to, but simply above or beyond, nature. Each of the three can present his position in a straightforward, relatively simple manner, using declarative sentences with a minimum of modifying clauses. Niebuhr would accuse each of oversimplifying the human situation. Brightman's categories of personality really presuppose a Biblical orientation. They have not been developed on the soil of non-Christian cultures, and when confronted by representatives of such cultures they lack power to convince by "reason." Barth's claim to be only the servant of Revelation reveals again and again that he reads the Bible through the spectacles of a philosophy of transcendence the more dangerous for not being recognized. Aquinas, in some of his more Augustinian statements, apparently admits that faith must precede reason, but even such admissions are never developed to a degree that overthrows his non-aggression accord between "nature" and "grace" in their supposedly separate spheres of influence.

The form of Niebuhr's exposition of the doctrine of man in the Gifford Lectures testifies to his conviction that experience and faith interpenetrate each other on every level. There is accordingly no presuppositionless inquiry into the human situation, nor on the other hand a purely revelational answer without organic connection with the structures of man and the fabric of history. The early chapters analyze the history of Western culture from Greece to our day, seeking to state the unsolved questions about man which rise in every period and thought system to plague him. While this cultural analysis precedes his detailed articulation of the Christian answers, it everywhere consciously presupposes that faith. This is at once more confusing than many other expositions of the Christian doctrine of man, but more honest because more faithful to the complex nature of the problem. To paraphrase a favorite Pauline quotation of Niebuhr's, the modern secular "Greeks" find the Christian faith "foolishness" and the Barthian "Jews" describe it as a "scandal," but on a deeper level it remains "the power and the wisdom of God." Perhaps one of Niebuhr's significant contributions will be his challenge to entrenched modern positions on the question of faith and experience or of revelation and reason. It cannot be claimed that he settles the issue, for he has not yet given us an exposition adequate to the intricacies of the problem, but his method of approach suggests an undercutting of the historic Protestant and Roman Catholic positions by carrying the problem to a deeper level. The dimensions for such a treatment are brilliantly sketched in his chapter "Coherence, Incoherence, and Christian Faith" in his most recent book *Christian Realism and Political Problems.*

III. APPROACH FROM AN ANALYSIS OF CULTURE

Niebuhr believes that Western culture in its modern view of man is heir to a commingling of two traditions, the classical and the Biblical. The dominant notes in the classical view are a rationalism which understands man from the uniqueness of his intellectual faculties, and a dualism, implicit in Aristotle and explicit in Plato, which tends to identify the body with evil and the mind or spirit with good. This generalization is not immediately supported by the evidence of Greek tragedy with its elements of Dionysian vitalism and its belief that man sins by pride. Nor is it clearly seen in the materialism of Democritus and Epicurus. But even here the understanding of nature is thoroughly rationalistic, as Stoicism again illustrates. The Greeks are unable to discover a meaning in history beyond a pattern of cyclic recurrence. This results in a pessimistic and melancholy attitude toward the responsibilities of the present which on the whole the Renaissance did not resurrect when it rehabilitated part of the classical view of man. It mixed a secularized transcript of the Christian belief in the meaningfulness of history with a revival of the classical anthropology of rational autonomy. Henceforth progress would be secured by human virtue and intelligence.

Niebuhr believes that the doctrine of creation is one root of the unique insight of Christianity into the human situation. Contrary to the usual picture in Greek thought of the divine as Mind giving form to pre-existent matter, Christianity affirms that God is both vitality and form, and, as the *ex nihilo* Creator, responsible for an order which is essentially good. Corollaries of this axiom of faith are an appreciation of the given unity of man as both body and spirit and of history as a meaningful sphere in which natural vitalities are being constantly directed and modified by human freedom. Second, the Christian faith seeks to understand man not so much from the uniqueness of his rational faculties as from an understanding of the nature of God in his historical self-revelation. To affirm that man is created "in the image of God" is to relate man to concepts of will and personality in God rather than to man's supposedly autonomous reason. On the one hand man is assigned the dignity of being a child of God and on the other it is realized that his sin derives not from his being limited, but from his proud unwillingness to accept his finiteness. Here the support for the dignity of man is not used to establish or guarantee his virtue, as is done sentimentally by simple Christian moralists and more ideologically by modern secularists who maintain claims for man's virtue rewritten on a non-theistic foundation. In other words, Niebuhr correlates the dignity of man not with his supposed virtue, but with the radical character of human freedom. With Pascal and Augustine, Niebuhr understands that the related problems of human creativity and destructiveness are rooted in the concept of creation in the image of God.

The modern view of man is a curious and unstable blending of these classical and Biblical perspectives. Three problems have proved insurmountable. First, the relating of vitality and form has been endlessly debated between naturalists and idealists, and more recently between the previous protagonists allied in a common rationalism and new challengers in the romanticists, with an unhappy political expression or caricature in fascism. Second, the problem of individuality has been no less perplexing. The Christian faith in its basic affirmation that man is created in the image of God roots this individuality in his highest relationship, but the Renaissance in its desire to overthrow all limitations upon man grounds its view of individuality upon "the infinite possibilities of the human spirit." The cultural reorientation that resulted from this movement shows that finally the self is lost in these abortive movements of liberation. This loss of the self can be traced in bourgeois culture, in naturalism, in idealism, and finally in romanticism. Their common failure to achieve their avowed aim of establishing human individuality on a sure foundation suggests that the Christian concept is more in tune with reality.

A third critical problem has been the attempt to explain away historical evil in terms of institutionalism or psychological structures of personality. Since it was usually assumed that man could change these elements at will, this easy optimistic view rejected the Christian understanding of original sin as touching all aspects of the self. The separate symptoms rather than the disease itself were studied in an isolating way. The self-righteousness which has attended some of these modern short-cuts to utopia has exacerbated the course of modern history and ought to have revealed the illusion of the simple perfectibility of man or of history as its own redeemer.

Niebuhr has been painting with a very broad brush on the canvas of Western cultural history. It is little wonder that specialists within some of these periods point out over-generalizations, if not some historical inaccuracies. They find more colors in the scene than those of the painter's palette, and protest that some areas of the canvas have been neglected whereas some others approach caricature. What Niebuhr is primarily concerned to establish (and here is the crux of the matter so often avoided by critics of his cultural survey) is that "both the majesty and the tragedy of human life exceed the dimension within which modern culture seeks to comprehend human existence."[1]

The theological significance of this masterful cultural approach to the doctrine of man is that Niebuhr has illuminated the self-refuting qualities of alternative explanations, and demonstrated in a preliminary way the remarkable relevance of the Christian explanation. The relevance is expressed in a framework that asserts both "majesty" and "tragedy" as realities organic to man on the basis of an

[1] *The Nature and Destiny of Man,* I, 122.

analysis of man in his historical relationships and on introspective evidence.

> The fact that man can transcend himself in infinite regression and cannot find the end of life except in God is the mark of his creativity and uniqueness; closely related to this capacity is his inclination to transmute his partial and finite self and his partial and finite values into the infinite good. Therein lies his sin.[2]

IV. APPROACH FROM REVELATION

The second source of Niebuhr's doctrine of man is revelation. It is intimately conjoined with the first source, an analysis of the human situation. Revelation is to be understood in a twofold manner: a revelation of God to the individual which is described in personal religious experience, and a revelation of God through social-historical experience. Concretely, this second type is Hebrew prophetism which prepares the way for the Christ who finally reveals the essential nature of man. The private revelation (Niebuhr also defines this as "general" revelation) requires the social-historical one (or the "special" revelation) to free it from individual caprice, just as the social-historical one presupposes the universality of the private one to give it credibility and rootage. Here general and special revelation have been related dialectically.

The transition from understanding man in the light of his self-knowledge to understanding him in the light of general revelation is a critical area in Niebuhr's thought. In reality they are opposite sides of the same coin, but it is just these changing angles of vision that are so irritating to many positivists and naturalists. They object to such philosophically problematic phrases as "man transcends himself" or "the self's capacity for self-transcendence."

But what does it mean to say that man transcends himself? In memory man can detach himself from his immediate environmental stimuli and call up for his special contemplation the drama of the ages. He can choose in his imagination to stand outside his world, his life, and even his reason. This quality of imagining indeterminate perspectives is more mysterious than what the rationalists call his reason because man can ask whether reason can comprehend the order of reality and whether such order as it may see comprehends the whole of reality. In other words, man's memory, his imagination,

[2] *Ibid.*, I, 122.

and his capacity for self-criticism are elements of general revelation. These elements hitherto defined in philosophical language are transposed into a religious key when Niebuhr describes personal religious experience.

> The general revelation of personal human experience, the sense of being confronted with a "wholly other" at the edge of human consciousness, contains three elements, two of which are not too sharply defined, while the third is not defined at all. The first is the sense of reverence for a majesty and of dependence upon an ultimate source of being. The second is the sense of moral obligation laid upon one from beyond oneself and of moral unworthiness before a judge. The third, most problematic of the elements in religious experience, is the longing for forgiveness.[3]

These three elements are hierarchically organized and receive clearer definition by the social-historical revelation of the Bible which reveals God respectively as Creator, Judge, and Redeemer. One of Niebuhr's strengths is the power of his analysis of Hebrew prophetism and messianism as he shows particularist or nationalistic perspectives in conflict with more universalistic ones. This contest culminates finally in the unsolved question of Hebrew religion as to whether there are resources of mercy in God capable of absorbing the condemnatory consequences of a divine justice that perceives the taint of corruption in the highest moral and cultural accomplishments of man.

V. CHRISTOLOGY AND THE DOCTRINE OF MAN

The Christian answer to this dilemma is expressed in its doctrines of atonement which are attempts to express "the good news . . . that God takes the sinfulness of man into Himself; and overcomes in His own heart what cannot be overcome in human life, since human life remains within the vicious circle of sinful self-glorification on every level of moral advance."[4]

Niebuhr's primary categories for his Christology are obviously Messianic-functional ones rather than Logos-incarnational ones. He believes that most of the fathers before Augustine were so preoccupied with the problem of finiteness—How can the infinite and eternal God reveal Himself to temporal and finite man? How can man escape death?—that they failed to reach the deeper Biblical problem of how a holy God can deal with sinful man. In his exposition of

[3] *Ibid.*, I, 131. [4] *Ibid.*, I, 142.

Jesus as offending contemporary messianism (and also some modern New Testament critics) by compounding Son of Man categories with the insights of the Suffering Servant, Niebuhr makes available his own categories of incarnation which deal more with "sacrificial love" as the locus of Christ's deity than with the classical "two natures in one person" terminology. Christ as the incarnation of "perfect love" reveals the essential nature of man as one created by God to live in love with his fellows.

Christ is the twofold revealer. He reveals the character of God in historical action. This gives added meaning to the view of man created in the image of God. Next, as "Second Adam" he reveals the essential nature of man. As "Adam" he reveals that man is created in love and for love (the perfection of Adam before the fall as redefined by Niebuhr), and as the "Second Adam" he reveals by the drama of the Cross that all men contradict their essential natures and that only the revelation of Christ which is the solution to the human dilemma fully reveals the depth of human self-contradiction. Otherwise the feeling of normality which we give to long-established and well acclimatized forms of sinfulness would blind us to the true dimensions of the problem.

> The revelation of God as redeemer accentuates a previous knowledge of God as judge, for the simple reason that the revelation of His redemptive love clarifies His character of Holiness, in terms of which human sin is judged. The anthropological consequences of this paradox are that faith in God's ultimate resolution of the contradiction in which man stands clarifies man's knowledge of that contradiction. He sees that his anxiety is due to his unbelief.[5]

Niebuhr uses his doctrine of Christology to throw light on man's situation both in its personal and in its social dimensions. Christ reveals the essential nature of man as love. The historical implications of this affirmation are that God's self-revelation meets the quest of culture for meaning in the dialectical relationship of question and answer. The question is asked in culture because there is a dim perception of the answer, but the actual answer is a threat to the security of the questioner.

> The fact that there can be no Christ without an expectation of Christ relates Christianity as founded in a unique revelation to the whole history of culture; the fact that the true Christ cannot be the Messiah who is expected separates Christianity from the history of culture.[6]

[5] *Ibid.*, I, 290.

[6] *Ibid.*, II, 16.

VI. MAN AS SINNER

Niebuhr's treatment of the doctrine of sin is so well known that only an outline is required here. There are some critics who know only this element in his thought. Evil remains basically irrational; if it could be explained man would not need God to redeem him. Recourse to the Devil as an explanation only pushes the problem back, although the symbol of the Devil gives dramatic expression to an insight of Christianity that human sinfulness is never simply an act of sheer defiance of God. Man has been tempted. There is an element of inevitability about man's precarious situation on the boundary between nature and spirit that tempts him to grasp at partial securities and to absolutize them. This unwillingness to accept his finiteness springs basically from unbelief, but finds its chief expression in pride—pride of power, pride of learning, pride of his goodness, and finally pride in a theology or in the very channels of grace in a religion which seeks to redeem man from pride. While sin is inevitable it is not thereby necessitated. Strict logicians find this distinction in words untenable, but Niebuhr appreciates keenly Augustine's battle against the tragic naturalism of the Manicheans every bit as much as the better known battle with Pelagius and his followers. Language is hard put to express this distinction in meaning. What exactly does "inevitable but not necessary" mean? Does it mean "statistically inevitable" (in the sense that many philosophers of science today would prefer the phrase "statistical averages" to the older concept of "laws of nature")? The reader senses a depth in the analysis here that corresponds to his self-understanding of the power of sin, but asks either for further definition or for a less obscure formula.

Anxiety, Niebuhr believes with Kierkegaard, may be described as the internal precondition of sin, but still man sins in freedom. Unlike Kierkegaard, he sees that while anxiety is the father of human destructiveness, it is also the mother of cultural creativity. To say that man sins in freedom means that he knows he is responsible for his actions. It is now necessary to qualify the statement that while man sins inevitably, he does not do so necessarily by the opposite horn of the dilemma that he remains responsible for his sin although not to such a degree (because of temptation, of psychological conditioning, and so on) that each act need be one of consciously wrong choice. Niebuhr recognizes that Reformation thought in its emphasis upon the universal sinfulness of man, when expressed rather inadequately in its doctrine of total depravity or in the destruction of the image of God after the fall, imperils the responsibility of man to make relative judgments between evils in history. He therefore pleads for a recognition of "the equality of sin" that also allows for the "inequality of guilt." It is not ontological fate but historical guilt that is the basis of man's alienation from God.

Niebuhr's phrase "the equality of sin and the inequality of guilt" seems to raise more questions than it solves. Perhaps it is wrong to ask how one can by some quantitative approach assert the "equality of sin" when the phrase may only be used, as the evidence in the passage would seem to indicate, to mean "all men are sinners." A more serious difficulty is the relation between sin and guilt when the latter is defined as follows:

> Guilt is distinguished from sin in that it represents the objective and historical consequences of sin, for which the sinner must be held responsible.[7]

But may there not be sins for which man feels or should feel guilty that have almost no determinable objective and historical consequences? What about bad motives for acts that happen to result in good consequences? Is there not here a need for further definition to relate degrees of responsibility to the persons concerned?

In Niebuhr's hands the doctrine of original sin is no excuse for complacency or for inactivity. It acts as a factor in puncturing man's inordinate tendency toward self-righteousness in his plans and activity. Niebuhr claims that the situation to which it is addressed is recognized by politicians and statesmen, although seldom by philosophers and moralists. Niebuhr offers it not so much as a doctrine of revelation as a transcript of experience when man looks at himself with his guards down. The doctrine is invested with political urgency in his defense of democracy.

> Man's capacity for justice makes democracy possible, but man's inclination to injustice makes democracy necessary.[8]

When pride issuing out of unbelief or faithlessness is regarded as the essential root of sin, it becomes possible to define sin vertically as separation from God. The horizontal dimensions of this sin in-

[7] *Ibid.*, I, 222.

[8] *The Children of Light and the Children of Darkness*, p. xi.

volve injustice to his fellow men and injury to the self in sensuality; that is, the self in its freedom gives undue devotion to some element of vitality within the self. Historic Christianity unfortunately has often been tempted to castigate more harshly the sins of the flesh than the more basic sin of pride.

If Niebuhr really regards "unbelief" as more basic than pride, it would seem justified to ask that this recognition on page 183 of Volume I of *The Nature and Destiny of Man* be developed to account for some human perversities quite inadequately explained by "pride" which in the subsequent exposition is really made the basic form of sin. There is a profundity in a common remark often heard about a person: "He ought to be a man. He ought to have more pride." Here the expressed desire is not that the person should exhibit a Promethean defiance of his creaturely status, but that he should at least live up to the responsibilities of that creaturehood. Niebuhr's categories fail adequately to account for the sins of the weak man as they do so forcefully for those of the strong man. This failure to be the man needs to be included in the Niebuhrian topography of sin. It is surely as common as our strategies of pride, and perhaps just as serious in God's eyes as the latter, because into this vacuum of weak irresponsibility and irresolution move the strong men of pride to bedevil our history.

VII. HUMAN SELF-CONTRADICTION

To affirm that the essential nature of man is existence in a state of love that was perfectly revealed in Christ, and then to describe the universality and inevitability of human sinfulness, is to pose a basic problem of how man's essential nature is related to his present contradiction of that nature. Historically Christianity has attempted too easy resolutions of this paradox by recourse to the Adam story and by a view of original justice as a quality possessed by Adam chronologically before his fall. In other words, a profound myth which describes something that is true vertically of all of us in every moment of our being has been "rationalized" by establishing a simple chronology and biology of sin in defiance of known facts. In Catholicism this abortive resolution of the problem took the form of the claim that before the fall Adam had possessed "superadded gifts" grafted upon his natural powers. The former, regarded as unessential to his nature, have been lost after the fall and need to be restored by the sacraments, whereas human nature itself has remained essentially the same after Adam as before. Reformation thought perceived that so optimistic a view of man opened the dike to a religion of self-righteousness, and by contrast asserted in various ways that man after the fall was totally corrupt, retaining only "relics" at best of the image of God, or in other versions unessential areas like "civil righteousness," naïvely regarded by Calvin as sound. Niebuhr believes first that a literalistic history or biology of sin leads only to cultural obscurantism and a false determinism, and second that even when this element is corrected both Catholicism and Protestantism fail to express the true dimensions of human self-contradiction. The one understates, the other overstates the problem.

In a brilliant analysis that undercuts both explanations Niebuhr asserts that there are two elements in the essential nature of man with their corresponding perfections. One consists of his natural endowments as a creature of nature, to which the associated term historically in Stoic and Christian thought has been "the natural law" or harmony of his impulses under a normal standard of social relations with his fellows. Thus there is tentative validity in the concept of "the natural law," but only tentative since the second element in his essential nature, namely, his being a creature of spirit and freedom, modifies the first and requires as its perfection what have traditionally been defined by Catholicism as the three theological virtues of faith, hope, and love. These last are by no means mere supplemental aspects; they are requirements of this freedom. Without faith in the providence of God man cannot be freed of the anxiety that drives him to sin; without hope he cannot face the future unafraid; without love he cannot relate himself creatively to his fellow men, for the self instinctively knows that beyond the norms of justice in any given situation there remains the imperative of a love which requires an I-Thou rather than an I-it relationship for its fulfillment. The present binding force of these "theological virtues" is testified to by the reality of conscience or by the sense of obligation.

> This character of the theological virtues as "law" to sinful man is perfectly revealed in the "thou shalt" of the law of love. . . . Such a commandment can be understood as stating an ultimate condition of complete harmony between the soul and God, its neighbor and its self in a situation in which this harmony is not a reality. If it were a reality the "thou shalt" would be meaningless. If there were not some possibility of sensing the

ultimate perfection in a state of sin the "thou shalt" would be irrelevant. . . . It is the sense that there ought not to be a sense of ought.[9]

Here is the point of contact for the evangelical call to repentance. Just as it is impossible to assign a locus to the residual health in a diseased organism, so it proves impossible to find some element in man, such as his reason or his will, which remains untouched by the fall. Figuratively one may describe the reality of the survival of the essential nature of man even in its state of contradiction by pointing to the self's "memory" at moments that love is its basic "law" in accordance with Paul's analysis: "So then it is no longer I that do it, but sin which dwells within me."[10]

> We have previously noted that the self which knows itself guilty is the transcendent self, or to speak more precisely, the self in the moment of transcending itself. The self in the moment of transcending itself exercises the self's capacity for infinite regression and makes the previous concretion of will its object. It is in this moment of self-transcendence that the consciousness and memory of original perfection arise.[11]

VIII. CHRIST AS POWER AND WISDOM

The preceding outline has developed Niebuhr's analysis of the human situation chiefly with respect to man's standing in contradiction to his essential nature of love as that nature has been perfectly revealed in Christ. The intellectual analysis needs supplementing by the recognition that the atoning work of Christ must be appropriated by "the existing individual" (Kierkegaard). It is this dimension of appropriation and of life in the light of Christ revealed as the Wisdom of God which also makes Christ the Power of God. In the understanding of the Bible a revelation of truth is also a revelation of grace.

Niebuhr's doctrine of grace is easily the most misunderstood area of his theology. One often hears comments such as these: "He believes in justification, but not in sanctification. He is too pessimistic about man. He accepts forgiving love, but not redeeming love. He does not understand the sacraments."

Each of those statements is wrong, but there is just enough submerged or partial truth in them to require serious attention in this analysis and perhaps some further development by Niebuhr in fu-

[9] Niebuhr, *The Nature and Destiny of Man,* I, 286, 293.
[10] Romans 7:17, R.S.V.
[11] *The Nature and Destiny of Man,* I, 277.

ture writing. Three layers can be discerned in these criticisms. Partly they are "dated." They result from the fact that Niebuhr's own pilgrimage in the faith began with a greater appreciation of that side of the Christian faith which shatters the idols of man's self-esteem and judges the "virtue" of man more severely than do the typical philosophies of our day. As a means of emancipation from modern ideologies, Niebuhr early emphasized the sin of man far beyond his appreciation of the Christian faith as furthering love, joy, and peace, the fruits of the Spirit. A simple counting of passages in the early works confirms this. But his subsequent "growth in grace" is often unfairly denied Niebuhr by those who, one suspects, may have read Volume I of the Gifford Lectures, but did not continue the study with the second volume two years later.

Second, these criticisms reveal an inability to understand Niebuhr's dialectical thought. After reading his analysis of grace as forgiveness and then as power, they either choose the first, as though it were meant as an exclusive alternative, or else they assume that Niebuhr's warning that corruptions are possible wherever grace is understood as power, particularly when ecclesiastical institutions claim a possession of grace, effectively cancels out the second dimension. Those who make these criticisms should perhaps not be judged too severely, for they are really only recapitulating in their persons the typical errors of traditional Christianity on these points.

> The Pauline emphasis upon forgiveness of past sins lies at the basis of the whole Catholic-Medieval interpretation of the relation of justification and sanctification, in which justification is made the prelude to subsequent sanctification, and in which the complex and paradoxical relation between the two is imperiled or destroyed, thus leading to new forms of self-righteousness.[12]

Third, these criticisms have considerable justice insofar as they are based upon a serious terminological mistake in Niebuhr's correlation of atonement with grace. In the Gifford Lectures he asserts that "sin is overcome in principle but not in fact. Love must continue to be suffering love rather than triumphant love."[13]

The word "fact" is extremely misleading here. It must be agreed that sin still exists in the world after the Cross, both in the unredeemed and the redeemed in such confusion (the wheat and the tares) as to require the symbols of the Second Coming of Christ and

[12] *Ibid.*, II, 105.

[13] *Ibid.*, II, 49.

of a Last Judgment before history itself is finally redeemed. In this sense, sin has not been completely, that is, "in fact," overcome. But the more common suggestion implied in these words, and an obvious misunderstanding of Niebuhr, is that the Cross does not now win any victories in history over sin. Such a view reduces the Atonement to the bare announcement of a "coming attraction" and would justify the charge that there is no doctrine of grace here. It is obvious from the whole presentation that Niebuhr does not himself so limit the Cross or so completely underrate the creative possibilities of sacrificial love, but a more dialectical statement of the problem is required than the misleading antithesis between "in principle" and " in fact."

IX. MAN SAVED BY GRACE

The intention of Niebuhr is to make the two-dimensional New Testament understanding of grace basic to his own exposition. An obvious question is whether he gives the New Testament doctrine of the Spirit enough consideration in his analysis of grace as power.

> The Christian gospel nevertheless enters the world with the proclamation that in Christ both "wisdom" and "power" are available to man; which is to say that not only has the true meaning of life been disclosed but also that resources have been made available to fulfill meaning. . . . The two emphases are contained in the double connotation of the word "grace" in the New Testament. Grace represents on the one hand the mercy and forgiveness of God by which He completes what man cannot complete and overcomes the sinful elements in all of man's achievements; Grace is the power of God *over* man. Grace is on the other hand the power of God *in* man; it represents an accession of resources, which man does not have of himself, enabling him to become what he truly ought to be.[14]

The creativity of Niebuhr's statement of grace (1) as a forgiveness which in the fruits of repentance brings new resources of fulfillment, and of grace (2) as a power which needs on every level forgiveness for the inevitable claims to possession or to a superior righteousness which the self or its institution will make, is illustrated by his exposition of Galatians 2:20. In this exposition, the "levels" of grace are correlated with the previous complex understanding of man's contradiction of his essential nature in terms of the historical action of God in the Cross.

"*I am crucified with Christ.*" Here is demanded a death of the

[14] *Ibid.*, II, 98–99.

old self centered upon its own concerns in such a way that no mere intellectual recognition of its plight can free the self to obey the law of its being; namely, realization in communion with others. "I can will what is right, but I cannot do it" (Romans 7:18b). The self must be shattered by being confronted with God, for "it is in Christ that the vague sense of the divine, which human life never loses, is crystallized into a revelation of a divine mercy and judgment. In that revelation fear of judgment and hope of mercy are so mingled that despair induces repentance and repentance hope."[15]

"Nevertheless I live." The self which must die to its sinful egocentricity is not simply destroyed in the interests of a *de novo* creation. It is born again in its essential nature as the "real" self, living in and for others in relationship to God, its true center of meaning. The new "I" is thus freed from demonic possession as a tool of nation, class, or race, and from the loss of its proper individuality in mystical schemes of redemption. Possession by the Holy Spirit is defined by Christ:

> He is the criterion of holiness because the revelation of God in Christ is on the one hand an historical focus of the divine, through which the mystery of the divine becomes morally and socially relevant to human nature, involved in finiteness and unable to comprehend the eternal. On the other hand it is the unique character of the revelation of God in Christ that it makes the divine and eternal known in history without giving any particular or partial force, value or vitality of history a sanctity or triumph which its finite and imperfect character does not deserve.[16]

"Yet not I, but Christ liveth in me." The negation of the previous clause that the self has been destroyed in the process of conversion or self-realization is here made subject to a further negation on a higher level. The meaning might simply be an expression of gratitude on the part of the self that wishes to attribute to Christ the whole work of redemption. But it might in addition be interpreted to mean that the new self perceives its accessions of divine help less as an accomplished reality than as an orientation toward Christ as norm in such a way that by divine mercy Christ's perfection is "imputed" to the self. The self is justified by the divine acceptance of its intentions rather than by its more ambiguous achievements. Here we are carried into the mysteries of Niebuhr's exposition of the doctrine of justification by faith which is so typical of his whole

[15] *Ibid.*, II, 109.

[16] *Ibid.*, II, 112.

thought. Often commentators have used Niebuhr's doctrine of justification by faith as the Archimedian position for explaining his whole thought. It must, however, be understood that Niebuhr is not simply reviving a past dogma without careful qualification and even considerable redefinition. He feels that the Protestant explication of this doctrine has suffered from special anti-Catholic animus, that Protestantism failed (in Tillich's phrase) to submit the doctrine of justification by faith to the experience of justification by faith, and that it has sometimes had the effect of relaxing moral imperatives and corroding the responsibility of the Christian to make responsible choices in history. In short, Niebuhr relates sanctification and justification in a dialectical relationship on every level of moral and religious advance, qualified only by his eschatological understanding of history.

X. MAN IN HISTORY

The preceding analysis of Niebuhr's doctrine of man has suffered some distortion in not being intimately conjoined at all points with his doctrine of history. Although it is beyond the limits of this chapter even to sketch the broad outlines of his understanding of history, it must be recognized that the fundamental contribution of Niebuhr to Christian anthropology is his understanding of the self in its historical relationships as expressed in the dramatic-historical world of the Bible. Here is a watershed between two colleagues who have influenced each other considerably. Tillich's doctrine of man seeks a foundation in ontological speculations which, while certainly represented in such Christian gnostics as Clement and Origen, are far removed from the naïvely dramatic language of the Bible. The crux of the matter is the phrase "naïvely dramatic." Can this Biblical-historical framework be translated into ontological propositions? Granted that the words "dramatic" and "historical" have ontological presuppositions, can they be "reduced" without essential loss? The ontological presuppositions may cry aloud for philosophical analysis, but the problem does not guarantee the results in any special instance or even that the attempt deserves success. One must acknowledge thankfully the architectonic genius of Tillich and the creativity of his system, but one may ask whether Niebuhr's less rigidly or even carefully defined dimensions of human selfhood are not more faithful to that revelation through history which the Christian faith sees in the drama of the birth, death, and resurrection of Christ. No ontological philosophy, even when it tries to incorporate a doctrine of history within its analysis, ever quite captures the authentic reality of selfhood dramatically portrayed in the Bible.

Continental theologians often find Niebuhr's treatment of the "Second Coming" as "Symbol" unsatisfying, and much remains to be done in relating this concept meaningfully to the present. In one area of eschatology he has made a considerable contribution. He gives a new urgency to the concept of the Resurrection of the Body as signifying the unitary apprehension of man as a creature of both nature and spirit. So organically related to both nature and spirit are man's freedom and individuality, that fulfillment must be pictured not as the freeing of an immortal soul from a finite body, but as a resurrection of body that will do justice to this rich view of human individuality by setting it in the context of a history redeemed by the Second Coming. Too often Christianity has treated its doctrine of man in individualistic terms, even on the levels of grace where the Church concept might be thought adequate to guard against this danger. The history of the types of grace analyzed and dispensed under institutional auspices betrays at base an incorrigible individualism. Niebuhr has succeeded in defining man in his historical relationships both in his lostness and in the requirements of a salvation that shall be social-historical as well as individual. This is an advance beyond the Reformation and Counter-Reformation controversies about grace, faith, and sanctification. His thought is no mere revival of "Reformationism."

XI. MAN AND THE CHURCH

At this very point of his greatest contribution there is a critical omission in Niebuhr's social picture of redemption. He articulates the relevance of Christian redemption for culture and civilization in their historical problems and he envisages in the "symbols" of the Second Coming and the Resurrection of the Body the final corporate or social redemption of history. But what of the Church which the New Testament presents as God's instrument for continuing his atoning work in Christ? Niebuhr is rightly critical of the sentimentalities, the tyrannies, the obscurantism, and the self-righteousness of the "churches" in history. For him, if we may invent a term, some elements in the Renaissance and modern secularism have been "hidden churches" in emancipating man from ecclesiastical sinfulness. He would reopen the debate between Reformation and Renaissance in the sense that the latter contributes to the understanding of development within history. Yet the historic fact remains that the Church or, more correctly, "the churches" have been the bearers of a revelation of Christ that has witnessed and does witness against the institution. More significantly, the Biblical drama itself presents a people of God in covenant relationship with Him, culminating in a new Israel of God. Its leader is the Christ whose body is the Church. It would be unfair to exaggerate this undeveloped area in his thought. There are suggestions in the Gifford Lectures about a reinterpretation of the sacraments along eschatological lines and statements about the Church in *Faith and History* that may well be expanded in the future. That he has a deep appreciation of the Church as the community of grace, open to the revelation of God, is clear from his prayers and his whole life.

XII. CONCLUDING STATEMENT

Niebuhr's sustained faithfulness to the Biblical presentation of the doctrine of man in its historical focus, his contributions to an understanding of the problem of faith and experience and of sin and grace beyond the entrenched positions of Catholicism and Protestantism, and his ability to invest Christian theology with relevance for the personal, political, and economic problems of our day entitle him to first place among Christian thinkers in America and to serious attention as a Christian apologist throughout the world by thoughtful Christians and secularists alike. The objections to and omissions in his thought suggested in this chapter come from one whose only defense is the rationalization of a hope that "they also serve who only stand and wait."

WILLIAM JOHN WOLF

DEPARTMENT OF THEOLOGY
EPISCOPAL THEOLOGICAL SCHOOL
CAMBRIDGE, MASSACHUSETTS

13

Paul Lehmann

THE CHRISTOLOGY OF REINHOLD NIEBUHR

13

THE CHRISTOLOGY OF REINHOLD NIEBUHR

CHRISTOLOGY is that branch of Christian theology which is concerned to explain and to interpret what Christian faith asserts about the person and the work of Jesus Christ. The doctrines which have traditionally served to express this faith are the *Incarnation* and the *Atonement*. The Christian doctrine of the Incarnation affirms that Jesus of Nazareth was God, embodied or incarnate in a human person, and is eternally the "only begotten Son of God." The Christian doctrine of the Atonement asserts that in and through His death and resurrection Jesus saved men from sin and death, restored them to the full and free relation with God which God intended for them, and gave to men the power to live new and fully human lives. Thus Jesus Christ is both God and Savior; His work and His person can be differentiated but not separated; and the task of Christology is to explain and to interpret the content, the interrelation, and the meaning of both.

I. GENERAL FEATURES OF NIEBUHR'S CHRISTOLOGICAL THINKING

Reinhold Niebuhr is not a systematic theologian, as he himself has often said.[1] At no point is this more apparent than at the point of his Christology. One looks in vain for a systematic consideration and elaboration of the Christological questions and answers. The lack of a systematic Christology is not a defect of Niebuhr's theology. It simply means that it is not necessary for every Christian thinker to be a systematic theologian and that the real concern and

[1] Most "systematically" perhaps in "Ten Years That Shook My World," *Christian Century*, Vol. LVI/1, No. 17, April, 1939, pp. 545ff.

contribution of Niebuhr's thought lie elsewhere. The great significance of Niebuhr's theological work is that he has attempted to overcome, and to a remarkable degree has succeeded in overcoming, the estrangement of the modern mind from the insights and content of the Christian faith. Niebuhr's achievement is due to the penetrating and creative movement of his thought from an analysis of the cultural and social *relevance* of traditional Christian faith to an analysis and demonstration (always with the full recognition that this cannot ultimately be done) of the *truth* of the Christian faith. It is to be expected, therefore, that Niebuhr's Christology should be involved in this general movement of his thought. Otherwise, indeed, his ideas about the person and work of Jesus Christ would not be integral to his theology as a whole.

By Reinhold Niebuhr's own admission, however, Christology has been and is the principal passion and purpose of his theological work. His theology, he once remarked, is actually intended to be nothing more than the analysis of the truth about *Christus pro nobis* and *Christus in nobis* in its significance for man.[2] If this is how Niebuhr himself views his literary labors, it is incumbent upon any interpretation of his thought to try to explore it from this point of view. The Christological fulcrum is not obvious. And yet, a rereading of his works, with his own key to them, has provided a fresh and rewarding discovery of an intrinsic unity. Christology is the leitmotiv of Reinhold Niebuhr's theology.

The movement of thought from the relevance to the truth of the Christian faith is really nothing other than the attempt to state the relevance and the truth of the insights which prompted the formulations concerning the person and work of Jesus Christ in orthodox Christian theology. The most explicit and elaborate statement of this Christological concern is in his latest systematic treatise, *Faith and History*.[3] Here the accent falls upon the relevance and the truth of the Incarnation and the Atonement for the culture, politics, and selfhood of modern man. But in the Gifford Lectures, which are his *magnum opus,* the mid-point as well as the turning point from

[2] Cf. Hans Hofmann, *Die Theologie Reinhold Niebuhrs* (Zürich, Zwingli Verlag, 1954), p. 235. Although principally a treatment of Niebuhr's doctrine of sin, Dr. Hofmann's monograph suggestively illuminates Niebuhr's work as a whole. It is gratifying to know that this indispensable source for Niebuhr interpretation is being made available in an English translation by Charles Scribner's Sons.

[3] See especially Chaps. IX–XI, XIII.

analytical to constructive argument is also Christological.[4] In a treatise on human nature and human destiny, one would not expect an extended treatment of Christology. What is important, however, is that the pivotal position in a discussion of the Christian view of man should be given to the specific connection between man and the person and work of Christ. The traditional theological distinction between the work of Christ "for us" (*pro nobis*) and the work of Christ "in us" (*in nobis*) is the crucial point in Niebuhr's exposition of Christian anthropology. The discussion does not make use of the traditional theological language, being concerned instead with the Biblical basis upon which the theological distinction rests. Thus, Niebuhr speaks about "grace" as "the power of God over man" and as "the power of God in man." But he regards "the double connotation of the word 'grace' in the New Testament" as the expression of the "two sides of the gospel." "The Christian gospel," says Niebuhr, "enters the world with the proclamation that in Christ both 'wisdom' and 'power' are available to man; which is to say that not only has the true meaning of life been disclosed but also that resources have been made available to fulfill that meaning."[5] Plainly, if unobtrusively, Niebuhr's account of Jesus Christ is the presupposition of his anthropology.

The Christology is even more concealed in his earliest writings. References to Jesus abound. But they are diffuse and imbedded in an intricate context of cultural, sociological, and ethical analyses. Niebuhr's first book has to do with religion and civilization.[6] But the argument again and again pivots around Jesus of Nazareth, and in terms which characterized the theological liberalism of the late nineteenth and early twentieth centuries. "The religion of Jesus," we are told, "is free of theological absurdities." "The significance of Jesus for the religious life of the western world is due to his attainment and incarnation of a spiritual and moral ideal of such absolute and transcendent nature that none of his followers have been able to compromise it by their practical adjustments to the social necessities of their day."[7] Remote as this way of speaking is from the orthodoxy which liberalism set out to correct, it must be regarded,

[4] *The Nature and Destiny of Man,* I, *Human Nature,* 1941; II, *Human Destiny,* 1943. See especially Vol. II, Chap. IV. The original two-volume edition of the Gifford Lectures has subsequently been published in a one-volume edition of several printings, 1949; latest printing, 1953.

[5] *Ibid.,* 98–99.

[6] *Does Civilization Need Religion?*

[7] *Ibid.,* pp. 73, 80.

in the light of Niebuhr's work as a whole, as seeking to express the orthodox concern for the centrality of Jesus Christ in Christian faith and thought. There is a neat hint in the Diary of the ambivalence of Niebuhr's thinking about Jesus and of a steady search for a fresh and meaningful position. "But for the life of me I can no more reduce Jesus to the status of a mere Galilean dreamer and teacher than I can accept the orthodox Christologies. The person who can make no distinction between a necessary symbolism and mythology seems to me no better than the wooden-headed conservative who insists that every bit of religious symbolism and poetry must be accepted literally and metaphysically."[8] The search for an alternative to these extremes becomes more and more articulate with each succeeding book.[9] The turning point comes with the publication of *Beyond Tragedy* in 1937. Here the "biblical view of life" is explicitly affirmed and the pivotal significance of the Cross, both for the human situation and as the clue to the person and work of Christ, is asserted.[10] From this point onward, Niebuhr's analyses gravitate more and more explicitly around a Christological center, and the Christological question becomes increasingly decisive for Niebuhr's account of the relevance and the truth of the Christian faith.

It is thus important for the understanding of the Christology of Reinhold Niebuhr to keep three general characteristics in mind. In the first place, Christology is *pivotal,* not *peripheral,* in Niebuhr's theology. Secondly, Niebuhr's ideas about the person and work of Jesus Christ are rather more *implicit* than *explicit,* though there is a general movement of his thought toward a more explicit affirmation of the central significance of Jesus Christ. And thirdly, Niebuhr's Christology is *reverse,* not *regular.* In common with the theological trend of the nineteenth century, Niebuhr reverses the direction of orthodox Christology, which characteristically moved from a consideration of Christ's person to an exposition of his saving work. But as Niebuhr's thought develops, he reverses the Christological orientation of theological liberalism. The theology of the nineteenth century abandoned the orthodox distinction between the person and the work of Christ as a scholastic construct and concentrated upon what in the tradition had been called "the work of

[8] *Leaves from the Notebook of a Tamed Cynic,* p. 120.

[9] So far as Niebuhr's developing Christology is concerned, exceptions must be made of *The Contribution of Religion to Social Work, Moral Man and Immoral Society,* and *The Irony of American History.*

[10] See especially the Preface and Chaps. I, IX, and X.

Christ." It is the "Jesus of history" rather than the "Christ of faith" who is the object of theological investigation. Niebuhr, without surrendering the "Jesus of history," and without returning to a scholastic Christological scheme, nevertheless comes at the end to the view that Jesus' relation to God is the basis of and the key to Jesus' historical significance. He writes:

The New Testament makes the startling claim that in Christ history has achieved both its end and a new beginning. The affirmation that Christ is the end of history signifies that in His life, death, and resurrection the meaning of man's historic existence is fulfilled. . . . The affirmation that in Christ there is a new beginning, that a "new age" has been initiated in the history of mankind, means that the wisdom of faith which apprehends the true meaning of life also contains within it the repentance which is the presupposition of the renewal of life. . . . Whether in the period when the Gospel of Christ was first proclaimed and accepted, or in our own day, the acceptance of such a gospel is always experienced as a miracle of revelation in the sense that the relation between God and man which it establishes is not the achievement of a rational analysis of life. Yet it is felt to be a new wisdom and power. From its standpoint it is possible to "make sense" out of life; whereas alternative approaches either destroy the sense of life entirely or make false sense of it.[11]

This is Niebuhr's way of saying that the proper understanding of the "Jesus of history" must *presuppose* not *precede* the apprehension of the heights and depths of the insights of the Christian faith.

It is this *reverse* aspect of Niebuhr's Christology which is the key to it. *His thought moves from the* Christus in nobis *to the* Christus pro nobis; *and only in the light of the latter does the Christological significance of what has preceded become plain.* From *Does Civilization Need Religion?* to *Beyond Tragedy* the major preoccupation is with the *Christus in nobis*. And from *Beyond Tragedy* to the latest volume[12] there is an increasingly articulate stress upon the *Christus pro nobis* which exposes not only the Christological concern of the early writings but also the Christological focus of Niebuhr's theology as a whole.

II. FROM CHRISTUS IN NOBIS TO CHRISTUS PRO NOBIS

In his early writings Niebuhr is chiefly concerned with the religion of Jesus, its contents, and its actual and possible role in per-

[11] *Faith and History*, pp. 139, 141.
[12] *Christian Realism and Political Problems.*

sonal and social life. The theological semantics of the phrase "the religion of Jesus" are as un-Christological as they could possibly be. The only link between this watchword of liberalism and traditional Christological thinking is that it tries to express what is important about Jesus of Nazareth. Niebuhr thinks within this framework. But from the first his attention is absorbed by a problem which foreshadows the reorientation of the later position.

The problem is the relation between "otherworldliness" and historical involvement, in Niebuhr's phrase, "concrete situations and material circumstances."[13] A tension permanently pervades his thought between two aspects of the religion of Jesus which he regards both as true to the genius of religion and to the personal and social life of man. After noting that a modern congregation would be shocked if it really grasped the significance of the Sermon on the Mount, Niebuhr writes:

> The modern Christian is inclined to destroy the force of the profound otherworldliness of such sentiments by reflecting that they represent an Oriental cast which is incidental and not essential to the gospel of Jesus. They are Oriental no doubt, but precisely because they are religious; and to regard them as incidental is to miss the whole meaning of the gospel. . . . For the absolute moral values incarnated in the personality of Jesus, which the West still reveres, are organically related to this otherworldliness. . . . The conclusion which emerges from such reflections is that the values of religion are conditioned and not absolute and that they attain their highest usefulness not when they subdue all other values but when they are in perpetual conflict with them, or it may be truer to say when they are coordinated with them. . . . Since man is a citizen of two worlds, he cannot afford to renounce his citizenship in either. He must work out his destiny both as a child of nature and as a servant of the absolute.[14]

This passage, from a chapter entitled "Transcending and Transforming the World," points to and points up the Christological correction that must be made in understanding Niebuhr's theology. On the face of it, these lines show how fully Niebuhr shared the theological outlook of the nineteenth century. The last sentence is almost a facsimile from a page of Ritschl. And the unabandoned preoccupation with the conditioned and co-ordinate character of religious values seems scarcely congenial to an evangelical understanding of Christianity, to say nothing of an orthodox Christology. Although

[13] *Does Civilization Need Religion?* pp. 171, 183.
[14] *Ibid.*, pp. 171–172, 185–186.

Niebuhr's subsequent rediscovery of Biblical faith brought into his writings a more traditional Biblical language and did indeed provide a dimension of depth to the religious insights which he sought to expound and establish, the shift of accent did not appear to have altered the early theological preoccupation and its framework. In the last analysis, he seems to be an unreconstructed liberal with a very, very low Christology indeed.

This appraisal of Niebuhr's theology is a misunderstanding. It is mistaken partly because it is too simple to do justice to the range and intricacy of his dialectical analyses. But it is also mistaken because it overlooks a remarkable connection between his early and later outlook and consequently obscures the crucial direction of his thought. This direction is *Christological.*

The passage cited immediately above expresses an uncertainty whether the "values of religion" are "in perpetual conflict with all other values" or "are coordinated with them." The latest book still maintains that "there is no simple solution for this problem."[15] But the problem is now stated in terms which presuppose more than a close approximation to the language and insights of the Bible. It may be that they presuppose a change of position, that the liberal theologian with a "Biblical hangover" has become the Biblical theologian with a "liberal hangover." On the contrary! A more careful reading of the text seems to me to disclose that the different way of stating the problem of the relation between the "values of religion" and "all other values" presupposes a clearer and more explicit grasp of what had been implicit all the while. The position has not been changed; it has been refined. The light has been set, not under a bushel but on a stand.

> In short, the situation is that the ultrarational pinnacles of Christian truth, embodying paradox and contradiction and straining at the limits of rationality, are made plausible when understood as the keys which make the drama of human life and history comprehensible and without which it is either given a too simple meaning or falls into meaninglessness. . . . The perennial question in Christian apologetics is how these validations of the truths of the Christian faith are to be related to the wisdom of the world, to the cultural disciplines which seek on various levels to find the congruities and coherences, the structures and forms of nature, life, and history.[16]

[15] *Christian Realism and Political Problems,* p. 199.
[16] *Ibid.,* pp. 185–186.

The "values of religion" in relation to "all other values" have become "the truths of the Christian faith . . . related . . . to the cultural disciplines which seek on various levels to find the congruities and coherences, the structures and forms of nature, life, and history." But what is significant is that this terminological shift presupposes a refinement of Christological thinking. Niebuhr thinks that "the ultrarational pinnacles of Christian truth" can be understood as the keys which make the drama of human life and history comprehensible" because of what Christian faith apprehends about the relation between Christ and the self. He says:

The Christian answer to the human predicament, a divine mercy toward man, revealed in Christ, which is at once a power enabling the self to realize itself truly beyond itself in love, and the forgiveness of God toward the self which even at its best remains in partial contradiction to the divine will, is an answer which grows out of, and which in turn helps to create, the radical Christian concept of human freedom. . . . The Christian doctrine of selfhood means that neither the life of the individual nor the total drama of man's existence upon earth can be conceived in strictly rational terms of coherence. Each is a drama of an engagement between the self and God and between mankind and God, in which all sorts of events may happen. . . . According to this answer, a suffering divine love is the final coherence of life. This love bears within itself the contradictions and cross-purposes made possible by human freedom. . . . Christian theology has sought through all the ages to make . . . the Doctrine of the Atonement . . . rationally explicable. This enterprise can never be completely successful, except in the sense that alternative propositions can be proved to be too simple solutions. Without the atonement all religious conceptions of justice degenerate into legalism and all conceptions of love into sentimentality.[17]

But this answer was already taking shape in Niebuhr's thought at the beginning. In exploring "A Philosophy for an Ethical Religion," he wrote:

In the early Christian church the naïve dualism of Jesus was given dramatic and dynamic force through his deification, so that he became, in a sense, the God of the ideal, the symbol of the redemptive force in life which is in conflict with evil. . . . Orthodox Christianity did indeed renounce the gnostic heresy which tried to give this implicit dualism explicit character by its distinction between the God who was revealed in Jesus and the God of creation. And history has justified the wisdom of its course.[18]

[17] *Ibid.*, pp. 182–185.
[18] *Does Civilization Need Religion?* pp. 198–199.

And in the "Conclusion," which follows this chapter and also ends the book, he wrote:

> There are resources in the Christian religion which make it the inevitable basis of any spiritual regeneration of Western civilization. . . . The task of redeeming Western society rests in a peculiar sense upon Christianity. . . . It has reduced the eternal conflict between self-assertion and self-denial to the paradox of self-assertion through self-denial and made the cross the symbol of life's highest achievement. . . . Its adoration of Jesus sometimes obscures the real genius of his life but cannot permanently destroy the fruitfulness of his inspiration. If there is any lack of identity between the Jesus of history and the Christ of religious experience, the Jesus of history is nevertheless more capable of giving historical reality to the *necessary* Christ idea than any character of history. . . . The God of our devotion is veritably revealed most adequately in the most perfect personality we know, as he is potentially revealed in all personal values; and his conflict with the inertia of the concrete and historical world is expressed most vividly in the cross of Christ. . . . The idea of a potent but yet suffering divine ideal which is defeated by the world but gains its victory in the defeat must remain basic in any morally creative world view.[19]

Of course this is liberalism. And what with "the most perfect personality we know," "the Christ idea," and a "suffering divine ideal," liberalism in a quite unblushing form. Yet it is surely plain that the central concern of the argument lies elsewhere. The central concern is the meaningfulness and the transforming power of Jesus Christ in the world in which the Cross occurred. Jesus Christ and His Cross—this is what the religion of Jesus is all about. This is what prompts Niebuhr's steady wrestling with the tension between "other-worldliness" and historical involvement. This is the source of the unyielding juxtaposition of Christianity and culture which provides the principal substance of Niebuhr's theology. And this is also the source of Niebuhr's initial and continuous effort to overcome the insufficiencies of orthodox and liberal theology alike. As he sees it, these insufficiencies are chiefly Christological, and he explores them under the aegis of a very evangelical Christology indeed. He wrote:

> It seems pathetic to me, that liberalism has too little appreciation of the tragedy of life to understand the cross and orthodoxy insists too much upon the absolute uniqueness of the sacrifice of Christ to make the preaching of the cross effective. . . . What makes this tragedy redemptive is that

[19] *Ibid.*, pp. 235–237. Italics mine.

the foolishness of love is revealed as wisdom in the end and its futility becomes the occasion for new moral striving.[20]

The work on ethics deliberately sets out to correct these defects. And here Niebuhr begins to draw more directly, though still very generally, upon the Bible. The ethic of Jesus is carefully analyzed with reference to its kinship with prophetic religion and its culmination in love as forgiveness.[21] To use Niebuhr's celebrated phrase, love in the ethic of Jesus is at once "an impossible possibility" and relevant "to the moral experience of mankind on every conceivable level."[22] The mistake of orthodoxy is to deny the genius of prophetic religion, which is to "insist on the organic relation between historic existence and that which is both the ground and the fulfillment of this existence, the transcendent."[23] The mistake of liberalism is that, in common with naturalism and secularism, it tries "to prove the relevance of the religious ideal . . . by reducing it to conformity with the prudential rules of conduct which the common sense of many generations and the experience of the ages have elaborated."[24] It is noteworthy that the discussion of the Christological question immediately precedes the discussion of "the real crux of the issue between essential Christianity and modern culture."[25] And once again the discussion turns upon the understanding of Jesus Christ and the Cross. Niebuhr declares:

In Christian theology, at its best, the revelation of Christ, the God-man, is a revelation of the paradoxical relation of the eternal to history, which it is the genius of mythical-prophetic religion to emphasize. Christ is thus the revelation of the very impossible possibility which the Sermon on the Mount elaborates in ethical terms. If Christian orthodoxy sometimes tends to resolve this paradox by the picture of a Christ who has been stripped of all qualities which relate him to man and history, Christian liberalism resolves it by reducing Christ to a figure of heroic love who reveals the full possibilities of human nature to us. In either case, the total human situation which the mythos of the Christ and the Cross illumines is obscured. . . . In genuine prophetic Christianity the moral qualities of the Christ are not only our hope, but our despair. Out of that despair arises a new hope centered in the revelation of God in Christ. In such faith, Christ and the Cross reveal not only the possibilities but the limits of human finitude in

[20] *Leaves from the Notebook of a Tamed Cynic*, pp. 85–86.
[21] *An Interpretation of Christian Ethics*, pp. 37, 223.
[22] *Ibid.*, pp. 118, 104. [23] *Ibid.*, p. 105. [24] *Ibid.*, p. 104.
[25] *Ibid.*, p. 121.

order that a more ultimate hope may arise from the contrite recognition of those limits. . . . Repentance is thus the gateway into the Kingdom of God.[26]

The "Christ-self" relation and the increasingly explicit adoption of justification by faith as a pivotal category of theological interpretation in the later works are more precisely Biblical than "the revelation of Christ [as] a revelation of the paradoxical relation of the eternal to history." Nevertheless, such a passage faithfully echoes Romans 5 and 6, and bears a striking resemblance to the paradoxical relation between despair and faith which marked Luther's attempt in his own day to give meaning and vitality to the gospel.

A still stronger statement of the central position of Jesus Christ and His Cross in Niebuhr's theology occurs at the close of the *Reflections*. Here again the dualism of the religion of Jesus is regarded both as the key to and the solution of the human situation in the world. And the insufficiencies of orthodox and liberal interpretations of Jesus are restated. The restatement, however, carries Niebuhr's Christology a step nearer to the creative orthodoxy which marks its culmination. The human situation is now characterized by "the tension between spirit and nature,"[27] and the truth and the relevance of the Christian religion in that situation are analyzed in terms of a theology of grace. The human situation is resolved in the experience of justification by grace. And this experience presupposes the traditional Christological thinking of the Church, especially of the Reformation, and illumines both the insights and the errors of this thinking.

Essentially the experience of grace in religion is the apprehension of the absolute from the perspective of the relative. The unachieved is in some sense felt to be achieved or realized. The sinner is "justified" even though his sin is not overcome. . . . In every life there must at least be times and seasons when the good is felt as a present possession and not as a far-off goal. The sinner must feel himself "justified," that is, he must feel that his imperfections are understood and sympathetically appreciated as well as challenged. Whenever he finds himself in a circle of love where he is "completely known and all forgiven" something of the mercy of God is revealed to him and he catches a glimpse of the very perfection which has eluded him. Perhaps the most sublime insight of Jewish prophets and the Christian gospel is the knowledge that since perfection is love, the apprehension of perfection is at once the means of seeing one's imperfection and the

[26] *Ibid.*, pp. 120–121. [27] *Reflections on the End of an Era*, p. 279.

consoling assurance of grace which makes this realization bearable. This ultimate paradox of high religion is not an invention of theologians or priests. It is constantly validated by the most searching experiences of life. . . .

The fact that Christian orthodoxy relates and fastens the experience of grace, which in the religion of Jesus is organically related to the total moral and religious experience in human life, to the one fact of the incarnation need not lead to a magical and unmoral interpretation of grace. Religious faith needs specific symbols; and the Jesus of history is a perfect symbol of the absolute in history because the perfect love to which pure spirit aspires is vividly realized in the drama of his life and cross. Thus a man becomes the symbol of God and the religious sense that the absolute invades the relative and the historical is adequately expressed. Naturally rational theology has difficulty in bringing the paradoxes of this mythological conception into the canons of rationality. In both orthodox and liberal theology the profound mythological conceptions of the incarnation and atonement are rationalized and their profundity is endangered by canons of logic and consistency. . . .

The idea of grace can be stated adequately only in mythical terms.[28]

This passage has been extensively cited because it serves both as a summary and a transition. As summary, it gathers up Niebuhr's early Christological position and shows how the concern for the truth and for the relevance of the Christian faith is both prompted by and pointed toward a remarkably evangelical view of the person and work of Jesus Christ. As transition, the passage marks the approach to the turning point from a less and less implicitly to a more and more explicitly evangelical Christology.

What we have seen is that Niebuhr from the first has concentrated upon the gulf between Christianity and contemporary culture and upon the anthropological consequences of that gulf. He is convinced that contemporary culture cannot resolve the human predicament because it lacks an adequate grasp of the human self and of the complexity and depth of its involvement in the world. He is also convinced that the Christian faith is both relevant and true because of this self-understanding. But neither orthodox nor liberal interpretations of the Christian faith have given relevant expression to the insights of Christian faith, so that its truth and power have been obscured. The principal reason for these errors is Christological. As Niebuhr sees it, the characteristic dualism of the religion of Jesus explains the tension between nature and spirit, ethical striving and

[28] *Ibid.*, pp. 281, 285, 287, 290.

personal reassurance which characterize the human situation. The focus of this explanation is the Cross—its occurrence and its symbolic significance. The Cross reveals Jesus of Nazareth as Son of God and Saviour, and validates the paradoxes of Christian faith and human experience.

Not the language but the *problem* with which Niebuhr wrestles, and the *direction* of his analysis, are in notable agreement with the Christology of the Reformation. "But what is the knowledge of Christ, unless to know the benefits of Christ, the promises which by the Gospel he has diffused into the world? And to know these benefits is properly and truly to believe in Christ, to believe that that which God has promised for Christ's sake, he will certainly fulfill."[29] It is not too much to say that Niebuhr's concern for the *relevance* of the Christian faith is a twentieth century version of the Reformers' insistence upon "the benefits of Christ" as the point of departure for a vital and meaningful Christian faith. For this reason, Niebuhr does his early Christological thinking in the context of Protestant Liberalism. Christologically speaking, Liberalism is the attempt to recover for modern man the meaning and the renewing power of what Jesus Christ has done in and to the human situation. For the same reason, Niebuhr engages from the first in the search for a more adequate context for his Christological thinking than that provided by Liberalism. And just as the Reformers moved from an appropriation of "the benefits of Christ" to a consideration and acceptance of "the truth of the gratuitous promise in Christ," so Niebuhr moves from the relevance to the *truth* of the Christian faith, and in so doing makes contemporary sense of the Christological insights of orthodoxy. Thus Niebuhr's claim concerning his Christology would seem to be substantiated. The Cross means that in his preoccupation with the relevance of Christianity, Niebuhr is really starting from and with "the benefits of Christ." It is this way of starting which gives contemporary meaning and effectiveness to the *Christus in nobis*.

[29] Philip Melanchthon, *Apology of the Augsburg Confession,* Chap. II, Art. iv, 101. The passage is quoted from the *Book of Concord,* ed. Henry Eyster Jacobs (Philadelphia: The United Lutheran Publishing House, 1911). Note also Calvin: "Now we shall have a complete definition of faith, if we say, that it is a steady and certain knowledge of the Divine benevolence towards us, which, being founded on the truth of the gratuitous promise in Christ, is both revealed to our minds, and confirmed to our hearts, by the Holy Spirit." *Institutes of the Christian Religion,* III, ii, 7 (Philadelphia, The Westminster Press, 1936). For expressions in similar vein from Luther, see Hugh Thompson Kerr, Jr., *A Compend of Luther's Theology* (Philadelphia, The Westminster Press, 1943), pp. 58–61.

Unlike the Christology of medieval and Protestant scholasticism, the Reformers broke fresh ground for understanding and interpreting the person and work of Jesus Christ by stressing the link between Christology and anthropology. Niebuhr's Christology stands in this tradition and shares its movement from the benefits to the promise, from the *Christus in nobis* to the *Christus pro nobis,* from what Christ is and does in and to us to what He does and is for us. As the passage from the *Reflections* suggests, Niebuhr gets across from the *Christus in nobis* to the *Christus pro nobis* with the help of such conceptions as "myth" and "symbol." And our next task is to try to follow this transition.

III. FROM CHRISTUS PRO NOBIS TO CHRISTUS IN NOBIS

The turning point in the theology of Reinhold Niebuhr is the point at which the concern for the relevance of Christianity is stated less and less with reference to the human situation to which the Christian faith is relevant and more and more with reference to the truth of the Christian faith by which the human situation is illumined and resolved. The intrinsic consistency between the later and the earlier treatises is provided by the way in which the substitutionary and the renewing significance of Jesus Christ and His Cross are linked. That the early attention to the Incarnation and Atonement is really a concern about the meaning and effectiveness of "Christ in us," that is, in personal human life and culture, is established and grounded by the increasing concern for the Christ who transcends and sustains the human situation in meaning and in power. And, conversely, Niebuhr thinks that the only way to give meaning and effectiveness to the "Christ for us" is through the continuous and diverse exposition of the inseparable and dialectical relation between "Christ for us" and "Christ in us."

In view of the gulf between Christianity and contemporary culture, the transforming and transcendent presence and power of Christ in and over the human situation involves an initial recovery of meaning. For Niebuhr this is not a matter of a more adequate rational interpretation of the person and work of Christ. It is a matter of an adequate mythological apprehension of revelation. He says:

> The Christian religion may be characterized as one which has transmuted primitive religious and artistic myths and symbols without fully rationalizing them. . . . We are deceivers, yet true, when we affirm that God became man to redeem the world from sin. . . . The dogmas which seek

to describe the relation of God the Father (the God who does not enter history) and God the Son (the God of history) all insist that the Son is equal to the Father and is yet not equal to Him. In the same way all the doctrines of the two natures of Christ assert that he is not less divine for being human and temporal and not less human and temporal for being fully divine. . . . The truth that the Word was made flesh outrages all the canons by which truth is usually judged. Yet it is the truth. The whole character of the Christian religion is involved in that affirmation. It asserts that God's word is relevant to human life. It declares that an event in history can be of such a character as to reveal the character of history itself; that without such a revelation the character of history cannot be known. It is not possible to arrive at an understanding of the meaning of life and history without such a revelation.[30]

It is this sharp juxtaposition of revelation and history, of theological affirmation and rational explanation, that leads Niebuhr to an increasing use of the term "myth." "Myth" is the conception by means of which the attempt is made to bring "the biblical view of life" and the meaningfulness of history together. And it is the explicit avowal of this attempt in *Beyond Tragedy* that marks this work as the turning point of his thinking and writing. "The thesis of these pages," he declares, is "that the biblical view of life is dialectical because it affirms the meaning of history and of man's natural existence on the one hand, and on the other insists that the centre, source and fulfillment of history lie beyond history. . . . An ancillary theme of these essays is . . . the necessary and perennially valid contribution of myth to the biblical world view."[31] And the crucial instance of the mythological interpretation of "the Christian view of history" is the Cross:

The idea of a meaningful history does not . . . explain the actual content of meaning. It is the thesis of these essays that the Christian view of history passes through the sense of the tragic to a hope and an assurance which is "beyond tragedy." The cross, which stands at the centre of the Christian world-view, reveals both the seriousness of human sin and the purpose and power of God to overcome it. . . . The Christian faith is centred in one who was born in a manger and who died upon the cross. This is really the source of the Christian transvaluation of all values. The Christian knows that the cross is the truth. In that standard he sees the ultimate success of what the world calls failure and the failure of what the world calls success.[32]

[30] *Beyond Tragedy*, pp. 7, 13–14.

[31] *Ibid.*, Preface, ix, x.

[32] *Ibid.*, p. x. The same point is made in *Christianity and Power Politics*, p. 213.

The clearest statement of what Niebuhr means by "myth" is in the Ethics:

> This is perhaps the most essential genius of myth, that it points to the timeless in time, to the ideal in the actual, but does not lift the temporal to the category of the eternal (as pantheism does), nor deny the significant glimpses of the eternal and the ideal in the temporal (as dualism does). When the mythical method is applied to the description of human character, its paradoxes disclose precisely the same relationships in human personality which myth reveals, and more consistent philosophies obscure, in the nature of the universe.[33]

It is not always clear from the use of this method whether myth is restricted to a method of interpretation merely or whether it is also a *category* of interpretation; whether "myth" and "symbol" are interchangeable or differentiable terms; and perhaps most important, whether "myth" expresses a precise or a loose relation between "idea" and "occurrence," "meaning" and "fact," "knowledge" and "reality." The prevailing tendency, however, seems to be to denote by the term "myth" a method of thinking especially suited to understand and to interpret the necessary connection[34] between historical experience and the ultimate mysteries of Biblical and Christian faith. "Symbols" are verbal (though not exclusively so) and chiefly Biblical and creedal formulations of mythical apprehension. They are, therefore, to be taken "seriously but not literally."[35] And since the real aim of the mythical method is to make effective sense of the connection between the "actual" and the ultimate mysteries of Christian faith, the focus of the analysis is the connection between "mystery and meaning."

> A genuine Christian faith must move between those who claim to know so much about the natural world that it ceases to point to any mystery beyond itself and those who claim to know so much about the mystery of the "unseen" world that all reverence for its secret and hidden character is dissipated. . . . A faith which resolves mystery too much denies the finiteness of all human knowledge, including the knowledge of faith. A faith which is overwhelmed by mystery denies the clues of divine meaning which

[33] *An Interpretation of Christian Ethics*, pp. 82–83.

[34] See above at Note 19, especially the italics.

[35] *The Nature and Destiny of Man*, II, 50. And again: "If the symbol is taken literally the dialectical conception of time and eternity is falsified and the ultimate vindication of God over history is reduced to a point in history. . . . On the other hand . . . all theologies which do not take these symbols seriously will be discovered upon close analysis not to take history seriously either."

shine through the perplexities of life. . . . The Christian faith is conscious of the penumbra of mystery which surrounds its conception of meaning. Yet . . . our faith cannot be identified with poetic forms of religion which worship mystery without any conception of meaning. . . . This . . . faith rests upon the belief that the divine is not mere mystery, the heart of it having been disclosed to those who are able to apprehend the divine disclosure in Christ. . . . (The meaning which has been disclosed is victorious over the mystery of existence.) . . . The Christian faith is the right expression of the greatness and the weakness of man in relation to the mystery and the meaning of life.[36]

In Niebuhr's theology the greatness and the weakness of man are related to the mystery and the meaning of life through the mythical apprehension of the divine disclosure in Christ. The symbol of the Cross is both the source and the substance of this apprehension. And the problem is to show how the Cross expresses the transcendent reality of Christ (*pro nobis*) and the transforming power of Christ (*in nobis*) in human nature and destiny. This problem is the central concern of the Gifford Lectures and of *Faith and History*.[37] The former, following the lead of *Beyond Tragedy*, accents "the perennially valid contribution of myth to the biblical world-view." The latter completes the argument of the Gifford Lectures by showing how the mythological apprehension of the Christian faith resolves the complex and fundamental problem of historical meaning.

After exploring the failure of classical and of modern culture adequately to comprehend "either the total stature of freedom in man or the complexity of the problem of evil in him,"[38] the Gifford Lectures turn to the truth and the relevance of a religion of revelation:

A religion of revelation is thus alone able to do justice to both the freedom and the finiteness of man and to understand the character of the evil in him. . . . The question is: is God merciful as well as just? And if He is

[36] Niebuhr, *Discerning the Signs of the Times* (New York: Charles Scribner's Sons, 1946). The passage is from a chapter entitled "Mystery and Meaning" which contains reflections upon 1 Corinthians 13:12: "For now we see through a glass, darkly; but then face to face: now I know in part; but then shall I know even as also I am known." The parenthetical sentence has been somewhat modified in the sequence of this citation but not so as to alter its meaning in the chapter.

[37] The core of the argument of *The Nature and Destiny of Man*, as well as the connecting link between the two volumes, is Vol. I, Chap. 5, especially Sec. iv; and Vol. II, Chap. 2, especially Sec. iii, and Chap. 3, especially Secs. ii and iii. The core of the argument of *Faith and History* is in Chaps. IX, X, XIII.

[38] *The Nature and Destiny of Man*, I, 131.

merciful, how is His mercy related to His justice? This is the question which hovers over the whole of Biblical religion. Because Christian faith believes the final answer to this ultimate question to be given in Christ, it regards the revelation in Christ a final revelation beyond which there can be no further essential revelation. . . . This revelation is final not only as a category of interpreting the total meaning of history but also as a solution for the problem of the uneasy conscience in each individual. . . . Christian faith sees in the Cross of Christ the assurance that judgment is not the final word of God to man. . . . The good news of the gospel is that God takes the sinfulness of man into Himself; and overcomes in His own heart what cannot be overcome in human life. . . . It is in answer to this central problem of history, as Biblical faith conceives it, that God speaks to man in the Incarnation; and the content of the revelation is an act of reconciliation in which the judgment of God upon the pride of man is not abrogated, in which the sin of man becomes the more sharply revealed and defined by the knowledge that God is Himself the victim of man's sin and pride.[39]

The Incarnation is the distinctive presupposition of the Atonement. The Atonement, with its anthropological corollary, Justification by Faith, is the distinctive content of the Incarnation and "an absolutely essential presupposition for the understanding of human nature and human history."[40] As Niebuhr sees it, this doctrine lost its commanding position both in patristic Christianity and in medieval Catholicism. "It emerged with elemental force in the Protestant Reformation to become the central truth of the Christian religion."[41] But this "Biblical-Protestant interpretation" of Christianity and of human nature and experience was lost to modern culture owing to "the virtual triumph of the Renaissance viewpoint over Reformation doctrine; and finally the disintegration of the Renaissance viewpoint." The Gifford Lectures offer a brilliant and incisive account of this development. But their main concern is with the truth and relevance of the doctrine of the Atonement. "This doctrine of Atonement and justification is the 'stone which the builders rejected' and which must be made 'the head of the corner.' "[42]

Niebuhr proceeds to do this necessary "rebuilding" by means of a mythical analysis of the Biblical-Protestant interpretation of Jesus Christ and His Cross. It is mythical because it points to "the ideal in the actual,"[43] or because, as he puts it in the Gifford Lectures,

[39] *Ibid.*, I, 127, 132, 142, 143, 147–148.

[40] *Ibid.*, I, 148. See also II, 55.

[41] *Ibid.*, I, 148.

[42] *Ibid.*, I, 148.

[43] See Note 33.

what "Christian faith discerns in Christ and the Cross" is the basis and meaning "of the possibilities and limits of history" which are both "the fruit of natural experience and a natural (rational) analysis of experience" and "the fruit of faith and revelation."[44] It is this mythical analysis which makes it possible to state what Christian faith discerns by starting either with a natural (rational) analysis of experience, or with "the revelation of Christ." It is also easy to forget that Niebuhr is thinking mythically and thus to conclude that his thought moves *in principle* from reason to faith, from history to gospel, from anthropology to Christology. But exactly the contrary is the case. Commenting upon St. Paul's account of "Christ crucified" as "the power of God and the wisdom of God,"[45] Niebuhr declares:

In these Pauline paradoxes we have a very exact and succinct definition of the relation of revelation to human culture. The truth which is revealed in the Cross is not a truth which could have been anticipated in human culture and it is not the culmination of human wisdom. The true Christ is not expected. All human wisdom seeks to complete itself from the basis of its partial perspective. . . . But on the other hand when the Christ is accepted, the truth embodied in him becomes the basis of a new wisdom. This is to say that while *Heilsgeschichte* is not merely an aspect of general history, nor its natural culmination, neither is it a completely separate history. Its revelations are what give history meaning. It is not true that life would be meaningless but for the revelations embodied in *Heilsgeschichte*. Life and history are filled with suggestions of meaning which point beyond themselves; and with corruptions of meaning due to premature solutions. The truth as apprehended by faith is not something which simple men believe upon authority and wiser men deduce from experience. For there is an element in the truth of faith which defies the wisdom of both wise and foolish, more particularly of the wise. But on the other hand, a truth of faith is not something which stands perpetually in contradiction to experience. On the contrary it illumines experience and is in turn validated by experience.[46]

Two symbols in particular express the way in which the truth revealed in the Cross becomes the basis of a new wisdom. The one is the affirmation of the Christian faith that Jesus is the "Son of God." The other is the Christian affirmation that Jesus is the "second Adam." When these two symbols are used to connect the Cross with human experience—specifically, the experience of the paradoxical relation of

[44] *The Nature and Destiny of Man*, II, 96–97. [45] I Corinthians 1:23, 24.
[46] *The Nature and Destiny of Man*, II, 62–63.

sacrificial to mutual love[47]—they are deprived of metaphysical and acquire historical meaning. Thus the deadening tendency in orthodox Christological thinking to end in speculative abstraction is avoided, and the unavoidable insights of orthodoxy leap into life.

Jesus Christ is the Son of God. This was the orthodox way of saying that Jesus was both divine and human, God and man; that the incarnation had really occurred in history and that it expressed the mystery of identity and differentiation between Jesus and God. Niebuhr accepts this Christology but emphasizes that its truth becomes meaningful with reference to the Cross. Apprehended with reference to the Cross, the symbol "Son of God" means that Christ is "the norm of human existence."[48] The norm of human existence is derived from the "ultimate relation of the divine to history." And the Cross defines this norm as love:

> The significance of the affirmation that God is revealed in Christ, and more particularly in his Cross, is that the love (agape) of God is conceived in terms which make the divine involvement in history a consequence of precisely the divine transcendence over the structures of history. The final majesty of God is contained not so much in His power *within* the structures as in the power of His freedom *over* the structures, that is, over the logos aspects of reality. This freedom is the power of mercy beyond judgment. By

[47] The following passage makes the point exactly, and offers a striking instance of Niebuhr's use of the mythical method. Having introduced the terms "Son of God" and "second Adam," Niebuhr declares: "The same Cross which symbolizes the love of God and reveals the divine perfection to be not incompatible with a suffering involvement in historical tragedy, also indicates that the perfection of man is not attainable in history. Sacrificial love transcends history. It does not transcend history as a thought transcends an act. It is an act in history; but it cannot justify itself in history. From the standpoint of history mutual love is the highest good. . . . The sacrifice of self for others is therefore a violation of natural standards of morals, as limited by historical existence. . . . Sacrificial love . . . is nevertheless the support of all historical ethics; for the self cannot achieve relations of mutual and reciprocal affection with others if its actions are dominated by the fear that they may not be reciprocated. Mutuality is not a possible achievement if it is made the intention and goal of any action. Sacrificial love is thus paradoxically related to mutual love; and this relation is an ethical counterpart of the general relation of super-history to history" (*ibid.*, II, 68–69). Niebuhr seems here to break new ground as regards the old and vexatious problem of the relation between revelation and reason, grace and nature, faith and history. The issue is not whether theological analysis rests upon an *analogy of being* or an *Anknüpfungspunkt* or even an *analogy of faith.* There must, of course, always be an *analogical* use of terms, as St. Thomas pointed out. But the real question is whether theological analysis presupposes a *mythical* apprehension of the divine activity in human history and experience.

[48] *Ibid.*, II, 74.

this freedom He involves Himself in the guilt and suffering of free men who have, in their freedom, come in conflict with the structural character of reality. The *agape* of God is thus at once the expression of both the final majesty of God and of His relation to history.[49]

The Cross, however, is the historical disclosure not only of the love of God but also of the love of Christ. Since the "Son of God" is crucified, the love of God in relation to history includes not only the paradox of majesty and mercy but also the paradox of power and goodness:

It is impossible to symbolize the divine goodness in history in any other way than by complete powerlessness. . . . The final majesty, the ultimate freedom, and the perfect disinterestedness of the divine love can have a counterpart in history only in a life which ends tragically, because it refuses to participate in the claims and counterclaims of historical existence. . . . The love of Christ, His disinterested and sacrificial *agape,* as the highest possibility of human existence, stands in paradoxical relation to the majesty of God.[50]

Thus the orthodox Christian assertion that Christ is both human and divine makes theological and human sense when understood in terms of "the paradoxical relation of a divine *agape,* which stoops to conquer, and the human *agape,* which rises above history in a sacrificial act."[51]

Jesus Christ is the "second Adam." According to orthodox Christology, the "second Adam" presupposes a "first Adam" so that what man really is and what he is destined to be are known and achieved only in Christ. Apprehended with reference to the Cross, this means that Christ is "the norm of human nature." The norm of human existence is that with reference to which man actually lives. The norm of human nature is "the final perfection of man in history"[52] with reference to which the full possibilities of being human are understood and achieved. Niebuhr analyzes these possibilities by showing how the doctrine of the "second Adam" meaningfully connects the ultimate and the original perfection of man;[53] how the doctrine de-

[49] *Ibid.,* II, 71. The underlining is mine, and calls attention to the movement of thought from *pro nobis* to *in nobis.*

[50] *Ibid.,* II, 72, 71. [51] *Ibid.,* II, 71. [52] *Ibid.,* II, 68.

[53] "To say that the innocency of Adam before the fall can be restored only in terms of the perfection of Christ is to assert that life *can approach its original innocency only by aspiring to its unlimited end.*" *Ibid.,* II, 77. Italics are in the text.

fines the possibilities and the limits of history;[54] and how the doctrine preserves the historical character of the perfection of history against attempts to surrender history to eternity in interpreting its fulfillment:[55]

The whole character of human history is thus implicitly defined in the Christian symbolism of the "first" and "second" Adam. To define the norm of history provisionally in terms of prehistoric innocency is to recognize that a part of the norm of man's historic existence lies in the harmonious relation of life to life in nature. To define it ultimately in terms of a sacrificial love which transcends history is to recognize the freedom of man over his own history without which historical creativity would be impossible. . . . The "essential," the normative man, is thus a "God-man" whose sacrificial love seeks conformity with and finds justification in, the divine and eternal *agape,* the ultimate and final harmony of life with life.[56]

The Cross as the meaning and fulfillment of "the whole character of human history" is expounded on a grand scale in Professor Niebuhr's latest systematic work. And with this more explicit elaboration, the central characteristic of his Christology becomes unmistakable. It now appears that the *developmental* movement of his thought from *Christus in nobis* to *Christus pro nobis* is substantiated by another movement of his thought from *Christus pro nobis* to *Christus in nobis.* Starting from the *Christus in nobis,* Niebuhr discovers the *Christus pro nobis.* Then he insists that the *Christus pro nobis* can be correctly stated only with reference to the *Christus in nobis.* What orthodox Christology tried to express in the doctrine of the substitutionary sacrifice of Christ, Niebuhr accepts and explores in its significance for man.

That the final clue to the mystery of the divine power is found in the suffering love of a man on the Cross is nct a proposition which follows logically

[54] Here the argument turns upon a fuller discussion of the relation of sacrificial to mutual love and centers upon the contention that Christian love is a real, although no simple, possibility in history, and that this possibility occurs only to the degree that it is inspired by the fact that the final meaning and perfection of life stand in contradiction to all historical approximations. *Ibid.*, II, 81–90.

[55] ". . . the Christian doctrine of an incarnated *Logos* who becomes the 'second Adam' is as rigorously opposed to dualistic doctrines which seek escape from history as to romantic and naturalistic ones in which history fulfills itself too simply." *Ibid.*, II, 91. The point is specifically applied to the problem of pacifism in *Christianity and Power Politics*, pp. 1–4.

[56] *Ibid.*, II, 80–81. The point is specifically applied to the problem of the creation of a world community in *The Children of Light and the Children of Darkness,* pp. 188–190.

from the observable facts of history. But there are no observable facts of history which can not be interpreted in its light. When so interpreted the confusions and catastrophes of history may become the source and renewal of life.[57]

As Niebuhr sees it, such an interpretation is possible because of what faith apprehends. What faith apprehends is what God is and does for man and in man in the death and resurrection of Jesus Christ. Once this has been apprehended, there is no facet or complexity of historical experience which is devoid of meaning or which deprives history of ultimate fulfillment. The mystery of the Atonement which is the truth of the gospel admits of "a limited rational validation."[58] This validation has a negative and a positive aspect:

Negatively, the Gospel must and can be validated by exploring the limits of historic forms of wisdom and virtue. Positively it is validated when the truth of faith is correlated with all truths which may be known by scientific and philosophical disciplines and proves itself a resource for coordinating them into a deeper and wider system of coherence.[59]

But no apologetic enterprise can be regarded as valid which weakens the priority and initiative of God's redemptive activity in Christ. A telling passage on the mystery and meaning of this activity may well conclude this exposition. After speaking of the content of the New Testament narrative of the Crucifixion and of its wider human and historical scope, Niebuhr says:

That love which could not maintain itself in history becomes the symbol both of the new beginning which a man could make if he subjected his life to the judgment of Christ, and of the mercy of God which alone could overcome the fateful impotence of man ever to achieve so perfect a love. In this double facet of the *Agape* of Christ is the point where a story in history becomes something more. It is recognized by the eyes of faith as the point where the heavens are opened and the divine mystery is disclosed and the love of God shines down upon him; and man is no longer afraid, even though he knows himself to be involved in the crucifixion. . . . Thus Biblical faith, which begins with a sense of mystery, embodying meaning, and moves to a sense of meaning in history which contains perplexity and ambiguity, ends by seeing human history perpetually, and on every level of its achievements, in contradiction to the divine. It sees the possibilities of new beginnings in history only upon the basis of the contrite recognition of this contradiction. Significantly, the same suffering love, the same *Agape* of Christ which reveals the divine mercy is also the norm of a new life.

[57] *Faith and History*, p. 137. [58] *Ibid.*, p. 152. [59] *Ibid.*, p. 152.

Men may have this new life if they discern what they are and what God is in this focal point of God's self-disclosure. Such a point in human history can be regarded both as the beginning of a new age for all mankind and as a new beginning for every individual man who is "called" by it, because both the individual and the collective realities of human existence are fully disclosed in it. If apprehended at all they are so apprehended that the old self, which makes itself its own end, is destroyed and a new self is born. That is why a true revelation of the divine is never merely wisdom but also power.[60]

IV. THE SIGNIFICANCE OF NIEBUHR'S CHRISTOLOGY

The Christology of Reinhold Niebuhr is an impressive and creative contemporary statement of the central insights and elements of orthodox Christian thinking about the nature and significance of the person and work of Jesus Christ. The literature confirms, moreover, Niebuhr's own estimate of the aim and substance of his theology as a whole. Christology is the key to the understanding and interpretation of his work.

For one thing, this Christology expresses the Christocentric understanding of New Testament Christianity as it came to light and life in the theology of the Reformation. The particular *historical* significance of Niebuhr's Christology is that it takes up the Reformers' concern for the personal-historical character of God's self-disclosure and self-giving in Christ (what they called "salvation by grace alone, by faith alone") and tries to give it contemporary actuality and meaning by rescuing it from the speculative abstractions and anthropological oversimplifications which had marked Christological thinking in the intervening centuries. In doing so, Niebuhr can be said to combine Luther's analysis of the "Christ-self" relation with Calvin's analysis of the "Christ-world" relation, and thus to provide the theology of the present with the possibility and the responsibility of working out a fully Protestant Christology.

The Christology that we have been examining has more than a historical importance. It has an impressive *systematic* importance as well. The anthropological orientation of these ideas about the person and work of Christ exposes the creative and indispensable connection between theology and ethics. Niebuhr is not writing systematic theology. But he is writing theological ethics. And what he demonstrates is that when Christian doctrine is considered in rela-

[60] *Ibid.*, pp. 143–144.

tion to ethics, the insights expressed in the doctrine take on reality and meaning and the concerns of ethics are given foundation and direction. Thus the orthodox doctrine of the person and work of Christ recovers a neglected ingredient and a creative method of analysis. Traditional Christology, for all its stress upon the human reality of the Incarnation and Atonement, has never satisfactorily related the human and the divine realities of the Christian revelation. The creative achievement of Niebuhr's Christology is that, without weakening the divine reality of the person and work of Christ, he steadily and illuminatingly insists upon its full human reality as well. This is a contribution to doctrinal theology of the first order. For it means that the relevance of Christianity is based upon its truth and the truth of Christianity is actual (that is, really true) in its relevance. Thus, it could be said that fresh ground is broken toward a fully adequate theological formulation of the person and work of Christ. The possibility is largely due to the use of a fresh theological method. The mythical method of theological analysis and exposition deserves continuing attention in contemporary theology. But it is not accidental that its effective application to the pivotal question of Christology in this instance should suggest, as already indicated, fresh possibilities for the solution of inescapable and yet stalemated theological puzzles.[61]

The celebrated opening of John Calvin's *Institutes of the Christian Religion* declares that "true and substantial wisdom consists principally in this: the knowledge of God and the knowledge of ourselves." Luther likewise was fond of insisting that "the Scripture beginneth very gently and leadeth us to Christ as to a man, and after that to a Lord of all Creation, and after that to a God. . . . We must begin at the bottom, and afterwards rise to the heights."[62] Niebuhr's Christology begins, if not gently, at least at the bottom—with the knowledge of ourselves. He does so partly because of what he had learned from the Reformers and partly because theology is nothing if not actual, and the actual theological situation in which he found himself was an acutely anthropological one. There is, however, no intrinsic prohibition against a Christology which starts with the *Christus in nobis*. This is the real meaning of Niebuhr's concern for the relevance

[61] See above, Note 47.

[62] Martin Luther, *Sermon on the Sunday after Pentecost, which is called Trinity Sunday*, EA / 2, 12, 412. The text on which Luther preached was John 3:1–15, the conversation between Jesus and Nicodemus.

of the Christian faith and certainly part of the secret of the power of this interpretation of the person and work of Christ to arrest the attention of an alienated generation. This Christology sets out the theology of the Cross not only faithfully but with communicative power.

The question, however, must be raised: Why is it that the central Christological concern of Reinhold Niebuhr's theology can be so tardily drawn to the attention of his contemporaries? This is, of course, partly due to its developmental character. There is nothing extraordinary about interpreting a man's thought in the light of its latest and maturest expression. Yet in this instance, the Christological concern is evident not only lately but from the first. Why is it that, if this is the case, the evidence was not more obvious? The answer is partly indicated by the consideration that in addition to Niebuhr's own development, the whole theological situation has altered, owing to influences which have also affected him. The dialectical theology has changed the understanding of the significance of theological liberalism. And what the dialectical theology does not account for may well be ascribed to the complex and tragic history of the twentieth century. But this cannot be the whole explanation for the elusive Christological emphasis of Niebuhr's early writings. The obscure Christological emphasis in these works is due, in the last analysis, not to the context of theological liberalism in which they are set, not to the prevailing theological climate which turned the attention of readers to other fresh and intriguing aspects of his thought. It is due to a particular oversight in the movement of these ideas from the *Christus in nobis* to the *Christus pro nobis* and back again. The oversight characterized both phases of this movement and points to the principal question that may be raised concerning this remarkable Christology.

To put the matter in a word: the question is whether this Christology is adequately trinitarian, or whether it is in the last analysis binitarian. That is, is it not almost wholly preoccupied with the relations between the Father and the Son to the exclusion of the relations between the Son and the Spirit? The Cross, which is apprehended and interpreted as the *basis* of a new wisdom and power, is not adequately apprehended and interpreted as *operative* wisdom and power. The case is persuasively made for the content of the mythical apprehensions of faith symbolized in and by the Cross and for the way in which these apprehensions resolve the problem of the self and of historical existence. But the power by which this wisdom and power effectually works is less persuasively set forth, indeed, almost not at all. There is a striking passage in *Faith and History* which discloses a glimpse of this problem and its marginal place in the Christological analysis as a whole:

> It is not possible to state the truth about God, as known from the standpoint of Christian faith, except in trinitarian terms. God was revealed in Christ in actual history. The Second Person of the Trinity thus defines that aspect of the divine power which is engaged in history, and which is known primarily by faith. . . . In the same manner, the doctrine of the Holy Spirit, as the third person of the Trinity is important, if we should understand that all forms of holiness and all signs of redemption in actual history are not merely extensions of human wisdom or human virtue but are the consequences of a radical break-through of the divine spirit through human self-sufficiency. Without relating these manifestations to God's nature, Christian faith degenerates into a shallow spiritualism. Yet this fact hardly justifies the long "filioque" controversy in Christian history in which theologians sought abortively to prove or to disprove that the Holy Spirit proceeded from only the Father or from both the Father and the Son.[63]

Certainly the efforts of the theologians have been abortive; and for the reasons which Niebuhr notes again and again and tries to correct. But there is perhaps another peril which arises from the inadequate consideration of the relations between the Spirit and the Father and the Son. And it may be that "this fact" does "justify the long *filioque* controversy in Christian history." The peril is that the mythical apprehensions of faith are deprived of the actuality of personal commitment and of transforming event. It is for this reason that the Reformers explicitly assign to the Holy Spirit the work of "energizing" and "enlightening" what has been apprehended "by grace alone, by faith alone." And however extended and futile the "filioque" controversy may be said to be, it does at least underline the point that unless the Spirit proceeds from the Father and from the Son there is no way of guaranteeing either the Christological substance of the apprehensions of faith or the personal character of the fulfillment of self and history symbolized in and by the Cross.

Despite its insistence upon the self-fulfillment made possible in

[63] Pp. 167–168. The "filioque" is, perhaps, implicit in the somewhat fuller discussion of the Holy Spirit in the Gifford Lectures, Vol. II, Chap. 4, especially pp. 98–115. But the context of the argument is a critique of mystic doctrines of the relation between "spirit" and "self" rather than a constructive trinitarianism.

and by the Cross of Christ, Niebuhr's Christological thinking does not sufficiently make room for the "Christ-self" relation as a relation of fulfillment in and through personal encounter. Despite its insistence upon the Cross as the standpoint from which it is possible to make sense out of the manifold and complex dynamic of history, Niebuhr's Christological thinking does not sufficiently stress "the mighty acts of God" as transforming events which, having actually occurred, serve as beacon lights in a sea of historical relativity whereby the channel to the fulfillment of human destiny is charted. The dynamic of history is rightly regarded as derived from the dialectical relation between the paradoxical activity of God and the tension between achievement and failure on every level of historical development. But the Incarnation and the Atonement express more than faith's apprehension of this dynamic. They point to the facts that something has occurred and does occur. God has become man. Jesus Christ has been crucified. In consequence of these events, other events happen which, though but signs, do demonstrate that history is not just *on the move* and the believer with it, but that history and the believer are going somewhere and that believers are to *take some stands* en route. In short, faith in Christ not only apprehends but also obeys. Sin is overcome not merely "in principle" but also "in fact."[64] Justification is not only a principle of meaning and a historical possibility. People are "in fact" justified, and the fruits of faith in sanctification, however tenuous, are actual human and historical realities.

Among the major unresolved problems of Christian thought and history, especially of the Reformation, are the problems of the relation of the gospel to culture and of the Holy Spirit to God's revelation in Christ and to the life of the believer. The Christology of Reinhold Niebuhr brings the Reformation abreast of itself and of the contemporary world because of the way in which it links justification by faith with the actual life of man, which the Incarnation and the

[64] Niebuhr rightly calls attention to the dangers in the Augustinian and Catholic acceptance of this point. And he does recognize that "if destruction of self-love 'in principle' does not also mean 'in fact' in some basic sense, what does it mean?" Yet the proper concern to avoid "a too simple statement" is not accompanied by a sufficient consideration of what, in the context of the dialectic of faith and history, "in fact" could mean. Once again he recognizes that the problem has to do with the spirit possessing the self and the Holy Spirit. But the preoccupation with the parallelism between the Father and the Son and the justice and mercy of God in forgiving love overshadows its consideration. The "first" and "second Adam" crowd out the "filioque." See *The Nature and Destiny of Man,* Vol. II, Chaps. IV and V; especially, pp. 137 and 112.

Atonement require. If this singular achievement should leave the other problem still unresolved, let it be remembered that the doctrine of the Holy Spirit is still waiting for the full creative attention of the Church. This doctrine promises to be in the foreground of contemporary theological reflection and debate. And toward the creative realization of this prospect, Niebuhr's Christology has already drawn suggestive boundaries and broken fertile ground.

Paul Lehmann

Stephen Colwell Professor of Applied Christianity
Princeton Theological Seminary
Princeton, New Jersey

14

Karl Löwith

HISTORY AND CHRISTIANITY

14

HISTORY AND CHRISTIANITY

MODERN man overestimates the significance of history within the totality of reality because he has lost the sense of human nature within nature at large. The natural universe of which we are a strange part is irreducible to universal history, for world history is never identical with the world. The term *Weltgeschichte* is the presumptuous result of modern historical thinking; and, if taken literally, it is a misconception of the universe, for the universality of history concerns only our historical world. The history of human civilization is something vanishing within the totality of the world. The historical world may or may not have a meaning and purpose; the quest for meaning and purpose is only meaningful if restricted to that which is conditioned and contrived by the purpose of a human or divine will.

If history has to be defined by and delimited to man's willful enterprise, the question about its meaning is in itself historically conditioned. It is a specifically Western concern which presupposes that history has a purpose as *telos* and *finis*. This belief in a final purpose has originated from the faith in the purposeful will of God with regard to his creation. With the secularization of the Christian theologies of history to the modern philosophies of history, the will of God became replaced by the will of man and divine Providence by human prevision. The possibility of a philosophy of history rests on secularized eschatology.

Neither classical philosophy nor Christian theology has asked our question about the meaning of history as the decisive scene of human existence and destiny. For the Greek historians history was governed by the laws of human nature, while Greek philosophers investigated that which is permanent.

For the Christian faith history is not an autonomous realm of human endeavor and progress but a realm of sin and death, and therefore in need of redemption. Within both perspectives the historical progress could not be experienced as all-important. The belief in the absolute relevance of history as such is the result of the emancipation of the modern historical consciousness from the foundation in and limitation by classical cosmology and Christian theology. Both restricted the experience of history and prevented its growing to indefinite dimensions.

Nothing in the New Testament warrants a conception of the new events that constituted early Christianity as the beginning of a new epoch of secular developments within a continuous process. For the early Christians the history of this world had rather come to an end, and Jesus himself was seen by them not as a world-historical link in the chain of historical happenings but as the unique redeemer. What really begins with the appearance of Jesus Christ is not a new epoch of secular history, called "Christian," but the beginning of an end. The Christian times are Christian only insofar as they are the last time. Because the Kingdom of God, moreover, is not to be realized in a continuous process of historical development, the eschatological history of salvation also cannot impart a new and progressive meaning to the history of the world, which is fulfilled by having reached its term. The "meaning" of the history of this world is fulfilled against itself because the story of salvation, as embodied in Jesus Christ, redeems and dismantles, as it were, the hopeless history of the world. In the perspective of the New Testament the history of the world entered into the eschatological substance of its unworldly message only insofar as the first generations after Christ were still involved in it, but without being of it.

Thus, if we venture to say that our modern historical consciousness is derived from Christianity, this can mean only that the eschatological outlook of the New Testament has opened the perspective toward a future fulfillment—originally beyond, and eventually within, historical existence. In consequence of the Christian consciousness we have a historical consciousness which is as Christian by derivation as it is non-Christian by consequence, because it lacks the belief that Christ is the beginning of an end and his life and death the final answer to an otherwise insoluble question. If we understand, as we must, Christianity in the sense of the New Testament and history in our modern sense, that is, as a continuous process of human action and secular developments, a "Christian history" is non-sense. The only, though weighty, excuse for this inconsistent compound of a Christian history is to be found in the fact that the history of the world has continued its course of sin and death in spite of the eschatological event, message, and consciousness. The world after Christ has assimilated the Christian perspective toward a goal and fulfillment and, at the same time, has discarded the living faith in an imminent *eschaton*. If the modern mind, concerned with the preservation and advance of the existing society, feels only the impracticability of such an eschatological outlook, it forgets that for the founders of the Christian religion, to whom the collapse of society was certain and imminent, it was, instead, practical good sense which dictated such a concentration upon ultimate issues and a corresponding indifference toward intermediate stages of worldly happenings.

The primitive faith of the early Christians believed that the Kingdom of God was at hand, and the early Christians were therefore unconcerned with the process and progress of the history of this world. The sophisticated faith of modern Christians is primarily concerned with the disorderly history of this world when confronting it ultimately with faith. Since the establishment of the Christian Church in the history of this world, the Christian faith has had to face the unbelief or the false beliefs of the world. The "and" between Faith and History indicates the problem of the relation between faith in things unseen and visible world history.

The primary question is, however, not how to answer a fixed question but how to pose the question itself. The answer which Niebuhr works out when asking about the relation between history and faith is predetermined by a question which implies that history and faith are *correlated as something provisional to something ultimate*. The Christian faith offers an answer to history at large and to the "special problems of our age." Hence follows the apologetic purpose of Niebuhr's book, which is, however, not a dogmatic defense against unbelief and false belief; rather it is itself essentially involved in the actual history of our world and in a historic perspective. Niebuhr is aware of the impossibility of erecting a "philosophy of history" on the foundation of faith, yet he attempts a Christian interpretation of history, taking history in the ordinary, non-theological sense of the word.

The apologetic purpose is carried through by an analysis of three approaches to the problem of history: Greek classical thought (which he dismisses as having no permanent relevance); Jewish-Christian faith; and the modern belief in history as such, that is, the assumption that the growth of man's power and freedom, in which Niebuhr also believes, will gradually resolve every human perplexity and eventually an indefinite progress will redeem history by itself. Niebuhr holds that there are obvious truths (in the plural) about life and history, discovered by modern sciences, and "provisional meanings" which, however, make sense only if they become completed and superseded by the final truth and meaning (in the singular) which is apprehended by faith. The modern, dynamic, and progressive view of history is, therefore, more closely related to the Christian sense of history than to the a-historical spirituality of Oriental and Greek thinking. Both the classical and the modern approach are inadequate, for the first reduces history "too simply" to natural recurrences and tragic fate, whereas the second is betrayed into illusions about the human situation which involves both a creature and a creator whose freedom is creative as well as destructive. The Christian faith prevents these provisional meanings from becoming absolutes and man's freedom from becoming *hybris*.

The revelation of Christ and faith in God's redemptive purpose are defined as both the fulfillment and the negation of all partial meanings in history, as they are "embodied" in national, imperial, and world-wide cultural destinies. In Niebuhr's presentation, the perplexing problem of how the Christian story of salvation is embodied in the history of the world seems to be resolved in a dialectical balance between the common experience of visible history and the individual experience of faith in things unseen by the rather conventional and unexamined assertion that there are "facets of the eternal in the flux of time." Tangents of moral meaning in history are supposed to point toward a supra-historical center. Being assured of this center of meaning and orientation by a faith which reduces the doctrines of creation, incarnation, resurrection, and consummation to mere "symbols" (which have, however, to be taken "seriously" but which would be embarrassing when taken literally), Niebuhr has little difficulty in asserting the superiority of the Christian interpretation: it is above the alternatives of despair and complacency, evolutionary optimism and defeatism, secularism and escapism, pietistic sectarianism and Catholic institutionalism, worldliness and asceticism, and so on. The Christian interpretation of history is more adequate than alternative interpretations because it is dialectically more comprehensive: "it comprehends all of life's antinomies and contradictions into a system of meaning." One wonders whether this criterion of the superiority of the Christian interpretation is not rather Hegelian than Christian. And if pride is sin, then this is the intellectual sin of dialectical comprehensiveness—that it cannot help being always superior to the too simple alternatives which will only *one* thing.

Faith and History leaves one with the general impression that the limits of man's virtue, wisdom, and power and the unresolved questions of the human enterprise exist only to be answered and completed by faith and religion. But one may question if the task of Christian apologetic is not "too simply" conceived, if it is worked out in this manner. For why should not the contradictions and ambiguities of our historical enterprise have to be endured with mature resignation instead of overcome and resolved "ultimately"? If, since Kant, philosophers make room for faith by subjecting the competence of reason to a philosophical criticism, they do not pretend to know the ultimate truth by revelation and faith. If theologians try to establish the truth of the Christian Gospel "at the very limits of all systems of meaning," and as the completion of provisional half-truths and meanings, they will have to demonstrate the validity of their apologetic on more than dialectic grounds.

Niebuhr distinguishes a negative and a positive apologetic task. The first consists in demonstrating that all worldly wisdom—be it optimistic or pessimistic, emphasizing either the dignity or the misery of man—gives an inadequate view of the total human situation. This "negative proof of the Christian truth" (it is actually only an intimation of its desirability) cannot be transmuted into a positive one. If there is a positive one, it must consist in "correlating" the truth apprehended by faith and repentance to truths about life and history gained in human experience. But the truth of faith, says Niebuhr, is incapable of simple correlation with any system of worldly experience. It cannot be explicated rationally in any worldly validation. The perfect goodness of Christ was validated by an obvious defeat in history, and no nation has ever been a saintly martyr-nation. But how can one then assert provisional meanings in the historical destinies of national and world-wide civilizations? And how can one simply say that the Biblical faith "must" be fruitful of genuine renewals of life in the historic, collective, human enterprise? Is human "life" at all identical with "history," and responsibility for one's neighbor with responsibility for history? And is responsibility at all an ultimate religious and not only a moral category? There is in man's attitude toward his fellow men a very real dialectic between quantity and quality which Niebuhr ignores because he conceives of history as a mere extension of human life and freedom, in spite of his insight that the realization of Christian love not only does not extend man's historic potentialities but makes historic survival even more problematic, "for it points to the fact that the highest form of human goodness embodies a heedlessness of self which endangers the self in its physical security." And yet Niebuhr insists that it is necessary to "incorporate" what is true in the modern discovery of a development in history into the final truth of the Christian Gospel. Thus, the intellectual power and versatility of *Faith and History* leave us with a profound ambiguity: the author of the book shares neither the modern, now obsolete, faith in history as such, nor the ancient faith in that Christ with whom the time was fulfilled, but makes an attempt to salvage by means of a liberal faith in symbols some fragments of the modern but shaken belief in the meaningfulness and purposefulness of the historical process.

Our critical thesis by which we judged Niebuhr's attempt to determine the "and" between "Faith and History" which separates God's redemptive purpose from the human adventure called history can be substantiated by a brief survey of some typical Christian positions with regard to the process of history. Those who have faith in Christ do not believe in the ultimate or provisional meaningfulness of history; rather they feel the radical *disproportion* between the history of the world and the succession of faith as implied in the story of the great flood.

The New Testament contains only one explicit reference to the world's history: it separates strictly what we owe to Caesar from what we owe to God. St. Paul develops for the first time a sort of theology of history by interpreting the succession of Gentiles as the providential fulfillment of the religious history of the Jews. This progress from the unbelieving Jews to the believing Gentiles refers, however, not to the process and progress of secular history but to the succession of faith. Augustine interprets the history of the world in relation to the purpose of God. The city of God and the city of Earth sometimes meet, but the story of salvation is, in principle, separated from the history of the world as truth (*veritas*) from vanity (*vanitas*) or faith from unbelief. Thomas does not deal at all with the historical process but follows instead the classical tradition by asking about the just political order, the justice of which cannot be understood historically but only morally and religiously. Luther compares the ups and downs of history with the vicissitudes of a tournament and its changing fortunes. Historically acting men are only "God's memory." To look behind the curtain of the visible scene of history in order to discover the real causes of the growth and decline of empires and nations is not a concern of faith in God's inscrutable will. When Melanchthon defended the cause of the reformation before the emperor, he was deeply disturbed about the possible historical consequences of his decisions. Luther wrote to him: "You are irritated by the unpredictable issue because it is beyond your grasp of understanding. But if you were able to understand it, I would not like to have any part in it and even less to be its head. God has put our cause under a viewpoint which you cannot realize by your rhetoric and philosophy, that is, on faith alone to which all things are subjected which are invisible and do not appear to the eyes. Those who try to make them visible, apparent, and intelligible will only earn distress." Faith cannot be represented to the world in terms of history but only in and by faith itself, regardless of the historical consequences which no man can anticipate and judge. Pascal's *Pensées* contain a single sentence on history: "The history of the church should rather be called the history of truth," for it seemed to him self-evident that true history is nothing else than the story of salvation as preached by the Church. The work of Kierkegaard is one coherent criticism of Hegel's identification of Christian faith and philosophical reason manifesting itself in the history of the world and of Christianity as a world-wide religion. Finally, a statement of K. Barth: "The story of salvation is not merely *one* story or the guiding thread within the tissue of all other stories, but the only authentical history which embraces all the others insofar as the story of salvation manifests itself in the others by way of hints or intimations."

All these Christian thinkers from the first century to the twentieth have, of course, experienced history even as we do, but none of them has tried to explicate the story of salvation in terms of the world's history. If it were possible to explicate the event of Christ in history and as history, this would imply the cancellation of the fundamental difference between the will of God and the will of man.

All that can be said in favor of relating the one to the other "history" is that, for the believer, profane history may have the character of a sign, visibly intimating that which is known only to faith in things unseen. Thus historical catastrophes can be interpreted as intimations of the last judgment, though the latter cannot be comprehended in terms of historical disasters. Theodor Haecker wrote in his diary of 1939–1945: "For the Christian believer there can be no doubt that the significance of external happenings can be shockingly different. By significance I understand the varying proximity or distance of the history of the world to the 'history' of the kingdom of God. A Christian cannot share Ranke's opinion that all epochs are equidistant from God. Or can one deny that Rome under Augustus, Palestine under Herod and Pilate were more intimately related to the story of salvation than Europe under Napoleon? . . . That our present history has such an intimate relation to the story of salvation, this belief many will share with me."

Even such a cautious statement is open to criticism, for the major proximity of "Rome under Augustus" to "Christ" is only historically a real proximity. From the viewpoint of faith, however, it is yet a semblance because the relation of the story of salvation to the history of the world cannot be fixed and defined by faith. The factual coincidence of Rome under Augustus with Christ does not exclude the possibility that God could have revealed himself a thousand years earlier or two thousand years later in Europe under Napoleon or in Russia under Stalin or in Germany under Hitler. And since the story of salvation does not refer to historical empires, nations, and civilizations but to each human soul, one cannot dismiss the thought that Christianity, that is, faith in Christ, is essentially indifferent over against world-historical differences, even over against the difference between civilization and barbarism. Both reveal under different circumstances the same human nature, though man appears better than he really is if orderly and civilized conditions do not put him to the test. Even atomic warfare would not change what human nature essentially is. "It will only put an end to a globe which we always knew was doomed to a bad end in any case. I am not sure that it would not be typical of human history if assuming that the world was bound some day to cease to be a possible habitation for living creatures—men should by their own contrivance hasten that end and anticipate the operation of nature or of time—because it is so much in the character of Divine judgement in history that men are made to execute it upon themselves."[1]

The missing link between "Faith *and* History" is perhaps something very positive because it is the Christian faith (as well as philosophical skepticism) which gives us that elasticity of mind which frees us from the historicism which is the typical dogmatism and obsession of our time. A wise historian and a Christian (something different from a "Christian historian") concludes his study on Christianity and History with the sentence: "Hold to Christ, and for the rest be totally uncommitted." It is more than doubtful whether a philosopher can offer an equally firm principle over against the predicament of human history. But even a philosopher may agree with Butterfield's sober statement that "when all is as remote as the tale of Troy, we are able at last perhaps to be a little sorry for everybody."

KARL LÖWITH

PHILOSOPHICAL SEMINAR
THE UNIVERSITY OF HEIDELBERG
GERMANY

[1] H. Butterfield, *Christianity and History* (New York: Charles Scribner's Sons, 1950), p. 66.

15

Robert E. Fitch

REINHOLD NIEBUHR'S PHILOSOPHY OF HISTORY

15

REINHOLD NIEBUHR'S PHILOSOPHY OF HISTORY

An inquiry into Niebuhr's philosophy of history must focus our attention on six volumes. The systematic statement of this philosophy is found in *Faith and History* (1949) and in *Human Destiny* (1943). There are two volumes of essays, *Beyond Tragedy* (1937) and *Discerning the Signs of the Times* (1946), which are important for the elaboration of some of his basic insights in this field. Finally, one must add *Reflections on the End of an Era* (1934) and *The Irony of American History* (1952) as instances of the practical application of his doctrine. However, all of his writings, whether published in books,[1] or scattered through various magazines, have some bearing on the problem.

In this essay it will be convenient to distinguish between Niebuhr's formal philosophy of history—under the rubric "Faith and History" —and his functioning philosophy of history—under the rubric "The Handles to History." The distinction is probably in equal parts real

[1] In this essay those books by Niebuhr which are cited are referred to by the initials of their titles, as follows:

BT: *Beyond Tragedy.*
CLCD: *The Children of Light and the Children of Darkness.*
CPP: *Christianity and Power Politics.*
CRPP: *Christian Realism and Political Problems.*
DST: *Discerning the Signs of the Times.*
FH: *Faith and History.*
HD: *Human Destiny,* Vol. II of *The Nature and Destiny of Man.*
HN: *Human Nature,* Vol. I of *The Nature and Destiny of Man.*
IAH: *The Irony of American History.*
ICE: *An Interpretation of Christian Ethics.*
LNTC: *Leaves from the Notebook of a Tamed Cynic.*
MMIS: *Moral Man and Immoral Society.*
REE: *Reflections on the End of an Era.*

and artificial. But it may help to illuminate the tension between the philosopher and the prophet in Reinhold Niebuhr—between the thinker who is speculating *about* history and the man of action who is operating *in* and *upon* history. This tension has some bearing on his belief about the coherence and the incoherence of history, as I shall discuss it under "The Mystery and the Meaning." It may also help to throw light upon the double impact that Niebuhr makes upon his readers and hearers—that of the bold and confident prophet of the Lord, and that of the skeptic and the pessimist. As far back as 1922 one of his parishioners in Detroit remarked to him on this difference between his Sunday morning mood and his Sunday evening mood.[2] It is necessary to attend both services to get the whole man.

I. FAITH AND HISTORY

Niebuhr's formal philosophy of history is pretty well stated in *Faith and History*. In summary, it may be presented as having a focal point, the revelatory event, and three radial propositions.

One basic proposition is that history has unity by faith but not by sight.[3] It has unity in virtue of our faith in the sovereignty of God over history. But there is no over-all structure—as in Hegel, Marx, Spengler, Toynbee—that can be elaborated by reason. Nor in a scene that is marked only by "tangents of coherence"[4] and by "tangents of moral meaning"[5] have we any empirical warrant for elaborating a historical order. History shows progress equally toward chaos and toward cosmos,[6] and its coherences and incoherences are so entangled with one another that we are unable to discern any clear and exact pattern of events. Indeed, the final coherence of life is found only in "a suffering divine love,"[7] which is apprehended by faith rather than by reason.

Another feature of the Christian doctrine, in contrast to secular philosophies, is that it affirms the ultimate character of sin and of evil in history.[8] This means that history cannot be redemptive, cannot be its own Christ. It has no order of progress that must eventually squeeze out sin. By the same token, man cannot be his own Christ or redeemer, cannot ever become the master of historical destiny.[9] With all his freedom, man is forever imprisoned in finitude and in particularity, through devices that are sexual, ethnic, linguistic, and even rational, and finally by the inescapable fact of his mortality.

[2] LNTC, 38–39. [3] FH, 107–119. [4] HD, 313. [5] FH, 132.
[6] ICE, 97–98. [7] CRPP, 184. [8] FH, VIII. [9] FH, V–VI.

To deny man's sin and finitude, and then to project some secular, this-worldly soteriology, is to generate some of the most terrible fanaticisms that history has known.

A third proposition is that history provides a disclosure of meaning but not a fulfillment of meaning. This mediates between classical philosophies, which deny all meaning to the temporal and seek escape to the eternal, and modern philosophies, which expect a total fulfillment in history. In one of Niebuhr's favorite metaphors, Man is a Moses[10] who has glimpsed the promised land from afar, and who has made some progress toward it on this earth, but who will not enter into it in history. The end of his life is a *finis*, an abrupt termination of his career in this world, but it is not the *telos*,[11] or true end, which takes him beyond history.

All of this comes to a focus in the doctrine of the revelatory event. "The Christian faith begins with, and is founded upon, the affirmation that the life, death, and resurrection of Christ represent an event in history, in and through which a disclosure of the whole meaning of history occurs."[12] We are enabled to apprehend the significance of this event primarily through the work of God's grace in us, but specifically through our own faith and repentance.[13] This apprehension calls for an act of the entire personality, and cannot be encompassed by the mere exercise of reason. Indeed, both the form and the content of the revelation are an affront to human dignity.[14] The form is a challenge to man's reason: it is a scandal to rationalism that the meaning of history should emerge from the core of a particular historical event. The content is a challenge to man's virtue: the agents in the crucifixion were the two highest achievements of human culture at that time—Roman law and Jewish religion.

This event has a positive function as a revelation of God's wisdom and truth, and of God's grace and power.[15] But what is perfect as given by God can be only imperfectly apprehended by man. God's grace shows itself, indeed, as power in man to do those things that he ought to do. But it shows itself also as mercy toward man for doing those things that he ought not to do, and for failing to do those things he ought to do. The justice that we achieve in history can be only a partial, tentative justice;[16] and the truth that we apprehend is always distorted by sin, so that man is an ambiguous creature

[10] ICE, 80; HD, 308; DST, 83.
[11] HD, 287.
[12] FH, 26.
[13] FH, 106, 151.
[14] FH, IX.
[15] HD, 54–67, and IV.
[16] HD, IX.

in the position of simultaneously having and not having the truth.[17]

The negative function of the revelatory event is that it stands in judgment upon all the idolatrous centers of meaning before which we worship.[18] These idolatrous centers may be secular in character—feudal, bourgeois, or Marxian. They may be Christian in character—Lutheran, Roman Catholic, Calvinist, Pietist. In either case they reflect the perennial human disposition to put our trust in the arm of flesh rather than to put our trust in God.

But how do we know that the revelation in Christ is not itself one more idolatrous center of meaning? Here Niebuhr calls our attention to the "history of expectation,"[19] and speaks of this event as "the last in a series of God's 'mighty acts,' "[20] but shows himself singularly unwilling to deal with the continuities in history that follow rather than precede the act. He does admit that, once we have apprehended this event by faith, then it may be susceptible of rational validation. But he himself expounds only the negative validation,[21] and contributes to the positive validation only a warning against three errors that may arise in the pursuit of it.[22] Quite recently, however, he has developed the doctrine that the real proof lies in the witness of a Christian life which shows the fruits of the Spirit. For at this point we are dealing with "a truth of faith; and it is validated by a witness of lives which have been obviously remade by the power of God's judgment and forgiveness."[23]

With regard to the formal philosophy of history—so cruelly compressed in this outline—I have at present only two questions to raise. First of all, if the Christian doctrine is a reminder of the ultimate character of sin and of evil in history, is it not also a revelation of an ultimate good? Niebuhr might reply that the sin is in man, but that the good is in the grace of God. Nevertheless, even though perfect love is defeated in history—as Niebuhr likes to remind us[24]—does it not also have its moments of triumph and its continuities of power? After the Resurrection there is Pentecost, and there is the "community of hopeful believers,"[25] and all these things are creative forces in history. At any rate those who accuse Niebuhr of an undue pessimism would like to hear him tell at least as much about God's

[17] HD, VIII. [18] BT, II, VI; FH, XII. [19] HD, 53.
[20] FH, 141. [21] FH, 152–165. [22] FH, 165–170.
[23] Concluding sentence of "The Christian Witness in a Secular Age," *Christian Century*, Vol. LXX, No. 29, July 22, 1953, p. 843.
[24] BT, 182; HD, 68; DST, 144; FH, 135, 143, 203.
[25] FH, 238.

"power in" man as he does about the need for God's "mercy toward" man. After all, there was a time in Niebuhr's ministry when he could exclaim—almost like Miranda in *The Tempest*—"There is so much that is good in human nature"![26]

The second question is whether, even on Niebuhr's own assumptions, he has given us an adequate verification of the revelatory event. The sentence quoted above, in which he speaks to the witness of lives which have been "obviously remade" by the power of God, reads like a final but desperate flourish of affirmation after all the qualifications which have preceded it. Indeed, in the main body of the article, he has already discussed five such qualifications to the witness. Generically it is imperfect because some sin remains in all of us. Specifically the imperfection is aggravated by the increasing complexity of moral problems, and by the increasing dominance of the group. The witness is made hazardous, moreover, by our tendency to a self-righteous conventionalism or legalism; and it can be corrupted when the final truth is used as an instrument of the final lie. In any case it is practically imperceptible, since those of a broken spirit and a contrite heart are known only to God. Thus the lives which have been remade by the power of God are not "obviously" so to our sight, and we are left with both a Church Invisible and a Witness Invisible.

II. THE HANDLES TO HISTORY

Let us turn now from the philosopher speculating about history to the prophet operating in and upon history. To some extent this is a change from the "Sunday evening mood" of skepticism and pessimism to the "Sunday morning mood" of bold affirmation. One surmises, indeed, that Niebuhr's reluctance to give us an adequate answer to our last two questions derives, not from any intellectual imbalance or dishonesty, but from a sensitive awareness that too confident an answer must lead to the peril of spiritual pride. The prophet, however, cannot be fretting always about the perils of his own pride. There must be a time when he speaks in the assurance that this is God's word and not just his own. He cannot always be meditating on the elusive, mysterious, and contradictory character of history. There must be a time when he takes hold of it with a firm grasp.

Niebuhr seems to have found four handles to history. Two of

[26] LNTC, 49.

these—symbolic events and polarities—have been a permanent part of his tool kit. A third, the Marxian dialectic, he once wielded fiercely, but with his hand protected by a glove of Christian insight. He dropped it when it appeared too crude for usefulness. The fourth, the irony of history, may have evolved out of the third, although one finds tentative uses of it quite early in his thought.

1. History, Symbols, and Revelatory Events.—While there is only one event in history which is *the* revelatory event, nevertheless, to the discerning eye, many events have their revelatory aspects. "There are moments in history which are more than mere historic moments; for in them a whole course of history is fulfilled. In them the seeming chaos of the past achieves its meaning; and the partial and particular aspects of life are illumined to become parts of a complete whole."[27] Indeed, anything in life may have a symbolic significance that is more than the obvious and immediate meaning.

The young pastor of a parish in Detroit is already sensitive to the rich texture of implications that can be found in any occurrence. In the *Leaves from the Notebook of a Tamed Cynic* he records the persons and events which he finds luminous with meaning: a dog with hair over its eyes, a revival meeting, children playing with a dangerous toy, the new Ford, Bishop M[cConnell], the parson's wedding fees, bayonet practice in the army, a hospital sickbed, the manipulations of the stock exchange, the Book of Common Prayer, a Packard car, a Good Friday service, a wife with an alcoholic husband, the difference between Los Angeles and Detroit,[28] the temptations of St. Anthony, a victory dinner in a financial campaign, a village parson, a convention of the American Federation of Labor, cigarette smoking among women, a Sunday-school class, a cathedral and a cocoa works, a healthy and hungry boy, a funeral, a portly and prosperous priest, a union Thanksgiving service, a drummer and two nuns, an every member canvass, the cross of Christ.

A good example of Niebuhr's ability to extract a rich texture of meaning out of one event can be found in his recent discussion of the coronation of Queen Elizabeth II of England.[29] He sees here a tribute to the permanent power of poetry in politics, and remarks that it appeals so much to Americans because we have banished

[27] DST, 96.

[28] LNTC, 82–84. But since Niebuhr wrote this in 1925, the spirit of Detroit has invaded and conquered the spirit of Los Angeles.

[29] "Coronation Afterthoughts," *Christian Century,* Vol. LXX, No. 26, July 1, 1953, pp. 771–772.

poetry from government. The event also exemplifies the force of unconscious and organic factors in history as against the conscious and the contractual: the British monarchy turned out better than the conscious intentions of either the monarchists or the anti-monarchists. After still further exegesis Niebuhr concludes that the Briton understands the imponderables of man's communal existence better than does any contemporary.

Niebuhr also finds that the symbols which are theological or Biblical are useful for interpreting history. Thus in the opening chapter of *Beyond Tragedy,* entitled "As Deceivers, Yet True," he presents his formal theory of the use of theological symbols, and goes on to discuss in detail the symbolism of the Creation, the Fall, the Incarnation, and the Atonement. In Chapter II of the same volume, he uses the Tower of Babel as a symbol of the sin of pride in history. In Chapter III he uses the Ark and the Temple as symbols of the contrast between the prophet and the priest—between the smug Solomon who built the temple, and the contrite David whose uneasy conscience would not let him build a temple. In Chapter IV, "Four Hundred to One," Micaiah is used as a symbol of the prophet who must speak against the world's vanity and love of false security. And in Chapter VI he uses a famous text from Jeremiah (17:5–9) to thunder against the human idols in which we have put our trust: the collective man of the Jews, the Roman man, the churchman of the Middle Ages, the pious man of the Reformation, the intelligent man of the Enlightenment, the intelligent-pious man of modern religious liberalism, the poor man of Marxism, the young man of the post World War I period. "Cursed be the man that trusteth in man, and maketh flesh his arm. . . . Blessed is the man that trusteth in the Lord, and whose hope the Lord is!"

At any rate the proliferation of symbols in Niebuhr's writings is incredible both for scope and for variety. There is no sign of his attempting to read tea leaves, but he can find significance in the peeling of an onion,[30] the Parousia,[31] the cedar of Lebanon,[32] the big city,[33] Jacob's ladder,[34] an automobile factory,[35] the wise and foolish virgins,[36] an expectant mother in hopeless travail,[37] Woodrow Wilson,[38] the Antichrist,[39] a cake and its icing,[40] the wheat and the

[30] BT, 262–263.
[31] HD, 290–291.
[32] DST, 57–58.
[33] LNTC, 116–117.
[34] HD, 230.
[35] LNTC, 78–79.
[36] DST, 94–95.
[37] DST, 39.
[38] LNTC, 22–23.
[39] HD, 316–319; FH, 126, 235.
[40] CRPP, 190.

tares,[41] the "aggression" of his one-year-old daughter against his five-year-old son,[42] the bodily resurrection,[43] seeing through a glass darkly,[44] murderers' row,[45] a Christian Endeavor Society,[46] a sick and unemployed old man,[47] the light which shineth in darkness,[48] the Red Cross,[49] four letters,[50] the ocean which is tumultuous on the surface but calm in its depths,[51] the building of a new church,[52] an envious beauty and her rival,[53] the Last Judgment.[54] Thus every event, every person, every idea, is revelatory of meaning.

2. *History and Polarities.*—History also has a structure of polarities, which are sometimes exalted to contradictions. This derives primarily from the amphibian character of man,[55] a creature of nature and of spirit, of necessity and of freedom. So Niebuhr sees man forever caught in some sort of "two-pronged predicament."[56]

Early in his career as a pastor in Detroit Niebuhr is exploring these polarities, and records them for us in the *Leaves from the Notebook of a Tamed Cynic:* Christian love—Aristotelian moderation; the prophet—the statesman; spontaneity—ritual; moral man—immoral society; the adoration of Christ—the emulation of Christ; innocence—virtue; tradition—experiment; trust—caution; conviction—humility; courage—patience; bitterness of the prophet—blandness of the pulpiteer; the comfort of life—the chaos of life; Christianity—secularism; disillusionment with others—disillusionment with self; mechanical interdependence of men—spiritual isolation of men; criticism—aspiration; religion and poetry—fundamentalism and science; speaking the plain truth—speaking the truth in love; faith—reason; saints—sinners; the panoply—the power; cowardice—inertia; principles—practice; the study—the pulpit.

However, since life is not reducible to any simple formula, these polarities may overlap and intersect one another in the most complicated manner. This can be seen by taking one of Niebuhr's basic categories—idealism, perfectionism, utopianism—and examining the antitheses, alternatives, and implications. Thus we get: idealism—

[41] FH, 231–234. [42] CPP, 13. [43] HD, 294–298.
[44] DST, 152–154, 159, 167, 171. [45] DST, 32.
[46] LNTC, 130–131. [47] LNTC, 149–150. [48] DST, 173.
[49] LNTC, 113. [50] CPP, 167–176. [51] DST, 194.
[52] LNTC, 34–35. [53] DST, 11. [54] HD, 291–294.
[55] DST, 129–130, 165.
[56] Last phrase of "Christianity and the Moral Law," *Christian Century,* Vol. LXX, No. 48, December 2, 1953, pp. 1386–1388.

realism;[57] idealism—nausea;[58] hypocritical idealism—irresponsible idealism;[59] idealism—sentimentalism and hypocrisy;[60] utopianism—cynicism;[61] utopianism of the radicals—hypocrisy of the Tories;[62] soft utopians—hard utopians;[63] utopians—mystics;[64] fanaticism and cruelty—inertia and opportunism;[65] perfectionism—expediency;[66] fanaticism and pride—skepticism and nihilism;[67] fanaticism and cowardice;[68] the brutal and the cynical—the sentimental and the hypocritical;[69] foolishness of the seer—wisdom of the statesman;[70] harmlessness of the dove—wisdom of the serpent.[71]

To be sure, some of these polarities have a more direct bearing than do others on his philosophy of history. There is one group, for instance, that revolves around the contrast of time and eternity:[72] time as the stage of history—time as the stuff of history;[73] knowledge of nature—knowledge of history;[74] this-worldliness—other-worldliness;[75] eternity as ground—eternity as end;[76] the old era—the new era;[77] the horizontal dimension—the vertical dimension;[78] finis—telos.[79] Another group may be related to the distinction between the disclosure of meaning and the fulfillment of meaning:[80] mystery—meaning;[81] having the truth—not having the truth;[82] grace as power in—grace as mercy toward;[83] chaos—cosmos;[84] man's involvement in history—man's transcendence over history;[85] unity by faith—unity by sight;[86] humor—faith;[87] peace of nature or of reason—peace of God.[88] In any comprehensive account of Niebuhr's philosophy of history, however, all the polarities exploited by him must find their place.

There are many other polarities that cannot be indicated here. In my most recent enumeration of them as found only in the books published by Niebuhr, I am able to list well over one hundred. For the present let me remark simply that, if history has only "tangents" of

[57] LNTC, 23, 104–106; CPP, 104; IAH, 40, 148.
[58] LNTC, 47–48. [59] IAH, 5. [60] LNTC, viii–ix.
[61] CPP, 61. [62] CPP, 141. [63] FH, 206–213.
[64] HD, 90–95; CLCD, 83. [65] MMIS, 221.
[66] MMIS, 266; REE, 262–263; HD, 88. [67] HD, 149, 236–239.
[68] LNTC, 167. [69] MMIS, 177. [70] MMIS, 258.
[71] CLCD, 40–41. [72] BT, IX; DST, VI. [73] FH, 35ff.
[74] HD, 7–11; DST, I [75] ICE, 31; DST, V. [76] HD, 299–301, 311.
[77] DST, III. [78] DST, VI.
[79] HD, 287–288; FH, 235–237. [80] HD, II.
[81] DST, IX; FH, VIII. [82] HD, VIII. [83] HD, IV.
[84] ICE, 97–98; HD, 169, 182, 315.
[85] HD, 1–3, 97, 128, 148, 214. [86] FH, 107–113.
[87] DST, VII. [88] DST, X.

meaning and of coherence, then Reinhold Niebuhr must have enough tangents by the tail to surround the circumference and to penetrate to the center of history.

3. *History and the Marxian Dialectic.*—There was a time, in the first half of the 1930's, when Reinhold Niebuhr took seriously the Marxian dialectic as applied to history. This concern shows itself in *Moral Man and Immoral Society* (1932) and in *Reflections on the End of an Era* (1934). The question is: Just to what extent did he embrace the Marxian analysis, and to what extent was his Marxism overborne by Christian insights?

In a recent article in the *Christian Century*, which *Time* magazine chose to celebrate as a recantation, Niebuhr tells us that he "used Marxist collectivism to counter liberal individualism, Marxist catastrophism to counter liberal optimism, and Marxist determinism to challenge liberal moralism and idealism."[89] In this mood he was able to declare that democracy alone could not effect the transition from capitalism to socialism,[90] and that our world "moves with inexorable logic toward collectivism."[91] He proclaimed "a new society such as the workers are destined to build,"[92] and affirmed "the inevitability of the reign of the workers,"[93] while he described these workers as "those who are destined to become the rulers of society"[94] and "fated to contend for a society which the logic of history affirms."[95] He assures us that "their victory is as certain as their revolt is inevitable when the time is ripe."[96] The era which is ending is the bourgeois era, and at the moment Niebuhr is convinced that this end is a *finis!*

Nevertheless, even here there are two factors in Niebuhr's thinking which qualify his Marxism. One factor may be labeled technically the philosophy of romantic organicism. Thus Niebuhr makes a brilliant critique of the mechanical character of a bourgeois culture.[97] But already he sees that Marxism fails to appreciate the organic unities of family, nation, and church—of religion, patriotism, and agrarian individualism.[98] And he gives expression prophetically to the fear that communism will merely substitute a mechanistic collectivism for the mechanistic individualism of capitalism.[99]

[89] "Communism and the Clergy," *Christian Century*, Vol. LXX, No. 33, Aug. 19, 1953, p. 937.

[90] REE, 80–81, 156–157. [91] REE, 238. [92] REE, 162.
[93] REE, 147. [94] REE, 148. [95] REE, 143.
[96] REE, 142. [97] REE, 70–74. [98] REE, XIII.
[99] REE, 93–94.

The other qualifying factor in Niebuhr's thinking comes from the perspective of Christian ethics. Thus he notes the egotism of the class which believes itself the most significant class for the future of history.[100] Since its members regard themselves as the instruments of a pure justice, their egotism will find expression in cruelty and vindictiveness.[101] Their cynicism makes them discount the moral and rational factors in social change,[102] and the cynicism coupled with the vindictiveness may even interfere with the establishment of the new society.[103] Indeed, there is no assurance that the new oligarchs, however great their sincerity, may not introduce a new pattern of inordinate privilege and power.[104]

The flowering of the ethical critique appears in a recently published essay entitled "Why Is Communism So Evil?"[105] There are four phases of the evil. Communism establishes an absolute monopoly of power—a monopoly which grows naturally out of the Marxian doctrine of the "dictatorship of the proletariat." Communism is made more dangerous than Nazism by its utopian illusions, which provide a moral façade for the most unscrupulous political policies. Communism believes in the transformation of society by a revolutionary act, after which man is no longer the creature but purely the creator of history, who not only proposes but also disposes. Finally, the pretension of scientific rationality in Marxism is an additional source of evil.

In summary: Niebuhr took from Marxism the "inexorable logic of history," the doctrine of class conflict, and the emphasis on the role of force. In a short time he was to repudiate this logic, or any other logic, of history; to reduce class conflict to a subordinate and instrumental concept; but to hold onto the factor of power and of force without any Marxian implications. The really extraordinary thing about this phase of his thought, however, is not the errors into which he was led by Marxism, but the astounding truth of the prophetic judgments he made from the perspective of Christian faith as they were to be verified by subsequent history. One can appreciate Niebuhr's revulsion against the communist categories, but that does not mean that history has no structure at all. What Niebuhr's own achievement at this point suggests is that the law of history is not a Marxian law: it is a moral law.

4. History and Irony.—As far back as his *Reflections on the End*

[100] MMIS, 156–157.
[101] REE, XIII.
[102] MMIS, 163, 167–168.
[103] MMIS, 157–158.
[104] REE, 245.
[105] CRPP, III.

of an Era (1934) Niebuhr had an intimation that the real dialectic of history is not Marxian but ironical. So he wrote: "One of the pathetic aspects of human history is that the instruments of judgment which it uses to destroy particular vices must belong to the same category of the vice to be able to destroy it. Thus some evil, which is to be destroyed, is always transferred to the instrument of its destruction and thereby perpetuated."[106] According to his later, more precise thinking, this would be, not one of the pathetic, but one of the ironic aspects of history. In another series of studies in politics (1944) he was to note how the creed of the children of light can become the instrument of the children of darkness.[107] Before that he had already explored the meaning of the category of tragedy as applied to history,[108] and then in *Discerning the Signs of the Times* (1946) he was to publish his essay on "Humour and Faith,"[109] which is certainly one of the most brilliant treatments of the subject in all literature. The maturing of his thought in this area, however, appeared in *The Irony of American History* (1952), which devoted the first and the last chapters to the interpretation of the theory of irony, and the intervening chapters to its application.

The major ironies revolve around virtue, power, security, and wisdom. America suffers the irony of Israel, in that our virtue and innocence have been insufficient to keep us from appearing most guilty before the rest of the world.[110] America suffers the irony of Babylon, in that our power does not save us from weakness, because we felt most confident when we were a young and relatively weak nation, but we are most frustrated by feelings of impotence now that our power is at its height.[111] The irony of security is that our virtue and prosperity do not appear to bring us an automatic happiness, and that there is no clear-cut course of action for maintaining our security in the future.[112] The irony of wisdom—in its outcome an "irony of success" rather than an "irony of failure"—lies in the triumph of experience over dogma, in the victory of American common sense over the foolishness of our official wise men.[113] There is a further irony in the fact that the Russian communists, who are our chief foes, represent an intensification of our own faults—our materialism and our confidence that we can be the masters of historical

106 REE, 94.
107 CLCD, 26, 32–34.
108 BT, especially VIII.
109 DST, VII.
110 IAH, 2, 4, II, VI.
111 IAH, 3, 12–13, IV, 162.
112 IAH, 7, III, VII.
113 IAH, 10–11, V.

destiny—and so have "transmuted ideals and hopes, which we most deeply cherish, into cruel realities which we most fervently abhor."[114]

But while Niebuhr's attention is focussed on the American scene in this book, he still takes space to dispose of the "irony of the poor" which is the Marxist delusion. "In the Marxist apocalypse one error is piled upon another with regard to the virtue of the poor. They are not only assumed to be completely disinterested or to have interests absolutely identical with the interests of the whole of mankind. But also no thought is given to the fact that if they become historically successful they will cease to be poor. Furthermore, the oligarchy which presumes to speak for the poor claims to participate in their supposed sanctity. To cap the mountain of errors, the poor, to whom all virtue is ascribed, are identified with the industrial proletariat. This latter error becomes a more and more vicious source of confusion as communism seeks to conquer great peasant civilizations."[115]

It is Niebuhr's suggestion in this book that Christian faith tends to make the ironic view of human evil in history the normative one.[116] This derives from the Christian conception of human freedom, according to which our creative powers are always subject to some abuse and corruption. It is also derived from the "faith that life has a center and source of meaning beyond the natural and social consequences which may be rationally discerned."[117] Thus man is ironic because he forgets that he is creature as well as creator.[118] When caught in the ironic situation, he may dissolve it through hatred and despair, or through contrition.[119] Of course, man's redemption from evil takes us beyond the limits of irony and of history. Nevertheless, within history the Christian interpretation of evil is consistently ironic. For we see that "the whole drama of human history is under the scrutiny of a divine judge who laughs at human pretensions without being hostile to human aspirations. The laughter at the pretensions is the divine judgment. The judgment is transmuted into mercy if it results in abating the pretensions and in prompting men to a contrite recognition of the vanity of their imagination."[120]

[114] IAH, 11.
[115] IAH, 165.
[116] IAH, 155.
[117] IAH, 168.
[118] IAH, 156.
[119] IAH, 168–169.
[120] IAH, 155.

III. THE MYSTERY AND THE MEANING

Every prophet who would speak to his own age must have an intuitive awareness of the mood of that age, and must even share in that mood to some extent. But if he is to be more than a prophet of Baal, if he is to be a prophet of the Lord, then he must have some perspective which lifts him above the prejudices of his time.

A part of Niebuhr's kinship with his own age lies in the radical relativism which pervades his cultural, historical, and ethical judgments. Like the great majority of secular prophets and social scientists today, he can appreciate the words of Nietzsche crying through the voice of his own *Zarathustra:* "O my brethren, is not everything at present in flux? Have not all railings and gangways fallen into the water? Who would still hold on to 'good' and 'evil'?"[121]

On the other hand, Niebuhr has a Christian perspective which finally emancipates him from pure relativism, and which raises his vision above that of the secular seers of the age. He believes by faith, if not by sight, that God is the Lord of history. He affirms categorically the commandments of God, no matter how much these may seem to trap man in an "impossible possibility." And he has confidence that in the grateful and contrite heart God's grace may bring to completion what man cannot finish.

Nevertheless, if I understand Niebuhr aright, while he accepts the moral law as God's commandment, he is not quite willing to insert the moral law *into history.*[122] At this point, it seems to me, he either repudiates or is reluctant to affirm a cardinal article of faith of the great Old Testament prophets in whose tradition he stands. Apart from his responsiveness to the *Zeitgeist,* there seem to be specific reasons for this extreme circumspection. He remembers St. Paul's revolt against legalism. He notes that Roman Catholic doctrine uses natural-law theory to give sanction to historically contingent elements. He once singed his fingertips—I cannot see that he really burned his fingers—in handling the Marxian dialectic for history. Also, on the deeper metaphysical level, he is convinced that history is hostile to absolutisms, and that it has in it irreducible aspects of

[121] Friedrich Nietzsche, *Thus Spake Zarathustra,* tr. Thomas Common, III–LVI–8 (New York: Modern Library, n.d.), p. 207.

[122] Cf. "Christianity and the Moral Law," *Christian Century,* Vol. LXX, No. 48, Dec. 2, 1953, pp. 1386–1388.

incoherence and of irrationality. With all of these scruples one may be in complete sympathy, and yet not accept the conclusion of historical relativism in ethics.

Indeed, there are four aspects of Niebuhr's own thought which provide the materials for a critical but affirmative reconstruction of the doctrine of a natural moral law. For one thing, the valuable insights and principles which Niebuhr allegedly got from beyond history[123] seem to me quite plainly to have been found in history. Where else, indeed, would he find them? It is possible, for instance, to take a whole series of propositions in his philosophy of history and to indicate their empirical origins and verification.[124] What is more important, the Christian revelation—whatever its origin—occurred in history, is connected with precedent and with subsequent history, and functions as a power in history. If then we may restore to history a large measure of the principles and patterns which have been arbitrarily taken away from it, we shall find that history has more structure and meaning than we supposed.

In the second place, we might invite Niebuhr to reconsider his earlier faith in a purely negative moral law of judgment in history. This is strongest in *Reflections on the End of an Era* (1934) when he can say that, amidst all the confusions of life, it is still "possible to discern the logic of an inexorable judgment upon evil."[125] It is still functioning in *Beyond Tragedy* (1937) when he can write, "Thus injustice is the social consequence of pride; and the inevitable fruit of injustice is self-destruction."[126] However, when we get down to *Faith and History* (1949), the qualifications begin to pile up.[127] "Moral judgments are executed in history; but never with precision.[128] . . . The virtuous and the innocent may, and frequently do, suffer more rather than less in the competitions of life and history, precisely because of their virtue."[129] Here I have only two remarks. In throwing out the Marxian dialectic, it was not necessary to throw out the prophetic idea of judgment in history. Again, if the righteous do suffer, that does not necessarily preclude a moral law in human affairs; it may simply deepen our understanding of the moral law.

[123] For instance, HN, 141: "It is, in fact, impossible to interpret history at all without a principle of interpretation which history as such does not yield."

[124] Cf. my "Reinhold Niebuhr as Prophet and as Philosopher," *Journal of Religion,* Vol. XXXII, No. 1, January, 1952, especially pp. 36–39.

[125] REE, 139.

[126] BT, 203.

[127] Cf. especially FH, VIII.

[128] FH, 129.

[129] FH, 131.

In the third place, we may invite Niebuhr to consider further the empirical bearings of his positive law of love. This law, he declares, is "indeed the law of life,"[130] and is also the "very law of history."[131] If it is not the only law of man's existence, it is still the "final law"[132] for man because of his condition of finiteness and freedom. As against unduly pessimistic theories of human nature, the requirements of the law of love must be affirmed; but against the various modern forms of utopianism, secular and religious, we are to be reminded that the law of love is "no simple possibility."[133] And yet while it has status as the "primary law"[134] of man's nature and of history, it is "not a norm of history"[135] in the sense that historical experience justifies it. But what kind of justification is Niebuhr looking for? Certainly not an absolute one!

In the fourth place, I may remark that the several "handles to history" which Niebuhr manipulates so effectively all add up to some kind of pattern of coherence. It is by means of symbols that we seize upon events in their unique individuality, and still exhibit the meanings which reach beyond that individuality. It is by means of the polarities, the dialectics, and the ironies, that we seize upon events in their recurrent aspects and take note, not of *the* structure of history, but of the plural and interlocking structures of history. The first tradition of insight is as old as the Hebrew prophets themselves. The second tradition of insight is as old as Plato, as vivid as Alexander Pope's *Essay on Man*, as vital as Pascal's *Pensées*, and as modern as Schelling and Hegel and Marx.

The gist of the matter, I think, is that Niebuhr still sees natural-law theory in the context of classical Greek and Roman Catholic metaphysics and of Newtonian mechanics. But if he were to probe for its implications in terms of his own pragmatism and of the postulates of modern theoretical physics, he might come out with something more affirmative. This modern theory of law would suggest that the principles of nature and the principles of history are not so radically divorced from one another as Niebuhr insists. Such a law would allow for flexibility as well as for precision, would combine the positive element of love with the negative element of judgment, would readily embrace the multifarious polarities and ironies of life, and, behind the competing but still cooperating impulses toward the creative and the discreative in man, would yet point to the

130 DST, 185. 131 HD, 49. 132 FH, 174.
133 HN, 296. 134 HD, 244. 135 HD, 96.

Christian revelation *in history* as the token of a God who, under the conditions of human freedom and finitude, is still both absolutely and empirically the Lord of that history.

IV. THE MAN AND THE MESSAGE

Reinhold Niebuhr likes to insist that what we deal with in any system of thought is not the product of a pure mind but the impact of a total self.[136] It may therefore be appropriate, in concluding this analysis, to consider the character of that self whose projections into history and about history and beyond history are the subject of this essay. To understand that self, I must insist that it is quite inadequate to engage in merely academic comparisons between his thought and the thought of other theologians. What is needed is the entire cultural context within which this self moves, and some sight upon the other selves to which this self has been related.

In any survey of the philosophy of history in the West, it seems to me that there are six figures which especially claim our attention. Three of them belong to a complex of secular and totalitarian thought. The other three belong to a complex of Christian, and eventually democratic, thought. Hegel, the philosophical idealist, is the father of the totalitarians. The child of his left hand is the communism of Karl Marx. The child of his right hand is the fascism of Oswald Spengler. Augustine is the father of the Christians, and, indeed, the originator of any sort of philosophy of history. The child of his left hand is Arnold Toynbee, with his "liberal" Christian outlook. The child of his right hand is Reinhold Niebuhr, with his "neo-orthodox" Christian outlook. Niebuhr is critically aware of his indebtedness to Augustine at this point,[137] and differs from his "liberal" confrere in a deeper awareness of the reality of sin and evil, and in a distrust of any rational structure into which history may be too easily strait-jacketed.

So far as Niebuhr's relation to the general history of philosophy is concerned, we may place him squarely in the great American tradition of pragmatism. He is the grateful heir of William James, and the understandably uncomfortable colleague of John Dewey. It was William James who ripped open the bandbox universe to give us a pluralistic universe,[138] and to affirm the potency therein of man's

[136] See especially CRPP, 92–93.
[137] Cf. CRPP, IX, "Augustine's Political Realism."
[138] Cf. CRPP, XI, "Coherence, Incoherence, and Christian Faith."

free will. It was John Dewey who put pragmatism under the discipline of experimental science, and celebrated the glories of freed intelligence. It is Reinhold Niebuhr who has given pragmatism breadth and depth and height of vision, richness and subtlety and scope of texture, by placing it within the heroic perspective of the Christian faith. Niebuhr cannot accept James's idolatry of the human will, or Dewey's idolatry of human intelligence. Niebuhr knows only one absolute: the God revealed in Jesus Christ. Nevertheless, for all the differences in sensitivity and in insight, these three men belong together, in methodology and in metaphysics, like variations upon a common theme.

However, if we think of Niebuhr as prophet rather than as philosopher, we must see him in another light. The philosopher moves from the particular to the universal; the business of the prophet is to exploit universals to cast light upon particulars. The prophet is the critic and interpreter of persons and events of his own age, in the light of his peculiar perspective. Here Niebuhr must be set in the company of an H. L. Mencken, a Walter Lippmann, a John Dewey, a Lewis Mumford. While he has been personally friendly to many a secular prophet, he has been distinguished from them by his use of the Christian rather than the secular perspective. One of the continuing themes of his discourse has been the way the "foolishness of God" sets at nought the "wisdom of man."[139] Objectively and pragmatically the interesting fact is that, while many a secular prophet has already fallen by the wayside, discredited or merely out of date, Niebuhr with his Christian perspective has been able to maintain a freshness and flexibility of insight which is neither withered by age nor made stale by custom.

It is also proper to put Niebuhr in the company of the more savage social critics and satirists. His early labeling of himself as a "tamed cynic" is not without significance. At the beginning of his career he had taken a vow not to be a "preacher of pretty sermons."[140] He had made the decision that, if he were forced to a

[139] Niebuhr's identification with the "eggheads" and the intelligentsia in the presidential election of 1952 must be viewed against the background of his lifelong polemic against them: cf. LNTC, 98–99; BT, X–XII; HD, 62–67; IAH, V; CRPP, 69–71, VI. Note that in the *Leaves,* in 1926, he compared his "young business men" favorably with "any faculty group in the country." To be sure, these young businessmen were members of the congregation of which he was the pastor.

[140] LNTC, 9.

choice of alternatives, he would prefer the bitterness of the prophet to the blandness of the pulpiteer.[141] All his life long he has thundered against the "deleterious sentimentalities"[142] of a liberal, rationalistic, and materialistic culture. At this point he is akin to an Elijah, a Swift, a Voltaire, a Nietzsche, a Carlyle, a Mencken; and like them he has visited the complacent iniquities of his generation with a derisive laughter[143] that had in it the sting of scorpions. Yet, unlike them, he has been indeed a *tamed* cynic—a cynic who could be disillusioned with himself as well as with others,[144] a cynic tamed by gratitude and contrition before a higher Judge than any merely mortal.

David Wesley Soper has ventured to call Niebuhr a "Lutheran Voltaire without a periwig."[145] The comparison is apt if one remembers in Voltaire not only the fighting man and the satirist but also the kindliness and the compassion. It is equally apt if one remembers the fury of the spirit in him as it consumed the frailty of the flesh. So there are moments when one thinks of Niebuhr as of that character in Dryden:

> A fiery soul, which, working out its way,
> Fretted the pigmy body to decay:
> And o'er-informed the tenement of clay.[146]

He has also been compared to an eagle and to an owl: to an eagle in his predatory and polemical aspects, to an owl in his imparting of warmth and of wisdom. He can be savage with an opponent; he can be tender with a person. He can set fire to a whole house if he thinks the foundations are rotten, and only a conflagration will purge the evil. He can refuse, though invited, to light a cigarette in a lady's parlor, lest the odor infect the lace curtains. Often he has spoken the truth with a fierce courage; sometimes he has spoken the truth in love; but just as often, though unheralded, he has been content to let truth rest in silence under the discipline of love.

ROBERT E. FITCH

PACIFIC SCHOOL OF RELIGION
BERKELEY, CALIFORNIA

141 LNTC, 88–89. 142 HD, 176. 143 Cf. DST, 116.
144 LNTC, 91.
145 David Wesley Soper, *Major Voices in American Theology* (Philadelphia: The Westminster Press, 1953), p. 49.
146 John Dryden, *Absalom and Achitophel,* Part I.

16

Paul Scherer

REINHOLD NIEBUHR—PREACHER

16

REINHOLD NIEBUHR—PREACHER

KARL BARTH has somewhere said that the whole task of Christian theology starts from and centers in proclamation, that is, in the heralding of God's Kingdom through word and sacrament. Certainly a good case could be made out for the contention that Reinhold Niebuhr owes his reputation as a theologian to his power as a preacher. As in the case of Luther, it is *because* he is a preacher that he is a theologian. During the thirteen years of his ministry in Detroit, theology became for him "the religious aspect of the whole life"; and he had to grapple with that in the pulpit. Undoubtedly the Church was "cultivating graces and preserving spiritual amenities in the more protected areas of society"; but its morality seemed to him anachronistic. It was not changing any of the brutal facts of modern industry by so much as a hair's breadth, for all its "homiletical spoutings"! Apparently it had neither the moral insight nor the courage to cope with the real problems. There was little evidence that it was even thinking about them.[1] So was he beginning to feel the pressure of his special vocation. Step by step his mind was being driven toward that realistic apprehension of the profound relevance of theology to the contemporary scene with which he has been preoccupied ever since, and which has been one of the main sources of his appeal. By the late twenties word had got around through the universities, and from such platforms as that of the Chicago Sunday Evening Club, that he was a preacher not to miss. Churches and auditoriums were crowded when it came his turn to appear. Lectureships were opened to him. And from hearing him, professors and students alike, doctors, lawyers, politicians, authors, editors, long unaccustomed to take seriously anything that emanated from the pulpit, began to read his books and discuss his theology. In his lectures and treatises he defined and made explicit

[1] *Leaves from the Notebook of a Tamed Cynic,* p. 79.

the content and the terms of man's encounter with the ultimate; in his sermons the terms and content of that encounter were beaten out on the anvil of Biblical revelation at the point of their deepest significance for human experience. Says one whose name is well known on both sides of the Atlantic, "I regard Reinhold Niebuhr as the most immediately influential force in American and British thinking in the last quarter-century." To that influence, adds another, his preaching was no postscript: it belongs to the body of the text.

Unfortunately most of his notes, especially for the period from 1946 to 1953, have not been subsequently written out, elaborated, and printed in the complete form of the delivered sermon. The only sources available to us are *Beyond Tragedy*[2] and *Discerning the Signs of the Times,* consisting in all of twenty-five sermonic essays, as he calls them, somewhat altered in transcription, yet amply representative of his university preaching. While they can scarcely be said to reflect the still more constructive and pastoral character of the sermons that marked the mid-century years, when his critical and polemical task was largely done, and he was free to shift from a preponderant emphasis on sin to an increasing stress on the grace of God and its power to refashion human life after the divine image, they are nevertheless sufficiently indicative of both substance and method to provide a sound basis for study and comment. To these have been added some few references to, and even quotations from, his other works; notably his *Leaves from the Notebook of a Tamed Cynic,* which (mistakenly, one is sure) he will not allow to be republished—on the ground that so much of it has been outgrown, and with too little appreciation of the fact that it charts the direction and lays down the lines of that growth with startling accuracy. Counsel has been taken, too, of many who from the beginning have been among his most discriminating listeners in lecture room and chapel. Their prompt and enthusiastic replies, often at considerable length, have in part been directly reproduced whenever occasion seemed to warrant it.

I. THE HISTORICAL AND THE TRANS-HISTORICAL: AN ORGANIC, DYNAMIC RELATION

Reinhold Niebuhr's conception of the function of the preacher belongs to the warp and woof of his own encounter with God and

[2] Published by Charles Scribner's Sons in 1937.

the Gospel. What has been said of his theology can be said with equal force of his preaching. As "his theology took shape under the pressure of social and economic issues," so his sermons, in which "every immediate problem is set in the context of the ultimate, and the ultimate reality is informed with concrete historic content by its relation to immediate social issues," faithfully reflect "the tension of daily experience."[3] At first glance it is evident that we are dealing with a man involved; involved not with the ultimate in the role of a theologian, not with the immediate in the role of a social and political revolutionary, but with both, as they stand "in an organic, dynamic relation," each with the other. It is not for nothing that he appeared at a time when it was desperately necessary for somebody to undermine the facile and never critically examined assumptions of modern culture, religious as well as secular; to criticize the presuppositions which made it impossible for man to hear the Gospel because they prevented his asking the profoundest questions; and to highlight "the perennial themes of the Christian faith . . . in terms of their special relevance to the thought and life" of the twentieth century.[4]

1. Prophetic.—It follows from what has been said that Dr. Niebuhr's preaching is best described as prophetic (interpretative) and apologetic, rather than as primarily kerygmatic. There are those who insist quite bluntly that his sermons usually take the form of "diagnosis, with five or ten minutes of the Gospel at the end"—if indeed that much. Such appraisals, relatively truer of the earlier than of the later period, would seem to do scant justice to the evangelical presuppositions which are always implicit in what he says, as they are implicit, *a minore ad majorem,* in the Sermon on the Mount, to the utter confusion of all simple-minded moralists! If they are not explicitly wrought out, they are nonetheless the last recourse of those who have in any real sense been caught in the toils of his inexorable analytical and interpretative insights; as they are the stumbling block of many of the "intellectuals," in the universities and elsewhere, who have felt themselves under necessity to come "thus far but no farther." Should the aim of every true preacher be not so much to secure a verdict—meretricious as that may prove, and impossible as it is for any respecter of persons—but to provide the

[3] D. R. Davies, *Reinhold Niebuhr: Prophet from America* (London: James Clarke & Co., Ltd.), pp. 11, 12, 38.

[4] *Discerning the Signs of the Times,* p. ix.

possibility of a free and untrammeled choice for or against God and his Christ, then the sermon where that choice at the last is inevitable has reached its mark. Granted for all our common purposes the desirability of a more balanced and detailed treatment of what goes by the name of "the positive aspects of the Gospel," its *what* and its *how,* the service which Reinhold Niebuhr has rendered his generation in bringing it within clear sight of the final alternative is yet quite incalculable.

What then is prophetic preaching? Let Niebuhr draw up his own definition of it. "It is the genius and the task of prophetic religion to insist on the organic relation between historic human existence and that which is both the ground and the fulfillment of this existence, the transcendent."[5] From the earliest through the latest of his published sermons, as of those never committed to writing, this is by far the most persistent theme-motif, to borrow a word from the musician's vocabulary. The "either/or" of the all too often otherworldliness of old-fashioned evangelicalism, against which the thisworldliness of twentieth-century Protestant liberalism stood in justifiable protest, is replaced by a "both/and" which has made of his theology, his doctrine of God and man, of sin and salvation, of justification by faith and of eschatology, a matter of the utmost "secular urgency and significance."[6]

2. *Demand.*—This relation between the historical and the transhistorical is to be understood first of all in terms of *demand:* the ceaseless exactions made by the absolute upon the relative, by the perfect upon the imperfect, by the "impossible" upon the "possible." The resulting ethical tension is never allowed to disappear for a moment in any premature relaxation of it. Far from being only the "answer," Christ becomes also the problem. "What shall I do then with Jesus which is called Christ?"[7] Facile solutions, the crying of "Peace, peace; when there is no peace,"[8] fulsome eulogies of Jesus Christ—all of them are not so much pious haberdashery as dread profanities to Niebuhr. "Be ye therefore perfect, even as your Father which is in heaven is perfect,"[9] tolls for him at once the death knell of selfrighteous complacency and rationalistic utopianism. His is a religious penetration which is bent upon disclosing life both on its heights and in its depths, confident that "a profound religion makes

[5] *An Interpretation of Christian Ethics,* p. 105.
[6] Davies, *op. cit.,* p. 21. [7] Matthew 27:22. [8] Jeremiah 6:14.
[9] Matthew 5:48.

a pure ethical passion possible and a pure ethical passion makes religion necessary."[10]

On the one hand is the Kingdom which is not of this world, and it threatens Pilate's kingdom far more than Pilate thinks. It is the Kingdom of truth, "a revelation of the fundamental pattern of life which sin has obscured and which Christ restores. . . . It is the picture of what this world ought to be. [It] is . . . not of this world, inasfar as the world is constantly denying the fundamental laws of human existence. Yet it is of this world. It is not some realm of eternal perfection which has nothing to do with historical existence. It constantly impinges upon man's every decision and is involved in every action." It is there "in man's uneasy conscience," its strange power manifest in the fact that "it does not ask to have its standards validated by worldly success," so that "its servants may not fight Pilate but . . . are able to defy Pilate," its triumph an assured and ultimate triumph. It is a Kingdom that "constantly enters the world" and "in every moment of existence" has its own way of conquering. Its truth condemns our lies; its pure justice indicts our injustice; its law of love reveals our selfishness; its vision of God discloses the true center and source of our existence. We may be disobedient to it; but we can never be as we *have* been.[11]

Over against the Kingdom which is not of this world is set the kingdom which is; namely, the domain of evil, with sin for its lord. The opposition between the two is not a simple opposition. Niebuhr is desperately intent on showing "how full of unrighteousness is all human righteousness. The Saviour of the world is not crucified by criminals or obviously evil people. . . . Jesus is destroyed by the chief priests and elders . . . his chief opponents are the best people of his day."[12] So it is that "when the Kingdom of God enters the world it is judged by the world and found to be dangerous."[13] Even when "the King and the Kingdom are accepted," when "the law of life is understood," a man cannot "simply live by it."[14] There is not, there never has been, there never will be any "final escape in historic existence from the contradictions in which human nature is involved,"[15] from the "conflict between the *is* and the *ought* of life, between the ideal possibilities to which freedom encourages man and the drive of egoism."[16] In short, there is no escape from the

[10] *Reflections on the End of an Era*, p. 281.
[11] *Beyond Tragedy*, pp. 273–286.
[12] *Ibid.*, p. 182.
[13] *Ibid.*
[14] *Ibid.*, p. 184.
[15] *Ibid.*, p. 187.
[16] *Ibid.*, pp. 137–138.

corruption of sin. That corruption is not "the consequence of a natural or cultural 'lag.'"[17] It is not due to ignorance.[18] "It arises from the very freedom of reason with which man is endowed," by which he is "able to throw the harmonies of nature out of joint,"[19] by making "himself, rather than God, the centre of existence."[20] "We can say it is due to the fact that man exists at the juncture of nature and spirit, of freedom and necessity. Being a weak creature, he is anxious for his life; and being a resourceful creature, armed with the guile of spirit, he seeks to overcome his insecurity by the various instruments which are placed at his disposal by the resources of his freedom. But inevitably the security which he seeks for himself is bought at the price of other men's security. Being an insignificant creature with suggestions of great significance in the stature of his freedom, man uses his strength to hide his weakness and thus falls into the evil of the lust for power and self-idolatry."[21] It is his "unbelief and pride which tempt [him] to sin,"[22] his inevitable though not necessary unwillingness"[23] to accept the peculiar weakness of his creaturely life, and "to find the ultimate source and end of his existence beyond himself."[24] It is in that sense, because evil presupposes itself, because it exists already in the very predisposition to it, that the idea of the fall of man achieves significance and relevance,[25] and his sin can be said to be "original." On any other basis history becomes an answerless riddle, and every attempt of science and philosophy to make sense of human existence refutes itself.

In such fashion, with ever recurring insistence, the relation between the historical and the trans-historical is shown to belong to the very constitution of the universe. Christian doctrine, therefore, which is the formulation, from revelatory fact and experience, of that organic relation (instead of having to do with some supernal realm of reality) is seen to be in its aspect of given-ness a revelation of the essential nature of things. It is more than relevant; apart from it life itself is irrelevant and man incredible. It is more than intellectually respectable; it is the indispensable prerequisite and "dominating principle of social criticism," cutting into "the pious complacen-

[17] *Discerning the Signs of the Times,* p. 43.
[18] *Ibid.,* p. 85.
[19] *Beyond Tragedy,* p. 11.
[20] *Ibid.*
[21] *Discerning the Signs of the Times,* p. 165.
[22] *Ibid.,* p. 166.
[23] *The Nature and Destiny of Man,* I, 150.
[24] *Ibid.,* I, 166.
[25] *Beyond Tragedy,* p. 12; *Discerning the Signs of the Times,* p. 166

cies" alike of bourgeois religion and of bourgeois politics, whether capitalist or socialist.[26]

3. Judgment and Mercy.—Further still, the relation of time and eternity, of God and the world, must be understood not only in terms of *demand* but also in terms of *judgment and mercy.* It is the theme of judgment that Niebuhr labors. It enters and re-enters, often unexpectedly, never quite able to resolve itself, as if we were dealing with some great fugue on the subject of God's Holy War. And may not one hazard the guess that this is precisely what life is? Here is that same curious interweaving of the human and the divine, in the course of which "history is forced partly to validate, though it usually defies, the standards of the Kingdom of God," and "the inequalities of nature . . . accentuated by human imagination . . . become intolerable and destroy themselves."[27] So is the judgment in store at the end of history anticipated by the judgments which are periodically executed in history: on the *noble,* who "sprinkle rose-water on the cesspools of injustice . . . clothe tyrannical power with broadcloth, . . . surround it with soft amenities, and fool themselves and others by their pretensions";[28] on the *wise,* "because they are not wise enough," or "because they are too wise," and in pride overreach themselves.[29] None is exempt: not the *strong,* who increase their power and seek to bring all of life under their dominion;[30] not the *weak* who will "sin when they become mighty" and "sin in prospect and imagination while they are weak."[31] It makes a difference whether men are good or evil; but evil and good alike stand under an ultimate judgment in every moment of time.[32] "All have sinned, and come short of the glory of God."[33] "There is no human vitality which is not subject to decay and no human virtue which is not subject to corruption."[34]

To Niebuhr this is no theory, no pious beating on the breast: each separate and specific count of the indictment is entered, and entered first against himself.[35] Not a sermon he has preached but has embodied the grace of genuine humility. However urgently he would enter his disclaimer, he must allow others at this point to speak for him. Here is one who does it: "In his visits to our college he has,

[26] Davies, *op. cit.*, p. 33.
[27] *Beyond Tragedy*, p. 200.
[28] *Ibid.*, p. 207.
[29] *Ibid.*, pp. 208–210.
[30] *Ibid.*, p. 221.
[31] *Ibid.*, p. 219.
[32] *Ibid.*, pp. 253ff.
[33] Rom. 3:23.
[34] *Beyond Tragedy*, p. 131.
[35] *Leaves from the Notebook of a Tamed Cynic*, pp. 166–167.

more often than otherwise, supplemented his sermons by a succession of informal conferences with groups of students or single individuals. His modesty and humility and utter unselfishness in these time-consuming meetings are matters of common knowledge. They have cost him heavily in his margins of time and strength." The secret of course lies in this, that the word God has given him to speak has from the very beginning addressed itself to him. One cannot help being profoundly aware of the autobiographical aspect of such sermons as "The Test of True Prophecy," "Childhood and Maturity," as indeed of many another. His is what D. R. Davies calls "a burdened utterance, for it tells of a doom which involves the prophet himself": with what incalculable consequences and implications for society it is one of Niebuhr's dominant purposes to explore and illumine.

Righteousness making its *demands* on the unrighteous; the arm of the Lord that is not shortened, executing its *judgments,* that men may be brought in contrition to humility and repentance; with the *mercy* which is "partly the fulfillment and partly the contradiction to the justice" that punishes, taking into itself the evil to smother it, and completing our incompleteness: until all the immediacies of human existence bear the seal—and reflect, each in its own way, the pattern—of the ultimate. It is here, as in music, that the conflict between the dominant and the tonic moves toward its resolution, and the kerygmatic note is struck: struck with authority, unfailingly struck, on stage or off, in front of the footlights or in the wings, and struck during the last six or seven years with increasing insistence and emphasis. If it is rarely developed into a major theme, the reason is not far to seek. For Niebuhr there can be no justification by faith until optimism breaks down, and men cease to trust in themselves that they are righteous. As unbelief is the root of sin, the secular and religious complacencies of which it is in part compounded have to be utterly shattered before there can be any of that "spiritual relaxation without which all moral striving generates a stinking sweat of self-righteousness and an alternation of fanatic illusions and fretful disillusionments."

4. Apologetic.—With the prophetic and interpretative task, therefore, which is the positive aspect of his apologetic, is inseparably bound *the negatively analytical and critical.* In what proportion may perhaps best be seen in the Lord's commission to Jeremiah: "See, I have this day set thee over the nations and over the kingdoms, to root out, and to pull down, and to destroy, and to throw down, to build, and to plant."[36] The steady drift of four hundred years toward the individualism, rationalism, and humanistic moralism of "bourgeois" religion, each of them a partial insight into reality, distorted and perverted by its pretensions toward the final and absolute, had to be stemmed somehow; to say nothing of the attendant flood of secularism, swelling through the social, economic, and political life of Western civilization, all covered over with the flotsam and jetsam of an enterprise which was once known as "inevitable progress," but was so obviously now coming to grief. If life, on pain of death, was not any longer to be allowed refuge behind its premature and therefore false securities, there could be little doubt as to what had to be done: done in this instance with a resolute, almost stubborn effort to be fair to both sides of every question; but done, and done first, and done thoroughly. The master of a college in one of the great universities writes of it vividly and in some detail: "In that hectic period of religious disillusionment that followed World War I, the young were at work removing the symbols of their fathers' faith from the mantelpiece, and consigning them to the cupboard. At first sight and hearing Niebuhr appealed to them as an earth-sent ally, in their efforts to destroy all evidences of an earlier trust in God, Whose Kingdom was just around the corner, and of the urbane belief in rational man's capacity to inherit the Kingdom here and now, with just a little more personal effort on man's part. Niebuhr's depiction of man as both a child of Heaven and a child of Hell, his focussing of attention on the dark, irrational forces by which men were driven, his continual barrage against human pretension and pride, his strictures against a complacent church, as the harmless adornment of a comfortable life: all this was a kind of tonic to the young in the 1920s and a bit later. It was an exhilarating experience for both young and old to hear him 'pour it on' of a Sunday morning, looking like a hawk and swooping upon his prey, hawk-fashion, to the accompaniment of wing-like gestures and torrential sentences. Here was something new and different in the pulpit—complete vitality of mind and body, words trying to catch up with ideas and therefore never obscuring them, deadpan humor oftentimes with a sting in it, and a sudden change of pace from direct address to a kind of dramatic dialogue between the preacher and God or the Devil. The remark of a chap who was very chary about churchgoing, but

[36] 1:10.

who never missed Niebuhr, is a fair summary of the pre-World War II impression that he created among his listeners: I feel as if I had been caught in an air-raid!"

Yet Niebuhr has never been a controversialist in his preaching. Matters under dispute draw his ire; his purpose is not to run headlong into them; rather is it to throw a clear light on the issues involved, and that in such a way as to make them "incidental to his interpretation of broad Christian teaching."

Perhaps it would be useful just to list, as one pages through the sermons, a few of the salient angles in the now crumbling wall of that defended city of man against which he has made his repeated and persistent assaults. In "As Deceivers, Yet True"[37] he deals chiefly with the error of literalism in confusing "myth" with history, and with the error of naturalistic philosophies in pretending to arrive at ultimate conclusions about the meaning of life. These are the major objectives, but with many a strategic position that has to be "mopped up" along the way, a fairly bewildering host of related fallacies: that the temporal and historical world is self-derived or self-explanatory; that God is the sum total of finite occasions and relationships (pantheism), or that the finite world is merely a corrupt emanation from the ideal and eternal (dualism); that the idea of causality is an adequate key to the understanding of creation (evolution), or even with Aristotle that some first cause which has no living relationship with the events of nature and history is the one and only sufficient premise; that the natural order is either of primary if not of exclusive significance (rationalistic materialism) or of none at all (theologism or occasionalism); that sin is due to the inertia of nature, or the hypertrophy of impulses, or to the defect of reason; that determinism is a sufficient explanation of the inevitability of sin; that induction from empirical facts can yield a conclusion about ultimate meaning; that the world is evil, because it does not conform to a rational idea of unity; that revelation is unnecessary, or that general revelation is enough; that man can either disregard or overcome his creatureliness; that there can be any satisfactory theory of the atonement, or any consequent rejection of the fact itself as absurd; that history is the record of the progressive triumph of good over evil; that a tragic view of life is either no more than one of two live options, or in itself must be regarded as final; that the transmutation of evil into good is not even a divine possi-

[37] In *Beyond Tragedy*, pp. 3ff.

bility; that either sectarian apocalypticism, with its chronological illusions, or proletarian apocalypticism, with its promises of unconditioned fulfillment in this life, may be substituted for the Biblical proclamation of God's ultimate triumph—potential in every moment of history, final at the end of history—which shall complete the human enterprise by the annihilation of the contradictions which sin has introduced. And all this is taken, not from twenty-five printed sermons, but from one—with no confusion of idea, no lack of clarity or of unified direction! No more conclusive demonstration could be given of the breadth and range of Niebuhr's thought. One of his colleagues asks at the close of a letter, "Has there been any preacher in our time who could speak so well to the intellectuals outside the church?" Add to the list of his other major objectives the culture that pretends to finality, and the righteousness that consciously or unconsciously assumes the aura of the absolute; the ready moral "solution" of life's profound dilemmas, and the oversimplification of its enigmas; the confusions of the orthodox, and the messianic illusions of the revolutionary, in whatever realm, religious, social, economic, political; the evils of pride and injustice, inseparable from the struggle for security and power; the perils of optimism and despair, of impersonal process and the escape into mysticism, of premature compromise and irresponsible detachment, of knowing too little and knowing too much: and the sum of it is an indictment which, as that same colleague has written, in its "understanding of the depths and concrete details of the human situation . . . is so unusual that it needs to have a place of its own."

II. PREACHING: A PART OF GOD'S REDEMPTIVE ACT

1. The Method of Approach.—In his choice of subjects Dr. Niebuhr has laid on himself certain limitations incident to the nature of the prophetic task which has been appointed him and to the size of the canvas on which he has been set to paint. His *métier* is to work not with miniatures but with murals. In them one has to deal with the spread of some vast engagement on many fronts, with the impact of worlds, with the panorama of a civilization, with maps of centuries and continents in high relief. The possibilities may be fewer in number, but how much grander in scope; so in music. Bach's *Art of the Fugue* employs no more than a single theme; but out of it have been developed nineteen compositions, all in D minor! Yet there is no lack of concreteness and detail in Niebuhr's work. What is so fascinating about his sermons, what rarely fails to hold his hearers spellbound, whether or not they fully understand him, is the almost endless variety of combinations and permutations, each of them sharply delineated, cameo-like, with which he elaborates the comparatively few central ideas that inform his preaching; often enough delivering what he has to say as if he had just arrived at it by some happy inspiration, and doing it with an explosive abruptness that seems to be the result of a kind of spontaneous internal combustion! It is to this, among those who have heard him most frequently, that reference is unfailingly made. Writes one, of a certain meeting that was held: "It was a brilliant Jewish jurist who suddenly said, 'What we need here is a teacher who can show his students *how his mind works*. . . . Reinhold Niebuhr does that better than any man I listen to: we need somebody here like him.'" Writes another: "One of our most critical faculty members goes so far as to say that of all our visiting preachers Niebuhr is the only one who interests him. By contrast the others seem to be doing homiletical 'stunts.' He seems to be thinking on the spot—thinking his own way into what is still for him an unsolved problem. Not that Niebuhr does not know precisely what he is going to say, or that his sermon is actually extempore. . . . But to a degree hardly matched by other preachers he does identify himself on the spot with what he is saying. His vitality and his own personal concern for his theme are contagious."

From the very start both the preacher and his hearers are inescapably involved. There is no dependence on any tawdry storytelling for the arousing of interest. Not that he makes no use of contemporary events, or of what he knows at the moment to be in the minds of the people who hear him: he does that with remarkable freshness, often with brilliant flashes of wit or humor. But he pays his congregations the compliment of believing that matters of obviously profound and vital concern need no more at the outset than to be announced: occasionally in a paragraph, more frequently as the first head of discourse; now and then with a striking sentence, always an anticipation of the whole progress of his thought, sometimes immediately relevant to the context of contemporary life, most often to the Biblical passage under consideration. And from that point on the development is allowed to proceed in whatever manner appears most congenial to the content. The form never seems to have been imposed; rather it emerges from Niebuhr's own keen insight into the ambivalences and ambiguities of human existence, even of truth itself. Throughout there is a deeper dialectic than thesis, antithesis, and synthesis can convey. Very little is simply stated, because very little can be simply stated if the statement is to prove adequate. Whether the order is determined roughly by chronological considerations, or by some necessary analysis of a given situation; whether it is suggested by the text, by some recapitulation of Christian doctrine, or in part at least by the paradoxical nature of reality itself, there is from beginning to end consistent, well marked, one is inclined to say inevitable movement: delayed at times, it may be, but never stultified, by a certain discursiveness; hastened here and there by a kind of kaleidoscopic merging of ideas, with leaps of intuition that are not always easy to follow. The integrating principle seems to be a sort of disciplined stream of consciousness, giving the impression that one is witnessing the very creative act itself, as he wrestles with his own thought, like some Jacob with an angel, protesting to it, as it tries to elude him in the shadows, lest the day should break. "I will not let thee go, except thou bless me." With the result, as often in the modern poets, that while meaning seems to accumulate with every step it is never fully disclosed until the last step is taken; and that step itself is scarcely ever more than a sometimes abrupt, always desperately earnest invitation to pilgrimage by a man who knows where it hurts, and knows toward what horizons the future lies. "And as he passed over Penuel the sun rose upon him, and he halted upon his thigh."[38]

Take as instance chosen almost at random, "The Ark and the Temple."[39] Here, without any preamble at all, we are at once introduced to (1) culture religion, the god of the ark which accompanies the warrior. Whereupon, over against it, and yet not unrelated, is set (2) the God of the prophets and of Christ, whose judgments upon the sins involved in our highest values bring princes to naught and make the judges of the world as vanity, rendering it impossible for men to extricate themselves so completely from the warfare of human existence as to be worthy of building a temple dedicated to him in whose bosom we learn the nothingness of all human victories. Such a temple has of necessity, therefore, to be built not by Solomon's goodness but by David's uneasy conscience, by the unworthiness which knows itself unworthy, being disturbed by the word of the eternal God. But let it be built (3) with no illusions!

[38] Gen. 32:26, 31.

[39] *Beyond Tragedy*, pp. 51ff.

The ark remains in the temple, where forever prophetic religion must speak an eternal "No" to all human pretensions, and priestly religion must point to the eternal in all human values, comprehending, as Lincoln did so profoundly, the meaning of human activities in the light of the so often inscrutable purposes of God. Little wonder that the "liberal" is likely to regard Niebuhr as a nihilist, while the nihilist is sure that he is a sanctifier of culture!

Or turn to his sermon on "The City Which Hath Foundations,"[40] which begins promptly with (1) the balance between the other-worldly and the this-worldly aspects of Biblical hope, between the historic fulfillments of freedom and brotherhood and those fulfillments which look beyond history. Certainly there are (2) possibilities in history of making actual what is potential, though every important realization is accompanied by equally significant frustrations. And (3) the frustration, by reason of man's finiteness and corruption, is as permanent an aspect of human existence as the realization. (4) These contradictions can be resolved only by faith, by an acknowledgment of the limits of human powers, and by the belief that the limits of human powers are not the limits of the meaning of existence. Consequently, (5) it is important to be more concerned with our duties than with the prospect of success in fulfilling them.

It is evident at a glance that the dialectical ("contrapuntal") pattern remains much the same from sermon to sermon, whatever the particular divisions may happen to be; but the upshot is not monotony, any more than it is in Bach or Mozart. As in all true art, elemental simplicities are elaborated into an enthralling web of relationships and implications, every one of them relevant. As he proceeds to uncover "the inadequacies of every alternative diagnosis and every alternative solution," it is as if a siren had suddenly begun to sound the alert; nobody knows precisely what presupposition, what habitual complacency, what cherished pretension will be shattered next! Drawing his illustrations least often perhaps from Scripture, more frequently from art and literature, but most of all from history, philosophy, and the contemporary scene, he somehow succeeds in lifting to the level of consciousness the shadowy and never fully apprehended awareness, even in the unthinking mind, of life's profound complexities, making articulate the inarticulate, giving shape and substance to the paradox which is already there in the stuff of human existence, laying its uneasy ghost by calling it

[40] *Discerning the Signs of the Times*, pp. 73ff.

from the tomb where men have tried to bury it out of sight and out of mind, loosing it and letting it go, in order that they may never again be so thoroughly disillusioned, seeing that now they have fewer illusions!

Evident too is the dilemma in which the hearer is left. It is the dilemma in which life itself leaves him, with no facile resolution available. Paul Tillich has said that the conventional sermon treats first of this troubled world, then proceeds to discredit the world's solutions, only to conclude by presenting Christ as the answer; whereas the Biblical order is quite the reverse! There every generation in its turn is confronted with the Christ of God, that in his light it may see the broken lights of all this world's wisdom, and know itself at the last to be troubled, far more deeply troubled than it had dreamed: the secular problem has now become a religious problem. Whichever pattern Niebuhr adopts, he knows how important that reversal is. In the sermon on Matthew 16:13–28,[41] he makes it explicit. We are brought from the paradox of suffering and triumph in the person of Christ to the mistaken messianic ideas of Jesus' time and of our own, after which we are faced with the inevitability of the cross, and with the strange coming of the son of man, both in history and at the end of history. Likely enough the usual treatment of such a passage would proceed from the perils of political messianism to the illusions of sectarian apocalypticism, with little if any realization of the measure of truth which each serves only to obscure or distort, closing on the note of redemption through suffering. It would perhaps be a neater package; but the neat package, gift-wrapped, is to Niebuhr an abomination. It is a betrayal of the facts. "Every easy assurance of triumph for the Kingdom of God falsifies the human situation and beguiles men into false conceptions of the tragedy of human existence."[42] If Dr. Niebuhr had rendered no other service than to disturb the conscience of both pulpit and pew at precisely that point, his contribution to American preaching would yet have been beyond reckoning. Here is the *justus et peccator* of the Reformation; Paul's "earnest expectation of the creature" which "waiteth for the manifestation of the sons of God";[43] the "we see not yet all things put under him" of Hebrews.[44] Anything else sounds like counterfeit coin, and is harder to pass off than most preachers think; this has the ring of the genu-

[41] "The Suffering Servant and the Son of Man," in *Beyond Tragedy*, pp. 175ff.
[42] *Ibid.*, p. 186. [43] Rom. 8:19. [44] Heb. 2:8.

ine. It is interesting and instructive to read, one after another, the last paragraph, even the last sentence, of each of the published sermons. Never is the tension relaxed, except insofar as is necessary to render it tolerable. Writes the dean of one university: "Tradition has it that it is more important to find a man who knows what your problem is than to find a man who knows what the answer is. Students recognize and respond to that quality in Niebuhr's preaching. They feel that he knows what the real problems of religion are, most particularly in these days. . . . In leaving his dual sermon-themes unresolved he invites his hearers to go on with the problem for themselves, and is, to this extent, preaching for them, not at them. His student hearers are not indifferent to the compliment he thus pays them."

2. *Servant of the Word.*—There can be no question that Dr. Niebuhr's preaching is Biblical preaching; not perhaps in the sense which that phrase commonly conveys, but in the sense that the content and burden of his utterance cannot possibly be understood in any other context than the Bible. He is of course a long sea mile away from being authoritarian in his view of Scripture; and yet Scripture, with an authority not imposed but intrinsic, lays upon him a living and compelling hand. What has already been said of his insistence on the organic relation between the historical and the trans-historical furnishes the clue to both his dependence and his freedom. God has revealed himself as Creator, Judge, and Redeemer, revealed himself supremely in Christ as prompting, answering to, and clarifying man's quest for the ultimate source of being, his realization of moral obligation and of moral unworthiness, and his longing for forgiveness.[45] To encounter this God in Christ, not as object but as subject, "a free self who speaks to us from beyond ourselves and discloses a truth which is beyond reason,"[46] is to come face to face with that Gospel for which the Old Testament prepared the way. As the transcendent is both the ground and the fulfillment of human existence, so the incontrovertible fact of revelation is both the ground and the fulfillment of Niebuhr's prophetic task. But because of the subtle interweaving in the Bible itself of the human and the divine, he is able to apprehend the Biblical revelation not as deposit, fossilized and static, but as present, organic reality. Unfail-

[45] *The Nature and Destiny of Man,* I, 1.

[46] Mary Frances Thelen, *Man as Sinner in Contemporary American Realistic Theology,* p. 90, quoted by Will Herberg.

ingly the Bible comes alive in his preaching. On the one hand, he can and does devote a whole sermon or sermons to an exposition of some Biblical passage, or of the Biblical faith; on the other, not only can he deal freely with the "mythological" element involved in Scripture and in Christian doctrine, but he can on occasion throw off the shackles of an accurate exegesis, find in a text what best suits his purpose,[47] and then plunge into some insight which, far from misconstruing the author's intent, illumines it! Such freedom, it should be added, while never "unchartered," was relatively more characteristic of the earlier years than of the later. In the sermon entitled "As Deceivers, Yet True,"[48] he makes explicit allowance for his use of Paul's answer to the charges bandied about by the congregation at Corinth, then goes on to speak of the deceptive symbols which the Christian faith employs to express the dimension of eternity in time! In "Zeal Without Knowledge,"[49] the apostle's question, with its echoes of Deuteronomy, "Who shall ascend into heaven? (that is, to bring Christ down from above) Or, Who shall descend into the deep? (that is, to bring up Christ again from the dead)"—intended only to stress, in view of the Incarnation and Ascension, the given-ness of that "righteousness which is of faith"—sums up for Niebuhr the "whole tragic self-destruction of humanistic idealism," which began "by protesting against orthodox Christianity's bringing 'Christ down from above,' " the "Church's claim that it has realised the transcendent possibility of life . . . incarnated in Christ," and "ends by seeking to 'bring Christ up from the dead,' " that is, by trying "to construct a Christ out of some human virtue or capacity." This is not exegesis. It is rather analogy. But it is suggestive, it is memorable, and it does illustrate—which is all it was meant to do! *Omne simile claudicat,* and religion is not science, poetry is not prose! If this kind of freedom is risky, and doubtless it is, it is yet deliberate with Niebuhr, not casual, as with so many others of his generation. And it is not undisciplined. There is the discipline of technical Biblical scholarship, which is one thing; and there is what someone has called the discipline of "an amazingly fruitful intuition about the meaning of the whole," which both is and is not another thing! It is primarily to the latter, to his fidelity without enslavement, that in Reinhold Niebuhr's case we are the more deeply indebted. Even "his detailed distortions are in harmony with some real facet of Christian truth."

[47] Cf. "Christianity and Tragedy," *Beyond Tragedy*, pp. 155ff.

[48] *Ibid.*, pp. 3ff.

[49] *Ibid.*, pp. 229f.

3. *The Ultimate Appeal.*—If the prime aim of the Christian preacher is to confront men with God in Christ, to make possible for them, insofar as he can, such a moment of untrammelled decision as every genuinely personal encounter provides, then that succinct phrase of the Air Force, "Mission accomplished," is the only over-all report which can be made of Niebuhr's preaching. Few of his published sermons convey the intimate and pastoral note which marks so many of those delivered at Union Seminary: they are set out on too broad a canvas for that. One must concede too, as is so often said of them, that they are addressed first and foremost to the mind, and only so to the will, with never anything that seems like a calculated attempt to involve the emotions. That no doubt is as it should be. People are not to be maneuvered. Why some superficial disturbance of the pulse beats, if only there is a deep probing that stirs hidden longings? There need be no momentary welling over of gratitude, no swift response of love, no sudden mounting up with wings as eagles, if only one may run and not be weary, walk and not faint. It is quite likely that Niebuhr himself feels the almost exclusively intellectual quality of his work to be something of a limitation in the pulpit. He writes of it from the earliest days of his ministry.[50] One can only answer that he is far more moving, and at deeper levels, than is at once evident from either the written or the spoken word. The very weakness of his strength is a virtue! There may be some who are blinded by the brilliance of the light; but as the eye grows accustomed to the unhindered view, may it not learn to see things steadily and to see them whole? "It is in relationships and in totalities that life's meaning is revealed," and the beauty which lies so close to tears![51]

Relatively more serious is the feeling one may have, reading and listening, that in the "place of meeting" between God and man, rendered so inevitable both by the content of Niebuhr's sermons and by the intense and honest sense of awe which marks their delivery, God as object occupies more room than God as subject. Here is the price which the "mystical" is bound to pay the analytical:[52] the "I-thou" all too often yields insensibly before the encroachments of *he* and *they*. There is more the announcement of a presence than an introduction of persons.[53] In the sermon on "The Power and

[50] *Leaves from the Notebook of a Tamed Cynic*, pp. 38–39, 67, 92–93, 132–133.

[51] *Ibid.*, pp. 58–59.

[52] *Ibid.*, p. 57.

[53] Yet see such passages as those in "Humour and Faith," pp. 127–128, and "Today, Tomorrow and the Eternal," in *Discerning the Signs of the Times.*

Weakness of God,"[54] while a thoroughly just criticism of Studdert-Kennedy's poem, "High and Lifted Up," is aptly entered into the record, there is yet about those quoted lines, even apart from the oft repeated pronouns *I* and *Thou,* a nuance of realization, a coming-toward of that Other, like a figure shaping itself out of the fog, which is measurably lacking in the sermon itself, vast and tender as it is. So with the sermon on "The Fulfilment of Life."[55] In the resurrection stories of the Fourth Gospel, which as Dr. Niebuhr points out is not so much history as interpretation of history, a woman cries out "Rabboni," a voice is heard saying, "Peace be unto you," and a man on his knees can think of nothing else but "My Lord and my God."[56] The meeting *is* the interpretation! But here is a sermon on the Christian world-view, not on immortality but on resurrection, in which the thought never really breaks through from the realm of idea into the place of which it is written, "That which was from the beginning, which we have heard, which we have seen with our eyes, which we have looked upon, and our hands have handled, of the Word of life . . . That . . . declare we unto you."[57] It remains true, nevertheless, that people are not cured of greed "by making them conscious of both the nature and the consequences of their expansive tendencies," nor "charmed into righteousness" by "the language of aspiration rather than that of criticism and command." They are not saved by contrition, even though completed by God's grace, nor "by hope and faith," nor by the humility out of which grows charity. They are saved as Peter was saved when he saw what there was to see in the face of Jesus Christ! To say as much is to do no more than to carry a few poor coals to Newcastle. Dr. Niebuhr knows all this, and gives convincing evidence of knowing it.[58] The only purpose which a listing of such phrases may serve is to point up the subtlety of the perils that beset every effort to communicate a Gospel which is not *about* Christ but identical with him. One of the most astonishing of the records that have to be set down of the apostle Paul is that under the same pressure of thought he succeeds, and without the intellectual martyrdom that witness so often exacts!

Perhaps not unrelated is the fact that the doctrine of the Holy Spirit, involving as it does the doctrines of sanctification and the Church, receives little attention in Dr. Niebuhr's sermons. It has

[54] *Ibid.*, pp. 132ff.
[55] *Beyond Tragedy,* pp. 289ff.
[56] John 20:16, 19, 28.
[57] I John 1:1, 3.
[58] *Beyond Tragedy,* pp. 156, 168, and, of course, particularly in his prayers.

been said of his preaching that it is a God-inspired *praeparatio evangelii;* that he "points to the Gospel, but does not set it forth." No doubt, as one of his friends expresses it, he is "afraid of the pious and hackneyed affirmations which usually pass for the preaching of the gospel, and thus may sometimes say too little. Although such themes as sanctification and the church are largely absent from his sermons, they stand in the wings, and one feels that he does not like to call them for a curtain bow over the footlights, because many would remember only the glitter and the grease, and forget the nerve of the act. While his sermons may not cover the whole range of the gospel, they never wander far from its core." His dealing with the Church as "that place in human society where men are disturbed by the word of the eternal God," and where "the word of mercy, reconciliation, and consolation is heard,"[59] together with the prospect of redemption, partial in time, complete in eternity, which he envisages for the individual and for society—these of themselves stand in rebuttal of the charge, sometimes entered against him, that the only grace he knows is the grace of justification rather than that of power; that ultimately he discounts and diminishes the Christian hope. For him it is in justification that the universe, and distortions of the power which he assumes, are corrected, but never absolutely. The very sense of sin is part of one's growth in grace, is how the pardon is fully apprehended. So that the question becomes by no means whether or not his view is pessimistic; the question is by all means whether or not the world is as he says, an arena of inevitable frustration, where a man's reach always exceeds his grasp. "Perplexed, but not in despair," he knows as few know what the Christian hope is, and what the odds against it are. It is what people are forever tempted to do with their "deliverances"—which is always the risk God has to run—that appals him. When the ark came to rest on Ararat, before the waters were abated, the dove could find no place for her foot; when the floods subsided, and everything seemed normal again, Noah got drunk! In *Reflections on the End of an Era*[60] is specifically set forth the dilemma between ethical tension and religious relaxation, a theme to be developed homiletically ten years later.[61] Neither the tension nor the relaxation is absent from Niebuhr's sermons; neither the

[59] *Ibid.*, p. 62 and *passim.*

[60] See Chap. XX, pp. 279ff.

[61] "Today, Tomorrow and the Eternal," in *Discerning the Signs of the Times,* pp. 94ff.

"Watch therefore" of Matthew 25:13, nor the "Take therefore no thought for the morrow" of Matthew 6:34.

Whether or not he has been making his way through the first two articles of The Apostles' Creed, and is now in process of exploring more fully the third, as many hope and believe to be the case, it can yet be said of him, as H. F. M. Prescott says of Malle and Wat in *The Man on a Donkey*:[62] "They crouched in the hillside, looking towards God, feeling God under their spread palms on the grass, and through the soles of their feet. Beyond, beyond, beyond, and beyond again, yet always that which went still beyond—God." And when Malle was asked about her visions, all she would say was, "There was a great wind of light blowing, and sore pain."[63]

PAUL SCHERER

UNION THEOLOGICAL SEMINARY
NEW YORK CITY

[62] P. 320.

[63] P. 338.

17

Henry Nelson Wieman

A RELIGIOUS NATURALIST LOOKS AT REINHOLD NIEBUHR

17

A RELIGIOUS NATURALIST LOOKS AT REINHOLD NIEBUHR

I. NIEBUHR'S PROBLEM

To understand a man, one must know the problem which he is trying to solve. If I understand Niebuhr, the problem with which he struggles might be stated thus: to direct man's faith to what alone can give ultimate and indestructible meaning to life when the illusions are cast off which conceal the truth about man's predicament. This predicament which man tries to conceal from his own eyes is a state of existence in which no adequate meaning can be found in actual events. Events in human life do develop meanings for the human mind for a season. But these meanings are always fragmentary and in conflict and in time fade out, giving place to others which are in turn overwhelmed. So, says Niebuhr, unless we can find a realm of meaning which transcends all this, overarching it, so to speak, as eternity over time, but not separable from time, man cannot find a greatness in life sufficient to make it worth his while. Towers of the human spirit can rise indefinitely, but always in the end they are torn down.

Only for man, not for any other creature, is such transcendent meaning a life-necessity. Man must have it because he can survey the past over long stretches of time and see the fate which has always fallen on the proudest structures. With this knowledge of the past man can anticipate the future indefinitely. But here begins the mischief. He cannot endure what he sees. So he falsifies the facts to keep up his courage. If he does not cast over them the mirage of illusion, this survey of the far past and this anticipation of the far future can yield no meaning sufficiently great and enduring to make life worth living.

It is a mark of human greatness that man cannot live for trivialities and futilities without casting over them some illusion. This inability of man to find any enduring satisfaction in the temporal process when freed from self-deception is, I believe, a part of what Niebuhr means when he says that the human spirit transcends self, nature, time and history.

Endowed with this transcending reach and with the ability to survey and judge the entire human situation, man must find a Majesty beyond the reach of human reason and exceeding the grasp of human imagination, if he is to be saved from despair on the one hand, and from all the pernicious devices by which he tries to conceal from himself his real predicament. As Niebuhr says, "Christianity measures the stature of man more highly and his virtue more severely than any alternative view."[1]

There is another mark of man's greatness or, as Niebuhr prefers to say, his transcendence. Man is so made that nothing can ultimately satisfy him except a society of perfect love. On the other hand, man is able to survey and appraise the whole movement of human history, and to foresee his own death. This combination—the imperative need for love and the survey of what the temporal world can yield—renders man anxious with an unendurable anxiety. It is unendurable in the sense that man cannot allow it to come fully into consciousness without despair. Hence he must either conceal the truth with illusions, or plunge to the depths of despair, or be possessed by a faith in the transcendent sovereignty of love.

This sovereignty of love found by way of faith but inaccessible to reason has been variously described by Niebuhr. The following is a typical statement:

> The Christian faith is the apprehension of the divine love and power which bears the whole human pilgrimage, shines through its enigmas and antinomies and is finally and definitively revealed in a drama in which suffering love gains triumph over sin and death. This revelation does not resolve all perplexities; but it does triumph over despair, and leads to the renewal of life from self-love to love. . . . The love toward God and neighbor, which is the final virtue of the Christian life, is rooted in an humble recognition of the fragmentary character of our own wisdom, virtue and power. The forgiveness which is the most perfect expression of that love, is prompted by a contrite recognition of the guilt with which our own virtue is tainted. Our faith in the faithfulness of God, and our hope in His triumph

[1] *The Nature and Destiny of Man*, I, 161.

over the tragic antinomies of life, do not annul, but rather transfigure, human wisdom. For they mark the limit of its power and purge it of its pretenses.[2]

I have stated what I understand to be Niebuhr's problem and the way he solves it. For the critical examination of Niebuhr's theology which is here undertaken it is important to note that this solution can be reached only by way of faith and not by reason. As we shall see, reason is definitely rejected not only as incompetent to reach this conclusion but as both corrupt and corrupting. Because my criticism of Niebuhr will center around this question of the nature and limits of reason, it is necessary to take a look at reason.

II. THE NATURE AND LIMITS OF REASON

The word "reason" has many different meanings. Niebuhr constantly refers to it, but to my knowledge never explains what he means by it. Examining the many contexts in which the word appears in his writings, I am sure that it must include, among other meanings, intellectual inquiry in the sense of distinguishing true from false propositions by: (1) observing under conditions more or less controlled the consequences predicted by the implications of the proposition in question; and (2) relating by way of logical coherence the given proposition with other propositions likewise tested.

This is the meaning of reason as I shall use it throughout this discussion. I fully recognize that it has other meanings also, but for the purposes of this discussion I shall use it in the sense indicated. It is the use of observation, inference, prediction, and logical coherence, for the attainment of knowledge and the solving of problems.

This kind of intellectual inquiry is never perfectly executed, and even if it were it would not be infallible. But it seems better fitted to detect and correct its own errors than any other alleged way of getting knowledge. Also, the limitations of this method of getting knowledge must be noted. It is limited not in the sense that there is another way to knowledge, but in a different sense.

Reason cannot create a new idea or proposition beyond the implication of the propositions already known. Yet new ideas in the form of innovating insights, problem-solving ideas, revolutionizing intuitions do emerge in the human mind. These newly generated

[2] *Faith and History*, pp. 233–234.

forms of thought and feeling and action are the materials with which reason must work. The work of reason is to test, classify, and interpret them. But reason cannot create if reason is understood in the sense here defined; namely, as a method for testing and classifying ideas and developing implications, and that only. These new insights are grist for the mill of reason; but the mill cannot create its own grist. This is just as true in physics and chemistry as it is in religious inquiry and artistic creation.

These innovating insights, whether in science or religion, whether in morals or art, whether in friendship and other interpersonal relations, whether in politics, government, or industry, although not the work of reason, must be subjected to the tests of reason. These innovating insights are produced by the creativity at work in human life which man cannot control except in the sense of providing conditions most favorable for it to occur. This creativity has brought forth higher ideals. By creating insights of appreciative and mutual understanding between individuals and peoples, it has widened and deepened friendship, love, and brotherhood among men. By insights created in science, common sense, and philosophy, it has expanded the range of what men can know, feel, and control. By insights in the field of art and in aesthetic experience of all manner of things, it has increased the variety of the vivifying contrasts of aesthetic quality accessible to human awareness. By insights in the field of government, politics, and other social relations, it has reduced authoritarian control and increased the mutual control of freedom which operates by way of appreciative understanding and mutual concern for one another's needs and interests between individuals and groups.

This creativity, I repeat, is not the work of reason. But all the new creations brought forth by this constructive transformation of the human mind must be subjected to the adjudication and testing of reason. This is the distinctive function of reason in human life, not to create but to test and organize, not to generate the visions but to distinguish and classify them. If this is not done by reason, the human mind cannot evaluate the new creation. It cannot tell how to interpret the new idea, whether to take it as a description of events, in which case it is empirical truth, or to take it as a work of pure fiction, or to adopt it as a moral ideal, or to enjoy it purely for its aesthetic value, or whatever. Only the tests of reason can adjudicate these questions concerning what creativity brings forth in the spiritual life of man. When reason is not properly applied to them, fictions are mistaken for facts, myths for historical events, fantasies for perceptions, visions for gods. All the wild illusions, insanities, obsessions, and horrors known to man take possession of him like evil spirits when the new creations brought forth by creativity are not subjected to the judgment of reason.

In human life this creativity is obstructed by many things. Infants up to the age of five or six seem to be richly endowed with it because in no other way could they have the many insights by which they discover the meaning of words and all the other innumerable meanings which they must acquire to participate in the culture. Even in these early years creativity is obstructed by fear, suppression, the arrogance and domination of associates—all producing a false and conventionalized and superimposed organization of the personality, suppressing and repressing the developments which might be creative. But after the age of six or seven, man is overwhelmed with these obstructions to creativity.

For the moment, and without further explanation, let us call these obstructions, so far as man is responsible for them, by the name of sin. In religion sin blocks the way to insight to a much greater degree than in the sciences because in religion one seeks to discover what can transform the organization of his personality and the order of his society so as to save man from his self-destructive tendencies and remake him into the best he can become. Since in religion one must seek for what will transform his own personality, and not merely for what will transform material things as in the physical sciences, it is obvious that one cannot undertake this religious search until he is profoundly aware of his need for transformation. On that account confession and repentance of sin is a necessary prior condition for religious discovery, as it is not in the arts and sciences to the same degree. One cannot confess sin if he is not aware of it; and he cannot even try to be aware of it if he has no sense of sin. This is the predicament of man in his religious search.

Niebuhr claims that reason is where sin exercises its corrupting power. This I believe is his most serious mistake, namely, his failure to trace sin to its deepest level in human life. Later we shall discuss this more fully. Here we are showing that the corruption of sin is at a deeper level in the personality than the level of reason. It obstructs creativity itself, before any of the insights can be produced upon which reason might work.

The blindness of sin can be overcome not by repudiating reason but by striving at every sacrifice to provide the conditions, both within the total existential self and in the environment, which will release creativity to bring forth the needed insight. It may be necessary to spend forty days and nights in the wilderness, searching the heart to cleanse it of vanity, complacency, prejudice, submission to accepted authorities, envy, selfish ambition, and everything in the human personality which is obstructive to the process which transforms the human mind so that it can discern what it has heretofore been unable to detect. But every new insight attained in this way or any other way must be tested by reason to discover if it is a new truth or a fiction or an ideal or a work of art or anything else. One major form of sin is to refuse to subject these new creations which emerge in the mind to the tests of reason, and to do this because the idea in this untested form satisfies a deep craving as it could not do if subjected to reason.

This brief sketch of the place of reason in religion is made in criticism of Niebuhr, who refuses to subject the faith and revelation to which he clings to the tests of reason because, he says, in the first place faith and revelation could not open the way to salvation if subjected to the tests of reason, and in the second place, because reason is corrupt. This rejection of reason and this appeal to faith and revelation beyond the reach of reason are what we examine next in Niebuhr's theology.

III. AUTHENTICATING RELIGIOUS BELIEF

Niebuhr claims to base his faith upon the Bible and calls it Biblical faith. But a careful examination shows that he corrects the Bible according to his own convictions. According to Niebuhr many truths of the Bible are presented in the form of myths. But myths are deceptive, he admits, and even Jesus and Paul were deceived by them, although he claims that he has penetrated the deception and found the hidden truth:

> But since myth is forced to state a paradoxical aspect of reality in terms of concepts connoting historical sequence, it always leads to historical illusions. Jesus, not less than Paul, was not free of these illusions.[3]

> The transcendent character of the love ideal was covert rather than overt in the words of Jesus because of the eschatological mold in which it was cast. Jesus thus made demands upon the human spirit which no finite man can fulfill, without explicitly admitting this situation.[4]

[3] *An Interpretation of Christian Ethics,* p. 57.
[4] *Ibid.,* p. 119.

He goes on to point out the errors of St. Paul.

Possibly St. Paul did not carry his own thought through to its ultimate conclusion and ages of Christian experience were required to disclose that a righteousness "by grace" may lead to new forms of Pharisaism if it does not recognize that forgiveness is as necessary at the end as at the beginning of the Christian life.[5]

These are only a few instances selected from the many in which Niebuhr corrects the errors of the Biblical authorities from Jesus down. I think Niebuhr is quite right in treating the Bible as he does. I am only trying to point out that Niebuhr's faith is determined by himself and not by the Bible. Niebuhr may be right and the Bible wrong, but I should like to hear what Jesus and Paul had to say in their own defense before pronouncing Niebuhr right and Jesus and Paul mistaken about the Christian faith. In sum, I demand that neither Niebuhr nor the Bible, but reason, adjudicate the truth.

But Niebuhr not only rejects the authority of the Bible, Jesus, and Paul; he also rejects reason. The following quotation states this very clearly:

. . . religious faith cannot be simply subordinated to reason or made to stand under its judgment. [When this is done] reason asks the question whether the God of religious faith is plausible. . . . Thus reason makes itself God.[6]

The obvious rejoinder is that when faith determines what God shall be without the tests of reason and in disagreement with Jesus, Paul, and other Biblical writers on certain points, and in disagreement on some point or other with every great Christian thinker, then faith "makes itself God" in a way more pernicious than if reason did so. It is more pernicious because, when reason is rejected on the one hand, and the Bible on the other, religious belief must be determined according to one's own personal judgment without the tests of reason. The only remaining way to determine what is true and what is false in religion is the method of pragmatic utility, made famous by William James in his "Will to Believe." Following quotations will show that Niebuhr uses this method, although he may not be conscious of so doing; and he does not hedge it about with protective devices set up by James.

By this method of pragmatic utility, when not protected as James

[5] *The Nature and Destiny of Man,* II, 105.
[6] *Ibid.*, I, 165–166.

protected it, one accepts as true those religious beliefs which seem to be the most useful in producing in human life the consequences which one wants to have produced. But nothing can corrupt religious faith so disastrously as this. This is the way in which rulers and politicians and cynics make use of religion for their own purposes. Certainly Niebuhr is not trying to use religion for his own purposes. He is doing the very best he can in service of the Christian faith. But his rejection of reason has brought on this tragic and inescapable fate. His method of pragmatic utility exposes religion to corruption worse than anything else can do.

This method of pragmatic utility for determining what religious beliefs shall be accepted is shown in the following quotations:

> . . . This is the final enigma of human existence for which there is no answer except by faith and hope; for all answers transcend the categories of human reason. Yet without these answers human life is threatened with scepticism and nihilism on the one hand, with fanaticism and pride on the other.[7]

Here the belief is held because of its pragmatic utility in saving man from skepticism, nihilism, fanaticism, and pride. Following is another quotation, defending another belief on these pragmatic grounds:

> Since supreme omnipotence and perfect holiness are incompatible attributes, there is a note of rational absurdity in all religion, which more rational types of theology attempted to eliminate. But they cannot succeed without sacrificing a measure of religious vitality.[8]

Here rational absurdity is accepted as true on the grounds that it is useful in generating religious vitality:

> Life has a center and source of meaning beyond the natural and social sequences which may be rationally discerned. This divine source and center must be discerned by faith because it is enveloped in mystery, though being the basis of meaning. So discerned, it yields a frame of meaning in which human freedom is real and valid and not merely tragic.[9]

Here the pragmatic utility of the belief is that it provides a frame of meaning which saves human freedom from being tragic and nothing more.

Niebuhr says that the most important truths which concern reli-

[7] *Ibid.*, II, 149. [8] *Moral Man and Immoral Society*, p. 53.
[9] *The Irony of American History*, p. 168.

gion must be put in the form of myths which are deceptive when you try to interpret them rationally because reason is corrupt and incompetent to find the truth in them. But Niebuhr claims to find the truth they contain by a method other than reason. Following is an example:

> The deceptions to which the idea of the fall give rise are many; and all of them have been the basis of error at some time or other in the history of Christian theology.[10]

Christian thinkers throughout our history have been deceived by this myth and others like it, says Niebuhr, because the truth in these myths involves intellectual absurdities. But Niebuhr claims to find the truth in them by accepting the intellectual absurdity and using reason only to find the belief which will be most useful in helping men to live in the way that Niebuhr thinks they should. My reply to Niebuhr and all theologians who do this is very simple. It is that nothing corrupts reason so much as to use the obscurity of a myth to get beliefs which are useful for producing results in human life or which are right and good in your own personal judgment.

Following is another example of this in Niebuhr's work:

> God became man to redeem the world from sin. The idea of eternity entering into time is intellectually absurd. The absurdity is proved to the hilt by all theological doctrines which seek to make it rational.[11]

This affirmation of faith, says Niebuhr, is "intellectually absurd," and therefore cannot be accepted on rational grounds. But he says it must be accepted on the grounds of pragmatic utility because, as he explains in following passages and throughout his writings, it saves us from the world-flight of mysticism and the prideful illusions of optimism.

The following passage shows how Niebuhr's rejection of reason leads him to strike a fatal blow at the very heart of religion, unintentional as this is:

> . . . man builds towers of the spirit from which he may survey larger horizons than those of class, race and nation.[12]

If Niebuhr had used reason to shape his religious beliefs instead of pragmatic utility, he would have found that man does not and

[10] *Beyond Tragedy,* p. 13. [11] *Ibid.,* p. 13. [12] *Ibid.,* p. 29.

cannot build towers of the spirit more lofty than those he happens to have at the time. There is a process of transformation, however, which works in human life and does do this. It generates new ideas in such form as to extend the range of what man can know, feel, and control, and carries this extension beyond any known limit when required conditions are present. Also, it generates appreciative understanding and mutual concern and thus has extended goodwill and brotherhood far beyond the bounds of the primitive tribe where this process of extension began. Also, it brings forth new and better ideals to condemn slavery, brigandage, and other evils sanctioned by older ideals. Also it creates mutual control as over against authoritarian control and when required conditions are present it extends this kind of democratic control to ever wider circles of politically associated individuals.

But all this is not the work of man for the following reasons. No man by his own efforts can get a new idea which has never yet entered his mind in faintest glimmer. No man or group of men can extend the range of their goodwill and brotherhood when their established sense of justice condemns such extension. No man or group can seek a higher ideal when it contradicts the ideal which they hold to be highest. No man or group can reduce authoritarian control and establish in its place mutual control unless among the people there is enough of that kind of free and open and full interchange which creates appreciative understanding and mutual concern for one another's needs and interests.

While man cannot do any of these things for himself, this kind of transformation has occurred in human life and history when required conditions were present. It has generated new ideas never before imagined; it has extended the bounds of brotherhood beyond the bounds previously established as right and just; it has brought forth ideals to contradict those previously established as the highest; it has pushed back the bonds of authoritarian control and released the freedom of mutual control.

Niebuhr fails to see that it is God who rears the highest towers of the human spirit and not man; it is God who lifts man to his supreme eminence and not the self-transcending powers of man. It is God if one seeks God not by choosing beliefs for their pragmatic utility but by using reason to search out what has such character and power in human life that it will save man from self-destruction and transform him into the best that human life can attain when required conditions are present.

If one applies the methods of reason he will see that what does all this is the kind of creative interchange above described. By way of this creativity one gets the unique and original view of the other person. By way of such creativity this original view of the other is integrated with your own with whatever modification of both views may be required for this combination of the two. By way of creativity this combination of diverse elements and viewpoints brings forth in your own mind a wider, richer view which is originally your own. By way of this creativity you communicate this wider, richer, and original view of your own to another, and so the process continues, provided that the required conditions are present.

But as each new and original idea emerges by way of this creativity, it must be subjected to the tests of observation, inference, prediction, and logical coherence to see what it is, whether a new empirical truth or a logical form or a work of art or a new technique for getting things done, or whatever it may be.

This creativity which works in human life is not of man. It is of God. In creating friendship and goodwill where there was none, in creating appreciative understanding and mutual concern between individuals and peoples, it is the power of God unto salvation revealed in Jesus Christ. But there is no way to distinguish it from other things in human life, nor find what conditions it must have to operate with saving power in the fateful age now upon us, nor even to find it as the revelation of God in Jesus Christ, except the method of observation, inference, prediction, and logical coherence.

Reason is the only way to get the knowledge which our faith must have to find for ourselves and to show to others what has such character and power in human life that it will save man from the self-destructive tendencies of sin and transform him into the best that human life can ever attain, provided that we accept it as Lord and Master of our lives, choosing always, at every time of choice and at any sacrifice, to do what it requires of us.

This rejection of God as a creativity at work in the midst of human life, attributing the attainment of higher levels of value to the initiative of man, is the basic difference between Niebuhr's theology and that of the religious naturalist. The sin of pride, says the religious naturalist, calling for confession and repentance, is this claim that man and not God rears the towers of the human spirit.

IV. PESSIMISM AND OPTIMISM IN NIEBUHR

I want to defend Niebuhr against two major criticisms frequently leveled against him: namely, (1) that he is too pessimistic; (2) that he unduly magnifies man's sin. I shall try to show that exactly the reverse of these criticisms is the truth of the matter. He is too optimistic and he does not get to the real depth of sin.

Niebuhr's optimism is expressed in terms of an ultimate outcome and also in terms of moral improvement in history. First, consider the ultimate outcome.

Niebuhr is sure that everything will work out all right in the end and that men will live in a realm of perfect love. To be sure, he says that this realm lies "beyond history." But on examination this is found to be a figure of speech. He writes:

> By the symbol of the resurrection the Christian faith hopes for an eternity which transfigures but does not annul the temporal process. . . . The symbol of the resurrection rejects the Platonic flight into an eternity of "pure" being. These eschatological symbols transcend the rational; but they do justice to the temporal and the eternal dimensions of man's historic existence. But Platonism and modern utopianism are only superficially, but not ultimately, more rational. For in elaborating frames of meaning in which eternity exists without time or time without eternity, they tear the two dimensions of human existence asunder.[13]

The continuance of man's individual existence in the temporal world, no matter how otherwise transfigured, is surely the continuation of history. If history is not the existence of individual men living in the temporal world, then what can history be? According to Niebuhr man in our own time transcends himself and nature and time and history even while also participating in all of these. Therefore the existence of man "beyond history" is not different from his existence in history in our time because even now he reaches into eternity. Doubtless Niebuhr means to say that "beyond history" the tension and conflict between the demands of eternity and the demands of time will no longer continue. But such a state of affairs is nothing else than history in Utopia.

The attainment of perfection in the future "beyond history" will not be accomplished by the power of man, says Niebuhr. But the utopians most severely criticized by Niebuhr, such as Herbert Spen-

[13] *Faith and History*, p. 237.

cer and Karl Marx, say the same. Not the power of man but some law, process or power in history beyond the power of man will produce the blessed outcome.

Let us now look at Niebuhr's belief in progress as it occurs in history. Many quotations can be cited.

> No absolute limit can be placed upon the degree to which human society can yet approximate the ideal (of perfect love).[14]

> The achievements of justice in history may rise in indeterminate degrees to find their fulfilment in a more perfect love and brotherhood; but each new level of fulfilment also contains elements which stand in contradiction to perfect love. There are therefore obligations to realize justice in indeterminate degrees; but none of the realizations can assure the serenity of perfect fulfilment. . . . Higher realizations of historic justice would be possible if it were more fully understood that all such realizations contain contradictions to, as well as approximations of, the ideal of love.[15]

Statements like the ones quoted are scattered throughout Niebuhr's writings. Some critics seem to think that he is a pessimist because he insists that no matter how good human life may become, it will always fall short of being a realm of perfect love, and evils will break out at every level of this approximation, to be fought and corrected. But surely a man is not a pessimist who makes such a claim. Niebuhr's constant insistence on the magnitude of evil in our present life may arise from the contrast between his vision of perfect love "beyond history" and human existence as it now is. But he repeatedly declares that in history as we now live it, human life can advance through indeterminate degrees of approximation toward perfect love, although never fully attaining it. What more can you ask of any sane optimist?

I shall try to show that this optimism of Niebuhr is unwarranted, not because such approximations in the direction of perfect love are impossible, but because Niebuhr does not recognize anything in human life which might produce them. Man cannot approximate, even by infinitesimal degrees, the ideal of perfect love in the ways in which Niebuhr says it must be done. Let us look at the ways in which Niebuhr says these approximations must be achieved.

First of all Niebuhr attributes to mere belief an inordinate and false power to transform life in the direction of perfect love:

[14] *An Interpretation of Christian Ethics,* p. 111.
[15] *The Nature and Destiny of Man,* II, 246.

Whenever men penetrate through the illusions and self-deceptions of life to confront this God, as revealed in Christ, finding his judgment upon their sin not less but more severe, because of the disclosure of the love which prompts it, they may be converted and renewed. History is thus a realm of endless possibilities of renewal and rebirth.[16]

Here it is said that the endless possibilities of history are made accessible to human striving all too simply and easily. The psychological effect of holding a belief about God and Christ does it, says Niebuhr. He repeatedly says that God revealed in Jesus Christ (and other beliefs mentioned) cannot refer to anything empirically and rationally discoverable in the events of history. All attempts to do so land in "logical absurdities." No actual process is going to achieve these endless possibilities in history except the human striving which results from holding these beliefs with deep conviction.

It is true that God appears in history in the form of the sacrificial love of Christ. But this love manifests God only because of its futility: ". . . the Christ who was powerless in history and in whom no particular cause or force in history triumphed or was vindicated."[17]

Besides this alleged power of belief to transform human life, there is God's grace. But when we examine Niebuhr's statements about God's grace we find that grace is equated (1) with the psychological effects of holding certain beliefs, and (2) with "the provisional coincidence between the interests of a ruling group within a nation and the interests of the total community, or [with] the coincidence between the interests of a powerful imperial community and the wider community of nations."[18]

Even Christ in us is not an actual power but only a hope, and therefore can operate only by way of the psychological effects of belief. "Christ in us is not a possession but a hope."[19]

If we examine any individual life, or any social achievement in history, it becomes apparent that there are infinite possibilities of organizing life from beyond the center of the self; and equally infinite possibilities of drawing the self back into the center of the organization. The former possibilities are always the fruit of grace (though frequently it is the "hidden Christ" and a grace which is not fully known which initiates the miracle). They are always the fruits of grace because any life which cannot "forget" itself and which merely makes brotherhood the instrument of its "happi-

[16] *Faith and History,* p. 28.
[17] *The Nature and Destiny of Man,* II, 145.
[18] *Faith and History,* p. 222.
[19] *The Nature and Destiny of Man,* II, 125.

ness" or its "perfection" cannot really escape the vicious circle of egocentricity.[20]

Here the grace of God is identified with man's ability to organize life beyond the center of self. It is not clear just how this is accomplished by the "hidden Christ," because the ability to organize after this fashion is dependent, according to Niebuhr, upon the humility and repentance for one's sin that arises from the belief that God was revealed in Christ as a God who not only judges our sin in all of its depth but also in love forgives if we repent. This alone can liberate man *from* overweening egocentricity and *unto* the love which forgives the evil in other men. Perhaps in the case of the hidden Christ it is some comparable belief which does the work. In any case God's grace in this instance is nothing more than man's ability to organize beyond the center of the self—as a consequence of accepting certain beliefs.

In all of Niebuhr's writings there seems to be no recognition of an actual power in the form of a temporal process other than man's power, which works to transform man in interpersonal relations in the direction of more perfect love. The only power for good which he recognizes is (1) what man himself can do when his mind is changed by accepting certain beliefs with his whole heart and (2) the provisional coincidence between the selfish strivings of powerful groups and the good of the community. If this is all there is in human life on which to count, Niebuhr's optimism is unjustified.

Niebuhr does certainly believe in God. Without doubt he is a theist. But for Niebuhr God's actual presence and power is at the ultimate source and the ultimate outcome of human life and history, except for the presence of God in Jesus Christ. For Niebuhr God is not to be found in the daily processes of human living. Even in Christ God was "powerless in history."[21]

V. THE DOCTRINE OF SIN

There is a second point on which I want to defend Niebuhr against his critics. It is the claim that he unduly magnifies human sin. Here again I shall try to show that the reverse is true. He does not recognize sin at its deepest and most sinister level. Following is Niebuhr's interpretation of sin:

[20] *Ibid.*, II, 123.

[21] *Ibid.*, II, 145.

> The abyss of meaninglessness yawns on the brink of all his mighty spiritual endeavors. Therefore man is tempted to deny the limited character of his knowledge and the finiteness of his perspectives. He pretends to have achieved a degree of knowledge which is beyond the limit of finite life. . . . It is always partly an effort to hide that ignorance by pretension.
>
> In short, man, being both free and bound, both limited and limitless, is anxious. Anxiety is the inevitable concomitant of the paradox of freedom and finiteness in which man is involved. Anxiety is the internal precondition of sin. It is the inevitable spiritual state of man, standing in the paradoxical situation of freedom and finiteness. Anxiety is the internal description of the state of temptation. It must not be identified with sin because there is always the ideal possibility that faith would purge anxiety of the tendency toward sinful self-assertion.[22]

Niebuhr denies that the anxiety issuing from man's refusal to commit himself completely to the power and goodness of God is sin. But if sin is alienation from God or departure from the way God would have us live, then this refusal to commit oneself in this way is sin; and the anxiety thus arising is the symptom of sin. Niebuhr says, No, it is not sin until it has issued in sinful self-assertion. But what is sinful self-assertion if it is not refusal to live as God would have us live; namely, in complete self-giving to God which would remove anxiety?

Niebuhr gives only two reasons for denying that sin begins at this deeper level where anxiety first arises. The first has been indicated. If sin is so understood, then it cannot begin with that particular kind of pride with which he has identified it throughout all his previous writings. But this begs the question. The second argument is that this existential anxiety arising from failure to give oneself over wholly to God cannot be separated from another kind of anxiety which is careful concern that one do his very best. But these two kinds of anxiety are utterly different. We should have two different words to indicate that they are almost diametrically opposites. If one is wholly committed to God he will be concerned and careful to do his best; but such concern is not at all the same kind of experience which one has when he sees that "the abyss of meaninglessness yawns on the brink of all his mighty spiritual endeavors."[23]

This failure of Niebuhr to get to the real depths of sin in human life issues in a serious error. If he recognized sin at this deeper level

[22] *Ibid.*, I, 182–183. [23] *Ibid.*

he would not claim, as he does, that man can be delivered from its deadly power by faith when faith refers merely to the psychological effects of holding certain beliefs. For Niebuhr there can be no other saving and transforming power because, in his teaching, God is not to be found in any actual process, but only "above the structure and forms of life."[24] Hence there is no access to God save by these beliefs. With God so interpreted there can be no deliverance from the deadly power of sin, if sin is this anxiety. Indeed, with Niebuhr's understanding of God and salvation, this anxiety is necessary and should be magnified in order to drive men to accept and hold tenaciously to the required beliefs which have no other authentication save the psychological effects upon the believer. Perhaps the whole tragedy of Niebuhr's heroic and mighty effort to show the way of salvation arises from his failure to get to the bottom of sin in human life.

Evil as well as good issues from the work of every man, and it is important that we distinguish between the two in order to guard against the one and promote the other. Therefore an examination of Niebuhr's work should conclude with some judgment on what is the major evil and what the major good resulting from his achievements.

VI. THE EVIL TO BE CORRECTED

Perhaps the clearest, briefest, and most recent expression of what I judge to be the major evil resulting from Niebuhr's theology is to be found in the *Christian Century* for July 22, 1953:

> In short, the proof that we encounter a God who is above the structures and forms of life . . . must be the witness of a life. . . . Reborn selves possessing the graces of "love, joy and peace" are the only effective witnesses that the Christian faith has rightly apprehended the dimension and the reality of both the divine and the human self. . . . But there is no rational proof that men encounter a divine judgment in this higher dimension. That is a truth of faith; and it is validated by a witness of lives which have been obviously remade by the power of God's judgment and forgiveness.

Note carefully the argument of this quotation. There is no persuasive evidence for belief in "a God beyond the structures and forms of life" except the transformed lives of those who hold this belief. But as soon as the Christian points to his own life of "love, joy and peace," or to that of his fellow believers, as evidence for the truth of his belief, he becomes guilty, according to Niebuhr's own teaching,

[24] "The Christian Witness in a Secular Age," *Christian Century*, July 22, 1953.

of "pride and pretension" unsurpassed in its "destructive nature . . . by any form of human evil which may appear in life and history." Following is his statement to this effect:

> . . . no grace of spirit can be made into a proof of virtue to be admired, and still be a true witness. . . . It is . . . silly for Christians to feel themselves morally superior by reason of their faith. . . . No one dares to name the members of the invisible church or try to separate them out from the whole church . . . because no one but God can look into the secret of the heart to see how honest our repentance has been. . . . The effort . . . to prove the truth of the gospel by pointing to a superior Christian virtue can easily result in a frantic respectability in comparison with which secular forms of goodness may show genuine marks of freedom and grace. . . . The destructive nature of such pride and pretension will be unsurpassed by any form of human evil which may appear in life and history.[25]

Here Niebuhr is saying that if we believe in "a God who is above the structures and forms of life" (and Niebuhr will consider no other) we can point to no convincing evidence to support such a belief except "the graces of love, joy and peace" appearing in those who belong to the invisible church. But if we try to make this evidence visible by pointing out the individuals who display these graces, we become guilty of "pride and pretension . . . unsurpassed in its destructive nature . . . by any form of human evil which may appear in life and history."

This is the trap of utter defeat into which Niebuhr's theology forces the Christian.

Certainly "lives which have been obviously remade" and "reborn selves possessing the graces" are evidence that something or other produces such lives. But the question at issue is this: Can we search and find "the structures and forms of life" which issue in reborn selves and lives remade? Or must we, as Niebuhr demands, repudiate as leading to the sources of this transformation, all such attempts now being conducted by the psychology of personality and allied studies of man? Must we insist, as Niebuhr does, that the source of the transformed life is "a God who is above the structures and forms of life"? If we adopt this alternative we are caught in the trap just described.

On the other hand, if we can find in the structures and forms of life what brings forth the reborn self, then we have found God by this kind of inquiry, if God is understood to be what brings forth

[25] *Ibid.*

such transformation. In this kind of inquiry the reborn self is the evidence that the process found in the structure of life does in truth produce the transformation. But in such case, the structure of this transforming process can be studied, noting its required conditions and all the gradations and degrees of approximation to "love, joy and peace" produced by it, even as psychotherapy and allied forms of inquiry are now doing.[26]

When this naturalistic approach is followed, the individual Christian is not forced to point to his own superior virtue or to that of his fellow believer to find the only evidence for God's transforming power. He can examine the structure of the process which transforms man and there find the evidence he seeks. It can be found in the lives of saints who profess no Christian beliefs as well as in those who do. Thus for the religious naturalist belief in the divine encounter does not depend on the superior humility and contriteness of himself or others who share his beliefs. If on the other hand, Niebuhr's theology is accepted, the Christian must do either of two things. Either he fails to find in himself the required humility and contriteness, and so proves that he did not encounter God; or, if he does find himself sufficiently humble and contrite to be the recipient of God's grace, he is guilty of the pride and pretension which Niebuhr rightly denounces as evil unsurpassed in its destructive nature. Thus does Niebuhr's theology force the Christian either to deny his faith or pervert it into one of the greatest evils in history.

VII. THE GOOD TO BE VALUED

Consider now the greatest good which, I believe, comes out of Niebuhr's work. It is the demonstration that all attempts to get any convincing evidence for belief in "a God beyond the structures and forms of life" are utterly futile. Niebuhr has a mind sufficiently penetrating and acute to see the error of all rational attempts to prove that such a Deity has being. Only by faith can one hold belief in such a God, and this faith is unsupported by any reliable evidence except the power of this belief to transform your life into love, joy and peace combined with a broken spirit and a contrite heart. But, as the argument just preceding demonstrates, you cannot even appeal to this

[26] To find the transforming power in a process having a characteristic structure does not deny man's freedom any more than finding it in a God beyond all structures. But space does not permit discussion of the problem of human freedom.

evidence without stultifying it and retransforming your life back into pride and pretension unsurpassed for destructive evil.

Thus does Niebuhr clear the ground for the only constructive approach to the great religious questions. The only constructive approach is by way of searching the temporal process, and not beyond it, for that form of this process which saves from evil and transforms into the best which man can ever become when he commits himself to it wholeheartedly and meets the other required conditions.

Niebuhr, better than any other known to me, has demonstrated that only two alternatives are open to religion. The one is commitment to what saves and transforms in the temporal process; the other is belief unsupported by rational and empirical evidence but held for its utility in helping us to keep on living when "the abyss of meaninglessness yawns on the brink of all [our] mightiest endeavors." Furthermore, Niebuhr has shown the self-defeating consequence of choosing the second alternative, leaving open only the first. But when we take this first alternative, reason must be our guide because there is no other way to search the temporal process for what in truth creates, sustains, and saves man, and transforms him into the best he can ever become. To be sure, reason can do nothing at all until creativity brings forth some insight or innovating idea to be tested and interpreted. But no such intuition can be accepted until it has been subjected to the test and interpretation of reason.

The basic and surest declaration of reason is that we give ourselves in faith to whatever in the temporal process has the character and power to save and transform, even before we know its specific character. This is necessary because otherwise creativity cannot generate the more profound and revealing insights, for reasons stated in the earlier part of this chapter.[27] Also, this reality in the temporal process, like every other, is always deeper and richer in content than any specific character attributed to it; and any description of it offered by reason may be infected with error. But always beyond the partial and distorted picture of this reality which reason and insight may provide at any given time is the reality itself, to be better understood as further insights disclose it. But these further insights must be subjected to the tests of reason, for otherwise they become illusions.

Mad illusion is the punishment for the sin of rejecting reason as supreme arbiter over intuition, mystic vision, alleged revelation, and all religious belief. Errors held subject to the tests of reason do not

[27] See pages 336–339 and 341–344.

lead to madness; but beliefs held because they protect from the abyss of meaninglessness are not subject to correction. They are held as neurotic beliefs are held, compulsively, because without them anxiety beyond endurance possesses the mind. Such beliefs not subject to reason become increasingly dangerous with the rising power of human action. In the age of atomic power they might issue in self-destructive madness.

With these considerations before us we reach the conclusion that reason must be the guide of faith. This conclusion issues from the theology of Reinhold Niebuhr even though it is almost diametrically opposed to what he intends to teach. But perhaps the greatest good issuing from the works of great men is other than they intend.

HENRY NELSON WIEMAN

THE DIVINITY SCHOOL
THE UNIVERSITY OF CHICAGO
CHICAGO, ILLINOIS

18

E. A. Burtt

SOME QUESTIONS ABOUT NIEBUHR'S THEOLOGY

18

SOME QUESTIONS ABOUT NIEBUHR'S THEOLOGY

REINHOLD NIEBUHR's theology has played a very significant rôle in contemporary Western thought. Since the bulk of this paper will consist in elaborating a few critical questions, I want to make clear at the start my agreement with those who believe that the world of Protestant theology could not well have done without him. He has punctured the false and perilous optimism characteristic of the era of Protestant liberalism, and has vividly revealed the limitations of a purely rationalistic approach to the problems of man's life and destiny. He has done this without falling into the anti-rationalism of Barth or the semi-fundamentalism of other dialectical theologians; he has placed his searching analyses in the setting of a broad perspective on the history of Western philosophy, but without dependence on the difficult ontological categories of his colleague Tillich. Many of his detailed discussions, in ethics, psychology, and political theory, as well as in the strictly theological field, are very keen contributions toward a penetrating and realistic understanding of the topics involved.

Niebuhr has done this, however, at a serious cost. In fact, the cost is so serious that in my judgment the main structure of his theological system will go down in history as of merely negative value. It clears the ground of varied obstructions and reveals some deceptive illusions to which many thinkers have succumbed. But it seems to me to lack two characteristics essential to any positive solution of the problems he has touched upon that can hope to endure—thoroughgoing respect for fact, and an inclusive philosophical perspective.

In saying what I am going to say about certain major features of his position, I do not know whether I am speaking for anyone besides myself. I should like to believe that at some points at least I speak for most philosophers who have taken note of Niebuhr's argument, and that at many points I speak for speculative thinkers with a special interest in the field of religion. But since my own philosophy represents no contemporary school, I shall make no claims. Many philosophers, I am sure, would be horrified at the extent of my agreement with Niebuhr. I agree with his contention that any adequate understanding in the field of religion must be more than intellectual, and must involve a "faith grounded in repentance."[1] As against the philosophers who talk about religion as though they thought this requirement could be sidestepped, I am on his side. But—and here the need mentioned above for unqualified respect for fact and for an inclusive perspective comes into the picture—Niebuhr appears unable to identify any human experience as "faith grounded in repentance" unless it assumes a specifically Christian form and expresses itself in his chosen categories. My criticisms will be focussed largely upon this kind of dogmatic limitation, and I am well aware that few of my philosophical colleagues are prepared to accompany me along this line of thought—not that they approve the limitation, but that they incline to admit no significant rôle for faith or repentance.

My concern is not to attack Niebuhr, but to elicit from him through this paper more explicit statements on some vital phases of his teaching. In the interest of such a clarification of what he really means to say, I shall couch my criticism not in the form of contrasting assertions, but in the form of a few questions. Each of the queries will be elaborated sufficiently, I hope, so that the orientation they express will be clear, and he will thus be in a position to answer frankly and freely when he makes his Reply.

The first of my questions has often been raised, but it needs to be raised again. It has to do with Niebuhr's frequent use of the phrase "the Biblical view" or "the Christian view"[2] when comparing a doctrine in which he believes with positions he holds to be false. This use of language cannot help making him appear to be indulging in an unconscious deception of himself and his readers. He seems to

[1] *Faith and History*, p. 151.

[2] This is done so frequently that references are probably needless. See *Faith and History*, Chaps. 7 and 8; *Nature and Destiny of Man*, Vol. I, Chaps. 1 and 5 *passim*.

wish to secure in this fashion, for his own interpretation of the Christian faith, the prestige and emotional appeal that to Christian readers are associated with the Bible and with the revered name of their religion. Now when we survey this procedure impartially, does it not betray the same kind of delusive pretense that he castigates so effectively, when engaged in by others in the history of Christian theology, as a form of intellectual and spiritual arrogance? If we take any major theological theme and examine the relevant facts objectively, do we not find, first, that in the Bible itself there is a diversity of beliefs with respect to that theme; and second, that Niebuhr's interpretation of any one of them is contradicted by many other interpretations that have just as good a claim as his own to constitute the "Biblical view"? Would it not be more honest, as well as modest, to make clear in every such situation that he is presenting one Biblical view among several, and that he is giving his own theory of it for which he claims no final adequacy as against the many other theories that have been proposed?

The point of this criticism is not to be met by asserting, as Niebuhr sometimes does, that St. Paul introduces into the New Testament a foreign note, expressing the Graeco-Hellenistic view rather than the Biblical one,[3] nor by a general admission that any thinker's interpretation of the message of the Bible may prove to stand in need of correction. The crucial point (to confine myself now to the first half of this query) is whether the evidence really supports the idea that there is any such thing as *the* Biblical view, and whether therefore any theology which assumes that there is does not inevitably project into the teachings of the Bible a selection, an emphasis, and an organizing unity that are in the theologian and not in the Bible. It is one thing to believe that one of the Biblical doctrines is more important and nearer the truth than others—no serious thinker who finds in the Bible any truth at all can do otherwise—but it is another thing to reject doctrines clearly taught in the Bible as "un-Biblical."

Take the very basic doctrine of sin, for example. There are many conceptions of sin in the Bible, as Niebuhr is disposed to recognize when he deals in systematic historical fashion with his question.[4] It is true that those views which have been subsequently influential fall for the most part under one or the other of two types. There is the view, prominent in almost all the Old Testament and implied by

[3] *The Nature and Destiny of Man,* I, 173–177, for example.
[4] *Ibid.*, I, 186ff.

many statements in the synoptic gospels, that the essence of sin is rebellious disobedience toward God. There is also the view, explicitly taught by St. Paul and implied in a few passages of the Johannine writings, that the root of sin lies in the lustful cravings of the flesh which war against the pure aspirations of spirit. Both these doctrines are clearly contained in the Bible, and there is no plausible way of reducing one to a species of the other—they express two basically divergent theories. How can one justify asserting that one of them is Biblical, the other not? Moreover, Niebuhr's own theory is obviously different from each of these. He presents it, to be sure, as a clarifying interpretation of the first of these two doctrines. But in the interest of honest impartiality it is essential to recognize that it moves in a framework of ideas that are not present in the Bible; they reflect what has transpired in psychological analysis and cosmology throughout the two millenniums that lie between the Biblical authors and today. In particular, they reflect much in the Augustinian and Calvinistic theories of human nature; and they represent an approving reaction to the psychology of Kierkegaard, which would locate the root of sin in man's emotion of "*Angst.*" There is much that is illuminating and challenging in Niebuhr's own emphasis on the rôle played in this situation by anxiety, arising from the tension between what he calls the "horizontal" and "vertical" dimensions of human nature. But it is a doctrine, not of the Biblical period but of the twentieth century, and just as plausible a harmony can be traced between other psychological doctrines of our time and important statements in the Bible as can be done in its case.

Why not, then, say openly and frankly: What I offer here is my own theory of sin, which seems to me in accord with the basic relevant facts of human experience, and in particular with certain teachings among those contained in the Bible? Does Niebuhr have some conviction about the Bible, and especially about its status as a unitary divine "revelation," which would be inconsistent with saying this, and with presenting his theology in the manner it would require? If so, it would help the rest of us understand his thought for him to express this conviction clearly in its relation to the question I have raised, and to indicate the evidence to which he would appeal for its support. In asking him to do this I do not mean to limit in any arbitrary way what is to be accepted as evidence in such a matter.

My second question has to do with the religious experience of repentance and forgiveness. No one who attempts to understand religion with appreciative sympathy can doubt the reality and religious importance of the experience which in Christian terminology is described in these words. To the individual who passes through it it is indeed a new birth. He feels himself to have been saved from the death that is the inevitable consequence of unresolved inner conflict to the new life of spiritual peace and oneness—oneness with himself, oneness with other persons, and oneness with God. And I agree with Niebuhr that no one can adequately understand such an experience unless in some real fashion he has gone through it himself; hence criticisms of any theological interpretation of it from a merely external standpoint are bound to be uncomprehending and may even be quite irrelevant.

But Niebuhr's analysis of this experience is not an intuitive reading of the plain facts of the experience itself; it is a questionable interpretation, reflecting a very limited perspective. His interpretation falls under the same general type that is exemplified in the theologies of Paul, Augustine, Calvin, and Kierkegaard, and is therefore supported by the major considerations that have led them to the doctrines they have championed. There are contrasting theories, however, as Niebuhr is well aware, which have been historically influential; these interpret the same facts in a quite different framework of psychological assumptions. Furthermore, contemporary psychiatry suggests a framework radically divergent from all of these but which may prove to make an indispensable contribution to their adequate understanding. The distinction between fact and theoretical interpretation is therefore vital. Considered apart from any explanatory scheme, with its distinctive metaphysical and anthropological presuppositions, what we have here is a human experience of transition from a state marked by conflict, feelings of guilt, a sense of helplessness (perhaps even despair) to a state of release from guilt, of achieved integrity, of strength, of happiness. Nothing could be more important for human sanity, growth, and moral well-being than to find out, as fully as possible, the essential conditions on which this experience depends, the various forms which it takes with different types of personality, which forms lead to the most constructive results from a personal and social standpoint, and the answers to other related problems. This enterprise would demand an open-minded and far-ranging inquiry, making use of the wealth of materials now available from the history of each of the great religions, from modern depth psychology, from the insights of the dramatists and poets, and from the autobiographies of tortured souls without limitation of time or place.

But instead of making the contribution that he might make toward such a desperately needed inquiry Niebuhr seems to assume, in a spirit of traditional Western dogmatism, that this experience only genuinely takes place when it occurs in a specifically Christian framework and when it is described in accordance with the theological presuppositions which seem to him sound. The most basic of these presuppositions is that all saving power which is revealed in the experience must be attributed to the transcendent divine and nothing but helpless dependence to the human participant.[5] He rejects, it is true, traditional doctrines of predestination; nonetheless the only positive rôle that he assigns to man is that of "opening the door" to the inflow of God's grace.

Let us consider this assumption and this presupposition. To maintain the former is surely to fly in the face of the facts of religious history, and can only be justified if Niebuhr is prepared to maintain that salvation *means* Christian salvation and means it alone. Is he ready to assert this? If so, how will he justify the dogma necessarily involved that what seems clearly to be a saving experience in the case of the Eastern saints is not genuine? That they, too, have experienced a release from inner conflict and have realized a power to love, is evident in the peace, joy, and benignity expressed on their faces, and also in their conduct. Because they have not been saved in the Christian way are we to affirm that they have not been saved at all, whatever the observable facts may be? And how will he justify the further dogma that even in its Christian form it is not true salvation unless it is felt to be only describable in the particular pattern of relationships that he prescribes? To insist that all transforming power in the experience of spiritual renewal must be attributed to divine grace is to interpret the entire process in terms of the emotion of despairing helplessness which is, to be sure, one phase of it in the case of many people. But this emotion is not the only important phase which it reveals, and to exaggerate its rôle in this way leads to the consequence that the continuity of selfhood which is present throughout the process is forgotten or misinterpreted. The theologian who fails at this vital point is almost certain either to assume that the converted self, being the direct creation of the divine love, is completely and magically safeguarded against all relics of its former nature, or else

[5] *Ibid.*, I, 142f., 147f., 136–141; Vol. II, Chap. 4 *passim.*

to encourage in it an excessive and continuing dependence on spiritual power from without—a dependence incompatible with the serene and stalwart self-respect that is an important part of true spiritual maturity. Niebuhr is careful to avoid the former danger; one of the greatest weaknesses of the type of theology he represents is that, in its understandable zeal to escape the evils of a childishly confident humanism, it falls right into the latter. Does he now acknowledge this? Will he avoid this danger hereafter?

Critical consideration of his treatment of sin and forgiveness leads to a third question, which has to do with his depreciation of the rôle of human reason in the process of growth toward spiritual freedom and perfection. To be sure, he does not share Barth's wholesale distrust of reason, and one must admit that it is not easy to debunk incisively the overweening liberal trust in reason without being tempted into the opposite extreme. But the human and religious stakes in this matter are very great. It is important that rationalists be brought to realize that in some sense reason needs to be criticized and corrected from beyond itself; Niebuhr is right in insisting on this. Otherwise, whatever happen to be our present presuppositions in logic and epistemology will be treated as absolutes, and whatever limitations they stand under will not be transcended or corrected. It is at least equally important, however, to interpret this situation in such a way that no encouragement is given to a blind irrationalism. Niebuhr's doctrine that reason belongs to the part of man that is ever ready to lead him astray, and hence that "spirit" (by which he is related to God) transcends reason as well as his natural vitalities,[6] leaves his followers in a serious danger on this point. If we are supposed, in our contrite self-condemnation, to stop being guided by a rational awareness of what is happening to us in relation to everything else in our experience, and to let God come in and take over, where is our safeguard against the always live possibility that it will be the devil instead of God who will take over? The young Nazis who followed Hitler repented of the support they had given to the German Republic; they stopped thinking with their minds and began under the spell of his fanaticism to "think with their blood." The world has witnessed the terrifying result. That which saves the Christian who abandons guidance by reason from falling into such antimoral darkness, if he is saved, is the fact that the God he feels himself confronted by in his moment of penitent despair is conceived to

[6] *Ibid.*, I, 1f., 3f., 13f., 112f., 125.

embody the ideal moral qualities of which man at his best is capable. But experience teaches that a Christian, like a Nazi, may not be saved from this tragic error, if he has been taught a relatively primitive notion of God or if the stress of his fearful and hostile emotions is strong enough to blot out from his mind the ideal component in the divine nature and leave a deity ready to support his fanatical passions. A criterion is indispensable if this peril is to be avoided; and whether we call it a "rational" criterion or not, it must at least be the expression of a stable and guiding awareness of the experience one is going through, in relation to its good and its evil possibilities. Does Niebuhr recognize this? If so, he must also recognize that there is not only a proper rôle for reason in the fields of science and history but likewise an indispensable rôle for it in the experience of conversion itself. And in this case he will see the need for a clarified doctrine (which so far as I know he has not yet developed) of such a relation between reason and spiritual faith as will provide this criterion, and show how it essentially functions in man's deepest religious experience of humble responsiveness to the forgiving grace of God. No room is left for such a doctrine when one's concept of reason reflects a too exclusive concern with the perils of intellectual pride. Will Niebuhr meet this need?

I have mentioned above the dogmatic claim for the truth of the Christian way of salvation as against the other religions, which is expressed in many of Niebuhr's statements and is implied in his treatment of religious topics throughout. This complacent narrowness of perspective affects his thinking in a yet more serious way than any thus far mentioned. His whole philosophy of history reflects the limited standpoint of Protestant Christianity, and the still more limited standpoint set by his own theological presuppositions. This is an astonishing matter when one surveys the course of world history as a whole and senses the manifold currents that are behind what is happening in the world scene today. Niebuhr almost completely ignores the powerful forces that have been at work, throughout the centuries, in the East, where between half and two-thirds of the human inhabitants of the planet live. He writes as though, so far as concerns the course of world history in the past, it has been entirely determined by the Greek, Hebrew, and medieval trends that have been influential in shaping the modern West; you would guess from his books that the only significant mood in history today is the despair and disillusionment that the typical Westerner feels as he senses the collapse of the scientific liberalism on which he has set his faith. But all this Occidental fumbling and fuming may turn out to be a relatively minor eddy in the total course of world history as viewed from a broader and more impartial perspective. Europe and her colonies may be just a rather queer offshoot of Asia, which in her massive solidity constitutes the real substance of the human enterprise on the surface of the planet; the kaleidoscopic and turbulent doings of the Western pigmies, which to a superficial view fill the arena of history with spectacular events, may be little more than a transitory effervescence in comparison with the slow and secular changes that go on in the giant cultures of the East. The contemporary mood which is truly creative and significant may not be at all the despairing weakness of the West, betraying itself clearly as such by its deepseated conflicts and its bumptious fearfulness. It may be the surge of new life and hope which fills the awakening peoples of Asia and Africa, bringing light to their eyes as they look forward to the future. They see the promise of a new era, sweeping away the injustices and deprivations of the past, spelling death to colonialism and to the callous landed aristocracy that has kept them in serfdom, generating confidence that they can synthesize the enduring value of their ancient cultures with the virtues of Western science and technology, and move toward a future of equalitarian opportunity and well-being such as they have never known.

To be sure, in suggesting this I may be going to the opposite extreme. I mention the possibility simply to show how pathetically provincial a philosophy of history is which blithely ignores the course of events in the East and treats it as though it were of no serious account. Doubtless the West cannot be ignored either. Whatever is sound in its science and its dynamic industry will be a heritage for the world culture of the future. And it may, through a hydrogen war, unleash an unprecedented catastrophe upon mankind, whose destructive agonies the East will have to share, at least in part. But the East can survive any such tragedy far more easily than the West. It could and would take the lead in shaping the wiser civilization of the future, while the remnants of Occidental culture are slowly picking their way out of the new epoch of barbarism into which they would have plunged. Will not Niebuhr rethink his philosophy of history, and his theological doctrines which are so intimately bound up with it, in terms of a broad perspective which realistically takes into account all these considerations? Otherwise they cannot hope to have the enduring relevance that he wishes them to have.

There are many aspects of his position which are of less general significance than the ones I have mentioned. It would be intriguing to examine several of these. However, I must not trespass upon space needed by my colleagues. Let me deal briefly with only one further matter. This is Niebuhr's conception of pacifism, as the expression of a spiritual commitment and as a social and political strategy. All of his references to pacifism that I have noted indicate that he conceives it essentially as a way of non-resistance to evil, expressing a naïve trust in the power of love. He ridicules pacifists for following such a program of futility in comparison with a readiness to fight against evil when that is the only realistic course by which to avoid the loss of hard-won freedoms.[7] Now there are pacifists of the sort he describes. But nothing could be a more serious distortion than to conceive pacifism as such in these terms. There is all the difference in the world between a philosophy of *non-resistance to evil* and a philosophy of *non-violent resistance* to evil. It is the latter for which the great exemplifiers of pacifism stand, not the former. The whole Gandhian movement in India, with its rejection of any program based on cowardice, and the pioneering Quakers of every generation since Fox in the West, with their readiness to accept all the perils that their non-pacifist fellows may have to meet but to accept them as a medium for the expression of love instead of hate, illustrate this latter philosophy. There is here no unrealistic submission to evil power; there is rather an uncompromising confrontation of it by the power of love, in the faith that even though one may be trampled on oneself by the blind violence of evil, the demonstration of such devoted courage will be more likely in the long run to serve the divine cause of unity and peace than multiplying the carnage of violence, with its further stimulation of the impulses to hate and vengeance. Pacifists are aware that the practice of such a philosophy may sometimes take mistaken forms, and that in any given case it may well seem to have been futile. But it comes nearer than anything else I know to being a significant expression of the "sublime madness" which at one stage of his career Niebuhr emphasized as necessary if love is to transcend prudential calculation, and provide a living force in human experience for the eliciting of self-giving in in-

[7] See, for example, *Faith and History*, pp. 184, 206ff.

dividual relationships and the progressive correction of justice in society.[8] Indeed, if it does not transcend such calculation it is not love at all, and cannot fulfill the creative rôle of awakening love in others—the distinctive rôle of religion at its best. According to Niebuhr, the heart of Christianity lies in the conviction that God, through love for man, freely takes upon Himself the suffering that is the blind and inevitable consequence of human sin. Are we not to identify ourselves with God in this creative rôle? And is the identification not to affect our behavior in the arena of politics? So far as the significant realities were concerned, Niebuhr's thinking in this area is uncomfortably close to the Lutheran separation of politics and religion which he rightly and severely condemns. If one is moved by the spirit of loving oneness with others, he cannot help expressing that spirit in whatever he does as a citizen, as fully as in any other arena of action. He should, of course, do so under the guidance of a wise understanding—especially an understanding of the limitations set for political action by the absence of faith in the power of love on the part of most of his fellow citizens. But this does not mean that he must surrender his own faith in favor of a "realistic" compromise with a strategy of action which is intrinsically evil, nor his willingness to suffer, if need be, for the sake of his commitment.

How far has Niebuhr abandoned his own earlier faith in the real power of love in history?

E. A. Burtt

Sage School of Philosophy
Cornell University
Ithaca, New York

[8] See his *Education Adequate for Modern Times* (New York: Association Press, 1931), pp. 54ff. In fact, this note is not entirely lost in his later writings; cf. *The Nature and Destiny of Man*, I, 295, for instance.

19

Gustave Weigel, S.J.

AUTHORITY IN THEOLOGY

19

AUTHORITY IN THEOLOGY

The Catholic theologian is attracted by and grateful to Reinhold Niebuhr. There are many reasons for this reaction. First, more than anyone else in the United States, Niebuhr has successfully challenged the moralistic optimism which used to permeate so much of American theology. Niebuhr powerfully helped to bring back the notion of sin which is the necessary background for the whole Christian message. He made the Christian stand before the congregation and confess that he is a sinner, for only the confessing sinner will "go down to his house justified." Second, Niebuhr insists on the inability of the natural to save man, and though his concept of the supernatural by no means coincides with its Catholic counterpart, yet the rhetoric of his doctrine sounds more like Catholic language than the theological idiom he has supplanted. Third, Niebuhr takes Catholic theology seriously and studies its answers to basic Christian problems, which many of his Protestant predecessors did not do. Moreover, critical though he is, Niebuhr yet shows a friendliness to Catholicism which Catholics do not always perceive in Protestant theologians. With Niebuhr a Catholic-Protestant dialogue is possible because he does not allow bitterness and hostility to poison the air of the encounter.

Yet in spite of the Catholic's spontaneous surrender to Professor Niebuhr's charm and verve, it would hardly be candid to pretend that a Catholic theologian is satisfied with all the approaches and viewpoints of Niebuhr. For if a Catholic should find himself in total agreement with Niebuhr, he would have ceased *ipso facto* to be a Catholic, since Niebuhr holds the Catholic position basically untenable, though he insists that it retains much which is genuinely Christian.

This is not the place to outline a systematic Catholic theology of the Gospel. Instead, it might be profitable to state those doctrines of Niebuhr which give a Catholic pause. Niebuhr's God seems to be very real indeed, but he is so utterly incomprehensible, so utterly other, that one wonders how Niebuhr can feel capable of making any affirmations about him at all. Of course, he would answer this wonderment by saying that religious truth is a symbolic, non-literal expression concerning reality beyond the limits of natural, communicable perception. This formula is as disturbing to the Catholic as the question it seeks to answer. It may readily be admitted that a great part of any perception cannot be communicated; that much of the content of a perceptive experience remains the luminous but exclusive possession of the subject; yet in any common perception a solid kernel permits of conceptual transference. Hence "existentialist" awareness which completely defies all valid conceptual expression must ultimately be reduced either to an unknowing or to incommunicable knowledge. But Professor Niebuhr is certainly striving to achieve something more than a *docta ignorantia,* and in his many moving books he is evidently trying to communicate something to his readers. Nor can he justify his brilliant essays at communication by professing to be only pointing to something ineffable through the use of gnostic symbols. A symbol is meaningful, at least vaguely so, and the test of all meaning is its conceptual validation. Common perceptions which wish to escape this test must remain suspect for all thinking men.

It is one thing to say that the linguistic media of a given point in time and space are inept or inadequate for the proper conceptual expression of new perceptions, but it is another thing to say that commonly achieved perceptions by their very structure totally exceed valid conceptualization. If a given language does not actually contain a sign for the content of a common perception, the potentiality of the language is still rich enough to permit the formation of an adequate sign. Such a sign evokes a concept. What else can it evoke?

Catholics believe not unreasonably that Professor Niebuhr knows God in the same manner they do, and when they listen to his descriptive phenomenology of the process in which they too have been involved, they are simply lost in the deep, dark woods of paradox. The Catholic knows that Niebuhr's discourse is really about the nature of analogy, a notion old in Catholic theology for many centuries but relatively new in Protestantism. Yet Thomas Aquinas, the first great exponent of a Christian theory of analogy, always supposed that analogy was an attribute of concepts. It is true that St. Thomas, in common with other Catholics, recognises one kind of perception which is truly incommunicable, and that is the uncommon perception of the mystic. This recognition is not helpful for the understanding of Niebuhr's doctrine, because he makes it patently clear that he is not talking about the mystical experience, if indeed he believes in it at all. The upshot of the matter is that the cautious Catholic, on confronting Niebuhr's approach to God, only shakes his head confusedly and says, "I do not understand."

In line with the thought of Barth, Brunner, and Tillich, Niebuhr insists that we can come to God only through revelation. It is hardly to the point to ask whether we can accept God's revelation unless we previously know that God exists, because Professor Niebuhr is not using the word "revelation" as the older theologians used it. For Niebuhr God reveals himself to us in personal encounter without propositions, and in that revelation we know him. Our transnatural envelopment by God is the primordial *prius* to the human achievement of God. The God-question cannot be raised unless God has revealed himself, and when it is then raised it is a pseudo-question. However, in the older tradition of revelation the conceptual contents of certain propositions were declared revealed, and Christians accepted them as true. Thus the one God was believed to be personally triune. One of the three persons became man so that he, Jesus of Nazareth, was *Deus de Deo, Lumen de Lumine, Deus verus de Deo vero*. Jesus, the unique God-man of history, died for our sins, rose again from the dead so that he was seen eating and heard speaking the Aramaic of his countrymen. This much at least was the common heritage of Christianity from the fourth to the eighteenth century. Protestants no less than Catholics held to these tenets, and they were willing to die and to kill for them.

Today Niebuhr tells us that the Trinity is a symbolic expression, meaningless if taken literally. Jesus of Nazareth was not literally divine nor could he be, for that is absurd and blasphemous, since the finite cannot be infinite. Jesus did not rise from the dead except in a gnostic, symbolic sense. The notion of a virgin birth of Jesus is also symbolically meaningful but literally nonsense. Jesus himself was subject to sin and error, as is every human being in history. He was clearly mistaken in his belief that he would come again to found a paradisiac era for humanity. Such propositions are not new in the recent history of Western thought. The Catholic is no longer amazed by them, for he hears them too often. What puzzles the Catholic is how such doctrine can be proposed as the genuine Christian message. It is obviously a frank negation of the clearly expressed beliefs of Christians for centuries.

Needless to say, Niebuhr has an answer for such a difficulty. He distinguishes between the permanently valid insights of Christianity and the conceptual formulations of these insights. The formulations are only stimulating pointers to man's perception of the divinity which is simply intolerant of valid conceptual expression, for all such expression is restricted to the order of the finite, which in Niebuhrian terminology is identical with the natural. The formulas of Christianity are not the heart of the matter. They are only ambiguous historical witnesses to something beyond the formulas which do not even attempt to express the great truths to which they can only point. Consequently Niebuhr regards himself as not demolishing Christianity but really defending its unshakable insights. This task demands that the carrier myths of Christian history be understood according to their relevant intent. The myths must be "reconstructed." Rudolf Bultmann would express this thought by saying that the gospel must be "demythologized."

Such a theory commits Niebuhr to the enterprise of reconstructing Christianity. He believes that the task is urgently necessary because the older constructions are no longer vitally pertinent. Christianity as reconstructed by the sixteenth century reform is in his mind practically dead, though some meager life can still be detected in it.[1] (This is affirmed in spite of the fact that there are millions of fervent fundamentalists all over the world.) As for the Catholic construction, which he considers hopelessly medieval, it has only "vestigial vitality."[2] (That alliteration is neat but it seems an inadequate description of one of the most palpable vitalities of our time.) A new construction is called for, and Niebuhr accepts the task resolutely.

The Protestant principle urges him on his way. The so-called prophetism of Protestantism, the very heart of its energy, is really reconstructionism. The reconstructionist sincerely believes that he is reforming the Church according to the genuine pattern of its being. Such was the conviction of Luther and Calvin, and it is the conviction of Niebuhr and Tillich, by whom Niebuhr is greatly influenced. The new reformers, however, meet with the surprising opposition of the stubborn sons of the first reform, for the orthodox evangelicals are

[1] *The Nature and Destiny of Man*, II, 183.
[2] *Ibid.*

more hostile to the principle of reform than the logic of their position warrants. The fundamentalists of the twentieth century arbitrarily restrict the applicability of the principle of reconstruction to the sixteenth century, because they have unwittingly remained in the postulational framework of discourse proper to that country. They refuse to see that Niebuhr and Tillich are today the genuine, and perhaps the only genuine, exponents of the reformers' dynamism.

It is this Protestantism in Niebuhr which inevitably enters him in the lists against the Catholic Church. As was said earlier, Niebuhr's opposition is not small, petty, or mean. It is kindly, consistent, and *prinzipiell.* He can and does admit that Catholicism retains much of the Christian gospel. He might even go as far as Tillich, who thinks that the Catholic Church has preserved the Christian substance more successfully than Protestantism has. Such recognitions do not involve the logical necessity of "becoming a Catholic"; they are merely the awareness and rediscovery of elements which must enter into a reconstruction significant for our time.

Niebuhr's most eloquent objection to the Catholic Church is that she is arrogant. Over and over again in his works this charge is explicitly made. In his well known article "The Pope's Domesticated God,"[3] he speaks of the "intolerable pretensions" of the papal spokesman of the Church. In that article Niebuhr asks Protestants to overcome their resentments when dealing with Catholicism and in consequence recognize that there is "Christian content" and "manifestations of grace" in the Catholic Church. Evidently he has done what he can to overcome such resentment in himself, but in spite of that, he can only consider the basic position of the Church "intolerable."

The pretensions of the Catholic Church are intolerable for Professor Niebuhr because his vision of the gospel excludes final authority in anything historical. God is alpha and omega, and only God is God. Everything else is finite, and certainly anything historical is finite. Jesus of Nazareth was finite, and the Catholic Church or any other church is yet more finite. The millennial Catholic doctrine that the finite and the infinite can be fused in history in a mysterious fashion through the infinite power of God is for Niebuhr absurd. The Catholic claim is, therefore, an intolerable pretension and its fruit is demonic arrogance.

Now one must be careful when making accusations of arrogance. The unthinking citizen can resent as an intrusion the entrance of an

[3] *Christian Century*, Vol. LXVII (1950), pp. 74–75.

unattractive human official into his seeming area of freedom, and declare the official's action arrogant. Yet in such a case it is not the official who is arrogant but rather the unsocial citizen. It is arrogant to reject the offices of a man empowered and obliged to do a certain task. In a purely *a priori* consideration, Niebuhr's accusation against the Catholic Church only presents us with the disjunction: either Niebuhr or the Catholic Church is arrogant. To know which of the two is the guilty and which the innocent, we must discover *a posteriori* which of the two oversteps the limits of competence.

As a Catholic sees it, Niebuhr's accusation, like any thesis, rests on assumptions. His basic assumption is that God is incomprehensible, although, Barth notwithstanding, there is a "point of contact" where God can be met, even though not known. The divine-human encounter leads man to have trust in the ultimate power which lies beyond power phenomena, because that power is wise. Trust in God's wisdom means trust in the moral meaningfulness of human life which is threatened with meaninglessness if it is considered only in the light either of naturalistic experience or of perfectionistic endeavor. For Niebuhr this trust in God is not justified by anything in nature or history, though both can lead man to the point where he can achieve contact with the wise and loving God. All this, I submit, is assumption. It derives neither from the notion of God nor from the belief of traditional Christianity. It is an uncritical surrender to the naturalistic dogma of our time, according to which meaningful knowledge must be restricted to the order of the phenomenal, which in turn must be submitted to some kind of controlled technique of description. Anything not adaptable to such a Procrustean bed cannot be known, though it can be the object of "faith." This "faith" is a voluntaristic stand which can be highly significant for human life, and therefore not unworthy of man's consideration. This doctrine is naturalistic empiricism. In accepting it tacitly, Niebuhr erects his religious vision to suit it. His point of departure is epistemological, not religious.

Niebuhr accepts these assumptions without criticism. He considers them the necessary background for any relevant dialogue with contemporary man. The Catholic believes that such a background renders the Christian explanation of reality impossible. The Catholic, no less than Professor Niebuhr, wishes to speak earnestly with contemporary society, but he feels that he will only falsify Christianity if he begins to explain it by accepting the basic scepticism of our culture.

Professor Niebuhr often speaks of taking Christian doctrine seriously, though not literally. A Catholic watching Niebuhr at work is inclined to believe that he takes it neither literally nor seriously. One is not serious in accepting a message if all the affirmatives of that message are turned into negatives on the assumption that the affirmations are unacceptable unless understood as negations. Christianity is an affirmation of the supernatural, and it is not taken seriously if depicted in any other way. Nor is the supernatural seriously affirmed by calling the postulates of moral action supernatural because they cannot be justified empirically. Yet it seems that this is all Niebuhr's supernaturalism means on ultimate analysis. In fact, a Catholic theologian slowly and reluctantly reaches the suspicion that Niebuhr is not so much interested in God as he is in man. Significantly his two *summae* deal professedly with human nature, human destiny, human history, and human culture. Nor can Niebuhr deal with anything higher, because he admits candidly that he knows God only insofar as he is a *concern of man.*

Not even Professor Niebuhr's strong insistence on human sinfulness seems to be a very serious consideration of sin. He points to the undisputed fact that every human action is the action of a self. This truth is restated in the truism that every action of man is selfish, which from then on is understood in a non-truistic sense. If morality is to be measured "purely," either by Kant's categorical imperative or Niebuhr's *agape,* then no human act can ever be thoroughly moral, because the motives of human action are so many since the urges for action are so many, and some of these urges are pre-moral. As the Scholastics put it, man is not a pure spirit, or, in Niebuhrian terminology, man is paradoxically rooted both in freedom and in nature.

As Professor Niebuhr readily admits, the selfish taint in all human action is recognized in Catholic moral theology, but he is not satisfied with this recognition. It is expressed in the Catholic distinction between mortal and venial sin. Such a distinction for Niebuhr is un-Christian because it makes room for human pride. At first sight this seems to be a rejection of the venial-sin conception, but by Niebuhr's theory of the moral ambiguity of all human actions he may be really denying the existence of mortal sin. He is never far from a belief in venial sin, for he teaches:

> . . . the new self is the Christ of intention rather than an actual achievement. It is the self only of faith, in the sense that its dominant purpose and intention are set in the direction of Christ as the norm. It is the self only

by grace, in the sense that the divine mercy "imputes" the perfection of Christ and accepts the self's intentions for achievements.[4]

Is this doctrine any different from the doctrine which he quotes from Calvin, and which he declares "comes rather close to the Catholic distinction between venial and mortal sins"?

Our carnal desires are daily more and more sanctified, that is, consecrated unto the Lord unto real purity of life, having our hearts moulded to obey his law so that our *prevailing inclination* is to submit to his will.[5]

In some respects Niebuhr's morality is "purer" than its Catholic counterpart because he derives no moral motivation from heaven and hell. He can do so because he sees in heaven, hell, and resurrection gnostic symbols of divine justice beyond history. He does not find in these terms any commitment to states of future existence, and he considers any attempt to see such content in the terms absurd.

It seems, in brief, that Niebuhrian theology is ultimately an affirmation of the absoluteness of the unknown God beyond history, with a thoroughgoing relativism for everything in history. This holds for doctrine and morality. Niebuhr's quarrel with the Catholic Church rises from the fact that she holds for absolutes in history. He recognizes that she makes this affirmation with reference to the absoluteness of God by claiming authority from him. Here Niebuhr is logically forced to protest from the premises of his own synthesis of Christian doctrine, for in that synthesis there is no room for anything absolute in history, so that absolute historic authority is absurd and a disgusting pretension.

A Catholic with gentle malice might ask Niebuhr if his transcendental principle of relativism is *absolutely* valid. Niebuhr has sought an answer to that question. He has found it in an explanation of Tillich which exempts the essential knowledge from the ambiguities of existential knowledge.[6] In other words, existential knowledge is defined as inevitably relative, and the case is closed. The cogency of this technique is hardly shattering.

Such displays of dialectical acrobatics intrigue the Catholic, who by long tradition is highly skilled in these arts. However, they do not still his primary question, which is a simple one: Is reconstruction a valid Christian enterprise? The reformers of the sixteenth century reconstructed the Christian message. They finally perceived what the

[4] *The Nature and Destiny of Man*, II, 114.
[5] *Ibid.*, II, 199–200.
[6] *Ibid.*, II, 217, Note 4.

Catholic Church saw from the beginning; namely, that it was a reconstruction. The reformers claimed the right to reconstruct because they supposed that they knew what the genuine Christian message was through the use of a source other than the Church. The Catholic Church from which they receded said then, as it says today, that there is no source of knowing what the Christian message is except the Church which formulated that message in human word and divinely inspired writings. These testimonies are valid only according to the intent it originally gave them and whose intent by God's assistance it abidingly knows. Other constructions of its words, literalistic or gnostic, are no longer the message of God but only human presumption or Biblicist idolatry. Professor Niebuhr thinks that the sixteenth century reconstruction, necessary in its day, is not suitable for our time, but he uses the same strategy which his (and my) forefathers used. Under the pressure of the *Zeitgeist* he has achieved a vision which he identifies with the essence of the Christian message, and he tells us the message is thus and so. His version of the message is quite different from the original construction and from the first reconstruction. Yet he offers us his version as the genuine thing, simultaneously assuring us that the other brands are stale and unprofitable.

God is God, and to him all men must bow. Man is man, finite, sinful, and fallible. If a man speaks to me of God in order to tell me what God is and what he wills, in piety and awe for the unseen God I must ask of that man: In whose name and by what authority do you speak? The question of authority simply cannot be evaded. To my question the Catholic Church gives a religious answer. It says that it speaks in God's holy name and by his absolute authority. Many cannot be persuaded of the validity of this claim, but at least the claim is religious. Professor Niebuhr gives a message different from that of the Church, but the only authority manifested is that of a fallible searcher for the truth of God. He refers me to the sources from which he has derived his doctrine by construction, but he has made that construction on his own authority. As a man subject to God and to God alone, I cannot accept such authority, for it does not claim to be divine. Humbly, Professor Niebuhr makes no claim to any authority at all, but an unauthorized statement is noncommittal and warrants no commitment either of essential or of existential man. By his principles Professor Niebuhr does not even claim to know much about God and his will. He only presents what he considers valid insights pertinent to our time. These insights are brilliantly and movingly expressed. They validly manifest one man's religious scheme of life. Can they guarantee the objective validity of the scheme itself?

GUSTAVE WEIGEL, S.J.

WOODSTOCK COLLEGE
WOODSTOCK, MARYLAND

20

Edward John Carnell

NIEBUHR'S CRITERIA OF VERIFICATION

20

NIEBUHR'S CRITERIA OF VERIFICATION

I. INTRODUCTION

REALIZING that bad subjectivity frequently travels under the name of good existentialism, Niebuhr cheerfully faces the problem of proof:

How is one to judge the eternal word and to know when the prejudice of an hour or the foolish opinion of a man has been falsely arrayed in the pretense of divine wisdom? The history of religion is full of the chronicles of both fools and knaves and our insane asylums still boast their due quotas of unhappy maniacs who think they are messiahs. By what criterion is one to discover what is true and what is false in the conflicting claims of competing messiahs and prophets?[1]

But Niebuhr refuses to cast pearls. Since chair-fast pedants frequently use questions of verification to evade spiritual commitment —their clamant cries for proof serving as cloaking for an indurated soul—Niebuhr dissipates no energy on an arid academicism. He deliberately etches a portrait of reality, transcendently persuasive if examined soulfully within D. H. Lawrence's "terrifying honesty," but tenuous and unconvincing if the self ensconces to the narrow corridors of its empirical life, limiting meaning to laboratory operations and gauging both the self and others with depersonalized objectivity. Christian faith is apposite only as one existentially accepts his bistratal milieu: body and soul, time and eternity, involvement and freedom; recognizing that his claim to natural security is interlarded with pretentious spiritual arrogance. Niebuhr is too moved by reality's dialectical complexity and man's impartible wholeness to offer Christian paradoxes on the platter of simple rational persuasion, take it or leave it. Academic noncommittalism is but the lengthening

[1] *Beyond Tragedy*, p. 93.

shadow of a turgid ego. Men who are too secure in themselves find the gospel irrelevant, and foolish because irrelevant.

II. PRE-SOTERIC PROOF

Convinced that too little commerce between nature and grace is dialectically as dissatisfying as too much, Niebuhr firmly disaffiliates himself from Kierkegaardian-Barthian discontinuity. Evidences for Christianity lie both "in" and "out" of grace. If the Gospel invades our experience in the manner of a cast stone, without reason or defense, Christian claims hold no antecedent advantage over non-Christian.

> The final truth about life is always an absurdity but it cannot be an absolute absurdity. It is an absurdity insofar as it must transcend the "system" of meaning which the human mind always prematurely constructs with itself as the centre. But it cannot be a complete absurdity or it could not achieve any credence. In this sense Kierkegaard goes too far.[2]

Like other time-eternity issues to pass across Niebuhr's desk, "common ground" is resolved by a "yes" and "no" held in "fear and trembling." "The truth contained in the Gospel is not found in human wisdom. Yet it may be found at the point where human wisdom and human goodness acknowledge their limits, and creative despair induces faith."[3] A penumbral zone of universal concrete reality borders revelation and culture, making minimal tests of competing religious claims possible and leaving all without excuse. An underprizing of man's native ability to assess, though not resolve, his moral predicament, inevitably corrupts the dialectic from the side of either nature or grace.

Affirmative pre-soteric proof swivels on the fixity of this one truth: namely, that human nature is tensionally mounted within an unconditioned obligation to fulfill the very moral law that involvement is impotent to actuate. Only as man consciously incarnates selfless love is he integral; yet each new effort at fulfillment betrays the self into something less than selfhood. Hence the antecedent persuasiveness of Christianity: *It is the only world view which defends hope in man and meaning in history within an honest acknowledgment that the libido is spiritually informed with law-defying vitalities not subject to mind.* Niebuhr's argument is as neat as that. Whenever one admits (*a*) that love is the law of life and (*b*) that inordinate affections transmute each level of fulfillment into a more refined base for

[2] *The Nature and Destiny of Man*, II, 38n.

[3] *Ibid.*, p. 206.

egoistic security, he must, if consistent, move on to Christianity. Niebuhr shows from individual and collective experience that man is inevitably, though not necessarily, a sinner, and that only Biblical theism convincingly resolves the law-sin dialectic. Until this Herculean literary effort is appreciated, affirmative pre-soteric proof, like the Cross itself, will remain foolish.

Ironically, this very honesty denudes prophetic insight of its power to persuade those who are too worldly wise to sense mind's role as a minion of vagrant impulse. When rationalists curtly dismiss the Cross, they think they act solely on the authority of a pure-metal use of reason; though in reality they are somewhat guided by the counsels of powerful personal interest. Pride prefers peace in sin rather than through the forgiveness of sin.

Negative pre-soteric proof turns on this: *that every effort to define the end of history from some perspective within history ends in a threat to both life and history.* Again, a very neat piece of persuasion. Niebuhr gauges the superiority of dialectical to non-dialectical insights by the degree that each defends (*a*) the intrinsic dignity of the individual and (*b*) a collective order wherein personal creativity and social justice enjoy fullest outlet. Nothing can preponderate these values, whether prophet's voice, confessional standards, or ecclesiastical tradition. "The final test of any religion must be its ability to prompt ethical action upon the basis of reverence for personality."[4]

This is the pith of the matter: If the distinctiveness of dialectical religion consists in the *exclusion* of any level on which freedom may enjoy an easy conscience, non-dialectical distinctiveness consists in its *inclusion*. In the stead of God who judges and forgives sinners from a perspective beyond history, some absolutized aspect of either form or vitality serves as a rallying point for the faithful on the one side, and a guide in eliminating nonconformists on the other. This results in either a premature flight from history or a Procrusteanizing of creativity to fit some individual or tribal virtue. The one leads to other-worldliness, the other to this-worldliness—equally noxious though not equally cynical, eventualities.

Other-worldliness abandons history's possibilities to a manageable "second best" in which a regnant caste of zealots or conceited philosopher-kings manacles the social order to personal interests: overlords who identify perfect social orderliness with the peaceful preservation of the *status quo,* as in Plato's pathetic stratification of life

[4] *Does Civilization Need Religion?* p. 31.

in the *Republic*, or the outraging of human dignity in Brahmanic and Buddhistic acosmic pantheism. "A human righteousness, which is not subjected to a purer righteousness than anything to be found in nature or history, must inevitably degenerate into a fanatic self-righteousness."[5] *This-worldliness* inflates hegemonic powers to exempt themselves and their cause from divine judgment by excluding some favorite virtue from the general ambiguity of history. Roman Catholicism sanctifies static feudal injustices on the confidence that, as "the continued incarnation of Jesus Christ," she is vested with perpetual divine authority over all human institutions. Protestantism recoils from medievalism, only to sanction dynamic injustices in a laissez-faire physiocracy that separates the proletariat from the ties of soil and fealty which held the feudal community together. Despotism replaces the milder claims of holy men with bold pretensions of racial homogeneity or utopianized versions of society; baiting its toadies with ridiculous promises and brutalizing malcontents with an iron fist. In brief: *non-dialectical ideologies inevitably defend some "party line" in which truth is selfishly tied in with the interests of the privileged*—an outraging of life's dignity at its core.

III. SOTERIC PROOF

Evidences "in grace" form no *arcanum*, accessible only to initiates and whispered among votaries in spiritual jargon, for Christianity fulfills rather than negates the general experience of the race. *Yes:* man is able to perceive the things of the Spirit, for he is made in the image of God; *no:* man is not able to perceive the things of the Spirit, for sin has corrupted the image. The one side safeguards responsibility and the other the universal need of the Cross. From this insight Niebuhr develops a dialecticized version of the relation between nature and grace: *Christian revelation preserves, even as false religions inevitably corrupt, the values of individual dignity and social justice which all men natively seek.* Proof "in grace" thus consists of no more than a cataloging of evidences to buttress this Christian claim. Whether such data are convincing will depend entirely on the degree to which an individual first understands and appreciates (*a*) his own longing for dignity and justice and (*b*) the tragic way that non-dialectical alternatives mismanage them. The Christian case is as follows:

Individual dignity: First, *the vicious circle of self-love is inter-*

[5] *Beyond Tragedy*, p. 242.

rupted. The self expires whenever it tries too desperately to rescue itself from within itself:

But the self lacks the faith and trust to subject itself to God. It seeks to establish itself independently. It seeks to find its life and thereby loses it. For the self which it asserts is less than the true self. It is the self in all the contingent and arbitrary factors of its immediate situation. By asserting these contingent and arbitrary factors of an immediate situation, the self loses its true self. It increases its insecurity because it gives its immediate necessities a consideration which they do not deserve and which they cannot have without disturbing the harmony of creation. By giving life a false centre, the self then destroys the real possibilities for itself and others. Hence the relation of injustice to pride, and the vicious circle of injustice, increasing as it does the insecurity which pride was intended to overcome.[6]

The Cross teaches men to save their life by losing it. Individuals neutralize anxiety's decaying effects by casting themselves on the mercy and love of a God who sublimates man's fragmentary existence within the security of the divine perspective. Second, *the sting of the law is removed.* Humility before God issues in the inner satisfaction that a just relationship maintains between God's judicial demands and the moral predicament of the sinner. Although conscience continues to remind man of his distance from life's norm, it is powerless to destroy confidence that life has meaning beyond this vale of tears:

The good news of the gospel is that God takes the sinfulness of man into Himself; and overcomes in His own heart what cannot be overcome in human life, since human life remains within the vicious circle of sinful self-glorification on every level of moral advance.[7]

Third, *evil is explained without dividing man against himself or history against its norm.* The Greeks glorify mind and undervalue body, unmindful that too much confidence in mind is itself part of man's evil. Kant unmasks the maxim-defying tendencies of radical evil, but he despairs of integrating this insight into the wider questions of the Critique. Idealism resolves the problem by winking at both the unity of will and the anchorage of mind in subrational impulse. Nietzsche canonizes man's robust capacity for self-deception by transmuting the "hidden lie" into the "honest lie."

All of these beliefs are pathetic alternatives to the Christian faith. They all come finally to the same thing. They do not believe that man remains a

[6] *The Nature and Destiny of Man*, I, 252. [7] *Ibid.*, I, 142.

tragic creature who needs the divine mercy as much at the end as at the beginning of his moral endeavors. They believe rather that there is some fairly easy way out of the human situation of "self-alienation."[8]

Without Christian insight into the height of man's freedom and the depth of his sin it is impossible to diagnose the true cause of history's sickness, for sin consistently places evil outside the self. Fourth, *universal history is established.* Since the temporal process is such a checkerwork of comforting regularity and distressing impertinence, historians either formulate a truncated philosophy from partial perspectives, or they despair altogether at finding unified meaning.

There are, in short, tangents of moral meaning in history; but there are no clear or exact patterns. The moral obscurities of history must either tempt men to the despairing conclusion that there is no meaning in the total historical enterprise and that history is merely a bewildering confusion of "death for the right cause, death for the wrong cause, paeans of victory and groans of defeat," or that it is under a sovereignty too mysterious to conform fully to the patterns of meaning which human beings are able to construct.[9]

Christian faith comes to history's moral ambiguity by way of judgment and forgiveness. Whenever a man turns from history's contradictions long enough to deal seriously with the contradictions in his own heart, he is introduced to a God wise enough to have a plan that transcends all rational systems devised within history.

A working social order: First, *an effective tie between persons is named.* Perfect justice is defended by a loving respect for the individual. Nuances of inequity can be detected only as the obligation of life to life flows from the infinite task of sacrificial love. "Love is thus the end term of any system of morals. It is the moral requirement in which all schemes of justice are fulfilled and negated."[10] When less than the intimacy of the whole person is accepted and defended, injustice becomes both natural and inevitable, with no checks against powermongers who make certain that others, never themselves, suffer the injustice. Second, *an effective motive in social action is named.* Love is easy when consanguinity and mutual interest prevail, but how shall it sustain its sweetness before an in-

[8] *Christianity and Power Politics*, p. 7. "The way of the wicked is like deep darkness; they do not know over what they stumble." Proverbs 4:19.

[9] *Faith and History*, p. 132.

[10] *The Nature and Destiny of Man*, I, 295.

corrigible, obdurate selfishness? If love must justify itself within the temporal process, it is engulfed with disappointment; but if love is abandoned, the norm of world brotherhood yields to the tyrannizing of life within calculated interests. Niebuhr rightly grounds the motive of love in Jesus Christ:

> We are to forgive because God forgives (Matt. 18:23); we are to love our enemies because God is impartial in his love. The points of reference are vertical and not horizontal. Neither natural impulses nor social consequences are taken into consideration.[11]

This insight, in turn, relieves the inner distresses which ensue whenever the self is consciously committed to futilitarian ends. Satisfaction with the right, while provisionally vindicated by love's rewards, is finally supported by filial pleasure toward God.

> The paradox of religion is that it serves the world best when it maintains its high disdain for the world's values. Its social usefulness is dependent upon its ability to maintain devotion to absolute moral and spiritual values without too much concern for their practical, even for their social usefulness.[12]

A working political order: First, *the collective ego is set under a principle of self-criticism.* Power is an "evil necessity"—necessary because of man's stubborn defense of interests, yet evil because it is an extension of partiality at the expense of perfect brotherhood.

> Perfect power and goodness can be united only in God, where the contest of life with life is transcended and where the possession of power does not lead to its misuse in the struggle for existence. In human history disinterested power is never as disinterested as it claims to be. It always insinuates something of the special interests of a participant in the struggle of life into the pretended position of disinterested preservation of justice.[13]

When force is not held as a sacred trust from God, wielders of power, whether autocratic or mobocratic, quickly fall prey to pride's counsel that *their* particular employment of power is a virtuous extension of divine right. "Man is always most inhuman, not when he is unconsciously driven by natural impulse, but when he imagines his natural impulses and his relative values to be the instruments of some absolute good."[14] Second, *perfect political ends are harmoni-*

[11] *An Interpretation of Christian Ethics,* p. 46.
[12] *Does Civilization Need Religion?* p. 77.
[13] *Discerning the Signs of the Times,* pp. 140–141.
[14] *Reflections on the End of an Era,* p. 171.

ously joined to realistic means. Marx shrewdly understands (*a*) that interests growing out of the division between "mine" and "thine" create history's sickness, and (*b*) that towering ideologies are consciously or unconsciously a partial rationalization of these interests. But his sagacity ends with the perversion that both the worker and his defenders are as innocent in their person as they are pure in their doctrine; and that proletarian resentments, not being part of the natural order, are deciduous affections that wither away with the complete socialization of property. "This is one reason, and perhaps the chief reason, why the communist alternative to the injustices of our civilization has universally created greater injustices and hatched more terrible tyrannies than previously known in history."[15] The only way to check this or any other political conceit is by a prophetic-dialectical religion that places the pretenses of the collective ego within the general ambiguity of history. Only Biblical insights can defend equality without creating a new caste of heavenly surrogates that confuse the perfection of the ideal with the perfection of their person. Democracy thus is relatively better than other political schemes, and that for three definite reasons:

> The first is that it assumes a source of authority from the standpoint of which the individual may defy the authorities of this world. . . . The second is an appreciation of the unique worth of the individual which makes it wrong to fit him into any political program as a mere instrument. . . . The third insight is the biblical insistence that the same radical freedom which makes man creative also makes him potentially destructive and dangerous, that the dignity of man and the misery of man therefore have the same root.[16]

A basis for tolerance: Here is the paradox of knowledge: Christian truth is final because it accepts the existential intimacy between interest and idea; yet part of this finality is its consistent denial that individuals may have final truth. Christian insight is not scepticism, yet it is. It is confidence "in faith," yet despair "in fact." Renaissance optimism embraces the scepticism, but rejects the faith, only to end by losing an integral element in tolerance.

> To meet the test it is necessary not merely to maintain a tolerant attitude towards those who hold beliefs other than our own. The test is twofold and includes both the ability to hold vital convictions which lead to action;

[15] *The Irony of American History*, p. 165.
[16] *Christian Realism and Political Problems*, p. 101.

and also the capacity to preserve the spirit of forgiveness towards those who offend us by holding to convictions which seem untrue to us.[17]

Scepticism issues in a provisional kindliness toward dissenters, but it is impotent to evaluate the fine shades of better and worse in life. The luxury of scepticism easily converts to the noxiousness of irresponsibility; which, in turn, makes the masses prey to a clever autocrat who tools his own finalities within either pragmatic expediency or tribal interest. Only Christian faith can cradle final truth within the humble denial that final truth can be had.

IV. CRITIQUE

Niebuhr cannot be evaluated with clinical objectivity. The most that one can do is to place oneself in the middle of the warmth and challenge of the system, sensitively matching Niebuhr's claims with the witness of reality itself. Critical estimates cannot be decisive; hence, a compromise which the reader must patiently accept.

I find the pre-soteric criteria entirely compelling. The more I ponder Niebuhr's arguments, the less successful is my escape from their force. But the soteric standards seem somewhat less than satisfying. Try as I may, in my most charitable moments of meditation, I am unable to avoid concluding that Niebuhr's theology rests on disappointing subjectivism and scepticism.

Subjectivism: Niebuhr eloquently assures us that "the suffering of God is . . . the voluntary acceptance by divine love of the consequence of sin",[18] but how is this claim proved? An examination of the fine print reveals that final authority for filial peace in God rests not on Christ or the apostolate but—surprisingly—on the subjective feeling of the penitent. "Whenever the power of sinful self-love is taken seriously there is a concomitant sense of gratitude in the experience of release from self. It is felt that this is a miracle which the self could not have accomplished."[19] But does this really end the matter? That the penitent may sense an inner peace which structurally resembles forgiveness, I do not question; but has Niebuhr given the *only* possible interpretation of this serenity? Psychology of religion abundantly witnesses to the inner deceptions of which

[17] *The Nature and Destiny of Man,* II, 219.

[18] *Ibid.,* II, 56.

[19] *Ibid.,* II, 115. "The sinner must feel himself 'justified,' that is, he must feel that his imperfections are understood and sympathetically appreciated as well as challenged." *Reflections on the End of an Era,* p. 285.

the human psyche is capable, especially when it is borne away in the partial madness of religious ecstasy. May not "peace of heart" actually represent an extension of self-sufficiency on a higher and more mysterious plane? Niebuhr is confident that inner manifestations of sin can be named, thus assuring an individual that his assuaged conscience represents a work of God and not the fruit of mystic, psychotherapeutic forces in the man himself. An appeal to the "experience of the race" strengthens Niebuhr's case verbally, though not factually, for if one individual can confuse strands of inner complacency with divine forgiveness, many can persist in the same error. Niebuhr cannot appeal to objective authority without conceding that the relation between time and eternity is not exclusively dialectical; yet apart from such an appeal, so it seems to me, a Luther can only answer an Eck by pointing to inner feelings which Eck would immediately equate with some extension of egoism. Hitler, we are informed, nursed a steady confidence that he was under the special protection of God. If so wretched a heart as his could be soothed, of what deceptions is the penitent capable, whose very posture of humility convinces the ego that the first step toward safety has been taken? Niebuhr's appeal to the Bible gives the impression of being lifted from the quagmire of subjectivism, and for this happy inconsistency I register thanks; but in such a case he solves the dialectical riddle by plowing with my heifer.

Scepticism: Insights of both Marx and depth psychology persuade Niebuhr that reason is too immersed in the vitalities and interests of life to be an innocent source of final truth. Name the conviction; it is conditioned by peculiar circumstances, "*as all convictions are.*"[20] "All human knowledge is tainted with an 'ideological' taint. It pretends to be more true than it is. It is finite knowledge, gained from a particular perspective; but it pretends to be final and ultimate knowledge."[21] This seems clear enough. Yet one is quite perplexed at the nonchalant way in which Niebuhr himself claims final truth. "The revelation of the Atonement is precisely a 'final' word because it discloses a transcendent divine mercy which represents the 'freedom' of God in quintessential terms: namely, God's freedom over His own law."[22] Niebuhr's main "finalities" include Christ, the Cross, the law of love, Renaissance optimism, and Reformation pes-

[20] *Moral Man and Immoral Society* (1947 edition), p. 166. Italics mine.
[21] *The Nature and Destiny of Man,* I, 194.
[22] *Ibid.,* II, 67.

simism. The reason that Niebuhr needs finalities is far more obvious to me than the justification of his simultaneous denial of and claim to final truth. Indeed, if the obligation to be tolerant is not final, it cannot consistently be argued that intolerance is normatively wrong for tomorrow; but how does Niebuhr prove its finality?

Closer inspection shows that when Niebuhr speaks of Christian insights as "final," he means to extend the claim only to a "knowledge of the limits of knowledge," a knowledge, in short, that suffers from no context, being directed toward the ground of being.[23] I am unpersuaded by this distinction. A "knowledge of the limits of knowledge" is hardly as rich as the assertion, "We must be tolerant because God, in Christ, has first been tolerant of us." The one is formal, the other factual. By drawing on such ontologic references as God's existence, nature, and will, Christian convictions are anchored in material truth. Whether or not Christ died for sins is partly a matter of historico-critical research. The transcendental significance of the Cross proceeds *through* these objective, contextual facts. It seems, despite all, that Niebuhr's defense of tolerance rests on the same scepticism that underlies bourgeois secularism.

I am not haggling over theological centesimals; I speak to questions which spell the gaining or losing of the Christian world view. Either tolerance rests on the scepticism that final truth cannot be had, and thus Christianity's objectivity is lost; or we widen our epistemology to include final, contextual knowledge of God, Christ, sin, grace, and forgiveness, and then the relation between time and eternity is no longer exclusively dialectical. Either the dialectic renders final truth invalid, or final truth renders the dialectic invalid. This is a forced option.

EDWARD JOHN CARNELL

DEPARTMENT OF APOLOGETICS
FULLER THEOLOGICAL SEMINARY
PASADENA, CALIFORNIA

[23] Cf. *Ibid.*, II, 217–218, Note 4.

21

Abraham I. Heschel

A HEBREW EVALUATION OF REINHOLD NIEBUHR

21

A HEBREW EVALUATION OF REINHOLD NIEBUHR

ONCE upon a time a king received a shocking report about the new harvest: whoever eats of the crop becomes mad. So he called together all his counselors. This was their decision: since no other food is available, we shall have to eat it, but we ought to know that we are mad. This parable by Rabbi Nahman of Bratslav (1772–1811) comes to my mind in opening an essay on the meaning of Reinhold Niebuhr to our generation. He reminds us what we are.

In boldness of penetration, depth of insight, fullness of vision and comprehensiveness, Reinhold Niebuhr's system excels everything which the whole of American theology has hitherto produced. A pioneer for his generation, he speaks of the eternal in a world of spiritual absenteeism, compelling it to listen to him. It is not easy to listen to him because he not only plants new truths but also roots out old errors, even the most comfortable and satisfying ones. Yet the degree to which Niebuhr does influence American thinking is one of the most significant facts of contemporary American history.

In an age that "has no vantage point from which to understand the predicament of modern man,"[1] Niebuhr not only helps many of his contemporaries to see through our delusions, deceptions, and pretensions; he also succeeds in recovering some of the insights of prophetic thinking that are of tremendous aid in understanding the central issues of existence from a religious perspective.[2]

In the following pages an attempt is made to examine some of Niebuhr's views in the light of Jewish thinking. We shall confine

[1] *Faith and History*, p. 9.

[2] "I have as a Christian theologian sought to strengthen the Hebraic-prophetic content of the Christian tradition." Reinhold Niebuhr, introduction to Waldo Frank's *The Jew in Our Time* (New York, 1944).

ourselves to a few aspects of his doctrine of evil, particularly those of common conviction and concern.

I

Niebuhr reminds us that "there is a mystery of evil in human life to which modern culture has been completely oblivious."[3]

It may have been possible prior to 1914 to believe with Herbert Spencer, who in his "Evanescence of Evil" asserted that "evil perpetually tends to disappear."[4] The certainty of evil's gradual extinction through the growth of culture and education was a part of the belief in the steady progress of mankind, of the belief in "redemption through progress." But the horrors through which we have lived in the past forty years have totally discredited such simple, easy-going optimism.

"He who is prudent will keep silent in such a time; for it is an evil time" (Amos 5:13). But Niebuhr is not prudent. The road to disaster is paved with pleasant illusions, and the way to deal with evil is not to ignore it. Indeed, the effort to minimize the power of evil has had fateful results in the past. It has not only weakened our alertness to the dangers of existence but also impaired our sense of guilt, our ability to repent, and our power to pray, "Forgive us for we have sinned."

Niebuhr's distinctive contribution to contemporary thinking lies in his comprehension of "the dimension of depth in life," in his tracing every problem with which he deals "to some ultimate origin." He stresses the antinomies and ambiguities of man's historic existence and denies that they can be overcome in history itself. He has shown that the tragic aspect of man cannot be reduced either to a psychological or to a biological quality; that it is rather an aspect of history, of the structure of existence. The question that is going to occupy us is to what degree Niebuhr's thought is within the Biblical and prophetic tradition.

[3] *An Interpretation of Christian Ethics*, p. 119.

[4] "All evil results from the non-adaptation of constitution to conditions. . . . Eventually true is it that evil perpetually tends to disappear. In virtue of an essential principle of life, this non-adaption of an organism to its conditions is ever being rectified; and modification or one or both continues until the adaption is complete. Whatever possesses vitality, from the elementary cell up to man himself, inclusive, obeys this law. . . This universal law of physical modification is the law of mental modification also. . . . Progress, therefore, is not an accident but a necessity. Evil and immorality must surely disappear; man must surely become perfect." Herbert Spencer, *Social Statics* (New York, 1897), pp. 28–32.

Many modern theologians have consistently maintained that the Bible stands for optimism, that pessimism is alien to its spirit.[5] There is, however, very little evidence to support such a view. With the exception of the first chapter of the Book of Genesis, the rest of the Bible does not cease to refer to the sorrow, sins, and evil of this world. As Maimonides pointed out (in a different context and order), the ideas that apply to the world in the state of its coming into being do not apply to the world that is in being. The design of the Creator was for a world that was to be good, very good; but then something mysterious happened, to which Jewish tradition alludes in many ways, and the picture of the world profoundly changed. When the prophets look at the world, behold "distress and darkness, the gloom of anguish" (Isaiah 8:22). When they look at the land, they find it "full of guilt against the Holy One of Israel" (Jeremiah 51:5). "O Lord, how long shall I cry for help, and Thou wilt not hear? Or cry to Thee 'violence!' and Thou wilt not save? Why dost Thou make me see wrongs and look upon trouble? Destruction and violence are before me; strife and contention arise. So the law is slacked and justice never goes forth. For the wicked surround the righteous, so justice goes forth perverted" (Habakkuk 1:2–4). This is a world in which the way of the wicked prosper and "all who are treacherous thrive" (Jeremiah 12:1); a world which made it possible for some people to maintain that "Everyone who does evil is good in the sight of the Lord, and He delights in them," and for others to ask, "Where is the God of justice?" (Malachi 2:17).

The Psalmist did not feel that this was a happy world when he prayed: "O God, do not keep silence; do not hold peace or be still, O God. For, lo, Thy enemies are in uproar; those who hate thee have raised their heads" (Psalms 83:2–3).

The terror and anguish that came upon the Psalmist were not caused by calamities in nature but by the wickedness of man, by the evil in history:

> Fearfulness and trembling come upon me,
> Horror has overwhelmed me.
> And I said, Oh that I had wings like a dove!
> Then would I fly away, and be at rest.
>
> Psalms 55:6–7.

[5] It was Schopenhauer who claimed that the Hebrew spirit was characteristically optimistic, whereas Christianity was pessimistic. *Die Welt als Wille und Vorstellung,* II, chap. 48; *Parerga and Paralipomena,* Gusbach ed., II, 397. *Sämtliche Werke,* Franenstadt ed., III, 712f.

These are the words of Moses in his last days: "I know how rebellious and stubborn you are. . . . I know after my death you will surely act corruptly, and turn aside from the way which I have commanded you; and in the days to come evil will befall you, because you will do what is evil in the sight of the Lord" (Deuteronomy 31:27–29). It is not a sweet picture of man that Isaiah paints, saying: "You have never heard, you have never known, from of old your ear has not been opened. For I knew that you would deal very treacherously, and that from birth you were called a rebel" (Isaiah 48:8).

There is one line that expresses the mood of the Jewish man throughout the ages: *"The earth is given into the hand of the wicked"* (Job 9:24).[6]

How does the world look in the eyes of God? Are we ever told that the Lord saw that the righteousness of man was great in the earth, and that He was glad to have made man on the earth? The general tone of the Biblical view of history is set after the first ten generations: "The Lord saw the wickedness of man was great in the earth and that every imagination of the thoughts of his heart was only evil continually. And the Lord was sorry that he made man on the earth, and it grieved Him to His heart" (Genesis 6:5–6; cf. 8:21). One great cry resounds throughout the Bible: The wickedness of man is great on the earth. It is voiced by the prophets; it is echoed by the Psalmist.

> The two dominant attitudes of prophetic faith are gratitude and contrition; gratitude for creation and contrition before judgment; or, in other words, confidence that life is good in spite of its evil and that it is evil in spite of good. In such faith both sentimentality and despair are avoided.[7]

The absence of the awareness of the mystery of evil is a tragic blindness of modern man. In his vocabulary the word is missing. But without an awareness of sin, without the fear of evil, there can be no repentance.

II

A major concern of Niebuhr's thinking is the problem of realism and the lack of realism in our contemporary "nominalistic" culture.

[6] Raba, in *Baba Bathra* 9a, referred to the end of the verse as denying Divine Providence.

[7] *An Interpretation of Christian Ethics*, p. 106.

An example of the sentimentality and unreality that dominate the political opinions of the liberal world is the belief that the power of man's lust and ambitions is no more than some subrational impulse, which can be managed with more astute social engineering or more psychiatric help. In contrast, Niebuhr insists that the freedom of the self is a radical one and is not easily brought under the control of reason, just as it is not easily kept within the confines of nature's harmonies.

The utopianism and deductive thinking of the modern mentality are best illustrated in its relation to the problem of egocentricity, the universality of which is "empirically respected by all men of affairs who are charged with any responsibility in business or government."[8] Yet academic empiricism continues to insist that the universal tendency to egocentricity is due to faulty education and that it could be overcome either by adequate psychiatric technique or social reforms.

The fact that the phenomenon of self-seeking may be related, not to specific forms of insecurity, but to the insecurity of life itself, seems to be obscured in even the most sophisticated psychological theory, which is why psychological theories are so irrelevant to political theory.

Such sentimentality and unreality have often been considered a distinctly Biblical attitude, while in truth the Bible constantly reminds us of man's frailty and unreliability. "All flesh is grass, and all the strength thereof is as the flower of the field. The grass withers, the flower fades . . . surely the people is grass" (Isaiah 40:6–7). "Put not your trust in princes, nor in the son of man, in whom there is no help" (Psalms 146:3). Isaiah calls upon us not to trust the world; the Psalmist tells us not to rely on man.

What the rabbis thought about the nature of man may be shown in the following comment. We read in Habakkuk 1:14, *And Thou makest man as the fishes of the sea, and as the creeping things, that have no ruler over them?* "Why is man here compared to the fishes of the sea? . . . Just as among fishes of the sea, the greater swallow up the smaller ones, so with men, were it not for fear of government, men would swallow each other alive. This is just what we have learned: Rabbi Hanina, the Deputy High Priest, said, 'Pray for the welfare of the government, for were it not for fear thereof, men would swallow each other alive.' "[9]

[8] *Christian Realism and Political Problems,* pp. 7–8.

[9] *Abodah Zarah* 3b–4a; see also *Aboth* III, 2.

According to Rabbi Jacob, "This world is like a vestibule before the world to come; prepare yourself in the vestibule, so that you may enter the banquet hall."[10] There is no reward for good deeds in this world.[11] The time for reward promised in the Bible is the life to come.[12] According to the Rav, "The world was created for the extremely pious or the extremely wicked, for men like Rabbi Hanina ben Dosa [a saint who lived in the first century of the common era] or for men like King Ahab; this world was created for the extremely wicked, the world to come was created for the extremely pious."[13] "In this world war and suffering, evil inclination, Satan, and the angel of death hold sway."[14]

In the Jewish mystical literature of the thirteenth century the doctrine is advanced that world history consists of seven periods (*shemitah*), each lasting seven thousand years, which in the Jubilee, the fifty thousandth year, will reach its culmination. The current period is one which is dominated by the divine quality of "stern judgment." In it the evil urge, licentiousness, arrogance, forgetfulness, and unholiness prevail.[15]

According to Rabbi Shneur Zalman of Ladi: "Anything that refuses to regard itself as nothing beside God but, on the contrary, asserts itself as an entity separate from God does not receive the light of its vitality from the inner holiness and essence of God." It receives the light of its vitality, so to speak, from the "hind-part" of his holiness, and only after it has gone through myriad channels of emanation and has been so obscured and contracted that it is capable of living "in exile," apart from God. And that is why this material world is called a "*world of shells*" (*kelipoth*), "*the other side*" (*sitra abra*). And this is why all the things that happen in this world are harsh and evil, and this is why the wicked prevail.[16]

The pious Jews put no trust in the secular world. "They realized quite well that the world was full of ordeals and dangers, that it contained Cain's jealousy of Abel, the cold malevolence of Sodom, and the hatred of Esau, but they also knew that there was in it the charity of Abraham and the tenderness of Rachel. Harassed and oppressed, they carried deep within their hearts a contempt for the

[10] *Aboth* 4:21. [11] *Erubin* 22a. [12] *Kiddushin* 39b.

[13] *Berachoth* 61b. This world is often compared to "night"; it is even called "the world of falsehood."

[14] *Midrash Vayosha, Beth Hamidrash,* ed. Jellinek, 2nd ed., Jerusalem, 1938, I, 55.

[15] *Temunah* (Koretz, 1784), p. 39b.

[16] Rabbi Shneur Zalman of Ladi, *Tanya,* p. 10b.

world,with its power and pomp, with its bustling and boasting. . . . They knew that the Jews were in exile, that the world was unredeemed."[17] Dazzled by the splendor of Western civilization, the modern Jew has been prone to forget that the world is unredeemed, and that God is in exile. The present generation which has witnessed the most unspeakable horrors committed by man and sponsored by an extremely civilized nation is beginning to realize how monstrous an illusion it was to substitute faith in man for faith in God.

We do not feel "at home" in the world. With the Psalmist we pray, "I am a stranger on earth, hide not Thy commandments from me" (119:19). Indeed, if not for our endless power to forget and our great ability to disregard, who could be at ease even for one moment in a lifetime? In the face of so much evil and suffering, of countless examples of failure to live up to the will of God, in a world where His will is defied, where His kingship is denied, who can fail to see the discrepancy between the world and the will of God?

And yet, just because of the realization of the power of evil, life in this world assumed unique significance and worth. Evil is not only a threat; it is also a challenge. It is precisely because of the task of fighting evil that life in this world is so preciously significant. True, there is no reward for good deeds in this world; yet this does not mean that the world is a prison. It is rather a prelude, a vestibule, a place of preparation, of initiation, of apprenticeship to a future life, where the guests prepare to enter *tricilinium,* or the banquet hall.[18] Life in this world is a time for action, for good works, for worship and sanctification, as eternity is a time for retribution. It is eve of the Sabbath, on which the repast is prepared for the Lord's day; it is the season of duty and submission, as the morrow shall be that of freedom from every law. More precious, therefore, than all of life to come is a single hour of life on earth—an hour of repentance and good deeds. Eternity gives only in the degree that it receives. This is why the book of Ecclesiastes pronounced the dead lion less happy than the living dog.[19]

III

Confusion of Good and Evil.—Niebuhr's central problem is not the problem of sin or the problem of evil. His problem is not good

[17] A. J. Heschel, *The Earth Is the Lord's* (New York, 1950), p. 96.
[18] *Aboth* 4:22.
[19] *Shabbat* 30a.

and evil, but the evil within the good, or more accurately the *confusion* of good and evil.

More frustrating than the fact that evil is real, mighty, and tempting is the fact that it thrives so well in the disguise of the good, and that it can draw its nutriment from the life of the holy. In this world, it seems, the holy and the unholy do not exist apart but are mixed, interrelated, and confounded; it is a world where idols are at home, and where even the worship of God may be alloyed with the worship of idols.

In Jewish mysticism we often come upon the view that in this world neither good nor evil exists in purity, and that there is no good without the admixture of evil nor evil without the admixture of good. The confusion of good and evil is the central problem of history and the ultimate issue of redemption. The confusion goes back to the very process of creation.

"When God came to create the world and reveal what was hidden in the depths and disclose light out of darkness, they were all wrapped in one another, and therefore light emerged from darkness and from the impenetrable came forth the profound. So, too, from good issues evil and from mercy issues judgement, and all are intertwined, the good impulse and the evil impulse."[20]

Ezekiel saw in his great vision that "a stormy wind came out of the north, and a great cloud, with brightness [*nogah*] round about it, and fire flashing forth continually" (1:4). He first beheld the powers of unholiness. A *great cloud* represents "the power of destruction"; "it is called *great,* on account of its darkness, which is so intense that it hides and makes invisible all the sources of light, thus overshadowing the whole world. The *fire flashing forth* indicates the fire rigorous of judgment that never departs from it. *With brightness round about it* . . . that is, although it is the very region of defilement, yet it is surrounded by a certain brightness . . . it possesses an aspect of holiness, and hence should not be treated with contempt, but should be allowed a part in the side of holiness."[21] Even Satan contains a particle of sanctity. In doing his ugly work as the seducer of man, his intention is "for the sake of heaven," for it is for a purpose such as this that he was created.[22]

[20] *Zohar,* III, 80b; see also I, 156a.

[21] *Ibid.,* II, 203a–203b; see pp. 69a–69b. The *kelipoth,* or the forces of the unholy, are unclean and harmful from the aspect of man. However, from the aspect of the holy, they exist because of the will of the Creator and for His sake. A spark of holiness abides in them and maintains them. Rabbi Abraham Azulai, *Or Hahamah* (Przemysl, 1897), II, 218a.

[22] *Baba Bathra* 16a.

The great saint Rabbi Hrish of Zydatschov once remarked to his disciple and nephew: "Even after I had reached the age of forty—the age of understanding—I was not sure whether my life was not immersed in that mire and confusion of good and evil [*nogah*]. . . . My son, every moment of my life I fear lest I am caught in that confusion."[23]

All of history is a sphere where good is mixed with evil. The supreme task of man, his share in redeeming the work of creation, consists in an effort to separate good from evil and evil from good. Since evil can only exist parasitically on good, it will cease to be when that separation will be accomplished. Redemption, therefore, is contingent upon the *separation* of good and evil.

IV

Most high religions make an effort to present the world and life as a unified whole and to regard all discord and incongruities as provisional or illusory. They seek a universal principle of meaning and are pantheistic either in the cosmic or in the acosmic sense. In contrast, the emphasis in Jewish mysticism is upon the contradictory, the paradoxical, and the unresolved mystery. The temporal world comes into existence through God's creation. "Thereby a realm of freedom and mystery is indicated beyond the capacity of reason to comprehend."[24] The final irrationality of the givenness of things is frankly accepted.

The pinnacles of faith embodying paradox and contradiction, and straining at the limits of rationality, are made plausible when understood as the keys which make the drama of human life comprehensible and without which it either is given a too simple meaning or falls into meaninglessness.

To Jewish tradition, too, paradox is an essential way of understanding the world, history, and nature. Tension, contrast, contradiction characterize all of reality. This is why, in the language of the *Zohar,* our universe is called *alma de-peruda,* "the world of separation." Strife, tension, and contradiction afflict all of life, including the study of the Torah; even the sages of the Talmud disagree on many details of the law. "God has also set one thing against the other; the good against the evil, and the evil against the good; good from good and evil from good; the good marks out the evil and the

[23] Rabbi Eisik Safran, *Zohar Hai,* I.

[24] *Christian Realism and Political Problems,* p. 181.

evil marks out the good; good is reserved for the good ones and evil is reserved for the evil ones."[25] The passage in Ecclesiastes 7:14, "God has made the one as well as the other," inspired a medieval Jewish author to compose a treatise (*Temuzah*) for the purpose of proving that contrast and contradiction are necessary to existence. "All things cleave to one another, the pure and the impure. There is no pure except through impurity; a mystery which is expressed in the words: *a clean thing out of an unclean* (Job 14:4). The brain is contained in a shell, a shell which will not be broken until that time when the dead shall rise again. Then will the shell be broken and the light shine out into the world from the brain, without any covering on it."[26] However, there is a polarity in everything except God. For all tension ends in God. He is beyond all dichotomies.

But it is true that not only the world He created but even His relation to the world is characterized by the polarity of justice and mercy, of law and love. When His justice is imposed, His mercy is afflicted.[27] Yet in His own being He is One. Thus the pinnacle of Jewish truth is a mystery of Divine unity. "Thou art One and none can penetrate . . . the mystery of Thy unfathomable unity" (Ibn Gabirol).

Evil, Niebuhr claims, is much more inextricably bound up with good than most psychological systems realize. There is an element of perversity in all human action; there is "the inevitability of sin in all human striving." "The corruption of evil is at the heart of human personality."[28] Thus "the supposedly objective and dispassionate ideas of the world of culture . . . are always subject to the corruption of man's spiritual pretension, to human sin."[29] This becomes manifest in the fact that "the tragedies in human history, the cruelties and fanaticisms, have not been caused by the criminals . . . but by the good people . . . by the idealists who did not understand the strange mixture of self-interest and ideals which is compounded in all human motives." Niebuhr warns, therefore, against making the cause of religion appear to be "a contest between God-fearing believers and unrighteous unbelievers." He points to the fact that Biblical religion has emphasized "the *inequality of guilt* just as much as the equality of sin." "Especially severe judgments fall upon the rich and the powerful, the mighty and the noble, the wise and

[25] *Yetsirah*, vi, 6. [26] *Zohar*, II, 69b. [27] See *Sanhedrin* 4:5.
[28] *Faith and History*, pp. 205, 122.
[29] *An Interpretation of Christian Ethics*, p. 123; see also p. 76.

the righteous."[30] Indeed, the most horrible manifestation of evil occurs when it acts in the guise of good. In dealing with the problem of evil religious living must include an effort in two directions: separation and purification. By separation is meant the detachment of good from evil; by purification is meant the elimination of evil from good.

Judaism is also aware of the danger of evil's intrusion into the instrument of good. Therefore at the great ritual on the Day of Atonement the high priest would cast lots upon the two goats: one lot for the Lord and the other lot for Azazel. He would lay both his hands upon the head of the goat, on which the lot fell for Azazel, "and confess over him all the iniquities of the children of Israel, all their transgressions, all their sins." While the purpose of the goat upon which the lot fell for the Lord was "to make atonement *for the holy place,* because of the uncleannesses of the children of Israel, and because of their transgressions, even all their sins; and so shall he do for the tent of meeting, that dwells with them in the midst of their uncleannesses."[31] At the most sacred day of the year the supreme task was *to atone for the holy.* It preceded the sacrifice, the purpose of which was to atone for the sins.

The ambiguity of human virtue has been a central issue in the lives of many Jewish thinkers, particularly in the history of Hasidism.

"God asks for the heart."[32] Yet our greatest failure is in the heart. "The heart is deceitful above all things, it is exceedingly weak—who can know it?" (Jeremiah 17:9). The regard for the ego permeates all our thinking. Is it ever possible to disentangle oneself from the intricate plexus of self-interests? Indeed, the demand to serve God in purity, selflessly, "for His sake," on the one hand, and the realization of our inability to detach ourselves from vested interests, represent the tragic tension in the life of piety.[33] In this sense, not only our evil deeds, but even our good deeds precipitate a problem.

What is our situation in trying to carry out the will of God? In addition to our being uncertain of whether our motivation—*prior to the act*—is pure, we are continually embarrassed *during the act* with "alien thoughts" which taint our consciousness with selfish intentions. And even following the act there is the danger of self-

[30] *The Nature and Destiny of Man,* I, 222ff.

[31] Leviticus 16:16.

[32] *Sanhedrin* 106b.

[33] The essence of idolatry is to regard something as a thing in itself, separated from the holiness of God. In other words, to worship an idol does not mean to deny God; it means not to deny the self. This is why pride is idolatry. *Tanya* 28b.

righteousness, vanity, and the sense of superiority, derived from what are supposed to be acts of dedication to God.

It is easier to discipline the body than to control the soul. The pious man knows that his inner life is full of pitfalls. The ego, the evil inclination, is constantly trying to enchant him. The temptations are fierce, yet his resistance is unyielding. And so he proves his spiritual strength and stands victorious, unconquerable. Does not his situation look glorious? But then the evil inclination employs a more subtle device, approaching him with congratulations: What a pious man you are! He begins to feel proud of himself. And there he is caught in the trap (Rabbi Raphael of Bersht).

"For there is not a righteous man upon this earth, that does good and sins not" (Ecclesiastes 7:20). The commentators take this verse to mean that even a righteous man sins on occasion, suggesting that his life is a mosaic of perfect deeds with a few sins strewn about. The Baal Shem, however, reads the verse: *For there is not a righteous man upon earth that does good and there is no sin in the good.* "It is impossible that the good should be free of self-interest."[34] Empirically, our spiritual situation looks hopeless: "We are all as an unclean thing, and all our deeds of righteousness are as filthy rags" (Isaiah 64:5).

"Even the good deeds we do are not pleasing but instead revolting. For we perform them out of the desire for self-aggrandizement and for pride, and in order to impress our neighbors."[35]

Who can be trustful of his good intention, knowing that under the cloak of *kavanah* there may hide a streak of vanity? Who can claim to have fulfilled even one *mitsvah* with perfect devotion? Said Rabbi Elimelech of Lizhensk to one of his disciples, "I am sixty years old, and I have not fulfilled one *mitsvah*."[36] *There is not a single mitsvah which we fulfill perfectly* . . . except circumcision and the Torah that we study in our childhood,[37] for these two acts are not infringed upon by "alien thoughts" or impure motivations.

The mind is never immune to alien intentions, and there seems to

[34] Rabbi Yaakob Yosef of Polnoye, *Toldoth Yaakov Yosef* (Lemburg, 1863), p. 150d.

[35] Rabbi David Kimhi, *Commentary on Isaiah, ad locum.* Similarly S. D. Luzatto in his commentary. Cf. N. J. Berlin, *Commentary on Sheeltoth,* Sec. 64, p. 420. According to *Sheeltoth* the meaning of the verse is that our deeds of righteousness are as a cloth put together in patches, not woven together properly.

[36] Rabbi Yaakob Aaron of Zalshin, *Beth Yaakov* (Pietrkov, 1899), p. 144; *Aboth* 2:20.

[37] *Midrash Tehillim,* 6, 1.

be no way of ever weeding them out completely. A Hassidic Rabbi was asked by his disciples, in the last hours of his life, whom they should choose as their master after his passing away. He said, "If someone should give you the way to eradicate 'alien thoughts,' know he is not your master."

We do not know with what we must serve until we arrive there (Exodus 10:26). "All our service, all the good deeds we are doing in this world, we do not know whether they are of any value, whether they are really pure, honest or done for the sake of heaven—until we arrive there—in the world to come, only there shall we learn what our service was here."[38]

The human will cannot circumvent the snare of the ego nor can the mind disentangle itself from the confusion of bias in which it is trapped. It often looks as if God's search for the righteous man will end in a cul-de-sac.[39]

Should we, then, despair because of our being unable to attain perfect purity? We should if perfection were our goal. Yet we are not obliged to be perfect once for all, but only to rise again and again. Perfection is divine, and to make it a goal of man is to call on man to be divine. All we can do is to try to wring our hearts clean in contrition. Contrition begins with a feeling of shame at our being incapable of disentanglement from the self. To be contrite at our failures is holier than to be complacent in perfection.

It is a problem of supreme gravity. If an act to be good must be done exclusively for the sake of God, are we ever able to do the good? Rabbi Nahman of Kossov gave an answer in the form of a parable. A stork fell into the mud and was unable to pull out his legs until an idea occurred to him. Does he not have a long beak? So he stuck his beak into the mud, leaned upon it, and pulled out his legs. But what was the use? His legs were out, but his beak was stuck. So another idea occurred to him. He stuck his legs into the mud and pulled out his beak. But what was the use? The legs were stuck in the mud. . . .

Such is exactly the condition of man. Succeeding in one way, he fails in another. We must constantly remember: We spoil, and God

[38] Rabbi Isaac Meir of Ger.

[39] Moments of despair were known to the prophets. Elijah, fleeing from Jezebel, fled to the wilderness, and there he sat down under a broom-tree and said, "It is enough; now, O Lord, take away my life, for I am not better than my fathers" (I Kings 19:4). Jeremiah exclaims, "Cursed be the day wherein I was born" (20:14). Cf. also Psalms 22, 39, 88; Job 9:21, 10:20f.; 14:6f.; Ecclesiastes 4:2.

restores. How ugly is the way in which we spoil, and how good and how beautiful is the way in which he restores!

And yet, Judaism insists upon the deed and hopes for the intention. Every morning a Jew prays, "Lord our God, make the words of Thy Torah pleasant in our mouth . . . so that we study Thy Torah for its own sake."

While constantly keeping the goal in mind, we are taught that for pedagogic reasons one must continue to observe the law even when one is not ready to fulfill it "for the sake of God." For the good, even though it is not done for its own sake, will teach us at the end how to act for the sake of God. We must continue to perform the sacred deeds even though we may be compelled to bribe the self with human incentives. Purity of motivation is the goal; constancy of action is the way.

The ego is redeemed by the absorbing power and the inexorable provocativeness of a just task which we face. It is the deed that carries us away, that transports the soul, proving to us that the greatest beauty grows at the greatest distance from the center of the ego.

Deeds that are set upon ideal goals, that are not performed with careless ease and routine but in exertion and submission to their ends, are stronger than the surprise and attack of caprice. Serving sacred goals may eventually change mean motives. For such deeds are exacting. Whatever our motive may be in beginning such an act, the act itself demands an undivided attention. Thus the desire for reward is not the driving force of the poet in his creative moments, and the pursuit of pleasure or profit is not the essence of a religious or moral act.

At the moment in which an artist is absorbed in playing a concerto, the thought of applause, fame, or remuneration is far from his mind. The complete attention of the artist, his whole being, is involved in the music. Should any extraneous thought enter his mind, it would arrest his concentration and mar the purity of his playing. The reward may have been on his mind when he negotiated with his agent, but during the performance it is only the music that claims his complete concentration.

Similar may be man's situation in carrying out a religious or moral act. Left alone the soul is subject to caprice. Yet there is a power in the deed that purifies desires. It is the act, life itself, that educates the will. The good motive comes into being while doing the good.

If the antecedent motive is sure of itself, the act will continue to unfold, and obtrusive intentions could even serve to invigorate the initial motive which may absorb the vigor of the intruder into its own strength. Man may be replete with ugly motives, but a deed and God are stronger than ugly motives. The redemptive power discharged in carrying out the good purifies the mind. The deed is wiser than the heart.

This, then, seems to be the attitude of Judaism. Though deeply aware of how impure and imperfect all our deeds are, the fact of our doing is cherished as the highest privilege, as a source of joy, as that which endows life with ultimate preciousness. We believe that moments lived in fellowship with God, acts fulfilled in imitation of God's will, never perish; the validity of the good remains regardless of all impurity.

V

Central to Niebuhr's thinking is the insight that "the possibilities of evil grow with the possibilities of good,"[40] and that "*every higher principle of order* to which the soul might attach itself, in the effort to rescue meaning from chaos, *is discovered*, upon analysis, *to have new possibilities of evil in it.*"[41]

That "the possibilities of evil grow with the possibilities of good" is an insight of which Jewish tradition was aware. The good is presumably used both in the worldly and in the spiritual sense. In the first sense, the idea is expressed by Hillel who used to say, "The more flesh, the more worms [in the grave]; the more property, the more anxiety" (*Aboth* 2, 7). According to rabbinic legends, the wantonness of the antediluvian generations was due "to the ideal conditions under which mankind lived before the Flood. They knew neither toil nor care, and as a consequence of their extraordinary prosperity they grew insolent. In their insolence they rose up against God."[42] In the Scriptural sense, the Talmud teaches that *the greater the man, the greater his evil inclination*,[43] for the evil inclination is more eager to attack "the great," "the scholars," than to attack the simple people.

However, Niebuhr speaks not only of "the possibilities of evil" in the good; he characterizes evil as an inevitable fact of human

[40] *An Interpretation of Christian Ethics*, p. 97.
[41] *Ibid.*, p. 68.
[42] Louis Ginzburg, *The Legends of the Jews,* I, 152f.; V, 173.
[43] *Sukkah* 52a; see also *Ecclesiastes Rabba,* 1, 16, and *Genesis Rabba,* 19, 3.

existence. Now, if every good action is liable to corruption, what would be the worth and relevance of the worship and service of God? Does not the grace of God consist precisely in its guarding the sacred acts from being vitiated by evil? It is profoundly true that goodness may turn to cruelty, piety to fanaticism, faith to arrogance. Yet this, we believe, is a perpetual possibility rather than a necessity, a threat rather than an inevitable result.

Biblical history bears witness to the constant corruption of man; *it does not, however, teach the inevitable corruptibility of the ultimate in the temporal process.* The holiness of Abraham, Isaac, and Jacob, and the humility of Moses are the rock on which they rely. *There are good moments in history that no subsequent evil may obliterate.* The Lord himself testified to it. The integrity of Job proved it. Abraham could not find ten righteous men in Sodom by whose merit the city would have been saved. Yet there is not a moment in history without thirty-six righteous men, unknown and hidden, by whose merit the world survives. We believe that there are corners full of light in a vastness that is dark, that unalloyed good moments are possible. It is, therefore, difficult from the point of view of Biblical theology to sustain Niebuhr's view, *plausible and profound as it is.*

If the nature of man were all we had, then surely there would be no hope for us left. But we also have the word of God, the commandment, the *mitsvah.* The central Biblical fact is *Sinai,* the covenant, the word of God. Sinai was superimposed on the failure of Adam. Is not the fact that we were given the knowledge of His will a sign of some ability to carry out His will? Does the word of God always remain a challenge, a gadfly? Is not the voice of God powerful enough to shake the wilderness of the soul, to strip the ego bare, to flash forth His will like fire, so that we all cry "Glory"?

To the Jew, Sinai is at stake in every act of man, and the supreme problem is not good and evil but God, and His commandment to love good and to hate evil. The central issue is not the sinfulness but the obligations of man.

While insisting upon the contrast between God's power and man's power, God's grace and human failure, Judaism stresses a third aspect, the *mitsvah.* It is a *mitsvah* that gives meaning to our existence. The *mitsvah,* the carrying out of a sacred deed, is given to us as a constant opportunity. Thus there are two poles of piety: the right and the wrong deed; *mitsvah* and sin. The overemphasis upon sin may lead to a deprecation of "works"; the overemphasis upon *mitsvah* may lead to self-righteousness. The first may result in a denial of the relevance of history and in an overly eschatological view; the second in a denial of messianism and a secular optimism. Against both dangers Judaism warns repeatedly.

We must never forget that we are always exposed to sin. "Be not sure of yourself till the day of your death," said Hillel.[44] We have been taught that one may be impregnated with the spirit of the holy all the days of his life, yet one moment of carelessness is sufficient to plunge into the abyss. *There is but one step between me and death* (I Samuel 20:3). On the other hand, we are taught to remember that we are always given the opportunity to serve Him. Significantly, Jewish tradition, while conscious of the possibilities of evil in the good, stresses the *possibilities of further good in the good.* Ben Azzai said, "Be eager to do a minor *mitsvah* and flee from transgression; for one *mitsvah* leads to [brings on] another *mitsvah,* and one transgression leads to another transgression; for the reward of a *mitsvah* is a *mitsvah,* and the reward of a transgression is a transgression."[45]

Judaism, in stressing the fundamental importance of the *mitsvah,* assumes that man is endowed with the ability to fulfill what God demands, at least to some degree. This may, indeed, be an article of prophetic faith: the belief in our ability to do His will. "For this commandment [*mitsvah*] which I command thee this day, it is not too hard for thee, neither is it far off. It is not in heaven, that thou shouldest say, Who shall go up for us to heaven and bring it unto us and make us hear it, that we may do it? Neither is it beyond the sea that thou shouldest say, Who shall go over the sea for us, and bring it unto us, and make us hear it, that we may do it? But the word is very nigh unto thee, in thy mouth and in thy heart, that thou mayest do it" (Deuteronomy 30:11–14). Man's actual failures rather than his essential inability to do the good are constantly stressed by Jewish tradition, which claims that man is able to acquire "merit" before God. The doctrine of merits implies the certainty that for all imperfection the worth of good deeds remains in all eternity.

It is true that the law of love, the demand for the impossible, and our constant failures and transgression create in us grief and a tension that may drive us to despair. Yet, is not the reality of God's

[44] *Aboth* 2:5. [45] *Ibid.,* 4:2.

love greater than the law of love? Will He not accept us in all our frailty and weakness? "For He knows our nature [*Yetsen*]; He remembers that we are dust" (Psalms 103:14).

"In liberal Christianity there is an implicit assumption that human nature has the resources to fulfill what the Gospel demands. The Kantian axiom, 'I ought, therefore I can,' is accepted as basic to all analyses of the moral situation. In classical Christianity the perfectionism of the Gospel stands in a much more difficult relation to the estimate of human resources. The love commandment stands in juxtaposition to the fact of sin. It helps, in fact, to create the consciousness of sin."[46]

Judaism, too, would reject the axiom, "I ought, therefore I can"; it would claim, instead, "Thou art commanded, therefore thou canst." It claims, as I have said, that man has the resources to fulfill what God commands, at least to some degree. On the other hand, we are continually warned lest we rely on man's own power and believe that the "indeterminate extension of human capacities would eventually alter the human situation." Our tradition does not believe that the good deeds alone will redeem history; it is the obedience to God that will make us worthy of being redeemed by God.

If Judaism had relied on the human resources for the good, on man's ability to fulfill what God demands, on man's power to achieve redemption, why did it insist upon the promise of messianic redemption? Indeed, messianism implies that any course of living, even the supreme human efforts, must fail in redeeming the world. In other words, history is not sufficient to itself.

Yet the Hebraic tradition insists upon the *mitsvah* as the instrument in dealing with evil. At the end of days, evil will be conquered all at once; in historic times evils must be conquered one by one.

A full appreciation of the significance of Reinhold Niebuhr will have to take into account not only his teachings but also his *religious epistemology*. It will, furthermore, turn not only to his books but also to his deeds. For all his profundity, his prophetic radicalism, his insights into the ultimate aspects of human destiny, his sense for the dimension of eternity, Niebuhr has maintained a concern for the immediate problems of justice and equity in human relations. His spirituality combines heaven and earth, as it were. It does not separate soul from body, or mind from unity of man's physical and spiritual life. His way is an example of one who does justly, loves

[46] *An Interpretation of Christian Ethics,* p. 65.

mercy, and walks humbly with his God, an example of the unity of worship and living. He reminds us that Evil will be conquered by the One, while he stirs us to help conquer evils one by one.

ABRAHAM I. HESCHEL

THE JEWISH THEOLOGICAL SEMINARY OF AMERICA
NEW YORK CITY, NEW YORK

22

Alexander J. Burnstein

NIEBUHR, SCRIPTURE, AND NORMATIVE JUDAISM

22

NIEBUHR, SCRIPTURE, AND NORMATIVE JUDAISM

It is not the purpose of this paper to enter into a critical examination of Niebuhr's doctrinal teaching, his Christological speculation or what he considers the Christian means of salvation, or his interpretation of Christian dogmatics; that is the job of Christian theologians, who are better qualified than I to assess such matters. I shall try rather to isolate and expound only those elements and qualities in his thought which challenge the views commonly held among believing Jews. Can Niebuhr's central theological ideas be consistently combined with the teachings of the Hebrew scriptures and normative Judaism? What are his views concerning man, the nature of human fallibility and human destiny, as compared with the ideas concerning the same subjects that rule the Jewish mind? How do they overlap? How are they different?

Let me begin with the most fundamental of Niebuhr's ideas, the doctrine of man as sinner, which dominates all his religious thinking; which is present, even when latent, in his earlier work, but which attains its fullest, clearest expression in the Gifford Lectures, where it is reaffirmed, strengthened, and counterpointed with opposing views. Niebuhr derives his basic teaching about man from man's ability to make himself the object of his thought:

> The human spirit has the special capacity of standing continuously outside itself in terms of indefinite regression. Consciousness is a capacity for surveying the world and determining action from a governing centre. Self-consciousness represents a further degree of transcendence in which the self makes itself its own object in such a way that the ego is finally always subject and not object. The self knows the world, insofar as it knows the world, because it stands outside both itself and the world, which means

that it cannot understand itself except as it is understood from beyond itself and the world.[1]

There is no need to trace here in detail the course of his argument. We need concern ourselves only with three affirmations which he makes about man, and which he takes pains to insist are inherent in the Christian tradition, or "Biblical religion." They may be briefly summarized as self-transcendence, finiteness, and corruption.

(1) Man is free. There is some constitutional kinship between God and man, as the Biblical saying that man is made "in the image of God" clearly indicates. At the same time (2) man is weak, dependent, "created," finite, mortal, limited by the "necessities and contingencies" of nature, like other biological organisms; and finally (3) man is unwilling "to acknowledge his dependence, to accept his finiteness and to admit his insecurity,"[2] and through overweening self-assertion made possible, nay inevitable, by the individual's misuse of freedom and his basic sense of insecurity together, he sins. Thus sin, according to Niebuhr, is inherent in the human situation, and is the necessary accompaniment of the disjunction in human experience.

Niebuhr finds that man is at all times living in a world that is impregnated with the scent of anxiety which emanates from the fundamental dichotomy of man's being, the continuous conflict between egotism and self-transcendence. Sin and its moral correlative, guilt, are intransigently part of the human predicament. Sin is a pervasive, driving force corrupting every faculty or motive of man's world. Using the Bible as his guide and as a point of departure, he develops his doctrine of sin in the Gifford Lectures, where he correctly relates it to the main teaching of the Scriptures: namely, that sin is rebellion against God, and pride is mankind's supreme vice.

Sin is, in short, the central, recurrent motif to which Niebuhr reverts in all of his writing. Yet when looking at the heights and depths of human folly, as Niebuhr so vividly describes it, we ask: Whence does the stubbornness of evil in the human situation stem? What is the ultimate origin of man's iniquity?

Niebuhr does not formulate his answer to these questions with any degree of accuracy. To avoid the dilemma of assigning the

[1] *The Nature and Destiny of Man,* I, 13–14.
[2] *Ibid.,* I, 150.

genesis of sin to human nature or to man's freedom directly, thus impugning God's goodness as Creator,[3] he asserts that its ultimate roots seem to lie beyond the human level and logical thought. For sin, he holds, with Kierkegaard, always implies "prior sin"[4]; even "Adam's sin" is not the first sin, but seems to point to sin running "farther back than human history." Here, then, lies the human dilemma: on the one side, man is confronted with the tendency to do evil which is inevitable, unavoidable; and on the other side, he is fully free and responsible for his sin.

In his discussion of sin and man's responsibility Niebuhr alludes to the role of Satan which the Judaeo-Christian tradition postulates as necessary, at least as a partial solution, for the problem of the existence of evil, which, while it cannot be assigned to God, does not spring from human nature considered most radically either. But Niebuhr does not accept the Biblical doctrine concerning the Devil, either as a myth or as a dogma, or as an extrinsic principle "of evil antecedent to any human action." He merely uses Satan as a paradigm, an illustration as to how the rebellious will of man operates.

Hence the paradox of man's constant predisposition to make the wrong choice, to put himself in God's place, as well as his moral accountability, remains unresolved and unexamined in Niebuhr's theology. He suggests that perhaps the ultimate source of evil is a primary datum which it is impossible to explain rationally or logically.[5] He hints that sin is something primordial. The fact remains, however, that sin assumes a peculiar status in Niebuhr's theology, and he leaves us guessing as to just how far sin is inevitable and how we can assign moral responsibility and irresponsibility to any individual.

Niebuhr's conception of sin has many virtues, for it acts as a healthy corrective to the many self-deceptions and fallacies that beset contemporary man. Yet it also has a great defect, for it makes into a major premise something that should be preliminary to a theory, or a fresh contemplation of the plight of man and his struggle for spiritual survival and perfectibility. It is this grim and gloomy view of man, and the great stress he places on man's inveterate liability to sin, that make his otherwise profound and stimulating teaching difficult to reconcile with the main stream of Biblical and Jewish religious thought.

For, apart from Jewish monotheism, the quality which most dis-

[3] *Ibid.*, I, 254, 260. [4] *Ibid.*, I, 251–252. [5] *Ibid.*, I, 262–263.

tinguishes even ancient Judaism from the dominant religious movements in the ancient Near East is the high estimate it placed upon the possibilities of human nature, and the unique importance and dignity with which it had endowed man in the cosmos.

Let it be admitted at the outset that Scripture was sharply aware of the tragic failings in man's habits, conditioning, and attitudes which had caused catastrophe upon catastrophe to come upon him. Surely no student of Scripture can deny the somber quality in the Biblical view of man, its undercurrent of sadness, the melancholy strain running through its pages, lush with man's disobedience to God, the venality, cupidity, corruption, violence, passions, and waywardness of the children of men. And who can fail to note the general indictment against man, the monumental disappointment voiced by his Creator when, having inventoried "the wickedness of man," he exclaims: "For that every imagination of the thoughts of his heart was only evil continually?"[6] Did not Jeremiah, who stands by no means alone among the prophets in reflecting upon man's persistent tendency to rationalize his malice and treachery, cry out in anguish: "The heart is deceitful above all things, and it is exceeding weak: who can know it?"[7]

And is not the account of man, as unfolded in the pages of Scripture, from his very appearance upon the stage of history, but the long record of man's persistent failures and tragic mistakes, resulting in a series of crises: the expulsion from the garden of Eden, the Flood, the tower of Babel, the cities of the Plain, the rejection of the theocracy, the captivities—do they not all tell the bitter story of man's involvement in sin and his betrayal of God's beneficent will? And do not such clearly formulated indictments of man as expressed or intimated in such statements as, "For there is not a righteous man upon earth, that doeth good, and sinneth not,"[8] or, "There is no man that sinneth not,"[9] and the long catalogue of sins included in the daily Jewish Prayer Book, and more particularly in the Al 'Het,' the great confessional recited on Yom Kippur, the Atonement Day—do they not all point up how deep-seated moral turpitude and evil are at the core of even the best of men?

When all this is said and brought into focus, however, we still have to take into serious account another and far more comprehensive evocative portrait of man which has its roots in the Bible;

[6] Genesis 6:5.
[7] Jeremiah 17:9; see also *ibid.*, 13:23; 16:12; Hosea 5:4; Ezekiel 14:3.
[8] Ecclesiastes 7:20.
[9] I Kings 8:46.

namely, that of a being who is created in the image of God (Genesis 1:26), who is capable of great deeds and words, and stands in unique relationship both to his spiritual and physical world and to that of his Maker. And, though there is a note of lyricism, a sort of poignancy, a compassionate understanding of his humble origin and mortality, an unmistakable tenderness about the fact that he is "formed of dust" and destined to "return unto dust," yet the author or authors of Scripture insist that man is more than flesh and bone, that there pulsates in him that "breath of life" which is his "portion from above" (Genesis 2:7 and 3:19; Job 31:2; 32:8).

In the order of creation man is thus both the last and the first; *condensed* earth (the name "Adam" being a derivative of *adamah*, earth) and part of heaven; closely related to the animals and yet differentiated from the animals by his inventiveness, his speech, and above all his intelligence, which enables him "to know good and evil" (Genesis 3:22); and the general implication of this exalted concept of man seems to be that it is this faculty of knowledge and discernment which man possesses that makes him free to choose between good and evil. It is through the assertion of his moral freedom, and by living in accordance with the Moral Law which God revealed to him, that man, a creature, becomes divine-like.

The one significant and dominant impression that emerges from a careful reading of the first three chapters of Genesis is that if taken either as a myth or as a dogma, a composite fusion of two separate accounts of creation or the product of a single mind, it is a hymn to man, who finds a special place in God's affection and care, and whose appearance upon the stage of history marks the climax of creation. In the words of a noted modern scholar: "If we examine the story in Genesis objectively we see that, while many elements go into the making up the whole picture, it's not so much an account of the 'Fall of Man' as the rise of man halfway to divinity. He obtained one of the two prerogatives or characteristics of the Gods: intelligence; but he was checked by God from obtaining immortality, which would have made man quite divine."[10] Insist though we may that this is the language of epic poetry, it must nevertheless stand as the major premise on which the Biblical estimate of man is built. For even the prophets, who took the most serious view of sin in all its

[10] Cyrus H. Gordon, *Introduction to Old Testament Times* (Ventnor, N.J., 1953), pp. 23–24. See also Fleming James, *Personalities of the Old Testament* (New York, 1947), pp. 201–207.

tragic diversity, in that they thought of it as rebellion, as treason rather than as transgression—even the prophets did not abandon the belief that man is by his natural endowment capable of attaining the highest good, and that the smoldering spark of the divine can be awakened in him by a change of heart, through repentance.

This exalted concept of the nature of man is implied in the whole idea of the "covenant" relationship between God and Israel, and lies at the heart of the Law of God, or the Torah. For the Hebrew word Torah, translated "law," is both an abstract and a concrete noun. It describes the way by which God's mind and will is disclosed to men, and the norms and forms of conduct He requires.[11] It is through the Torah that God speaks to men, and it is through "the knowledge of the Lord," accessible to all men, and through the love of God that expresses itself in right conduct toward his fellowman, that man has kinship with his Creator.

It is noteworthy that no Biblical poet or prophet or psalmist (or any authoritative exponent of Judaism, for that matter) sets the awful grandeur and majesty of God against the thought of man's littleness in order to make man feel puny, unimportant, and of little worth. On the contrary, all the great Biblical writers and masterly interpreters of Judaism stress God's greatness and universal sovereignty over Nature and man, not to make man feel small and petty, but to make man aware of God's beneficence in nature, His faithful providence, and His constant love especially toward those who are humble, weak, and distressed.[12]

Nowhere in Jewish Scripture is there an attempt to describe man as a loathsome creature, made for inevitable sinning. Nor is there a single psalm meant to lower man's dignity and to produce the mood of dejection or self-depreciation. Even the much debated Psalm 51, where the author dwells with great poignancy on his deeply ingrained tendency to sin, and directly and movingly complains: "Behold I was shapen in iniquity; and in sin did my mother conceive me"—even here man's dignity is not denied, and in the end the psalmist derives comfort from the thought that God will grant him "a clean heart" and "a steadfast spirit." Finally, the contrast and yet the intimate relationship that exist between God and man is perhaps best brought out in that magnificent passage in the 40th chapter of Isaiah, where the prophet celebrates the might and transcendent

[11] Micah 6:8; Amos 4:13; Psalms 19:8–12, also 119.
[12] Job 38:31, 32; Psalms 113; 145; 146:8–9; 147:3.

power of God; even here the nearness to God is revealingly expressed. In dramatic, majestic words the prophet exalts the God who "comprehended the dust of the earth in a measure, and weighed the mountains in scales, and the hills in a balance," so that to Him the "nations are as a drop of a bucket," and "the small dust of the balance:" and that "He taketh up the isles as a very little thing." But the passage is introduced by the verse, "He shall feed his flock like a shepherd: He shall gather the lambs with His Arm, and carry them in His Bosom." And the touching chapter concludes with the glorious and transforming words: "They that wait upon the Lord shall renew their strength; they shall mount up with wings as eagles; they shall run, and not be weary; and they shall walk, and not faint." In short, this mighty Lord, whom it is absurd to try to imprison in a piece of wood or metal, is one who in creation and in providence and in all the vast ways of the divine activity is at the disposal of those who trust in Him.

As Dr. Irwin, in writing about the very high position ancient Israel assigned to man, puts it: "God was exalted, yet He was not separated from man. God and man were alike in nature. Even if man's frailties were such as to make the resemblance a caricature, nonetheless he was in the image of God.[13] Indeed, it may confidently be asserted that this arch-image of man, carrying within himself the impress of the divine, has had the greatest impact on Jewish feeling and thinking and has deeply colored the texture of the Jewish mind throughout the ages, and this without nullifying the sordid aspects of human nature or minimizing the grave flaws and curious weaknesses that so frequently blur this portrait of man. This picture of man, with his amazing capacity for good or evil, grew out of a particular conception of man, his possibilities, and his destiny. It is predicated on the presupposition that man is essentially a free agent. Man can will what he really wants to will, and insofar as his conduct is concerned it is his peculiar prerogative to exercise freedom of choice. He is a creature who can say "yes" to God. He is a creature who can say "no" to God. He is a responsible being who can, by obedience to the word of God and His Torah, make God's will his own. He has the power to resist evil, overcome temptation, and choose the

[13] William A. Irwin, "The Hebrews," in *The Intellectual Adventure of Ancient Man* (Chicago: University of Chicago Press, 1946), pp. 262–263. A brilliant and convincing study.

good; or, having stumbled, he can raise himself above his habitual tendency to sin. It is always possible for man, for all his tragic moral blunders and mistaken choices, to break through again to a new and fresh response to the call of the divine within him, and man can, whether by reason or by a change of heart and feeling, find his way to God. Teshubah (penitence), a process of return or renewal, is always possible.

Does not the very fact of the "covenant," the agreement into which God and Israel had entered, presuppose the idea that man has the power and the capacity to obey or disobey God's law? That man is free to resist evil and choose good is explicitly proclaimed in the Book of Deuteronomy, where we hear Moses saying: "I call heaven and earth to witness against you this day, that I have set before thee life and death, the blessing and the curse; therefore choose life, that thou mayest live, thou and thy seed."[14] Again, at the end of his career Joshua declares: "And if it seem evil unto you to serve the Lord, choose you this day whom ye will serve; whether the Gods which your father served that were beyond the River, or the Gods of the Amorites, in whose land ye dwell."[15]

Every prophetic pronouncement, warning, and condemnation has implicit in it the thought that man is free to act and free to refrain. Every prophetic appeal summoning men to "return," to repent, is predicated on the premise that despite his strong and deeply ingrained tendency to sin, man could, if he tried hard enough, seek after righteousness, and thus realize the destiny granted by the divine will. The very purpose of the existence of the Torah, which the Jew regarded as the expression of the will of God, is that men may choose to obey it.

If we look at the whole body of post-Biblical literature, covering many centuries, we find the belief in man's inner freedom asserted implicitly and explicitly. It is most neatly and emphatically phrased in Ben Sira: "God made man in the beginning, and left him in the hands of his own decision."[16] The rabbis, who were not prepossessed by philosophical speculations, never wrangled over the doctrine of free will but accepted it unconditionally, as is evident from their often-quoted, undisputed maxim, "All is in the hands of God except the fear of God."[17] And even the more metaphysically-minded Jewish

[14] Deuteronomy 30:19; 11:26.
[15] Joshua 24:15.
[16] *Ben Sira* 15:14.
[17] *Berachoth* 33.

philosophers, from Philo Judaeus to Maimonides, Gersonides, Herman Cohen, and Martin Buber—all repeatedly and vigorously have professed it.

While Niebuhr and normative Judaism are virtually at one in accepting freedom as an objective existential fact, they differ in the conclusion or inferences they draw from this essential factor in man's makeup. The key to their divergence lies in their attitude toward man and his cosmic setting.

Niebuhr's root assumption, as we have already indicated, is that man ultimately lives in a double environment, the world of "eternity and time." Unlike the bird and the beast, to which the world offers the smooth caress of an environment whole and total as the womb, man is a creature "who is involved in flux but who is also conscious of the fact that he is so involved, and hence cannot be totally involved. A spirit who can set time, nature, the world, and being *per se* into juxtaposition to himself and inquire after the meaning of these things, proves that in some sense he stands outside and beyond time."[18]

In Niebuhr's view there is an unending conflict and a continuing tension at the base of life itself which points to a fundamental duality in man. Man's inner life is not a uniform, harmonious, and homogeneous world. It consists of forces in battle array, a confused mass of energies and vitalities struggling for ascendancy, a battlefield of varied desires and ideas, where the essential relation is that of tension and conflict between person and person and between man and his universe, a conflict which can be reduced, explained, if not completely resolved, only if we grasp the validity and the universal implications of the Christian view of man. It is Christianity, he insists, which provides man with the necessary vantage point from which to measure "both freedom and involvement without invalidating either," and the Christian myths, though they cannot and should not be accepted literally, express ultimate truths concerning man and his cosmic setting.

There is a further insight which Niebuhr derives from the Christian tradition, and which is assigned a special place and pressed into the foreground of his thinking: namely, the doctrines of Original Sin and the Fall. And this element, a pivotal point in his theology which he shares with most of the neo-Reformationists, is quite irreconcilable with the main trend of Jewish religious teaching.

[18] *The Nature and Destiny of Man,* I, 124.

Here too Niebuhr frankly rejects the traditional interpretation of these doctrines. He regards them no longer as events in the past but as true expressions, in a symbolic form, of the ultimate but neglected truths about mankind's universal, inevitable, and incorrigible tendency to sin. In the light of this insight sin is centered in human existence. It has its roots in "man's unwillingness to acknowledge his finiteness."[19] It is the acid that corrodes even the ethical and religious principles which men profess, and which can never be completely eradicated because of the structural incapacity of the will to do other than sin. In brief, man in his essential nature is a sinner, yet at the same time he is free and responsible. Here is a paradox, a contradiction at the core of life itself which we may not be able to resolve logically, but which nonetheless is psychologically true. Besides, not only is man a sinner, but what makes him a singular sinner is the fact that he is conscious of his guilt. For Niebuhr, departing from the traditional interpretation given to the concept of *justitia originalis,* sin finds its locus in man's freedom rather than in a prehistoric event in the past. "Original righteousness" thus becomes, in Niebuhr's teaching, the moral imperative, the awareness of obligation to do justly and to love God and man that speaks to us through the voice of conscience and is borne in upon us by means of memory in our lofty moments of self-transcendence.

The over-all portrait of man as it emerges, then, from Niebuhr's writings is that of a creature, dark and shadowed by sin, weak and wholly impotent to control the ungovernable tendency to self-love, yet lured on by a sense of *justitia originalis* which he can never hope to embody in life and history; a being strangely at odds with himself and the world he inhabits, haunted by the spectre of remorse and guilt, caught in a web of dialectical tensions between finity and infinity, history and eternity, which are not merely unresolved in human experience but which are ultimately unresolvable.

Despairing of man's basic incapacity to realize the moral ideal within the framework of historic experience, Niebuhr sees no hope in history, which is an "interim" for man; but there is hope in the *telos* which is grounded beyond history and which sums up all that we mean when we say that history has a universal purpose or goal. Christ, the wisdom of God, is the *telos* of history, as well as the norm, the standard of absolute, selfless love and perfection. The *agape,* the perfect love of Christ, can only serve as an ideal to beckon and inspire

[19] *Faith and History,* p. 118; also *The Nature and Destiny of Man,* I, 179–180.

men to nobler actions in their difficult struggle to achieve the good; but, owing to the corruptive tendencies in man, it can never be absorbed or fulfilled in the realm of history. The *finis* and *telos*, dramatically represented by the Christian tradition in the concept of the coming of Christ and in the Parousia, the second coming of Christ, according to Niebuhr, come to teach us that the completion and the fulfillment of the moral ideal are to be sought "not within history" but at the end of history.[20]

Niebuhr's philosophy of history logically reaches an impasse. This is expressed in his own words: "The Christian philosophy of history is rational, therefore, only in the sense that it is possible to prove that alternatives to it fail to do justice to all aspects of human existence; and that the basic presuppositions of the Christian faith, though transcending reason, make it possible to give an account of life and history in which all facts and antinomies are apprehended."[21]

What Niebuhr does is to infuse or inject into the stream of history an arbitrary or subjective set of standards and meanings and insights, which a whole cluster of Christian dogmas, such as justification by faith, "beyond time," the doctrine of the resurrection of the body, and so on, suggest or yield to him, and in terms of which he attempts to decipher the deeper implications of the historical process.

Now this interpretation of man and history, anchored as it is in the Christian faith, may prove of extreme interest and importance to those who share the same tradition, and may help them to see more clearly, more fully, and more nearly as a whole the ultimate purpose of history. But what about those who are not reared in this particular brand of faith and who cannot profit by the secret lessons which the Christian dogmas are supposed to impart? Are they doomed to eternal blindness?

Turning from this sketchy, but I hope not distorted description of Niebuhr's ideas concerning man and his relation to history, let us look for a moment at the divergent estimate of man developed and set forth by the ancient rabbis, the great molders of the Jewish tradition.

The conquest of evil by good, the rabbis recognized, is a long, rough-hewn, incessant uphill struggle, and a host of subtle insights and a variety of more explicit prayers and affirmations scattered throughout rabbinic literature may be gleaned to show how keenly

[20] *The Nature and Destiny of Man*, I, 287–290; also *Faith and History*, p. 235.
[21] *Faith and History*, p. 138.

perceptive they were of the anguishes and stresses of the conflict between good and evil in the life of man;[22] yet equally patent to any student is the special emphasis Israel's teachers placed upon the fact that man can subdue the evil within him, particularly when to man's own endeavor is added the supporting grace of God. Man, they remind us, has within him the necessary freedom and the spiritual defenses which, if marshaled properly, can prevail against the strongest forces of evil (*Jalkut Shimoni* [Job] 901), and in one striking passage they emphatically state:

"Should you say that the evil impulse is not in your power, I [God] have declared unto you in Scripture, 'Unto thee is its desire, but *thou* mayest rule over it' " (*Genesis Rabbah* 22, 15).

Furthermore, through unswerving determination, moral apprehension, the zealous study of the Torah, and through active devotion to the doing of good deeds, man can not only curb the violent passions and impulses that surge within him, but he can convert them to the service of goodness and God. The rabbis, it may be inferred, believed that the very natural impulses and vitalities, so frequently destructive to man's will and spirit, can be tamed, disciplined, and transmuted into that which is good. A splendid illustration of this is to be found in the teaching of the *Mishnah* (*Berachoth* 9, 5; also *Sifre on Deuteronomy* 6, 5; *Friedmann* 73a), where the rabbis, basing their interpretation on Deuteronomy 6:5, "Thou shalt love the Lord thy God with thy whole heart," deduce the doctrine that one must love God with both the *Yezarim*, the evil one as well as the good one. In a word, the entire personality of man is to be enlisted in the service and in the love of the Highest.

So it is, the rabbis observed, that the bigger the man, the bigger may be his temptation; and the truly great and upright men in history are those who have wrestled with the evil *Yezer*, a mighty foe within man, and have proved themselves the masters, and not the creatures, of their *Yezer* (*Sukkah* 52a,b).

Much of what takes place in the hearts and minds of the illustrious, the rabbis held, is also exhibited, on a minor scale to be sure, in the hearts and souls of all men. We too, whether we fully realize

[22] Mark the sad, rueful note in the maxim of Simeon Ben Pazzi (*Berachoth* 6/a): "Woe is to me from [my responsibility to] my Creator, woe to me from [my struggle with] my inclination." For many other sayings about the menacing nature of the *Yezer Hara*, see *Kiddushin* 30a; *Sukka* 52; also noteworthy is the touching prayer (*Berachoth* 60b) which found its way into the daily Prayer Book: "Subdue our inclination that it may submit itself to Thee." See also *Berachoth* 17a.

it or not, are engaged in an unending struggle betwen light and darkness, right and wrong. Ominous and seemingly inexhaustible are the forces of evil that are within man and outside him, but greater still, the rabbis sturdily maintained, are the forces that make for good in the common man and in the world about him. Such were the indivisible, constituent elements of the composite, classic Jewish picture of man.

To recapitulate: along with ideas stressing the persistent moral failures, cruelties, and corruptions of men, there is another equally dominant, and perhaps theologically more important, current of thought which frequently accompanies them, providing a substratum of radiance, a glow of light and hope to historic Judaism's vision of man: namely, a mighty belief in the latent potentialities for good that inhere in the human heart. Indeed, what makes the student of rabbinic literature wonder is the amazing fact that the rabbis, who knew the full terror of the world and apprehended so well the strange aberrations and infirmities of the human mind and will, could yet cling so tenaciously to an earnest faith in man himself, in his power to overcome the errors and moral deficiencies of his nature, in his ability to make heroic responses of a high order to the furtherance of God's laws, plans, and purposes. The rabbis knew that man, having stumbled and fallen, could by his own resolve right himself, rise above the impediments which are constantly besetting him, and renew the sense of contact with the living and ever compassionate God.

This basic belief in the potential goodness of man lies at the core of the concept of *teshubah,* generally translated "repentance," which conceals the real intent or connotation of the Hebrew original; literally and significantly the term means "return," a derivative from the verbal root *"shub,"* to return, and denotes the deliberate turning from sin and returning to God. It is a word rich in overtones and in all sorts of suggestions. It is not merely remorse, regret, or the lash of moral condemnation which we experience when we commit a sinful act, nor is it to be identified with the sudden change of heart, the wild leap of faith, the immense alteration in the self brought about by certain types of religious conversion or the mystic's immediate, intuitive sense of the Divine, though the concept of the *teshubah* may include all of these elements as parts of its rich complexity. But it includes very much besides. It is a continuous, arduous, life-long process of directing one's "heart to heaven" which must be arduously pursued, rather than an irruptive, ecstatic state, if man is to achieve a life of integration with the Divine and a harmonious relationship with himself and his fellow men. In brief, *teshubah,* as the rabbis conceived it, is an activity of the soul, an insight, a power, a gift from God granted to every normal human being which he can and must cultivate and foster as a part of the soul's purification, elevation, and health, not only during the penitential season but day by day, sincerely and contritely. This is strikingly voiced in the prayer offered by the observant Jew thrice daily: "Cause us to return, O our Father, unto thy Law; draw us near, O our King, unto Thy service, and bring us back in perfect repentance unto Thy presence. Blessed art Thou, O Lord, who delightest that man should return to the right way" (Daily Prayer Book, p. 46).[23]

These, then, are the two focal points around which this concept of *teshubah,* the lodestar of Jewish theology, revolves:

1. A confidence in man's potentialities for greatness, as well as a fixed trust in man's power to deliver himself from the thraldom of sin and self-love through a steady concentration of the will on God's righteous purpose and the human welfare which is dear to God.

2. A positive belief in the goodness of God who "knoweth our frame," as the rabbis translated it, "our *Yezer,* our evil inclinations," and "like as a father pitieth his children," so our Father in Heaven—an appellation of God which is prominent even in early rabbinic literature—yearns for the return of His erring children, and is ever near and ready to forgive the penitent sinners and receive them back into His endless lovingkindness.[24]

It is this kindlier and more charitable view of man—a master-belief rather than the result of any kind of discursive analysis, bound up as it was with an overwhelming faith in the sovereignty and goodness of God working in and through history—that made the rabbis so astonishingly hopeful as to the fate of man and the ulti-

[23] For many splendid rabbinic comments on the value and importance of *teshubah,* see *Mishnah, Yoma* 8, 9; *Mishnah Aboth* 2, 5; also *Talmud, Yoma* 86a, b; *Berachoth* 34b; *Rosh Hashanah* 16a; notably, *Midrash Deut. Rabbah,* Chap. II, a chapter replete with many rich and provocative ideas concerning *teshubah,* some of which have been incorporated in the Day of Atonement liturgy. See also *Abot de Rabbi Nathan,* Chap. 15; see also Maimonides' admirable exposition of the doctrine in *Mishnah Torah* (The Code), chapter on Repentance.

[24] For a clear and interesting study of the concept of God as Father not only of Israel but of the world in early rabbinic thought, see A. Marmorstein, *The Old Rabbinic Doctrine of God,* I, *The Names of God* (London, 1927), pp. 56–61.

mate end of history on this earth. This teaching, behind which stands that Biblical covenant relationship between God and Israel never forgotten by the Jews, generated a mood, a state of mind quite general, if not universal, among the rabbis, which differs radically from that of Niebuhr: namely, that man, despite his frequent waywardness and grave moral lapses, can reach greatness and nobility by action and by a religious softening and ripening of the heart, and that man is capable of realizing a universal kingdom of righteousness and peace among individuals and nations. It is this sympathetic assessment of the character of man as a whole, which sprang from a deep sense of the moral integrity of God who rules and determines the destiny of men and nations, that infiltrated and inspired Judaism's interpretation of the great processes of history as the unfolding of the divine purpose, a movement toward the ultimate triumph of righteousness and holiness, and never allowed eschatological visions to deform or shake the traditional Jewish trust in a worthy dénouement of the human drama within time.[25]

It is only in the light of this theocentric context, where the doctrine of man is closely linked with the unity, creativity, and goodness of God, who is near and readily accessible through a life of righteousness, that we can understand why the mood and the thought-tone of traditional Jewish teaching remained radiant and soberly optimistic even with regard to this world, and why the rabbis in their ultimate appraisal of the human potential arrived at a verdict which is at variance with the predominantly mordant view of man and the community to be found in the writings of Niebuhr.

This essay has left out of account many important questions that may be raised. I should like at least to mention a few of them. I have said nothing about Niebuhr's tendency to regard law or the code-making capacity in man as the product of wrongdoing which is engendered by his insatiable lust for power and domination; the vagaries, incongruities, self-deceptions, and infirmities of the human mind which betray its incapacity to serve as a rational tool of analysis; the ever recurrent drama of the moral struggle between immediate, tentative, and ultimate values grounded in eternity, which

[25] For a perceptive, well documented essay on the early rabbinic interpretation of history, see Nahum Robert Glatzer, *Untersuchungen zur Geschichte der Tannaiten* (Schocken Verlag: Berlin, Lehre 1933).

For an adequate though far from convincing presentation of the significance of apocalypticism, see Joshua Bloch on *Apocalyptic in Judaism* (Dropsie College for Hebrew and Cognate Learning: Philadelphia, 1952).

cannot be resolved by reason but which can only be expressed in terms of transcendence.

Here and there, in widely scattered passages throughout his copious descriptions of the human situation, Niebuhr does take cognizance of the actuality of "man's capacity for justice," of which he says that it "makes democracy possible" at the same time that "his inclination to injustice makes democracy necessary."[26] And in another passage he goes so far as to state: "Against pessimistic theories of human nature which affirm the total depravity of man it is important to assert the continued presence in man of the *justitia originalis.*"

This passage, among many others that may be adduced, shows clearly that original righteousness is, according to Niebuhr, a part of universal experience. But beyond that there is also implicit in it the idea that original righteousness is not so much an intuition, an insight leading to ethical conduct, or, to use a Talmudic phrase, "a good intention that bears fruit in good deeds,"[27] but rather a kind of celestial censor which we carry within us, always ready to deplore our defections and moral lapses from the ideal of perfection, and which is within man even while it is beyond him. Since our performances in the actual world can never be squared with any ideal of right exemplified in the realm of eternity, there is a rift, a schism in the consciousness of man which can only partly be healed by a new orientation toward ultimate reality; and it is Christianity above all that can save us from the torturing burden of guilt and anxiety, which arises to plague us constantly.

Finally we must ask: Which of the two essentially divergent estimates of man is more adequate and accurate? Here I find the mental picture of man, drawn from the reservoir of the Jewish religious tradition, the more temperate, comprehensive, and balanced; whereas Niebuhr's portrait of man, perhaps influenced by the idiom of his own tradition, is one-sidedly heavy and irretrievably dark. The fallacy of Niebuhr's root conception of man is not, in this writer's opinion, that it is pessimistic (there is also an occasional note of pessimism to be found in the Bible and in rabbinic literature), but rather that in underscoring man's frightening iniquity and

[26] *The Children of Light and the Children of Darkness,* p. xi, quoted by the late and very much lamented Rabbi Milton Steinberg in his brilliant essay entitled "The Theological Issues of the Hour," Rabbinical Assembly of America *Proceedings,* 1949, v, XIII.

[27] *Kidd.,* 40a.

spiritual impotence Niebuhr overlooks man's extraordinary capacity for good and glosses over the element of growth, development, and progress which is a datum of human history.

Having made these criticisms of Niebuhr's world-view, we cannot help admiring the tremendous contribution he has already made to our understanding of the place and power of evil in man and society, a truth which the ancient Jewish teachers grasped but which the contemporary Jew has frequently forgotten.

The best tribute which we can all pay to this great and challenging teacher is to revaluate and rethink the human issues at stake, the problems which he has raised, and to emulate his intellectual honesty and courage in answering them. May he continue his vigorous activity for many, many years to come!

ALEXANDER J. BURNSTEIN

RABBI: MILLINERY CENTER SYNAGOGUE
NEW YORK CITY

III

REPLY TO INTERPRETATION AND CRITICISM BY REINHOLD NIEBUHR

REPLY

I SHALL try to answer my various critics as best I can, but not before expressing my gratitude to them for subjecting my thought to such careful scrutiny and sympathetic consideration. I have learned much from their criticisms. I also must express the constant embarrassment which I felt in reading their criticisms, because they were asked to consider a system of thought which does not deserve the attention which they were asked to give it. I felt this embarrassment particularly in reading those criticisms which accurately and sympathetically traced my inconstant shifting of viewpoints, particularly in political theory. I was aware constantly of the problem of why any one should pay any more attention to what I have to say than to what I once said and have since repudiated or amended.

PROFESSORS BRUNNER AND TILLICH

Emil Brunner's generous essay with its one complaint against me gives me the opportunity to make some amends for a grievous omission in my *The Nature and Destiny of Man.* I read Brunner's book some time before giving my lectures, and profited greatly from his analysis of the doctrine of sin in his *Man in Revolt.* Subsequently I became involved in tracing the doctrine through as much of history as I could encompass. In the process I lost sight of Brunner and did not refer to his work, though, as he confesses, I had written appreciatively to him about the book. It was a grievous error not to acknowledge my debt to him, though my omission was occasioned by finding no specific agreement or disagreement with him which would require a footnote. I may say that Brunner's whole theological position is close to mine and that it is one to which I am more indebted than any other. I say this though in recent years our respective treatment of the ethical problem has diverged rather widely, through his increasing adoption, and my increasing rejection, of the concept of "Natural Law."

Before engaging in a debate with my friend Paul Tillich, I want to express my gratitude to him for the education I received at his hands in two decades of teaching on the same faculty. Tillich is a great metaphysician, but he will not think too much of my gratitude because he feels that I have not learned the philosophical lessons too well.

The point at issue between us is the old and yet ever new problem of the relation of faith to reason. I think that is what he means by saying that I have inadequate epistemology. I can find no way of proving by any epistemological method that God, the creator, is revealed as forgiving love in the drama of Christ's life, death, and resurrection. Upon that faith the Christian Church is founded. I think this faith may be validated in experience. It is the key which resolves the divine mystery into meaning and makes sense out of life. But I know of no way of inducing this faith by purely rational arguments. Tillich thinks my difficulty is that I have confused the modern idea of reason ("calculating reason") with the classical type of reason ("*logos* type"). This is a serious misunderstanding on Tillich's part. It is with the classical rationalism that I am chiefly concerned. I do not depreciate it. I know that God must be reason or have reason of the type Aristotle ascribes to the divine. The human self also has this *logos* type of reason as part of its unique creative power. But the self has a freedom which cannot be equated with this reason; and God has freedom beyond the rational structure. The Bible attributes the power of creation to him. Tillich says he must have "the power of being." I agree; but I think the idea of creation points to a mystery beyond any system of rational intelligibility. If we try to incorporate this mystery into a system of rational intelligibility, the "power of being" is interpreted as a vast reservoir of potentiality. The idea of God as primarily the structure of things attributes creative force to form, as contrasted with the formless stuff. It is quite true that whenever we speak of "being" we speak ontologically. But since ontology is the "science of being," it has its limitations in describing any being or being *per se* which contains mysteries and meanings which are not within the limits of reason. Among these are both the human self in its mystery of freedom within and beyond the rational structure of mind, and the divine mystery which certainly implies the "power of being"; but the mystery of God's creative power is certainly beyond the limits of a rational ontology.

Professor Tillich thinks that my trouble is that I have capitulated to a Hebraic mode of thought in preference to the Hellenic. But my thesis is simply that both modes of thought are necessary. Without the Hellenic understanding of *logos*, of structure, of form, we could not understand anything at all because every being and being *per se* certainly have structures. Therefore the Hellenic component of our culture generated our sciences and philosophies. My point is simply that when we deal with aspects of reality which exhibit a freedom above and beyond structures, we must resort to the Hebraic dramatic and historical way of apprehending reality. Both the divine and the human self belong to this category. Tillich rightly contends that every kind of freedom is involved in "destiny." Very true. But if philosophers try to comprehend the patterns of historical destiny within a framework of ontology, they make nonsense of history, as in the case of Hegel. History certainly contains patterns of destiny. But these patterns are not in the strict sense subject to ontological inquiry. For nothing in history follows "in a necessary manner," that is, either logically or in terms of efficient cause, which could be proved "necessary" by scientific verification.

Professor Tillich suggests that what he regards as my errors are derived from my preoccupation with the nature of the self. That is indeed the cause of the difference between our respective viewpoints. I do not believe that ontological categories can do justice to the freedom either of the divine or of the human person, or to the unity of the person in his involvement in and transcendence over the temporal flux or that the sin of man and the forgiveness by God of man's sin or the dramatic variety of man's history can be comprehended in ontological categories. If it is "supernaturalistic" to affirm that faith discerns the key to specific meaning above the categories of philosophy, ontological or epistemological, then I must plead guilty of being a supernaturalist. The whole of the Bible is an exposition of this kind of supernaturalism. If we are embarrassed by this and try to interpret Biblical religion in other terms, we end in changing the very character of the Christian faith.

PROFESSORS BENNETT AND RAMSEY

Professor Bennett, after a very thorough analysis of the history of my social theories, points to the fact that I have recently come to some conclusions which have been defined as conservative. Professor Bennett is careful to point out what kind of conservatism I espouse. I don't want to challenge his very fair conclusions at all, but merely underline his judgment that any conservatism which is merely interested in the preservation of some *status quo* would be anathema for any one who had drawn inspiration from the Old Testament prophets. American conservatism, which is nothing more than a decadent liberalism, would be doubly unacceptable. My conservatism relates to an increasing appreciation of the organic factors in social life in contrast to the tendencies stemming from the Enlightenment which blind modern men to the significance of these organic factors, and treat the human community and its instruments of order and justice as if they were purely artifacts. I believe that, ultimately considered, this is a religious issue. For the extreme voluntarism is related to lack of appreciation of the providential elements in community building. It derives from a failure of modern man to realize how much he is a creature in the historical process, though he is undoubtedly also a creator. I believe that Communistic voluntarism is merely the end product of this attitude toward historical responsibilities and this inability to recognize the limits of all human contrivances.

Professor Ramsey has subjected my conceptions of the relation of love to law to searching examination and criticism, from which I have greatly profited. I will eliminate some of the points of difference between us, first by unqualifiedly accepting one of his criticisms as valid. He rightly charges me with interpreting love "beyond" the law in both the subjective and the objective sphere. He rightly insists that love transcends law only in the subjective sphere, when the conflict between duty and inclination is overcome. I accept his criticism that love is never beyond law in the objective sphere. I tried to make the transcendence of love over law to mean the indeterminacy of love as against the determinate obligations which are defined in natural law. I still think that this is a valid point, but I should not have tried to cover it with the idea of "love beyond law."

I should like to eliminate another area of difference by failing to support any idea which I propounded in my early work, *An Interpretation of Christian Ethics,* which he criticizes. It is of course perfectly legitimate to hold an author accountable for his various works. But I was only dimly feeling my way in this book toward a realistic and valid Christian ethic. I disavowed some of my ideas and amended others in later works, which roughly represent my present position. I am not therefore able to defend, or interested in defending, any position I took in *An Interpretation of Christian Ethics.*

The elimination of these points of difference leaves still the basic point of Professor Ramsey's criticism of my thought. He thinks that I do not do justice to "natural law" concepts as defining the essential structure of human existence. I may have been too critical of natural law concepts, but I do not think that Professor Ramsey really deals, except by implication, with the two main points of my criticisms of classical, catholic, and modern natural-law concepts. The one point is that these concepts do not allow for the historical character of human existence. They are rooted in a classical rationalism which did not understand history. They therefore do not understand the uniqueness of historical occasion or the historical biases which creep into the definitions of natural law. This criticism is not met by calling attention to the distinction between the *jus natura,* the *jus gentium,* and the *jus civilis.* Of course, every natural law theory allows for the application of general principles to particular situations. But the question is whether its general principles are not too inflexible on the one hand and their definition too historically conditioned on the other hand. How, for instance, can one declare property to be a right according to natural law when the institution of property represents such various types of power and responsibility in various historical settings? Professor Ramsey dismisses the charge of relativism or affinity with modern existentialism against me. He knows that I believe in an "essential" nature of man. But there would have been no reason for this defense if it had been fully considered that what I was trying to deal with was the problem of the historical elaboration of man's essential nature on the one hand, and of the historical bias which crept into the definition of that essential nature on the other hand.

The other point of my criticism of natural law concepts is the tendency to make the law of love an addendum to the natural law, so that the one defines the determinate possibilities and the other the indeterminate possibilities of good. My point is that it is not possible to draw a neat line between determinate and indeterminate possibilities. Justice is an application of the law of love. The rules are not absolute but relative. They are applications of the law of love and do not have independence apart from it. They would be independent only if they were founded in an "essential" social structure. If the illusions of classical rationalism are dispelled, it will be seen that it is not possible to define an essential structure of community except the law of love.

I make these criticisms of natural law concepts without challenging in any way the idea that there is an essential nature of man to which man must conform. But a part of that essential nature is his freedom, for which love is the only law.

"FRIENDLY CRITICS"

A special section of this rejoinder to criticisms must be devoted to my friendly critics who have been so diligent in tracing my pilgrimage that they have let my record damn me more than anything they might have said either by condoning or by emphasizing my stupidities. I refer particularly to the analysis of my political and social thought by Professors Bennett, Thompson, and Schlesinger. This analysis proves that I had used Marxist instruments to extricate myself from what I regarded as the illusions of liberalism, and that I clung to shreds of Marxist dogma long after I had supposed myself critical of Marxist illusions. Professor Thompson thinks I was rather late in arriving at the idea that prudence as well as justice must be a norm of statesmanship. And Professor Schlesinger proves conclusively that the political philosophy at which I arrived in my chapter entitled "The Triumph of Experience over Dogma" in my *Irony of American History* was a long-delayed explication of earlier presuppositions in my thought. I can only plead guilty. It is rather embarrassing to retrace one's pilgrimage and even more embarrassing to have it subjected to friendly or critical analysis, because it becomes so apparent that one was incredibly stupid in slowly arriving at a position which now seems valid but which required all the tragedies of history to clarify in one's own mind. Besides throwing doubt upon the reliability of the person thus examined, it prompts me to view the ephemeral character of all our convictions. I will read these chapters in this book whenever I am tempted to impatience with some young student who is hesitant to disavow what I now recognize to be illusions.

I shall begin with those critics who are in general agreement with me but who offer peripheral criticisms of my thought. I can accept most of these criticisms without argument either because I had changed my position on the relevant issue before the criticism or because my critics persuaded me.

In regard to Professor Kroner's sympathetic account of the movement of my thought, I have only a slight amendment to suggest, and that is that I was first influenced not so much by the Reformers as by the study of St. Augustine.

Professor Wolf makes some very telling criticisms on peripheral points which I must heartily accept. He is right in criticizing my idea of "equality of sin and inequality of guilt" as elaborated in *The Nature and Destiny of Man*. I have been convinced for some time that this was an error. I sought to do justice to the fact that there is in fact great distinction between forms of evil, that the saint and the criminal are not at all alike but that yet in the ultimate instance it is true that "In God's sight no man living is justified." It is not, however, adequate to explain this situation in quantitative terms. I remain baffled in my search for an adequate description of the situation which will allow for discriminate judgments between good and evil on the one hand, and which will, on the other, preserve the Biblical affirmation that all men fall short before God's judgment.

I have the same attitude toward his criticism of my formula "redeemed in principle but not in fact." My friend Professor Kroner long ago convinced me that this was an inadequate way of doing justice to the fact that there is sin in the life of the redeemed, that is, to the Reformation principle *justus et peccator simul*. It is inadequate because it does not describe the real sanctification which takes place in conversion when the soul turns from itself to God.

I am not so sure that I would want to accept his criticism of my attitude toward the Church without at least a motion of defense. I think I have increasingly recognized the value of the Church as a community of grace which, despite historic corruptions, has the "oracles of God," as St. Paul said about Israel. The Church is the one place in history where life is kept open for the final word of God's judgment to break the pride of men and for the word of God's mercy to lift up the brokenhearted. Inasmuch as this has been only a growing recognition, Professor Wolf's criticism is justified. But when I see how much new evil comes into life through the pretension of the religious community, through its conventional and graceless legalism and through religious fanaticism, I am concerned that my growing appreciation of the Church should not betray me into this complacency.

Professor Richardson really disagrees with me on only one point: the subject of miracles, on which he is an authority. He is not sure that he disagrees with me but he suspects me of holding a position similar to that of Bultmann, with whom he disagrees. I do not think that Bultmann makes a sufficient distinction between the prescientific myths and what I have elsewhere defined as the myths of permanent validity, without which it is not possible to describe the ultimate realities in conditions of the temporal world. But this distinction would not, I am sure, satisfy Professor Richardson. For he seems to hold that the essential Biblical picture of God's creation, judgment, and redemption is dependent upon faith in miracles. He declares, "God did create the world," even though the creation myths are prescientific. I would add that the idea of creation is valid beyond any concepts of natural or rational causation. It points to a mystery of divine freedom beyond all schemes of rational intelligibility. Professor Richardson adds, "and Man did fall from grace," but it is not clear whether he holds that idea valid only in relation to the Fall as an actual historical event. I think the idea of the Fall is essential to the Christian message and to an understanding of the human situation; but I do not think its validity depends upon the idea of the Fall as a historical event. I would add, "and God was in Christ reconciling the world unto Himself"; but I do not think that this revelation gains its validity from the story of the virgin birth. The problem of the resurrection of Christ is of course more crucial. It is the only point where there is a real issue. I cannot follow Professor Richardson, however, when he gives the assurance that modern historical scholarship does not call this "miracle" into question. My impression was that historical scholarship seemed to indicate that the story of the empty tomb was an afterthought and that the really attested historical fact was the experience of the risen Christ among his various disciples. I accept that fact together with the certainty that the Church was founded upon the assurance that Christ was indeed risen. Again, I do not think that the failure to regard the story of the empty tomb as well authenticated changes the Biblical message as much as Professor Richardson thinks, or that it reduces the Christian faith merely to a philosophy. The Christian faith will never be that as long as it grasps by faith the "mighty acts of God" as points of illumination in which the purposes of God are revealed within the flux of history.

Professor Lehmann has given an appreciative account of the centrality of my Christological interest and of the development of my thought in the direction of a more adequate Christology than the old liberalism with which I began. I can only concur in his conclusions and confess to the shortcomings which he implies but does not explicitly state. The situation is that I have come gradually to realize that it is possible to look at the human situation without illusion and without despair only from the standpoint of the Christ-revelation. It has come to be more and more the ultimate truth. If it is reduced to something other than its Scriptural content, if, for instance, Jesus is revered as an exemplary man and example, all the confusions and sentimentalities of secular idealism are multiplied. I have come to know with Pascal that only in "simplicity of the Gospel" is it possible to measure the full "dignity" and the "misery" of man. Thus the Christological center of my thought has become more explicit and more important. But, as Professor Lehmann declares, I have never pretended to be a theologian, and so I have elaborated the Christological theme only in the context of inquiries about human nature and human history.

Professor Lehmann makes one explicit criticism. He thinks my approach does not do justice to the divine initiative and to "God's mighty acts." I wonder whether this criticism may not be due to my use of "myth" in describing the transcendent significance of Jesus. The word has subjective and skeptical connotations. I am sorry I ever used it, particularly since the project for "demythologizing" the Bible has been undertaken and bids fair to reduce the Biblical revelation to eternally valid truths without any existential encounters between God and man.

Professor Löwith's criticism succinctly explicates the difference between our conceptions, as developed more fully in his *Meaning of History* and my *Faith and History*. The difference is essentially that Professor Löwith finds no tangents of meaning in the historical drama which are clarified by Christian revelation. He seems to me to be saying that the drama is "full of sound and fury, signifying nothing," and that only revelation and salvation rescue life from meaninglessness. I know how easily any "Christian" interpretation of history can give it false meanings, analogous to the false meanings elaborated by Hegel or other philosophers. I know that Christ is the "light that shineth in darkness." The question between us is how absolute the darkness is. If it is as dark as he assumes, there cannot be any relevance between faith and our life as historical creatures. Professor Löwith says that responsibility is a moral and not a religious category. Is this distinction absolute? Is there no wisdom in the Christian faith which might prevent a powerful nation and a secure culture from plunging into catastrophe by its pride? Or which would prevent individual Christians from fleeing into complete irresponsibility about the fate of their civilization?

We ought to be quite clear what is at stake in this issue. If we declare "history" to be totally meaningless, we also absolve the individual of responsibility for the health of the various collective enterprises, cultures, and civilizations which make up the stuff of history. The Christian faith is reduced to a purely individual transcendence over a very inscrutable collective life. I cannot see this as the meaning of New Testament faith, even though "world history" is not specifically mentioned in the Bible. Incidentally, it is worth remembering that the Bible contains both Old and New Testaments. In the Old Testament the prophets are certainly concerned with the sovereignty of God over the history of all the nations, and over the problem of whether the historical drama has any meaning. They assert that it has meaning which will be clarified in the Messianic Age.

In regard to Professor Fitch's criticism of my position on the moral law, which he thinks unduly critical of "natural law" concepts, I can only say that I agree with him perfectly that the criticism must be directed only against too detailed and too inflexible "rules" of conduct, and not against certain abiding principles of justice. I had sought to make this distinction, but my polemic against rigid natural-law conceptions may have obscured my point.

My colleague, Professor Scherer, attributes so much more homiletical skill to me than I possess that I am inclined to accept any criticisms of my method out of hand. I think, for instance, that he is right in suggesting that I have, in the past at least, placed so much emphasis on the analysis of the human situation that I did not have time to preach a positive answer to the human predicament. Also, I dwelt so extensively upon the divine judgment that the divine mercy came short. In my own mind these emphases seemed important at the time because for a good part of my ministry the state of our culture was such that the Christian faith was regarded as completely irrelevant. I sought to establish its relevance by these analyses and therefore became preoccupied with the apologetic task and temper akin to Schleiermacher's address on religion to its intellectual despisers. I think now that a more positive message would have been preferable, though I still don't know how one may strike a right balance between the task of finding the "point of contact" and preaching the Gospel. Dr. Scherer is also critical of the freedom of my interpretation of Scripture. I don't think I ever used allegory in my interpretation and I was equally critical of far-fetched analogies. But I admit that the Pauline text, "as deceivers, yet true," did not originally contemplate the problem of the element of deception in religious symbols. That may be stretching a text too far. I confess that a revered colleague and chief, Dr. Henry Sloane Coffin, through his very Biblical sermons, which availed themselves of quite free interpretations of text, particularly from the Old Testament, may have influenced me in this regard, though I must not make him responsible for any of my failings.

"SUBSTANTIVE CRITICISMS"

Professor Williams thinks my characterizations of "liberalism" and "liberal Christianity" are too sweeping and inexact, and he is right; because I did define liberalism too consistently in terms of its American versions. Liberalism placed its confidence in the virtue of rational man and in the fact of historical development. These two facets of liberalism were not identical but they were interlaced. In America liberalism was usually associated with a historical optimism which was not characteristic, for instance, of the theology of Albrecht Ritschl, who was a theological offshoot of Kantian philosophy. When Professor Williams names names I am embarrassed. For instance, he names Professor Hocking as "liberal," and I have never had any consciousness of any serious difference with Professor Hocking's viewpoint, though his thought developed more in the context of an idealistic philosophy while I became increasingly oriented by Biblical modes of thought. On the other hand, if Professor Williams cites the thought of the distinguished "religious naturalist" Professor Wieman to disprove my accusation that liberalism is too optimistic about human nature, he is in error. Professor Wieman is indeed no optimist, but I don't think that Professor Williams considers sufficiently my thesis that while the prevailing mood of modern culture is optimistic, there is a subordinate mood of pessimism, illustrated, for instance, in one facet of Freud's thought. I sought to expound Pascal's thesis that the "philosophers" either tell man about his "dignity" and tempt him to pride, or they see his "misery" and drive him to despair.

There are a series of criticisms by Professor Williams which have to do with the relation between the eschatological and the historical in Christian thought. These criticisms are probably substantive rather than peripheral. I think Professor Williams misconceives my position. He thinks I ascribe meaning only to the "ultimate" and look too much beyond history rather than in history, and that ethically I make too sharp a distinction between "sacrificial" and "mutual" love. All the points are various aspects of the same problem. Professor Williams thinks they mean an attack by me upon the inclination of liberalism to find "meaning" in the ongoing tasks and processes of history. My point, on the other hand, is that the whole of modern culture tries too desperately to contain the ultimate within the fragmentary tasks and possibilities of history. I have never criticized a statesman for responsibly seeking to maintain a tolerable peace or establish a tolerable justice. I have criticized the Christian perfectionist who either claimed that these tasks could be accomplished more perfectly by the "love method" or who have sought to prove that their love was "perfect," even if they had to disavow responsibilities to preserve its perfection. I have never insisted on a sharp distinction between sacrificial love and mutual love, that is, between the love which is, and which is not, reciprocated and historically justified. I have only criticized the tendency to identify these two facets of love completely, so that the New Testament ethic is reduced to the limits of a prudential ethic, according to which we are counseled to forgive our foe because he will then cease to be our foe; and are promised that if suffering love becomes sufficiently general it will cease to be "suffering" and change society into a harmony of life in which no one need suffer. The relation between sacrificial love and mutual love contains the issue of the relation between the eschatological and the historical in a nutshell. Love, heedless of the self, must be the initiator of any reciprocal love. Otherwise the calculation of mutual advantages makes love impossible. But heedless love usually wins a response of love. That is a symbol of the moral content of history. But this response cannot be guaranteed, as modern thought sought erroneously to guarantee it. That is symbolic of the "tragic" dimension of history and a proof that the meaning of life always transcends the fulfillments of meaning in history. That is why Christian faith is "eschatological" and has a touch of "otherworldliness," which one cannot eliminate by trying to contain all facets of meaning in the processes of history.

I do not know whether Professor Carnell would regard his criticism of my thought as substantive; but I do not, because he agrees with me up to the point of verifying the Christian faith in the experience of redemption. He is afraid that at that point I become "subjective" because I regard the experience of divine judgment and forgiveness as validated by the actual fruits of "love, joy and peace" and the grace of a new life in Christ which issues from this experience. This is an important issue. I don't think Professor Carnell's apprehensions about subjectivism are justified because, if I understand the matter correctly, subjectivism means that one finds "God" in the deepest level of selfhood and takes divine forgiveness to mean some kind of "self-acceptance." I believe this kind of "subjectivism" has corrupted much of liberal Christianity and that it is important to insist on the Biblical idea that the soul encounters God as the "divine other," if not the "wholly other." The personal encounter in religious experience is determined by the pattern set in the revelation in Christ and would not be conceivable without this revelation. The experience is "subjective" only in the sense that the forgiveness of God must be appropriated in repentance, trust, and commitment, involving the whole of the self. Any liberalism which transmutes the experience into a philosophical proposition which can be intellectually accepted, and any Biblicism which changes belief from repentance and commitment to the mere acceptance of historical propositions, equally rob the experience of its resource of "wisdom and power."

Professor Carnell is concerned to know upon what basis one can maintain the absoluteness of the Christian faith while recognizing the relativity of any formulation of the meaning of the faith and the corruption of the experience to which it may be subject. My answer is that the faith proves its absoluteness precisely where its insights make it possible to detect the relativity of the interpretations and to question the validity of any claim, including our own, that we have been redeemed. At those points it is proved that faith has discerned and is in contact with the "true" God and not with some idol of our imagination.

I appreciate Father Weigel's friendly essay the more because my frequent accusations against what seems to me to be the "pretension" and the "intolerance" of the Church must seem very trying. Father Weigel neatly brings the whole issue to a head in his statement that either the Church or I am arrogant and one must take one's choice between the pretension of the private individual and that of a great historic institution which has been the treasury of the "oracles of God." This is a "palpable hit" which may well leave the private critic reeling.

Of course, every individual is in the same predicament with regard to this contrast and what is at stake is the whole Reformation insistence on the right of private judgment and on the "priesthood of all believers." Luther was certainly very impertinent and arrogant when he defied the Church; and every Catholic history has enlarged upon the degree of Luther's arrogance.

Father Weigel, however, believes Protestants of our day are in an even more precarious position than the Reformers because we do not regard the Bible as so absolute an authority as the Reformers did. I would question whether there is much difference between Luther's position that the "Bible is the cradle of Christ," and therefore authoritative for us, and our position. I acknowledge, however, that the difference between Calvinistic conceptions and our own is considerable. But even the most extreme fundamentalist exercises the right of interpreting and applying Scripture, and in that sense is involved in the hazard of private judgment. On the other hand the Catholic Church has, by the assertion of the authority of the Church in all matters of doctrine, maintained a monolithic unity which must be, in some respects, the envy of all Christians, particularly when they survey the chaotic condition of our denominational life and are also compelled to concede that the substance of the Christian truth is dissipated from time to time to such an extent by the capitulation of Christian people and their leaders to every form of popular culture which strikes the imagination as plausible in a particular era and then vanishes again. Thus Protestantism has been affected by various philosophies, Kantian, Hegelian, or Marxist; and by the determinism of psychological and social sciences in such a way that the truth of the Gospel has been greatly imperiled. In comparison, the Catholic Church has always preserved some substance of the Gospel truth. We Protestants must concede this advantage and recognize that the Church is in consequence always a genuine source of grace to individual souls, whatever might be the corruptions which are consequent upon its collective arrogance. But we Protestants are not merely capricious and arrogant if we nevertheless refuse to purchase this unity and this preservation of the kernel of the Gospel at the price demanded. That price is to lift a historic institution into a trans-historic reality, making the claim of speaking for God, of being privy to the divine will, and of dispensing the divine grace. That claim is in our opinion a very great heresy, perhaps as great as the more overt heresies which destroy the substance of the Gospel truth in Protestantism. It prevents the Church from recognizing that there is a very great difference between the Biblical affirmation that the Church is the "body of Christ" and the claim that it is an extension of the "Incarnation." The second assertion leaves out of account the actuality that the Church, no less than the individual, is subject to the fact that there is "a law in its members which wars against the law that is in its mind." I need not enlarge upon the baneful consequences which follow upon the pretension of absolute authority and the possession of absolute truth in various fields, including the fields of politics and morals, in which the Church, an interested party in the contests of history, claims to be a transcendent god-like force only intent upon arbitrating these conflicts of interests. It is a significant fact that the Catholic Church in particular, and the Christian Church in general, have never fully understood or heeded the prophetic affirmation that "judgment begins in the house of God." No matter, therefore, how much we may admire or envy the Catholic Church, we are prepared to pay the price necessary for the freedom of the individual conscience and the freedom to contradict even a very imposing institution, suggesting that it is in danger of ascribing human prejudices to the divine.

I don't think that the danger of individual pretension and arrogance is quite as great as Father Weigel suggests. All who have become Christian will find their own convictions formed by the witness of the whole Christian Church through the ages, beginning with the witness of Scripture, including, of course, the Scripture which gives us the witness of the Church before the Church; namely, Israel. A responsible theologian, as distinguished from an irresponsible speculator, will think and live within the discipline of this Church, though he will feel free to correct what seem to him to be errors of the past. He will be under the corresponding hazard of propagating more grievous errors than he may have corrected.

The growth of the ecumenical movement among the non-Roman churches proves that the confusion of liberty is being overcome and that it is possible to exercise liberty in faith within a very broad consensus. This movement will not of itself prevent essential heresy from arising, by which I mean positions which challenge the very substance of the Gospel message. But an ecumenical consensus will gradually eliminate the local and parochial corruptions which have been introduced into Christian history by particular events, partial emphases, and undue preoccupation with portions of the Gospel message. It should be mentioned in conclusion that any lingering envy which many of us may have had for the Roman Catholic unity has recently been dispelled by the consistent effort of the Church to change the very basis of the Gospel message and to exalt the Virgin Mary until she has become a virtual replacement for the Holy Spirit in the Trinity.

There is no resolution of the conflict between these two forms of Christianity. From the standpoint of Catholicism, Protestantism is corrupted by anarchy, and the Gospel is endangered by all kinds of heresies at the fringes of its life. From the standpoint of Protestantism, the Catholic Church has an impressive trans-national unity and preserves some of the essential affirmations of the Gospel. But the price of this unity is an assertion which we must regard as essentially heretical: it is the affirmation that the Church, a historical institution, is divine. The distance between God and man, of which the prophets were so conscious, is thus obscured. Catholics must undoubtedly find our various heresies very trying. But we must confess on our part that it is not easy to be confronted on every hand with the claims of absolute truth and sometimes by the pretensions of superior virtue and justice.

I must add that I am puzzled by Father Weigel's assertion that I believe in the Trinity and in the Divinity of Christ "symbolically but not literally." I do not know how it is possible to believe in anything pertaining to God and eternity "literally." But I do not equate "symbolically" with "subjectively." Father Weigel cannot be expected to follow all the nuances of Protestant theology. Therefore he equates my ideas with those of Bultmann. I think on the other hand that Bultmann does not distinguish rigorously between pre-scientific myths and permanently valid symbols.

I suppose the most substantive differences in this volume are between my thought and that of Professor Wieman. I suspect that he would be ready to admit that he disagrees not so much with my particular interpretation of the Christian faith as with any classical statement of that faith, which he views from the standpoint of what he defines as "religious naturalism."

Before stating the crux of the differences between us, I should like to clear up some misconceptions in Professor Wieman's mind in regard to my position. I have never maintained that the corruption of sin is "in reason." I have asserted that it is in the self and that a self-centered self is able to use reason for its own ends; which is why there is no protection in reason as such against sin. I have also not been scornful of reason in all of its aspects in reaching the truth. I have agreed with Kant in finding logic a provisional instrument of morals insofar as the logical principle in reason may prompt the self to consider its ends in terms of their relationship with a total and coherent system of ends. Naturally I would not dispense with every analytical power of reason to analyze and chart the coherences and sequences of every type of reality. Professor Wieman has unconsciously misconceived all of these emphases because of a preconception that anyone who is critical of "reason" must be an obscurantist who trusts "blind faith" in place of reason. My criticisms against rationalism have been on two points: that it regards reason as the source of virtue and by inference places the source of evil in the subrational vitalities of the self. This error, derived originally from classical interpretations, is at the basis of many Christian and non-Christian heresies in the interpretation of man. The fundamental Biblical, and I think true, proposition about man's evil is that its root is in the self and not in the mind or in the body. When Augustine places it in the self's will, he insists also that the self expresses itself in its will.

Professor Wieman is also in error in suggesting that I have a purely "utilitarian" attitude toward faith. He thinks this is dangerous, though he is not warning against the particular "utility" which interests me. I confess that I do not quite know what he means by "utilitarian." Is it, for instance, "utilitarian" to use an instrument for the achievement of truth?

But perhaps it is better to get at the crux of the disagreement between us, for these incidental differences or misconceptions are but facets of the underlying disagreement. Professor Wieman believes in God. That is, he believes in a "process" which he call "God." He is a very religious man; and he has a religious attitude toward this process. I should prefer less reverence toward the process, for it is in fact ambiguous; and there is no room in it either for the human or for the divine person. Professor Wieman identifies this process with "nature," but that is only because all modern naturalism defines every form of reality as "nature." Neither Professor Wieman nor other modern naturalists would reduce the whole drama of history to natural process as simply as the French Enlightenment did. But they do not understand the distinctive character of the human person, particularly its radical freedom over natural necessity. They therefore do not understand why coherence should not be a final test of truth. Incidentally, Professor Wieman's statement that I have a completely incomprehensible faith in a God "above the structures of existence" does not quite get at the heart of the matter. God is certainly in the structures and temporal processes just as the human person is "in" its organism. But both the human and the divine person possess a freedom over and above the processes and structures. That is why we as persons know each other partly by making a "scientific" analysis of the processes which bear us; but it is also why we do not know each other as persons who are more than temporal processes except by faith and love, and why we cannot know God except in the same terms.

The trouble with religious naturalism is not only that it obscures the whole mystery of the divine, the mystery of creativity and grace, but that it also falsifies the whole drama of human history with its increasing heights of good and evil and in the paradoxical relation of persons to this drama. For persons are both the creatures and the creators of the process. Professor Wieman is under the impression that a classical Christian faith is merely a crude, pre-scientific way of looking at the world, God, and the self. He, with the help of modern science and the ontology of Dewey and Whitehead (more Dewey than Whitehead, for Whitehead did understand the mystery of creation beyond the temporal process and consequently agonized about the relation of the "primordial" to the "consequent" God), will construct a more adequate view of God and the world. He will define either the temporal process itself as God, or that part of it which is value-creating. Since Hitler's day he is not so certain that the process of "integration" is of itself "value-creating."

No one could deny that this picture of the self and of God, of the world and of history is more "rational" than the Christian picture in the sense that its coherences are neater and that its mystery has been abolished from the realm of meaning, the latter being reduced to rational intelligibility on the lowest level of a scientific account of "nature."

The only trouble with the picture is that all significant truths and facts about man and God, about the nobility and the misery of human freedom, and about the judgment and mercy of God, are left out of the picture. Thus a culture which prides itself on its "empiricism" obscures and denies every "fact" which does not fit into its frame of meaning. The frame of meaning is determined on the one hand by the concept of "nature" or the "temporal process," and on the other hand by the so-called "scientific method" which ironically enough is meant to ascertain the "facts." Unfortunately, there are some "facts" which escape the "method." The irrationality of this cult of "reason" is that it merely denies the reality of any fact which does not fit into its conception of rational coherence.

I appreciate Professor Burtt's friendly questions to me and I shall try to answer them in order. The questions are put from the standpoint of a sensitive religious syncretism, partly influenced by Professor Burtt's sympathy for Buddhism, the study of which has engaged him so much.

Professor Burtt wants to know how I can speak of a "Biblical" view of God or of man or of sin when the Bible has many layers of truth and sometimes conflicting ideas. I would not deny this, but I believe nevertheless that there is a "Biblical" faith of great consistency and uniqueness which must be distinguished from both classical rationalism and Oriental mysticism. Professer Burtt raises the question whether there is a Biblical view of sin, and points to the fact that there are at least two views, one of them being derived from the body-spirit dualism, which attributes evil to the body. This is a shrewd question because there is, in fact, a subordinate dualism in the history of Christian thought which attributes evil to the body and regards ascetic flagellations of physical passion as means of salvation. Professor Burtt thinks this dualism is derived from the Pauline concept of the "flesh warring against the spirit." I think he is in error in this contention. At least the best Biblical scholarship seems agreed that Paul means by "carnally minded" the self seeking itself. The two great Pauline theologians of Christian history, Augustine and Luther, certainly never interpreted the Pauline concepts in terms of Platonic dualism, whether they defined sin as *amor sui* or as *concupiscentia*, as self-love or as lust. Even lust, according to Luther, is not simply physical passion but self-regard. I think there is a consistent interpretation of sin in the Bible from the story of the Fall through the prophets to the Pauline definition in Romans I: "They [men] change the glory of the incorruptible God into the image of corruptible man and worship the creature rather than the Creator." This consistent interpretation does not, of course, exclude the fact that a subordinate interpretation, drawn from body-mind dualism, has always persisted in Christian thought and that it was partially nourished by Pauline concepts of the flesh warring against the spirit.

Professor Burtt also questions me about the fact that I assume the Christian revelation as the source of truth and am not therefore able to do justice to the truth in other religions. I would say in answer that every religious or philosophical faith is an existential commitment. This commitment must not be restrictive so that it would prevent us from recognizing truth and grace in other lives with other commitments. I believe him when he finds the Buddhism which he has studied generating love perhaps more gracious in specific instances than any love manifested in a Christian's life. But there is still the question of truth; and if one believes, one is bound to testify to the truth. I believe that the Christian faith illumines the truth about man and God; about man's freedom, responsibility and sin; and about the grace which makes the freedom tolerable and which overcomes the sin. This I hold to be the truth in comparison with the Buddhist faith which ultimately involves the annulment of the ego as the way of salvation.

His final question has to do with my opposition to pacifism. He thinks that Eastern thought will correct the dynamism of Western life and will show that Western life has not sufficiently incorporated the love ethic. I have spent a good part of my life validating the love ethic as final on the one hand, and trying to prove on the other hand that it must and can include all the discriminate judgments and commitments which we may broadly define as commitments in the cause of justice. That these commitments may involve us at times in war, and that at all times they involve us in moral ambiguity, must be recognized if an ethic of justice is not to degenerate into a merely political ethic. On the other hand I am certain that an ethic of love which dispenses with the structures and commitments of justice is ultimately irrelevant to the collective life of man. I do not think that Gandhi, to whom Burtt refers, has taught us anything new on this perplexing problem. He made the pretension of sainthood into an instrument of political power. That may have seemed plausible in the environment of India, but it must be ultimately intolerable anywhere.

Fortunately, we have two contributions from Jewish sources. Rabbi Burnstein finds my interpretation of human nature at variance with "normative Judaism." I suspect that he interprets "normative Judaism" in its modern optimistic version not dissimilar from what many Christians would call the optimism of "normative Christianity." If Dr. Heschel had not contributed his paper, I should have been inclined to question Rabbi Burnstein on his interpretation of the Psalms and the Prophets, but not to challenge him on the interpretation of human nature in Judaism; however, Dr. Heschel has in my opinion refuted his position and has piled up a great deal of evidence which has been very instructive to me on the similarities between Christianity and Judaism on this issue, even in the post-Biblical period.

I am deeply grateful to all the contributors to this volume for the great care that they have taken in analyzing various facets of my thought, and for the fairness that they have shown in criticizing it. I sincerely hope that I have learned a great deal from their analyses and their criticism, and that if I have a few years of creative work left, my thought may reveal the profit which I have gained from their criticism.

REINHOLD NIEBUHR

UNION THEOLOGICAL SEMINARY
NEW YORK CITY

IV

BIBLIOGRAPHY OF THE WRITINGS OF REINHOLD NIEBUHR

BIBLIOGRAPHY OF THE WRITINGS OF REINHOLD NIEBUHR

Reinhold Niebuhr's works prior to 1956, as listed in the first edition of this book, were voluminous. They included fifteen books and a great body of occasional writings published in more than seventy magazines and journals. Professor D. B. Robertson of Berea College prepared that first bibliography, and he has now brought it up to date (in this edition), i.e., to the time of Niebuhr's death. With a record of reviews, translations, etc., a complete bibliography constitutes a small book in itself. Indeed, just that was published by G. K. Hall & Company of Boston, Massachusetts but is now out of stock. This makes the present bibliography below all the more valuable. Professor Robertson points out that lack of space in this book requires the omission of a number of items, e.g., the titles of editorials that appeared in *Radical Religion, Christianity and Society*, and *Christianity and Crisis*, as well as the weekly column Niebuhr wrote for Religious News Service. We are grateful for this first complete though necessarily selective bibliography.

C. W. K.

BOOKS BY REINHOLD NIEBUHR

Does Civilization Need Religion? A Study in the Social Resources and Limitations of Religion in Modern Life (New York: The Macmillan Company, 1927).

Leaves from the Notebook of a Tamed Cynic (Chicago: Willett, Clark & Colby, 1929).

The Contribution of Religion to Social Work (New York: Columbia University Press, 1932).

Moral Man and Immoral Society: A Study in Ethics and Politics (New York: Charles Scribner's Sons, 1932).

Reflections on the End of an Era (New York: Charles Scribner's Sons, 1934).

An Interpretation of Christian Ethics (New York: Harper & Brothers, 1935).

Beyond Tragedy: Essays on the Christian Interpretation of History (New York: Charles Scribner's Sons, 1937).

Christianity and Power Politics (New York: Charles Scribner's Sons, 1940).

The Nature and Destiny of Man: A Christian Interpretation, Vol. I, *Human Nature* (New York: Charles Scribner's Sons, 1941).

The Nature and Destiny of Man: A Christian Interpretation, Vol. II, *Human Destiny* (New York: Charles Scribner's Sons, 1943). (Since 1949 Scribner's has been printing a one-volume edition of these Gifford Lectures.)

The Children of Light and the Children of Darkness: A Vindication of Democracy and a Critique of Its Traditional Defense (New York: Charles Scribner's Sons, 1944).

Discerning the Signs of the Times: Sermons for Today and Tomorrow (New York: Charles Scribner's Sons, 1946).

Faith and History: A Comparison of Christian and Modern Views of History (New York: Charles Scribner's Sons, 1949).

The Irony of American History (New York: Charles Scribner's Sons, 1952).

Christian Realism and Political Problems (New York: Charles Scribner's Sons, 1953).

The Self and the Dramas of History (New York: Charles Scribner's Sons, 1955).

Pious and Secular America. New York: Charles Scribner's Sons, 1958.

The Structure of Nations and Empires, A Study of the Recurring Patterns and Problems of the Political Order in Relation to the Unique Problems of the Nuclear Age. New York: Charles Scribner's Sons, 1959.

A Nation So Conceived, Reflections on the History of America from Its Early Visions to Its Present Power (with Alan Heimert). New York: Charles Scribner's Sons, 1963.

Man's Nature and His Communities, Essays on the Dynamics and Enigmas of Man's Personal and Social Existence. New York: Charles Scribner's Sons, 1965.

The Democratic Experience, Past and Prospects (with Paul E. Sigmund). New York: Frederick A. Praeger, 1969.

ESSAYS AND ARTICLES BY REINHOLD NIEBUHR

Journal Abbreviations

NR	*The New Republic*	RR	*Radical Religion*
WT	*The World Tomorrow*	CS	*Christianity and Society*
N	*The Nation*	CC	*Christianity and Crisis*
CCY	*The Christian Century*	NL	*The New Leader*

1916

"Failure of German-Americanism," *Atlantic Monthly* (July, 1916), Vol. 118, pp. 13–18.

"The Nation's Crime Against the Individual," *Atlantic Monthly* (Nov., 1916), Vol. 118, pp. 609–614.

1920

"The Church and the Industrial Crisis," *The Biblical World* (Nov., 1920), 54, 588–592.

"Religion's Limitations," *The World Tomorrow* (March, 1920), 3, 77–79.

1921

"Heroes and Hero Worship," *The Nation* (Feb. 23, 1921), 112, 293–294.

1922

"The Church and the Middle Class," *The Christian Century* (Dec. 7, 1922), 39, 1513–1515.

1923

"The Paradox of Institutions," *The World Tomorrow* (Aug., 1923), 6, 231–232.

"Protestantism in Germany," *The Christian Century* (Oct. 4, 1923), 40, 1258–1260.

"Wanted: A Christian Morality," *The Christian Century* (Feb. 15, 1923), 40, 201–203.

"Youth Movement of Germany," *The Christian Century* (Nov. 1, 1923), 40, 1396–1397.

1924

"Christianity and Contemporary Politics," *The Christian Century* (April 17, 1924), 41, 498–501.

"European Reform and American Reform: How They Differ," *The Christian Century* (Aug. 28, 1924), 41, 1108–1110.

"The German Klan," *The Christian Century* (Oct. 16, 1924), 41, 1330–1331.

"Is Protestantism Self-Deceived?" *The Christian Century* (Dec. 25, 1924), 41, 1661–1662.

"What Are the Churches Advertising?" *The Christian Century* (Nov. 27, 1924), 41, 1532–1533.

1925

"Can Christianity Survive?" *Atlantic Monthly* (Jan., 1925), 135, 84–88.

"Can Schweitzer Save Us from Russell?" *The Christian Century* (Sept. 3, 1925), 42, 1093–1095.

"Capitalism: Protestant Offspring," *The Christian Century* (May 7, 1925), 42, 600–601.

"Germany and Modern Civilization," *Atlantic Monthly* (June, 1925), 135, 843–848.

"Shall We Proclaim the Truth or Search for It?" *The Christian Century* (March 12, 1925), 42, 344–346.

1926

"Does Religion Quiet or Disquiet?" *The World Tomorrow* (Nov., 1926), 9, 220–221.

"How Philanthropic Is Henry Ford?" *The Christian Century* (Dec. 9, 1926), 43, 1516–1517.

"Our Secularized Civilization," *The Christian Century* (April 22, 1926), 43, 508–510.

"Puritanism and Prosperity," *Atlantic Monthly* (June, 1926), 137, 721–725.

"Reverend Doctor Silke," *The Christian Century* (March 11, 1926), 43, 316–318.

"The Threat of the R.O.T.C.," *The World Tomorrow* (Oct., 1926), 9, 154–156.

1927

"Beauty as a Substitute for Righteousness," *The Christian Century* (Sept. 29, 1927), 44, 1133–1134.

"A Critique of Pacifism," *Atlantic Monthly* (May, 1927), 139, 637–641.

"Ford's Five-Day Week Shrinks," *The Christian Century* (June 9, 1927), 44, 713–714.

"Missions and World Peace," *The World Tomorrow* (April, 1927), 10, 170–171.

"The Practical Unbelief of Modern Civilization," in *Religion on the Campus*, ed. by F. P. Miller, New York: Association Press, 1927.

"A Religion Worth Fighting For," *Survey* (Aug. 1, 1927), 58, 444–446.

"Students and the Religion of Today," in *A Survey of Our Student Life and of the Present Religious Situation As It Affects American Students*, by

Reinhold Niebuhr, Bruce Curry, and G. A. Studdert-Kennedy, at the National Student Conference, Milwaukee, Dec. 28, 1926–Jan. 1, 1927.

"To Whom Shall We Go?—Sermon," *The Christian Century* (March 10, 1927), 44, 299–301.

"Why I Am Not a Christian," *The Christian Century* (Dec. 15, 1927), 44, 1482–1483.

1928

"Barth—Apostle of the Absolute," *The Christian Century* (Dec. 13, 1928), 45, 1523–1524.

"The Confession of a Tired Radical," *The Christian Century* (Aug. 30, 1928), 45, 1046–1047.

"Oriental vs. Occidental Strategy of Life," *The World Tomorrow* (Jan., 1928), 11, 21–23.

"Pacifism and the Use of Force," *The World Tomorrow* (May, 1928), 11, 218–220.

"Protestantism and Prohibition," *The New Republic* (Oct. 24, 1928), 56, 265–267.

"What the War Did to My Mind," *The Christian Century* (Sept. 27, 1928), 45, 1161–1163.

"Why We Need a New Economic Order," *The World Tomorrow* (Oct., 1928), 11, 395–398.

"Would Jesus Be a Churchman Today?" *The World Tomorrow* (Dec., 1928), 11, 492–494.

1929

"Christianity and Redemption," in *Whither Christianity?* pp. 110–122, ed. by L. H. Hough (New York: Harpers, 1929).

"It Was a Sermon on Love," *The Christian Century* (Dec. 11, 1929), 46, 1540–1542.

"The Minister as an Expert," in *Effective Preaching*, pp. 81–92 (Boston University School of Theology, Conference on Preaching, 1929).

"The Perils of American-European Relationships," in J. H. Holmes, the Community Pulpit Series, No. 11, 1928–1929.

"Political Action and Social Change," *The World Tomorrow* (Dec., 1929), 12, 491–493.

"Religion and Moral Experience," in pamphlet entitled "What Religion Means to Me," by Reinhold Niebuhr, H. E. Fosdick, A. B. Curry, E. F. Tittle, *et al.* (New York: Doubleday, Doran & Co., 1929).

"Senator Norris and His Clerical Critic," *The World Tomorrow* (April, 1929), 12, 169–170.

"The Terrible Beauty of the Cross," *The Christian Century* (March 21, 1929), 46, 386–388.

"The Unethical Character of Modern Civilization," in J. H. Holmes, the Community Pulpit Series, No. 10, 1928–1929.

"The Unhappy Intellectuals," *Atlantic Monthly* (June, 1929), 143, 790–794.

"The Use of Force," in *Pacifism in the Modern World*, ed. by Devere Allen (New York: Doubleday, Doran & Co., 1929).

"We Are Being Driven," *The Christian Century* (May 1, 1929), 46, 578–579.

"Would Jesus Be a Modernist Today?" *The World Tomorrow* (March, 1929), 12, 122–124.

1930

"At Oberammergau," *The Christian Century* (Aug. 13, 1930), 47, 983–984.

"Awkward Imperialists," *Atlantic Monthly* (May, 1930), 145, 670–675.

"Christian Faith in the Modern World," Introduction to *Ventures in Belief*, ed. by H. P. Van Dusen (New York: Charles Scribner's Sons, 1930).

"Church Currents in Germany," *The Christian Century* (Aug. 6, 1930), 47, 959–960.

"Church in Russia," *The Christian Century* (Sept. 24, 1930), 47, 1144-1146.

"Europe's Religious Pessimism," *The Christian Century* (Aug. 27, 1930), 47, 1031–1033.

"The German Crisis," *The Nation* (Oct. 1, 1930), 131, pp. 358, 360.

"Germany Wrestles with Her Debts," *The Christian Century* (July 30, 1930), 47, 935–936.

"Glimpses of the Southland," *The Christian Century* (July 16, 1930), 47, 893–894.

"If You Were President—How Would You Proclaim Thanksgiving?" *The Christian Century* (Nov. 26, 1930), 47, 1452.

"Is Stewardship Ethical?" *The Christian Century* (April 30, 1930), 47, 555–557.

"The Land of Extremes," *The Christian Century* (Oct. 15, 1930), 47, 1241–1243.

"Mechanical Men in a Mechanical Age," *The World Tomorrow* (Dec., 1930), 13, 492–495.

"Political Action and Social Change," in *A New Economic Order*, ed. by Kirby Page (New York: Harcourt, Brace & Co., 1930).

"The Preaching of Repentance," *The Christian Century* (June 18, 1930), 47, 779–781.

"Russia Makes the Machine Its God," *The Christian Century* (Sept. 10, 1930), 47, 1080–1081.

"Russian Efficiency," *The Christian Century* (Oct. 1, 1930), 47, 1178–1180.

"Russia's Tractor Revolution," *The Christian Century* (Sept. 17, 1930), 47, 1111–1112.

"The Speculation Mania," *The World Tomorrow* (Jan., 1930), 13, 25–27.

"The Spirit of Life," *Addresses and Proceedings of The National Educational Association of the United States,* 1930, pp. 610–618.

1931

"An American Approach to the Christian Message," in *A Traffic in Knowledge*, ed. by W. A. Visser 'T Hooft, pp. 54–85 (London: S.C.M. Press, 1931).

"A Comment on 'Barthianism and the Kingdom,'" an article by E. G. Homrighausen, *The Christian Century* (July 15, 1931), 48, 924–925.

"The Common Root of Joy and Pain," in *What Can Students Believe?* pp. 129–138, ed. by E. M. McKee (New York: R. R. Smith, 1931).

"Crisis in British Socialism," *The Christian Century* (Sept. 30, 1931), 48, 1202–1204.

"The Crisis of Society," *The Congregationalist and Herald of Gospel Liberty* (Aug. 27, 1931), 116, 1157–1159. Also published in *The Christian* (Sept. 5, 1931), 7, 682–684.

"Economic Perils to World Peace," *The World Tomorrow* (May, 1931), 14, 154–156.

"Let Liberal Churches Stop Fooling Themselves!" *The Christian Century* (March 25, 1931), 48, 402–404.

"Making Peace with Russia," *The World Tomorrow* (Nov., 1931), 14, 354–355.

"Property and the Ethical Life," *The World Tomorrow* (Jan., 1931), 14, 19–21.

"Radicalism and Religion," *The World Tomorrow* (Oct., 1931), 14, 324–327.

"The Religion of Communism," *Atlantic Monthly* (April, 1931), 147, 462–470.

"Socialism and Christianity," *The Christian Century* (Aug. 19, 1931), 48, 1038–1040.

"Toward a New Economic Society: A Program for Students by a Commission," Introduction by Reinhold Niebuhr, Student Christian Association Movement, Economics Commission, F. A. Henderson, Chairman (New York: Eddy & Page, c. 1931).

"The Weakness of the Modern Church," *The Christian Herald* (May, 1931), 10, 42–43.

"What Chance Has Gandhi?" *The Christian Century* (Oct. 14, 1931), 48, 1274–1276.

"When the Virtues are Vices," *The Christian Century* (Jan. 21, 1931), 48, 114–115.

1932

"Catastrophe or Social Control: The Alternatives for America," *Harper's* (June, 1932), 165, 114–118.

"The Ethic of Jesus and the Social Problem," *Religion in Life* (Spring, 1932), 1, 198–209.

"Germany—Prophecy of Western Civilization," *The Christian Century* (March 2, 1932), 49, 287–289.

"Is Peace or Justice the Goal? *The World Tomorrow* (Sept. 21, 1932), 15, 275–277.

"Moralists and Politics," *The Christian Century* (July 6, 1932), 49, 857–859.

"Must We Do Nothing?" A critique of article by H. Richard Niebuhr entitled "The Grace of Doing Nothing," *The Christian Century* (March 30, 1932), 49, 415–417.

"Perils of American Power," *Atlantic Monthly* (Jan., 1932), 149, 90–96.

"Religion and the Class War in Kentucky," *The Christian Century* (May 18, 1932); 49, 637–638.

"The Stakes in the Election," *The Christian Century* (Nov. 9, 1932), 49, 1379–1381.

1933

"After Capitalism—What?" *The World Tomorrow* (March 1, 1933), 16, 203–205.

"A Christian Philosophy of Compromise," *The Christian Century* (June 7, 1933), 50, 746–748. Discussion continued in issues of July 26 and Aug. 9.

"A Christmas Service in Retrospect," *The Christian Century* (Jan. 4, 1933), 50, 13–14.

"An Editorial Conversation" (with C. C. Morrison), *The Christian Century* (July 26, 1933), 50, 950–951. Continued in issue of Aug. 9, pp. 1006–1008.

"The Germans: Unhappy Philosophers in Politics," *The American Scholar* (Oct., 1933), 2, 409–419.

"Germany Must Be Told!" *The Christian Century* (Aug. 9, 1933), 50, 1014–1015.

"Hitlerism—A Devil's Brew," *The World Tomorrow* (April 19, 1933), 16, 369–370.

"Human Nature and Social Change," *The Christian Century* (March 15, 1933), 50, 363–364.

"Making Radicalism Effective," *The World Tomorrow* (Dec. 21, 1933), 16, 682–684.

"Marxism and Religion," *The World Tomorrow* (March 15, 1933), 16, 253–255.

"Nationalism, Socialism and Christianity," *The World Tomorrow* (Aug., 1933), 16, 469–470.

"A New Strategy for Socialists," *The World Tomorrow* (Aug. 31, 1933), 16, 490–492.

"Notes from a Berlin Diary," *The Christian Century* (July 5, 1933), 50, 872–873.

"Notes from a London Diary," *The Christian Century* (July 12 and 19, 1933), 50, 903–904; 927–929.

"The Opposition in Germany," *The New Republic* (June 28, 1933), 75, 169–171.

"Optimism and Utopianism," *The World Tomorrow* (Feb. 22, 1933), 16, 179–180.

"Religion and the New Germany," *The Christian Century* (June 28, 1933), 50, 843–845.

"A Reorientation of Radicalism," *The World Tomorrow* (July, 1933), 16, 443–444.

"Why German Socialism Crashed," *The Christian Century* (April 5, 1933), 50, 451–453.

1934

"Barthianism and Political Reaction," *The Christian Century* (June 6, 1934), 51, 757–759.

"The Church and Political Action," *The Christian Century* (Aug. 1, 1934), 51, 992–994.

"Churches in Germany," *The American Scholar* (Summer, 1934), 3, 344–351.

"Comment on an Appeal to the Socialist Party," *The World Tomorrow* (April 12, 1934), 17, 185–186.

"Comment on 'The Christian Cult of Violence,'" an article by Jerome Davis, *Religion in Life* (Summer, 1934), 3, 439–441.

"The Fellowship of Socialist Christians," *The World Tomorrow* (June 14, 1934), 17, 297–298.

"The Problem of Communist Religion," *The World Tomorrow* (July 26, 1934), 17, 378–379.

"Religion as a Source of Radicalism," *The Christian Century* (April 11, 1934), 51, 491–494.

"Shall We Seek World Peace or the Peace of America?" *The World Tomorrow* (March 15, 1934), 17, 132–133.

"Study in Black and White: A Reply" (to an article by E. E. Voelkel with the title "Study in Black and White"), *The Christian Century* (June 20, 1934), 51, 837.

"When Will Christians Stop Fooling Themselves?" *The Christian Century* (May 16, 1934), 51, 658–660.

"Why I Leave the F.O.R.," *The Christian Century* (Jan. 3, 1934), 51, 17–19.

1935

"Christianity in Its Relation to the Perennial and the Contemporary Man," *Religion in Life* (Autumn, 1935), 4, 551–558.

"Don't Preach Ideals in a Vacuum," *The American Friend* (May 30, 1935), 23, 208–209.

"Marx, Barth and Israel's Prophets," *The Christian Century* (Jan. 30, 1935), 52, 138–140.

"The Pathos of Liberalism," *The Nation* (Sept. 11, 1935), 141, 303–304.

"Radical Religion," *Radical Religion* (Autumn, 1935), 1, 3–5.

"Is Religion Counter-Revolutionary," *Radical Religion* (Autumn, 1935), 1, 14–20.

"The Revival of Feudalism," *Harper's* (March, 1935), 170, 483–488.

"The Revolutionary Moment," *The American Socialist Quarterly* (June, 1935), 4, 8–13.

"Our Romantic Radicals," *The Christian Century* (April 10, 1935), 52, 474–476.

"Sects and Churches," *The Christian Century* (July 3, 1935), 52, 885–887.

"Is Social Conflict Inevitable?" *Scribner's* (Sept., 1935), 98, 66–69.

1936

"Arrogance in the Name of Christ," *The Christian Century* (Sept. 2, 1936), 53, 1157–1158.

"Britain Bewildered," *The Christian Century* (Aug. 12, 1936), 53, 1081–1082.

"Christian Politics and Communist Religion," in *Christianity and the Social Revolution,* ed. by John Lewis (New York: Charles Scribner's Sons, 1936).

"Christianity and Communism—Social Justice," *Spectator* (Nov. 6, 1936), 157, 802–803.

"Doom and Dawn," Reinhold Niebuhr and Sherwood Eddy (New York: Kirby Page, 1936).

"The English Church—An American View," *Spectator* (Sept. 4, 1936), 157, 373–374.

"English and German Mentality—A Study in National Traits," *Christendom* (Spring, 1936), 1, 465–476.

"German Church Girds for Battle," *The Christian Century* (Aug. 26, 1936), 53, 1129–1130.

"The Idea of Progress and Socialism," *Radical Religion* (Spring, 1936), 1, 27–29.

"Moralistic Preaching," *The Christian Century* (July 15, 1936), 53, 985–987.

"Must Radicals Be Atheists?" *Common Sense* (July, 1936), 5, 11–13.

"Pacifism Against the Wall," *The American Scholar* (Spring, 1936), 5, 133–141.

"Pacifism and Sanctions," A Symposium by J. N. Sayre and Reinhold Niebuhr, *Radical Religion* (Winter, 1936), 1, 27–30.

"The Radical Minister and His Church," *Radical Religion* (Winter, 1936), 2, 25–27.

"The Secular and the Religious," *The Christian Century* (Nov. 4, 1936), 53, 1452–1454.

"Sunday Morning Debate," *The Christian Century* (April 22, 1936), 53, 595–597.

"Which Way, Great Britain?—Will It Be France or Germany? War or Peace?" *Current History* (Nov., 1936), 45, 35–39.

1937

"America and the War in China," *The Christian Century* (Sept. 29, 1937), 54, 1195–1196.

"The Catholic Heresy," *The Christian Century* (Dec. 8, 1937), 54, 1524–1525.

"Catholicism and Anarchism in Spain," *Radical Religion* (Spring, 1937), 2, 25–28.

"The Contribution of Paul Tillich," *Religion in Life* (Autumn, 1937), 6, 574–581.

Do the State and Nation Belong to God or the Devil? (Burge Memorial Lecture) (London: S.C.M. Press, 1937).

"European Impressions," *Radical Religion* (Autumn, 1937), 2, 31–33.

"Japan and the Christian Conscience," *The Christian Century* (Nov. 10, 1937), 54, 1390–1391.

"Meditations from Mississippi," *The Christian Century* (Feb. 10, 1937), 54, 183–184.

"Pawns for Fascism—Our Lower Middle Class," *The American Scholar* (Spring, 1937), 6, 145–152.

"Pius XI and His Successor," *The Nation* (Jan. 30, 1937), 144, 120–122.

"Social Justice," in *Christianity and Communism*, ed. by Henry W. Harris (Oxford: Basil Blackwell, 1937).

"The Truth in Myths," in *The Nature of Religious Experience*, Essays in Honor of D. C. Macintosh (New York: Harper & Brothers, 1937).

1938

"Christian Faith and the Common Life," in *Christian Faith and the Common Life* (Oxford Conference Series, Vol. 4) (London: George Allen & Unwin, Ltd., 1938).

"The Creed of Modern Christian Socialists," *Radical Religion* (Spring, 1938), 3, 13–18.

"The *London Times* and the Crisis," *Radical Religion* (Winter, 1938), 4, 29–32.

"The Protestant Opposition Movement in Germany, 1934–37," *Friends of Europe*, 1937.

"The Return to Primitive Religion," *Christendom* (Winter, 1938), 3, 1–8.

"Russia and Karl Marx," *The Nation* (May 7, 1938), 146, 530–531.

"Will of God and the Van Zeeland Report," *The Christian Century* (Dec. 14, 1938), 55, 1549–1550.

1939

"The British Conscience," *The Nation* (Aug. 26, 1939), 149, 219–221.

"Germans and Nazis," *Spectator* (Sept. 22, 1939), 163, 401–402.

"Leaves from the Notebook of a War-Bound American," *The Christian Century* (Oct. 25, Nov. 15, Dec. 6, 27, 1939), 56, 1298–1299, 1405–1406, 1502–1503, 1607–1608.

"Ten Years That Shook My World," *The Christian Century* (April 26, 1939), 56, 542–546. Fourteenth article in a series on "How My Mind Has Changed in This Decade."

1940

"Christian Faith and Natural Law," *Theology* (Feb., 1940), 40, 86–94.

"Christian Moralism in America," *Radical Religion* (Winter, 1940), 5, 16–20.

"Europe's Catastrophe and the Christian Faith" (London: Nisbet & Co., Ltd., 1940).

"Let Him Who Is Without Sin," *Union Review* (March, 1940), 1, 9–11, 25.

"An Open Letter to Richard Roberts," *Christianity and Society* (Summer, 1940), 5, 30–33.

"Politics and the Christian Ethic," *Christianity and Society* (Spring, 1940), 5, 24–28.

"To Prevent the Triumph of an Intolerable Tyranny" (third in a series on the question "If America is drawn into the war, can you, as a Christian, participate in it or support it?"), *The Christian Century* (Dec. 18, 1940), 57, 1578–1580.

"A Reply to Professor Macintosh," *Review of Religion* (March, 1940), 4, 304–308.

1941

"Allied Peace Aims," *Christianity and Crisis* (June 30, 1941), 1, 1–2.

"America and the Enslaved Nations," *Christianity and Crisis* (Oct. 6, 1941), 1, 1–2.

"America and the Peace After the War," *Christianity and Crisis* (March 24, 1941), 1, 1–2.

"American Doldrums," *Christianity and Crisis* (Sept. 22, 1941), 1, 1–2.

"America's Last Chance," *Christianity and Crisis* (July 14, 1941), 1, 1–2.

"Armistice Day 1941," *Christianity and Crisis* (Nov. 17, 1941), 1, 1–2.

"The Christian Faith and the World Crisis," *Christianity and Crisis* (Feb. 10, 1941), 1, 4–6.

"Christmas Light on History," *Christianity and Crisis* (Dec. 29, 1941), 1, 1–2.

"Church and State in America," *Christianity and Crisis* (Dec. 15, 1941), 1, 1–2.

"The City of Man: A Declaration on World Democracy," Committee of Fifteen: Reinhold Niebuhr, H. Agar, F. Aydelotte, G. A. Borgese, *et al.* (New York: Viking Press, 1941).

"The Crisis," *Christianity and Crisis* (Feb. 10, 1941), 1, 1–2.

"The Crisis Deepens," *Christianity and Crisis* (May 5, 1941), 1, 1–2.

"Crisis in the Far East," *Christianity and Crisis* (March 10, 1941), 1, 1–2.

"Fighting Chance for a Sick Society," *The Nation* (Supplement) (March 22, 1941), 152, 357–360.

"An Ineffectual Sermon on Love," *Christianity and Crisis* (Dec. 15, 1941), 1, 2–3.

"Just or Holy?" *Christianity and Crisis* (Nov. 3, 1941), 1, 1–2.

"Labor and Defense," *Christianity and Crisis* (April 21, 1941), 1, 1–2.

"The Mirage of Mediation," *Christianity and Crisis* (July 28, 1941), 1, 1–2.

"Momentous Decision by Narrow Margin," *Christianity and Crisis* (Dec. 1, 1941), 1, 1–2.

"The Necessity of Decision," *Christianity and Crisis* (June 2, 1941), 1, 1–2.

"A Negotiated Peace," *Christianity and Crisis* (April 7, 1941), 1, 1–2.

"New Allies, Old Issues," *The Nation* (July 19, 1941), 153, 50–52.

"Pacifism and America First," *Christianity and Crisis* (June 16, 1941), 1, 2–5.

"The President and the People," *Christianity and Crisis* (June 16, 1941), 1, 1–2.

"The Providence of God and the Defence of Civilization," *The Christian News-Letter* (May 21, 1941), Supplement 82.

"Reflections on the World Situation," *Christianity and Crisis* (April 21, 1941), 1, 2–3.

"Religion and Action," in *Religion and the Modern World,* pp. 89–108, University of Pennsylvania Bicentennial Conference (Philadelphia: University of Pennsylvania Press, 1941). Republished in *Science and Man,* ed. by Ruth N. Anshen (New York: Harcourt, Brace & Co., 1942).

"Repeal the Neutrality Act!" *Christianity and Crisis* (Oct. 20, 1941), 1, 1–2.

"The Russians and Our Interdependence," *Christianity and Crisis* (Aug. 25, 1941), 1, 1–2.

"We Are at War," *Christianity and Crisis* (Dec. 29, 1941), 1, 2–3.

"What Is at Stake?" *Christianity and Crisis* (May 19, 1941), 1, 1–2.

"Whosoever Will Save His Life," *Christianity and Crisis* (Feb. 24, 1941), 1, 1–2.

1942

"Amidst Encircling Gloom," *Christianity and Crisis* (March 9, 1942), 2, 1–2.

"The Anglo-Russian Pact," *Christianity and Crisis* (June 29, 1942), 2, 2–3.

"Civil Liberties in Wartime," *Christianity and Crisis* (Feb. 23, 1942), 2, 1–2.

"Common Council for United Nations," *Christianity and Crisis* (Oct. 5, 1942), 2, 1–2.

"Does the Church Pray?" *Christianity and Crisis* (June 15, 1942), 2, 3–4.

"The End of the Beginning," *Christianity and Crisis* (Nov. 30, 1942), 2, 1–2.

"The Evacuation of Japanese Citizens," *Christianity and Crisis* (May 18, 1942), 2, 2–5.

"A Faith for History's Greatest Crisis," *Fortune* (July, 1942), 26, 99–100, 122, 125–126, 128, 131.

"The Germans and the Nazis," *The Nation* (April 4, 1942), 154, 398–400. Review article of several books on the subject.

"Jews After the War," *The Nation* (Feb. 21 and 28, 1942), 154, 214–216 and 253–255.

"The Limits of Liberty," *The Nation* (Jan. 24, 1942), 154, 86–88.

"Love Your Enemies," *Christianity and Society* (Autumn, 1942), 7, 35–37.

"Our Responsibilities in 1942," *Christianity and Crisis* (Jan. 12, 1942), 1, 1–2.

"Plans for World Reorganization," *Christianity and Crisis* (Oct. 19, 1942), 2, 3–6.

"Preaching in War-Time," *Christianity and Crisis* (Feb. 9, 1942), 2, 1–2.

"The Role of Prophetic Religion in the World Crisis," in *Men of Tomorrow*, ed. by T. H. Johnson (New York: G. P. Putnam's Sons, 1942).

"Russia's Partnership in War and Peace," *Christianity and Crisis* (Feb. 23, 1942), 2, 2–3.

"The Spirit and the Body in War," *Christianity and Crisis* (Aug. 10, 1942), 2, 1–2.

"The Unity of History," *Christianity and Crisis* (May 4, 1942), 2, 1–2.

1943

"American Power and World Responsibility," *Christianity and Crisis* (April 5, 1943), 3, 2–4.

"American Trends," *Spectator* (Dec. 17, 1943), 171, 573.

"Anglo-Saxon Destiny and Responsibility," *Christianity and Crisis* (Oct. 4, 1943), 3, 2–4.

"The Editor's Report on Britain," *Christianity and Crisis* (June 28, 1943), 3, 4–6.

"Educational and Religious Barrenness," *Christianity and Crisis* (Aug. 9, 1943), 3, 1–2.

"England Teaches Its Soldiers," *The Nation* (Aug. 21, 1943), 157, 208–210.

"Factors of Cohesion," *Spectator* (June 18, 1943), 170, 562–563.

"Fourth Term for Roosevelt," *New Statesman and Nation* (May 15, 1943), 25, 315–316.

"Great Britain's Post-War Role," *The Nation* (July 10, 1943), 157, 39–40.

"Is Peace Being Made?" *Christianity and Crisis* (Dec. 27, 1943), 3, 2.

"A Just World Power," *Current Religious Thought* (Oct., 1943), 3, 11–13.

"Letter from Britain," *Christianity and Crisis* (July 12, 1943), 3, 2.

"Marxism in Eclipse," *Spectator* (June 4, 1943), 170, 518–519.

"National Power and the Organization of the Peace," *The American Teacher* (April, 1943), 27, 23–26.

"The Perils of Our Foreign Policy," *Christianity and Society* (Spring, 1943), 8, 18–21.

"Pillars of Peace," *Spectator* (Oct. 22, 1943), 171, 378.

"Politics and the Children of Light," *Christianity and Crisis* (Nov. 29, 1943), 3, 2.

"The Politics of North Africa," *Christianity and Crisis* (Feb. 22, 1943), 3, 2.

"Politics and Religion in Britain," *Christianity and Crisis* (July 26, 1943), 3, 2–3.

"Russia and the Christian World," *Christian News-Letter* (Aug. 25, 1943), Supplement 189.

"Russia and the West," *The Nation* (Jan. 16, 1943), 156, 82–84.

"Russia and the West II," *The Nation* (Jan. 23, 1943), 156, 124–125.

"Tensions in British Politics," *The Nation* (June 26, 1943), 156, 889–890.

"The Timeless Christian Message and Its Immediate Meaning," *Current Religious Thought* (March, 1943), 3, 10–14.

"Understanding England," *The Nation* (Aug. 14, 1943), 157, 175–177.

"The United Nations and World Organization," *Christianity and Crisis* (Jan. 25, 1943), 2, 1–2.

"We Are in Peril," *Christianity and Crisis* (Oct. 18, 1943), 3, 2–3.

"Who Wants the Hapsburg Monarchy?" *Christianity and Crisis* (Jan. 11, 1943), 2, 2–3.

1944

"Airplanes Are Not Enough," *Christianity and Crisis* (Feb. 7, 1944), 4, 1–2.

"Archbishop Temple," *Christianity and Crisis* (Nov. 13, 1944), 4, 1.

"The Basis of World Order," *The Nation* (Oct. 21, 1944), 159, 489.

"The Christian Faith and the German Problem," *The Student Movement* (Oct., 1944), 47, 6–8.

"The Christian Perspective on the World Crisis," *Christianity and Crisis* (May 1, 1944), 4, 2–5.

"The Climax of the War," *Christianity and Crisis* (May 29, 1944), 4, 1–2.

"Critical Analysis of the Dumbarton Oaks Proposals," *Post-War World* (Dec. 15, 1944), 2, 1, 3.

"Democratic Goals and World Order," *The New Leader* (Sept. 23, 1944), 27, 4–5.

"Dr. William Temple and His Britain," *The Nation* (Nov. 11, 1944), 159, 584–586.

"Dumbarton Oaks" (editorial), *Christianity and Society* (Winter, 1944), 10, 3–4.

"Election Insights on Our Civilization" (editorial), *Christianity and Society* (Winter, 1944), 10, 6–7.

"The German Problem," *Christianity and Crisis* (Jan. 10, 1944), 3, 2–4.

"Is the Bombing Necessary?" *Christianity and Crisis* (April 3, 1944), 4, 1–2.

"Prayer and Global Civilization," *Christianity and Crisis* (Sept. 18, 1944), 4, 1–2.

"Roosevelt's Chances," *Spectator* (Aug. 25, 1944), 173, 166.

"Russia and the Peace," *Christianity and Crisis* (Nov. 13, 1944), 4, 2–4.

"Stones from a Glass House," *Christianity and Crisis* (Oct. 16, 1944), 4, 1–2.

"Unity and Depth of Our Culture," *Sewanee Review* (April–June, 1944), 52, 193–198.

"World War III Ahead?" *The Nation* (March 25, 1944), 158, 356–358.

1945

"Anglo-Saxon Tensions," *Spectator* (Feb. 16, 1945), 174, 142.

"The Atomic Issue," *Christianity and Crisis* (Oct. 15, 1945), 5, 5–7.

"Changing and Abiding Elements in the Human Situation," *Current Religious Thought* (June, 1945), 5, 23–28.

"Christian Faith and the Race Problem," *Christianity and Society* (Spring, 1945), 10, 21–24.

"The Conference of the 'Big Three,'" *Christianity and Crisis* (March 5, 1945), 5, 1–2.

"The Contribution of Religion to Cultural Unity," Hazen Pamphlets, No. 13, 1945.

"The Death of a Martyr" (Dietrich Bonhoeffer), *Christianity and Crisis* (June 25, 1945), 5, 6–7.

"The Death of the President," *Christianity and Crisis* (April 30, 1945), 5, 4–6.

"Is This 'Peace in Our Time'?" *The Nation* (April 7, 1945), 160, 382–384.

"A Lecture to Liberals," *The Nation* (Nov. 10, 1945), 161, 491–493.

"Our Relations to Japan," *Christianity and Crisis* (Sept. 17, 1945), 5, 5–7.

"Russia and the Peace," *Social Progress* (Jan., 1945), 35, 8–9, 22–23.

"Soberness in Victory," *Christianity and Crisis* (May 28, 1945), 5, 1–2.

"Theologian and Church Statesman," in *This Ministry: The Contribution of Henry S. Coffin* (New York: Scribner's, 1945).

"The Vengeance of Victors," *Christianity and Crisis* (Nov. 26, 1945), 5, 1–2.

"Which Question Comes First for the Church?" *Christianity and Crisis* (Nov. 12, 1945), 5, 1–2.

"The Widow's Mite," *Christianity and Crisis* (Feb. 5, 1945), 5, 1–2.

"Will America Back Out? Our Stake in Europe's Future," *The Nation* (Jan. 13, 1945), 160, 42–43.

"Will Civilization Survive Technics?" *Commentary* (Dec. 1945), 1, 2–8.

"World Community and World Government," *Christianity and Crisis* (March 4, 1945), 6, 5–6.

1946

"American Liberals and British Labor," *The Nation* (June 8, 1946), 162, 682–684.

"As Others See Us," *Christianity and Crisis* (Dec. 9, 1946), 6, 4–6.

"The Conflict Between Nations and Nations and Between Nations and God," *Christianity and Crisis* (Aug. 5, 1946), 6, 2–4.

"Dietrich Bonhoeffer," *Union Seminary Quarterly Review* (March, 1946), 1, 3.

"The Ecumenical Issue in the United States," *Theology Today* (Jan., 1946), 2, 525–536.

"Europe, Russia and America," *The Nation* (Sept. 14, 1946), 163, 288–289.

"The Fight For Germany," *Life* (Oct. 21, 1946), 21, 65–72.

"I Was An Hungred and Ye Gave Me No Meat!" *Christianity and Crisis* (Jan. 7, 1946), 5, 5–6.

"Man's Defiance of God," *Current Religious Thought* (March, 1946), 6, 5–8.

"Mr. Wallace's Errors," *Christianity and Crisis* (Oct. 28, 1946), 6, 1–2.

"The Myth of World Government," *The Nation* (March 16, 1946), 162, 312–314.

"The Nation in Peril," *Christianity and Crisis* (July 22, 1946), 6, 1.

"New View of Palestine," *Spectator* (Aug. 16, 1946), 177, 162.

"Our Relations with Russia," in *Christianity Takes a Stand*, ed. by Bishop William Scarlett (New York: Penguin Books, Inc., 1946).

"Palestine: British-American Dilemma," *The Nation* (Aug. 31, 1946), 163, 238–239.

"Positive Defense," *Christianity and Crisis* (April 29, 1946), 6, 1–2.

"A Problem of Evangelical Christianity," *Christianity and Crisis* (May 13, 1946), 6, 5–6.

"The Religious Level of the World Crisis," *Christianity and Crisis* (Jan. 21, 1946), 5, 4–7. Originally published in *The Christian News-Letter*.

"A Report on Germany," *Christianity and Crisis* (Oct. 14, 1946), 6, 6–7.

"Victors' Justice," *Common Sense* (Jan., 1946), 15, 6–9.

"Will Germany Go Communist?" *The Nation* (Oct. 5, 1946), 163, 371–373.

1947

"American Power and European Health," *Christianity and Crisis* (June 9, 1947), 7, 1–2.

"American Scene," *Spectator* (Feb. 14, 1947), 178, 198.

"America's Precarious Eminence," *The Virginia Quarterly Review* (Autumn, 1947), 23, 481–490.

"Democracy as a Religion," *Christianity and Crisis* (Aug. 4, 1947), 7, 1–2.

"The Dilemma of Modern Man," *The Nation* (Feb. 22, 1947), 164, 205–209.

"Dishonest Praise," *Basic* (April, 1947), 1, 27–28.

"European Impressions," *Christianity and Crisis* (May 12, 1947), 7, 2–4.

"Labor Coalition in Holland," *The Nation* (April 19, 1947), 164, 447–448.

"The Marshall Plan," *Christianity and Crisis* (Oct. 13, 1947), 7, 2.

"The Organization of the Liberal Movement," *Christianity and Society* (Spring, 1947), 12, 8–10.

"Our Chances for Peace," *Christianity and Crisis* (Feb. 17, 1947), 7, 1–2.

"Our Relations to Catholicism," *Christianity and Crisis* (Sept. 15, 1947), 7, 5–7.

"The Reunion of the Church Through the Renewal of the Churches," *Christianity and Crisis* (Nov. 24, 1947), 7, 5–7.

"The Tension Between Marxism and Christianity on the Continent," *Christianity and Society* (Summer, 1947), 12, 9–11.

"They All Fear America," *The Christian Century* (Aug. 20, 1947), 64, 993–994.

1948

"Amid Encircling Gloom," *Christianity and Crisis* (April 12, 1948), 8, 41–42.

"Babel and Pentecost," *Christianity and Crisis* (Oct. 4, 1948), 8, 121–122.

"Can the Church Give a 'Moral Lead'?" *Christianity and Crisis* (Aug. 2, 1948), 8, 105–106.

"Can We Avoid Catastrophe?" *The Christian Century* (May 26, 1948), 65, 504–506.

"Churches and Society," *New Statesman and Nation* (Sept. 18, 1948), 36, 232–233.

"The Federation of Western Europe," *Christianity and Crisis* (March 1, 1948), 8, 17–18.

"For Peace We Must Risk War," *Life* (Sept. 20, 1948), 25, 38–39.

"The Godly and the Godless," *Christianity and Crisis* (Dec. 13, 1948), 8, 161–162.

"God's Design and the Present Disorder of Civilization," introductory statement to Vol. III of the Amsterdam studies, *The Church and the Disorder of Society* (New York: Harper & Brothers, 1948).

"The Impact of Protestantism Today," *Atlantic* (Feb., 1948), 181, 57–62.

"One World or None," *Christianity and Crisis* (Feb. 16, 1948), 8, 9–10.

"Our Spiritual Pilgrimage from a Century of Hope to a Century of Perplexity," *Current Religious Thought* (Nov., 1948), 8, 20–27.

"The Presidential Campaign," *Christianity and Crisis* (Nov. 1, 1948), 8, 137–138.

"Protestantism in a Disordered World," a report on the First World Council of Churches, *The Nation* (Sept. 18, 1948), 167, 311–313.

"Sex Standards in America," *Christianity and Crisis* (May 24, 1948), 8, 65–66.

"The Sickness of American Culture," *The Nation* (March 6, 1948), 166, 267–270.

"The Situation in U.S.A.," Chap. 6, Vol. III, Amsterdam studies, *The Church and the Disorder of Society* (New York: Harper & Brothers, 1948).

"Two Forms of Tyranny," *Christianity and Crisis* (Feb. 2, 1948), 8, 3–5.

"We Are Men and Not God," *The Christian Century* (Oct. 27, 1948), 55, 1138–1140.

"The World Council at Amsterdam," *Christianity and Crisis* (Sept. 20, 1948), 8, 114–116. Same appeared in *Union Seminary Quarterly Review* (Nov., 1948), 4, 11–14.

"The World Council at Amsterdam," *The Pastor* (Dec., 1948), 12, 4–5.

1949

"An Answer to Karl Barth," *The Christian Century* (Feb. 23, 1949), 56, 234–236.

"The Cult of Freedom in America," *Christianity and Crisis* (Feb. 7, 1949), 9, 4–7.

"Hazards and Resources," *The Virginia Quarterly Review* (Spring, 1949), 25, 194–204.

"The Illusion of World Government," *Foreign Affairs* (April, 1949), 27, 379–388. Reprinted as a pamphlet by the Graphics Group (Whitestone, New York, 1949).

"The North Atlantic Pact," *Christianity and Crisis* (May 30, 1949), 9, 65–66.

"Peace Through Cultural Coöperation," *Christianity and Crisis* (Oct. 17, 1949), 9, 131–133.

"Providence and Human Decisions," *Christianity and Crisis* (Jan. 24, 1949), 8, 185–186.

"Religion and Modern Knowledge," in *Man's Destiny in Eternity*, the Garvin Lectures (Boston: Beacon Press, 1949).

"The Rising Catholic-Protestant Tension," *Christianity and Crisis* (Aug. 8, 1949), 9, 106–108.

"The Russian Idea," *Religion in Life* (Spring, 1949), 18, 239–242. A review article of Berdyaev's *The Russian Idea.*

"The Second Focus of the Fellowship (of Socialist Christians)," *Christianity and Society* (Winter, 1949–50), 15, 21–22.

"The Spirit and the Mechanism of Partnership," *Christianity and Crisis* (Oct. 3, 1949), 9, 121–122.

"Streaks of Dawn in the Night," *Christianity and Crisis* (Dec. 12, 1949), 9, 162–164.

1950

"The Captive Churches," *Christianity and Crisis* (Nov. 13, 1950), 10, 145–146.

"The Christian Conscience and Atomic War," *Christianity and Crisis* (Dec. 11, 1950), 10, 161.

"The Conditions of Our Survival," *The Virginia Quarterly Review* (Autumn, 1950), 26, 481–492.

"The False Defense of Christianity," *Christianity and Crisis* (June 12, 1950), 10, 73–74.

"Halfway to What?" An answer to critics of the "Welfare State," *The Nation* (Jan. 14, 1950), 170, 26–28.

"Has the Church Any Authority?" *Christianity and Crisis* (April 3, 1950), 10, 35–36.

"The Increasing Isolation of the Catholic Church," *Christianity and Crisis* (Sept. 18, 1950), 10, 113–114.

"Is There a Revival of Religion?" *The New York Times Magazine* (Nov. 19, 1950), Sec. 6, p. 13.

"The Pope's Domesticated God," *The Christian Century* (Jan. 18, 1950), 67, 74–75.

"A Protest Against a Dilemma's Two Horns," *World Politics* (April, 1950), 2, 338–344.

"The Relevance of Reformation Doctrine in Our Day," in *The Heritage of the Reformation,* ed. by E. J. F. Arndt (New York: R. R. Smith, 1950).

"Should We Be Consistent?" *Christianity and Crisis* (Feb. 6, 1950), 10, 1–2.

"The Theory and Practice of UNESCO," *International Organization* (Feb., 1950), 4, 3–11.

"Utilitarian Christianity and the World Crisis," *Christianity and Crisis* (May 29, 1950), 10, 66–69.

"The World Council and the Peace Issue," *Christianity and Crisis* (Aug. 7, 1950), 10, 107–108.

1951

"American Conservatism and the World Crisis: a Study in Vacillation," *The Yale Review* (March, 1951), 40, 385–399.

"The Peril of War and the Prospects of Peace," *Christianity and Crisis* (Oct. 15, 1951), 11, 129–130.

"Ten Fateful Years," *Christianity and Crisis* (Feb. 5, 1951), 11, 1–4.

"Transatlantic Tension," *The Reporter* (Sept. 18, 1951), 5, 14–16.

"The Two Dimensions of the Struggle," *Christianity and Crisis* (May 28, 1951), 11, 65–66.

"The Weakness of Common Worship in American Protestantism," *Christianity and Crisis* (May 28, 1951), 11, 68–70.

1952

"Biblical Thought and Ontological Speculation in Tillich's Theology," in *The Theology of Paul Tillich*, Vol. I of The Library of Living Theology, ed. by Kegley & Bretall (New York: The Macmillan Company, 1952).

"Catholics and Politics: Some Misconceptions," *The Reporter* (Jan. 22, 1952), 6, 9–11. Reprinted in *Christianity and Crisis* (June 23, 1952), 12, 83–85.

"Christian Faith and Political Controversy," *Christianity and Crisis* (July 21, 1952), 12, 97–98.

"The Importance of the Religious Dimension," *Christian Action* (May, 1952), 2, 1.

"Love and Law in Protestantism and Catholicism," *The Journal of Religious Thought* (Spring–Summer, 1952), 9, 95–111.

"The Moral Implications of Loyalty to the United Nations," Hazen Pamphlets, No. 29, 1952.

"Our Country and Our Culture: A Symposium," *Partisan Review* (May–June, 1952), 19, 301–303.

"Prayer and Politics," *Christianity and Crisis* (Oct. 27, 1952), 12, 138–139.

"The Protestant Clergy and U.S. Politics," *The Reporter* (Feb. 19, 1952), 6, 24–27.

"The Republican Split on Foreign Policy," *The New Leader* (May 12, 1952), 35, 16–17.

"The Republican Victory," *Christianity and Crisis* (Nov. 24, 1952), 12, 153–154.

"Whither the National Council?" *Christianity and Crisis* (Jan. 7, 1952), 11, 1–2.

1953

"American Attitudes on World Organization: Comment," *Public Opinion Quarterly* (Winter, 1953–54), 17, 435–438.

"The Anomaly of European Socialism," *The Yale Review* (Winter, 1953), 42, 161–167.

"Christian Faith and the Economic Life of Liberal Society," in *Goals of Economic Life*, ed. by A. Dudley Ward (New York: Harper & Brothers, 1953).

"Christian Faith and Social Action," in *Christian Faith and Social Action*, ed. by John Hutchison (New York: Charles Scribner's Sons, 1953).

"The Christian Witness in a Secular Age," *The Christian Century* (July 22, 1953), 70, 840–843.

"Christianity and the Moral Law," *The Christian Century* (Dec. 2, 1953), 70, 1386–1388.

"The Church Speaks to the Nation," *Christianity and Crisis* (Nov. 30, 1953), 13, 153–154.

"Coercion, Self-Interest, and Love," in Kenneth E. Boulding's *The Organizational Revolution* (New York: Harper & Brothers, 1953).

"Communism and the Clergy," *The Christian Century* (Aug. 19, 1953), 70, 936–937.

"Coronation Afterthoughts," *The Christian Century* (July 1, 1953), 70, 771–772.

"Democracy, Secularism, and Christianity," *Christianity and Crisis* (March 2, 1953), 13, 19–20, 24.

"The Evil of the Communist Idea," *The New Leader* (June 8, 1953), 36, 16–18. Published as a chapter in *Christian Realism and Political Problems.*

"The French Do Not Like Us. The Roots of Anti-American Sentiment in France," *Christianity and Society* (Winter, 1953–54), 19, 9–12.

"Hope Needs Faith and Love," *The Ecumenical Review* (July, 1953), 5, 358–363.

"A Protestant Looks at Catholics," *The Commonweal* (May 8, 1953), 58, 117–120. Published as a chapter in *Catholicism in America* (New York: Harcourt, Brace, & Co., 1954).

"Sex and Religion in the Kinsey Report," *Christianity and Crisis* (Nov. 2, 1953), 13, 138–141. A chapter in the symposium entitled: *An Analysis of the Kinsey Reports on Sexual Behavior in the Human Male and Female* (New York: E. P. Dutton Co., 1954).

"The Significance of Dr. Fosdick in American Religious Thought," *The Union Seminary Quarterly Review* (May, 1953), 8, 3–6. Same published in *The Christian Century* (June 3, 1953), 70, 657–658, under the title "Fosdick: Theologian and Preacher."

"Sorrow and Joy According to the Christian Faith," *Current Religious Thought* (January–February, 1953), 13, 7–11.

"We Stand Alone," *Christianity and Crisis* (Sept. 21, 1953), 13, 113–114.

1954

"Alternatives to the H-Bomb" (Symposium), *The New Leader* (Aug. 2, 1954), 37, 12–14.

"America and the Asians," *The New Leader* (May 31, 1954), 37, 3–4.

"American Leadership in the Cold War," *Christianity and Crisis* (Oct. 18, 1954), 14, 129–130.

"Beria and McCarthy," *The New Leader* (Jan. 4, 1954), 37, 3–4.

"The Case for Coexistence," *The New Leader* (Oct. 4, 1954), 37, 5–6.

"The Catholic Hierarchy's Analysis of the Ills of Our Day," *Christianity and Crisis,* 14, 171–173.

"Christ the Hope of the World—What Has History to Say?" *Religion in Life* (Summer, 1954), 23, 334–340. Also published in *Christianity and Crisis* (Aug. 9, 1954), 14, 108–111, under the title "The Theme of Evanston."

"Christ vs. Socrates," *The Saturday Review* (Dec. 18, 1954), 37, 7–8, 37–39.

"Co-existence or Total War," *The Christian Century* (Aug. 18, 1954), 71, 971–973.

"The Commitment of the Self and the Freedom of the Mind," in *Religion and Freedom of Thought,* by Perry Miller, Robert C. Calhoun, Nathan M. Pusey, and R. N. (New York: Doubleday & Co., Inc., 1954).

"Democracy and the Party Spirit," *The New Leader* (Mar. 15, 1954), 37, 3–5.

"Frustrations of American Power," *The New Leader* (Nov. 29, 1954), 37, 7–8.

"Ideals and Basic Law," *The New Leader* (Nov. 1, 1954), 37, 11.

"Ike's First Year," *The New Leader* (Feb. 8, 1954), 37, 3–5.

"Is History Predictable?" *Atlantic* (July, 1954), 194, 69–72.

"Learning from History," *The New Leader* (May 10, 1954), 37, 3–4.

"More on Kinsey," *Christianity and Crisis* (Jan. 11, 1954), 13, 182–183.

"Our Dependence on God," an address written for delivery at the Evanston Assembly of the World Council, *The Christian Century* (Sept. 1, 1954), 71, 1034–1037.

"The Peril of Complacency in Our Nation," *Christianity and Crisis* (Feb. 8, 1954), 14, 1–2.

"The Significance of the Growth of 'Christian Action,'" *Christianity and Crisis* (March 2, 1954), 14, 30–32.

"The Supreme Court on Segregation in the Schools," *Christianity and Crisis* (June 14, 1954), 14, 75–77.

"The Tyranny of Science," *Theology Today* (Jan., 1954), 10, 464–473.

"Why They Dislike America," *The New Leader* (Apr. 12, 1954), 37, 3–5.

1955

"The Anatomy of American Nationalism," *The New Leader* (Feb. 28, 1955), 38, 16–17.

"Buchmanism Under Scrutiny," *Christianity and Crisis* (May 16, 1955), 15, 62, 64.

"Conversation: On the International Affairs Report from the Evanston Assembly of the World Council of Churches," (R. N. and R. M. Fagley), *Christianity and Society* (Spring, 1955), 20, 7–8.

"The Fate of European Socialism," *The New Leader* (June 20, 1955), 38, 6–8.

"God Wills Both Justice and Peace," (Angus Dun and R. N.), *Christianity and Crisis* (June 13, 1955), 15, 75–78.

"Law and Grace in Christianity and Secularism," *Christianity and Crisis* (June 27, 1955), 15, 81–82.

"Liberalism: Illusions and Realities," *New Republic* (July 4, 1955), 133, 11–13.

"Limitations of the Scientific Method: An Answer to Pierre Auger," *Bulletin of the Atomic Scientists* (March, 1955), 11, 87.

"The Limits of Military Power," *The New Leader* (May 30, 1955), 38, 16–17.

"The Meaning of Labor Unity," *The New Leader* (Mar. 28, 1955), 38, 8–9.

"Nobody Predicted Today," *The New Leader* (Jan. 3, 1955), 38, 9–10.

"Our Fifteenth Birthday" (anniversary issue of *Christianity and Crisis*), *Christianity and Crisis* (Feb. 7, 1955), 15, 1–3.

"Religiosity and the Christian Faith," *Christianity and Crisis* (Jan. 24, 1955), 14, 185–186.

"The Sources of American Prestige," *The New Leader* (Jan. 31, 1955), 38, 6–8.

"Winston Churchill and Great Britain," *Christianity and Crisis* (May 2, 1955), 15, 51–52.

1956

"Biblical Religion and Ontological Speculation in Tillich's Theology," in *The Theology of Paul Tillich*. Edited by C.W. Kegley and R.W. Bretall. New York: Macmillan, pp. 216–27.

"The Cause and Cure of the American Psychosis." *The American Scholar*, 21, no. 1 (Winter), 11–20.

"The Christian Life and an Economy of Abundance." *Union Seminary Quarterly Review*, 11, no. 2 (January), 25–31.

"Clericalism in Europe." NL, 39, no. 1 (January 2), 17–18.

"The Crisis in the Suez Canal." CC, 16, no. 15 (September 17), 113–14.

"The Ethics of Loyalty (A Summary)." *Confluence*, 3, no. 4 (December), 480–89.

"Foreword," to *Dying We Live*. Edited by H. Gollwitzer, Käthe Kuhn, and R. Schneider. New York: Pantheon, pp. xiii–xix.

"Ike Is No Sure Thing." NL, 39, no. 11 (March 12), 3–4.

"The Indeterminate Possibilities for Good and Evil," in *Sermons from an Ecumenical Pulpit*. Edited by Max Daskam. Boston: Starr King Press, pp. 15–26.

"Is There a Right and Wrong Way to Pray?" *McCalls,* 83, no. 12 (September), 29. Also printed by Good Reading Rack Service, 1957.

"Literalism, Individualism and Billy Graham." CCY, 73, no. 21 (May 23), 640–42.

"Love and Law." *The Pulpit,* 27, no. 1 (January), 19–23. From sermons honoring Charles Clayton Morrison.

"The Middle East and Hungary." NL, 39, no. 48 (November 26), 7–8.

"Mideast Impasse: Is There a Way Out?" NL, 39, no. 23 (June 4), 9–10.

"New Hopes for Peace in the Middle East." CC, 16, no. 9 (May 28), 65–66.

"The New International Situation." CC, 16, no. 19 (November 12), 150–51.

"Nikita Khrushchev's Meditation on Josef Stalin." CC, 16, no. 12 (July 9), 89–90.

"Our Moral and Spiritual Resources for International Cooperation." *Social Action,* 22, no. 6 (February), 5–24.

"Proposal to Billy Graham." CCY, 73, no. 32 (August 8), 921–22.

"A Qualified Faith." NR, 134, no. 7 (February 13), 14–15.

"School, Church, and the Ordeals of Integration." CC, 16, no. 16 (October 1), 121–22.

"Seven Great Errors in U.S. Foreign Policy." NL, 39, no. 52 (December 24–31), 3–5.

"Stalin—Deity or Demon." CC, 16, no. 6 (April 16), 42–43.

"A Theologian's Comments on the Negro in America." *The Reporter,* 15, no. 9 (November 29), 24–25.

"There Is No Peace." CC, 16, no. 16 (November 26), 121–22.

"The Tyrant as Symbol of Community." NL, 39, no. 21 (May 21), 13–14.

"Why Ike Is in Trouble." NL, 39, no. 39 (September 24), 3–5.

1957

"After Comment, the Deluge." CCY, 74, no. 36 (September 4), 1034–35. Attacks by correspondents on *Life* article on Billy Graham.

"The Anglo-Saxon Alliance." CC, 17, no. 8 (May 13), 58–59.

"Barth on Hungary—An Exchange." CCY, 74, no. 15 (April 10), 454–55. Reprinted in *Essays in Applied Christianity.*

"The Cardinal and the Commissar." NL, 40, no. 42 (October 21), 5–6. The curious alliance which has developed between the church and the Communist State.

"China and the United Nations." *Journal of International Affairs,* 11, no. 2 (1957), 187–89.

"The Civil Rights Bill." NL, 40, no. 37 (September 16), 9–11.

"The Conquest of Space." NL, 40, no. 47 (November 25), 7–8.

"The Decline of Britain and France." CC, 17, no. 2 (February 18), 10–11.

"Democracy and Foreign Policy." NL, 40, no. 14 (April 8), 9–11.

"The Dismal Prospects for Disarmament." CC, 17, no. 15 (September 16), 113–14.

"The Eisenhower Doctrine." NL, 40, no. 5 (February 4), 8–10.

"Eisenhower's Theory of Power and Morals." NL, 40, no. 10 (March 11), 3–4.

"Filling the Middle East Vacuum." CC, 16, no. 24 (January 21), 189–90.

"The Heresy of Mao Tse-Tung." CC, 17, no. 11 (June 24), 82–83.

"Higher Education in America." *Confluence*, 6, no. 1 (Spring), 3–14.

"Hoffa and the Teamsters." CC, 17, no. 18 (October 28), 137–38.

"Human Creativity and Self-Concern in Freud's Thought," in *Freud and the 20th Century*. Edited by Benjamin N. Nelson. New York: Meridian Books, pp. 259–76.

"Liberty and Equality." *The Yale Review*, 47, no. 1 (September), 1–14.

"Neither Adam Smith nor Karl Marx." NL, 40, no. 51 (December 23), 8–9.

"The New British Strategy." CC, 17, no. 7 (April 29), 50–51.

"On Freedom, Virtue and Faith," in *This Is My Philosophy*. Edited by Whit Burnett. New York: Harper and Brothers, pp. 262–86.

"Our Stake Is in the State of Israel." NR, 136, no. 5 (February 4), 9–12.

"Piety and Secularism in America." *Atlantic Monthly*, 200, no. 5 (November), 180–84.

"Power and Prestige in Empires and Alliances." NL, 40, no. 20 (May 20), 16–18.

"The President's Budget." CC, 17, no. 10 (June 10), 73–74.

"The 'Right to Work' Laws." CC, 17, no. 4 (March 18), 25–26.

"The Security and Hazard of the Christian Ministry." *Union Seminary Quarterly Review*, 13, no. 1 (November), 19–23.

"The Situation in the Middle East." CC, 17, no. 6 (April 15), 42–43.

"The Teamsters and Labor's Future." NL, 40, no. 34 (August 26), 3–5.

"Theology and Political Thought in the Western World." *The Ecumenical Review*, 9, no. 3 (April), 253–62.

"Triumph of a 'Backward' Technology." CC, 17, no. 20 (November 25), 153–54.

"The Two Sources of Western Culture," in *The Christian Idea of Education*. Edited by Edmund Fuller. New Haven: Yale University Press, pp. 237–54.

"The U.N. Is Not a World Government." *The Reporter,* 16, no. 5 (March 7), 30–32.

"Why Is Barth Silent on Hungary?" CCY, 74, no. 4 (January 23), 108–10.

1958

"After Sputnik and Explorer." CC, 18, no. 4 (March 17), 29–30.

"Christianity and Darwin's Revolution," in *A Book that Shook the World: Anniversary Essays on Charles Darwin's* Origin of Species. Pittsburgh: The University of Pittsburgh Press, pp. 30–37.

"Disaster in United States Foreign Policy." CC, 18, no. 5 (September 15), 117–18.

"The Disaster of U.S. Policy." NL, 41, no. 30 (August 18–25), 8–9.

"Discriminate Justice in Technical Society." NL, 41, no. 3 (January 20), 13–14.

"France's Malady." NL, 41, no. 13 (March 31), 17–18.

"Freedom," in *A Handbook of Christian Theology.* Edited by Marvin Halverson. New York: Meridian Books, pp. 139–41.

"The Gospel in Future America." CCY, 75, no. 25 (June 18), 712–16.

"Implications for the Elections." CC, 18, no. 20 (November 24), 161–62.

"The Janus Face of American Diplomacy." NL, 41, no. 8 (February 24), 16–17.

"Mr. Eisenhower and the State of the Union." CC, 18, no. 1 (February 3), 2–3.

"The Moral Insecurity of Our Security." CC, 17, no. 23 (January 6), 177–78.

"A Note on Pluralism," in *Religion in America.* Edited by John Cogley. New York: Meridian Books, pp. 42–50.

"Personalities and Social Forces." NL, 41, no. 44 (December 1), 7–8.

"A Predicament We Share with Russia." NL, 41, no. 16 (April 21), 10–11.

"The Relations of Christians and Jews." *CCAR Journal* [Central Conference of American Rabbis], no. 21 (April), 18–32.

"A Rich Nation in a Poor World." CC, 18, no. 5 (March 31), 38–39.

"The Self," in *A Handbook of Christian Theology.* Edited by Marvin Halverson. New York: Meridian Books, pp. 342–45.

"Sin," in *A Handbook of Christian Theology.* Edited by Marvin Halverson. New York: Meridian Books, pp. 348–51.

"The Situation in the Middle East." CC, 18, no. 14 (August 4), 109–10.

"The States' Rights Crisis." NL, 41, no. 35 (September 29), 6–7.

"Uneasy Peace or Catastrophe." CC, 18, no. 7 (April 28), 54–55.

"Walter Rauschenbusch in Historical Perspective." *Religion in Life*, 27, no. 4 (Autumn), 527–36.

"Why We Are Losing to the Russians." NL, 41, no. 2 (January 13), 6–7.

"Will DeGaulle Save France?" NL, 41, no. 26 (June 30), 6–7.

1959

"The Art of the Possible." NL, 42, no. 34 (September 21), 3–4.

" 'Balance of Terror': Credit and Debit." NL, 42, no. 29 (August 3–10), 4–5.

"Barth's East German Letter." CCY, 76, no. 6 (February 11), 167–68.

"Biblical Faith and Socialism: A Critical Appraisal," in *Religion and Culture: Essays in Honor of Paul Tillich.* Edited by Walter Liebrecht. New York: Harper and Brothers, pp. 44–57.

"The Church in the World." *Theology Today,* 15, no. 4 (January), 542–48.

"Civil Rights and the Filibuster." CC, 19, no. 1 (February 2), 2–3.

"Coexistence Under a Nuclear Stalemate." CC, 19, no. 15 (September 21), 121–22.

"The Cold War and Nuclear Dilemma." *Cross Currents,* 9, no. 3 (Summer), 212–24.

"The Dangers of the Nuclear Test Bans." NL, 42, no. 23 (June 8), 11–12.

"A Decade of Dizzy and Rapid Change." CC, 19, no. 22 (December 28), 191–92.

"DeGaulle Balance Sheet." NL, 42, no. 14 (April 6), 6–7.

"The Democratic Elite and American Foreign Policy," in *Walter Lippmann and His Time.* Edited by Marquis W. Childs. New York: Harcourt Brace Jovanovich, pp. 168–88.

"Education and the World Scene." *Daedalus,* 88, no. 1 (Winter), 107–20.

"From Progress to Perplexity," in *The Search for America.* Edited by Huston Smith. Englewood Cliffs, N.J.: Prentice-Hall, pp. 135–46.

"Geneva: Preface and Problems." CC, 19, no. 10 (June 8), 78–79.

"The Image of America." NL, 42, no. 8 (February 23), 8–10. Discussion of why Lincoln achieved supremacy over all other heroes in the national pantheon.

"A Khrushchev Visit to America?" CC, 19, no. 14 (August 3), 113–14.

"The Long Haul of Co-existence." CC, 19, no. 20 (November 30), 172–73.

"The Long Ordeal of Co-existence." NR, 140, no. 13 (March 30), 10–12.

"Macmillan and the Peace." NL, 42, no. 19 (May 11), 8–9.

"Mr. Khrushchev and Post-Stalin Russia." CC, 19, no. 3 (March 2), 17–18.

"Modern Answers to an Enigma." *Life,* 46, no. 20 (May 18), 135, 137. Discussion of MacLeish's *J.B.*

"Moral and Political Judgments of Christians." CC, 19, no. 12 (July 6), 99–103.

"Morality," in *The Search for America.* Edited by Huston Smith. Englewood Cliffs, N.J.: Prentice-Hall, pp. 147–53.

"The New Nations: Seeds, Buds and Flowers." CC, 19, no. 5 (March 30), 34–35.

"Power and Ideology in National and International Affairs," in *Theoretical Aspects of International Relations.* Edited by W.T.R. Fox. Notre Dame: The University of Notre Dame Press, pp. 107–18. Reprinted in *Faith and Politics.*

"The Problem of a Protestant Social Ethic." *Union Seminary Quarterly Review,* 15, no. 1 (November), 1–11.

"Steel Strike: Glory of an Open Society." CC, 19, no. 17 (October 19), 145–46.

"The Test of Christian Faith Today." CCY, 76, no. 43 (October 28), 1239–43.

1960

"Berlin, Disarmament and the Summit." CC, 20, no. 2 (February 22), 10–11.

"Catholics and the Presidency." NL, 43, no. 19 (May 9), 3–4.

"Catholics and the State." NR, 143, no. 17 (October 17), 13–15.

"The Changing United Nations." CC, 20, no. 16 (October 3), 133–34.

"The Christian Moral Witness and Some Disciplines of Modern Culture." *Pastoral Psychology,* 11, no. 101 (February), 45–54.

"A Christian View of the Future." Interview by Henry Brandon. *Harper's Magazine,* 221, no. 1327 (December), 71–77.

"The Church and the South African Tragedy." CC, 20, no. 7 (May 2), 53–54.

"Cold Comfort of a 'Mystic Unity.'" CC, 20, no. 8 (May 16), 65–66. The Dutch Reformed Church of South Africa and its racial views.

"The Eisenhower Era." NL, 43, no. 38 (October 3), 3–4.

"The Election and the Next President." CC, 20, no. 20 (November 28), 169–70.

"The Election—The Religious Issue." NL, 43, no. 48 (December 12), 3–4.

"'End of an Era' for Organized Labor." NL, 43, no. 1 (January 4), 15–16.

"The Failure of U.S. Diplomacy." NL, 43, no. 31 (August 1–8), 6–7.

"First Steps Toward a New Diplomacy." NL, 43, no. 25 (June 20), 7–8.

"France's Fifth Republic and Its General." NL, 43, no. 7 (February 15), 12–13.

"Imperialism in Perspective." NL, 43, no. 44 (November 14), 7–8.

"Khrushchev's Rumanian Rhapsody." CC, 20, no. 12 (July 11), 98–99.

"National Goals and Purposes." CC, 20, no. 22 (December 26), 191–92.

"The Negro Dilemma." NL, 43, no. 15 (April 11), 13–14.

"The President's Triumphal Journey." CC, 19, no. 23 (January 11), 202–3.

"The Problem of a Protestant Political Ethic." CCY, 77, no. 38 (September 21), 1085–87.

"The Quality of Our Lives." CCY, 77, no. 19 (May 11), 568–72. In the series "How My Mind Has Changed."

"Religion and Politics," in *Religion and Politics.* Edited by Peter H. Odegard. New York: Oceana Publications, pp. 107–12.

"The Religious Issue." NL, 43, no. 48 (December 12), 3–4.

"The Religious Traditions of Our Nation." *The Saturday Evening Post,* 233, no. 4 (July 23), 26–27, 45, 48.

1961

"Berlin and Prestige in Europe." NR, 145, no. 12 (September 18), 17–19.

"Christianity and Darwin's Revolution," in *A Book that Shook the World: Anniversary Essays on Charles Darwin's* Origin of Species. Pittsburgh: The University of Pittsburgh Press, pp. 30–37.

"Communist Dogma and Latin America." NL, 44, no. 22 (May 29), 17–18.

"Democracy's Foreign Policy Dilemma." NL, 44, no. 34 (October 2), 22–23.

"The Eichmann Trial." CC, 21, no. 5 (April 3), 47–48.

"The Eternal Church and the Modern World." CCY, 78, no. 38 (September 20), 1105–8.

"The Gravity of Our Contest with Communism." CC, 21, no. 13 (July 24), 129–30.

"How My Mind Has Changed," in *How My Mind Has Changed.* Edited by Harold E. Fey. New York: Meridian Books, pp. 116–32.

"Laos and Cuba: Problems for Review." CC, 20, no. 24 (January 23), 209–10.

"Mistaken Venture." NL, 44, no. 18 (May 1), 3–4. Assessment of the Bay of Pigs.

"The Montgomery Savagery." CC, 21, no. 10 (June 12), 102–3.

"The New Feudalism." NL, 44, no. 31 (August 28), 13–14. Hoffa's succession to presidency of the Teamsters.

"On Ambitious Politicians." NR, 144, no. 9 (February 27), 14–15.

"Persuasion, Politics and Power," in *The Agreeable Autocracies: A Series of Conversations on American Institutions.* Edited by Joseph P. Lyford. New York: Oceana Publications, pp. 128–41.

"Present Heritage of the Long Encounter Between Christian Faith and Western Civilization." *The Harvard Divinity Bulletin,* 26, no. 1 (October), 1–11.

"President Kennedy's Cuban Venture." CC, 21, no. 8 (May 15), 69–70.

"Prospects for the South." NL, 44, no. 25 (June 19), 3–4.

"Reflections on Democracy as an Alternative to Communism." *Columbia University Forum,* 4, no. 3 (Summer), 10–18.

"The Resumption of Nuclear Testing." CC, 21, no. 16 (October 2), 161–62.

"Rising Hopes for Arms Control." CC, 21, no. 3 (March 6), 21–22.

"The Rising Tide of Color." NL, 44, no. 4 (January 23), 16–17.

"School Aid, the President and the Hierarchy." NL, 44, no. 12 (March 20), 8–9.

"Tractors for Freedom." CC, 21, no. 11 (June 26), 109–10.

"The Unintended Virtues of an Open Society." CC, 21, no. 13 (July 24), 132–38.

"The U.N.: An End to Illusions." NL, 44, no. 9 (February 27), 3–4.

"Well-Tempered Evangelism." NR, 144, no. 26 (June 26), 11–12. Limitations of liberal democracy in much of the world.

1962

"Algeria: Political Heights and Depths." CC, 22, no. 12 (July 9), 117–18.

"The Alternatives to Communism." NR, 147, no. 14 (October 1), 15–16.

"American Hegemony and the Prospects for Peace." *The Annals,* 342 (July), 154–60.

"Boulder in the Currents." *The Spectator,* 209, no. 7006 (October 5), 488, 490.

"Can Democracy Work?" NL, 45, no. 11 (May 28), 8–9.

"The Case for Congo Unity." NL, 45, no. 1 (January 8), 3–4.

"The Concept of 'Order of Creation' in Emil Brunner's Social Ethic," in *The Theology of Emil Brunner.* Edited by Charles W. Kegley. New York: Macmillan, pp. 265–71.

"Cuba: Avoiding the Holocaust." CC, 22, no. 20 (November 26), 204–5.

"The Cuban Crisis in Retrospect." NL, 45, no. 25 (December 10), 8–9.

"Despair Can Be a Source of Danger." *Vogue,* 139, no. 1 (January 1), 70–71.

"A Dissenting Opinion." NL, 45, no. 14 (July 9), 3–4. On the Supreme Court's "Regents' Prayer" decision.

"Elections at Mid-Term." NL, 45, no. 22 (October 29), 19–20.

"Internationalism and DeGaulle's Nationalism." CC, 22, no. 10 (June 11), 98–99.

"The Intractability of Race Prejudice." CC, 22, no. 18 (October 29), 181.

"One Year of the New Frontier." CC, 22, no. 1 (February 5), 1–2.

"Our Latin American Policy." CC, 22, no. 5 (April 2), 42–43.

"Our Stake in the Common Market." CC, 22, no. 2 (February 19), 13–14.

"A Plea for Tolerance." *The Atlantic Monthly,* 210, no. 2 (August), 72–77. Part of a symposium on "The Roman Catholic Church in America."

"President Kennedy's Defeats and Victories." CC, 22, no. 14 (August 6), 133–34.

"The Problem of the Modern Church: Triviality." CC, 22, no. 21 (December 10), 223–26, 228.

"The Regents' Prayer Decision." CC, 22, no. 13 (July 23), 125–26.

"U.S. Steel and the U.S.A." CC, 22, no. 8 (May 14), 69–70.

"Woe Unto Them that Spoil." CC, 22, no. 16 (October 1), 159–60.

1963

"Advent of Compulsory Arbitration." CC, 23, no. 16 (September 30), 166–67.

"America the Smug." *The Saturday Evening Post,* 236, no. 40 (November 16), 12, 17.

"The Christian and the Cold War." *The Lutheran,* NS 1, no. 3 (January 30), 6–8.

"The Clay Committee Report." CC, 23, no. 7 (April 29), 65–67.

"The Crisis in American Protestantism." CCY, 80, no. 49 (December 4), 1498–1501.

"The Development of a Social Ethic in the Ecumenical Movement," in *The Sufficiency of God, Essays on the Ecumenical Hope* (in honor of W.A. Visser't Hooft). Edited by Robert C. Mackie and Charles C. West. Philadelphia: Westminster Press, pp. 111–28.

"Dilemma of U.S. Power." NL, 46, no. 24 (November 25), 11–12.

"Federal Aid to Education: A Call to Action." CC, 23, no. 18 (October 28), 189–91.

"History's Limitations in the Nuclear Age." NL, 46, no. 3 (February 4), 18–19.

"How Liberal Is the Pope?" NL, 46, no. 15 (July 22), 10–11.

"The Mounting Racial Crisis." CC, 23, no. 12 (July 8), 121–22.

"Pacem in Terris: Two Views" (with John Bennett). CC, 23, no. 8 (May 13), 81, 83.

"The Peril of a New Napoleon." CC, 23, no. 3 (March 4), 22–23.

"The Problem of South Vietnam." CC, 23, no. 14 (August 5), 142–43.

"The Religious Situation in America," in *Religion and Contemporary Society*. Edited by Harold Stahmer. New York: Macmillan, pp. 145–55.

"Revolution in an Open Society." NL, 46, no. 11 (May 27), 7–8.

"A Tentative Assessment." NL, 46, no. 25 (December 9), 7–8. In a series of articles on "The Kennedy Legacy."

1964

"After the Second Session." NL, 47, no. 2 (January 20), 11–12. The Vatican Council.

"Christian Attitudes Toward Sex and Family." CC, 24, no. 7 (April 27), 73–75.

"The End of an Era." CC, 24, no. 9 (May 25), 96–97. Unions and industrial automation.

"Further Reactions to Vatican II." CC, 23, no. 24 (January 20), 259–60.

"The Giant and the Dwarf." CC, 24, no. 1 (February 3), 1–2. Considers the issues separating the U.S. and Panama, on the occasion of the riots in Panama.

"Goldwater vs. History." NL, 47, no. 22 (October 26), 16–17.

"Johnson and the Myths of Democracy." NL, 47, no. 11 (May 25), 18–20.

"Man, the Unregenerate Tribalist." CC, 24, no. 12 (July 6), 133–34.

"The Panama Crisis." NR, 150, no. 5 (February 1), 5–6.

"The Politics of Nostalgia." NL, 47, no. 14 (July 20), 3–4.

"Prayer and Justice in School and Nation." CC, 24, no. 9 (May 25), 93, 95–97.

"President Johnson's Foreign Policy." CC, 24, no. 4 (March 16), 31–32.

"Prisoner of the South." NL, 47, no. 9 (April 27), 16–17. Senators Fulbright and Russell.

"Protestant Individualism and the Goldwater Movement." CC, 24, no. 21 (December 14), 248–50.

"The Struggle for Justice." NL, 47, no. 14 (July 6), 10–11.

"Triumph of Primitivism." NL, 47, no. 16 (August 17), 5–6. Implications of Republican nomination of Goldwater.

1965

"Adlai Stevenson: 1900–1965." CC, 25, no. 14 (August 9), 169–70.

"Caribbean Blunder." CC, 25, no. 9 (May 31), 113–14.

"Consensus at the Price of Flexibility." NL, 48, no. 19 (September 27), 18–20. Attacking Johnson's support of the Vietnam war "by consensus."

"The Drama of the Vatican Council." CC, 24, no. 23 (January 11), 275–76.

"The Fateful Triangle." NL, 48, no. 1 (January 4), 18–20. Russia, China and the U.S. will determine peace for a long time.

"Felix Frankfurter—In Memoriam." CC, 25, no. 5 (April 5), 69–70.

"Lessons of the Detroit Experience." CCY, 82, no. 16 (April 21), 487–90.

"Martin Buber: 1878–1965." CC, 25, no. 12 (July 12), 146–47.

"Norman Thomas: Incarnate Conscience." CC, 24, no. 23 (January 11), 271–72. On the occasion of his eightieth birthday.

"Paul Tillich in Memoriam." *Union Seminary Quarterly Review,* 21, no. 1 (November), 11.

"Pretense and Power." NL, 48, no. 5 (March 1), 6–7.

"Prospects of the Johnson Era." CC, 25, no. 2 (February 22), 13–14.

"The Religion of Abraham Lincoln." CCY, 82, no. 6 (February 10), 172–75.

"Roosevelt and Johnson: A Contrast in Foreign Policy." NL, 48, no. 15 (July 19), 5–8.

"Senator Fulbright's Achievement." CC, 25, no. 17 (October 18), 209–10.

"Some Things I Have Learned." *The Saturday Review,* 48, no. 45 (November 6), 63–64.

"Vietnam: An Insoluble Problem." CC, 25, no. 1 (February 8), 1–2.

"Winston Churchill and Great Britain." CC, 25, no. 1 (February 8), 8–10.

1966

"The Army in the New Nations." CC, 26, no. 7 (May 2), 83–84.

"A Christian Journal Confronts Mankind's Continuing Crisis." CC, 26, no. 2 (February 21), 11–13.

"The CIA: Tool or Policy-Maker?" CC, 26, no. 9 (May 30), 105–6.

"Faith as the Sense of Meaning in Human Existence." CC, 26, no. 10 (June 13), 127–31. Observations on the "death of God" theologians.

"An Interview with Reinhold Niebuhr." By John Cogley. *McCall's,* 93, no. 5 (February), 90–91, 166–71.

"An Interview with Reinhold Niebuhr." By Patrick Granfield. *Commonweal,* 85, no. 11 (December 16), 315–21.

"The Peace Offensive" (with Ursula M. Niebuhr). CC, 25, no. 24 (January 24), 301–2.

"The President on 'The Arrogance of Power.'" CC, 26, no. 10 (June 13), 125–26.

"Reinhold Niebuhr Discusses the War in Vietnam." NR, 154, no. 5 (January 29), 15–16. Answers to questions posed by *The New Republic.*

"Some Things I Have Learned," in *What I Have Learned, A Saturday Review Book.* New York: Simon & Schuster, pp. 233–49.

"To America and Back," in *I Knew Dietrich Bonhoeffer.* Edited by Wolf-Dieter Zimmermann and G. Smith. New York: Harper & Row, p. 165.

"The Unresolved Religious Problem in Christian-Jewish Relations." CC, 26, no. 21 (December 12), 279–83.

"Vietnam and the Imperial Conflict." NL, 49, no. 12 (June 6), 15–18.

"Vietnam: The Tide Begins to Turn." CC, 26, no. 17 (October 17), 221–23.

1967

"David and Goliath." CC, 27, no. 11 (June 26), 141–42. On the six-day war.

"The Ethics of War and Peace in the Nuclear Age" (with Hans Morgenthau). *War/Peace Report,* 7, no. 2 (February), 3–8.

Does Civilization Need Religion? A Study of the Social Resources and Limitations of Religion in Modern Life. New York: The Macmillan Company, 1927.

Leaves from the Notebook of a Tamed Cynic. New York: Willett, Clark and Company, 1929.

The Contribution of Religion to Social Work. New York: Columbia University Press, 1932. Reprinted by AMS Press, Inc., 1971.

Moral Man and Immoral Society, A Study in Ethics and Politics. New York: Charles Scribner's Sons, 1932.

Reflections on the End of an Era. New York: Charles Scribner's Sons, 1934.

An Interpretation of Christian Ethics. New York: Harper and Brothers, 1935.

Beyond Tragedy, Essays on the Christian Interpretation of History. New York: Charles Scribner's Sons, 1937.

Christianity and Power Politics. New York: Charles Scribner's Sons, 1940.

The Nature and Destiny of Man, Volume I. New York: Charles Scribner's Sons, 1941.

The Nature and Destiny of Man, Volume II. New York: Charles Scribner's Sons, 1943.

The Children of Light and the Children of Darkness, A Vindication of Democracy and a Critique of Its Traditional Defense. New York: Charles Scribner's Sons, 1944.

Discerning the Signs of the Times, Sermons for Today and Tomorrow. New York: Charles Scribner's Sons, 1946.

Faith and History, A Comparison of Christian and Modern Views of History. New York: Charles Scribner's Sons, 1949.

The Irony of American History. New York: Charles Scribner's Sons, 1952.

Christian Realism and Political Problems. New York: Charles Scribner's Sons, 1953.

The Self and the Dramas of History. New York: Charles Scribner's Sons, 1955.

"Foreign Policy in a New Context." NL, 50, no. 5 (February 27), 17–19.

"An Interview with Reinhold Niebuhr," in *Theologians at Work.* By Patrick Granfield. New York: Macmillan, pp. 51–68. Originally published in *Commonweal* (December 16, 1966).

"Our Schizoid Vietnam Policy." CC, 26, no. 24 (January 23), 313–14.

"Politics, Patriotism and Integrity." CC, 27, no. 4 (March 20), 45–46.

"The Social Myths of the 'Cold War.'" *Journal of International Affairs,* 21, no. 1 (1967), 40–56.

"The Vietnam Elections." CC, 27, no. 15 (September 18), 199–200.

"Vietnam: Study in Ironies." NR, 156, no. 25 (June 24), 11–12.

"Without 'Advice and Consent.'" NL, 50, no. 17 (August 28), 5–6. President Johnson and the Vietnam War.

"Words for the Memorial Service of Dr. Harry F. Ward." *The Union Seminary Tower,* 14, no. 1 (Winter), 1.

1968

"Fighting an Intractable Dwarf." NL, 51, no. 15 (August 5), 12–13.

"Foreword," to *The Religious Situation: 1968.* Edited by Donald Cutler. Boston: Beacon Press, pp. ix–xv.

"Ideology vs. Power." NL, 51, no. 22 (November 18), 16–17.

"A Question of Priorities." NL, 51, no. 2 (January 15), 9–11.

"A Time for Reassessment." CC, 28, no. 5 (April 1), 55–56. On the Vietnam War.

1969

"An Interview with Reinhold Niebuhr." By Ronald H. Stone. CC, 29, no. 4 (March 17), 48–52.

"The King's Chapel and the King's Court." CC, 29, no. 14 (August 4), 211–13. Official worship at the White House.

"The President's Error." CC, 29, no. 15 (September 15), 227–28.

"Toward Intra-Christian Endeavors." CCY, 86, no. 53 (December 31), 1662–67.

1970

"Indicting Two Generations." NL, 53, no. 19 (October 5), 13–14. The workers' discontent of the 1930s and student discontent today.

"John Coleman Bennett: Theologian, Churchman, and Educator," in *Theology and Church in Times of Change*. Essays in Honor of John Coleman Bennett. Edited by E.L. Long and Robert T. Handy. Philadelphia: Westminster Press, pp. 233–36.

"The Presidency and the Irony of American History." CC, 30, no. 6 (April 13), 70–72.

1971

"Mission and Opportunity; Religion in a Pluralistic Culture," in *Social Responsibility in an Age of Revolution*. Edited by Louis Finkelstein. New York: Jewish Theological Seminary, pp. 177–211.

"Without Consensus There Is No Consent." *The Center Magazine*, 4, no. 4 (July/August), 2–9.

1972

The Reminiscences of Reinhold Niebuhr. New York: Columbia University Oral History Research Office.

1973

"Germany." *Worldview*, 16, no. 6 (June), 13–18. Prepared for publication about 1962; now published for the first time.

1974

"Britain." *Worldview*, 17, no. 7 (July), 30–33. Published here for the first time.

SUBJECT INDEX

NAME INDEX